A-

Key to Map Pages		
Large Scale City Centre		
Map Pages	6-125	
Postcode Map	126-127	

		128-221
	erest	
Index to Hospitals & Hospices		222-224

REFERENCE

Motorway	**M57**
A Road	**A59**
Tunnel	
B Road	**B5180**
Dual Carriageway	
One-way Street	
Traffic flow on A Roads is also indicated by a heavy line on the driver's left.	
Road Under Construction	
Opening dates are correct at the time of publication.	
Proposed Road	
Restricted Access	
Pedestrianized Road	
Track / Footpath	
Residential Walkway	
Railway	Station Level Crossing Tunnel
Built-up Area	MANOR ST
Local Authority Boundary	
Posttown Boundary	
Postcode Boundary (within Posttown)	
Map Continuation	60 Large Scale City Centre 4

Airport	✈
Car Park (selected)	🅿
Church or Chapel	†
Cycleway (selected)	
Fire Station	■
Hospital	Ⓗ
House Numbers (A & B Roads only)	13 8
Information Centre	🄸
National Grid Reference	445
Park & Ride	Marshalls Cross P+R
Police Station	▲
Post Office	★
Safety Camera with Speed Limit	(30)
Fixed cameras and long term road works cameras. Symbols do not indicate camera direction.	
Toilet:	
without facilities for the Disabled	▽
with facilities for the Disabled	▽
Disabled use only	▽
Viewpoint	⁂ ✵
Educational Establishment	■
Hospital or Healthcare Building	■
Industrial Building	▦
Leisure or Recreational Facility	■
Place of Interest	■
Public Building	■
Shopping Centre or Market	■
Other Selected Buildings	☐

SCALE

Map Pages 6-125 1:18,103	Map Pages 4-5 1:9,051
0 ¼ ½ Mile	0 ⅛ ¼ Mile
0 250 500 750 Metres	0 100 200 300 Metres
3½ inches (8.89 cm) to 1 mile 5.52 cm to 1 km	7 inches (17.78 cm) to 1 mile 11.05 cm to 1 km

Copyright of Geographers' A-Z Map Company Limited

Fairfield Road, Borough Green, Sevenoaks, Kent TN15 8PP
Telephone: 01732 781000 (Enquiries & Trade Sales)
01732 783422 (Retail Sales)
www.az.co.uk
Copyright © Geographers' A-Z Map Co. Ltd.
Edition 6 2013

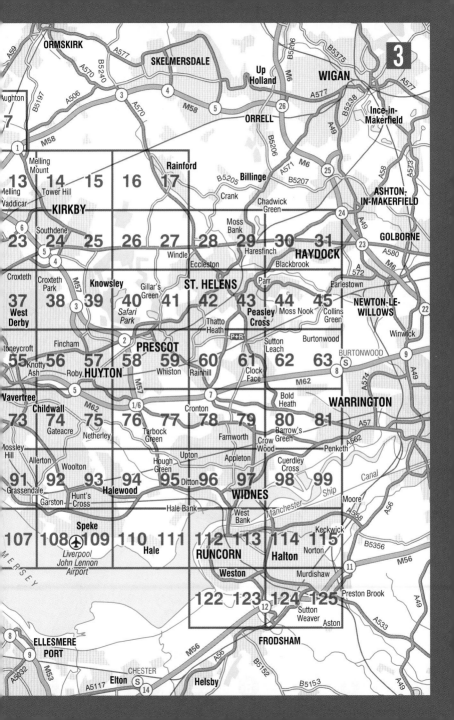

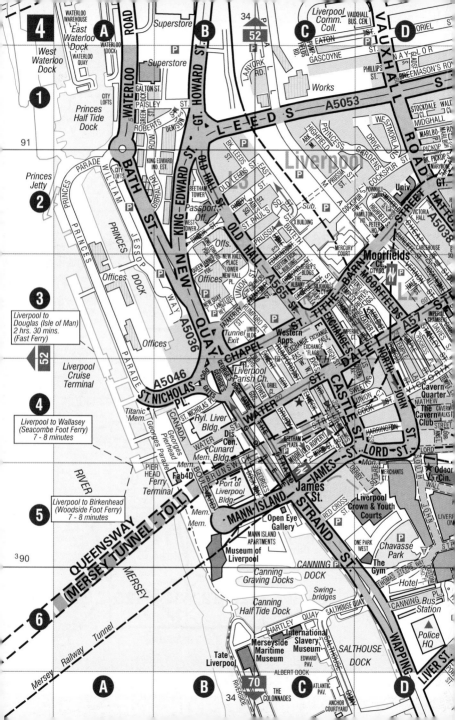

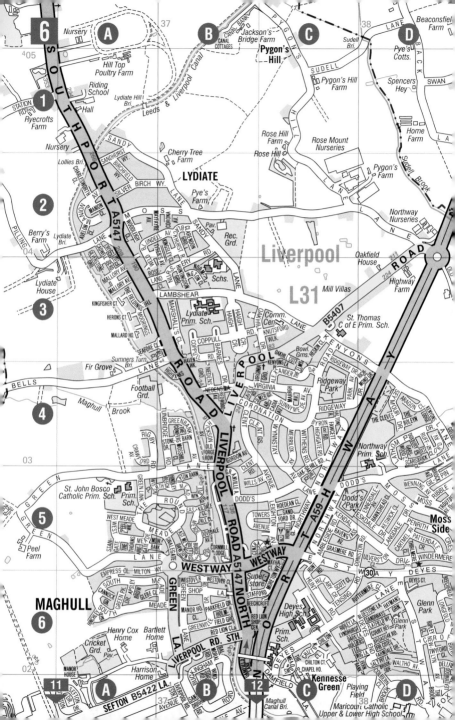

E F G H 9

MOSS LANE B5193 A565 INCE LANE 02

Trap Plantation Sunnyfield Farm Border Plantation 33

High Farm St. Mary's Catholic Prim. Sch. Sunnyfields Bens Gorse St. Joseph's Hospice 1

Delph Farm DELPH BACK Kennel Plantation Thornton Wood

LANE LITTLE CROSBY Church Wood Chet Centre Crosby Hall Bens Gorse Belt

Well Farm White House Farm Model Farm The Vista Moor Hey Plantation 2 Cottage Farm VIRGIN'S INCE

LITTLE LANE BACK LA. Liverpool

Burying Ground Plantation 0.1 LANE

Liverpool CROSBY Holy Family Catholic High School 3 Sports Ground LA.

Playing Fields St. Michael's C of E High School Sports Ground Running Track Cricket Grounds Crosby High Sch. Moor Park Pav. Tennis Cts. Pav. Pav.

MANOR DR. ANDREWS DR. SUNNINGDALE DR. PRESTWICK DR. ROEHAMPTON DR. ST. MICHAEL'S ROAD BOUNDARY B5193 RD. OAKLANDS MILL LONGFIELD BARN. CROFT HALSALL CT. VILLIERS AV. AVENUE CHESTNUT BEECH The Stables MORET CT.

COLLEGE ROAD CAMBRIDGE ROAD BERWICK SHERWOOD ENNISMORE BERKELEY RD. CAMBRIDGE RD. Prim. Sch. GREAT CROSBY MANOR FARWAYS HAIGH AV. MANOR RD. ROAD FORD MILLER AV. Prim. Sch. WILLOW MAYFAIR AV. DE VILLIERS AV. AVON WOODLAND RD. PARK AV. ESPLEN AV. POPLAR AV. SYCAMORE AV. ELM Tithebarn A565 COPPICE MANORS CT. ELMWOOD HILLCREST GREENWAY ROSEMOR 83 400

LINDEN AV. ELTON NORTH ROAD MERE PK. VICTORIA RD. CHATER GRA. KINGS RD. CARLTON TER. VICTORIA SANDAL WOODS RICHMOND RD. VALE MOOR MOOR HO. THE BYWAY WINMILL WK. CHRETWOOD HIGH FIELD GR. ROWAN MOOR CT. FORFIELD HILLCREST DR. NEWBOROUGH LUPTON LYNDHURST BELLAIR

ASHBOURNE HOME AV. THE CROFT DROP RD. ALEXANDRA RD. REGENT PRINCES AV. LUKE'S RD. HARRINGTON RD. VALE ENFIELD QUEENS AV. ASCOT PK. MOORSIDE Bowl. Grn. Forefield Jun. Sch. Moorside Park TREVOR DRIVE

FIRE STA. Alexandra Pk. ALEXANDRA ROAD CORONATION Lib. CORONATION ROAD Coronation Park CLAREMONT RD. EVEREST RD. FAIRHOLME THE PRECINCT Prim. Sch. ROSEDALE CT. SEAFIELD AV. MOORGATE ORCHARD AV. NORTHERN AV. LANE VOGAN AV. WYLVA AV.

MERSEY BLUNDELLSANDS NIBLEY RD. LOTHIAN RD. VERMONT RD. KIMBERLEY DR. Crossroads Cen. York YORK RD. Sch. St. AGNES ROAD WARWICK RD. BROMPTON KINGSWOOD Marine AFC (The Arriva Stadium) WOODVILLE WINCHESTER BELVEDERE R. The Mews PRESELAND RD. MOORGATE MELROSE AV. BALMORAL AV. STIRLING BLAIR INDUSTRIAL ESTATE STACEY RD. KERSHAW AV. MORNINGSIDE STALEY AV. CARRICK 6

HARLECH RD. CAVENDISH RD. JUBILEE SUNNYDALE MYERS ROAD WEST DRIVE BENNETT Merchant Taylors' Boys' Sch. Sacred Heart Catholic Coll. MILLERSTAIN Nazareth Ho. Sch. ROTHESAY CATHNESS DR. STRATHMORE BROWNMOOR Ten. Cts. GRASMERE DERWENT RD. 399

E F 19 G H 33 Bowl. Grns. 32 MORNINGTON AV. GROSVENOR AV. DUDDING

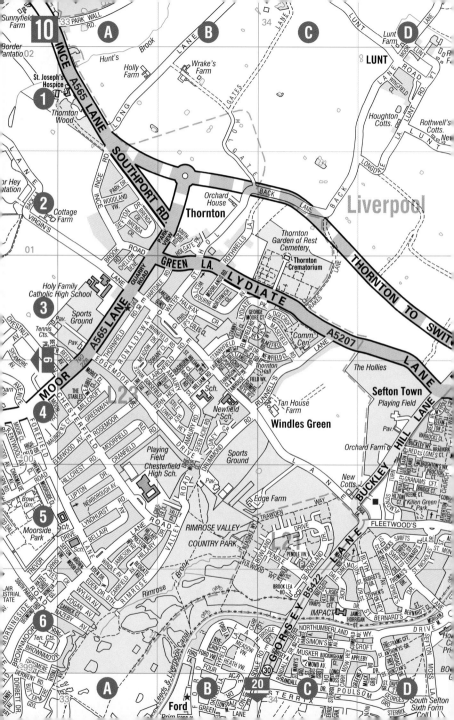

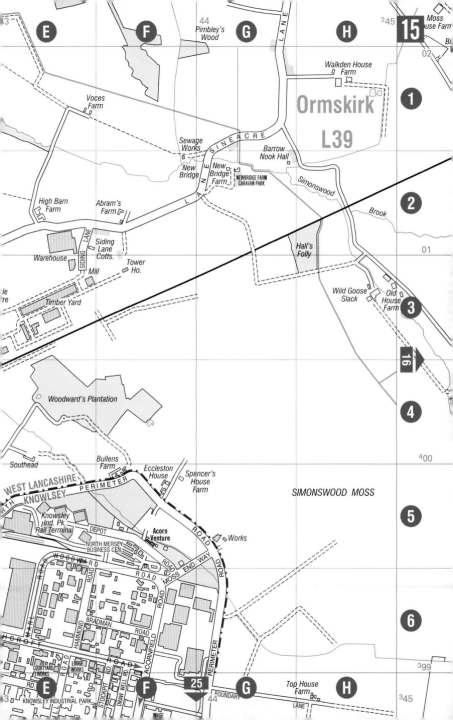

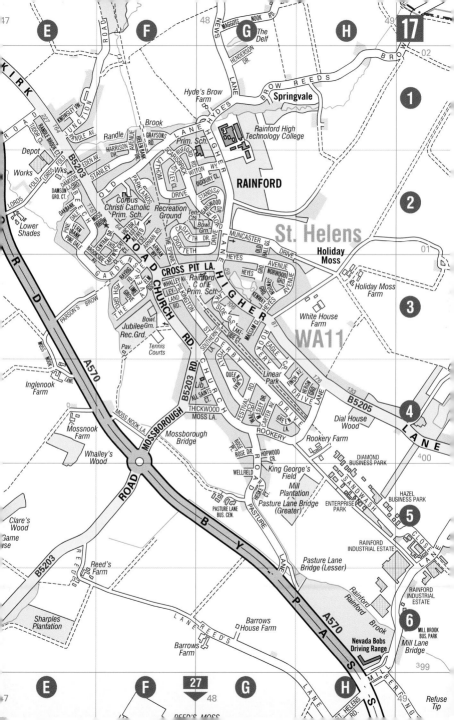

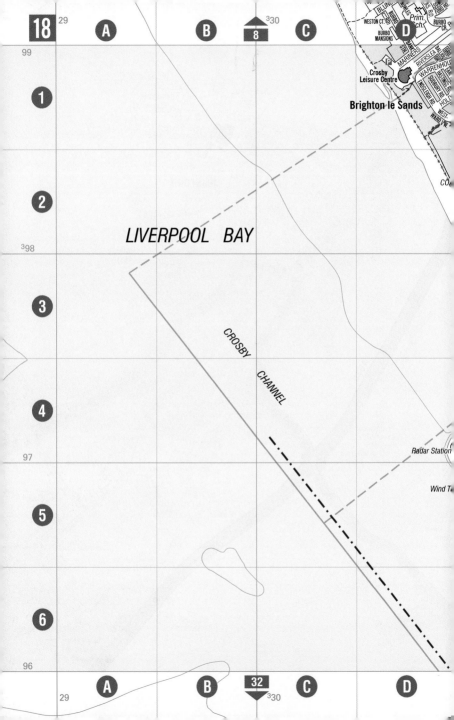

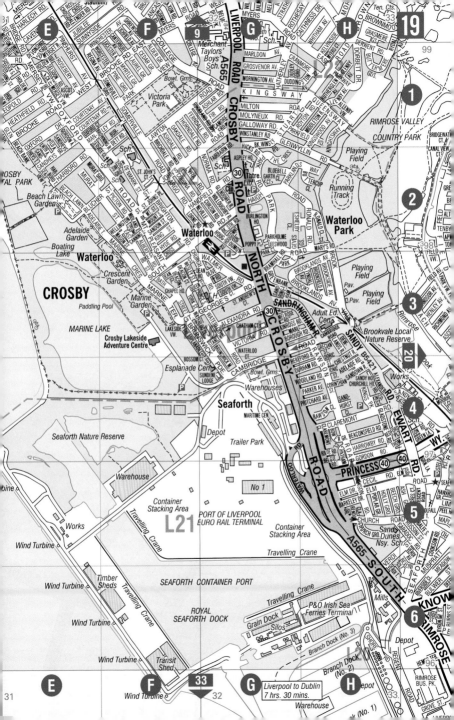

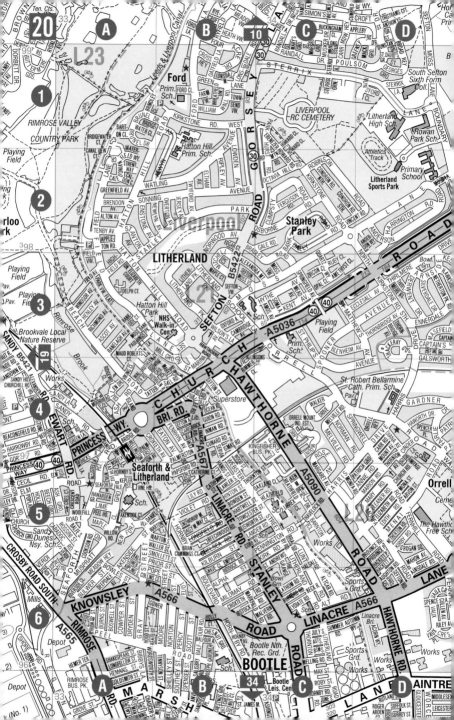

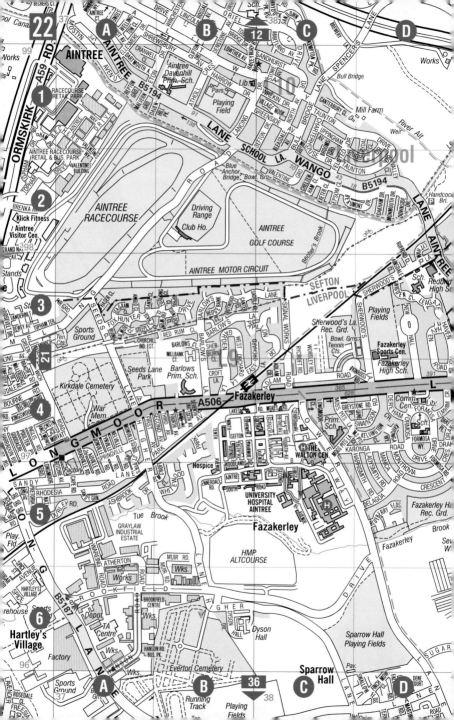

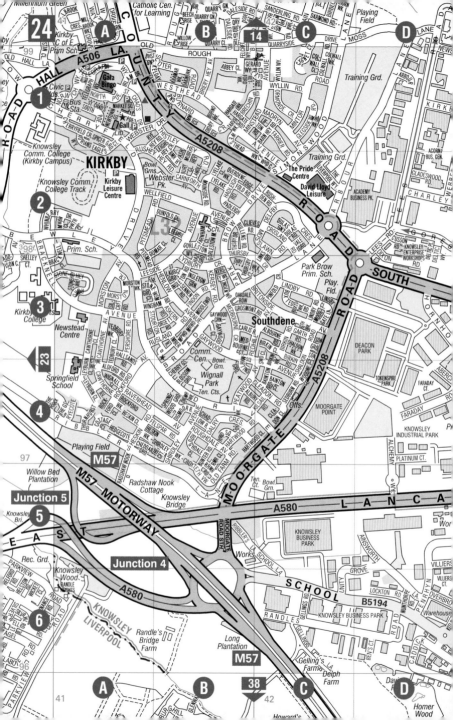

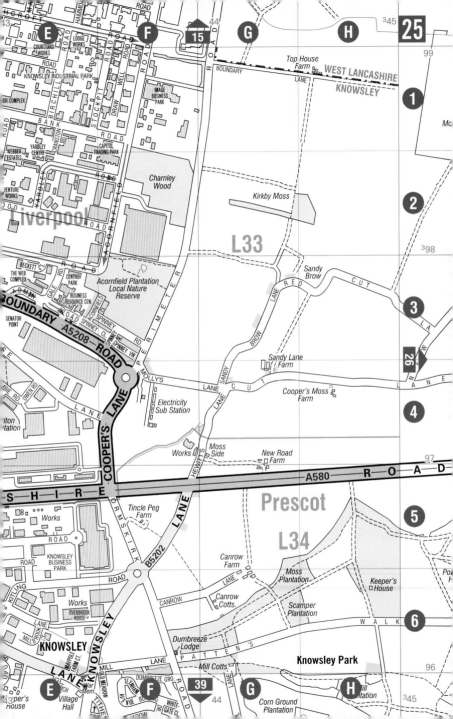

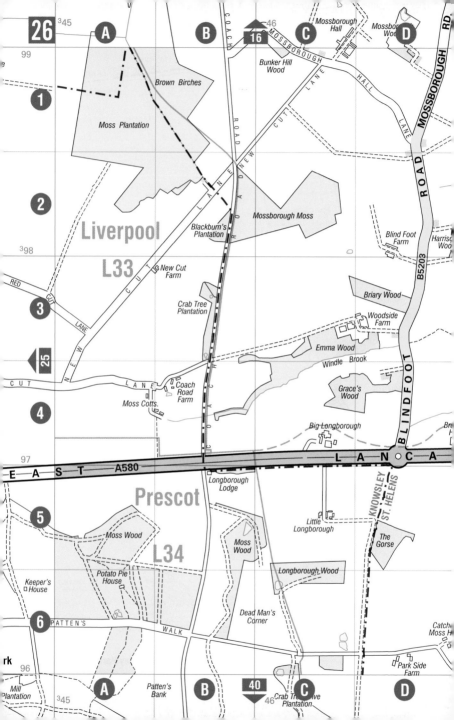

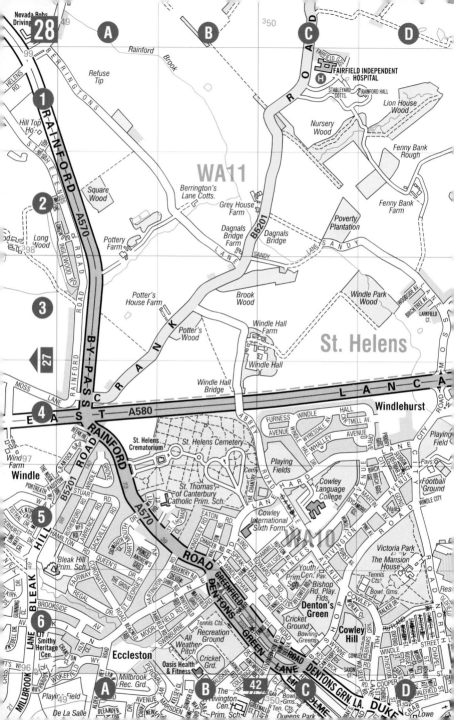

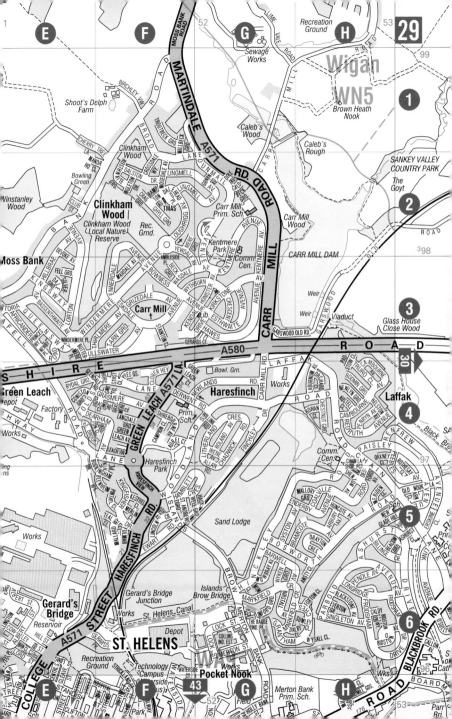

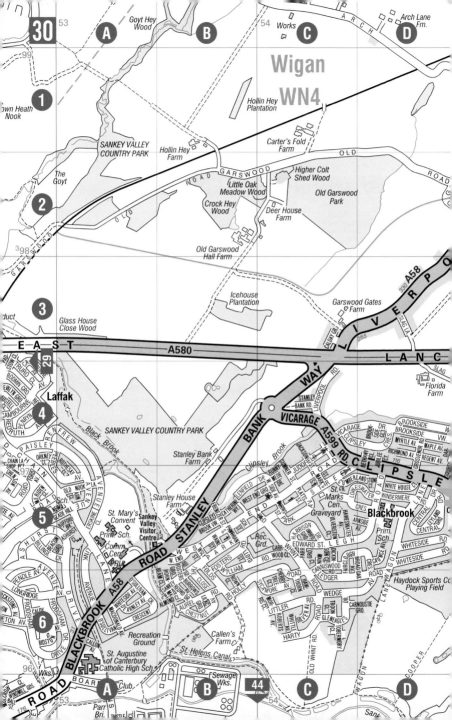

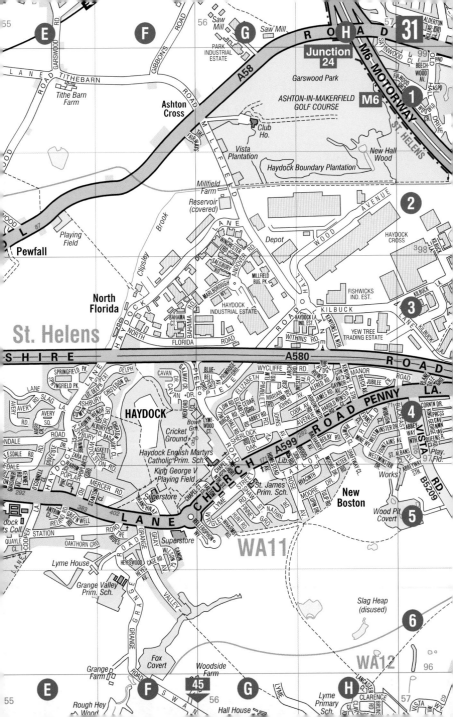

Wind Turbine
F TRANSIT Shed
19
G
Branch Dock (No. 3)
H

Wind Turbine

GLADSTONE DOCK

Branch Dock (No. 2)

Depot

Warehouse

Branch Dock (No. 1)

Travelling Crane

Travelling Cranes

Bootle

1 LIVERPOOL INTERMOD. FREEPORT TERMINA

Lighthouse

Gladstone Lock

Liverpool to Dublin
7 hrs. 30 mins.

Coal Terminal

L20   Hornby Dock

West Hornby Dock

2

Branch Dock (No. 3)

Branch Dock (No. 2)

ALEXANDRA DOCK

3

LANGTON DOCK

34

Brockle... Dock

4

94

SEFTON
WIRRAL

R I V E R

erch Rock

Breakwater

SEFTON
LIVERPOOL

5

NEW BRIGHTON

Tower Grounds

Comm. Cen. Vale Park

M E R S E Y

6

93

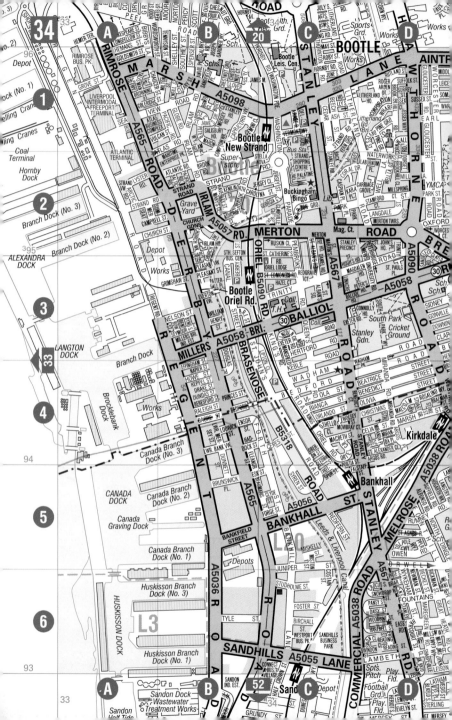

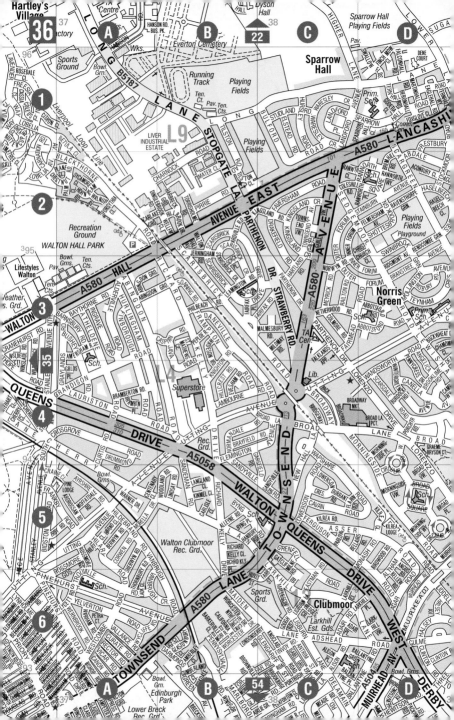

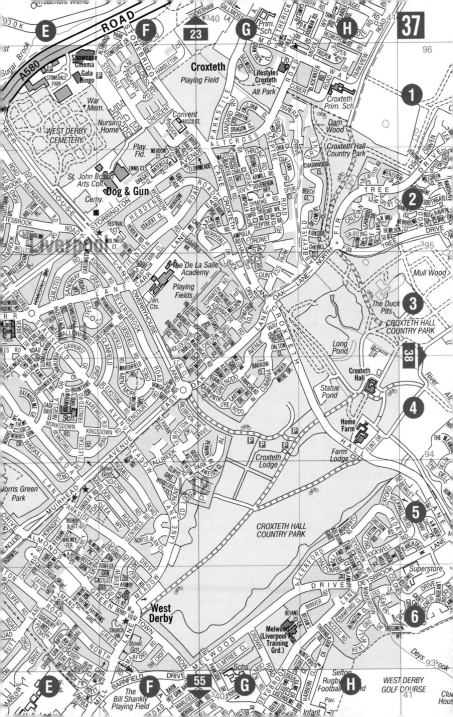

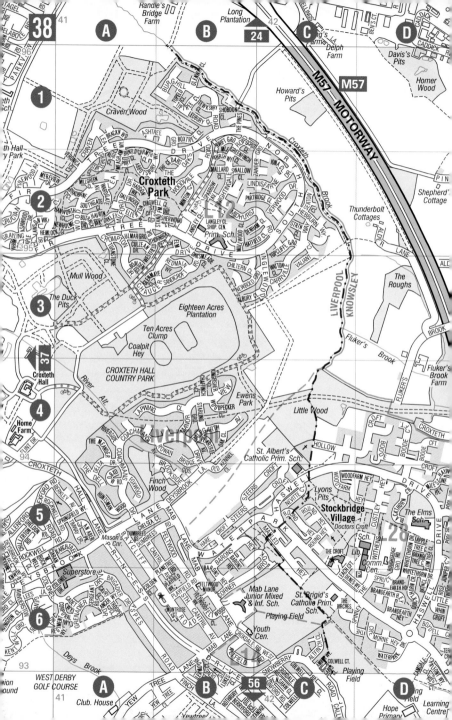

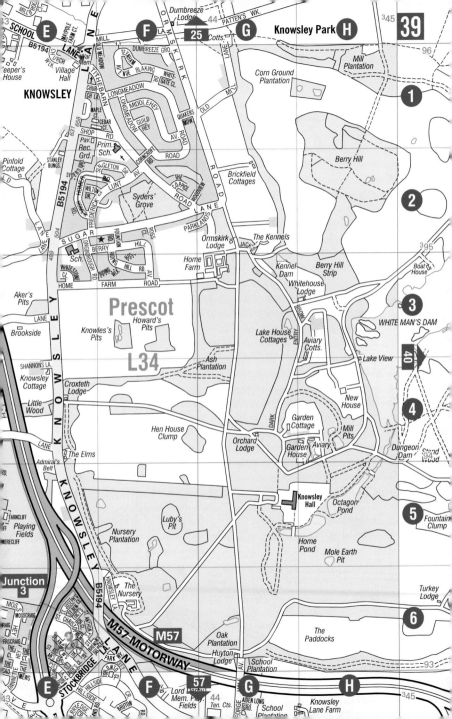

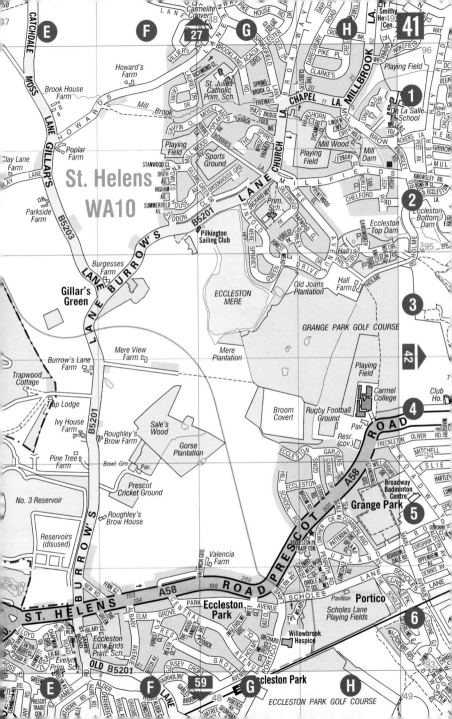

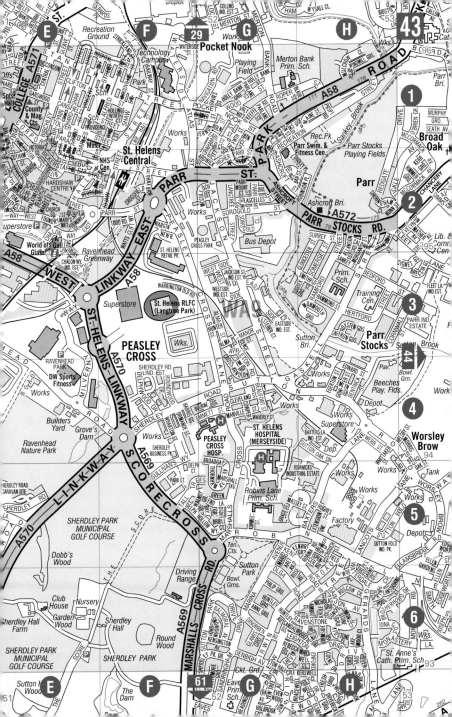

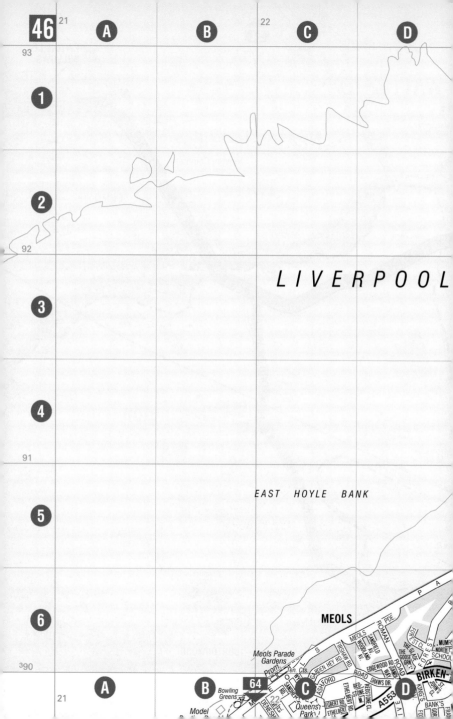

A B 22 C D

93

1

2

92

LIVERPOOL

3

4

91

5

EAST HOYLE BANK

6

MEOLS

Meols Parade
Gardens
Prom. Ten. Cts.

390

21

A B **64** C D

22

Bowling
Greens

Model

93

1

2

92

3

48

BAY

WALLASEY EMBANKMENT

4 Lea
Light

Greenacres

Lingham
Farm 91

NORTH WIRRAL COASTAL PARK

Eve-a-lyn
Farm

Parkfield
House

5 wage
Pumping Station

Park Lane
HOLIDAY HOMES

Parkfields

Refuse Tip

WIRRAL BEACH
CARAVAN PARK

Arrowe Brook

Coastguard
Station

ve Point

SEABANK
COTTAGE

CURLEW

NEWLYN

DALE DR.

Wirral

Great Meols
Prim.
Sch.

Rec.

Sewage Works

MILHOUS TERN

6

Great Meols

CH47

The Birket

Greenwood

CLEVELEY

DERWENT

390

Works

LIVERPOOL BAY

Breakwater

Club House

Caravan Park

CASTLEFIELDS

LEA

MURRAYFIELD

WALLASEY EMBANKMENT

Moreton Common

Leasowe Common

LEASOWE ROAD LEA

SHANNON RD.
LAGAN CAUSEWAY HO.
HO.

Rugby Football Grounds

WAKEFIELD

MURRAYFIELD

RAVENHEAD

Pasture Farm

Leasowe Lighthouse

Caravan Site

Greenacres

The Birket

Lingham Farm

PASTURE ROAD

DITTON

LEASOWE OAKMERE CT.
GDNS.
CASTLEGRANGE CASTLEFORD

THE SANDY HILLS

ARNWORTH
CRONTON

THE BEECHES
HEATH
FIELD CT.
MARSH
CASTLE
STAKES

CHELTENHAM CRES.
EPSOM RD.
NEWBURY WY.
EPSOM CT.
DUNSTALL CL.
CROWMERE CL.
ELMTREE CL.
GOODWOOD DR.

BLACKHEATH DR.
REC. GRD.
GREEN HEATH WY.
FARNSIDE
REEDS

Ditton Lane Nature Area

★ Reeds B.

Eve-a-lyn Farm

Lingham Farm

TARRAN WY. NTH.

TARRAN WAY
TARRAN WAY WEST
TARRAN WAY STH.
TARRAN DR.

Bowl. Grn.

Play. Fld.

Sewage Pumping Station

Refuse Tip

Moreton Hills Golf Centre

Play Field

Works

Moreton

Leasowe

Pasture Rd. Bri.

SUNNYSIDE

PASTURE ROAD A551

REEDVILLE GRO.
ROSSALL
AVENUE

Wirral

Arrowe Brook

CURLEW CT.
CURLEW WY.
BRADMAN RD.
GLACIER RD.
LINGHAM LANE

BERRYLANDS
MEADFOOT RD.
BRAMBLE
HARVEST

HEATHMOOR
FLAXHILL

FORTUNE WY.
WESTWAY
WESTWAY

PASTURE CRES.
EASTWAY
DANGER

SUNFIELD RD.
LONGBARD RD.
SAXON

MOORETON

PASTURE ROAD HOYLAKE A553

WASTDALE
BERMUDA
HARDIE AV.

ELEANOR RD.
HEATHER DRIVE
HARVEST LANE

FELICITY GRO.
MARYLAND LANE
BERRYLANDS

MAURICE JONES COURT

DUDLEY CL.
Comm. Cen.
Offs.
Club

Eastway Prim. Sch.

BLUNDELLS

DANESWELL

Prim. Sch.

TERN
WASTDALE
BELFRY CL.
ESKDALE
MORPETH CL.

EGREMONT
DRIVE
MEADOW
ESTHER

Bowling Greens

Lingham Prim. Sch.
Comm. Cen.
MILLINGTON

Running Track

Pav.

Lingham Park

WIMBRICK

CHAPEL HILL

GARRICK AV.
HAIG AV.

³²⁵

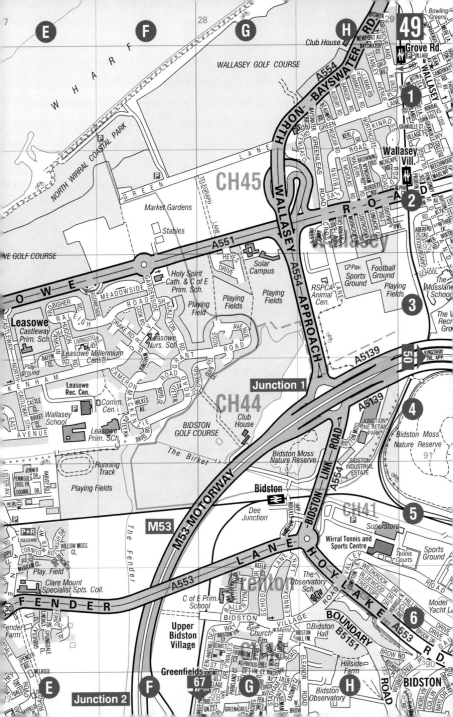

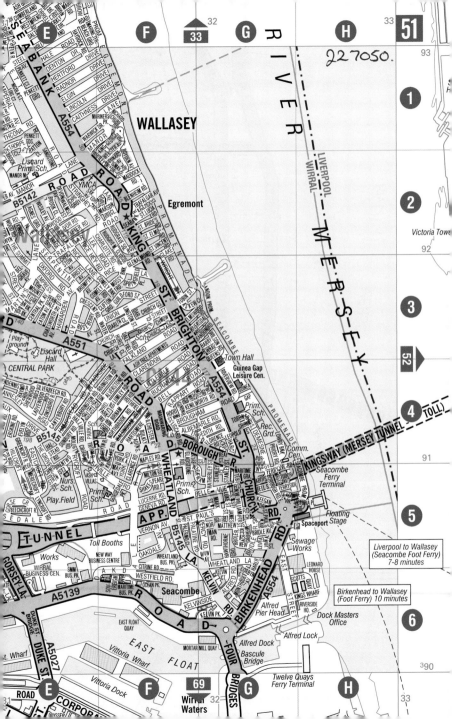

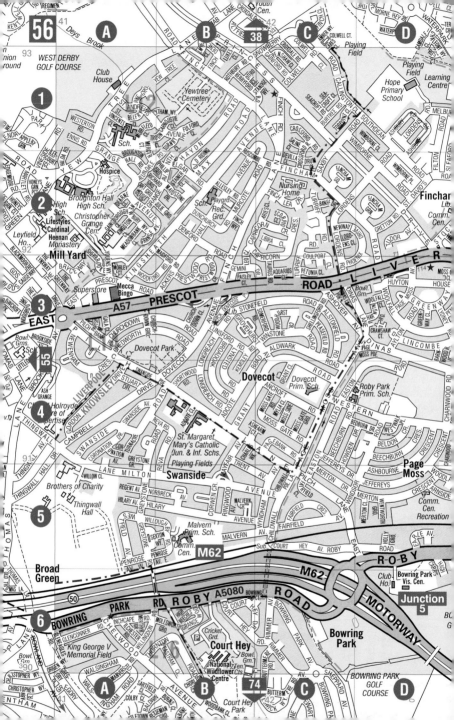

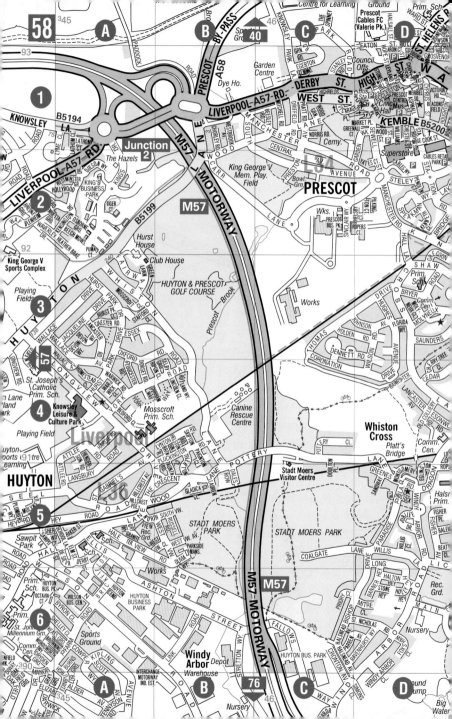

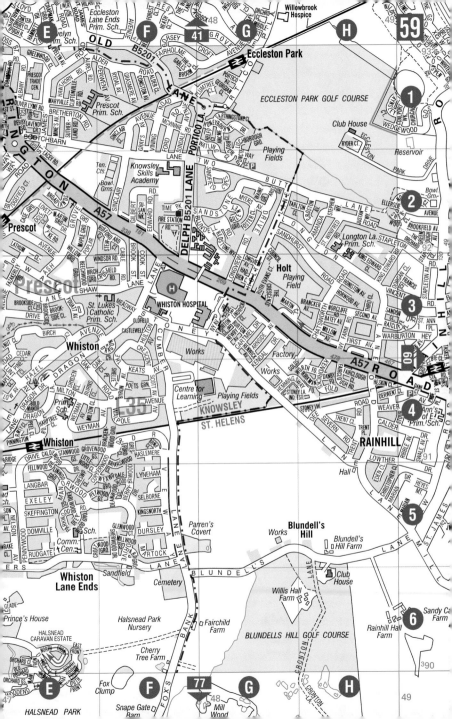

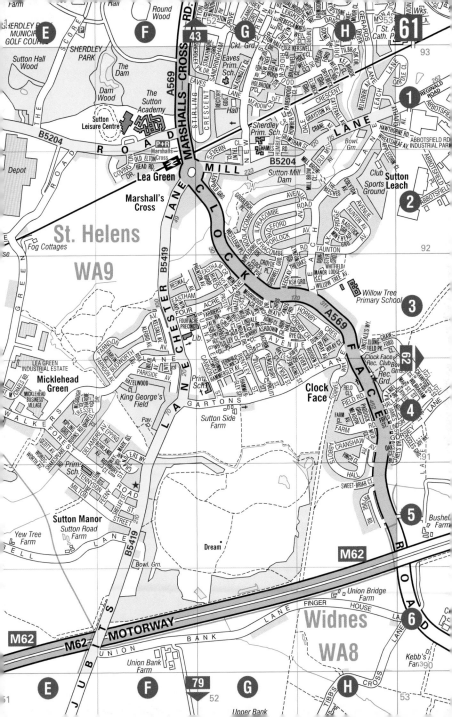

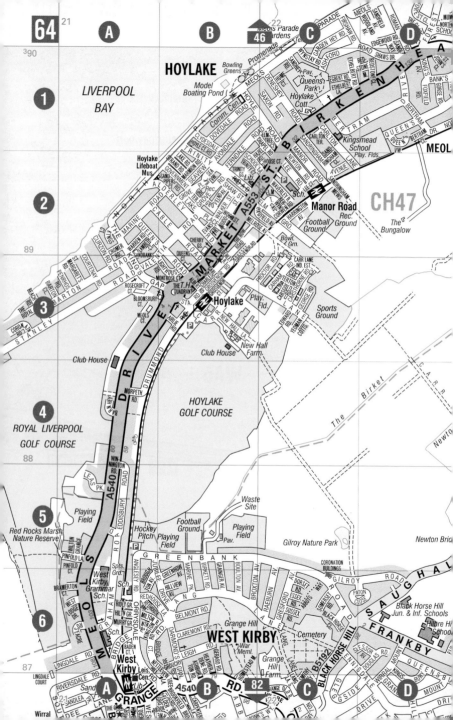

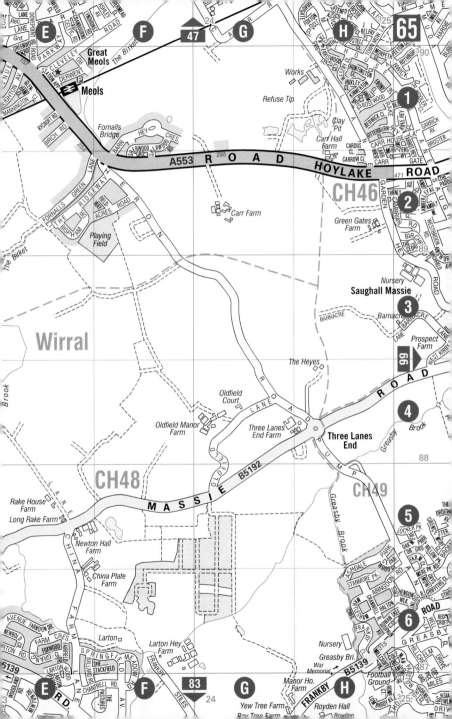

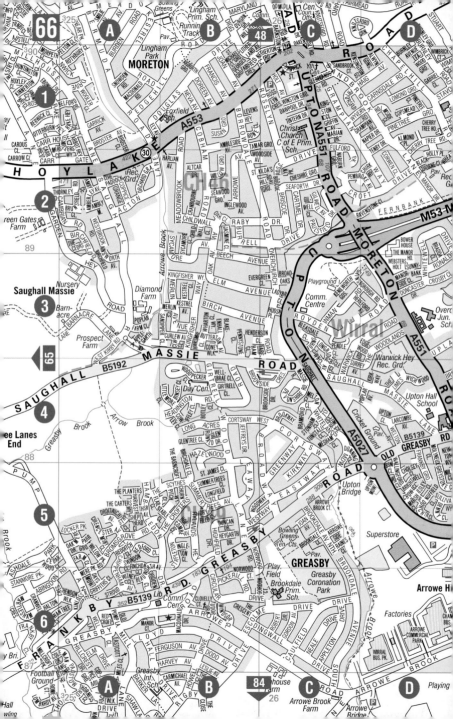

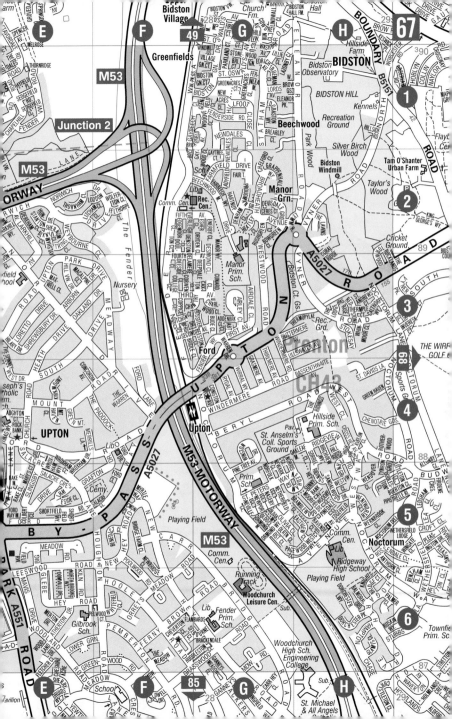

A Birkenhead to: Belfast 8 hrs.

B Mem. Museum of Liverpool

James St.

Mann Is. Gall.

Crown Ct.

C WALL ST. SCHOOL

COLLEGE

D Earts St.

390

1

Birkenhead to: Belfast 8 hrs.

52 Canning Graving Docks

Canning Half Tide Dock

SALT HOUSE

Hartley Quay

Hotel

Bus Sta.

Police HQ

HANOVER

PARK

JAMES ST.

Liver St.

QUEENSWAY (MERSEY TUNNEL - TOLL)

MERSEY RAILWAY TUNNEL

Tate Liverpool

4

LIVERPOOL

Mus. Edward Pav.

ATLANTIC PAV.

Albert Dock

Britannia Pav.

The Beatles Story

W A P P I N G

ST. JAM

WAPPING DOCK

Birkenhead to Wallasey (Foot Ferry) 10 minutes

Liverpool to Birkenhead (Woodside Foot Ferry) 7-8 minutes

TV Studio

GOWER

Duke's Dock

Royal Quay

N. Quay

E. Quay

W. Quay

S. Quay

Wapping Quay

Wapping Dock Wharf

JAMAICA ST.

CHALONER ST.

Warehouse

BLUNDELL

PACIFIC ROAD

WOODSIDE BUS.

Ferry Terminal

U-boat Story

2

Great Western House

Echo Arena

Hotel

BT Convention Cen

Monarchs Quay

Queens Quay

Queen's Wapping Bridge

Gala Leo Casino

Queen's Dock

Liverpool Watersports Cen.

PARLIAMENT

SEFTON

BIRKENHEAD

Rosebrae Court

Landsdowne House

Kingfisher House

Connaught Ho.

Half-tide Wharf

Customs & Excise

PARADE

Coburg Dock (Marina)

GRANARY WY.

STANHOPE

3

Monk's Ferry

St. Mary's Tower

Birkenhead Priory

69

Graving Dock

Ind. Est.

Abbots Quay

MARINERS WHARF

COBURG

Brunswick Dock (Marina)

QUEBEC QUAYS

R I V E R

A5036

4

Graving Docks

Outer Basin

L I V E R P O O L   W I R R A L

HMS Eaglet

Brunswick Enterprise Cen.

ATLANTIC

88

5

Maritime Business Park

Shipbuilding & Engineering Works

M E R S E Y

TV Studio

Wk

CH41

CAMPBELTOWN

6

TRANMERE

Tranmere Beach

Floating Stage

Pier

Floating Stage

VANGUARD

CH42

OIL TERMINAL

A41

ROCK BY-PASS

A41

A

Rock Ferry

Royal Mersey Yacht Club

B Rock Ferry Pier

88

34

C

D

BEDFORD

87

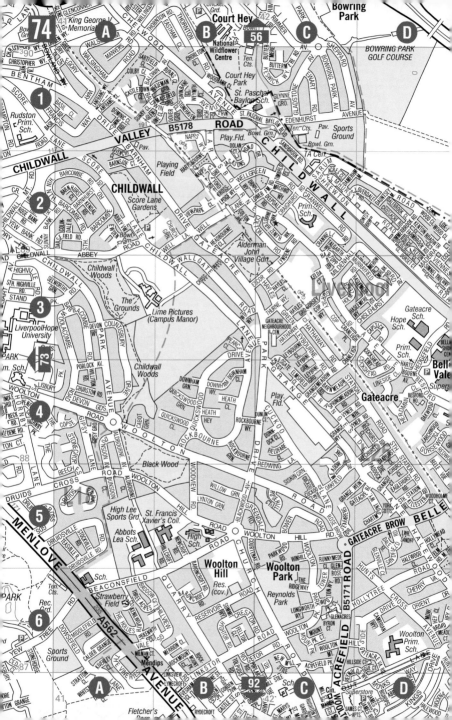

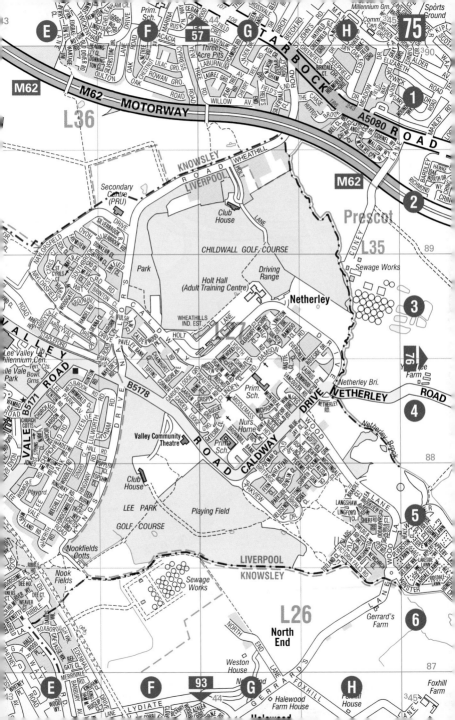

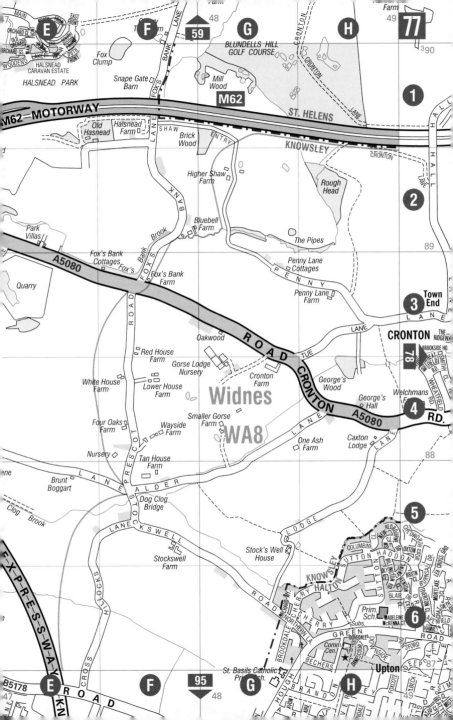

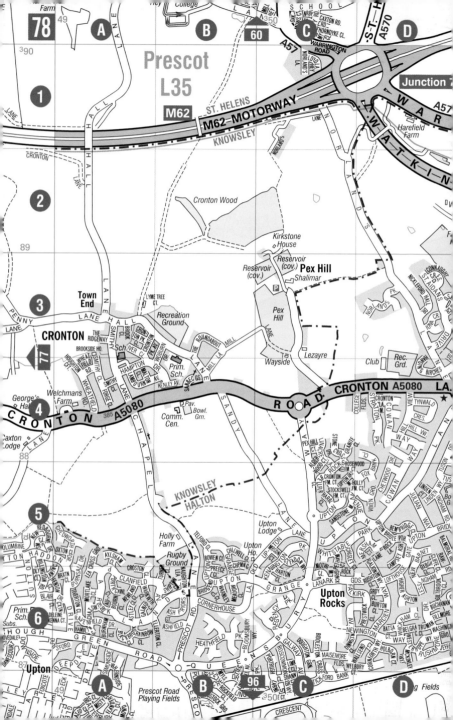

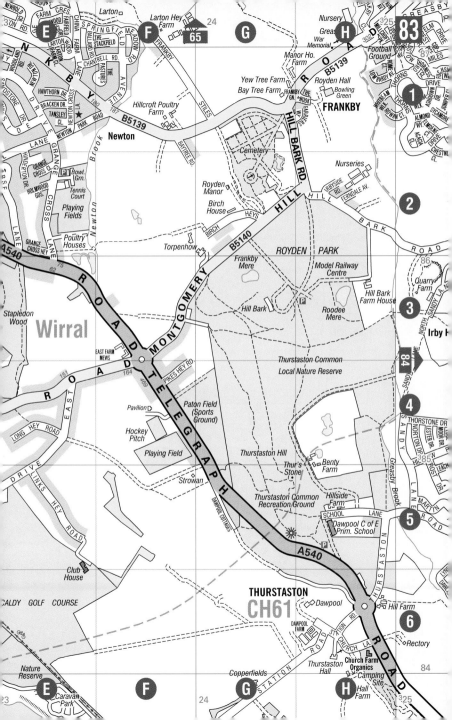

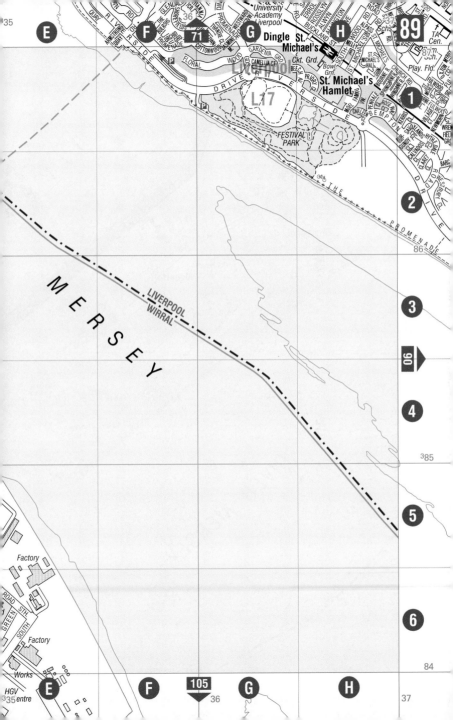

MERSEY

LIVERPOOL
WIRRAL

University
Academy
Liverpool

Dingle St.
Michael's

St. Michael's
Hamlet

Ckt. Grd.

Bowl.
Grn.

St.
Michael's
Hall

Play. Fld.

FESTIVAL
PARK

L17

Factory

Factory

Works

HGV
Centre

E F G H

71 36 89

105 36 37

385

86

90

84

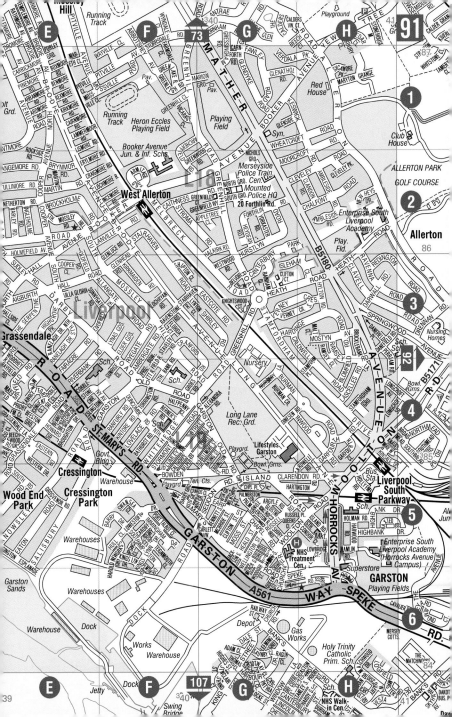

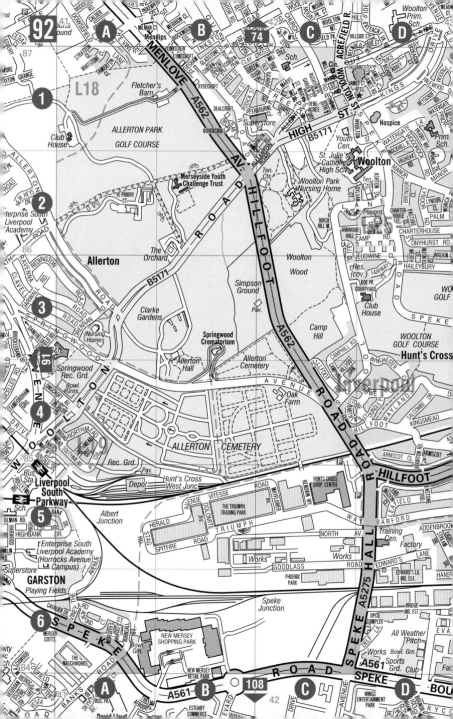

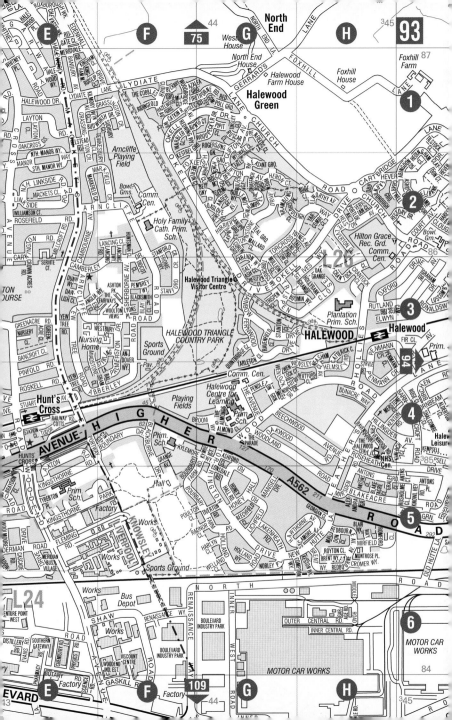

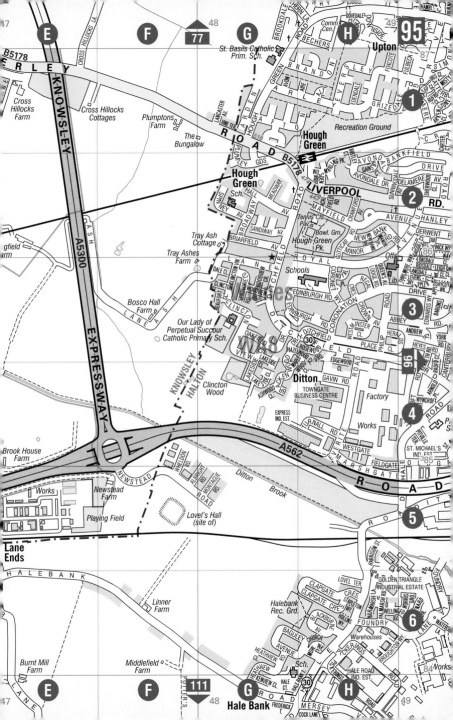

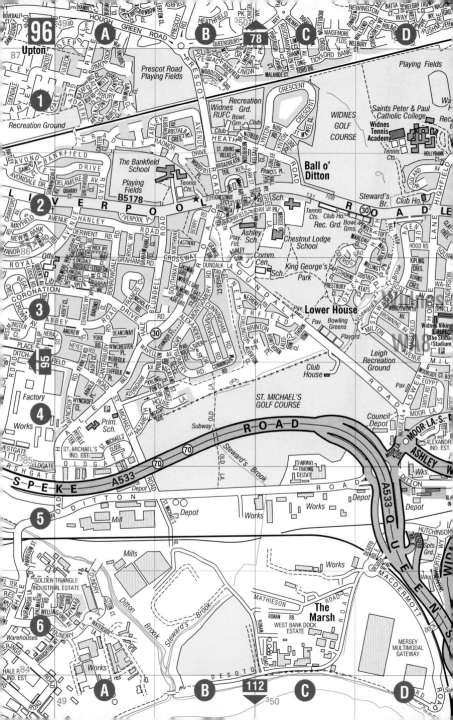

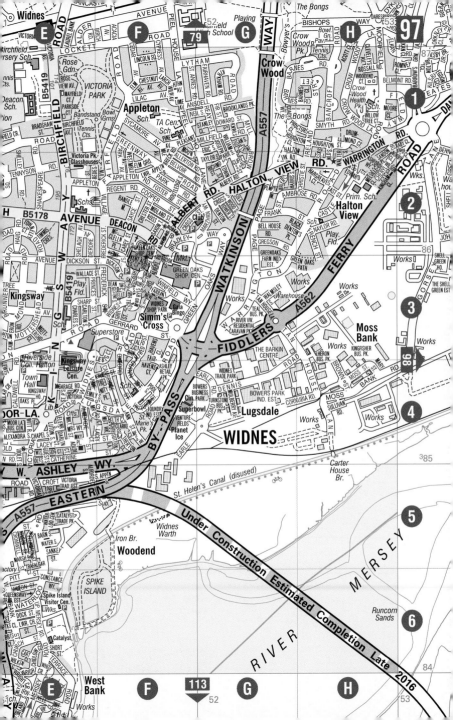

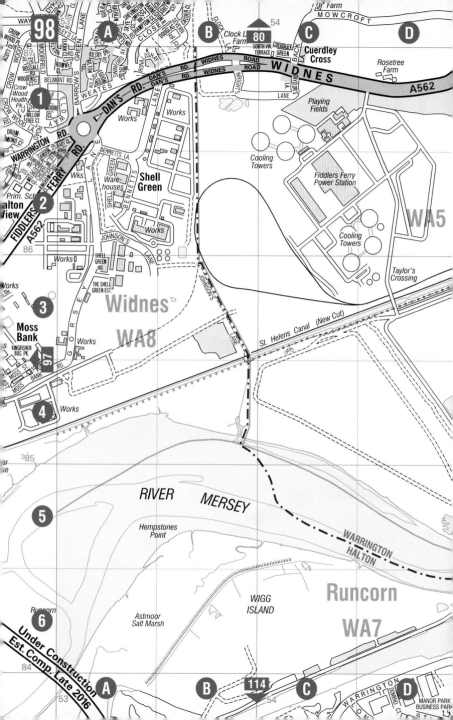

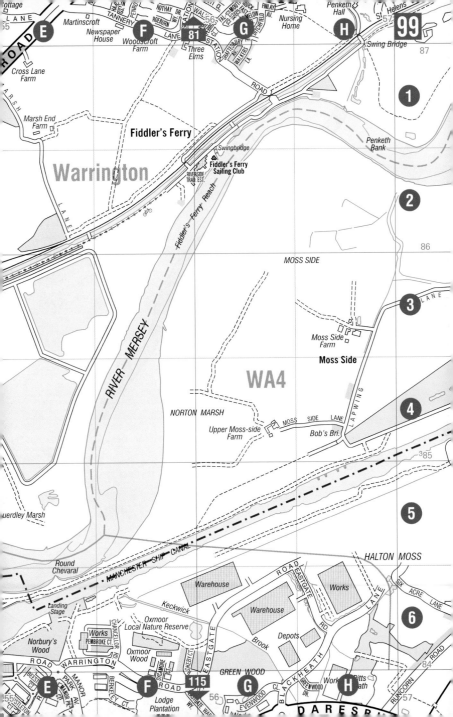

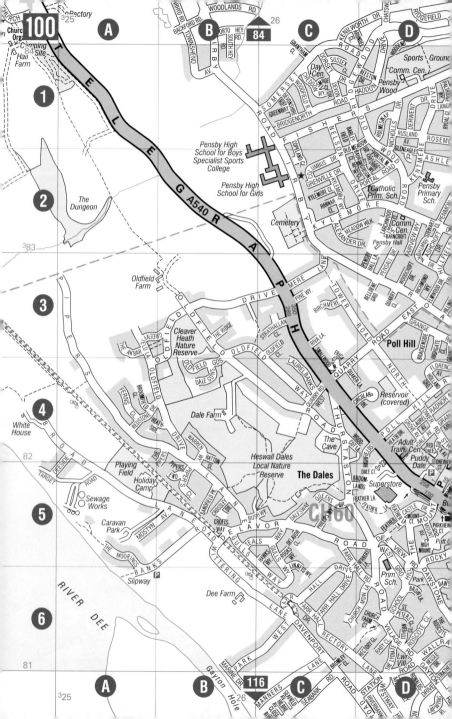

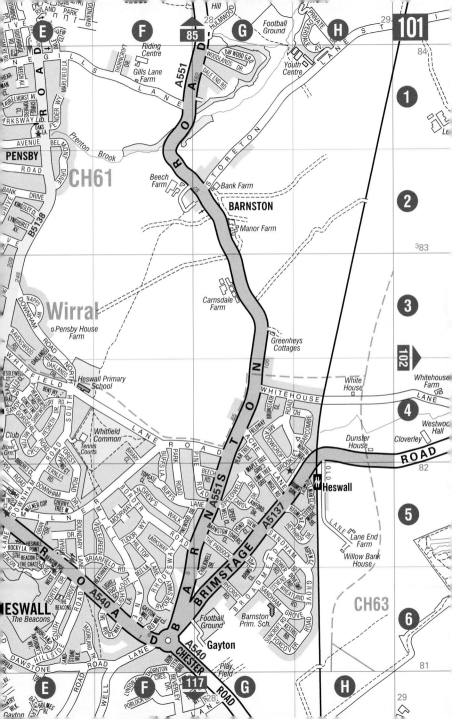

A   B   90   C   D

84

1

2

³83

3

105

4

82

5

6

Eastham
Locks

en Elizabeth II
Dock

RIVER

A   B   38   C   D

37

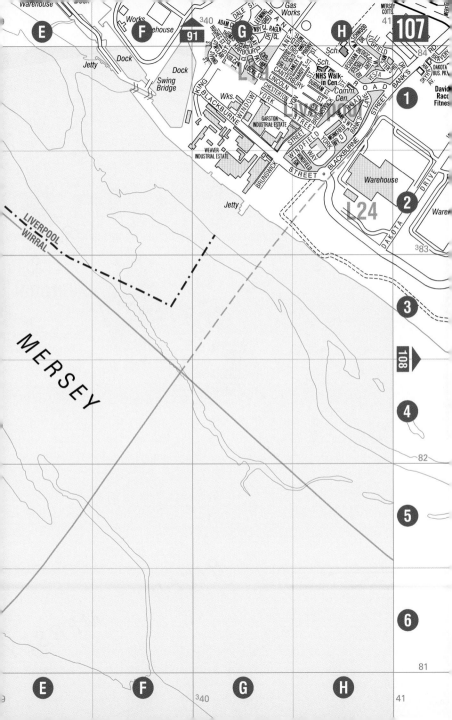

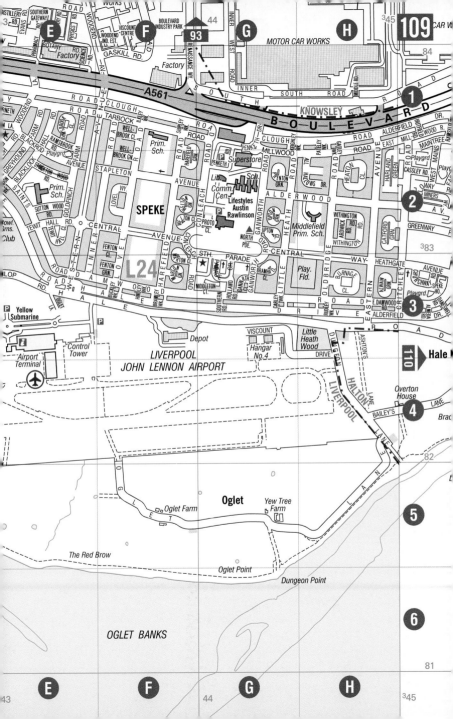

E **F** **95** **48** **G** **H** **111**

Burnt Mill Farm

Midd' Farm

CARR

LANE

POTTER'S

HALEBANK

Heathview RD

AVENUE

BAGULEY

CHURCH

Warehouses

Works

84

Heathview

KENVIEW CL.

Sch.

HALE CT.

HALE BANK T.

30

MERSEY VIEW ROAD

PICKERINGS

HALE ROAD IND. EST.

BROAD

Hale Bank

ROAD

FREDERICK T.

COCK LANE ENDS

Depots

1

Hope Farm

LANE

POTTER'S LA.

ROAD

Shore House

Pickerings Pasture Visitor Centre

Widnes

Little Boar's Wood

GARNETT'S

Pickerings Pasture Local Nature Reserve

LA.

WA8

Keepers Cottage

2

Big Boar's Wood

Ram's

Brook

Sewage Works

³83

iss Green

Marsh Bri.

LANE   HALE   GATE

Hale Gate Farm

3

TOWN

GODS...

BROOK

Hale Duck Decoy

Hale Gate Marsh

112

Decoy Marsh

HALE

Play. Fld.

Parsonage Grn.

4

Manor Farm

WITHIN

82

RIVER MERSEY

Pav.

Church Willow Bed

WAY   WITHIN   WY.

5

Willow Bed

CHURCH

Old Pits

ROAD

6

81

ighthouse

LIGHTHOUSE

E   **F**   **G**   **H**

Hale Head

17   48   49

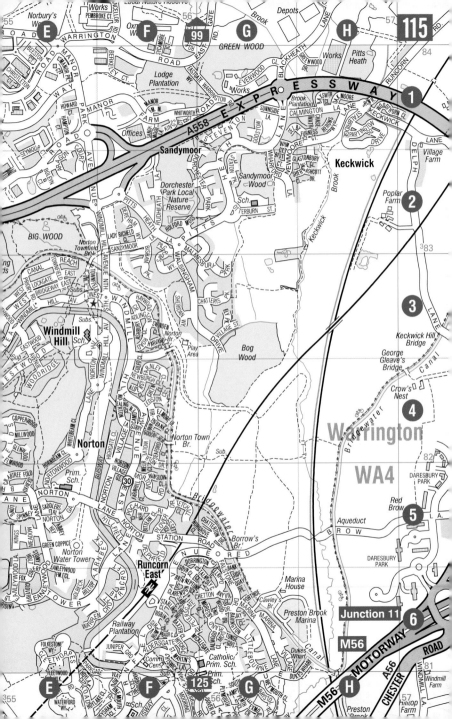

81

1

2

³80

3

4

79

5

6

78

³25

26

A
B
C
D

26
100

GAYTON HOLE
MARINE DR
PARK
WEST

MANNERS ROAD
DAVENPORT LANE
RECTORY
RECTORY CL
RABY CT
VILLAGE
ROSCO
WALLRA
ROAD
THE
HEYWORTH
ROMULUS WAY
KAPWING DR
STRATHAVEN
LANE
BROMILEY CL
STATION ROAD
MEADWAY
PARKTON DRIVE

SEABANK
RIVERBANK CL
HIND

P RIVERBANK

Wirral

CH60

COTTAGE DR WEST
COTTAGE DR
COTTAGE DR EAST

LILLYFIELD
LONG

WOODBURN DR

GAYTON SANDS

RIVER DEE

GAYTON SANDS
NATURE RESERVE

81

HESWALL

E F **101** G H 28 29

Gayton

Play Field

Gayton

CHESTER ROAD A540

Bridges House Farm

New Hall Farm
NEW HALL MANOR

Crows Nest

1

CHESTER HIGH ROAD

2

380

Club House

Gayton Hall

Gayton Wood

HESWALL GOLF COURSE

Lyndale Farm

The Runnell

The Runnell

3

118

Backwood Hall Farm

Backwood Hall

West Point

Leighton Hall Farm

Lone Acres

Ashfield Hall Farm

4

WIRRAL CHESHIRE WEST and CHESTER

The Lodge

LEIGHTON RD.

Leighton House

Neston

Hydestyle House

Leighton Brow

CH64

79

Nursery

Woodcote

Brook House

5

CLAY INDUST

LONGACRE

Household Waste Site

FAIRHOLME AV.

BOATHOUSE LANE

WOOD LANE

BROOK LA.

Windy Knowe

TURNERS VW.

Parkgate

THE PARADE B5135

NORTH HO.

TITHEBARN

Moorings Cl.

Mealor's Weint

Deeside Ct.

Mostyn Sq.

Pine Hey

Paddock Dr.

LEIGHTON ROAD

THE PINE HEY

Leigh Chase

New Heyes

Mill Cft.

6

78

LIVERPOOL RD.

Playg.

Parkgate Prim. Sch.

Sports Ground

Spinney

NESTON

Hall

Earle Cres.

WOOD LANDS

E F **G** H
27 28 STATION ROAD 29

Crkt. Grd

Grenfell Ct.

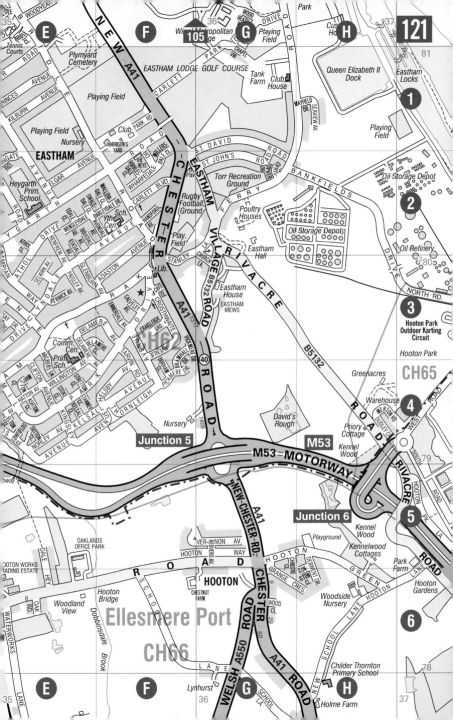

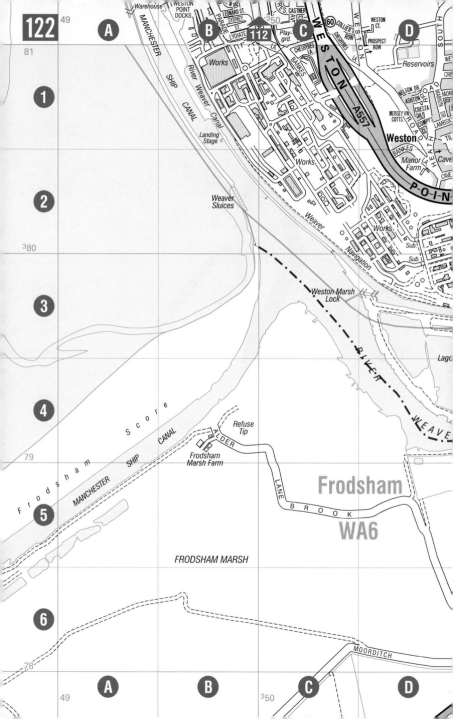

Frodsham

WA6

FRODSHAM MARSH

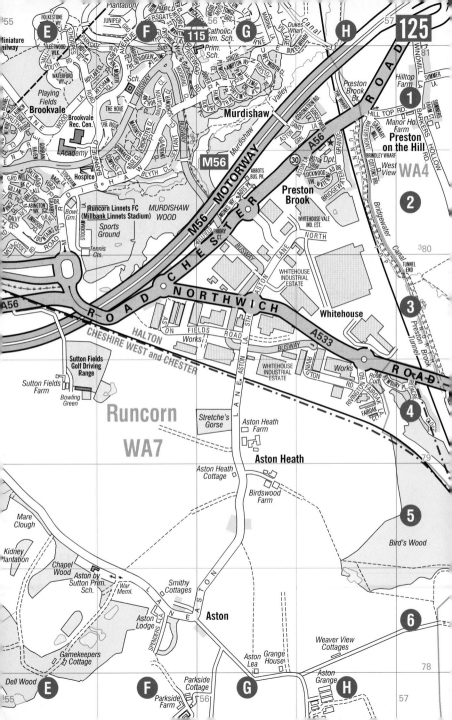

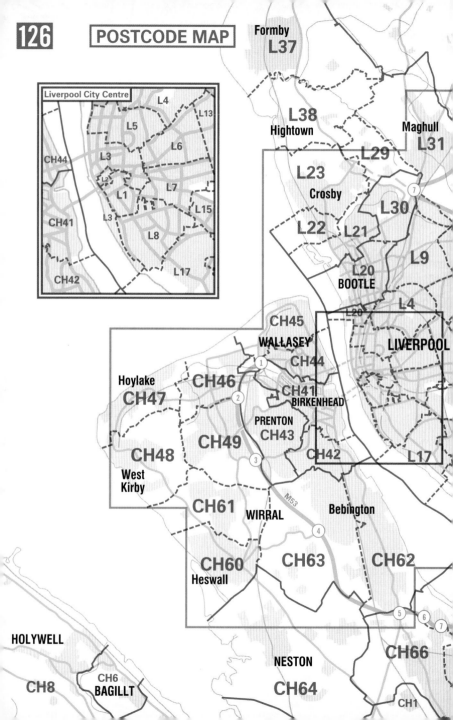

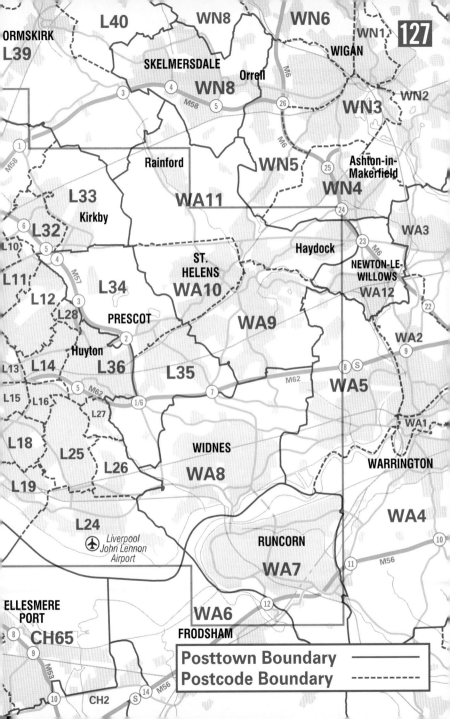

INDEX

Including Streets, Places & Areas, Industrial Estates,
Selected Flats & Walkways, Stations and Selected Places of Interest.

HOW TO USE THIS INDEX

1. Each street name is followed by its Postcode District, then by its Locality abbreviation(s) and then by its map reference;
   e.g. **Abberley Rd.** L25: Hunts X . . . .4E **93** is in the L25 Postcode District and the Hunts Cross Locality and is to be found in
   square 4E on page **93**. The page number is shown in bold type.

2. A strict alphabetical order is followed in which Av., Rd., St., etc. (though abbreviated) are read in full and as part of the street name;
   e.g. **Ashcombe Rd.** appears after **Ash Cl.** but before **Ash Cres.**

3. Streets and a selection of flats and walkways that cannot be shown on the mapping, appear in the index with the thoroughfare to which
   they are connected shown in brackets; e.g. **Acresfield** L13: Liv . . . .5F **55** (off Broad Grn. Rd.)

4. Addresses that are in more than one part are referred to as not continuous.

5. Places and areas are shown in the index in BLUE TYPE and the map reference is to the actual map square in which the town centre or
   area is located and not to the place name shown on the map; e.g. **AINTREE** 6A **12**

6. An example of a selected place of interest is **Halton Castle** 4B **114**

7. An example of a station is **Aigburth Station (Rail)** . . . .3C **90**, also included is **Park & Ride**.
   e.g. **Leasowe (Park & Ride)** 5E **49**

8. Map references for entries that appear on large scale pages **4** & **5** are shown first, with small scale map references shown in brackets;
   e.g. **Bath St.** L3: Liv 2A **4** (5B **52**)

GENERAL ABBREVIATIONS

All. : Alley	**Est.** : Estate	**Pde.** : Parade
App. : Approach	**Fld.** : Field	**Pk.** : Park
Arc. : Arcade	**Flds.** : Fields	**Pas.** : Passage
Av. : Avenue	**Gdn.** : Garden	**Pav.** : Pavilion
Bk. : Back	**Gdns.** : Gardens	**Pl.** : Place
Blvd. : Boulevard	**Ga.** : Gate	**Pct.** : Precinct
Bri. : Bridge	**Gt.** : Great	**Prom.** : Promenade
B'way. : Broadway	**Grn.** : Green	**Res.** : Residential
Bldg. : Building	**Gro.** : Grove	**Ri.** : Rise
Bldgs. : Buildings	**Hgts.** : Heights	**Rd.** : Road
Bungs. : Bungalows	**Ho.** : House	**Shop.** : Shopping
Bus. : Business	**Ind.** : Industrial	**Sth.** : South
C'way. : Causeway	**Info.** : Information	**Sq.** : Square
Cen. : Centre	**Intl.** : International	**Sta.** : Station
Chu. : Church	**La.** : Lane	**St.** : Street
Cl. : Close	**Lit.** : Little	**Ter.** : Terrace
Comn. : Common	**Lwr.** : Lower	**Twr.** : Tower
Cnr. : Corner	**Mnr.** : Manor	**Trad.** : Trading
Cott. : Cottage	**Mans.** : Mansions	**Up.** : Upper
Cotts. : Cottages	**Mkt.** : Market	**Va.** : Vale
Ct. : Court	**Mdw.** : Meadow	**Vw.** : View
Cres. : Crescent	**Mdws.** : Meadows	**Vs.** : Villas
Cft. : Croft	**M.** : Mews	**Vis.** : Visitors
Dr. : Drive	**Mt.** : Mount	**Wlk.** : Walk
E. : East	**Mus.** : Museum	**W.** : West
Ent. : Enterprise	**Nth.** : North	**Yd.** : Yard

LOCALITY ABBREVIATIONS

Aig : **Aigburth**	Caldy : **Caldy**	Garst : **Garston**
Ain : **Aintree**	Cas : **Castlefields**	Garsw : **Garswood**
Aller : **Allerton**	Chil T : **Childer Thornton**	Gate : **Gateacre**
Ash M : **Ashton-in-Makerfield**	Child : **Childwall**	Gras : **Grassendale**
Ast : **Astmoor**	Clau : **Claughton**	Grea : **Greasby**
Aston : **Aston**	Clftn : **Clifton**	Gt San : **Great Sankey**
Augh : **Aughton**	Clock F : **Clock Face**	Hale : **Hale**
Barn : **Barnston**	Coll G : **Collins Green**	Hale B : **Hale Bank**
Beb : **Bebington**	Crank : **Crank**	Halew : **Halewood**
Beech : **Beechwood**	Cron : **Cronton**	Halt : **Halton**
Bic : **Bickerstaffe**	Crosb : **Crosby**	Hay : **Haydock**
Bid : **Bidston**	Crox : **Croxteth**	Hesw : **Heswall**
Bil : **Billinge**	Cuerd : **Cuerdley**	Hghr B : **Higher Bebington**
Birke : **Birkenhead**	Dares : **Daresbury**	Hoot : **Hooton**
Blun : **Blundellsands**	Dutt : **Dutton**	Hoy : **Hoylake**
Bold : **Bold**	East : **Eastham**	Hunts X : **Hunts Cross**
Bold H : **Bold Heath**	Eccl : **Eccleston**	Huy : **Huyton**
Boot : **Bootle**	Eccl P : **Eccleston Park**	Ince B : **Ince Blundell**
Brim : **Brimstage**	Ell P : **Ellesmere Port**	Irby : **Irby**
Broad G : **Broad Green**	Faz : **Fazakerley**	Kirkb : **Kirkby**
Brom : **Bromborough**	Ford : **Ford**	Kirkd : **Kirkdale**
Brook : **Brookvale**	Frank : **Frankby**	Knott A : **Knotty Ash**
Burtw : **Burtonwood**	Frod : **Frodsham**	Know : **Knowsley**

Know I : **Knowsley Industrial Park**
Know P : **Knowsley Park**
Leas : **Leasowe**
Lith : **Litherland**
Lit C : **Little Crosby**
Liv : **Liverpool**
Lyd : **Lydiate**
Mag : **Maghull**
Manor P : **Manor Park**
Mell : **Melling**
Meols : **Meols**
Moore : **Moore**
More : **Moreton**
Moss H : **Mossley Hill**
Murd : **Murdishaw**
Nest : **Neston**
N'ley : **Netherley**
N'ton : **Netherton**
New B : **New Brighton**
New F : **New Ferry**
Newt W : **Newton-le-Willows**
Noct : **Noctorum**
Norr G : **Norris Green**
Nort : **Norton**
Oxton : **Oxton**

Pal F : **Palace Fields**
Park : **Parkgate**
Penk : **Penketh**
Pens : **Pensby**
Port S : **Port Sunlight**
Pren : **Prenton**
Presc : **Prescot**
Pres B : **Preston Brook**
Pres H : **Preston on the Hill**
Raby : **Raby**
Raby M : **Raby Mere**
Rainf : **Rainford**
Rainh : **Rainhill**
Roby : **Roby**
Rock F : **Rock Ferry**
Run : **Runcorn**
St H : **St Helens**
Sea : **Seaforth**
Seft : **Sefton**
Sim : **Simonswood**
Speke : **Speke**
Spit : **Spital**
Stockb V : **Stockbridge Village**
Store : **Storeton**
Sut L : **Sutton Leach**

Sut M : **Sutton Manor**
Sut W : **Sutton Weaver**
Tar G : **Tarbock Green**
Thing : **Thingwall**
Thorn : **Thornton**
Thorn H : **Thornton Hough**
Thurs : **Thurstaston**
Tran : **Tranmere**
Upton : **Upton**
Wall : **Wallasey**
Walt : **Walton**
Water : **Waterloo**
Wav : **Wavertree**
W Der : **West Derby**
W Kir : **West Kirby**
Westb : **Westbrook**
West : **Weston**
West P : **Weston Point**
Whis : **Whiston**
Wid : **Widnes**
Will : **Willaston**
Windle : **Windle**
Wind H : **Windmill Hill**
Woodc : **Woodchurch**
Woolt : **Woolton**

---

20 Forthlin Road
(Childhood Home of Paul McCartney)
. . . . .2G **91**

A

Abacus Rd. L13: Liv 3E **55**
Abberley Cl. WA10: St H 2D **42**
Abberley Rd. L25: Hunts X 4H **93**
Abberton Pk. L30: N'ton 4G **11**
Abbey Cl. CH41: Birke 4H **69**
  L33: Kirkb 1B **24**
  WA8: Wid 3A **96**
Abbey Ct. L25: Woolt 1D **92**
Abbeyfield Dr. L12: Crox 3H **37**
Abbeygate Apartments L15: Wav . .2D **72**
Abbey Hey WA7: Nort 5E **115**
Abbey M. L8: Liv 4H **71**
Abbeymill Ct. L15: Wav 2E **73**
Abbey Rd. CH48: W Kir 1B **82**
  L6: Liv 1A **54**
  WA8: Wid 3H **95**
  WA10: St H 4B **28**
  WA11: Hay 4G **31**
Abbeystead Av. L30: N'ton 2G **21**
Abbeystead Rd. L15: Wav 1F **73**
Abbey St. CH41: Birke 4H **69**
Abbeyvale Dr. L25: Gate 3E **75**
Abbey Vw. L16: Child 2A **74**
Abbeyway Nth. WA11: Hay 4H **31**
Abbeyway Sth. WA11: Hay 5H **31**
Abbeywood Gro. L35: Whis 5F **59**
Abbot Cl. CH43: Bid 3G **67**
Abbotsbury Way L12: Crox 2A **38**
Abbots Bus. Pk. WA7: Pres B 2G **125**
Abbots Dr. CH63: Beb 6H **87**
Abbotsfield Rd. WA9: Bold, St H 1A **62**
  (not continuous)
Abbotsfield Rd. Ind. Est.
  WA9: St H 1A **62**
Abbotsford Ct. L23: Blun 6E **9**
Abbotsford Gdns. L23: Crosb 6E **9**
Abbotsford Rd. L11: Norr G 3D **36**
  L23: Blun 6E **9**
Abbotsford St. CH44: Wall 5G **51**
Abbots Hall Av. WA9: Clock F 4H **61**
Abbots Pk. WA7: Pres B 2G **125**
Abbots Quay CH41: Birke 3A **70**
Abbots Way CH48: W Kir 6C **64**
  CH64: Nest 6A **118**
Abbott Dr. L20: Boot 6E **21**
Abbotts Cl. L18: Moss H 6F **73**
  WA7: Run 5E **113**

Abbottsleay Av. L18: Moss H 6F **73**
Abdale Rd. L11: Norr G 2D **36**
Abercrombie Rd. L33: Know I 4D **24**
Abercromby Sq. L7: Liv 1F **71**
Aberdale Rd. L13: Liv 4F **55**
Aberdeen St. CH41: Birke 2E **69**
Aberford Av. CH45: Wall 2A **50**
Abergele Rd. L13: Liv 5D **54**
Aber St. L6: Liv 4G **53**
Abingdon Gro. L4: Walt 3A **36**
  L26: Halew 2A **94**
Abingdon Rd. CH49: Grea 6H **65**
  L4: Walt 3A **36**
Abington Wlk. WA7: Brook 2E **125**
Abney Cl. L7: Liv 1H **71**
Aboyne Cl. L9: Walt 1G **35**
Abram St. L5: Liv 2E **53**
Abyssinia Cl. L15: Wav 2C **72**
Acacia Av. L36: Huy 6F **57**
  WA8: Wid 6F **79**
Acacia Cl. CH49: Grea 1A **84**
  CH48: W Kir 1A **82**
  L9: Ain 5H **21**
  WA7: Run 5G **113**
Acacia Gro. CH44: Wall 5G **51**
  CH42: Tran 5G **69**
  L9: Ain 6G **55**
  WA7: Eccl 1G **41**
Acacia St. WA12: Newt W 1H **45**
Academy Bus. Pk. L33: Know I 2D **24**
Acanthus Rd. L13: Liv 3E **55**
Access Rd. L12: W Der 6H **37**
Acer Leigh L17: Aig 1B **90**
Acheson Rd. L13: Liv 1C **54**
Achilles Ct. WA7: Cas 3C **114**
Ackers Hall Av. L14: Knott A 3B **56**
Ackers La. L23: Lit C 2E **9**
  WA10: St H 1A **42**
Ackers Rd. CH49: Woodc 1G **85**
Ackers St. L34: Presc 1D **58**
Acland Rd. CH44: Wall 3D **50**
Aconbury Cl. L11: Norr G 2D **36**
Aconbury Pl. L11: Norr G 2D **36**
Acorn Bus. Cen. L33: Know I 1D **24**
Acorn Cl. CH63: Hghr B 5F **87**
  WA9: Clock F 3G **61**
Acorn Ct. L8: Liv 3F **71**
Acornfield Cl. L33: Know I 1E **25**
Acornfield Plantation Local Nature Reserve
  . . . . .3F **25**
Acornfield Rd. L33: Know I 2F **25**
Acorn Venture 5F **15**
Acrefield Cl. CH42: Tran 2D **86**
Acrefield Pk. L25: Woolt 6C **74**
Acrefield Rd. CH42: Tran 2D **86**
  L25: Woolt 6C **74**
  WA8: Wid 2H **95**
Acre Grn. L26: Halew 5A **94**

Acre La. CH60: Hesw 4G **101**
  CH62: Brom 5C **104**
  CH63: Brom 6C **104**
Acres Cl. L25: Gate 2C **74**
Acresfield L13: Liv 5F **55**
  (off Broad Grn. Rd.)
Acresgate Ct. L25: Gate 4C **74**
Acres Rd. CH47: Meols 2F **65**
  CH63: Beb 5H **87**
Acreville Rd. CH63: Beb 6H **87**
Acton Cl. WA11: Hay 5E **31**
Acton Gro. L6: Liv 1A **54**
Acton La. CH46: More 2A **66**
Acton Rake L30: N'ton 4D **10**
  (off Higher End Pk.)
Acton Rd. CH42: Rock F 2A **88**
  L32: Kirkb 1G **23**
  WA5: Burtw 1G **63**
Acton Way L7: Liv 1A **72**
Acuba Gro. CH42: Tran 5G **69**
Acuba Rd. L15: Wav 6G **55**
Adair Pl. L13: Liv 6C **36**
Adair Rd. L13: Liv 6C **36**
Adam Cl. L19: Garst 6G **91**
Adamson Ho. WA7: Run 2C **112**
Adamson St. L7: Liv 5B **54**
Adam St. L5: Liv 1F **53**
Adaston Av. CH62: East 3F **121**
Adcote Cl. L14: Knott A 4B **56**
Adcote Rd. L14: Knott A 4B **56**
Addenbrook Cl. CH43: Bid 3G **67**
Addenbrooke Dr. L24: Speke 5D **92**
Adderley Cl. WA7: Run 4G **113**
Adderley St. L7: Liv 5H **53**
Addingham Av. WA8: Wid 4A **96**
Addingham Rd.
  L18: Moss H 4F **73**
Addington St. CH44: Wall 4F **51**
Addison Cl. L32: Kirkb 3H **23**
Addison Sq. WA8: Wid 2E **97**
Addison St. L3: Liv 1E **5** (4D **52**)
  L20: Boot 6A **20**
Addison Way L3: Liv 1E **5** (4D **52**)
Adelaide Av. WA9: St H 6C **42**
Adelaide Ct. WA8: Wid 4E **97**
Adelaide Pl. L5: Liv 3E **53**
Adelaide Rd. CH42: Tran 5E **69**
  L7: Liv 5H **53**
  (not continuous)
  L21: Sea 4H **19**
Adelaide St. CH44: Wall 4D **50**
Adelaide Ter. L22: Water 2E **19**
Adela Rd. WA7: Nort 3D **112**
Adele Thompson Dr. L8: Liv 2G **71**
Adelphi St. CH41: Birke 3G **69**
Adkins St. L5: Liv 1G **53**
Adlam Cres. L9: Faz 4C **22**

Adlam Rd. L9: Faz 4C 22
   L10: Faz 4C 22
Adler Way L3: Liv 6F 71
Adlington Ho. L3: Liv 1E 5
Adlington Rd. WA7: Wind H 3F 115
Adlington St. L3: Liv 1E 5
Admin Rd. L33: Know I 3E 25
Admiral Gro. L8: Liv 4G 71
   (off High Pk. St.)
Admirals Quay L23: Blun 5C 8
Admiral St. L8: Liv 4G 71
Admiral Way L30: Boot 3E 21
Adrian's Way L32: Kirkb 1A 24
Adshead Rd. L13: Liv 6C 36
Adswood Rd. L36: Huy 4G 57
Aerial Extreme
   Knowsley 6B 40
Aerodrome, The L24: Speke 1A 108
Africander Rd. WA11: St H 3E 29
Afton WA8: Wid 1G 95
Agar Rd. L11: Norr G 6D 36
Agate St. L5: Liv 2G 53
Agincourt Rd. L12: W Der 2G 55
Agnes Gro. CH44: Wall 2E 51
Agnes Jones Ho. L8: Liv 1F 71
Agnes Rd. CH42: Tran 6G 69
   L23: Blun 6E 9
Agnes St. WA9: Clock F 4G 61
Agnes Way L7: Liv 6H 53
Agulnek Ct. L18: Moss H 6D 72
Aiden Long Gro. L34: Know P 1G 57
AIGBURTH .3C 90
Aigburth Dr. L17: Aig 4A 72
Aigburth Gro. CH46: More 1B 66
Aigburth Hall Av. L19: Aig 3D 90
Aigburth Hall Rd. L19: Aig 3E 91
Aigburth Ho. L17: Aig 6C 72
Aigburth Rd. L17: Aig 5H 71
   L19: Aig, Gras 2C 90
Aigburth Station (Rail) 3C 90
Aigburth St. L7: Liv 1H 71
AIGBURTH VALE 6C 72
Aigburth Va. L17: Aig 4A 72
   (not continuous)
   L18: Moss H 6C 72
Ailsa Rd. CH45: Wall 2C 50
Ainley St. WA7: Brook 2C 124
Ainsdale Cl. CH61: Thing 6E 85
   CH63: Brom 2C 120
   L10: Faz 3D 22
   WA5: Penk 5H 81
Ainsdale Rd. L20: Boot 6D 20
Ainsworth Av. CH46: More 2A 66
Ainsworth La. L34: Know 5D 24
Ainsworth Rd. WA10: St H 6B 28
Ainsworth St. L3: Liv 4H 5 (6E 53)
AINTREE 6A 12
Aintree Cl. CH46: Leas 4D 48
Aintree Ct. L10: Ain 6A 12
Aintree Golf Course 2B 22
Aintree La. L10: Ain 6A 12
   L10: Faz 2D 22
Aintree Motor Circuit 3B 22
Aintree Racecourse 2A 22
Aintree Racecourse Retail & Business Pk.
   L9: Ain 2H 21
Aintree Rd. L9: Ain 5B 22
   L20: Boot 1D 34
Aintree Station (Rail) 3H 21
Aintree Visitor Cen. &
   Grand National Experience 2H 21
Aintree Way L9: Ain 1A 22
Airdale Cl. CH43: Bid 3G 67
Airdale Rd. L15: Wav 3D 72
Airdrie Cl. CH62: East 4D 120
Aire WA8: Wid 1H 95
Airedale Cl. WA5: Gt San 2H 81
Airegate L31: Mag 5A 6
Airlie Gro. L13: Liv 1B 54
Airlie Rd. CH47: Hoy 3B 64
Aisthorpe Gro. L31: Mag 2B 12
Akbar, The CH60: Hesw 3A 100
Akenside St. L20: Boot 5A 20

Akenside St. L20: Boot 5A 20
Alabama Way CH41: Birke 3H 69
Alamein Rd. L36: Huy 3F 57
Alan's Way L33: Kirkb 4A 14
Alaska M. WA5: Gt San 2H 81
Alastair Cres. CH43: Pren 2B 86
Alban Rd. L16: Child 1H 73
Albany, The L3: Liv 3C 4
Albany Av. L34: Eccl P 6F 41
Albany Rd. CH42: Rock F 1G 87
   L7: Liv 5G 53
   L9: Ain 4H 21
   L13: Liv 4A 54
   L34: Presc 1E 59
Albany Ter. WA7: Run 3E 113
Albemarle Rd. CH44: Wall 4F 51
Alberta Gro. L34: Presc 2H 57
Albert Ct. WA8: Wid 6F 97
   (off Albert Rd.)
Albert Dock L3: Liv 6C 4 (1C 70)
Albert Dock Vis. Cen. 1C 70
Albert Dr. L9: Walt 5F 21
   WA5: Gt San 3F 81
Albert Edward Rd. L7: Liv 5G 53
   (not continuous)
Albert Gro. L15: Wav 1E 73
   L23: Crosb 6D 8
Albert Pk. L17: Aig 4H 71
Albert Rd. CH42: Tran 5E 69
   CH47: Hoy 3B 64
   CH48: W Kir 1A 82
   L13: Liv 1B 54
   L22: Water 2F 19
   WA8: Wid 3F 97
Albert Row WA6: Frod 6F 123
Albert Schweitzer Av.
   L30: N'ton 6F 11
Albert Sq. WA8: Wid 3F 97
Albert St. CH45: New B 4E 33
   L7: Liv 6G 53
   WA7: Run 3E 113
   WA10: St H 6E 29
Albert Ter. WA5: Coll G 4G 45
Albion Pl. CH45: New B 5D 32
Albion St. CH41: Birke 3H 69
   (not continuous)
   CH45: New B 5C 32
   L5: Liv 1E 53
   WA10: St H 2C 42
   (not continuous)
Albourne Rd. L32: Kirkb 3C 24
Albright Rd. WA8: Wid 5F 95
Albury Cl. L12: Crox 3B 38
   WA11: Hay 4E 31
Albury Rd. L32: Kirkb 4B 24
Alcester Rd. L12: W Der 1G 55
Alchemy Way L33: Know I 4D 24
Alcock St. WA7: Run 2E 113
Aldams Gro. L4: Kirkd 4E 35
Aldbourne Av. L25: Woolt 4A 74
Aldbourne Cl. L25: Woolt 5A 74
Alder Av. L36: Huy 1A 76
   WA8: Wid 6E 79
Alderbank Rd. WA5: Gt San 3H 81
Alder Cl. L34: Presc 1F 59
Alder Cres. L32: Kirkb 6H 13
Alderfield Dr. L24: Speke 1H 109
Alder Gro. L22: Water 1F 19
Alder Hey Rd. WA10: St H 2A 42
Alder La. L34: Know 2D 38
   (not continuous)
   WA5: Burtw 6H 45
   WA6: Frod 4B 122
   WA8: Cron 5F 77
Alderley Av. CH41: Birke 2B 68
Alderley Rd. CH44: Wall 4D 50
   CH47: Hoy 1C 64
Alderman Rd. L24: Speke 5E 93
Alderney Rd. L5: Liv 1C 52
Alder Rd. CH63: Hghr B 1F 103
   L12: W Der 4B 36
   L34: Presc 1F 59
Aldersey Cl. WA7: Wind H 4F 115
Aldersey St. L3: Liv 4D 52

Aldersgate CH42: Rock F 1H 87
Aldersgate Av. WA7: Murd 6F 115
Aldersgate Dr. L26: Halew 5A 94
Alderson Rd. L15: Wav 2B 72
Alderton Cl. L26: Halew 4A 94
Alderton Dr. WN4: Ash M 1H 31
Alderville Rd. L4: Walt 3A 36
Alderwood Av. L24: Speke 2G 109
Alderwood Ct. WA8: Wid 5C 78
Alderwood Lodge L24: Speke 2A 110
   (off East Mains)
Aldford Cl. CH43: Oxton 1A 86
   CH63: Brom 1B 120
Aldford Rd. L32: Kirkb 4A 24
Aldridge Cl. L12: Crox 2A 38
Aldridge Dr. WA5: Burtw 6H 45
Aldrins La. L30: N'ton 5F 11
Aldwark Rd. L14: Knott A 3C 56
Aldwych Rd. L12: W Der 1G 55
Aldykes L31: Mag 1C 12
Alexander Ct. CH61: Pens 2C 100
   L31: Lyd 4C 6
   WA8: Wid 3B 96
Alexander Fleming Av. L30: N'ton . . .5F 11
Alexander Grn. L36: Huy 3G 57
Alexander Ho. L21: Sea 4H 19
   L34: Presc 6D 40
   (off Rio Ct.)
Alexander Wlk. L4: Walt 5F 35
   (off Florence St.)
Alexander Way L8: Liv 5F 71
   (off Park Hill Rd.)
Alexander Wharf L31: Mag 6B 6
   (off Damfield La.)
Alexandra Cl. L6: Liv 4H 53
Alexandra Ct. CH45: New B 5C 32
   (off Alexandra Rd.)
   L23: Crosb 5F 9
   WA9: St H 5B 42
   (off Carnarvon St.)
Alexandra Dr. CH42: Rock F 2G 87
   L17: Aig 5H 71
   L20: Boot 5E 21
   WA10: St H 4B 42
   (not continuous)
Alexandra Grn. L17: Aig 5H 71
Alexandra Gro. L26: Halew 5H 93
   WA7: Run 4G 113
Alexandra Ho. L17: Aig 5H 71
Alexandra Ind. Est. WA8: Wid 4D 96
Alexandra M. WA6: Frod 6F 123
Alexandra Mt. L21: Lith 3B 20
Alexandra Pk. L17: Aig 6H 71
Alexandra Rd. CH43: Oxton 4E 69
   CH45: New B 5C 32
   CH48: W Kir 2A 82
   L7: Liv 1A 72
   L13: Liv 5E 55
   L19: Garst 4G 91
   L22: Water 3G 19
   L23: Crosb 5F 9
Alexandra St. WA8: Wid 4E 97
   WA10: St H 4B 42
Alexandra Ter. L8: Liv 2F 71
   (off Princes Rd.)
Alexandra Vs. L21: Lith 3B 20
   (off Alexandra Mt.)
Alex Cl. L8: Liv 3F 71
Alfonso Rd. L4: Kirkd 5D 34
Alford Av. WA9: Sut M 3F 61
Alforde St. WA8: Wid 4E 97
   (not continuous)
Alfred St. L7: Liv 5C 54
Alfred Cl. WA8: Wid 3F 97
Alfred M. L1: Liv 2E 71
Alfred Rd. CH43: Oxton 4E 69
   CH44: Wall 6G 51
   WA11: Hay 4H 31
Alfred Stocks Ct. L8: Liv 6G 71
   (off Turner Cl.)
Alfred St. L15: Wav 1B 72
   WA8: Wid 3F 97
   WA10: St H 1F 43
   WA11: Rainf 2F 17

Alfriston Rd. L12: W Der 1G 55
Algernon St. WA7: Run 2D 112
Alice Ct. WA8: Wid 1E 113
Alice St. WA9: St H 5A 44
Alicia Wlk. L10: Faz 4F 23
Alison Av. CH42: Rock F 6H 69
Alison Pl. L13: Liv 6C 36
Alison Rd. L13: Liv 6C 36
Alistair Dr. CH63: Brom 2C 120
Allangate Cl. CH49: Grea 1A 84
Allangate Rd. L19: Gras 3F 91
Allan Rd. WA11: St H 4G 29
Allanson St. WA9: St H 2H 43
Allcot Av. CH42: Tran 1F 87
Allenby Av. L23: Crosb 1H 19
Allenby Sq. L13: Liv 5E 55
Allendale WA7: Pal F 1D 124
Allendale Av. L9: Ain 4H 21
   L35: Rainh 4B 60
Allengate L23: Crosb 4G 9
Allen Rd. WA7: West P 6B 112
Allerford Rd. L12: W Der 6G 37
ALLERTON .3H 91
Allerton Beeches
   L18: Moss H 6G 73
Allerton Dr. L18: Moss H 5F 73
Allerton Gro. CH42: Tran 6G 69
Allerton Park Golf Course 1A 92
Allerton Rd. CH42: Tran 6F 69
   CH45: Wall 1C 50
   L18: Aller, Moss H 4E 73
   L25: Woolt 2B 92
   WA8: Wid 2F 97
Allesley Rd. L14: Knott A 2B 56
Alleyne Rd. L4: Walt 5B 36
All Hallows Dr. L24: Speke 2H 109
Allington St. L17: Aig 6H 71
Allinsons Ct. L21: Lith 3B 20
Allonby Cl. CH43: Noct 5A 68
Allport La. CH62: Brom 5D 104
   (not continuous)
Allport La. Pct. CH62: Brom 4D 104
Allport Rd. CH62: Brom 1C 120
   CH63: Brom 1C 120
Allports, The CH62: Brom 6D 104
All Saints Cl. L30: N'ton 6E 11
All Saints Ct. WA11: Rainf 4G 17
All Saints Rd. L24: Speke 2E 109
Allysum Ct. WA7: Beech 3B 124
Alma Cl. L10: Faz 4F 23
Almacs Cl. L23: Blun 6D 8
Alman Ct. L17: Aig 6H 71
   (off Bryanston Rd.)
Alma Pl. WA9: St H 3G 43
Alma Rd. L17: Aig 3C 90
Alma St. CH41: Birke 3G 69
   CH62: New F 4A 88
   WA9: St H 3G 43
Alma Ter. L15: Wav 1D 72
   (off Sandown La.)
Almeda Rd. L24: Speke 3A 110
Almond Av. L30: N'ton 6C 10
   WA7: Run 5G 113
Almond Cl. L26: Halew 4G 93
   WA11: Hay 6B 30
Almond Ct. L19: Garst 6A 92
Almond Dr. WA5: Burtw 1H 63
Almond Gro. WA8: Wid 3B 96
Almond Pl. CH46: More 1D 66
Almonds, The L26: Halew 4G 93
Almond's Grn. L12: W Der 5E 37
Almond's Gro. L12: W Der 5E 37
Almond's Pk. L12: W Der 5E 37
Almonds Turn L30: N'ton 5D 10
Almond Tree Cl. L24: Hale 4E 111
Almond Way CH49: Grea 1A 84
Alness Dr. L35: Rainh 5B 60
Alnwick Dr. CH46: More 1H 65
Aloeswood Cl. L6: Liv 2H 53
Alpass Rd. L17: Aig 6H 71
Alpha Ct. CH45: Wall 2A 50
Alpha Dr. CH42: Rock F 2A 88
Alpha St. L21: Lith 6B 20
Alpine Cl. WA10: St H 1A 42

Alresford Rd. L19: Aig 3D 90
Alroy Rd. L4: Walt 6G 35
Alscot Av. L10: Faz 4E 23
Alscot Cl. L31: Mag 1B 12
Alston Cl. CH62: Brom 4C 104
Alstonfield Rd. L14: Knott A 3C 56
Alston M. WA10: St H 6H 41
Alston Rd. L17: Aig 3C 90
Alt Av. WA8: Wid 1H 95
Alt Av. L31: Mag 2A 12
Altbridge Pk. L11: Crox 2G 37
   (not continuous)
Altbridge Rd. L36: Huy 2F 57
Altcar Av. L15: Wav 2B 72
Altcar Dr. CH46: More 2B 66
Altcar Rd. L20: Boot 6C 20
Altcross Rd. L11: Crox 1G 37
Altcross Way L11: Crox 1G 37
Altfield Rd. L14: Knott A 6B 38
Altfinch Cl. L14: Knott A 6C 38
Altham Rd. L11: Norr G 6D 36
Althorp St. L8: Liv 6F 71
Altmoor Rd. L36: Huy 1F 57
Alton Av. L21: Lith 2A 20
Alton Rd. CH43: Oxton 4C 68
   L6: Liv 2B 54
Alt Rd. L20: Boot 6C 20
   L36: Huy .4G 57
Alt Side Ct. L10: Faz 4F 23
Alt St. L8: Liv 2H 71
Altway L10: Ain 6A 12
Altway Ct. L10: Ain 6A 12
   (off Altway)
Alundale Ct. L20: Boot 2C 34
   (off Clairville Cl.)
Alundale Rd. L12: W Der 2A 56
Alvanley Grn. L32: Kirkb 1G 23
Alvanley Pl. CH43: Oxton 3E 69
Alvanley Rd. L12: W Der 2G 55
   L32: Kirkb 1G 23
Alva Rd. L35: Rainh 5B 60
Alvega Cl. CH62: New F 4C 88
Alverstone Av. CH41: Birke 2B 68
Alverstone Cl. WA5: Gt San 2E 81
Alverstone Rd. CH44: Wall 4F 51
   L18: Moss H 4D 72
Alverton Cl. WA8: Wid 3B 96
Alvina La. L4: Walt 6E 35
   L33: Kirkb 4C 14
Alwain Grn. L24: Speke 3H 109
Alwen St. CH41: Birke 6B 50
Alwyn Av. L21: Lith 2B 20
Alwyn Cl. L17: Aig 6H 71
Alwyn Gdns. CH46: More 1D 66
Alwyn St. L17: Aig 6H 71
Amanda Av. L10: Faz 4F 23
   L35: Rainh 2H 59
Amanda Way L31: Mell 5F 13
Amaury Cl. L23: Thorn 4B 10
Amaury Rd. L23: Thorn 4B 10
Ambassador Dr. L26: Halew 2A 94
Ambergate Cl. WA9: St H 6H 43
Ambergate Rd. L19: Gras 4F 91
Amberley Av. CH46: More 2A 66
Amberley Cl. CH46: More 2A 66
   L6: Liv 6B 36
Amberley St. L8: Liv 2G 71
Amber Way L14: Knott A 6C 38
Ambleside Av. CH46: More 1B 66
Ambleside Cl. CH61: Thing 5E 85
   CH62: Brom 6E 105
   WA7: Beech 2A 124
Ambleside Dr. L33: Kirkb 5H 13
Ambleside Pl. WA11: St H 2F 29
Ambleside Rd. L18: Aller 2H 91
   L31: Mag 5C 6
Amelia Cl. L6: Liv 4F 53
   WA8: Wid 5F 79
Amersham Rd. L4: Walt 3A 36
   (not continuous)
Amery Gro. CH42: Tran 1E 87
Amethyst Cl. L6: Liv 3H 53
   L21: Lith 3C 20
Amherst Rd. L17: Aig 1A 90

Amidian Ct. CH44: Wall 4D 50
   (off Poulton Rd.)
Amity St. L8: Liv 4F 71
Amos Av. L21: Lith 3C 20
Ampleforth Cl. L32: Kirkb 2G 23
Ampthill Rd. L17: Aig 1A 90
Ampulla Rd. L11: Crox 2G 37
Amy Wlk. L10: Faz 4F 23
Ancaster Rd. L17: Aig 1A 90
Ancholme Rd. L35: Whis 1G 59
Anchorage, The L3: Liv 3D 70
Anchorage La. L18: Moss H 6C 72
Anchor Cl. WA7: Murd 1F 125
Anchor Courtyard L3: Liv 6C 4
Ancient Mdws. L9: Ain 4H 21
Ancroft Rd. L14: Knott A 4C 56
Ancrum Rd. L33: Kirkb 3H 13
Anders Dr. L33: Kirkb 4C 14
Anderson Cl. CH61: Irby 5E 85
   L35: Rainh 6B 60
Anderson Cl. CH62: Brom 1D 120
Anderson Rd. L21: Lith 2D 20
Anderson St. L5: Liv 1E 53
   (not continuous)
Anderson Trad. Est. WA8: Wid 5E 97
   (off Croft St.)
Anderson Way L21: Lith 2D 20
Anderton Ter. L36: Roby 5E 57
Andover Rd. WA11: Hay 6A 30
Andover Way L25: Hunts X 3F 93
Andrew Av. L31: Mell 6F 13
Andrew Cl. WA8: Wid 3A 96
Andrew Ho. L8: Liv 2F 71
   (off Birley Cl.)
Andrew St. L4: Walt 4F 35
Andrew's Wlk. CH60: Hesw 5F 101
Andromeda Way WA9: Bold 6D 44
Anemone Way WA9: Bold 6C 44
ANFIELD 6G 35
Anfield 6G 35
Anfield Ct. L4: Walt 6G 35
Anfield Crematorium L4: Walt 5H 35
Anfield Rd. L4: Walt 6F 35
Angela St. L7: Liv 1H 71
Angelica Dr. L11: Norr G 3D 36
Angelica Rd. L32: Kirkb 5B 14
Angers La. L31: Mell 3F 13
Anglesea Rd. L9: Walt 2G 35
Anglesea Way L8: Liv 5F 71
Anglesey Rd. CH44: Wall 2D 50
   CH48: W Kir 5A 64
Anglezark Cl. L7: Liv 5H 53
Anglia Way L25: Hunts X 3E 93
Anglican Cl. L8: Liv 2E 71
   (off Blair St.)
Anglo Cl. L9: Ain 3A 22
Angus Rd. CH63: Brom 1C 120
   L11: Norr G 5D 36
Annandale Cl. L33: Kirkb 3H 13
Ann Conway Ho. L15: Wav 2C 72
   (off Garmoyle Cl.)
Anne Gro. WA9: St H 6G 43
Annerley St. L7: Liv 1A 72
Annesley Rd. CH44: Wall 4E 51
   L17: Aig .1A 90
Anne St. WA9: Clock F 4H 61
Annie Rd. L20: Boot 5D 20
Ann St. WA7: Run 2F 113
Ann St. W. WA8: Wid 4F 97
Anscot Av. CH63: Beb 5H 87
Ansdell Dr. WA10: Eccl 6H 27
Ansdell Rd. WA8: Wid 1F 97
Ansdell Vs. Rd. L35: Rainh 3G 60
Anson St. L3: Liv 3H 5 (5F 53)
Anstey Cl. CH46: More 6H 47
Anstey Rd. L13: Liv 4F 55
Ansty Cl. WA11: St H 6H 29
Anthony's Way CH60: Hesw 6E 101
Anthorn Cl. CH43: Noct 5H 67
Antonio St. L20: Boot 4D 34
Antons Cl. L26: Halew 5H 93
Antons Ct. L26: Halew 5A 94
Antons Rd. CH61: Pens 6E 85
   L26: Halew 5H 93

Antrim Cl. WA11: Hay 5E 31
Antrim St. L13: Liv 6C 36
Anvil Cl. L20: Boot 1B 34
Anzacs, The CH62: Port S 5C 88
Anzio Rd. L36: Huy 3F 57
Apex Ct. CH62: Brom 4E 105
Apollo Ct. CH44: Wall 2F 51
(off Rudgrave Sq.)
Apollo Cres. L33: Kirkb 5A 14
Apollo Way L6: Liv 2H 53
L30: N'ton 5F 11
Apostles Way L33: Kirkb 4H 13
Appin Rd. CH41: Birke 4G 69
Appleby Cl. WA8: Wid 3A 96
Appleby Dr. L30: N'ton 6C 10
Appleby Grn. L12: W Der 1H 55
Appleby Gro. CH62: Brom 1D 120
Appleby Lawn L27: N'ley 5A 76
Appleby Rd. L33: Kirkb 5A 14
Appleby Wlk. L27: N'ley 5A 76
WA8: Wid 3A 96
Applecorn Cl. WA9: Sut L 1H 61
Apple Ct. L6: Liv 4H 53
(off Coleridge St.)
Appledore Ct. L24: Speke 1D 108
Appledore Gro. WA9: Sut L 3G 61
Applegarth CH46: More 3A 66
APPLETON 1F 97
Appleton Dr. CH49: Grea 6C 66
Appleton Rd. L4: Walt 4H 35
L21: Lith .2A 20
L32: Kirkb 5A 14
WA8: Wid 2F 97
WA9: St H 3G 43
Appleton St. WA8: Wid 5F 97
Appleton Village WA8: Wid 2E 97
Apple Tree Cl. L24: Hale 4E 111
L28: Stockb V 5D 38
Appletree Cl. L18: Aller 2G 91
Applewood Ct. L26: Halew 2A 94
Applewood Gro. L26: Halew 2A 94
April Gro. L6: Liv 2B 54
April Ri. L30: N'ton 6E 11
Apsley Av. CH45: Wall 1D 50
Apsley Brow L31: Mag 6A 6
Apsley Gro. CH63: Beb 5A 88
Apsley Rd. CH62: New F 3B 88
L12: W Der 1G 55
Aquarius Cl. L14: Knott A 3C 56
Arabis Gdns. WA9: Bold 6D 44
Aragon Cl. L31: Mag 4D 6
Aragon Ct. WA7: Manor P 2E 115
Aran Cl. L24: Hale 3D 110
Arborn Dr. CH49: Upton 3E 67
Arbour Ct. L33: Know I 1D 24
Arbour La. L33: Know I 2C 24
Arbury Av. WA11: St H 5H 29
Arcadia Av. L31: Lyd 4C 6
Archbishop Warlock Ct. L3: Liv 3C 52
Archbrook M. L13: Liv 2C 54
(off Sutton St.)
Archer Cl. L4: Kirkd 6E 35
Archerfield Rd. L18: Aller 1F 91
Archer Gro. WA9: St H 1A 44
Archers Ct. CH49: Woodc 1E 85
(off Childwall Grn.)
Archers Cft. CH62: Brom 4D 104
Archers Fold L31: Mell 5F 13
Archers Grn. CH62: East 3E 121
Archer St. L4: Kirkd 6E 35
Archers Way CH49: Woodc 1E 85
Arch La. WN4: Garsw 1D 30
Arch Vw. Cres. L1: Liv 1E 71
Archway Rd. L36: Huy 5F 57
Arctic Rd. L20: Boot 2A 34
Arden WA8: Wid 1G 95
Ardennes Rd. L36: Huy 4G 57
Arderne Cl. CH63: Spit 3B 104
Ardleigh Cl. L13: Liv 5D 54
Ardleigh Gro. L13: Liv 5D 54
Ardleigh Pl. L13: Liv 5D 54
Ardleigh Rd. L13: Liv 5C 54
Ardmore Rd. L18: Moss H 1E 91
Ardrossan Rd. L4: Walt 5A 36

Ardville Rd. L11: Norr G 2B 36
Ardwick Rd. L24: Speke 2H 109
Ardwick St. WA9: St H 2G 43
Argo Rd. L22: Water 2F 19
Argos Pl. L20: Kirkd 4D 34
Argos Rd. L20: Kirkd 4D 34
Argyle Ct. L1: Liv 6E 5
Argyle Rd. L4: Walt 1H 53
L19: Garst 5G 91
Argyle St. CH41: Birke 3G 69
L1: Liv 6E 5 (1D 70)
WA10: St H 6D 28
Argyle St. Sth.
CH41: Birke 4G 69
Argyll Av. CH62: East 3D 120
Aries Cl. L14: Knott A 2C 56
Ariss Gro. L35: Whis 2G 59
Arkenstone Cl. WA8: Wid 1A 96
Arkle Rd. CH43: Bid 1B 68
Arkles La. L4: Walt 1G 53
Arkles Rd. L4: Walt 1G 53
Arklow Dr. L24: Hale 3D 110
Arkwood Cl. CH62: Spit 2C 104
Arkwright Cl. WA7: Ast 2B 114
Arkwright Rd. WA7: Ast 2B 114
Arlescourt Rd. L12: W Der 2G 55
Arley Cl. CH43: Bid 3G 67
Arley Dr. WA8: Wid 1G 95
Arley St. L3: Liv 3C 52
Arlington Av. L18: Moss H 4D 72
Arlington Ct. CH43: Oxton 4B 68
Arlington Dr. WA5: Penk 5G 81
Arlington Rd. CH45: Wall 1A 50
Armill Rd. L11: Crox 2G 37
Armitage Gdns. L18: Aller 2F 91
Armley Rd. L4: Walt 6H 35
Armour Gro. L13: Liv 5E 55
Armoury, The L12: W Der 6F 37
Armscot Cl. L25: Hunts X 4D 92
Armscot Pl. L25: Hunts X 4D 92
Armstrong Quay L3: Liv 6F 71
Arncliffe Dr. WA5: Burtw 1H 63
Arncliffe Rd.
L25: Hunts X, Woolt 2E 93
Arndale WA7: Beech 2A 124
Arnhem Rd. L36: Huy 3G 57
Arnian Rd. WA11: Rainf 2F 17
Arnian Way WA11: Rainf 2F 17
Arno Ct. CH43: Oxton 6D 68
Arnold Av. WA10: St H 6B 28
Arnold Cl. WA9: St H 4G 43
Arnold Cres. L8: Liv 3G 71
Arnold Gro. L15: Wav 1E 73
Arnold Pl. WA8: Wid 4A 96
Arnold St. CH45: Wall 2D 50
Arno Rd. CH43: Oxton 6D 68
Arnot Cl. WA10: St H 6D 28
Arnot St. L4: Walt 4F 35
Arnot Way CH63: Hghr B 5F 87
Arnside L21: Lith 3D 20
Arnside Av. L35: Rainh 3G 59
WA11: Hay 5D 30
Arnside Rd. CH43: Oxton 5C 68
CH45: Wall 2D 50
L7: Liv 6A 54
L36: Huy .2D 56
Aron Cl. L34: Presc 1D 58
Arrad Ho. L7: Liv 1F 71
(off Arrad St.)
Arrad St. L7: Liv 1F 71
Arran Cl. WA11: St H 5A 30
Arranmore Rd. L18: Moss H 1E 91
Arriva Stadium, The 2E 43
Arrivato Plaza WA10: St H 2F 43
(off Hall St.)
Arrowe Av. CH46: More 2B 66
Arrowe Brook Cl. CH49: Grea 5C 66
Arrowe Brook La. CH49: Grea 2B 84
Arrowe Brook Rd. CH49: Woodc 1D 84
Arrowe Commercial Pk.
CH49: Upton 6D 66
Arrowe Country Pk. 2D 84

Arrowe Ct. CH49: Woodc 1E 85
(off Childwall Grn.)
ARROWE HILL 6D 66
Arrowe Park Golf Course 3E 85
Arrowe Pk. Rd.
CH49: Upton, Woodc 4E 67
Arrowe Rd. CH49: Grea 6B 66
Arrowe Side CH49: Grea 5C 66
Arrowsmith Rd. WA11: Hay 4H 31
Art Ho. Sq. L1: Liv 6G 5
Arthur St. CH41: Birke 2E 69
(not continuous)
L9: Walt 2F 35
L19: Garst 6H 91
WA7: Run 3E 113
Arundel Av. CH45: Wall 1B 50
L8: Liv 3A 72
L17: Liv 3A 72
Arundel Cl. CH61: Pens 6C 84
L8: Liv 3G 71
Arundell Cl. WA5: Burtw 1H 63
Arundel St. L4: Walt 4E 35
Arvon St. L20: Boot 5D 20
Asbridge St. L8: Liv 3H 71
Asbury Cl. L18: Aller 6H 73
Asbury Rd. CH45: Wall 1H 49
Ascot Av. L21: Lith 3A 20
WA7: Run 1F 123
Ascot Dr. CH63: Beb 6H 87
L33: Kirkb 4A 14
Ascot Gro. CH63: Beb 6H 87
Ascot Pk. L23: Crosb 5H 9
Ascot Vw. L22: Water 1E 19
Ascroft Rd. L9: Ain 3H 21
Ashbank Rd. L11: Norr G 3E 37
Ashbourne Av. L23: Blun 5E 9
L30: N'ton 1E 21
WA7: Run 1F 123
Ashbourne Cres. L36: Huy 5D 56
Ashbourne Rd. L17: Aig 1A 90
Ashbrook Av. WA7: Sut W 3A 124
Ashbrook Dr. L9: Ain 5A 22
Ashbrook Ter. CH63: Beb 5A 88
Ashburn Av. L33: Kirkb 5A 14
Ashburnham Way L3: Liv 4E 53
Ashburton Av. CH43: Clau 3B 68
Ashburton Rd. CH43: Clau 3A 68
CH44: Wall 3D 50
CH48: W Kir 6B 64
Ashbury Cl. L14: Knott A 1D 56
WA7: Wind H 3F 115
Ashbury Dr. WA11: Hay 4E 31
Ashby Rd. L14: Knott A 1D 56
Ashby Cl. CH46: More 6H 47
Ash Cl. L15: Wav 1C 72
Ashcombe Rd. L14: Knott A 4G 55
Ash Cres. L36: Huy 1G 75
Ashcroft CH61: Hesw 2D 100
Ashcroft Rd. L33: Know I 6D 14
Ashcroft St. L20: Boot 2B 34
WA9: St H 2G 43
(not continuous)
Ashdale L36: Huy 5F 57
Ashdale Pk. CH49: Grea 6H 65
Ashdale Rd. L9: Walt 1G 35
L18: Moss H 4E 73
L22: Water 1F 19
Ashdown Cres. WA9: Clock F 3G 61
Ashdown Dr. CH49: Grea 1A 84
Ashdown Gro. L26: Halew 2A 94
Ashfarm Ct. L14: Knott A 4B 56
Ashfield L15: Wav 1B 72
L35: Rainh 4B 60
Ashfield Ct. WA10: St H 2D 42
(off Glover St.)
Ashfield Cres. CH62: Brom 5D 104
Ashfield Rd. CH62: Brom 5C 104
L17: Aig 1B 90
Ashfield St. L5: Liv 2C 52
Ashford Cl. L26: Halew 4G 93
Ashford Rd. CH41: Birke 5E 69
CH47: Meols 1C 64
Ashford Way WA8: Wid 2H 97
Ash Grange L14: Knott A 4H 55

Ash Gro. CH45: New B 6E 33
  L15: Wav 1B 72
  L21: Sea 5A 20
  L35: Presc .3E 59
  WA7: Run 5G 113
  WA8: Wid .3B 96
  WA9: Clock F 3G 61
  WA11: Rainf 3F 17
Ash La. WA8: Wid 2E 95
Ashlar Gro. L17: Aig 1C 90
Ashlar Rd. L17: Aig 1C 90
  L22: Water .1G 19
Ashlea Rd. CH61: Pens 2D 100
Ashleigh Rd. L31: Mag 2D 12
Ashley Av. CH47: Meols 6F 47
Ashley Bus. Cen. L34: Presc 1E 59
                         (off East St.)
Ashley Cl. L33: Kirkb 4A 14
  L35: Rainh .5B 60
Ashley Grn. WA8: Wid 2B 96
Ashley Retail Pk. WA8: Wid 4F 97
Ashley Rd. WA7: Run 3H 113
Ashley St. CH42: Rock F 1H 87
Ashley Way WA8: Wid 5E 97
Ashley Way W. WA8: Wid 4D 96
Ashmore Cl. CH48: Caldy 5C 82
Ashmuir Hey L32: Kirkb 2B 24
Ashover Av. L14: Knott A 3C 56
Ash Priors WA8: Wid 6B 78
Ashridge St. WA7: Run 2D 112
Ash Rd. CH42: Tran 5F 69
  CH63: Hghr B 4H 87
  L21: Lith 4A 20
  WA5: Penk 5H 81
  WA11: Hay .4G 31
Ash St. L20: Boot 1C 34
Ashton Av. L35: Rainh 6A 60
Ashton Cl. CH62: East 4E 121
  WA6: Frod 6H 123
  WA7: West 1D 122
Ashton Ct. CH48: W Kir 2A 82
  WA6: Frod 6G 123
ASHTON CROSS 1F 31
Ashton Dr. CH48: W Kir 2A 82
  L25: Hunts X 4D 92
  WA6: Frod 5G 123
Ashton-in-Makerfield Golf Course 1G 31
Ashton Pk. L25: Hunts X 3F 93
ASHTON'S GREEN 2B 44
Ashtons Grn. Dr. WA9: St H 3B 44
Ashton's La. L24: Hale 3H 109
Ashton Sq. L25: Woolt 2D 92
Ashton St. L3: Liv 5F 53
  L13: Liv 4E 55
Ash Tree Apartments
  CH44: Wall 4F 51
Ashtree Gro. L12: Crox 1A 38
Ashurst Cl. L25: Gate 5D 74
  WA11: St H 5A 30
Ashurst Dr. WA11: St H 5H 29
Ash Va. L15: Wav 1C 72
Ash Vs. CH44: Wall 5E 51
Ashville Ind. Est. WA7: Sut W 4A 124
Ashville Point WA7: Sut W 4A 124
Ashville Rd. CH41: Birke 3C 68
  CH43: Clau 3C 68
  CH44: Wall 5F 51
Ashville Way WA7: Sut W 4A 124
Ashwater Rd. L12: W Der 3G 37
Ashway CH60: Hesw 1F 117
Ashwell St. L8: Liv 2E 71
Ashwood Cl. L27: N'ley 4G 75
  L33: Kirkb .4A 14
  WA8: Wid .4G 95
Ashwood Cl. CH43: Bid 6G 49
Ashwood Dr. L12: Crox 2H 37
Askern Rd. L32: Kirkb 3B 24
Askett Cl. WA11: Hay 4F 31
Askew Cl. CH44: Wall 3F 51
Askew St. L4: Walt 4F 35
Askham Cl. L8: Liv 2H 71
Aspen Cl. CH60: Hesw 5H 101
  L33: Kirkb .3B 14
Aspendale Rd. CH42: Tran 5F 69

Aspen Gdns. WA9: St H 1A 60
Aspen Gro. L8: Liv 3A 72
Aspenwood WN4: Ash M 1H 31
Aspes Rd. L12: W Der 6A 38
Aspinall St. CH41: Birke 2E 69
  L34: Presc .1D 58
Aspley Ho. L22: Water 2G 19
Asquith Av. CH41: Birke 2D 68
Asser Rd. L11: Norr G 5C 36
Assheton Wlk. L24: Hale 3E 111
Assissian Cres. L30: N'ton 5E 11
Aster Av. WA5: Penk 5H 81
Aster Cres. WA7: Beech 2B 124
Aster Dr. L33: Kirkb 4H 13
Asterfield Av. CH63: Hghr B 4G 87
Aster Rd. WA11: Hay 4H 31
Astley Cl. WA8: Wid 6A 78
  WA11: Rainf 2F 17
Astley Rd. L36: Huy 1G 57
ASTMOOR 2B 114
Astmoor Bri. La. WA7: Cas 3B 114
Astmoor Ind. Est. WA7: Ast 2B 114
                     (Brindley Rd.)
  WA7: Ast .3B 114
                     (Goddard Rd.)
Astmoor La. WA7: Ast 2G 113
  WA7: Cas .3B 114
Astmoor Rd. WA7: Ast 2G 113
Astmoor Spine Rd. WA7: Ast 2C 114
ASTON 6G 125
Aston Cl. CH43: Oxton 6B 68
Aston Flds. Rd.
  WA7: Pres B 3F 125
Aston Forge WA7: Pres B 2H 125
Aston Grn. WA7: Pres B 1G 125
ASTON HEATH 4G 125
Aston La. WA7: Aston, Sut W 4C 124
  WA7: Pres B 2H 125
Aston La. Nth.
  WA7: Pres B 3G 125
Aston La. Sth. WA7: Pres B 4G 125
Aston St. L19: Garst 6H 91
Astonwood Rd. CH42: Tran 6F 69
Astor St. L4: Walt 3F 35
Atheldene Rd. L4: Walt 3A 36
Athelstan Cl. CH62: Brom 4D 104
Atherton Cl. L5: Liv 2E 53
Atherton Ct. CH45: New B 5C 32
               (off Alexandra Rd.)
Atherton Dr. CH45: Woodc 6E 67
Atherton Ho. CH45: New B 5D 32
Atherton Rake L30: N'ton 5D 10
Atherton Rd. L9: Ain 5A 22
Atherton St. CH45: New B 4C 32
  L34: Presc .1D 58
  WA10: St H 6D 28
Athol Cl. CH62: East 2E 121
  WA12: Newt W 1H 45
Athol Dr. CH62: East 3E 121
Atholl Cres. L10: Ain 1B 22
Athol St. CH41: Birke 2G 69
  L5: Liv 2C 52
           (Bangor St., not continuous)
  L5: Liv 2B 52
          (Denbigh St., not continuous)
Atkinson Gro. L36: Huy 3H 57
Atlanta Ct. L33: Kirkb 3H 13
Atlantic Pav. L3: Liv 6C 4 (1C 70)
Atlantic Point L3: Liv 1E 5 (4D 52)
Atlantic Rd. L20: Boot 2B 34
Atlantic Terminal L20: Boot 2A 34
Atlantic Way L3: Liv 4D 70
  L30: Boot .3E 21
Atlas Bus. Complex L20: Boot 1A 34
Atlas Rd. L20: Boot 1B 34
Atlas St. WA9: St H 1F 43
Atterbury Cl. WA8: Wid 1A 96
Atterbury St. L8: Liv 4E 71
Attle Rd. L36: Huy 4A 58
Attwood St. L4: Walt 6F 35
Atwell St. L6: Liv 3G 53
Aubourn Cl. WA8: Wid 6A 78
Auburn Rd. CH45: Wall 6C 32
  L13: Liv 1C 54

Aubynes, The CH45: Wall 6A 32
Auckland Rd. L18: Moss H 4E 73
Audlem Av. CH43: Oxton 6B 68
Audlem Cl. WA7: Sut W 3B 124
Audley St. L3: Liv 2H 5 (5E 53)
Audre Cl. WA5: Gt San 3F 81
Audrey Wlk. L10: Faz 4F 23
AUGHTON 1F 7
Aughton Ct. CH49: Upton 4E 67
Aughton Rd. L20: Boot 6D 20
Augusta Cl. L13: Liv 5E 55
August Rd. L6: Liv 2B 54
August St. L20: Boot 6C 20
Aukland Gro. WA9: St H 1B 60
Aurorean Cl. L27: N'ley 3F 75
Austell Cl. WA11: St H 4H 29
Austin Av. WA10: St H 5A 42
Austin Cl. L32: Kirkb 6H 13
Austin St. CH44: Wall 5C 50
Autumn Gro. CH42: Rock F 3G 87
Autumn Way L20: Boot 6C 20
  WA9: Clock F 4G 61
Avalon Cl. WA7: Cas 4C 114
Avalon Ter. L20: Boot 1B 34
               (off Tennyson St.)
Avebury Cl. WA8: Wid 6A 80
Avelon Cl. CH43: Noct 4H 67
  L31: Lyd 2A 6
Avenue, The CH62: Brom 5C 104
  L19: Garst .6A 92
  L26: Halew .4G 93
  L36: Huy 4G 57
  WA11: Rainf 3F 17
Avery Cres. WA11: Hay 4E 31
Avery Rd. WA11: Hay 4E 31
Avery Sq. WA11: Hay 4E 31
Aviary Ct. L9: Walt 5F 21
                 (off Dove Rd.)
Aviemore Rd. L13: Liv 4D 54
Avington Cl. L12: W Der 6H 37
Avis Wlk. L10: Faz 4F 23
Avolon Rd. L12: W Der 2H 55
Avon WA8: Wid 1G 95
Avon Av. WA5: Penk 5G 81
Avon Cl. L4: Kirkd 5E 35
  L33: Kirkb .3B 14
Avon Ct. L23: Crosb 4G 9
Avondale Av. CH46: More 6D 48
  CH62: East 2F 121
  L31: Mag 1A 12
Avondale Dr. WA8: Wid 2H 95
Avondale Rd. CH47: Hoy 2B 64
  L15: Wav 3C 72
  WA11: Hay .4E 31
Avonmore Av. L18: Moss H 6E 73
Avon St. CH41: Birke 6B 50
  L6: Liv 2H 53
Awelon Cl. L12: W Der 5G 37
Awesome Walls Climbing Cen. . . .2B 52
Axbridge Av. WA9: Sut L 1H 61
Axholme Cl. CH61: Thing 6F 85
Axholme Rd. CH61: Thing 6E 85
Ayala Cl. L9: Walt 4F 21
Aycliffe Rd. WA9: St H 1B 60
Aycliffe Wlk. WA8: Wid 3A 96
Aylesbury Av. CH43: Oxton 1A 86
Aylesbury Rd. CH45: New B 6E 33
Aylesford Rd. L13: Liv 4E 55
Aylsham Cl. WA8: Wid 5A 78
Aylsham Dr. CH49: Upton 2E 67
Aylton Rd. L36: Huy 3D 56
Aylward Pl. L20: Boot 1A 34
                 (off Glover Pl.)
Aynsley Ct. WA9: St H 1H 59
Ayres Ct. WA9: St H 6C 42
Ayr Rd. L4: Walt 3G 35
Ayrshire Gdns. WA10: St H 3C 42
Ayrshire Rd. L4: Walt 5A 36
Ayrton Ho. L8: Liv 5F 71
              (off Commerce Way)
Aysgarth Av. L12: W Der 1G 55
Aysgarth Rd. CH45: Wall 1B 50
Ayton La. L16: Child 2G 73

Azalea Gdns. WA9: Bold 6C 44
Azalea Gro. L26: Halew 1F 93
   WA7: Beech 3B 124

B

Babbacombe Rd. L16: Child 3A 74
   WA5: Penk 5G 81
Bk. Barlow La. L4: Kirkd 5E 35
Bk. Beau St. L5: Liv 3E 53
Bk. Bedford St. L7: Liv 1F 71
   (off Cambridge St.)
Bk. Belmont Rd. L6: Liv 2H 53
Bk. Berry St. L1: Liv 6G 5
Bk. Blackfield Ter. L4: Kirkd 6D 34
Bk. Bold St. L1: Liv 5G 5
Bk. Boundary Cl. L5: Kirkd 1D 52
Bk. Bridge Rd. L23: Blun 6E 9
   (off Riverslea Rd.)
Bk. Bridport St. L3: Liv 3G 5
Back Broadway L11: Norr G 4C 36
Bk. Canning St. L8: Liv 1F 71
Bk. Catharine St. L8: Liv 1F 71
   (off Little St Bride St.)
Bk. Chadwick Mt. L5: Liv 6E 35
Bk. Chatham Pl. L7: Liv 6H 53
   (off Queensland St.)
Bk. Colquitt St. L1: Liv 6G 5 (1E 71)
Bk. Commutation Row L3: Liv 2G 5
Bk. Dovecot Pl. L14: Knott A 3B 56
Bk. Egerton St. Nth. L8: Liv 2F 71
   (off Egerton St.)
Bk. Egerton St. Sth. L8: Liv 2F 71
   (off Egerton St.)
Bk. Falkner St. Sth. L8: Liv 1G 71
Backford Cl. CH43: Oxton 6A 68
   WA7: Brook 2E 125
Backford Rd. CH61: Irby 6B 84
Bk. Gillmoss La. L11: Crox 5G 23
Bk. Granton Rd. L5: Liv 1G 53
   (off Salisbury Rd.)
Bk. Guilford St. L6: Liv 4F 53
Bk. Hadfield Pl. L25: Woolt 1C 92
   (off Church Rd.)
Bk. High St. L25: Woolt 1C 92
   (off High St.)
   WA7: Run 3E 113
Bk. Holland Pl. L7: Liv 6H 53
   (off Wavertree Rd.)
Bk. Hope Pl. L1: Liv 6H 5
Bk. Huskisson St. L8: Liv 2F 71
Bk. Irvine St. L7: Liv 6G 53
   (off Up. Mason St.)
Bk. Kelvin Gro. L8: Liv 3G 71
   (off Kelvin Gro.)
Bk. Knight St. L1: Liv 6G 5
Back La. L23: Lit C 1G 9
   L29: Seft, Thorn 2C 10
   L39: Augh 1D 6
   WA5: Coll G 6F 45
   WA5: Cuerd 1C 98
Bk. Langham St. L4: Walt 5F 35
Bk. Leeds St. L3: Liv 1B 4 (4B 52)
Bk. Legh St. WA12: Newt W 2H 45
Bk. Lime St. L1: Liv 4F 5
Bk. Little Canning St. L8: Liv 2F 71
   (off Lit. Canning St.)
Bk. Luton Gro. L4: Walt 5F 35
Bk. Market St. WA12: Newt W 1H 45
Bk. Maryland St. L1: Liv 6H 5
Bk. Menai St. CH41: Birke 3E 69
Bk. Mersey Vw. L22: Water 1E 19
Bk. Mount St. L22: Water 2F 19
Bk. Mulberry St. L7: Liv 1F 71
Bk. Oliver St. CH41: Birke 3G 69
   (off Argyle St.)
Bk. Orford St. L15: Wav 1D 72
   (off Sandown La.)
Bk. Percy St. L8: Liv 2F 71
   (off Percy St.)
Bk. Pickop St. L3: Liv 2D 4
Bk. Price St. CH41: Birke 2F 69
Bk. Renshaw St. L1: Liv 5G 5 (6E 53)

Bk. Rockfield Rd. L4: Walt 6F 35
   (off Blessington Rd.)
Back St Bride St. L8: Liv 1F 71
   (off Little St Bride St.)
Bk. Sandon St. L8: Liv 2F 71
Bk. Sandown La. L15: Wav 1D 72
   (off Sandown La.)
Bk. Seaman Rd. L15: Wav 2C 72
   (off Seaman Rd.)
Back Seaview CH47: Hoy 2B 64
Bk. Seel St. L1: Liv 6F 5
Bk. Sir Howard St. L8: Liv 1F 71
   (off Sir Howard St.)
Bk. South Rd. L22: Water 2G 19
Bk. Stanley Rd. L20: Boot 2C 34
Bk. Towerlands St. L7: Liv 6H 53
   (off Church Mt.)
Bk. Wellesley Rd. L8: Liv 6H 53
   (off The Elms)
Bk. Westminster Rd. L4: Kirkd 5E 35
Bk. Windsor Vw. L8: Liv 2H 71
   (off Lodge La.)
Bk. Winstanley Rd. L22: Water 1G 19
Badbury Cl. WA11: Hay 4F 31
Badby Wood L33: Kirkb 5B 14
Baddow Cft. L25: Woolt 6A 74
Baden Ct. CH48: W Kir 6A 64
Baden Ho. L13: Liv 4F 55
Baden Rd. L13: Liv 4F 55
Bader Cl. CH61: Pens 2C 100
Badger Cl. WA7: Pal F 1C 124
Badger's Set CH48: Caldy 5D 82
Badger Way CH43: Pren 3A 86
Badminton St. L8: Liv 6F 71
Baffin Cl. CH46: Leas 3E 49
Bagnall St. L4: Walt 6G 35
Bagot St. L15: Wav 2B 72
Baguley Av. WA8: Hale B 6G 95
Bahama Cl. WA11: Hay 3F 31
Bahama Rd. WA11: Hay 3F 31
Bailey Cl. L20: Boot 4E 21
Bailey Dr. L20: Boot 5E 21
Baileys Cl. WA8: Wid 4E 79
Bailey's La. L24: Hale 4H 109
   L24: Speke 2C 108
   L26: Halew 3A 94
Bailey St. L1: Liv 1E 71
Bailey Way L31: Mag 2A 12
Bainbridge Cres. WA5: Gt San 1G 81
Bainton Cl. L32: Kirkb 4C 24
Bainton Rd. L32: Kirkb 4C 24
Baker Rd. WA7: West P 6B 112
Bakers Grn. Rd. L36: Huy 3G 57
Baker St. L6: Liv 4G 53
   L36: Huy 5A 58
   WA9: St H 2G 43
Baker Way L6: Liv 4G 53
Bakewell Gro. L9: Ain 4H 21
Bakewell Rd. WA5: Burtw 6H 45
Bala Gro. CH44: Wall 4C 50
Bala St. L4: Walt 1H 53
Balcarres Av. L18: Moss H 4D 72
Baldwin Av. L16: Child 1A 74
Baldwin St. WA10: St H 1E 43
Bales, The L30: N'ton 5G 11
Balfe St. L21: Sea 5A 20
Balfour Av. L20: Boot 6B 20
Balfour Rd. CH43: Oxton 4D 68
   CH44: Wall 5C 50
   L20: Boot 6B 20
Balfour St. L4: Walt 6F 35
   WA7: Run 4D 112
   WA10: St H 2B 42
Balham Cl. WA8: Wid 5E 79
Balharry Av. WA11: Hay 4H 31
Balker Dr. WA10: St H 6D 28
Balkan Rd. L18: Moss H 6G 73
Ballantyne Dr. CH43: Bid 6G 49
Ballantyne Gro. L13: Liv 6C 36
   L20: Boot 5E 21
Ballantyne Pl. L13: Liv 6C 36
Ballantyne Rd. L13: Liv 1C 54
Ballantyne Wlk. CH43: Bid 6G 49

Ballard Rd. CH48: W Kir 6E 65
Ball Av. CH45: New B 5C 32
Balliol Cl. CH43: Bid 6G 49
Balliol Gro. L23: Blun 1D 18
Balliol Ho. L20: Boot 3C 34
Balliol Rd. L20: Boot 3C 34
BALL O' DITTON 2C 96
Ball Path WA8: Wid 2D 96
Ball Path Way WA8: Wid 2C 96
Ball's Rd. CH43: Oxton 5D 68
Balls Rd. E. CH41: Birke 4E 69
Ball St. WA9: St H 1H 43
Balmer St. WA9: St H 5B 42
Balmoral Av. L23: Crosb 6G 9
   WA9: St H 6G 43
Balmoral Cl. L33: Kirkb 4A 14
Balmoral Ct. L13: Liv 2C 54
Balmoral Gdns. CH43: Pren 2B 86
Balmoral Gro. CH43: Noct 6H 67
Balmoral Rd. CH45: New B 4E 33
   L6: Liv 3A 54
   L9: Walt 5G 21
   L31: Mag 6B 6
   WA8: Wid 5D 78
Balmoral Way L34: Presc 2H 57
Balm St. L7: Liv 5H 53
Balniel St. WA9: Clock F 4H 61
Balsham Cl. L25: Hunts X 4F 93
Baltic Rd. L20: Boot 2B 34
Baltic St. L4: Walt 6G 35
Baltimore St. L1: Liv 6H 5 (1E 71)
Bamboo Cl. L27: N'ley 3G 75
Bamford Cl. WA7: Run 6G 113
Bamford Dr. L6: Liv 3G 53
Bampton Av. WA11: St H 2F 29
Bampton Rd. L16: Child 1H 73
Banbury Av. L25: Woolt 1E 93
Banbury Ct. L20: Boot 1D 34
   (off Worcester Rd.)
Banbury Way CH43: Oxton 1A 86
Bancroft Cl. L25: Hunts X 3E 93
Bancroft Rd. WA8: Wid 1H 97
Bandon Cl. L24: Hale 3D 110
Banff Av. CH63: East 2D 120
Bangor Rd. CH45: Wall 1H 49
Bangor St. L5: Liv 2C 52
Bankburn Rd. L13: Liv 1C 54
Bank Dene CH42: Rock F 3A 88
Bankes La. WA7: West 2D 122
   WA7: West P 1C 122
Bankfield Ct. CH62: Brom 2F 105
   L13: Liv 2D 54
Bankfield Rd. L13: Liv 1D 54
   WA8: Wid 2H 95
Bankfields Dr. CH62: East 2H 121
Bankfield St. L20: Boot 5B 34
Bank Gdns. WA5: Penk 5G 81
Bankhall La. L20: Kirkd 5C 34
Bankhall Station (Rail) 5C 34
Bankhall St. L20: Kirkd 5C 34
Bankland Rd. L13: Liv 2D 54
Bank La. L31: Mell 2G 13
   L33: Kirkb 2G 13
Bank Rd. L20: Boot 2B 34
Banks, The CH45: Wall 6A 32
Bank's Av. CH47: Meols 1D 64
Bankside WA7: Pres B 6G 115
Bankside Cl. L21: Lith 3A 20
Bankside Rd. CH42: Rock F 3H 87
Bank's La. L19: Garst 1H 107
   L24: Speke 3B 108
Banks Rd. CH48: W Kir 1A 82
   CH60: Hesw 6A 100
   L19: Garst 6G 91
Bank St. CH41: Birke 3G 69
   WA8: Wid 1E 113
   WA10: St H 2C 42
   WA12: Newt W 2H 45
Bank's Way L19: Garst 1H 107
Bankville Rd. CH42: Tran 6G 69
Banner Hey L35: Whis 6D 58
Bannerman St. L7: Liv 1B 72
Banner St. L15: Wav 2C 72
   WA10: St H 2D 42

Banner Wlk. *WA10: St H* 2D *42*
               (off Banner St.)
Banning Cl. CH41: Birke 2F 69
Banstead Gro. L15: Wav 2F 73
Barbara Av. L10: Faz 4E 23
Barbara St. WA9: Clock F 4A 62
Barberry Cl. CH46: More 1H 65
Barberry Cres. L30: N'ton 5G 11
Barber St. WA9: St H 1G 43
Barbondale Cl. WA5: Gt San 2H 81
Barbour Dr. L20: Boot 5E 21
Barbrook Way L9: Walt 2H 35
Barchester Dr. L17: Aig 2A 90
Barclay St. L8: Liv 5F 71
Barcombe Rd. CH60: Hesw 4H 101
Bardley Cres. L35: Tar G 2A 76
Bardon Cl. L25: Gate 4E 75
Bardsay Rd. L4: Walt 4F 35
Barford Cl. CH43: Bid 3F 67
Barford Grange CH64: Will 6B 120
Barford Rd. L25: Hunts X 5D 92
   L36: Huy 1H 57
Bargate Water WA9: St H 1B 60
Barge Ind. Pk., The WA9: St H 6G 29
Barington Dr. WA7: Murd 6G 115
Barkbeth Rd. L36: Huy 2E 57
Barkbeth Wlk. L36: Huy 2E 57
Barkeley Dr. L21: Sea 5H 19
Barker Cl. L36: Huy 1H 75
Barker La. CH49: Grea 1A 84
            (not continuous)
Barker Rd. CH61: Irby 5D 84
Barkers Hollow Rd.
   WA4: Dutt, Pres H 1H 125
Barkerville Cl. L13: Liv 6B 36
Barker Way L6: Liv 2H 53
Barkhill Rd. L17: Aig 2D 90
Barkin Cen., The WA8: Wid 3G 97
Barkis Cl. L8: Liv 4F 71
Bark Rd. L21: Lith 2C 20
Barleyfield CH61: Pens 1C 100
Barlow Av. CH63: Beb 5A 88
Barlow Gro. WA9: St H 3C 44
Barlow La. L4: Kirkd 5E 35
Barlows Cl. L9: Ain 3B 22
Barlow's La. L9: Ain 3B 22
Barlow St. L4: Kirkd 5E 35
Barmouth Rd. CH45: Wall 1H 49
Barmouth Way L5: Liv 2C 52
Barnacre Dr. CH64: Park 5F 117
Barnacre La. CH46: More 3H 65
Barnard Rd. CH43: Oxton 4D 68
Barn Cl. L30: N'ton 5G 11
Barncroft CH61: Pens 2D 100
   WA7: Run 6F 115
Barncroft, The CH49: Grea 5B 66
Barncroft Pl. L23: Crosb 3G 9
Barncroft Rd. L26: Halew 4A 94
Barndale Rd. L18: Moss H 5D 72
Barnes Cl. L33: Kirkb 3A 14
   WA8: Wid 1H 97
Barnes Dr. L31: Lyd 3B 6
Barnes Grn. CH63: Spit 3A 104
Barnes Rd. WA8: Wid 1G 97
Barnes St. L6: Liv 2G 53
Barneston Rd. WA8: Wid 6A 80
Barnet Cl. L7: Liv 1A 72
Barnett Av. WA12: Newt W 2G 45
Barnfield Cl. CH47: Meols 6E 47
   L12: W Der 1F 55
   L30: N'ton 1E 21
Barnfield Dr. L12: W Der 1F 55
Barnham Cl. L24: Speke 1D 108
Barnham Dr. L16: Child 2A 74
Barn Hey CH47: Hoy 4A 64
Barn Hey Cres. CH47: Meols 1F 65
Barn Hey Grn. L12: W Der 1F 55
Barn Hey Rd. L33: Kirkb 1C 24
Barnhill Rd. L15: Wav 3E 73
Barnhurst Cl. L16: Child 2A 74
Barnhurst Rd. L16: Child 2A 74
Barn La. WA5: Burtw 2H 63
Barnmeadow Rd. L25: Gate 4C 74

Barnsbury Rd. L4: Walt 3A 36
Barnsdale Av. CH61: Thing 6F 85
Barnstaple Cl. L16: Child 2A 74
Barnstaple Way WA5: Penk 5G 81
BARNSTON 2G 101
Barnston La. CH46: More 6C 48
Barnston Rd. CH60: Hesw 6F 101
   CH61: Barn, Thing 4F 85
   L9: Ain 4H 21
Barnston Towers Cl. CH60: Hesw .5G 101
Barnstream Cl. L27: N'ley 3E 75
Barn St. WA8: Wid 5E 97
Barnwell Av. CH44: Wall 2D 50
Barnwood Rd. L36: Huy 3D 56
Baroncroft Rd. L25: Woolt 5B 74
Barons Cl. WA7: Cas 4B 114
   WA8: Wid 3A 96
Barons Hey L28: Stockb V 5B 38
Barren Gro. CH43: Oxton 5D 68
Barrington Rd. CH44: Wall 4E 51
   L15: Wav 3C 72
Barrow Cl. L12: W Der 4G 37
Barrowfield Rd. WA10: Eccl 6G 27
Barrow Hall La. WA5: Gt San 2G 81
Barrows Cotts. L35: Whis 4E 59
             (off Cross La.)
BARROW'S GREEN 5H 79
Barrow's Grn. La. WA8: Wid 1A 98
Barrow's Row WA8: Wid 5F 79
Barrow St. WA10: St H 2E 43
Barry Dr. L19: Garst 5F 91
Barrymore Rd. L13: Liv 4D 54
   WA7: Run 6F 113
Barrymore Way CH63: Brom 1B 120
Bartholomew Cl. L35: Rainh 6C 60
Bartlegate Cl. WA7: Brook 2D 124
Bartlett St. L15: Wav 2C 72
Barton Cl. CH47: Hoy 3A 64
   L21: Lith 1A 20
   WA7: Murd 6F 115
Barton Hey Dr. CH48: Caldy 5C 82
Barton Rd. CH47: Hoy 3A 64
   L9: Walt 1F 35
Barton St. CH41: Birke 3E 69
            (not continuous)
Barwell Av. WA11: St H 5G 29
Basil Cl. L16: Child 1A 74
Basildon Cl. WA9: St H 6D 42
Basil Grange Apartments
   L12: W Der 2E 55
            (off North Dr.)
Basil Rd. L16: Child 1H 73
Basing St. L19: Garst 4G 91
Baskervyle Cl. CH60: Hesw 1E 117
Baskervyle Rd. CH60: Hesw 1E 117
Basnett St. L1: Liv 4E 5 (6D 52)
Bassendale Rd. CH62: Brom 3E 105
Bassenthwaite Av. CH43: Noct 4H 67
   L33: Kirkb 5H 13
   WA11: St H 3E 29
Bates Cres. WA10: St H 5B 42
Batey Av. L35: Rainh 3H 59
Batherton Cl. WA8: Wid 4F 97
Bathgate Way L33: Kirkb 3H 13
Bath St. CH62: Port S 6B 88
   L3: Liv 2A 4 (5B 52)
   L22: Water 3F 19
   WA10: St H 2D 42
Bathurst Rd. L19: Gras 4F 91
Batley St. L13: Liv 4E 55
Battenberg St. L7: Liv 5G 53
Battersea Rd. WA8: Wid 6D 78
Battery Cl. L17: Aig 1A 90
Baucher Dr. L20: Boot 4E 21
Baumville Dr. CH63: Spit 3H 103
Baxter Cl. WA7: Murd 6F 115
           (not continuous)
Baxters La. WA9: St H 5H 43
Baxters La. Ind. Est. WA9: St H 4H 43
Baycliffe Cl. WA7: Beech 2H 123
Baycliff Rd. L12: W Der 5A 38
Bayfield Rd. L19: Gras 4E 91

Bayhorse La. L3: Liv 2H 5 (5F 53)
Baynard Dr. WA8: Hale B 6A 96
Baysdale Cl. L8: Liv 5G 71
Bayswater Cl. WA7: Nort 1H 115
Bayswater Ct. CH45: Wall 1H 49
Bayswater Gdns. CH45: Wall 6A 32
Bayswater Rd. CH45: Wall 1H 49
Baythorne Rd. L4: Walt 3A 36
Bay Tree Gro. WA9: St H 5G 43
Baytree Gro. L31: Mell 6E 13
Baytree Rd. CH42: Tran 6G 69
   CH48: Frank 1F 83
Bay Vw. Dr. CH45: Wall 6A 32
Bayvil Cl. WA7: Murd 6G 115
Beach Bank L22: Water 1E 19
Beachcroft Rd. CH47: Meols 6E 47
Beach Gro. CH45: Wall 6E 33
Beach Lawn L22: Water 2E 19
Beach Rd. CH47: Hoy 3A 64
   L21: Lith 3A 20
Beach Wlk. CH48: W Kir 3B 82
Beacon Ct. CH60: Hesw 5E 101
Beacon Dr. CH48: W Kir 1C 82
Beacon Gro. WA11: St H 5H 29
Beacon Hill Vw. WA7: West P 6B 112
Beacon Ho. L5: Liv 3E 53
           (off Portland Pl.)
Beacon La. CH60: Hesw 5E 101
   L5: Liv .1F 53
Beacon Pde. CH60: Hesw 5E 101
Beacons, The CH60: Hesw 6E 101
Beaconsfield L34: Presc 1D 58
Beaconsfield Cl. CH42: Tran 6H 69
Beaconsfield Cres. WA8: Wid 5E 79
Beaconsfield Gro. WA8: Wid 5F 79
Beaconsfield Rd. CH62: New F 4B 88
   L21: Sea 4H 19
   L25: Woolt 6A 74
   WA7: Run 5C 112
   WA8: Wid 6F 79
   WA10: St H 6A 28
Beaconsfield St. L8: Liv 3G 71
Beaconsfield Ter. L19: Garst 5F 91
          (off St Mary's Rd.)
Beacon Sports Hall, The 1E 43
Beadnell Dr. WA5: Penk 6G 81
Beames Cl. L7: Liv 6A 54
Beamish Cl. WA9: St H 3C 60
Beamont St. WA8: Wid 1E 113
Beatles Story, The 1C 70
Beatrice Av. CH63: Hghr B 4G 87
Beatrice St. L20: Boot 4D 34
Beattock Cl. L33: Kirkb 3H 13
Beatty Cl. CH48: Caldy 5C 82
   L35: Whis 5D 58
Beatty Rd. L13: Liv 4E 55
Beauclair Dr. L15: Wav 2F 73
Beaufort Cl. WA7: Run 6F 113
   WA8: Wid 3G 95
Beaufort Dr. CH44: Wall 2A 50
Beaufort Rd. CH41: Birke 6B 50
Beaufort St. L8: Liv 3E 71
            (Hill St.)
   L8: Liv .3E 71
           (Mann St.)
   L8: Liv .4E 71
       (Northumberland St.)
   WA8: Wid 4G 43
Beaumaris Ct. CH43: Oxton 4D 68
Beaumaris Dr. CH61: Thing 5F 85
Beaumaris Rd. CH45: Wall 1H 49
Beaumaris St. L20: Kirkd 5C 34
           (not continuous)
Beaumaris Way WA7: Cas 3B 114
Beaumont Av. WA10: St H 1B 42
Beaumont Dr. L10: Ain 2C 22
Beaumont St. L8: Liv 2H 71
Beau St. L3: Liv 3E 53
Beauworth Av. CH49: Grea 6A 66
Beaver Gro. L9: Ain 5G 21
BEBINGTON 5A 88
Bebington Rd. CH42: Rock F, Tran 1F 87
   CH62: New F 5A 88
   CH63: Beb 5A 88

Bebington Station (Rail) 4A 88
Bechers WA8: Wid 6H 77
Bechers Bus. Cen. L30: N'ton 1G 21
Bechers Ct. L30: N'ton 6H 11
Bechers Dr. L10: Faz 1A 22
Bechers Row L9: Walt 5F 21
Beck Cl. L10: Faz 4F 23
Beckenham Av. L18: Moss H 4D 72
Beckenham Cl. WA8: Wid 5H 79
Beckenham Rd. CH45: New B 4A 32
Becket St. L4: Kirkd 6D 34
(not continuous)
Beckett Cl. L33: Know I 3E 25
Beckett Gro. CH63: Hghr B 4F 87
Beckinsale Cl. L26: Halew 2A 94
Beck Rd. L20: Boot 6C 20
Beckwith Ct. CH41: Birke 1E 69
(off Beckwith St.)
Beckwith St. CH41: Birke 1D 68
L1: Liv 6E 5 (1D 70)
Beckwith St. E. CH41: Birke 2F 69
Becky St. L6: Liv 2H 53
Becontree Rd. L12: W Der 3H 55
Bective St. L7: Liv 1A 72
Bedale Wlk. L33: Kirkb 6B 14
Bedburn Dr. L36: Huy 4D 56
Bede Cl. L33: Kirkb 3A 14
Bedford Av. CH42: Rock F 2G 87
L31: Mell 3D 12
Bedford Cl. L7: Liv 1F 71
L36: Huy 4A 58
Bedford Ct. CH42: Rock F 1H 87
L7: Liv 2F 71
(off Bedford St. Sth.)
Bedford Dr. CH42: Rock F 2F 87
Bedford Pl. CH42: Rock F 1A 88
L20: Boot 4B 34
L21: Sea .4H 19
Bedford Rd. CH42: Rock F 1H 87
CH45: Wall 1D 50
L4: Walt .3D 34
L20: Boot 4C 34
Bedford Rd. E. CH42: Rock F 1A 88
Bedford St. WA9: St H 3H 43
Bedford St. Nth. L7: Liv 6F 53
Bedford St. Sth. L7: Liv 1F 71
(not continuous)
Bedford Wlk. L7: Liv 1F 71
(off Bedford Cl.)
Beecham Cl. L36: Huy 6F 57
Beech Av. CH49: Upton 3B 66
CH61: Pens 1E 101
L17: Aig .1H 89
L23: Crosb 3A 10
L31: Mell .6F 13
L34: Eccl P 6F 41
WA5: Penk 6E 81
WA9: Clock F 3G 61
WA11: Hay 4H 31
Beechbank Rd. L18: Moss H 4C 72
Beechburn Cres. L36: Huy 4D 56
Beechburn Rd. L36: Huy 4C 56
Beech Cl. L12: Crox 2H 37
L32: Kirkb 6G 13
Beech Ct. CH42: Tran 5F 69
L18: Moss H 6G 73
Beechcroft L31: Mag 6B 6
Beechcroft Rd. CH44: Wall 5E 51
Beechdale Rd. L18: Moss H 5E 73
Beechdene Rd. L4: Walt 6H 35
Beeches, The
CH42: Rock F 2A 88
CH46: Leas 4C 48
L18: Moss H 4H 73
WA8: Wid 5H 79
(off Hampton Ct. Way)
WA9: Sut L 2H 61
Beechfield L31: Mag 6D 6
L36: Roby 5E 57
(off Church Rd.)
Beechfield Cl. CH60: Hesw 6E 101
L26: Halew 5G 93
Beechfield Rd. L18: Moss H 5H 73

Beech Gdns. WA7: Run 5G 113
(off Beech Rd.)
WA11: Rainf 2E 17
Beech Grn. L12: W Der 5E 37
Beech Gro. L9: Ain 5H 21
L21: Sea .5H 19
L30: N'ton 1G 21
Beech Hey La. CH64: Will 6B 120
Beechill Cl. L25: Gate 5E 75
Beech La. L18: Moss H 4G 73
Beech Lawn L19: Gras 4D 90
Beech Mdws. L27: Presc 2A 58
Beech Mt. L7: Liv 5A 54
Beech Pk. L12: W Der 1E 55
L23: Crosb 3H 9
Beech Ri. L33: Kirkb 6B 14
Beech Rd. CH42: Tran 5E 69
CH60: Hesw 5G 101
CH63: Hghr B 4H 87
L4: Walt .3G 35
L36: Huy .6G 57
L39: Augh .1F 7
WA7: Run 5G 113
WA7: Sut W 3D 124
Beech St. L7: Liv 5A 54
L20: Boot 1C 34
WA10: St H 5B 42
Beech Ter. L7: Liv 5A 54
Beech Tree Ct. L19: Gras 4D 90
(off Beechwood Rd.)
Beechtree Rd. L15: Wav 6F 55
Beechurst Cl. L25: Gate 4D 74
Beechurst Rd. L25: Gate 4D 74
Beechwalk, The L14: Knott A 3F 55
Beechway CH63: Beb 2H 103
L31: Mag .5G 7
Beechway Av. L31: Mag 5G 7
BEECHWOOD
CH43 . . . . .1G 67
WA7 . . . . .2A 124
Beechwood Av. CH45: Wall 2A 50
L26: Halew 4G 93
L35: Gt San 4H 81
WA7: Beech 1G 123
WN4: Ash M 1H 31
Beechwood Cl. L19: Gras 4E 91
WA9: Clock F 4G 61
Beechwood Ct. CH49: Woodc 2F 85
(off Childwall Grn.)
L31: Mag .6E 7
(off Deyes La.)
Beechwood Dr. CH43: Bid 2G 67
Beechwood Gdns. L19: Gras 4D 90
Beechwood Grn. L19: Gras 4E 91
Beechwood Recreation Cen. 2G 67
Beechwood Rd. CH62: Brom 5C 104
L19: Gras 4D 90
L21: Lith .5B 20
Beechwood Rd. Sth. L19: Gras 5D 90
Beesands Cl. L27: N'ley 5H 75
Beesley Rd. L34: Presc 1C 58
Beeston Cl. CH43: Bid 3G 67
Beeston Ct. WA7: Manor P 1E 115
Beeston Dr. CH61: Pens 1D 100
L30: N'ton 4H 11
Beeston Gro. L19: Gras 4E 91
Beeston St. L4: Kirkd 5E 35
Beetham Plaza L2: Liv 4C 4
Beetham Twr. L3: Liv 2B 4
Beetham Way L33: Kirkb 6B 14
Beilby Rd. WA11: Hay 4H 31
Beldale Pk. L32: Kirkb 5G 13
Beldon Cres. L36: Huy 4D 56
Belem Cl. L17: Aig 4A 72
Belem Twr. L17: Aig 4A 72
Belfast Rd. L13: Liv 4F 55
Belfield Cres. L36: Huy 6G 57
Belfield Dr. CH43: Oxton 6D 68
Belford Dr. CH46: More 1A 66
Belfort Rd. L25: Gate 5D 74
Belfry Cl. CH46: More 6H 47
L12: W Der 1A 56

Belgrave Av. CH44: Wall 3E 51
Belgrave Cl. WA8: Wid 6A 80
Belgrave Rd. L17: Aig 6H 71
L21: Sea .4H 19
Belgrave St. CH44: Wall 2D 50
Belgravia Ct. WA8: Wid 6D 78
Belhaven Rd. L18: Moss H 4D 72
Belladonna Rd. L11: Norr G 4E 37
Bellair Av. L23: Crosb 5A 10
Bellairs Rd. L11: Norr G 5C 36
Bellamy Rd. L4: Walt 3E 35
Bell Cl. L36: Huy 1H 75
Belldene Gro. CH61: Hesw 3D 100
Bellefield Av. L12: W Der 1F 55
Bellerophon Way WA11: Hay 5G 31
BELLE VALE 4E 75
Belle Va. Rd. L25: Gate 5D 74
Belle Va. Shop. Cen. L25: Gate 3D 74
Belle Vue Rd. CH44: Wall 5G 51
L25: Gate .5D 74
Bellew Rd. L11: Norr G 6D 36
Bellfield Cres. L45: New B 5C 32
Bellflower Cl. WA8: Wid 5C 78
Bell Ho. Rd. WA8: Wid 2G 97
Bellingham Dr. WA7: Run 5E 113
Bellini Cl. L21: Sea 5A 20
Bell La. L35: Rainh 5E 61
WA9: Sut M 5E 61
Bellmore St. L19: Garst 4G 91
Bell Rd. CH44: Wall 4F 51
Bell's Cl. L31: Lyd 3B 6
Bells La. L31: Lyd 4A 6
Bell St. L13: Liv 4E 55
Belltower La. L7: Liv 5H 53
Bellward Cl. CH63: Spit 3H 103
Belmont CH41: Birke 4E 69
Belmont Av. CH62: Brom 4C 104
Belmont Cres. WA5: Gt San 3H 81
Belmont Dr. CH61: Pens 1E 101
L6: Liv 2A 54
Belmont Gro. CH43: Oxton 4E 69
L6: Liv 2A 54
Belmont Pl. L19: Garst 5G 91
(off Shrewsbury Rd.)
Belmont Rd. CH45: New B 4D 32
CH48: W Kir 6B 64
L6: Liv 2H 53
WA8: Wid 1H 97
Belmont St. WA10: St H 2B 42
Belmont Vw. L6: Liv 2A 54
(off W. Derby Rd.)
Beloe St. L8: Liv 5F 71
Belper St. L19: Garst 5F 91
Belsford Way L24: Speke 1D 108
Belsdon Rd. L16: Child 1H 73
Belton Rd. L36: Huy 1F 57
(not continuous)
Belvedere WA7: Run 2E 113
(off Cooper St.)
Belvedere Av. WA9: Sut L 1H 61
Belvedere Cl. L34: Presc 6E 41
(off Marlborough Rd.)
WA6: Frod 6G 123
Belvidere Ct. CH49: Woodc 2E 85
(off Childwall Grn.)
Belvidere Pk. L23: Crosb 6G 9
Belvidere Rd. CH45: Wall 1B 50
L8: Liv 4G 71
L23: Crosb .6F 9
Belvoir Rd. L18: Aller 3G 91
WA8: Wid 2F 97
Bembridge Cl. WA5: Gt San 2E 81
WA8: Wid 5D 78
Bempton Rd. L17: Aig 1H 89
Benbow Cl. CH43: Bid 1B 68
Benbow St. L20: Boot 3B 34
Benedict Cl. CH49: Woodc 5F 67
Benedict Ct. L20: Boot 4C 34
Benedict St. L20: Boot 4D 34
Benfleet Ho. L19: Aig 4D 90
(off The Spinnakers)
Benledi St. L5: Liv 2D 52
Benmore Rd. L18: Moss H 1E 91

Bennet's La. CH47: Meols 5E **47**
Bennetts Hill CH43: Oxton 5D **68**
Bennetts La. WA8: Wid 1A **90**
Bennett St. L19: Garst 5G **91**
Bennett Wlk. CH61: Pens 2D **100**
Ben Nevis Rd. CH42: Tran 1F **87**
Bennison Dr. L19: Gras 4E **91**
Ben's Ct. L34: Know 6D **24**
Benson Cl. CH49: Upton 5D **66**
Benson St. L1: Liv 5G **5** (6E **53**)
Bentfield L17: Aig 3D **90**
Bentfield Cl. CH63: Hghr B 4F **87**
Bentfield Gdns. CH63: Hghr B 4F **87**
Bentham Cl. CH43: Noct 6A **68**
Bentham Dr. L16: Child 1H **73**
Bentinck Cl. CH41: Birke 3E **69**
Bentinck Pl. CH41: Birke 3E **69**
Bentinck St. CH41: Birke 3E **69**
        (not continuous)
L5: Liv .2B **52**
WA7: Run 2D **112**
WA9: St H 4H **43**
Bentley Rd. CH43: Oxton 5D **68**
CH61: Pens 6D **84**
L8: Liv .3H **71**
Bentley St. WA9: Clock F 4G **61**
Benton Cl. L5: Liv 1D **52**
Bentley Cl. CH63: Hghr B 1G **103**
Benty Farm Gro. CH61: Pens 6E **85**
Benty Heath La. CH64: Will 4G **119**
CH66: Hoot 4B **120**
Benwick Rd. L32: Kirkb 1F **23**
Berbice Rd. L18: Moss H 4E **73**
Beresford Av. CH63: Beb 4A **88**
Beresford Cl. CH43: Oxton 4C **68**
Beresford Dr. CH43: Oxton 4C **68**
CH63: Beb 4A **88**
        (off Beresford Av.)
Beresford Rd. CH43: Oxton 4B **68**
CH45: Wall 6B **32**
L8: Liv .5F **71**
Beresford St. L5: Liv 3E **53**
L20: Boot 4B **34**
WA9: St H 6C **42**
Berey's Bldgs. L3: Liv 3C **4**
Bergen Cl. L20: Boot 3E **35**
Berkeley Av. CH43: Pren 2B **86**
Berkeley Cl. CH49: Woodc 1E **85**
        (off Childwall Grn.)
WA7: Manor P 1F **115**
WA12: Newt W 1H **45**
Berkeley Dr. CH45: New B 6E **33**
Berkeley Rd. L23: Crosb 4E **9**
Berkeswell Rd. L11: Norr G 4E **37**
Berkley Av. L12: W Der 5A **38**
Berkley Cl. L8: Liv 3F **71**
Berkley St. L8: Liv 2F **71**
Berkshire Gdns. WA10: St H 3D **42**
Bermondsey Gro. WA8: Wid 5H **79**
Bermuda Rd. CH46: More 6A **48**
Bernard Av. CH45: New B 6E **33**
Berner's Rd. L19: Gras 4F **91**
Berner St. CH41: Birke 1F **69**
Berrington Av. L25: Woolt 1C **92**
Berringtons La. WA11: Rainf 1H **27**
Berryedge Cres. L36: Huy 1E **57**
Berryford Rd. L14: Knott A 1B **56**
Berry Hill Av. L34: Know 2F **39**
Berrylands Cl. CH46: More 6B **48**
Berrylands Rd. CH46: More 6B **48**
Berry Rd. WA8: Wid 2B **96**
Berrys La. WA9: St H 4B **44**
Berry St. L1: Liv 6G **5** (1E **71**)
L20: Boot 3B **34**
Berry St. Ind. Est. L20: Boot 2B **34**
        (off Berry St.)
Berrywood Dr. L35: Whis 5F **59**
Bertha Gdns. CH41: Birke 1B **68**
Bertha St. CH41: Birke 1B **68**
Bertram Cl. CH47: Meols 1D **64**
Bertram Dr. CH47: Meols 1C **64**
Bertram Dr. Nth. CH47: Meols 1D **64**
Bertram Rd. L17: Aig 5A **72**

Bertram St. WA12: Newt W 2H **45**
Berwick Av. CH62: East 3E **121**
Berwick Cl. CH46: More 1H **65**
L6: Liv .3A **54**
Berwick Dr. L23: Crosb 4E **9**
Berwick St. L6: Liv 3H **53**
Berwyn Av. CH47: Hoy 2C **64**
CH61: Thing 5E **85**
Berwyn Blvd. CH63: Hghr B 3G **87**
Berwyn Dr. CH61: Hesw 3D **100**
Berwyn Gro. WA9: St H 2B **44**
Berwyn Rd. CH44: Wall 2E **51**
L4: Walt 5A **36**
Beryl Rd. CH43: Noct 4G **67**
Beryl St. L13: Liv 6E **55**
Beryl Wlk. L10: Faz 4F **23**
Besford Ho. L25: Gate 4D **74**
Besford Rd. L25: Gate 4D **74**
Bessborough Rd.
CH43: Oxton 5D **68**
Bessbrook Rd. L17: Aig 1C **90**
Bessemer St. L8: Liv 5F **71**
Beta Cl. CH62: New F 4A **88**
Betchworth Cres. WA7: Beech 1H **123**
Bethany Cl. WA11: Hay 4D **30**
Bethany Cres. CH63: Beb 6H **87**
Bethel Gro. L17: Liv 3B **72**
Betjeman Gro. L16: Child 1B **74**
Betony Cl. L26: Halew 2G **93**
Bettisfield Av. CH62: Brom 2D **120**
Betula Cl. L9: Walt 1A **36**
Bevan Cl. WA9: St H 1B **60**
Bevan's La. L12: W Der 6H **37**
Bevan Way L12: W Der 6G **37**
Bevan Way WA8: Wid 6F **79**
Beverley Dr. CH60: Hesw 1F **117**
Beverley Gdns. CH61: Thing 5F **85**
Beverley Rd. CH45: Wall 1B **50**
CH62: New F 3B **88**
L15: Wav 3E **73**
Beversbrook Rd. L11: Norr G 3F **37**
Bevington Bush L3: Liv 4D **52**
Bevington Hill L3: Liv 3D **52**
Bevington St. L3: Liv 3D **52**
Bevyl Rd. CH64: Park 5F **117**
Bewey Cl. L8: Liv 5E **71**
Bewley Dr. L32: Kirkb 2H **23**
Bewsey St. WA10: St H 4B **42**
Bexhill Cl. L24: Speke 1D **108**
Bexhill Gdns. WA9: St H 1A **60**
Bianca St. L20: Boot 4C **34**
Bibbys La. L20: Boot 6A **20**
Bibby St. L13: Liv 4D **54**
Bickerstaffe St. L3: Liv 4E **53**
WA10: St H 2E **43**
Bickerton Av. CH63: Hghr B 3F **87**
Bickerton St. L17: Aig 6A **72**
Bickley Cl. WA7: Run 4G **113**
Bidder St. L3: Liv 1H **5** (4E **53**)
Biddleston Cross WA8: Wid 6C **78**
Bideford Av. WA9: Sut L 2G **61**
Bideford Rd. WA5: Penk 5G **81**
BIDSTON .1H **67**
Bidston Av. CH41: Birke 2A **68**
CH45: Wall 1A **50**
WA11: St H 6H **29**
Bidston Ct. CH43: Noct 2A **68**
Bidston Golf Course 4G **49**
Bidston Grn. Ct. CH43: Bid 1G **67**
Bidston Grn. Dr. CH43: Bid 1G **67**
Bidston Hall Farm CH43: Bid 6G **49**
Bidston Ind. Est. CH44: Wall 4H **49**
Bidston Link Rd. CH43: Bid 5H **49**
CH44: Wall 5H **49**
Bidston Moss CH44: Wall 4H **49**
Bidston Moss Nature Reserve 4A **50**
Bidston Rd. CH43: Clau, Oxton 3A **68**
L4: Walt 5H **35**
Bidston Station (Rail) 5G **49**
Bidston Sta. App. CH43: Bid 5G **49**
Bidston Vw. CH43: Bid 6G **49**
Bidston Village Rd. CH43: Bid 6G **49**
Bidston Way WA11: St H 6H **29**

Bidston Windmill 2H **67**
Bigdale Dr. L33: Kirkb 6B **14**
Bigham Rd. L6: Liv 4A **54**
Biglands Dr. L36: Huy 1H **75**
Big Meadow Rd. CH49: Woodc 5E **67**
Billinge Cres. WA11: St H 5H **29**
Billingham Rd. WA9: St H 6B **42**
Billings Cl. L5: Kirkd 1D **52**
Billington Cl. WA5: Gt San 1G **81**
Billington Rd. WA8: Wid 5H **77**
Bilston Rd. L17: Aig 3C **90**
Bilton Cl. WA8: Wid 1A **98**
Bingley Rd. L4: Walt 6H **35**
Binns Rd. L7: Liv 5C **54**
L13: Liv 5C **54**
Binns Rd. Ind. Est. L13: Liv 6D **54**
Binns Way L13: Liv 6D **54**
Binsey Cl. CH49: Upton 4B **66**
Birbeck Rd. L33: Kirkb 6C **14**
Birbeck Wlk. L33: Kirkb 6C **14**
Birchall St. L20: Kirkd 6C **34**
Birch Av. CH49: Upton 3B **66**
L9: Ain .5H **21**
WA10: St H 5D **28**
Birch Cl. CH43: Oxton 6D **68**
L31: Mag 6E **7**
L35: Whis 3E **59**
Birch Ct. L8: Liv 5G **71**
        (off Weller Way)
Birch Cres. WA12: Newt W 1H **45**
Birchdale Cl. CH49: Grea 4B **66**
Birchdale Rd. L9: Walt 1G **35**
L22: Water 1F **19**
Birchen Rd. L26: Halew 4A **94**
Birches, The CH44: Wall 5G **51**
CH64: Nest 5B **118**
L28: Stockb V 6C **38**
Birches Cl. CH60: Hesw 5E **101**
Birchfield CH46: More 2A **66**
Birchfield Av. WA8: Wid 1E **97**
Birchfield Cl. CH46: More 3A **66**
L7: Liv .5C **54**
Birchfield Rd. L4: Walt 3G **35**
L7: Liv .5C **54**
WA8: Wid 4E **79**
Birchfield St. L3: Liv 1H **5** (4E **53**)
WA9: St H 6B **42**
Birchfield Way L31: Lyd 2A **6**
Birch Gdns. WA10: St H 5D **28**
Birch Gro. CH45: New B 6E **33**
L15: Wav 6E **55**
L35: Presc 3E **59**
L36: Huy 5F **57**
Birch Heys CH48: Frank 2G **83**
Birch Hill M. L25: Woolt 2C **92**
Birchill Rd. L33: Know I 1E **25**
Birchley St. WA10: St H 1E **43**
Birchley Vw. WA11: St H 1F **29**
Birchmere CH60: Hesw 3C **100**
Birchmuir Hey L32: Kirkb 2B **24**
Birchridge Cl. CH62: Spit 3C **104**
Birch Rd. CH43: Oxton 6D **68**
CH47: Meols 1E **65**
CH63: Beb 1A **104**
L36: Huy 6G **57**
WA7: Run 5F **113**
WA8: Wid 6F **79**
WA11: Hay 4G **31**
Birch St. L5: Liv 2B **52**
Birch Tree Av. WA11: St H 3D **28**
Birch Tree Ct. L12: W Der 1E **55**
Birchtree Dr. L31: Mell 6E **13**
Birchtree Rd. L17: Aig 6C **72**
Birchview Way CH43: Noct 4H **67**
Birchway CH60: Hesw 1G **117**
Birchwood Av. CH41: Birke 2G **69**
Birchwood Cl. CH41: Birke 2F **69**
Birchwood Way L33: Kirkb 4C **14**
Bird St. L7: Liv 2A **72**
Birdwood Rd. L11: Norr G 5D **36**
Birkdale Av. CH63: Brom 1C **120**
Birkdale Cl. L6: Liv 1B **54**
L36: Roby 6E **57**
Birkdale Ct. L36: Huy 1H **75**

Birkdale Rd. WA5: Penk 5H **81**
  WA8: Wid 4F **79**
BIRKENHEAD 3H **69**
Birkenhead Central Station (Rail) . . .4G **69**
Birkenhead North Station (Rail) . . .6B **50**
Birkenhead Park Station (Rail) 1D **68**
Birkenhead Priory 3H **69**
Birkenhead Rd. CH44: Wall 6G **51**
  CH47: Hoy, Meols 1C **64**
  CH64: Will 5F **119**
Birkenshaw Av. L23: Blun 4D **8**
Birket Av. CH46: Leas 4D **48**
Birket Cl. CH46: Leas 4E **49**
Birket Dr. WA8: Wid 3E **79**
Birket Ho. CH41: Birke 2F **69**
Birket Sq. CH46: Leas 4D **48**
Birkett Rd. CH42: Rock F 2G **87**
  CH48: W Kir 5B **64**
Birkett St. L3: Liv 1G **5** (4E **53**)
Birkin Cl. L32: Kirkb 3C **24**
Birkin Rd. L32: Kirkb 3C **24**
Birkin Wlk. L32: Kirkb 3C **24**
Birley Cl. L8: Liv 2F **71**
Birnam Dr. L35: Rainh 5B **60**
Birnam Rd. CH44: Wall 4F **51**
Birstall Av. WA11: St H 6G **29**
Birstall Ct. WA7: Run 6H **113**
Birstall Rd. L6: Liv 4H **53**
Birt Cl. L8: Liv 2H **71**
Birtley Ct. WA8: Wid 2H **95**
Bisham Pk. WA7: Nort 2F **115**
Bishopdale Cl. WA5: Gt San 2H **81**
Bishopdale Dr. L35: Rainh 4B **60**
Bishop Dr. L35: Whis 6C **58**
Bishopgate St. L15: Wav 1C **72**
Bishop Reeves Rd.
  WA11: Hay 4G **31**
Bishop Rd. CH44: Wall 5D **50**
  L6: Liv .6A **36**
  WA10: St H 6C **28**
Bishops Ct. CH43: Oxton 6D **68**
  L12: W Der 5E **37**
  L25: Woolt 1D **92**
Bishop Sheppard Ct. L3: Liv 3C **52**
Bishops Way WA8: Wid 6H **79**
Bisley St. CH45: Wall 2D **50**
  L15: Wav 2C **72**
Bispham Dr. CH47: Meols 2E **65**
Bispham Ho. L3: Liv 1E **5**
Bittern Cl. WA7: Nort 5F **115**
Bixteth St. L3: Liv 2C **4** (5C **52**)
BLACKBROOK 5C **30**
Blackbrook Cl. L9: Walt 2G **35**
  WA8: Wid 6A **78**
Blackbrook Rd. WA11: St H 6A **30**
Blackburne Av. WA8: Hale B 6H **95**
Blackburne Dr. L25: Hunts X 4F **93**
Blackburne Pl. L8: Liv 1F **71**
Blackburne St. L19: Garst 1G **107**
Blackburne Ter. *L8: Liv* 1F **71**
    (off Blackburne Pl.)
Black Cat Ind. Est. WA8: Wid 5D **96**
Black Denton's Pl. WA8: Wid 2G **97**
Blackdown Gro. WA9: St H 3B **44**
Blackfield St. L5: Kirkd 1D **52**
Blackheath Dr. CH46: Leas 4D **48**
Blackheath La. WA7: Manor P 1G **115**
Black Horse Cl. CH48: W Kir 6C **64**
Black Horse Hill CH48: W Kir 1C **82**
Black Horse La. L13: Liv 3F **55**
  WA8: Wid 4E **79**
Black Horse Pl. L13: Liv 4F **55**
Blackhorse St. WA9: St H 1H **43**
Blackhurst Rd. L31: Lyd 2B **6**
Blackley Gro. L33: Kirkb 3C **14**
Blacklock Hall Rd. L24: Speke 2E **109**
Blacklow Brow L36: Huy 5F **57**
Blackmoor Dr. L12: W Der 1G **55**
Blackpool St. CH41: Birke 4G **69**
Blackrod Av. L24: Speke 1E **109**
Blacksmith Pl. L25: Hunts X 3F **93**
Blackstock St. *L30: N'ton* 5D **10**
    (off Granams Cft.)

Blackstock St. L3: Liv 4C **52**
Blackstone Av. WA11: St H 6H **29**
Blackstone St. L5: Liv 1B **52**
Blackthorn Cres.
  L28: Stockb V 5D **38**
Blackthorne Cl. CH46: More 2D **66**
Blackthorne Rd. L9: Walt 2A **36**
Blackwater Rd. L11: Crox 1H **37**
Blackwood Av. L25: Woolt 5B **74**
Blackwood Ct. *L16: Child* 3G **73**
    (off Woolton Rd.)
Blair Cl. CH43: Clau 3D **68**
Blair Dr. WA8: Wid 6H **77**
Blair Ind. Est. L23: Crosb 6H **9**
Blair Pk. CH63: Spit 2B **104**
Blair St. L8: Liv 2E **71**
Blair Wlk. L26: Halew 5H **93**
Blakeacre Cl. L26: Halew 5H **93**
Blakeacre Rd. L26: Halew 5H **93**
Blakefield Rd. L23: Thorn 3C **10**
Blakeley Brow CH63: Raby M 1A **120**
Blakeley Ct. CH63: Raby M 1A **120**
Blakeley Dell CH63: Raby M 1B **120**
Blakeley Dene CH63: Raby M 6B **104**
Blakeley Rd. CH63: Raby M 6A **104**
Blakeney Cl. CH49: Upton 2E **67**
Blakenhall Way CH49: Upton 3B **66**
Blaking Dr. L34: Know 1F **39**
Blantyre Rd. L15: Wav 3C **72**
Blantyre St. WA7: Run 2D **112**
Blay Cl. L25: Hunts X 3F **93**
Blaydon Cl. L30: N'ton 2G **21**
Blaydon Gro. WA9: St H 6B **42**
Blaydon Wlk. CH43: Clau 3A **68**
Bleak Hill Cl. WA10: Windle 4A **28**
Bleak Hill Rd.
  WA10: Eccl, Windle 6H **27**
Bleasdale Av. L10: Ain 1C **22**
Bleasdale Cl. CH49: Upton 3C **66**
Bleasdale Rd. L18: Moss H 5F **73**
Bleasdale Way L21: Ford 5B **10**
Blenheim Av. L21: Lith 3C **20**
Blenheim Dr. L34: Presc 2H **57**
Blenheim Rd. CH44: Wall 2F **51**
  L18: Moss H 4D **72**
  L5: Liv .3C **52**
Blenheim Way L24: Speke 2D **108**
  WA11: St H 5F **29**
Blessington Rd. L4: Walt 6F **35**
Bletchley Av. CH44: Wall 3B **50**
Bligh St. L15: Wav 2C **72**
Blindfoot Rd. WA11: Rainf 4D **26**
Blisworth St. L21: Lith 5B **20**
Blithedale Ct. *CH42: Rock F* 2A **88**
    (off The Hawthornes)
Blomfield Rd. L19: Aller 4H **91**
Bloomfield Grn. L17: Aig 5A **72**
Bloomsbury Ct. CH47: Hoy 3A **64**
Bloomsbury Way WA8: Wid 6B **78**
Blossom Gro. L32: Kirkb 4B **24**
Blossom St. L20: Boot 6C **20**
Blucher St. L22: Water 2E **19**
Bluebell Av. CH41: Birke 1B **68**
  WA11: Hay 4G **31**
Bluebell Cl. L22: Water 2G **19**
  L32: Kirkb 5A **14**
Bluebell Ct. WA7: Beech 3B **124**
Blue Bell La. L36: Huy 3G **57**
Bluebell La. CH64: Nest 6E **119**
Blueberry Flds. L10: Faz 5D **22**
Bluecoat, The 5E **5** (6D **52**)
Bluecoat Chambers L1: Liv 5E **5**
Bluefields St. L8: Liv 2F **71**
Blue Hatch WA6: Frod 6G **123**
Blue Jay Cl. L27: N'ley 4G **75**
Blue Ridge Cl. WA5: Gt San 2G **81**
Bluestone La. L31: Mag 6D **6**
Bluewood Dr. CH41: Birke 6H **49**
Blundell Rd. L35: Whis 2G **59**
  WA8: Wid 3A **96**
BLUNDELLSANDS 6D **8**
Blundellsands Classic L23: Blun 6D **8**
Blundellsands Rd. E. *L23: Blun* 6D **8**
    (off Blundellsands Rd. W.)

Blundellsands & Crosby Station (Rail)
  . . . . .5E **9**
Blundellsands Rd. E. L23: Blun 5E **9**
Blundellsands Rd. W.
  L23: Blun 6D **8**
Blundells Dr. CH46: More 6C **48**
BLUNDELL'S HILL 5H **59**
Blundells Hill Golf Course 6H **59**
Blundell's La. L35: Rainh 6G **59**
Blundell St. L1: Liv 2D **70**
Blyth Cl. WA7: Murd 2F **125**
Blythe Av. WA8: Wid 5F **79**
Blyth Hey L30: N'ton 5D **10**
Blyth Rd. CH63: Brom 6C **104**
Blythswood St. L17: Aig 6H **71**
BMB Ind. Pk. CH44: Wall 4B **50**
Boaler St. L6: Liv 4G **53**
Boaler St. Ind. Est. *L6: Liv* 4H **53**
    (off Boaler St.)
Boardmans La. WA9: St H 1A **44**
  WA11: St H 1A **44**
Boathouse La. CH64: Park 5F **117**
Bobbies La. WA10: Eccl 1H **41**
Bob Paisley Ct. *L5: Liv* 1G **53**
    (off Adkins St.)
Bodden St. WA9: Clock F 3H **61**
Bodley St. L4: Walt 6F **35**
Bodmin Cl. WA7: Brook 1D **124**
Bodmin Gro. WA11: St H 4H **29**
Bodmin Rd. L4: Walt 4F **35**
Bodmin Way L26: Halew 3G **93**
Bognor Cl. L24: Speke 1D **108**
Bolan St. L13: Liv 4E **55**
BOLD 6D **44**
Bold Bus. Cen. WA9: Bold 6D **44**
Bolden Cl. L30: N'ton 2F **21**
Bolde Way CH63: Spit 4A **104**
BOLD HEATH 2A **80**
Bold Ind. Est. WA8: Wid 4G **79**
Bold Ind. Pk. WA9: Bold 1D **62**
Bold La. L39: Augh 1F **7**
  WA5: Coll G 6D **44**
  WA9: Bold 6D **44**
Bold Manor L35: Whis 4E **59**
Bold Pl. L1: Liv 6H **5**
Bold Rd. WA9: St H 6B **44**
Bold St. L1: Liv 5F **5** (6D **52**)
  WA7: Run 2F **113**
  WA8: Wid 4E **97**
  WA10: St H 2D **42**
Boleyn, The L31: Mag 4D **6**
Boleyn Ct. WA7: Manor P 2E **115**
Bolingbroke La. WA8: Wid 5A **80**
Bollin Ct. WA8: Wid 4F **79**
Bollington Cl. CH43: Oxton 6B **68**
Bolton Av. L32: Kirkb 1G **23**
Bolton Cl. WA9: St H 1G **43**
Bolton Rd. CH62: Port S 6B **88**
Bolton Rd. E. CH62: Port S 5C **88**
Bolton St. L3: Liv 4G **5** (6E **53**)
  WA9: St H 1G **43**
    (not continuous)
Bolton Wlk. L32: Kirkb 1G **23**
Bonchurch Dr. L15: Wav 6D **54**
Bond St. L3: Liv 3D **52**
  L34: Presc 1D **58**
Bonnington Av. L23: Crosb 4E **9**
Bonnington Cl. WA10: St H 2A **42**
Bonsall Rd. L12: W Der 1F **55**
Boode Cft. L28: Stockb V 4D **38**
Booker Av. L18: Moss H, Aller 2E **91**
Booth St. L13: Liv 4E **55**
  WA9: St H 6B **42**
Boothwood Cl. L7: Liv 6H **53**
BOOTLE 2C **34**
Bootle Leisure Cen. 1C **34**
Bootle Municipal Golf Course 2E **21**
Bootle New Strand Station (Rail) . . .1C **34**
Bootle Oriel Road Station (Rail) 3B **34**
Borax St. L13: Liv 5E **55**
Bordehill Gdns. L12: W Der 5H **37**
Border Rd. CH60: Hesw 5F **101**
Border Way L15: Wav 1E **53**
Borella Rd. L13: Liv 1D **54**

Borough Pavement CH41: Birke 3G 69
Borough Pl. *CH41: Birke* *3G 69*
(off Grange Rd. E.)
Borough Rd. CH41: Birke 6E 69
  CH42: Rock F, Tran 6E 69
  CH44: Wall 4F 51
  WA10: St H 3C 42
Borough Rd. E. CH41: Birke 3G 69
  CH44: Wall 5G 51
Borough Way CH44: Wall 5G 51
Borrowdale Rd. CH46: More 1B 66
  CH63: Beb 1G 103
  L15: Wav 3C 72
  WA8: Wid 3A 96
  WA10: St H 5H 41
Bosco Ct. L11: Crox 1F 37
Boscow Cres. WA9: St H 6H 43
Bosnia St. L8: Liv 6G 71
Bossom Ct. L22: Water 4F 19
Bostock St. L5: Liv 2D 52
Boston Av. WA7: Run 5F 113
Boston Blvd. WA5: Gt San 2H 81
Boswall Rd. CH43: Pren 2B 86
Boswell St. L8: Liv 2A 72
  L20: Boot 6A 20
Bosworth Cl. CH63: Spit 3H 103
Bosworth Rd. WA11: St H 5G 29
Botanic Est. L7: Liv 6B 54
Botanic Gro. L7: Liv 6A 54
Botanic Pl. L7: Liv 5A 54
Botanic Rd. L7: Liv 6A 54
Botany Rd. L24: Speke 6E 93
Botley Cl. CH49: Upton 4B 66
Boulevard L6: Liv 3B 54
Boulevard, The L8: Liv 3G 71
  L12: W Der 3G 37
Boulevard Industry Pk. L24: Halew ...6F 93
(not continuous)
Boulton Av. CH48: W Kir 5B 64
  CH62: New F 3B 88
Boundary Ct. WA10: St H 1C 42
Boundary Dr. L23: Crosb 3F 9
  L25: Hunts X 4F 93
Boundary Farm Rd. L26: Halew 5F 93
Boundary La. CH60: Hesw 5E 101
  L6: Liv 3H 53
  L33: Kirkb 1G 25
Boundary Rd. CH43: Bid, Noct 6H 49
  CH48: W Kir 3D 82
  CH62: Port S 4B 88
  L21: Lith 1D 20
(not continuous)
  L36: Huy 1H 75
  WA10: St H 2C 42
Boundary Stone La. WA8: Wid 5A 80
Boundary St. L5: Liv 1B 52
Boundary St. E. L5: Liv 1E 53
Boundary Wlk. L36: Huy 1A 76
Bourne Gdns. WA9: St H 4G 43
Bournemouth Cl. WA7: Murd 1F 125
Bourne St. L6: Liv 4H 53
Bourton Rd. L25: Hunts X 4D 92
Bousfield St. L4: Walt 6E 35
Bowden Cl. L12: Crox 3A 38
Bowden Rd. CH45: Wall 1C 50
  L19: Garst 5F 91
Bowden St. L21: Lith 5B 20
Bowdon Cl. WA10: Eccl 3H 41
Bowen Cl. WA8: Wid 5B 78
Bower Gro. L21: Sea 4H 19
Bower Ho. CH49: Upton 2D 66
Bower Rd. CH60: Hesw 5G 101
  L25: Woolt 5C 74
  L36: Huy 3G 57
Bowers Bus. Pk. WA8: Wid 4G 97
Bowers Pk. Ind. Est. WA8: Wid 4G 97
Bower St. WA8: Wid 2G 97
Bowfell Cl. CH62: East 4D 120
Bowfield Rd. L19: Gras 4F 91
Bowgreen Cl. CH43: Bid 2G 67
BOWKER'S GREEN 2H 7
Bowker's Grn. La. L39: Augh, Bic ...2H 7
Bowl, The
  Bromborough 3E 105

Bowland Av. L16: Child 6H 55
  WA9: Sut M 4F 61
Bowland Cl. CH62: Brom 4D 104
  WA7: Beech 2A 124
Bowland Dr. L21: Ford 5C 10
Bowles St. L20: Boot 6A 20
Bowls Rd. L13: Liv 2D 54
Bowmore Way L7: Liv 1A 72
Bowness Av. CH43: Pren 1C 86
  CH63: Brom 2C 120
  WA11: St H 3F 29
Bowood Ct. L8: Liv 6F 71
Bowring Ct. L14: Broad G 6B 56
Bowring Dr. CH64: Park 6F 117
BOWRING PARK 6C 56
Bowring Pk. Av. L16: Child 6C 56
Bowring Park Golf Course 6D 56
Bowring Pk. Rd. L14: Broad G 6G 55
Bowring Park Vis. Cen. 6D 56
Bowscale Cl. CH49: Upton 4C 66
Boxdale Cl. L18: Moss H 5E 73
Boxdale Rd. L18: Moss H 5E 73
Boxgrove Cl. WA8: Wid 6F 79
Boxmoor Rd. L18: Moss H 1E 91
Boxtree Cl. L12: Crox 1B 38
Boxwood Cl. L36: Roby 5E 57
Boxwood Gdns. WA9: St H 6A 44
Boycott St. L5: Liv 1G 53
Boyd Cl. CH46: Leas 4F 49
Boydell Cl. L28: Stockb V 6D 38
Boyer Av. L31: Mag 2B 12
Boyes Brow L33: Kirkb 5H 13
Boyes Cl. L31: Mag 2B 12
Boyton Ct. L7: Liv 1A 72
Brabant Rd. L17: Aig 2C 90
Braby Rd. L21: Lith 5C 20
Bracewell Cl. WA9: St H 1G 61
Bracken Ct. WA9: Clock F 5G 61
Brackendale CH49: Woodc 6G 67
  WA7: Run 5H 113
Brackendale Av. L9: Ain 4H 21
Bracken Dr. CH48: W Kir 1E 83
Brackenhurst Dr. CH45: New B 6E 33
Brackenhurst Grn. L33: Kirkb 1A 24
Bracken La. CH63: Hghr B 6F 87
Brackenside CH60: Hesw 3D 100
Bracken Wlk. *L32: Kirkb* *2H 23*
(off Wervin Rd.)
Bracken Way L12: W Der 2E 55
Bracken Wood L12: Crox 1A 38
Brackenwood Dr. WA8: Wid 4G 95
Brackenwood Golf Course 6F 87
Brackenwood Gro. L35: Whis 4F 59
Brackenwood Rd. CH63: Hghr B ...1F 103
Brackley Cl. CH44: Wall 4C 50
  WA7: Run 2D 112
Brackley St. WA7: Run 2D 112
Bracknell Av. L32: Kirkb 2H 23
Bracknell Cl. L32: Kirkb 3H 23
Bradda Cl. CH49: Upton 2D 66
Bradden Av. L13: Liv 2C 54
Bradden Cl. CH63: Spit 3B 104
Braddan Av. L13: Liv 2C 54
Bradewell Cl. L4: Kirkd 5E 35
Bradewell St. L4: Kirkd 5E 35
Bradfield Av. L10: Ain 6A 12
Bradfield St. L7: Liv 5A 54
Bradgate Cl. CH46: More 6H 47
Bradkirk Ct. L30: N'ton 4D 10
Bradley Fold L36: Huy 1A 76
Bradley La. WA5: Burtw 3H 45
Bradley Rd. L21: Lith 2B 20
Bradley Way WA8: Wid 2F 97
Bradman Cl. CH45: Wall 2D 50
Bradman Rd. CH46: More 6A 48
  L33: Know I 6E 15
Bradmoor Rd. CH62: Brom 5D 104
Bradshaw Cl. WA10: St H 1B 42
Bradshaw St. WA8: Wid 1E 97
Bradshaw Wlk. *L20: Boot* *1B 34*
(off St James Dr.)
Bradstone Cl. L10: Faz 5F 23

Bradville Rd. L9: Ain 4A 22
Bradwell Cl. CH48: W Kir 1D 82
Braehaven Rd. CH45: New B 6E 33
Braemar Cl. L35: Whis 4F 59
Braemar Ho. CH43: Oxton 4B 68
Braemar St. L20: Kirkd 4D 34
Braemore Rd. CH44: Wall 3B 50
Braeside Gdns. CH49: Upton 4D 66
Brae St. L7: Liv 5H 53
Brahms Cl. L8: Liv 3H 71
Braid St. CH41: Birke 1F 69
Braidwood Ct. *CH41: Birke* *4E 69*
(off Mount Gro.)
Brainerd St. L13: Liv 2C 54
Braithwaite Cl. L35: Rainh 4A 60
  WA7: Beech 1H 123
Brakedale Cl. L27: N'ley 5H 75
Bramberton Pl. L4: Walt 4A 36
Bramberton Rd. L4: Walt 4A 36
Bramble Av. CH41: Birke 1B 68
Bramble Cl. WA5: Penk 6G 81
Brambles, The WA5: Burtw 6H 45
Bramble Way CH46: More 5B 48
  WA7: Beech 3A 124
Bramblewood Cl. CH43: Noct 5H 67
  L27: N'ley 4G 75
Brambling Cl. WA7: Beech 2A 124
Brambling Pk. L26: Halew 2G 93
Bramcote Av. WA11: St H 5G 29
Bramcote Cl. L33: Kirkb 5C 14
Bramcote Rd. L33: Kirkb 5B 14
Bramcote Wlk. L33: Kirkb 5B 14
Bramerton Ct. CH48: W Kir 6A 64
Bramford Cl. CH49: Upton 4C 66
Bramhall Cl. CH48: W Kir 1D 82
  L24: Speke 3G 109
Bramhall Dr. CH62: East 4F 121
Bramhall Rd. L22: Water 3G 19
Bramhope Pk. L12: W Der 6H 37
Bramley Av. CH63: Hghr B 4G 87
Bramley Cl. L27: N'ley 4F 75
Bramleys, The L31: Mag 2A 12
Bramley Wlk. L24: Speke 3F 109
Bramley Way L32: Kirkb 6G 13
Brampton Ct. L32: Kirkb 5A 14
Brampton Ct. WA9: St H 2D 44
Brampton Dr. L8: Liv 1G 71
Bramwell Av. CH43: Pren 2C 86
Bramwell St. WA9: St H 1A 44
Branchway WA11: Hay 5F 31
Brancker Av. L35: Rainh 3H 59
Brancote Ct. CH43: Clau 3B 68
  CH62: Brom 6D 104
Brancote Mt. CH43: Clau 3B 68
Brancote Rd. CH43: Clau 3B 68
Brandearth Hey L28: Stockb V 6D 38
Brandearth Ho. L28: Stockb V 6D 38
Brandon WA8: Wid 1H 95
Brandon St. CH41: Birke 3H 69
Brandreth Cl. L35: Rainh 4A 60
Branfield Cl. L12: Crox 2A 38
Bransdale Cl. WA5: Gt San 2H 81
Branstree Av. L11: Norr G 3D 36
Branthwaite Cres. L11: Norr G 3E 37
Branthwaite Gro. L11: Norr G 4E 37
Brasenose Rd. L20: Boot 3B 34
  L8: Liv 3E 71
Brassey St. CH41: Birke 1D 68
  L8: Liv 3E 71
Brattan Rd. CH41: Birke 5E 69
Braunton Rd. CH45: Wall 1C 50
  L17: Aig 3C 90
Bravery Ct. L19: Speke 1A 108
Braybrooke Rd. L11: Norr G 2E 37
Bray Cl. WA7: Beech 1H 123
Braydon Cl. L25: Hunts X 5E 93
Brayfield Rd. L4: Walt 4B 36
Bray Rd. L24: Speke 1E 109
Bray St. CH41: Birke 1D 68
Brearley Cl. CH43: Bid 1G 67
Breccia Gdns. WA9: St H 3A 44
Brechin Rd. L33: Kirkb 1B 24
Breckfield Pl. L5: Liv 2F 53
Breckfield Rd. Nth. L5: Liv 1F 53

Breckfield Rd. Sth. L6: Liv 2G 53
Breck Pl. CH44: Wall 4C 50
Breck Rd. CH44: Wall 3B 50
   L4: Walt 3F 53
   L5: Liv 3F 53
   WA8: Wid .2F 97
Breckside Av. CH44: Wall 3A 50
Breckside Pk. L6: Liv 1A 54
Brecon Av. L30: N'ton 2F 21
Brecon Rd. CH42: Tran 2E 87
Brecon St. L6: Liv 4H 53
Brecon Wlk. L30: N'ton 2G 21
                   (off Durham Av.)
Breeze Cl. L9: Walt 2F 35
Breeze Hill L9: Walt 3F 35
   L20: Boot .2D 34
Breezehill Cl. CH64: Nest 6B 118
Breezehill Rd. CH64: Nest 6B 118
Breeze La. L9: Walt 2F 35
Brelade Rd. L13: Liv 3D 54
Bremhill Rd. L11: Norr G 2D 36
Bremner Cl. L7: Liv 6A 54
Brenda Cres. L23: Thorn 2A 10
Brendale Av. L31: Mag 1A 12
Brendan's Way L30: N'ton 6E 11
Brendon Av. L21: Lith 2A 20
Brendon Gro. WA9: St H 1C 44
Brendor Rd. L25: Woolt 2D 92
Brenig St. CH41: Birke 6B 50
Brenka Av. L9: Ain 2H 21
Brentfield WA8: Wid 1B 96
Brent Way L26: Halew 5H 93
                (not continuous)
Brentwood Av. L17: Aig 6A 72
   L23: Crosb 4H 9
Brentwood Cl. WA10: Eccl 2H 41
Brentwood Ct. CH49: Woodc 1E 85
            (off Childwall Grn.)
Brentwood Gro. L33: Kirkb 3A 14
Brentwood St. CH44: Wall 4E 51
   L15: Wav .3E 73
Brereton Av. CH63: Beb 5A 88
   L15: Wav .3E 73
Brereton Cl. WA7: Cas 5C 114
               (not continuous)
Bretherton Ct. L35: Rainh 3A 60
              (off Ratcliffe Pl.)
Bretherton Rd. L34: Presc 1E 59
Bretlands Rd. L23: Thorn 3B 10
Brett Cl. L33: Kirkb 4H 13
Brett St. CH41: Birke 1D 68
Brewery La. L31: Mell 5C 12
                (not continuous)
Brewster St. L4: Kirkd 4E 35
   L20: Boot .4E 35
Breydon Gdns. WA9: St H 1C 60
Brian Av. CH61: Irby 5D 84
Brian Cummings Ct.
   L21: Lith 5B 20
Briardale Rd. CH42: Tran 5E 69
   CH44: Wall 5G 51
   CH63: Hghr B 4H 87
   CH64: Will .6A 120
   L18: Moss H 4D 72
Briar Dr. CH60: Hesw 5E 101
   L36: Huy 5F 57
Briarfield Av. WA8: Wid 2G 95
Briarfield Rd. CH60: Hesw 5E 101
Briars Cl. L35: Rainh 6B 60
Briars Grn. WA10: St H 6D 28
Briars La. L31: Mag 6D 6
Briar St. L4: Kirkd 6D 34
Briarswood Cl. CH42: Rock F 3H 87
   L35: Whis .4F 59
Briarwood L23: Blun 3D 8
   WA7: Nort .5D 114
Briarwood Rd. L17: Aig 6C 72
Briary Cl. CH60: Hesw 4F 101
Brickfields L36: Huy 6A 58
Brick St. L1: Liv 2D 70
   WA12: Newt W 2H 45
Brickwall Grn. L29: Seft 2F 11
Brickwall La. L29: Seft 4E 11
Bride St. L4: Walt 3F 35
Bridewell Cl. WA8: Wid 6F 79

Bridge Ct. CH48: W Kir 6A 64
   L30: N'ton 5D 10
Bridge Cft. L21: Ford 6C 10
Bridgecroft Rd. CH45: Wall 1D 50
Bridge Farm Cl.
   CH49: Woodc 5F 67
Bridge Farm Dr. L31: Mag 5E 7
Bridgefield Cl. L25: Gate 2D 74
Bridgefield Ct. L34: Presc 2E 59
Bridgeford Av. L12: W Der 6E 37
Bridge Gdns. L12: W Der 4B 38
Bridgehouse La. L10: Faz 5E 23
Bridge Ind. Est. L24: Speke 6D 92
Bridge La. L30: N'ton 5D 10
   WA6: Frod 6G 123
Bridge La. M. WA6: Frod 6H 123
Bridgeman St. WA10: St H 2B 42
                (not continuous)
Bridgemere Cl. L7: Liv 4B 54
Bridgemere Ho. L17: Aig 1B 90
Bridgemill Cl. L27: N'ley 5H 75
Bridgend Cl. WA8: Wid 6B 78
Bridgenorth Rd. CH61: Pens 1C 100
Bridge Retail Pk. WA7: Run 3E 113
Bridge Rd. CH48: W Kir 6A 64
   L7: Liv 1B 72
   L18: Moss H 6E 73
   L21: Lith 4A 20
                (not continuous)
   L23: Blun .6E 9
   L31: Mag .2B 12
   L34: Presc 2D 58
   L36: Roby .5E 57
   WA9: Clock F 5H 61
Bridges La. L29: Seft 2F 11
Bridge St. CH41: Birke 2G 69
                (not continuous)
   CH62: Port S 6B 88
                (not continuous)
   L20: Boot .3B 34
   WA7: Run 3F 113
   WA10: St H 2E 43
Bridge Vw. Cl. WA8: Wid 1E 113
Bridge Vw. Dr. L33: Kirkb 5B 14
Bridge Wlk. WA7: Pal F 6B 114
        (off Halton Lea Shop. Cen.)
Bridgewater Ct. L21: Lith 1A 20
   WA6: Frod 6G 123
Bridgewater Ct. L21: Lith 1A 20
Bridgewater Grange WA7: Pres B 2H 125
Bridgewater Ho. WA7: Run 2C 112
Bridgewater St. L1: Liv 2D 70
   WA7: Run 2E 113
Bridgewater Way L36: Huy 1A 76
Bridgeway L11: Norr G 4C 36
Bridgeway E. WA7: Wind H 3E 115
Bridgeway W. WA7: Wind H 3D 114
Bridle Av. CH44: Wall 5G 51
Bridle Cl. CH43: Bid 3F 67
   CH62: Brom 6E 105
Bridle Ct. WA9: St H 5G 43
Bridle Pk. CH62: Brom 6E 105
Bridle Rd. CH44: Wall 5G 51
   CH62: Brom, East 6E 105
   L30: N'ton 3E 21
Bridle Ind. Est. L30: N'ton 3F 21
Bridle Way L30: N'ton 3F 21
   L33: Kirkb .3H 13
Bridport St. L3: Liv 3G 5 (5E 53)
Brierfield Rd. L15: Wav 3D 72
Brierley Cl. L30: N'ton 5H 11
               (off Beeston Dr.)
Brierley Ter. WA8: Wid 2G 97
Briery Hey Av. L33: Kirkb 1B 24
Brigadier Dr. L12: W Der 6A 38
Brightgate Cl. L7: Liv 1H 71
BRIGHTON LE SANDS 1D 18
Brighton Rd. L22: Water 2F 19
   L36: Huy 4B 58
Brighton St. CH44: Wall 3F 51
Brighton Va. L22: Water 1E 19
Bright St. CH41: Birke 3E 69
                (not continuous)
   L6: Liv 4G 53

Brightwell Cl. CH49: Upton 5D 66
   WA5: Gt San 4G 81
Brill St. CH41: Birke 1D 68
Brimelow Cres. WA5: Penk 6G 81
BRIMSTAGE 3D 102
Brimstage Av. CH63: Hghr B 3F 87
Brimstage Cl. CH60: Hesw 6G 101
Brimstage Grn. CH60: Hesw 5H 101
Brimstage Hall 3C 102
Brimstage Hall Courtyard
   CH63: Brim 3C 102
Brimstage La.
   CH63: Brim, Store 3D 102
Brimstage Rd. CH60: Hesw 6G 101
   CH63: Beb, Brim, Hghr B 6G 101
   L4: Walt 3E 35
Brimstage St. CH41: Birke 4E 69
Brindley, The .3E 113
Brindley Cl. L21: Lith 1A 20
Brindley Rd. L32: Kirkb 1G 23
   WA7: Ast .2B 114
   WA9: St H 1A 62
Brindley St. L8: Liv 3D 70
   WA7: Run 2D 112
Brindley Wharf WA4: Pres H 2H 125
Brinley Cl. CH62: Brom 2D 120
Brinton Cl. L27: N'ley 3E 75
   WA8: Wid .3B 96
Brisbane Av. CH45: New B 5C 32
Brisbane St. WA9: St H 6B 42
Briscoe Av. CH46: More 2C 66
Briscoe Dr. CH46: More 2C 66
Bristol Av. CH44: Wall 3E 51
   WA7: Murd 1G 125
Bristol Rd. L15: Wav 3E 73
Britannia Av. L15: Wav 2B 72
Britannia Cres. L8: Liv 6F 71
Britannia Ho. CH41: Birke 3H 69
Britannia Pav. L3: Liv 1C 70
Britannia Rd. CH45: Wall 3C 50
Britonside Av. L32: Kirkb 3C 24
Brittarge Brow L27: N'ley 5G 75
Britten Cl. L8: Liv 3H 71
Broadacre Cl. L18: Moss H 4H 73
Broadbelt St. L4: Walt 3F 35
Broadfield Av. CH43: Bid 1F 67
Broadfield Cl. CH43: Bid 2F 67
Broadfields WA7: Nort 5E 115
Broadgate Av. WA9: St H 4G 43
BROAD GREEN 6H 55
Broad Grn. Rd. L13: Liv 4E 55
Broad Green Station (Rail) 6H 55
Broadheath Av. CH43: Bid 2G 67
Broadheath Ter. WA8: Wid 2B 96
Broad Hey L30: N'ton 6D 10
Broad Hey Cl. L25: Woolt 6D 74
Broadhurst St. L17: Aig 6A 72
Broadlands L35: Presc 2E 59
Broad La. Pct. L11: Norr G 4D 36
Broadleaf Rd. L19: Gras 4D 90
Broadmead CH60: Hesw 6G 101
   L19: Aller .4A 92
BROAD OAK .1B 44
Broad Oak Av. WA5: Penk 5G 81
   WA11: Hay 5C 30
Broad Oak Rd. WA9: St H 2A 44
Broadoak Rd. L14: Knott A 3B 56
   L31: Mag .6D 6
Broadoaks CH49: Upton 3C 66
Broad Pl. L11: Norr G 5D 36
Broads, The WA9: St H 1C 60
Broad Sq. L11: Norr G 5D 36
Broadstone Dr. CH63: Spit 3H 103
Broad Vw. L11: Norr G 5D 36
Broadway CH45: Wall 2B 50
   CH49: Grea 4C 66
   CH63: Hghr B 4F 87
   L9: Ain 4C 22

Broadway L11: Norr G 4C **36**
    WA8: Wid .2G **95**
    WA10: Eccl 1G **41**
    WA10: St H 5A **42**
Broadway Av. CH45: Wall 2B **50**
Broadway Badminton Cen. 5H **41**
Broadway Mkt. L11: Norr G 4C **36**
Broadwood Av. L31: Mag 2A **12**
Broadwood St. L25: Wav 2C **72**
Brock Av. L31: Mag 5D **6**
Brockenhurst Rd. L9: Walt 6G **21**
Brock Gdns. L24: Hale 3E **111**
Brock Hall Cl. WA9: Clock F 3G **61**
Brockhall Cl. L35: Whis 1G **59**
Brockholme Rd. L18: Moss H 2E **91**
Brocklebank La. L19: Aller 3H **91**
Brockley Av. CH45: New B 4D **32**
Brock St. L4: Kirkd 5E **35**
Brodie Av. L18: Moss H 6E **73**
    L19: Aig, Aller 2F **91**
BROMBOROUGH 5C **104**
Bromborough Golf Course 2B **120**
BROMBOROUGH POOL 6D **88**
BROMBOROUGH PORT 2E **105**
Bromborough Rake Station (Rail) . . .5C **104**
Bromborough Rd. CH63: Beb 6A **88**
Bromborough Station (Rail) 6C **104**
Bromborough Village Rd.
    CH62: Brom 4E **105**
Brome Way CH63: Spit 3B **104**
Bromilow Rd. WA9: St H 3B **44**
Bromley Av. L18: Moss H 4D **72**
Bromley Cl. CH60: Hesw 6C **100**
    L26: Halew 2A **94**
Bromley Rd. CH45: New B 6C **32**
Brompton Av. CH44: Wall 3E **51**
    L17: Liv 4A **72**
    L23: Crosb 6E **9**
    L33: Kirkb 4C **14**
Brompton Ct. L17: Liv 4A **72**
Brompton Ho. L17: Aig 4B **72**
Bromsgrove Rd. CH49: Grea 5A **66**
Bromyard Cl. L20: Boot 1B **34**
Bronington Av. CH62: Brom 1D **120**
Bronshill Ct. L23: Blun 5C **8**
Bronte Cl. L23: Blun 5D **8**
Bronte St. L3: Liv 3H **5**
    WA10: St H 1B **42**
Brook, The L31: Mag 1C **12**
Brookbank Ct. L10: Faz 4F **23**
Brookbridge Rd. L13: Liv 1C **54**
Brook Cl. CH44: Wall 2E **51**
    WA8: Cron 3A **78**
Brookdale WA8: Wid 6G **77**
Brookdale Av. Nth. CH49: Grea 5C **66**
Brookdale Av. Sth. CH49: Grea 5C **66**
Brookdale Cl. CH49: Grea 5C **66**
Brookdale Rd. L15: Wav 3C **72**
Brook Dr. WA5: Gt San 4H **81**
Brook End WA9: St H 4C **44**
Brooke Rd. E. L22: Water 1F **19**
Brooke Rd. W. L22: Water 1E **19**
Brookfield Av. L22: Water 3H **19**
    L23: Crosb 6F **9**
    L35: Rainh 2A **60**
    WA7: Run 3A **114**
Brookfield Cen. L9: Ain 6A **22**
Brookfield Dr. L9: Ain, Faz 6A **22**
Brookfield Gdns. CH48: W Kir 1B **82**
Brookfield Ho. L36: Huy 4G **57**
Brookfield La. L39: Augh 1F **7**
Brookfield Rd. CH48: W Kir 1B **82**
BROOKFIELDS GREEN 2F **7**
Brook Furlong WA6: Frod 5C **122**
Brook Hey Ct. CH64: Park 5F **117**
Brook Hey Dr. L33: Kirkb 5B **14**
Brook Hey Wlk. L33: Kirkb 6C **14**
Brookhill Cl. L20: Boot 2D **34**
Brookhill Rd. L20: Boot 1D **34**
Brookhouse Gro. WA10: Eccl 2G **41**
BROOKHURST 2C **120**
Brookhurst Av. CH62: East 1C **120**
    CH63: Brom, East 1C **120**
Brookhurst Cl. CH63: Brom 2C **120**

Brookhurst Rd. CH63: Brom 1C **120**
Brookland La. WA9: St H 3C **44**
Brookland Rd. CH41: Birke 4F **69**
Brookland Rd. E. L13: Liv 4E **55**
Brookland Rd. W. L13: Liv 4E **55**
Brooklands CH41: Birke 2F **69**
    L17: Aig 1B **90**
Brooklands, The L36: Huy 6G **57**
Brooklands Av. L22: Water 3H **19**
Brooklands Dr. L31: Mag 1B **12**
Brooklands Gdns. CH64: Park 6G **117**
Brooklands Pk. WA8: Wid 1G **97**
Brooklands Rd. CH64: Park 6G **117**
    WA10: Eccl 3A **42**
Brook La. CH64: Park 5G **117**
Brook Lea Ho. L21: Ford 6C **10**
Brooklet Rd. CH60: Hesw 5G **101**
Brooklime Rd. L11: Norr G 4D **36**
Brook Mdw. CH61: Irby 4C **84**
Brook Pk. L31: Mag 2A **12**
Brook Rd. L9: Walt 1G **35**
    L20: Boot .2B **34**
    L23: Thorn 3A **10**
    L31: Mag .1C **12**
Brooks, The WA11: St H 4E **29**
Brooks All. L1: Liv 5E **5** (6D **52**)
Brookside L12: W Der 5B **38**
    L31: Mag 6D **6**
Brookside Av. L14: Knott A 4H **55**
    L22: Water 3H **19**
    WA10: Eccl 6H **27**
    WA11: Rainf 2E **17**
Brookside Cl. L35: Presc 3E **59**
    WA11: Hay 4D **30**
Brookside Ct. L23: Crosb 5G **9**
    L35: Presc 3E **59**
Brookside Cres. CH49: Upton 4B **66**
Brookside Dr. CH49: Upton 4C **66**
Brookside Rd. L35: Presc 3E **59**
Brookside Vw. WA11: Hay 4D **30**
Brookside Way WA11: Hay 4D **30**
Brook St. CH41: Birke 1E **69**
    CH62: Port S 5A **88**
    L3: Liv 2B **4** (5B **52**)
    L35: Whis .2F **59**
    WA7: Run 3E **113**
        (not continuous)
    WA8: Wid .3F **97**
    WA10: St H 2E **43**
Brook St. E. CH41: Birke 2G **69**
Brook Ter. CH48: W Kir 1A **82**
    WA7: Run 4A **114**
Brookthorpe Cl. CH45: Wall 1E **51**
BROOKVALE 1E **125**
Brook Va. L22: Water 3H **19**
Brookvale Av. Nth. WA7: Brook 1D **124**
Brookvale Av. Sth. WA7: Brook 1D **124**
Brookvale Cl. WA5: Burtw 1H **63**
Brookvale Local Nature Reserve . . .3H **19**
Brookvale Recreation Cen. 1E **125**
Brookview Cl. L27: N'ley 5H **75**
Brook Wlk. CH61: Irby 4B **84**
Brookward Cl. L32: Kirkb 5B **14**
Brookway CH43: Pren 2A **86**
    CH45: Wall 2C **50**
    CH49: Grea 4C **66**
Brookway La. WA9: St H 4B **44**
Brookwood Rd. L36: Huy 3G **57**
Broom Cl. L34: Eccl P 1F **59**
Broome Ct. WA7: Brook 1D **124**
Broomfield Cl. CH60: Hesw 4A **100**
Broomfield Gdns. L9: Walt 6F **21**
Broomfield Rd. L9: Walt 6F **21**
        (not continuous)
Broom Hill CH43: Clau 2B **68**
Broomhill Cl. L27: N'ley 3E **75**
Broomlands CH60: Hesw 5D **100**
Broomleigh Cl. L35: Hghr B 6F **87**
Broom Rd. WA10: St H 5H **41**
Brooms Gro. L10: Ain 1C **22**
Broom Way L26: Halew 4G **93**
Broseley Av. CH62: Brom 4C **104**
Broster Av. CH46: More 1A **66**
Broster Cl. CH46: More 1A **66**

Brosters La. CH47: Meols 1D **64**
Brotherhood Dr. WA9: St H 6H **43**
Brotherton Cl. CH62: Brom 4C **104**
Brotherton Park &
    Dibbinsdale Local Nature Reserve
    . . . . .3C **104**
Brougham Av. CH41: Tran 5H **69**
Brougham Rd. CH44: Wall 4F **51**
Brougham Ter. L6: Liv 4G **53**
        (off W. Derby Rd.)
Broughton Av. CH48: W Kir 6A **64**
Broughton Dr. L19: Gras 4E **91**
Broughton Hall Rd. L12: W Der 2A **56**
Broughton Rd. CH44: Wall 4D **50**
Broughton Way WA8: Hale B 6H **95**
BROW, THE 4B **114**
Brow La. CH60: Hesw 6D **100**
Brownbill Bank L27: N'ley 4G **75**
BROWN EDGE 6B **42**
Browning Av. CH42: Rock F 2H **87**
    WA8: Wid .3D **96**
Browning Cl. L36: Huy 6H **57**
Browning Rd. CH45: Wall 2H **49**
    L13: Liv 1D **54**
    L22: Water 1F **19**
Browning St. L20: Boot 1A **34**
Brownlow Arc. WA10: St H 2E **43**
Brownlow Hill L3: Liv 4G **5** (6E **53**)
Brownlow Rd. CH62: New F 4B **88**
Brownlow St. L3: Liv 6F **53**
Brownmoor Cl. L23: Crosb 5A **10**
Brownmoor La. L23: Crosb 6H **9**
Brownmoor Pk. L23: Crosb 6H **9**
Brown's La. L30: N'ton 6F **11**
Brown St. WA8: Wid 4H **97**
Brownville Rd. L13: Liv 6B **36**
Brow Rd. CH43: Bid 6H **49**
Brow Side L5: Liv 3F **53**
Broxholme Way L31: Mag 2B **12**
Broxton Av. CH43: Pren 1B **86**
    CH48: W Kir 6B **64**
Broxton Cl. WA8: Wid 6A **78**
Broxton Rd. CH45: Wall 1B **50**
Broxton St. L15: Wav 1C **72**
Bruce Cres. CH63: Brom 1C **120**
Bruce St. L8: Liv 5G **71**
    WA10: St H 2C **42**
Brunel Dr. L21: Lith 1A **20**
Brunel M. L6: Liv 2G **53**
Brunel Rd. CH62: Brom 4F **105**
Brunner Rd. WA8: Wid 3E **97**
Brunsborough Cl. CH62: Brom 1C **120**
Brunsfield Cl. CH46: More 2A **66**
Brunstath Cl. CH60: Hesw 4G **101**
Brunswick WA7: Run 2E **113**
Brunswick Bus. Pk. L3: Liv 4D **70**
        (not continuous)
Brunswick Cl. L4: Kirkd 5E **35**
Brunswick Ct. CH41: Birke 2G **69**
        (off Brunswick M.)
Brunswick Ent. Cen. L3: Liv 4D **70**
Brunswick M. CH41: Birke 2G **69**
    L22: Water 3G **19**
Brunswick Pde. L22: Water 3F **19**
Brunswick Pl. L20: Kirkd 5B **34**
Brunswick Rd. L6: Liv 4F **53**
    WA12: Newt W 1H **45**
Brunswick Station (Rail) 5E **71**
Brunswick St. L2: Liv 5B **4** (6C **52**)
    L3: Liv 5B **4** (6B **52**)
    L19: Garst 2G **107**
        (not continuous)
    WA9: St H .2C **44**
Brunswick Way L3: Liv 4D **70**
Brunt La. L19: Aller 4A **92**
Brushford Cl. L12: W Der 3F **37**
Bruton Rd. L36: Huy 1F **57**
        (not continuous)
Bryanston Rd. CH42: Tran 1C **86**
    L17: Aig 6H **71**
Bryant Rd. L21: Lith 5B **20**
Bryce Cl. CH62: Brom 2C **104**
Bryce Dr. CH62: Brom 2C **104**
Bryce Wlk. CH62: Brom 1C **104**

Bryceway, The L12: Knott A 3H 55
Brydges St. L7: Liv 6G 53
Bryer Rd. L35: Presc 3D 58
Bryn Bank CH44: Wall 3E 51
Brynmor Rd. L18: Moss H 2E 91
Brynmoss Av. CH44: Wall 3B 50
Brynn St. WA8: Wid 3F 97
WA10: St H 1E 43
Bryony Way CH42: Rock F 3H 87
Brythen St. L1: Liv 4F 5 (6D 52)
BT Convention Cen. 2C 70
Buccleuch St. CH41: Birke 6B 50
Buchanan Cl. WA8: Wid 6D 78
Buchanan Rd. CH44: Wall 4F 51
L9: Walt 2F 35
Buckfast Av. WA11: Hay 4H 31
Buckfast Cl. L30: N'ton 5F 11
WA5: Penk 6G 81
Buckfast Ct. WA7: Nort 2G 115
Buckingham Av. CH43: Clau 2B 68
CH63: Hghr B 4G 87
L17: Liv 3B 72
WA8: Wid 5E 79
Buckingham Bingo
  Bootle 2C 34
Buckingham Cl. L30: N'ton 6C 10
WA10: St H 3C 42
Buckingham Ct. L33: Kirkb 6B 14
Buckingham Dr. WA11: St H 4E 29
Buckingham Ho. L17: Aig 4B 72
Buckingham Gdns. WA9: St H 1A 60
Buckingham Rd. CH44: Wall 3B 50
L9: Walt 5G 21
L13: Liv 1B 54
L31: Mag 1A 12
Buckingham St. L5: Liv 2E 53
Buckland Cl. WA8: Wid 4B 96
Buckland Dr. CH63: Spit 3H 103
Buckland St. L17: Aig 6H 71
Buckley Hill La. L29: Seft 5D 10
Buckley Wlk. L24: Speke 3F 109
Buckley Way L30: N'ton 4D 10
Buckthorn Cl. L28: Stockb V 6D 38
Buckthorn Gdns. WA9: St H 1A 60
Bude Cl. CH43: Bid 3G 67
Bude Ho. CH43: Bid 3G 67
                          (off Bude Cl.)
Bude Rd. WA8: Wid 1C 96
Budworth Av. WA8: Wid 1B 96
WA9: Sut M 4F 61
Budworth Cl. CH43: Oxton 5A 68
WA7: Run 6H 113
Budworth Ct. CH43: Oxton 4B 68
Budworth Dr. L25: Woolt 1E 93
Budworth Rd. CH43: Noct, Oxton 5A 68
Buerton Cl. CH43: Noct 5A 68
Buffs La. CH60: Hesw 4F 101
Buildwas Rd. CH64: Nest 5A 118
Bulford Rd. L9: Faz 1C 36
Bulkeley Rd. CH44: Wall 4F 51
Bull Bri. La. L10: Ain 1C 22
Bullens Rd. L4: Walt 5F 35
L32: Kirkb 2B 24
Bullfinch Cl. L26: Halew 2G 93
Bull La. L9: Ain 4H 21
L9: Walt 5F 21
Bullrush Dr. CH46: More 5E 49
Bulrushes, The L17: Aig 6F 71
Bulwer St. CH42: Rock F 1H 87
L5: Liv 2G 53
L20: Boot 6A 20
Bunbury Dr. WA7: Run 1G 123
Bundoran Rd. L17: Aig 1C 90
Bunter Rd. L32: Kirkb 4B 24
Bunting Ct. L26: Halew 1F 93
Burbo Bank Rd. L23: Blun 5C 8
Burbo Bank Rd. Nth. L23: Blun 4B 8
Burbo Bank Rd. Sth. L23: Blun 6D 8
Burbo Cres. L23: Blun 6D 8
Burbo Mans. L23: Blun 6D 8
Burbo Point L23: Blun 3C 8
Burbo Way CH45: Wall 5A 32
Burden Rd. CH46: More 1A 66
Burdett Av. CH63: Spit 3H 103

Burdett Cl. CH63: Spit 3A 104
Burdett Rd. CH45: Wall 2H 49
L22: Water 1F 19
Burdett St. L17: Aig 6A 72
Burdock Rd. L11: Norr G 4D 36
Burford Av. CH44: Wall 4B 50
Burford Rd. L16: Child 6G 55
Burgess Gdns. L31: Mag 5B 6
Burgess St. L3: Liv 2H 5 (5E 53)
Burghill Rd. L12: Crox 1B 38
Burgundy Cl. L17: Aig 1A 90
Burland Cl. WA7: Run 4D 112
Burland Rd. L26: Halew 5A 94
Burleigh M. L5: Liv 1F 53
                   (off Burleigh Rd. Sth.)
Burleigh Rd. Nth. L5: Liv 1F 53
Burleigh Rd. Sth. L5: Liv 1F 53
Burley Cl. L32: Kirkb 2B 24
Burlingham Av. CH48: W Kir 2D 82
Burlington Ho. L22: Water 2G 19
Burlington Rd. CH45: New B 4D 32
Burlington St. CH41: Birke 3G 69
L3: Liv 3C 52
Burman Cres. L19: Garst 4G 91
Burman Rd. L19: Garst 4G 91
Burmarsh La. WA8: Hale B 6H 95
Burnage Av. WA9: Clock F 3G 61
Burnage Cl. L24: Speke 3H 109
Burnand St. L4: Walt 6F 35
Burnard Cl. L33: Kirkb 1B 24
Burnard Cres. L33: Kirkb 1B 24
Burnard Wlk. L33: Kirkb 1B 24
Burnell Cl. WA10: St H 2D 42
Burnet Rd. L5: Liv 1G 53
Burnham Cl. WA5: Penk 4H 81
WA8: Wid 6A 78
Burnham Rd. L18: Moss H 6G 73
Burnie Av. L20: Boot 6E 21
Burnley Av. CH46: More 1D 66
Burnley Cl. L6: Liv 3G 53
Burnley Gro. CH46: More 6D 48
Burnley Rd. CH46: More 6D 48
Burnsall Dr. WA8: Wid 6A 78
Burnsall St. L19: Garst 6A 92
Burns Av. CH45: Wall 2C 50
Burns Cl. L16: Child 1B 74
L35: Whis 4E 59
Burns Cres. WA8: Wid 3D 96
Burns Gro. L36: Huy 6A 58
Burnside Av. CH44: Wall 5D 50
Burnside Rd. CH44: Wall 5D 50
Burns Rd. WA9: Sut M 4E 61
Burns St. L20: Boot 6A 20
Burnt Ash Cl. L19: Gras 4D 90
Burnthwaite Rd.
  L14: Knott A 4G 55
Burnt Mill La. WA8: Hale B 6D 94
Burrell Cl. CH42: Tran 2E 87
Burrell Ct. CH42: Tran 2E 87
Burrell Dr. CH46: More 2B 66
Burrell Rd. CH42: Tran 2E 87
Burrell St. L4: Walt 5F 35
Burroughs Gdns. L3: Liv 3D 52
Burrow's Av. WA11: Hay 6B 30
Burrows Ct. L3: Liv 3C 52
WA9: St H 2A 44
                      (off Chancery La.)
Burrow's La. L34: Eccl P 6E 41
WA10: Eccl 3F 41
Burrows St. WA11: Hay 5C 30
Burton Av. CH45: Wall 2A 50
L35: Rainh 3G 59
Burton Cl. L1: Liv 1D 70
L35: Rainh 3G 59
WA8: Wid 6D 78
Burtonhead Ct. WA9: St H 4F 43
                        (off Harris Gdns.)
Burtonhead Rd. WA9: St H 3D 42
WA10: St H 3D 42
Burton St. L5: Kirkd 1C 52
Burtons Way L32: Kirkb 3G 23
BURTONWOOD 1G 63
Burtonwood Cotts. WA9: St H 3E 45
Burtonwood Ind. Cen. WA5: Burtw 6H 45

Burtonwood Rd.
  WA5: Burtw, Gt San, Westb
                         . . . . .3H 63 & 5H 63
Burtree Rd. L14: Knott A 1C 56
Burwain Ho. L19: Aig 4D 90
Burwell Cl. L33: Kirkb 6C 14
Burwen Dr. L9: Walt 5F 21
Busby's Cotts. CH45: New B 5D 32
Bushell Ct. CH43: Oxton 5C 68
Bushel's Dr. WA9: Clock F 4H 61
Bushey Rd. L4: Walt 3A 36
Bushley Cl. L20: Boot 1B 34
Bush Way CH60: Hesw 5B 100
Business Resource Cen.
  L33: Know I 3E 25
Butchers La. L39: Augh 2E 7
Bute St. L5: Liv 4E 53
                           (not continuous)
Butleigh Rd. L36: Huy 2F 57
Butler Cres. L6: Liv 4H 53
Butler St. L6: Liv 3H 53
Buttercup Cl. CH46: More 5E 49
L22: Water 2H 19
Buttercup Way L9: Walt 1H 35
Butterfield St. L4: Walt 6F 35
Buttermere Av. CH43: Noct 3G 67
WA11: St H 3E 29
Buttermere Cl. L31: Mag 6D 6
L33: Kirkb 5H 13
Buttermere Ct. CH41: Birke 4E 69
                       (off Penrith St.)
Buttermere Gdns. L23: Crosb 1H 19
Buttermere Gro. WA7: Beech 2H 123
Buttermere Rd. L16: Child 1C 74
Buttermere St. L8: Liv 2H 71
Butterton Av. CH49: Upton 3B 66
Butterwick Dr. L12: Crox 2A 38
Buxted Rd. L32: Kirkb 3C 24
Buxted Wlk. L32: Kirkb 3C 24
Buxton La. CH44: Wall 2A 50
Buxton Rd. CH42: Rock F 1A 88
Byerley St. CH44: Wall 4F 51
Byland Cl. WA8: Wid 4G 79
Byles St. L8: Liv 5G 71
Byng Pl. L4: Walt 5B 36
Byng Rd. L4: Walt 5B 36
Byng St. L20: Boot 3B 34
By-Pass, The L23: Crosb 5G 9
Byrne Av. CH42: Rock F 2H 87
Byrne Avenue Baths 2H 87
Byrom St. L3: Liv 2F 5 (5D 52)
Byron Av. L12: W Der 6E 37
L35: Whis 4F 59
Byron Cl. CH43: Pren 3B 86
L36: Huy 6A 58
WA10: St H 6E 29
Byron Ct. L25: Woolt 6C 74
Byron Rd. L23: Blun 5E 9
L31: Lyd 4C 6
Byron St. L19: Garst 6G 91
L20: Boot 6A 20
WA7: Run 4E 113
Byron Ter. L23: Blun 5D 8
Byton Wlk. L33: Kirkb 5C 14
Bywater Way L10: Faz 4F 23
Byway, The L23: Crosb 4G 9

C

CABBAGE HALL 1H 53
Cabes Cl. L14: Knott A 6C 38
Cablehouse L2: Liv 2D 4
Cable Rd. CH47: Hoy 2A 64
L35: Presc 2F 59
Cables Retail Pk. L34: Presc 2D 58
Cable Yard, The L2: Liv 2D 4
                        (off Cheapside)
Cabot Grn. L25: Woolt 4A 74
Cadbury Cl. L12: W Der 3F 37
Caddick Rd. L34: Know 6D 24
Cadet Way L12: W Der 6A 38
Cadnam Rd. L25: Gate 4F 75

Cadogan St. L15: Wav 1B 72
Cadwell Rd. L31: Lyd 2A 6
Caernarvon Cl. CH49: Upton 3E 67
   WA7: Cas .3B 114
Caernarvon Ct. CH63: Beb 1H 103
Caerwys Gro. CH42: Tran 5G 69
Caesars Cl. WA7: Cas 3A 114
Cainfield Wlk. L4: Kirkd 6D 34
   (off Upperbrook St.)
Cains Brewery 3E 71
Caird St. L6: Liv 4G 53
Cairn Ct. WA9: St H 5B 42
Cairnmore Rd. L18: Moss H 1E 91
Cairns St. L8: Liv 3G 71
Cairo St. L4: Kirkd 4E 35
   WA10: St H 4B 42
Caithness Ct. WA7: Run 3F 113
Caithness Dr. CH45: Wall 1E 51
   L23: Crosb .6H 9
Caithness Gdns. CH43: Pren 2B 86
Caithness Rd. L18: Aller 2F 91
Calcott Rake L30: N'ton 5E 11
   (not continuous)
Calday Grange Cl. CH48: W Kir 2D 82
Calday Grange Swimming Pool 1D 82
Calday Gro. WA11: Hay 3C 30
Caldbeck Gro. WA11: St H 2G 29
Caldbeck Rd. CH62: Brom 3D 104
Calder Av. CH43: Pren 1C 86
Calder Cl. L33: Kirkb 3C 14
   WA8: Wid 6B 80
Calder Dr. L18: Moss H 4G 73
   L31: Mag 5E 7
   L35: Rainh .4H 59
Calder Edge L18: Moss H 5G 73
Calderfield Rd. L18: Moss H 4H 73
Calder Grange L18: Aller 6A 74
Calderhurst Dr. WA10: Windle 5H 27
Calder Pk. Ct. L18: Moss H 5H 73
Calder Rd. CH63: Hghr B 6F 87
   L5: Liv 1F 53
Calders, The L18: Moss H 6G 73
Calderstones Av. L18: Moss H 4G 73
Calderstones Cl. L18: Moss H 5G 73
Calderstones Park 6G 73
Calderstones Rd. L18: Moss H 5F 73
Calders Vw. Ct. L18: Moss H 6G 73
Calderwood Pk. L27: N'ley 3F 75
Caldicott Av. CH62: Brom 6D 104
Caldon Cl. L21: Lith 2A 20
Caldway Dr. L27: N'ley 3F 75
Caldwell Cl. L33: Kirkb 5B 14
Caldwell Dr. CH49: Woodc 1F 85
Caldwell Rd. L19: Aller 3G 91
   WA8: Wid 4E 97
Caldwell St. WA9: St H 2H 43
CALDY 4D 82
Caldy Chase Dr. CH48: Caldy 4D 82
Caldy Ct. CH48: W Kir 2B 82
Caldy Golf Course 6E 83
Caldy Gro. WA11: St H 6H 29
Caldy Pk. CH48: W Kir 3C 82
Caldy Rd. CH45: Wall 2D 50
   CH48: Caldy, W Kir 2B 82
   L9: Ain 4G 21
Caldy Wood CH48: Caldy 4D 82
Caldywood Dr. L35: Whis 4E 59
Caledonian Cres. L21: Lith 2A 20
Caledonia St. L7: Liv 6H 5 (1F 71)
Calgarth Rd. L36: Huy 2E 57
Calgary Way L36: Huy 2E 57
California Rd. L13: Liv 6B 36
Callaghan Cl. L5: Liv 2D 52
Callander Rd. L6: Liv 4B 54
Callard Cl. L27: N'ley 3E 75
Callestock Cl. L11: Crox 6H 23
Callington Cl. L14: Knott A 1C 56
Callon Av. WA11: St H 6A 30
Callow Rd. L15: Wav 2B 72
Calmet Cl. L5: Liv 1E 53
Calmington La. WA7: Nort 1H 115
Calne Cl. CH61: Irby 4B 84
Calstock Cl. WA5: Penk 6G 81

Calthorpe St. L19: Garst 5F 91
Calthorpe Way CH43: Noct 3H 67
Calton Av. L18: Moss H 4E 73
Calvados Cl. L17: Aig 2A 90
Calveley Av. CH62: East 3F 121
Calveley Cl. CH43: Oxton 6A 68
Calveley Gro. L26: Halew 5A 94
Calverley Cl. WA7: Brook 2E 125
Calvers WA7: Halt 4A 114
Camberley Dr. L25: Hunts X 3E 93
Camberwell Pk. Rd. WA8: Wid 5H 79
Camborne Av. L25: Woolt 2E 93
Camborne Cl. WA7: Brook 1E 125
Camborne Rd. WA5: Burtw 1H 63
Cambourne Av. WA11: St H 4H 29
Cambrian Cl. CH46: More 2H 65
   (off Cambrian Rd.)
Cambrian Rd. CH46: More 2A 66
Cambrian Way L25: Woolt 6D 74
Cambria St. Nth. L6: Liv 4H 53
Cambria St. Sth. L6: Liv 4H 53
Cambridge Av. L21: Lith 3B 20
   L23: Crosb .5F 9
Cambridge Ct. L7: Liv 1F 71
Cambridge Dr. L23: Crosb 4E 9
   L26: Halew .3H 93
Cambridge Rd. CH42: Tran 1D 86
   CH45: New B 6D 32
   CH62: Brom 5E 105
   L9: Ain 3H 21
   L20: Boot 3D 34
   L21: Sea 3H 19
   L22: Water .4G 19
   L23: Crosb .5F 9
   WA10: St H 1C 42
Cambridge St. L7: Liv 1F 71
   (not continuous)
   L15: Wav 1B 72
   (not continuous)
   L34: Presc .1D 58
   WA7: Run .3G 113
   WA8: Wid 4F 97
Camdale Cl. L28: Stockb V 6D 38
Camden Cl. CH49: Woodc 5F 67
Camden Cl. WA7: Nort 4F 115
Camden Pl. CH41: Birke 3G 69
Camden St. L3: Liv 2G 5 (5E 53)
Camelford Rd. L11: Crox 6H 23
Camellia Ct. L17: Aig 1G 89
Camellia Gdns. WA9: Bold 6D 44
Camelot Cl. WA12: Newt W 1H 45
Camelot Ter. L20: Boot 1B 34
   (off Tennyson St.)
Camelot Way WA7: Cas 5C 114
Cameo Cl. L6: Liv 3H 53
Cameron Av. WA7: Run 5C 112
Cameron Rd. CH46: Leas 4F 49
   WA8: Wid 3E 97
Cameron St. L7: Liv 5A 54
Cammell Ct. CH43: Clau 3D 68
Campbell Av. WA7: Run 5E 113
Campbell Cl. WA7: Run 5E 113
Campbell Cres. L33: Kirkb 3H 13
   WA5: Gt San 3H 81
Campbell Dr. L14: Broad G 4A 56
Campbell Sq. L1: Liv 6E 5
Campbell St. L1: Liv 6E 5 (1D 70)
   L20: Boot 2A 34
   WA10: St H 1C 42
Campbeltown Rd. CH41: Tran 5H 69
Camperdown St. CH41: Birke 3H 69
Camphill Rd. L25: Woolt 3C 92
Campion Way L25: Woolt 4D 36
Campion Cl. WA11: St H 4F 29
Campion Gro. L32: Kirkb 5B 14
Campion Way L36: Huy 2H 75
Camp Rd. L25: Woolt 2D 92
Campsey Ash WA8: Wid 5D 78
Campus Dr. WA7: Run 3C 112
Camrose Cl. WA7: Run 1G 123
Cam St. L25: Woolt 1B 92
Canada Blvd. L3: Liv 4B 4 (6B 52)
Canal Bank L31: Lyd 1B 6
Canal Cotts. L31: Lyd 1B 6

Canal Reach WA7: Wind H 3E 115
Canal Side WA7: West P 6B 112
Canalside Gro. L5: Liv 2C 52
Canal St. L20: Boot 3B 34
   WA7: Run .3F 113
   WA10: St H .3D 42
   WA12: Newt W 2H 45
Canal Vw. L31: Mell 6E 13
Canal Vw. Ct. L21: Lith 2A 20
Canberra Av. WA9: St H 6C 42
Canberra La. L11: Crox 6G 23
Candia Towers L5: Liv 1E 53
   (off Jason St.)
Canella Av. L11: Norr G 4D 36
Cannell Ct. WA7: Pal F 1C 124
Canning Pl. L1: Liv 6D 4 (1C 70)
Canning St. CH41: Birke 2G 69
   L8: Liv 1F 71
   L22: Water .2F 19
Canniswood Rd. WA11: Hay 5C 30
Cannock Grn. L31: Mag 6A 6
Cannonbury Cl. WA7: Halt 5C 114
Cannon Hill CH43: Clau 3D 68
Cannon Mt. CH43: Clau 3D 68
Cannon St. WA9: Clock F 4G 61
Canon Rd. L6: Liv 6A 36
Canon St. WA7: Run 2E 113
Canon Wilson Cl. WA11: Hay 5F 31
Canova Cl. L27: N'ley 5H 75
   (off Victoria Falls Rd.)
Canrow La. L34: Know 6F 25
Cansfield St. WA10: St H 1E 43
Canterbury Av. L22: Water 6F 9
Canterbury Cl. L10: Ain 1C 22
   L34: Presc .6E 41
Canterbury Pk. L18: Aller 3G 91
Canterbury Rd. CH42: Rock F 2A 88
   CH44: Wall .4E 51
   WA8: Wid 4A 96
Canterbury St. L3: Liv 1H 5 (4E 53)
   L19: Garst 1G 107
   WA10: St H .6C 28
Canterbury Way L3: Liv 1H 5 (4F 53)
   L30: N'ton .5F 11
Canter Cl. L9: Ain 3B 22
Cantley Cl. WA7: Beech 1H 123
Cantsfield St. L7: Liv 2A 72
Canvey Cl. L15: Wav 2F 73
Capella Cl. L17: Aig 4C 90
Cape Rd. L9: Ain 5A 22
Capesthorne Cl. WA8: Wid 3C 96
Capital Gate L3: Liv 5F 53
Capitol Trad. Pk. L33: Know I 1F 25
Caplin Cl. L33: Kirkb 3A 14
Capper Gro. L36: Huy 4G 57
Capricorn Cres. L14: Knott A 2B 56
Capricorn Way L20: Boot 1B 34
Capstick Cres. L25: Gate 3D 74
Captain Charles Jones Wlk.
   CH45: Wall .1F 51
   (off Webster Av.)
Captains Cl. L30: Boot 3D 20
Captain's La. L30: Boot 3D 20
Caradoc Rd. L21: Sea 5A 20
Caraway Cl. L23: Thorn 4B 10
   (off Tanhouse Rd.)
Caraway Gro. WA10: St H 1B 42
Carbis Cl. L10: Faz 5E 23
Carden Cl. L4: Kirkd 6E 35
Cardeston Cl. WA7: Sut W 4B 124
Cardiff Way L19: Garst 5F 91
Cardigan Av. CH41: Birke 3F 69
Cardigan Cl. WA10: St H 3D 42
Cardigan Rd. CH45: New B 6D 32
Cardigan St. L15: Wav 1B 72
Cardigan Way L6: Liv 3H 53
   L30: N'ton .5H 11
Cardus Cl. CH46: More 1H 65
Cardwell Rd. L19: Garst 5H 91
Cardwell St. L7: Liv 1G 71
Carey Av. CH63: Hghr B 5F 87
Carey St. WA8: Wid 2F 97
Carfax Rd. L33: Kirkb 5C 14
Cargill Gro. CH42: Rock F 3B 88

Carham Rd. CH47: Hoy 3C 64
Carillion Cl. L11: Crox 2G 37
Carina Ct. L17: Aig 4D 90
Carisbrooke Cl. CH48: Caldy 3C 82
Carisbrooke Pl. L4: Kirkd 4F 35
Carisbrooke Rd. L4: Kirkd, Walt 3E 35
　　L20: Boot 2E 35
Carkington Rd. L25: Woolt 2E 93
Carlake Gro. L9: Ain 2A 36
Carland Cl. L10: Faz 5F 23
Carlaw Rd. CH42: Tran 1C 86
Carleen Cl. L17: Aig 1H 89
Carlett Blvd. CH62: East 2F 121
Carlett Pk. CH62: East 1F 121
Carlett Vw. L19: Garst 5G 91
Carley Wlk. L24: Speke 3G 109
Carlile Way L33: Kirkb 3B 14
Carlingford Cl. L8: Liv 2G 71
Carlisle Av. L30: N'ton 2F 21
Carlisle Cl. L4: Walt 5B 36
Carlisle M. CH43: Oxton 4E 69
Carlis Rd. L32: Kirkb 3B 24
Carlow Cl. L24: Hale 3C 110
Carlow St. WA10: St H 4B 42
Carlsruhe Ct. L8: Liv 4G 71
Carl's Way L33: Kirkb 3C 14
Carlton Av. WA7: Run 3H 113
Carlton Bingo Club 5F 21
Carlton Cl. CH64: Park 5G 117
Carlton La. CH47: Meols 1C 64
　　L13: Liv .3E 55
Carlton Little Theatre 4E 69
Carlton Mt. CH42: Tran 6G 69
Carlton Rd. CH42: Tran 5E 69
　　CH45: New B 5D 32
　　CH63: Beb 1B 104
Carlton St. L3: Liv 3B 52
　　L34: Presc 1D 58
　　WA8: Wid 3E 97
　　WA10: St H 2C 42
Carlton Ter. CH47: Meols 1C 64
　　L23: Crosb 5F 9
Carlyon Way L26: Halew 3G 93
Carmarthen Cres. L8: Liv 3D 70
Carmel Cl. CH45: New B 5D 32
Carmel Ct. WA8: Wid 5F 79
Carmelite Cres. WA10: Eccl 6G 27
Carmen Wlk. L7: Liv 1H 71
Carmichael Av. CH49: Grea 1B 84
Carnaby Cl. L36: Huy 1A 76
Carnarvon Ct. L9: Walt 2F 35
Carnarvon Rd. L9: Walt 2F 35
Carnarvon St. WA9: St H 5B 42
Carnatic Cl. L18: Moss H 6D 72
Carnatic Ct. L18: Moss H 6C 72
Carnatic Rd. L18: Moss H 6C 72
Carnation Rd. L9: Walt 2H 35
Carnegie Av. L23: Crosb 6F 9
Carnegie Cres. WA9: St H 5A 44
Carnegie Rd. L13: Liv 3C 54
Carnforth Av. L32: Kirkb 2B 24
Carnforth Cl. CH41: Birke 4E 69
　　L12: W Der 4G 37
Carnforth Rd. L18: Moss H 1G 91
Carno St. L15: Wav 1C 72
Carnoustie Cl. CH46: More 6H 47
　　L12: W Der 1B 56
Carnoustie Gro. WA11: Hay 6C 30
Carnsdale Rd. CH46: More 1D 66
Carol Dr. CH60: Hesw 5G 101
Carole Cl. WA9: Sut L 1A 62
Carolina St. L20: Boot 2B 34
Caroline Pl. CH43: Oxton 4D 68
Caroline St. WA8: Wid 4F 97
Caronia St. L19: Garst 6G 91
Carpathia St. L19: Garst 1G 107
Carpenter's La. CH48: W Kir 1B 82
Carpenters Row L1: Liv 6E 5 (1D 70)
Carraige Gro. L20: Boot 2D 34
Carraway Rd. L11: Crox 5G 23
Carr Bri. Rd. CH49: Woodc 5F 67
Carr Cl. L11: Norr G 3F 37
Carr Cft. L21: Ford 6B 10
Carrfield Av. L23: Crosb 6A 10

Carrfield Wlk. L11: Norr G 2F 37
Carr Gate CH46: More 2H 65
Carr Hey CH46: More 2H 65
Carr Hey Ct. CH49: Woodc 1G 85
Carr Ho. La. CH46: More 1H 65
Carriage Dr. L24: Hale 4D 110
Carrick Ct. L23: Crosb 6A 10
Carrickmore Av. L18: Moss H 1E 91
Carrington Rd. CH45: Wall 1E 51
Carrington St. CH41: Birke 1C 68
Carr La. CH46: More 6F 47
　　CH47: Hoy 3B 64
　　CH47: Meols 6F 47
　　CH48: W Kir 4D 64
　　L11: Norr G 3D 36
　　L24: Hale 3D 110
　　L34: Presc 2B 58
　　L36: Roby 6E 57
　　WA8: Hale B 6E 95
Carr La. E. L11: Norr G 3F 37
Carr La. Ind. Est. CH47: Hoy 3C 64
Carr Mdw. Hey L30: N'ton 1C 20
CARR MILL .3F 29
Carr Mill Rd. WA11: St H 4G 29
　　WN5: Bil .2G 29
Carrock Rd. CH62: Brom 3E 105
Carr Rd. CH46: More 2H 65
Carr Rd. L20: Boot 4D 20
Carrs Ter. L35: Whis 4D 58
Carr St. WA10: St H 6B 28
Carruthers St. L3: Liv 4C 52
Carrville Way L12: Crox 3C 38
Carrwood Cl. WA11: Hay 5C 30
Carsdale Rd. L18: Moss H 4E 73
Carsgoe Rd. CH47: Hoy 3C 64
Carsington Rd. L11: Norr G 3F 37
Carstairs Rd. L6: Liv 3B 54
Carsthorne Rd. CH47: Hoy 3C 64
Cartbridge La. L26: Halew 2H 93
Carter Av. WA11: Rainf 4G 17
Carters, The CH49: Grea 5A 66
　　L30: N'ton 5G 11
Carter St. L8: Liv 2F 71
Carterton Rd. CH47: Hoy 3C 64
Cartmel Av. L31: Mag 5D 6
Cartmel Cl. CH41: Birke 4E 69
　　L36: Huy .3F 57
Cartmel Dr. CH46: More 2C 66
　　L12: W Der 4G 37
　　L35: Rainh 3G 59
Cartmell Av. WA10: St H 4C 28
Cartmell Cl. WA7: Run 1F 123
Cartmel Rd. L36: Huy 2E 57
Cartmel Ter. L11: Norr G 2F 37
Cartmel Way L36: Huy 3E 57
Cartwright Cl. WA11: Rainf 3F 17
Cartwright Ct. WA11: Rainf 2F 17
Cartwrights Farm Rd. L24: Speke 1C 108
Cartwright St. WA7: Run 3G 113
Carver St. L3: Liv 1H 5 (4F 53)
Caryl Gro. L8: Liv 5E 71
Caryl St. L8: Liv 4E 71
　　　　　　　　　　　　　　(Atterbury St.)
　　L8: Liv 4E 71
　　　　　　　　　　　　　　　　(Park St.)
　　L8: Liv 3D 70
　　　　　　　　　　　　　　　(Stanhope St.)
Casbah Cl. L12: W Der 1F 55
Cascade Rd. L24: Speke 5E 93
Case Gro. L35: Presc 2E 59
Case Rd. WA11: Hay 5F 31
Cases St. L1: Liv 4F 5 (6D 52)
Cashel Rd. CH41: Birke 5D 50
Caspian Pl. L20: Boot 2C 34
Caspian Rd. L4: Walt 3B 36
Cassia Cl. L9: Walt 1H 35
Cassino Rd. L36: Huy 4G 57
Cassio St. L20: Boot 3E 35
Cassley Rd. L24: Speke 2A 110
Cassville Rd. L18: Moss H 3E 73
Castell Gro. WA10: St H 2D 42
Castle Av. WA9: St H 2A 44
Castlebridge Ct. CH42: Rock F 2H 87
　　　　　　　　　　　　(off Old Chester Rd.)

Castle Cl. CH46: Leas 4E 49
Castle Ct. CH48: W Kir 2B 82
Castle Dr. CH60: Hesw 5D 100
Castlefield Cl. L12: W Der 6E 37
Castlefield Rd. L12: W Der 6E 37
CASTLEFIELDS 3C 114
Castlefields Av. E. WA7: Cas 4C 114
Castlefields Av. Nth. WA7: Cas 3A 114
Castlefields Av. Sth. WA7: Cas 4B 114
Castleford Ri. CH46: Leas 4C 48
Castleford St. L15: Wav 2E 73
Castlegate Gro. L12: W Der 6F 37
Castlegrange Cl. CH46: Leas 3C 48
Castleheath Cl. CH46: Leas 4C 48
Castle Hill L2: Liv 4C 4
Castle Keep L12: W Der 6F 37
Castle Mt. CH60: Hesw 5D 100
　　　　　　　　　　　　　　(off the Mount)
Castle Ri. WA7: Run 3H 113
Castle Rd. CH45: Wall 1C 50
　　WA7: Halt 5B 114
Castlesite Rd. L12: W Der 5F 37
Castle St. CH41: Birke 3H 69
　　L2: Liv 4C 4 (6C 52)
　　L25: Woolt 1B 92
　　WA8: Wid .3D 96
Castleton Dr. L30: N'ton 5H 11
Castletown Cl. L16: Child 1A 74
Castleview Rd. L12: W Der 6F 37
Castleway Nth. CH46: Leas 3E 49
Castleway Sth. CH46: Leas 4E 49
Castlewell L35: Whis 3F 59
Castlewood Rd. L6: Liv 2H 53
Castner Av. WA7: West P 6C 112
Castner Ct. WA7: West P 6C 112
Castor St. L6: Liv 2H 53
Catalyst Science Discovery Cen. 6E 97
Catalyst Trade Pk. WA8: Wid 5E 97
Catchdale Moss La.
　　WA10: Eccl 5E 27
Catford Cl. WA8: Wid 1A 96
Catford Grn. L24: Speke 2H 109
Catharine St. L8: Liv 1F 71
Cathcart St. CH41: Birke 2F 69
Cathedral Cl. L1: Liv 2E 71
Cathedral Ct. L1: Liv 2F 71
　　　　　　　　　　　　　(off Gambier Ter.)
Cathedral Ga. L1: Liv 1E 71
Cathedral Rd. L6: Liv 1A 54
Cathedral Wlk. L3: Liv 5H 5 (6F 53)
Catherine St. L21: Lith 5B 20
Catherine St. CH41: Birke 3F 69
　　L21: Lith .5B 20
　　WA8: Wid .4E 97
Catherine Way WA11: Hay 5B 30
Catkin Rd. L26: Halew 1F 93
Catonfield Rd. L18: Moss H 4H 73
Catterall Av. WA9: Sut L 1H 61
Catterick Cl. L26: Halew 3H 93
Caulfield Dr. CH49: Grea 6C 66
Caunce Av. WA11: Hay 5D 30
Causeway, The CH62: Port S 6B 88
　　L12: W Der 3H 55
Causeway Cl. CH62: Port S 5B 88
Causeway Ho. CH46: Leas 3C 48
Cavalier Dr. L19: Garst 6H 91
Cavalry Cl. L12: W Der 6A 38
Cavan Dr. WA11: Hay 4F 31
Cavan Rd. L11: Norr G 5C 36
Cavell Cl. L25: Woolt 2C 92
Cavendish Dr. CH42: Rock F 2F 87
　　L9: Walt 2G 35
Cavendish Farm Rd.
　　WA7: West 2D 122
　　　　　　　　　　　　　　(not continuous)
Cavendish Gdns. L8: Liv 4G 71
Cavendish Rd. CH41: Birke 2D 68
　　CH45: New B 4D 32
　　L23: Blun 3F 9
Cavendish St. CH41: Birke 1D 68
　　WA7: Run 3D 112
　　　　　　　　　　　　　　(not continuous)
Cavern Club, The 4D 4

Cavern Ct. *L6: Liv* 4H *53*
(off Coleridge St.)
Cavern Quarter 4D 4
Cavern Walks L2: Liv 4D 4
Cawdor St. L8: Liv 3G 71
WA7: Run 2D 112
Cawfield Av. WA8: Wid 2B 96
Cawley St. WA7: Run 4E 113
Cawthorne Av. L32: Kirkb 3A 24
Cawthorne Cl. L32: Kirkb 3A 24
Cawthorne Wlk. L32: Kirkb 4A 24
Caxton Cl. CH43: Bid 3G 67
WA8: Wid 6A 78
Caxton Rd. L35: Rainh 6C 60
Cazneau St. L3: Liv 4D 52
Cearns Rd. CH43: Oxton 4C 68
Cecil Dr. WA10: Eccl 6G 27
Cecil Rd. CH42: Tran 1D 86
CH45: Wall 3C 50
CH62: New F 3B 88
L21: Sea 5H 19
Cecil St. L15: Wav 1B 72
WA9: St H 6B 44
Cedar Av. CH63: Hghr B 1G 103
WA7: Run 6G 113
WA7: Sut W 3D 124
WA8: Wid 1F 97
Cedar Cl. L18: Aller 6H 73
L35: Whis 3E 59
Cedar Ct. L34: Know 1F 39
Cedar Cres. L36: Huy 6F 57
Cedardale Pk. WA8: Wid 5A 80
Cedardale Rd. L9: Walt 1G 35
Cedar Gro. L8: Liv 3A 72
L22: Water 1F 19
L31: Mag 3B 12
WA11: Hay 4G 31
Cedar Rd. L9: Ain 5H 21
L35: Whis 4D 58
WA5: Gt San 3H 81
Cedars, The CH46: More 2A 66
L12: Crox 2B 38
Cedar St. CH41: Birke 4F 69
L20: Boot 1C 34
WA10: St H 3B 42
Cedar Ter. *L8: Liv* *3A 72*
(off Cedar Gro.)
Cedarway CH60: Hesw 2F 117
Cedarwood Cl. CH49: Grea 5H 65
Cedarwood Ct. L36: Huy 1G 75
Celandine Way WA9: Bold 6D 44
Celebration Dr. L6: Liv 2A 54
Celendine Cl. L15: Wav 1C 72
Celia St. L20: Kirkd 4D 34
Celtic Rd. CH47: Meols 6E 47
Celtic St. L8: Liv 3G 71
Celt St. L6: Liv 3H 53
Cemaes Cl. L5: Liv 2C 52
Centenary Cl. L4: Walt 5A 36
Centenary Ho. WA7: Run 5G 113
Central Av. CH62: Brom 4C 104
L24: Speke 2F 109
L34: Eccl P 6F 41
L34: Presc 1C 58
Central Bldgs. *L23: Crosb* *5G 9*
(off Church Rd.)
Central Dr. L12: W Der 2F 55
WA11: Hay 5D 30
WA11: Rainf 2F 17
Central Expressway WA7: Run 6A 114
Central Gdns. L1: Liv 5G 5
Central Pk. Av. CH44: Wall 3E 51
Central Rd. CH62: Port S 5B 88
(Osborne Ct.)
CH62: Port S 6B 88
(Wood St.)
Central Shop. Cen. L1: Liv 5F 5 (6D 52)
Central Sq. L31: Mag 5B 6
Central Station (Rail) 5F 5 (6D 52)
Central St. WA10: St H 1E 43
Central Way L24: Speke 2G 109
Centreville Rd. L18: Moss H 3E 73
Centre Way L36: Huy 5G 57
Centro Pk. L33: Know I 3E 25

Centurion Cl. CH47: Meols 6E 47
Centurion Dr. CH47: Meols 6E 47
Centurion Row WA7: Cas 3B 114
Century Bldgs. L3: Liv 5D 70
Century Rd. L23: Crosb 5F 9
Ceres Ct. CH43: Bid 2G 67
Ceres St. L20: Kirkd 4C 34
Cestrian Dr. CH61: Thing 6E 85
Chadlow Rd. L32: Kirkb 4B 24
Chadwell Rd. L33: Kirkb 5B 14
Chadwick Av. WA8: Wid 6G 79
Chadwick Ct. Ind. Cen.
L3: Liv 3B 52
Chadwick Rd. WA7: Ast 2A 114
WA11: St H 4G 29
Chadwick Rd. CH46: More 1C 66
L3: Liv 3B 52
Chadwick Way L33: Kirkb 3A 14
Chaffinch Cl. L12: W Der 4B 38
Chaffinch Glade L26: Halew 2G 93
Chainhurst Cl. L27: N'ley 3F 75
Chain La. WA11: St H 4H 29
Chain La. Shop. Pct.
WA11: St H 4H 29
Chain Wlk. WA10: St H 2A 42
Chalfont Cl. L18: Aller 2H 91
Chalfont Way L28: Stockb 6D 38
Chalgrave Cl. WA8: Wid 6B 80
Chalice Way L11: Crox 2G 37
Chalkley Cl. CH42: Tran 1E 87
Chalkwell Dr. CH60: Hesw 6G 101
Challis St. CH41: Birke 6A 50
Challoner Cl. L36: Huy 1H 75
Chaloner Gro. L19: Gras 5D 90
Chaloner St. L3: Liv 2D 70
Chalon Way E. WA10: St H 2E 43
Chalon Way Ind. Est.
WA10: St H 3E 43
Chalon Way W. WA10: St H 2D 42
Chamberlain Dr. L33: Kirkb 4B 14
Chamberlain St. CH41: Tran 5G 69
CH44: Wall 5C 50
WA10: St H 2B 42
Chamomile Cl. L11: Norr G 3D 36
Champions Bus. Pk. CH49: Upton 6D 66
Chancellor Ct. L8: Liv 1G 71
Chancellor Rd. WA7: Manor P 6F 99
Chancel St. L4: Kirkd 6D 34
Chancery La. WA9: St H 2A 44
Chandlers Ct. WA7: Run 4C 112
Chandlers Way WA9: Sut M 4F 61
Chandos St. L7: Liv 6H 53
Change La. CH64: Will 6B 120
Changford Grn. L33: Kirkb 6C 14
Changford Rd. L33: Kirkb 5C 14
Channel, The CH45: Wall 5A 32
Channell Rd. L6: Liv 4A 54
Channel Reach L23: Blun 6D 8
Channel Rd. L23: Blun 6D 8
Chantrell Rd. CH48: W Kir 1E 83
Chantry, The WA10: St H 5B 28
Chantry Cl. CH43: Bid 3F 67
Chantry Wlk. CH60: Hesw 1E 117
Chapel Av. L9: Walt 5G 21
Chapelcroft Ct. L12: W Der 1G 55
Chapelfields WA6: Frod 6E 123
Chapel Gdns. L5: Liv 2D 52
Chapelhill Rd. CH46: More 1D 66
Chapel Ho. L22: Water 3F 19
L31: Mag 6C 6
Chapel La. L30: N'ton 4F 11
L31: Mell 5E 13
L35: Rainh 6C 60
WA5: Burtw 1G 63
WA8: Cron, Wid 4A 78
WA10: Eccl 1H 41
Chapel Pl. L19: Garst 5G 91
L25: Woolt 1C 92
Chapel Rd. CH47: Hoy 1C 64
L6: Liv 1A 54
L19: Garst 5G 91
(not continuous)
WA5: Penk 6G 81
Chapelside Cl. WA5: Gt San 3H 81

Chapel St. L3: Liv 3B 4 (5B 52)
L34: Presc 1D 58
WA8: Wid 4E 97
WA10: St H 6D 28
WA11: Hay 5F 31
(not continuous)
Chapel Ter. L20: Boot 2B 34
Chapel Vw. CH62: East 1G 121
Chapel Yd. *L15: Wav* *2E 73*
(off Waterloo St.)
Chapman Cl. L8: Liv 4E 71
WA8: Wid 5B 78
Chapman Gro. L34: Presc 6E 41
Chardstock Dr. L25: Gate 5E 75
Charing Cross CH41: Birke 4F 69
Charlcombe St. CH42: Tran 5F 69
Charlecote St. L8: Liv 6F 71
Charles Av. WA5: Gt San 3H 81
Charles Berrington Rd. L15: Wav 3E 73
Charles Best Grn. *L30: N'ton* *5F 11*
(off Albert Schweitzer Av.)
Charles Rd. CH47: Hoy 3B 64
Charles St. CH41: Birke 2F 69
WA8: Wid 3E 97
WA10: St H 1E 43
Charleston Rd. L8: Liv 5F 71
Charlesville CH43: Oxton 4D 68
Charlesville CH43: Oxton 4D 68
Charles Wlk. L14: Broad G 4B 56
Charlesworth Cl. L31: Lyd 2A 6
Charlotte Rd. L33: Know I 2D 24
Charlock Cl. L30: N'ton 5G 11
Charlotte Rd. CH44: Wall 2F 51
Charlotte's Mdw. CH63: Beb 1A 104
Charlotte Wlk. WA8: Wid 4F 97
Charlotte Way L1: Liv 4F 5
Charlton Cl. WA7: Pal F 6C 114
Charlton Ct. CH43: Clau 3B 68
L25: Hunts X 4F 93
Charlton Pl. L13: Liv 6E 55
Charlton Rd. L13: Liv 6E 55
Charlwood Av. L36: Huy 6G 57
Charlwood Cl. CH43: Bid 3G 67
Charmalue Av. L23: Crosb 5H 9
Charmouth Cl. L12: Crox 2A 38
Charnley Dr. L15: Wav 1G 73
Charnock Av. WA12: Newt W 2H 45
Charnock Rd. L9: Ain 2B 36
Charnwood Cl. L12: Crox 2H 37
Charnwood Rd. L36: Huy 4D 56
Charnwood St. WA9: St H 1A 44
Charon Way WA5: Westb 4H 63
Charter Ho. *CH44: Wall* *3F 51*
(off Church St.)
Charterhouse Cl. L25: Woolt 2D 92
Charterhouse Dr. L10: Ain 1C 22
Charterhouse Rd. L25: Woolt 2D 92
Chartmount Way L25: Gate 5D 74
Chartwell Gro. L26: Halew 2H 93
Chase, The CH60: Hesw 5E 101
CH63: Brom 2C 120
L36: Huy 1H 75
Chaser Cl. L9: Ain 3A 22
Chasewater WA7: Nort 1H 115
Chase Way L5: Liv 3E 53
Chatbrook Cl. L17: Aig 4D 90
Chater Cl. *L35: Whis* *1G 59*
(off Watling Way)
Chatham Cl. L21: Sea 4H 19
Chatham Ct. L22: Water 3G 19
Chatham Pl. L7: Liv 6H 53
Chatham Rd. CH42: Rock F 1A 88
Chatham St. L7: Liv 1F 71
L8: Liv 1F 71
Chatsworth Av. CH44: Wall 3E 51
L9: Walt 6F 21
Chatsworth Dr. L7: Liv 6H 53
WA8: Wid 6A 78
Chatsworth Rd. CH42: Rock F 1A 88
CH61: Pens 6D 84
L35: Rainh 3H 59
Chatteris Ct. *WA10: St H* *4B 42*
(off Bewsey St.)
Chatteris Pk. WA7: Nort 3G 115

Chatterton Dr.—Churchfields

Chatterton Dr. WA7: Murd 5G **115**
Chatterton Rd. L14: Knott A 3G **55**
Chaucer Dr. L12: Crox 3A **38**
Chaucer Rd. WA10: St H 5B **28**
Chaucer St. L3: Liv 4D **52**
L20: Boot 1A **34**
WA7: Run 4E **113**
Cheadle Av. L13: Liv 4D **54**
Cheapside L2: Liv 2D **4** (5C **52**)
Cheapside All. L2: Liv 3D **4**
Cheddar Cl. L25: Woolt 1B **92**
Cheddar Gro. L32: Kirkb 4A **24**
WA5: Burtw 6H **45**
Cheddon Way CH61: Pens 1C **100**
Chedworth Dr. WA8: Wid 5A **78**
Chedworth Rd. L14: Knott A 3A **56**
Cheldon Rd. L12: W Der 3G **37**
Chelford Cl. CH43: Bid 2G **67**
Chelford Rd. WA10: Eccl 2H **41**
Chellow Dene L23: Thorn 3A **10**
Chelmsford Cl. *L4: Kirkd* *6D* ***34***
(off Harcourt St.)
Chelsea Ct. L12: W Der 5A **38**
Chelsea Lea L9: Walt 5F **21**
Chelsea Rd. L9: Walt 5G **21**
L21: Lith 5B **20**
Cheltenham Av. L17: Liv 3B **72**
Cheltenham Cl. L10: Ain 2C **22**
WA5: Gt San 1H **81**
Cheltenham Cres. CH46: Leas 4C **48**
L36: Roby 6F **57**
WA7: Run 1F **123**
Cheltenham Rd. CH45: Wall 1A **50**
Chelwood Av. L16: Child 6A **56**
Chemistry Rd. L24: Speke 6E **93**
Chenotrie Gdns. CH43: Noct 4H **67**
Chepstow Av. CH44: Wall 3E **51**
Chepstow St. L4: Walt 4E **35**
Chequers Gdns. L19: Aig 3D **90**
Cheriton Av. CH48: W Kir 1D **82**
Cheriton Cl. L26: Halew 3G **93**
Chermside Rd. L17: Aig 2C **90**
Cherry Av. L4: Walt 4H **35**
Cherrybank CH44: Wall 5D **50**
Cherry Blossom Rd. WA7: Beech 3B **124**
Cherry Cl. L4: Walt 4H **35**
WA12: Newt W 1H **45**
Cherrydale Rd. L18: Moss H 5E **73**
Cherryfield Cres. L32: Kirkb 1A **24**
Cherryfield Dr. L32: Kirkb 1H **23**
Cherry Gdns. CH47: Hoy 2B **64**
L32: Kirkb 4B **24**
Cherry La. L4: Walt 4H **35**
Cherry Sq. CH44: Wall 3D **50**
Cherry Sutton WA8: Wid 6G **77**
Cherry Tree Av. WA5: Penk 5H **81**
WA7: Run 5G **113**
Cherry Tree Cl. L24: Hale 4E **111**
L35: Whis 4D **58**
WA11: Hay 6C **30**
Cherry Tree Dr. WA9: St H 3C **44**
Cherry Tree Ho. CH46: More 1D **66**
Cherry Tree La. WA11: St H 1E **29**
Cherry Tree M. CH60: Hesw 5E **101**
Cherry Tree Rd. CH46: More 1D **66**
L36: Huy 1G **75**
Cherry Va. L25: Woolt 6D **74**
Cherry Vw. L33: Kirkb 4C **14**
Cherrywood Av. L26: Halew 2B **94**
Cheryl Dr. WA8: Wid 2H **97**
Cheshire Acre CH49: Woodc 6E **67**
Cheshire Av. L10: Faz 4F **23**
Cheshire Gdns. WA10: St H 3C **42**
Cheshire Gro. CH46: More 2C **66**
Cheshire Way CH61: Pens 2D **100**
Cheshyre Dr. WA7: Halt 4B **114**
Cheshyres La. WA7: West, West P 1C **122**
(not continuous)
Chesnell Gro. L33: Kirkb 4C **14**
Chesney Cl. L8: Liv 3E **71**
Chesnut Gro. CH42: Tran 5F **69**
L20: Boot 6B **20**
(not continuous)
Chesnut Rd. L21: Sea 4H **19**
Chester Av. L30: N'ton 2F **21**
Chester Cl. L23: Crosb 5B **10**
WA7: Cas 3C **114**
Chester Ct. CH63: Beb 1H **103**
Chesterfield Dr. L33: Kirkb 4A **14**
Chesterfield Rd. CH62: East 3D **120**
L23: Crosb 4A **10**
Chesterfield St. L8: Liv 2E **71**
Chester High Rd. CH64: Nest 2H **117**
Chester La. WA9: Sut M, St H 3F **61**
Chester Rd. CH60: Hesw 6F **101**
CH66: Chil T, Hoot 6G **121**
L6: Liv 2B **54**
L36: Huy 3A **58**
WA4: Dares 3F **125**
WA7: Sut W, Pres B 5B **124**
Chester St. CH41: Birke 3H **69**
CH44: Wall 4C **50**
L8: Liv 2E **71**
L34: Presc 1D **58**
WA8: Wid 2F **97**
Chesterton St. L19: Garst 1G **107**
Chester Wlk. *L36: Huy* *3A* ***58***
(off Chester Rd.)
Chestnut Av. L23: Crosb 3H **9**
L36: Huy 1F **75**
WA5: Gt San 3H **81**
WA8: Wid 1F **97**
WA11: Hay 6B **30**
Chestnut Cl. CH49: Grea 2A **84**
L35: Whis 3E **59**
Chestnut Ct. L20: Boot 1B **34**
WA8: Wid 2B **96**
Chestnut Farm CH66: Hoot 6G **121**
Chestnut Gro. CH62: Brom 5C **104**
L15: Wav 1D **72**
WA11: St H 4H **29**
Chestnut Ho. *L20: Boot* *1B* ***34***
(off St James Dr.)
Chestnut Rd. L9: Walt 2H **35**
Chestnuts, The CH64: Will 6H **119**
Chestnut Wlk. L31: Mell 5E **13**
Cheswood Cl. L35: Whis 5E **59**
Cheswood Ct. *CH49: Woodc* *1E* ***85***
(off Childwall Grn.)
Chetton Dr. WA7: Murd 6G **115**
Chetwood Av. L23: Crosb 4H **9**
Chetwood Dr. WA8: Wid 5D **78**
Chetwynd Cl. CH43: Oxton 5B **68**
Chetwynd Rd. CH43: Oxton 4C **68**
Chetwynd St. L17: Aig 6H **71**
Chevasse Wlk. L25: Woolt 6E **75**
Cheverton Cl. CH49: Woodc 6F **67**
Chevin Rd. L9: Walt 6G **21**
Cheviot Av. WA9: St H 2B **44**
Cheviot Cl. CH42: Tran 2F **87**
Cheviot Rd. CH42: Tran 2E **87**
L7: Liv 5C **54**
Cheviot Way L33: Kirkb 3B **14**
Cheyne Cl. L23: Blun 6C **8**
Cheyne Gdns. L19: Aig 3D **90**
Cheyne Wlk. WA9: St H 1D **60**
Chichester Cl. L15: Wav 1B **72**
WA7: Murd 1F **125**
Chidden Cl. CH49: Grea 6A **66**
Chidlow Cl. WA8: Wid 6E **97**
Chigwell Cl. L12: Crox 2A **38**
Chilcott Rd. L14: Knott A 4G **55**
Childers St. L13: Liv 4E **55**
CHILDWALL 2A **74**
Childwall Abbey Rd. L16: Child 3H **73**
Childwall Av. CH46: More 2B **66**
L15: Wav 2B **72**
Childwall Bank Rd. L16: Child 2H **73**
Childwall Cl. CH46: More 2B **66**
Childwall Cres. L16: Child 2H **73**
Childwall Fiveways L15: Wav 2G **73**
Childwall Golf Course **2G 75**
Childwall Grn. CH49: Woodc 1E **85**
Childwall La. L14: Broad G 5C **56**
L16: Child 3B **74**
L25: Child 3B **74**
Childwall Mt. Rd. L16: Child 2H **73**
Childwall Pde. L14: Broad G 5C **56**
Childwall Pk. Av. L16: Child 3H **73**
Childwall Priory Rd. L16: Child 2H **73**
Childwall Rd. L15: Wav 2E **73**
Childwall Valley Rd. L16: Child 2H **73**
L25: Gate 2C **74**
L27: N'ley 2C **74**
Chilhem Cl. L8: Liv 5F **71**
Chilington Av. WA8: Wid 3B **96**
Chillerton Rd. L12: W Der 5H **37**
Chillingham St. L8: Liv 6G **71**
Chiltern Cl. L12: Crox 3B **38**
L32: Kirkb 5G **13**
Chiltern Dr. L32: Kirkb 5G **13**
Chiltern Rd. CH42: Tran 2E **87**
WA9: St H 2B **44**
Chilton Cl. L31: Mag 6C **6**
Chilton Ct. L31: Mag 6C **6**
Chilton M. L31: Mag 6C **6**
Chilwell Cl. WA8: Wid 5B **78**
China Farm La. CH48: W Kir 5E **65**
Chippenham Av. CH49: Grea 5A **66**
Chirkdale St. L4: Kirkd 4E **35**
(not continuous)
Chirk Way CH46: More 2D **66**
Chirton Cl. WA11: Hay 4F **31**
Chisenhale St. L3: Liv 3C **52**
Chisledon Cl. WA11: Hay 4F **31**
Chislehurst Av. L25: Gate 3D **74**
Chislet Ct. WA8: Wid 5C **78**
Chisnall Av. WA10: St H 1A **42**
Chiswell St. L7: Liv 5A **54**
Chiswick Cl. WA7: Murd 6F **115**
Cholmondeley Rd. CH48: W Kir 1B **82**
WA7: Clftn 3H **123**
Cholmondeley St. WA8: Wid 1E **113**
Cholsey Cl. CH49: Upton 5D **66**
Chorley Rd. L34: Presc 1B **58**
Chorley's La. WA8: Wid 6H **79**
Chorley St. WA10: St H 1D **42**
Chorley Way CH63: Spit 4A **104**
Chorlton Cl. L16: Child 1B **74**
WA7: Wind H 4F **115**
Chorlton Gro. CH45: Wall 2H **49**
Christchurch Cl. L11: Norr G 2D **36**
Christchurch Rd. CH43: Oxton 5D **68**
Christian St. L3: Liv 1F **5** (4E **53**)
Christie Cl. CH66: Hoot 5G **121**
Christie St. WA8: Wid 2H **97**
Christleton Cl. CH43: Oxton 1H **85**
Christleton Ct. WA7: Manor P 1E **115**
Christmas St. L20: Kirkd 4D **34**
Christopher Cl. L16: Child 1H **73**
L35: Rainh 5H **59**
Christopher Dr. CH62: East 2G **121**
Christophers Cl. CH61: Pens 1E **101**
Christopher St. L4: Walt 5F **35**
Christopher Taylor Ho. L31: Mag 1B **12**
Christopher Way L16: Child 1H **73**
Christowe Wlk. *L11: Crox* *6G* ***23***
(off Kennford Rd.)
Chris Ward Cl. L7: Liv 6A **54**
Chudleigh Cl. L26: Halew 2G **93**
Chudleigh Rd. L13: Liv 4D **54**
Chung Hok Ho. *L1: Liv* *2E* ***71***
(off Pine M.)
Church All. L1: Liv 5E **5** (6D **52**)
Church Av. L9: Ain 4H **21**
Church Cl. CH44: Wall 3F **51**
Church Cotts. L25: Gate 4E **75**
Church Cres. CH44: Wall 5G **51**
Churchdown Cl. L14: Knott A 3B **56**
Churchdown Gro. L14: Knott A 3A **56**
Churchdown Rd. L14: Knott A 3A **56**
Church Dr. CH62: Port S 5B **88**
Church End L24: Hale 4D **110**
Church End M. L24: Hale 4E **111**
Church Farm CH63: Beb 6A **88**
Church Farm Ct. CH60: Hesw 6D **100**
Church Farm Organics **6H 83**
Churchfield Ct. *L25: Gate* *5E* ***75***
(off Jones Farm Rd.)
Churchfield Rd. L25: Gate 4E **75**
Churchfields WA8: Wid 4F **79**
WA9: Clock F 3G **61**

Church Flats. L4: Walt 3F **35**
Church Gdns. CH44: Wall 3F **51**
L20: Boot 2B **34**
Church Grn. L16: Child 2B **74**
L32: Kirkb 6A **14**
Church Gro. L21: Sea 5H **19**
Church Hill CH45: Wall 2B **50**
Churchill Av. CH41: Birke 2D **68**
Churchill Gdns. WA9: St H 1A **60**
Churchill Gro. CH44: Wall 2E **51**
Churchill Ho. L21: Sea 4H **19**
Churchill Ind. Est. L9: Ain 3A **22**
Churchill Mans. WA7: Run 2E **113**
(off Cooper St.)
Churchill Way Nth. L3: Liv 2E **5** (5D **52**)
Churchill Way Sth.
L3: Liv 3E **5** (5D **52**)
Churchlands CH44: Wall 5G **51**
(off Bridle Rd.)
Church La. CH44: Wall 3F **51**
(not continuous)
CH49: Woodc 1F **85**
CH61: Thurs 6H **83**
CH62: Brom 4D **104**
CH62: East 3G **121**
L4: Walt 3F **35**
L17: Aig 2C **90**
L34: Know 1E **39**
L39: Augh 1F **7**
WA10: Eccl 2G **41**
Churchmeadow Cl. CH44: Wall 3F **51**
Church Mdw. La. CH60: Hesw 6C **100**
Church Mdw. Wlk. WA8: Hale B 6H **95**
Church M. CH42: Rock F 2A **88**
Church Mt. L7: Liv 6H **53**
Church Rd. CH42: Tran 1F **87**
CH44: Wall 5G **51**
CH48: W Kir 2A **82**
CH49: Upton 4E **67**
CH63: Beb 2A **104**
CH63: Thorn H 1D **118**
L4: Walt 3G **35**
L13: Liv 5D **54**
L15: Wav 3E **73**
L19: Garst 6G **91**
L20: Boot 5D **20**
L21: Lith 4B **20**
(not continuous)
L21: Sea 5H **19**
L22: Water 3F **19**
L23: Crosb 5F **9**
L24: Hale 4E **111**
L25: Woolt 5B **74**
L26: Halew 1G **93**
L31: Mag 2B **12**
L36: Roby 5E **57**
WA11: Hay 5G **31**
WA11: Rainf 3F **17**
Church Rd. Nth. L15: Wav 2E **73**
Church Rd. Sth. L25: Woolt 1C **92**
Church Rd. W. L4: Walt 3F **35**
Church Sq. CH62: Brom 4D **104**
WA9: St H 2E **43**
Church St. CH41: Birke 3H **69**
(not continuous)
CH44: Wall 3F **51**
L1: Liv 4E **5** (6D **52**)
L20: Boot 2A **34**
L34: Presc 1D **58**
WA7: Run 2E **113**
WA8: Wid 6E **97**
WA10: St H 2E **43**
Church Ter. CH42: Tran 6F **69**
Church Vw. L12: W Der 6F **37**
L20: Boot 2B **34**
Churchview Rd. CH41: Birke 1D **68**
Church Wlk. CH48: W Kir 2B **82**
L20: Boot 2B **34**
L34: Know 1E **39**
WA10: Eccl 1G **41**
Churchward Ct. L25: Woolt 1C **92**
(off Garden St.)
Church Way L30: N'ton 5D **10**
L32: Kirkb 6A **14**

Churchway Rd. L24: Speke 3A **110**
Churchwood Cl. CH62: Brom 4D **104**
Churchwood Ct. CH49: Woodc 2F **85**
(off Childwall Grn.)
Churnet St. L4: Kirkd 5E **35**
Churn Way CH49: Grea 5B **66**
Churston Rd. L16: Child 4A **74**
Churton Av. CH43: Oxton 6B **68**
Churton Ct. L6: Liv 4G **53**
Ciaran Cl. L12: W Der 5H **37**
Cicely St. L7: Liv 6H **53**
Cinder La. L18: Moss H 4G **73**
L20: Boot 4D **20**
Cineworld Cinema
Halton Lea 6A **114**
Liverpool 6D **54**
St Helens 2D **42**
Cinnamon Building, The L1: Liv 6F **5**
Circle 109 L1: Liv 6F **5**
Circular Dr. CH49: Grea 6B **66**
CH60: Hesw 4D **100**
CH62: Port S 4B **88**
Circular Rd. CH41: Birke 4F **69**
Circular Rd. E. L11: Norr G 5D **36**
Circular Rd. W. L11: Norr G 5D **36**
Cirencester Av. CH49: Grea 5A **66**
CISS GREEN 3D **110**
Citadel, The
St Helens 2E **43**
(off Waterloo St.)
Citrine Rd. CH44: Wall 5F **51**
Citron Cl. L9: Walt 1H **35**
City Gdns. WA10: St H 4D **28**
City Lofts L3: Liv 1A **4**
(Waterloo Rd.)
L3: Liv .2A **4**
(William Jessop Way)
City Rd. L4: Walt 4F **35**
WA10: St H 4D **28**
City Sq. L2: Liv 3D **4**
Civic Cl. CH63: Beb 6A **88**
Civic Way CH63: Beb 6A **88**
L36: Huy 5G **57**
Civil & Family Court
Liverpool 3D **4** (5C **52**)
Clairville Cl. L20: Boot 2C **34**
Clairville Ct. L20: Boot 2C **34**
(off Clairville Cl.)
Clairville Way L13: Liv 2C **54**
Clamley Ct. L24: Speke 2A **110**
Clamley Gdns. L24: Hale 3E **111**
Clandon Rd. L18: Aller 2H **91**
Clanfield Av. WA8: Wid 6A **78**
Clanfield Rd. L11: Norr G 3F **37**
Clapgate Cres. WA8: Hale B 6H **95**
Clapham Rd. L4: Walt 1H **53**
Clare Cl. WA9: St H 6C **42**
Clare Cres. CH44: Wall 3B **50**
Claremont Av. L31: Mag 1H **11**
WA8: Wid 5G **79**
Claremont Cl. L21: Sea 4H **19**
Claremont Ct. CH45: Wall 1B **50**
Claremont Dr. WA8: Wid 5F **79**
Claremont Rd. CH48: W Kir 6B **64**
L15: Wav 3C **72**
L21: Sea 4H **19**
L23: Crosb 5G **9**
WA7: Run 3F **113**
Claremont Way CH63: Hghr B 3F **87**
Claremount Dr. CH63: Beb 1H **103**
Claremount Rd. CH44: Wall 6B **32**
CH45: Wall 6B **32**
Clarence Av. WA5: Gt San 3F **81**
WA8: Wid 5E **79**
Clarence Cl. WA9: St H 3G **43**
Clarence Rd. CH42: Tran 6E **69**
CH44: Wall 5F **51**
Clarence St. L3: Liv 4H **5** (6E **53**)
WA7: Run 2D **112**
WA12: Newt W 1H **45**
Clarence Ter. WA7: Run 2E **113**
Clarendon Cl. CH43: Oxton 4E **69**
WA7: Murd 6F **115**
Clarendon Gro. L31: Lyd 2B **6**

Clarendon Rd. CH44: Wall 4F **51**
L6: Liv .1A **54**
L19: Garst 5G **91**
L21: Sea 5H **19**
Clare Rd. L20: Boot 3D **34**
Claret Cl. L17: Aig 2A **90**
Clare Wlk. L10: Faz 4F **23**
Clare Way CH45: Wall 2B **50**
Claribel St. L8: Liv 3G **71**
Clarke Av. CH42: Rock F 1G **87**
Clarke Gdns. WA8: Wid 4F **97**
Clarke's Cres. WA10: Eccl 1H **41**
Clarks Ter. WA7: West P 5B **112**
Classic Rd. L13: Liv 3E **55**
Clatterbridge Rd. CH63: Spit 6F **103**
Claude Rd. L6: Liv 1A **54**
CLAUGHTON 2B **68**
Claughton Cl. L7: Liv 6A **54**
Claughton Dr. CH44: Wall 4D **50**
Claughton Firs CH43: Oxton 5D **68**
Claughton Grn. CH43: Oxton 4C **68**
Claughton Pl. CH41: Birke 3E **69**
Claughton Rd. CH41: Birke 3E **69**
Claughton St. WA9: St H 1E **43**
Clavell Rd. L19: Aller 3H **91**
Claverton Cl. WA7: Run 1F **123**
Clay Cross Rd. L25: Woolt 1B **92**
Claydon Ct. L26: Halew 2A **94**
Clayfield Cl. L20: Boot 3D **34**
Clayford Cres. L14: Knott A 3F **55**
Clayford Pl. L14: Knott A 3F **55**
Clayford Rd. L14: Knott A 3G **55**
Clayford Way L14: Knott A 3G **55**
Clayhill Ind. Est. CH64: Nest 5A **118**
Clayhill Light Ind. Pk. CH64: Nest . . .5A **118**
Clay La. WA5: Burtw 1G **63**
WA10: Eccl 2E **41**
Claypole Cl. L7: Liv 1A **72**
Clay St. L3: Liv 3B **52**
Clayton Cl. WA10: St H 2C **42**
Clayton Cres. WA7: Run 4D **112**
WA8: Wid 2D **96**
Clayton La. CH44: Wall 5C **50**
Clayton Pl. CH41: Birke 4E **69**
Clayton Sq. L1: Liv 4F **5**
Clayton Sq. Shop. Cen.
L1: Liv 4F **5** (6D **52**)
Clayton St. CH41: Birke 4E **69**
Cleadon Cl. L32: Kirkb 4C **24**
Cleadon Rd. L32: Kirkb 4C **24**
Cleadon Way WA8: Wid 5C **78**
Clearwater Cl. L7: Liv 5H **53**
Cleary St. L20: Boot 1B **34**
Cleaver Heath Nature Reserve 3B **100**
Clee Hill Rd. CH42: Tran 2E **87**
Cleethorpes Rd. WA7: Murd 6E **115**
Clegg St. L5: Liv 3E **53**
Clematis Rd. L27: N'ley 3G **75**
Clement Gdns. L3: Liv 3C **52**
Clementina Rd. L23: Blun 5D **8**
Clements Way L33: Kirkb 4H **13**
Clemmey Dr. L20: Boot 5E **21**
Clent Av. L31: Lyd, Mag 4B **6**
Clent Gdns. L31: Lyd 4B **6**
Clent Rd. L31: Mag 4B **6**
Cleopas St. L8: Liv 5F **71**
Cleveland Cl. L32: Kirkb 5H **13**
Cleveland Sq. L1: Liv 6E **5** (1D **70**)
Cleveland St. CH41: Birke 1E **69**
WA9: St H 4G **43**
Cleveley Pk. L18: Aller 2H **91**
Cleveley Rd. CH47: Meols 1E **65**
L18: Aller 2H **91**
Cleveleys Av. WA8: Wid 1H **97**
Cleves, The L31: Mag 4D **6**
Clevelands Rd. L32: Kirkb 2B **24**
Clieves Rd. L32: Kirkb 2B **24**
Cliff, The CH45: New B 5B **32**
Cliff Dr. CH44: Wall 2F **51**
Cliffe St. WA8: Wid 2F **97**
Clifford Rd. CH44: Wall 4E **51**
WA5: Penk 5H **81**
Clifford St. CH41: Birke 1C **68**
L3: Liv 2H **5** (5E **53**)
Cliff Rd. CH44: Wall 4B **50**

Cliff St. L7: Liv 5A **54**
CLIFTON 3H **123**
Clifton Av. CH62: East 4E **121**
  L23: Crosb *4G 9*
           (off Liverpool Rd.)
  L26: Halew 1G **93**
Clifton Ct. CH41: Birke 4F **69**
  L19: Aller 3G **91**
  WA7: Run 1F **123**
Clifton Cres. CH41: Birke 3G **69**
  WA6: Frod 6G **123**
Clifton Dr. L10: Ain 1B **22**
Clifton Ga. *CH41: Birke* *4G 69*
           (off Clifton Rd.)
Clifton Gro. CH44: Wall 3F **51**
  L5: Liv 3E **53**
Clifton La. WA7: Clftn 3H **123**
  WA7: Sut W 4A **124**
CLIFTON PARK 4F **69**
Clifton Rd. CH41: Birke 4F **69**
  L6: Liv 2B **54**
  WA7: Run 6E **113**
  WA7: Sut W 4A **124**
Clifton Rd. E. L6: Liv 2B **54**
Clifton St. L19: Garst 5G **91**
  WA10: St H 1E **43**
Cliftonville Rd. L34: Presc 1E **59**
Clincton Cl. WA8: Wid 3G **95**
Clincton Vw. WA8: Wid 3G **95**
CLINKHAM WOOD 2F **29**
Clinkham Wood Local Nature Reserve
  . . . . .2E **29**
Clinton Pl. L12: W Der 6D **36**
Clinton Rd. L12: W Der 6D **36**
Clint Rd. L7: Liv 6A **54**
Clint Rd. W. L7: Liv 6A **54**
Clint Way *L7: Liv* *6A 54*
           (off Clint Rd.)
Clipper Vw. CH62: New F 3C **88**
Clipsley Brook Vw. WA11: Hay 5B **30**
Clipsley Cres. WA11: Hay 4C **30**
Clipsley La. WA11: Hay 5D **30**
Clive Rd. CH43: Oxton 5E **69**
CLOCK FACE 4H **61**
Clock Face Colliery Country Pk. 3B **62**
Clock Face Pde. WA9: Sut L 3G **61**
Clock Face Rd.
  WA8: Bold H, Clock F 6A **62**
  WA9: Clock F 2G **61**
Clock La. WA5: Cuerd 6B **80**
Clocktower Dr. L9: Walt 2F **35**
Clock Twr. St. WA10: St H 2D **42**
Cloisters, The L23: Crosb 6F **9**
  WA10: Eccl 1H **41**
Clorain Cl. L33: Kirkb 6C **14**
Clorain Rd. L33: Kirkb 6C **14**
Close, The CH49: Grea 1B **84**
  CH61: Irby 5B **84**
  CH63: Hghr B 2F **87**
  L9: Walt 1F **35**
  L23: Crosb 6F **9**
  L28: Stockb V 6E **39**
  WA10: Eccl 6G **27**
  WA11: Hay 6B **30**
Closeburn Av. CH60: Hesw 1C **116**
Close St. WA9: St H 6C **42**
Cloudberry Cl. L27: N'ley 3G **75**
Clough, The WA7: Halt 4B **114**
Clough Rd. L24: Speke 1F **109**
           (not continuous)
  L26: Halew 2A **94**
Clovelly Av. WA5: Gt San 2G **81**
  WA9: St H 1A **62**
Clovelly Ct. CH49: Grea 6B **66**
Clovelly Gro. WA7: Brook 2D **124**
Clovelly Rd. L4: Walt 1H **53**
Clover Av. L26: Halew 1F **93**
Clover Ct. WA7: Brook 2D **124**
Cloverdale Rd. L25: Gate 2D **74**
Clover Dr. CH41: Birke 6A **50**
Cloverfield WA7: Nort 6E **115**
Clover Hey WA11: St H 4F **29**
Club 3000 Bingo
  Huyton 5G **57**

CLUBMOOR 6C **36**
Club St. WA11: St H 2E **29**
Clwyd Gro. L12: W Der 5F **37**
Clwyd St. CH41: Birke 3F **69**
  CH45: New B 6C **32**
Clyde Rd. L7: Liv 5C **54**
Clydesdale Rd. CH44: Wall 4A **51**
  CH47: Hoy 1B **64**
Clyde St. CH42: Rock F 1H **87**
  L20: Kirkd 5C **34**
Coach Ho. Ct. L29: Seft 3E **11**
Coach Ho. M. L22: Water 2F **19**
  L25: Woolt 6E **75**
Coachmans Dr. L12: W Der 4A **38**
Coach Rd. L39: Bic 1A **16**
  WA11: Rainf, Kirkb 4B **16**
Coady Way WA8: Wid 1G **97**
Coalbrookdale Rd.
  CH64: Nest 5B **118**
Coalgate La. L35: Whis 5C **58**
Coalport Wlk. WA9: St H 1A **60**
Coal St. L3: Liv 3G 5 (5E **53**)
Coalville Rd. WA11: St H 5H **29**
Coastal Dr. CH45: Wall 5A **32**
Coastal Point *CH46: Leas* *3C 48*
        (off Leasowe Rd.)
Coastguard La. CH64: Park 6F **117**
Cobb Av. L21: Lith 5B **20**
Cobbles, The L26: Halew 1F **93**
Cobblestone Cnr. L19: Gras 4E **91**
Cobden Av. CH42: Tran 6H **69**
Cobden Cl. CH42: Tran 6H **69**
Cobden Ct. CH42: Tran 6H **69**
Cobden Pl. CH42: Tran 6H **69**
  L25: Woolt 1B **92**
Cobden St. L6: Liv 4F **53**
  L25: Woolt 1B **92**
           (not continuous)
Cobden Vw. L25: Woolt 1B **92**
Cobham Av. L9: Walt 5F **21**
Cobham Rd. CH46: More 1B **66**
Cobham Wlk. L30: N'ton 5D **10**
Coburg St. CH41: Birke 3F **69**
Coburg Wharf L3: Liv 3C **70**
Cochrane St. L5: Liv 2F **53**
Cockburn St. L8: Liv 5F **71**
Cockerell Cl. L4: Walt 4H **35**
Cockerham Way L11: Crox 6F **23**
Cock Glade L35: Whis 6D **58**
Cocklake La. L24: Hale 4D **110**
Cock La. Ends WA8: Hale B 1H **111**
Cockspur St. L3: Liv 2D 4 (5C **52**)
Cockspur St. W. L3: Liv 2C 4 (5C **52**)
Coerton Rd. L9: Ain 4H **21**
Cokers, The CH42: Rock F 3G **87**
Colbern Cl. L31: Mag 1C **12**
Colbert Cl. CH49: Upton 5E **67**
Colby Cl. L16: Child 1A **74**
Colden Cl. L12: W Der 6A **38**
Colebrooke Rd. L17: Aig 6H **71**
Coleman Dr. CH49: Grea 6H **65**
Colemere Dr. CH61: Thing 5F **85**
Coleridge Av. WA10: St H 1B **42**
Coleridge Ct. L32: Kirkb 3H **23**
Coleridge Dr. CH62: New F 4A **88**
Coleridge Gro. WA8: Wid 2C **96**
Coleridge St. L6: Liv 4H **53**
  L20: Boot 1A **34**
Colesborne Rd. L11: Norr G 3F **37**
Coles Cres. L23: Thorn 3B **10**
Coleshill Rd. L11: Norr G 2C **36**
Cole St. CH43: Oxton 3E **69**
Colette Rd. L10: Faz 4F **23**
Colin Cl. L36: Roby 6E **57**
Colindale Rd. L16: Child 2A **74**
Colin Dr. L3: Liv 2C **52**
Colinton St. L15: Wav 1C **72**
College Av. L23: Crosb 6F **9**
College Cl. CH43: Bid 1A **68**
  CH45: Wall 1A **50**
College Ct. L12: W Der 2E **55**
College Dr. CH63: Beb 4A **88**

College Flds. L36: Huy 6G **57**
  WA8: Wid 4D **78**
College Grn. Flats L23: Crosb 6F **9**
College La. L1: Liv 5E 5 (6D **52**)
College Rd. L23: Crosb 5E **9**
College Rd. Nth. L23: Blun 4E **9**
College St. WA10: St H 1E **43**
           (not continuous)
College St. Nth. L6: Liv 4F **53**
College St. Sth. L6: Liv 4F **53**
College Vw. L36: Huy 5G **57**
Collegiate, The *L6: Liv* *4F 53*
           (off Shaw St.)
Collier's Row WA7: West 6C **112**
Collier St. WA7: Run 2D **112**
Colliford Way L6: Liv 3G **53**
Collingwood Cl. L4: Kirkd 5D **34**
Collingwood Rd. CH63: Beb 1B **104**
Collin Rd. CH43: Bid 1A **68**
Collins Cl. L20: Boot 6A **20**
COLLINS GREEN 4F **45**
Collins Grn. La. WA5: Coll G 4G **45**
Collins Ind. Est. WA9: St H 6G **29**
Colmoor Cl. L33: Kirkb 3B **14**
Colmore Av. CH63: Spit 4H **103**
Colmore Rd. L11: Norr G 3C **36**
Colne Dr. WA9: St H 6H **43**
Colne Rd. WA5: Burtw 1H **63**
Colonel Dr. L12: W Der 6A **38**
Colonnades, The L3: Liv 6C 4 (1B **70**)
Colquitt St. L1: Liv 6G 5 (1E **71**)
Coltart Rd. L8: Liv 3H **71**
Colton Rd. L25: Gate 2C **74**
Colton Wlk. L25: Gate 2B **74**
Columban Cl. L30: N'ton 6E **11**
Columbia Hall *WA8: Wid* *2F 97*
         (off Frederick St.)
Columbia La. CH43: Oxton 5D **68**
Columbia Rd. CH43: Oxton 5D **68**
  L4: Walt 3G **35**
  L34: Presc 1E **59**
Columbine Cl. L31: Mell 6E **13**
  WA8: Wid 5H **77**
Columbine Way WA9: Bold 6D **44**
Columbus Dr. CH61: Pens 2C **100**
Columbus Quay L3: Liv 6E **71**
Columbus Way *L21: Lith* *4B 20*
         (off Bridge Rd.)
Column Rd. CH48: Caldy, W Kir 1C **82**
Colville Rd. CH44: Wall 3C **50**
Colville St. L15: Wav 1C **72**
Colwall Cl. L33: Kirkb 1C **24**
Colwall Rd. L33: Kirkb 1C **24**
Colwall Wlk. L33: Kirkb 1C **24**
Colwell Cl. L14: Knott A 6C **38**
Colwell Ct. L14: Knott A 6C **38**
Colwell Rd. L14: Knott A 6C **38**
Colworth Rd. L24: Speke 1D **108**
Colwyn Rd. L13: Liv 5D **54**
Colwyn St. CH41: Birke 1C **68**
Colyton Av. WA9: Sut L 2H **61**
Combermere St. L8: Liv 3F **71**
  L15: Wav 1B **72**
Comely Av. CH44: Wall 3E **51**
Comely Bank Rd. CH44: Wall 3F **51**
Comer Gdns. L31: Lyd 4C **6**
Comfrey Gro. L26: Halew 1G **93**
Commerce Way L8: Liv 2H **71**
Commercial Rd. CH62: Brom 2E **105**
  L5: Kirkd 1C **52**
Common, The WA7: Halt 5C **114**
Commonfield Rd. CH49: Woodc 2F **85**
Common Rd. WA12: Newt W 2G **45**
Common St. WA9: St H 6B **42**
  WA12: Newt W 2G **45**
Commutation Row L3: Liv 2G 5 (5E **53**)
Company's Cl. WA7: West 1D **122**
Compass Cl. WA7: Murd 2F **125**
Compass Ct. CH45: Wall 5B **32**
Compton Cl. WA11: Hay 4E **31**
Compton Rd. CH41: Birke 6H **49**
  L6: Liv 3G **53**
Compton Wlk. L20: Boot 1B **34**
Compton Way L26: Halew 5H **93**

Comus St. L3: Liv 1F **5** (4D **52**)
Concert Sq. L1: Liv 5F **5**
Concert St. L1: Liv 5F **5** (6D **52**)
Concordia Av. CH49: Upton 4E **67**
Concourse Way WA9: St H 3B **44**
Condor Cl. L19: Garst 5H **91**
Condron Rd. Nth. L21: Lith 2C **20**
Condron Rd. Sth. L21: Lith 2C **20**
Coney Cres. L23: Thorn 4B **10**
Coney Gro. WA7: Brook 2D **124**
Coney La. L35: Tar G 2H **75**
    L36: Huy 2H **75**
Coney Wlk. CH49: Upton 3B **66**
Congress Gdns. WA9: St H 6B **42**
Conifer Cl. L9: Walt 2H **35**
    L33: Kirkb 4A **14**
Conifer Gro. WA5: Gt San 2H **81**
Conifers, The L31: Mag 4B **6**
Coningsby Dr. CH45: Wall 3C **50**
Coningsby Rd. L4: Walt 6G **35**
Coniston Av. CH43: Noct 4G **67**
    CH45: Wall 6A **32**
    CH63: East 3C **120**
    L34: Presc 1F **59**
    WA5: Penk 5F **81**
Coniston Cl. CH66: Hoot 6H **121**
    L9: Ain 4H **21**
    L33: Kirkb 5H **13**
    WA7: Beech 1H **123**
Coniston Dr. WA6: Frod 6H **123**
Coniston Gro. WA11: St H 4E **29**
Coniston Ho. L17: Aig 1C **90**
Coniston Rd. CH61: Irby 5B **84**
    L31: Mag 5D **6**
Coniston St. L5: Liv 1G **53**
Conleach Rd. L24: Speke 2G **109**
Connaught Cl. CH41: Birke 1C **68**
Connaught Cres. WA8: Wid 3D **78**
Connaught Ho. CH41: Birke 3A **70**
Connaught Rd. L7: Liv 5G **53**
    (not continuous)
Connaught Way CH41: Birke 1C **68**
Connect Bus. Village L5: Kirkd 6C **34**
Connolly Av. L20: Boot 6E **21**
Connolly Ho. L20: Boot 3D **34**
Consett Rd. WA9: St H 1B **60**
Constables Cl. WA7: Cas 4C **114**
Constance St. L3: Liv 2H **5** (5F **53**)
    WA10: St H 3B **42**
Constance Way WA8: Wid 6E **97**
Constantine Av. CH60: Hesw 4E **101**
Convent Cl. CH42: Tran 7F **69**
    L19: Gras 4E **91**
Conville Blvd. CH63: Hghr B 3G **87**
Conway Cl. CH63: Hghr B 6F **87**
    L33: Kirkb 4H **13**
    WA5: Gt San 3H **81**
Conway Ct. CH63: Beb 1H **103**
Conway Dr. CH41: Birke 3F **69**
Conway Ho. L6: Liv 3A **54**
Conway Lodge L5: Liv 2E **53**
Conway Park Station (Rail) 2G **69**
Conway St. CH41: Birke 2F **69**
    (not continuous)
    L5: Liv 2E **53**
    WA10: St H 3B **42**
Conwy Ct. WA7: Cas 3C **114**
Conwy Dr. L6: Liv 2H **53**
Coogee Av. WA5: Gt San 2G **81**
Cook Av. WA11: Hay 4G **31**
Cookes Cl. CH64: Nest 6A **118**
Cook Rd. CH46: Leas 3F **49**
Cooks Ct. L23: Crosb 4F **9**
Cookson Rd. L21: Sea 5A **20**
Cookson St. L1: Liv 2E **71**
Cooks Rd. L23: Crosb 4F **9**
Cook St. CH41: Birke 4F **69**
    L2: Liv 4D **4** (6C **52**)
    L34: Presc 1D **58**
    L35: Whis 3F **59**
Coombe Dr. WA7: Run 5D **112**
Coombe Rd. CH61: Irby 4C **84**
Cooperage Cl. L8: Liv 5E **71**
Cooper Av. WA12: Newt W 2H **45**

Cooper Av. Nth. L18: Moss H 2E **91**
Cooper Av. Sth. L19: Aig 2E **91**
Cooper Cl. L19: Aig 3E **91**
Cooper La. WA11: Hay 1D **44**
Cooper's La. L33: Know I 5F **25**
Coopers Row L22: Water 3G **19**
    (off Brunswick Pde.)
Cooper St. WA7: Run 2E **113**
    WA8: Wid 2F **97**
    WA10: St H 1D **42**
Copeland Cl. CH61: Pens 1C **100**
Copeland Gro. WA7: Beech 2A **124**
Copperas Hill L3: Liv 4G **5** (6E **53**)
Copperas St. WA10: St H 2D **42**
Copperfield Cl. L8: Liv 4F **71**
Copperwood WA7: Nort 4E **115**
Copperwood Dr. L35: Whis 5E **59**
Coppice, The CH45: Wall 6C **32**
    L4: Walt 1A **54**
    L34: Know 2F **39**
Coppice Cl. CH43: Bid 3F **67**
    WA7: Cas 4D **114**
Coppice Cres. L36: Huy 3H **57**
Coppice Grange CH46: More 2A **66**
Coppice Gro. CH49: Grea 1A **84**
Coppice La. L35: Tar G 2B **76**
Copplehouse Ct. L10: Faz 4E **23**
    (off Copplehouse La.)
Copplehouse La. L10: Faz 4E **23**
Coppull Rd. L31: Lyd 3B **6**
Copse, The L12: Moss H 4H **73**
    L25: Woolt 2D **92**
    WA7: Pal F 1C **124**
    (not continuous)
Copse Gro. CH61: Irby 4C **84**
Copsmead CH46: More 1D **66**
Copthorne Rd. L32: Kirkb 1F **23**
Copthorne Wlk. L32: Kirkb 1F **23**
Copy Cl. L30: N'ton 4F **11**
Copy La. L30: N'ton 4F **11**
Copy Way L30: N'ton 4F **11**
Coral Av. L36: Huy 4F **57**
    WA9: St H 6D **42**
Coral Cl. L32: Kirkb 1G **23**
Coral Dr. L20: Boot 2C **34**
Coral Ridge CH43: Bid 2H **67**
Coral St. L13: Liv 6E **55**
Corbet Cl. L32: Kirkb 1G **23**
Corbet Wlk. L32: Kirkb 1G **23**
Corbridge Rd. L16: Child 2G **73**
Corbyn St. CH44: Wall 6G **51**
Corfu St. CH41: Birke 3E **69**
Coriander La. L11: Norr G 4E **37**
Corinthian Av. L13: Liv 3E **55**
Corinthian St. CH42: Rock F 1H **87**
    L21: Sea 4H **19**
Corinth Twr. L5: Liv 1E **53**
    (off Anderson St.)
Corinto St. L8: Liv 2F **71**
Corkdale Rd. L9: Walt 6H **21**
Cormorant Cen., The WA7: Run . . .3C **112**
Cormorant Ct. CH45: Wall 5A **32**
Cormorant Dr. WA7: Run 3C **112**
Corncroft Rd. L34: Know 2F **39**
Corndale Rd. L18: Moss H 5E **73**
Cornelius Dr. CH61: Pens 6D **84**
Cornel Way L36: Huy 1H **75**
Corner Brook L28: Stockb V 6B **38**
Cornerhouse La. WA8: Wid 6B **78**
Cornett Rd. L9: Ain 4H **21**
Corney St. L7: Liv 2A **72**
Cornfield Cl. CH49: Woodc 1G **85**
Cornfields Cl. L19: Garst 5F **91**
Cornflower Way CH46: More 5E **49**
Cornforth Way WA8: Wid 6D **78**
Cornhill L1: Liv 1D **70**
Cornice Rd. L13: Liv 3E **55**
Cornmill Lodge L31: Mag 5B **6**
Corn St. L8: Liv 4E **71**
Cornubia Rd. WA8: Wid 4G **97**
Cornwall Av. WA7: Run 3E **113**
Cornwall Cl. WA7: Cas 4B **114**
Cornwall Ct. CH63: Beb 1H **103**

Cornwall Dr. CH43: Pren 2C **86**
Cornwallis St. L1: Liv 6G **5** (1D **70**)
    (not continuous)
Cornwall Rd. L20: Boot 1D **34**
    WA8: Wid 6F **79**
Cornwall St. WA9: St H 3H **43**
Cornwell Cl. CH62: New F 3B **88**
Cornwood Cl. L25: Gate 2D **74**
Corona Av. L31: Lyd 2B **6**
Corona Rd. CH62: Port S 5C **88**
    L13: Liv 3E **55**
    L22: Water 2F **19**
Coronation Av. CH45: New B 6D **32**
    L14: Broad G 4A **56**
Coronation Bldgs. CH45: Wall 2D **50**
    (off Wallasey Rd.)
    CH48: W Kir 5C **64**
Coronation Dr. CH62: Brom 2D **104**
    L14: Broad G 4A **56**
    L23: Crosb 6F **9**
    L35: Presc 5D **58**
    WA5: Penk 5H **81**
    WA6: Frod 6H **123**
    WA8: Wid 3H **95**
    WA11: Hay 4H **31**
Coronation Ho. WA7: Run 5G **113**
Coronation Rd. CH47: Hoy 3A **64**
    L23: Crosb 6F **9**
    L31: Lyd 4B **6**
    WA7: Pres B 1H **125**
    WA7: Run 4F **113**
    WA10: Windle 6A **28**
Coroner's La. WA8: Wid 4E **79**
Coronet Rd. L11: Crox 2G **37**
Coronet Way WA8: Wid 3H **95**
Corporal Way L12: W Der 6A **38**
Corporation Rd. CH41: Birke 1B **68**
Corporation St. WA9: St H 1E **43**
    WA10: St H 1E **43**
    (not continuous)
Corporation Wharf L20: Boot 1D **34**
Corrie Dr. CH63: Beb 1H **103**
Corsewall St. L7: Liv 1B **72**
Corsican Gdns. WA9: St H 4B **44**
Cortsway CH49: Grea 4C **66**
Cortsway W. CH49: Grea 4B **66**
Corwen Cl. CH43: Bid 3F **67**
    CH46: More 2D **66**
Corwen Cres. L14: Broad G 5B **56**
Corwen Dr. L30: N'ton 5H **11**
Corwen Rd. CH47: Hoy 2A **64**
    L4: Walt 5A **36**
Cosgrove Cl. L6: Liv 6B **36**
Coslett Dr. WA10: St H 2A **42**
Costain St. L20: Kirkd 6C **34**
Cote Lea Ct. WA7: Pal F 1B **124**
Cotham St. WA10: St H 2E **43**
Coton Way L32: Kirkb 6G **13**
Cotsford Cl. L36: Huy 3E **57**
Cotsford Pl. L36: Huy 3E **57**
Cotsford Rd. L36: Huy 3E **57**
Cotsford Way L36: Huy 3E **57**
Cotswold Gro. WA9: St H 2C **44**
Cotswold Rd. CH42: Tran 2E **87**
Cotswolds Cres. L26: Halew 4G **93**
Cotswold St. L7: Liv 5H **53**
Cottage Cl. CH63: Brom 2C **120**
    L33: Kirkb 4A **24**
Cottage Dr. E. CH60: Hesw 2D **116**
Cottage Dr. W. CH60: Hesw 2D **116**
Cottage La. CH60: Hesw 2D **116**
Cottage Pl. WA9: Clock F 3G **61**
Cottage St. CH41: Birke 2F **69**
Cottenham St. L6: Liv 4H **53**
Cotterdale Cl. WA5: Gt San 2H **81**
    WA9: St H 1G **61**
Cotterill WA7: Run 5H **113**
Cottesbrook Cl. L11: Norr G 2E **37**
Cottesbrook Pl. L11: Norr G 2E **37**
Cottesbrook Rd. L11: Norr G 2E **37**
Cottesmore Dr. CH60: Hesw 5H **101**
Cotton Exchange Bldg. L3: Liv 3C **4**
Cotton La. WA7: Run 5H **113**
Cottons Bri. WA4: Pres H 2H **125**

Cotton St.—Cronton Rd.

Cotton St. L3: Liv 3B 52
Cotton Ter. WA9: St H 5B 44
Cottonwood L17: Aig 6F 71
Cottrell Cl. L19: Garst 1G 107
Coulport Cl. L14: Knott A 3C 56
Coulsdon Pl. L8: Liv 5G 71
Coulthard Rd.
   CH42: Rock F 3A 88
Coulton Rd. WA8: Wid 6A 80
Council St. L35: Rainh 3G 59
Countess Pk. L11: Crox 3G 37
Countisbury Dr. L16: Child 3A 74
County Court
   Birkenhead 3H 69
   St Helens 1E 43
County Dr. WA10: St H 3C 42
County Rd. L4: Walt 4F 35
   L32: Kirkb 5A 14
Court, The CH63: Beb 1A 104
   L28: Stockb V 6E 39
Court Av. L26: Halew 2A 94
Courtenay Av. L22: Water 1E 19
Courtenay Rd. CH47: Hoy 3A 64
   L22: Water 1E 19
   L25: Woolt 5B 74
Courtfields Cl. L12: W Der 2F 55
COURT HEY 6B 56
Court Hey L31: Mag 6D 6
Court Hey Av. L36: Roby 5C 56
Court Hey Dr. L16: Child 6B 56
Court Hey Pk. 1B 74
Court Hey Rd. L16: Child 6B 56
Courthope Rd. L4: Walt 3H 35
Courtier Cl. L5: Liv 3E 53
Courtland Rd. L18: Moss H 4F 73
Courtney Av. CH44: Wall 4C 50
Courtney Rd. CH42: Rock F 3A 88
Courtyard, The L18: Moss H 6D 72
Courtyard Works
   L33: Know I 6E 15
Covent Gdn. L2: Liv 3C 4 (6C 52)
Coventry Av. L30: N'ton 2F 21
Coventry Rd. L15: Wav 3E 73
Coventry St. CH41: Birke 6C 50
Coverdale Av. L35: Rainh 4B 60
Coverdale Cl. WA5: Gt San 2H 81
Coverside CH48: W Kir 1D 82
Covington Dr. WA9: St H 2F 61
Cowan Dr. L6: Liv 3G 53
Cowan Way WA8: Wid 4D 78
Cowdrey Av. CH43: Bid 6G 49
Cow Hey La. WA7: Clftn 2E 123
   (not continuous)
Cowley Cl. CH49: Upton 4B 66
Cowley Ct. WA10: St H 6C 28
COWLEY HILL 6D 28
Cowley Hill La. WA10: St H 6D 28
Cowley Rd. L4: Walt 4F 35
Cowley St. WA10: St H 6E 29
Cowper Rd. L13: Liv 4F 55
Cowper St. L20: Boot 6A 20
   WA9: St H 4G 43
Cowper Way L36: Huy 6A 58
Coxheath CH42: Rock F 2A 88
Coylton Av. L35: Rainh 5B 60
Crab St. WA10: St H 1D 42
Crab Tree Cl. L24: Hale 3E 111
Crabtree Cl. L27: N'ley 4G 75
Crabtree Fold WA7: Nort 5E 115
Cradley WA8: Wid 1A 96
Crag Gro. WA11: St H 2F 29
Craigburn Rd. L13: Liv 1C 54
Craighurst Rd. L25: Gate 2C 74
Craigleigh Gro. CH62: East 3F 121
Craigmore Rd. L18: Moss H 2E 91
Craigside Av. L12: W Der 6E 37
Craigs Rd. L13: Liv 1C 54
Craigwood Way L36: Huy 4D 56
Craine Cl. L4: Walt 5H 35
Cramond Av. L18: Moss H 4D 72
Cranage Cl. WA7: Run 6H 113
Cranberry Cl. L27: N'ley 3G 75
   WA10: St H 6D 28
Cranborne Rd. L15: Wav 2B 72

Cranbourne Av. CH41: Birke 2C 68
   CH46: More 2B 66
   CH47: Meols 6E 47
Crane Av. WA9: Sut L 1H 61
Cranehurst Rd. L4: Walt 3H 35
Cranfield Rd. L23: Crosb 4A 10
Cranford Cl. CH62: East 3F 121
Cranford Rd. L19: Gras 3F 91
Cranford St. CH44: Wall 5E 51
Crank Rd. WA11: Crank, St H 4A 28
Cranleigh Gdns. L23: Crosb 5F 9
Cranleigh Pl. L25: Gate 3C 74
Cranleigh Rd. L25: Gate 3C 74
Cranmer St. L5: Liv 2C 52
   (not continuous)
Cranmore Av. L23: Crosb 1G 19
Cranshaw Av. WA9: Clock F 4H 61
Cranshaw La. WA8: Wid 4F 79
Cranston Cl. WA10: St H 6A 28
Cranston Rd. L33: Know I 1E 25
Crantock Cl. L11: Crox 1G 37
   L26: Halew 3H 93
Crantock Gro. WA10: Windle 4A 28
Cranwell Cl. L10: Ain 1A 22
Cranwell Rd. CH49: Grea 6H 65
   L25: Gate 2C 74
Cranwell Wlk. L25: Gate 2C 74
   (off Cranwell Rd.)
Crask Wlk. L33: Kirkb 5B 14
Craven Cl. CH41: Birke 3F 69
Craven Lea L12: Crox 2A 38
Craven Rd. L12: W Der 6G 37
   L35: Rainh 4A 60
Craven St. CH41: Birke 3E 69
   L3: Liv 2H 5 (5E 53)
Cravenwood Rd. L26: Halew 4H 93
Crawford Av. L18: Moss H 4D 72
   L31: Mag 4A 6
   WA8: Wid 2H 95
Crawford Cl. L12: W Der 6H 37
   WA9: Clock F 3H 61
Crawford Dr. L15: Wav 6E 55
Crawford Pk. L18: Moss H 6D 72
Crawford Pl. WA7: Run 1F 123
Crawford St. WA9: Clock F 3A 62
Crawford Way L7: Liv 5D 54
Crawshaw Ct. L36: Huy 3D 56
Crediton Cl. L11: Crox 6G 23
Creek, The CH45: Wall 5A 32
Cremona Cnr. L22: Water 2G 19
   (off South Rd.)
Cremorne Hey L28: Stockb V 6D 38
Crescent, The CH48: W Kir 1A 82
   CH49: Grea 6B 66
   CH60: Hesw 1F 117
   CH61: Pens 5D 84
   CH63: Hghr B 6D 87
   L20: Boot 5E 21
   L22: Water 2G 19
   L23: Thorn 3A 10
   L24: Speke 1E 109
   L31: Mag 2A 12
   L35: Whis 3F 59
   L36: Huy 5A 58
Crescent Ct. L21: Sea 5A 20
Crescent Rd. CH44: Wall 3E 51
   L9: Walt 6H 21
   L21: Sea 5A 20
   L23: Blun 4D 8
Crescent Row WA7: Run 3D 112
   (off Hankey St.)
Crescents, The L35: Rainh 3G 59
Cressida Av. CH63: Hghr B 4G 87
Cressingham Rd. CH45: New B 5D 32
Cressington Av. CH42: Tran 2F 87
Cressington Esplanade L19: Gras 5E 91
CRESSINGTON PARK 4E 91
Cressington Station (Rail) 4E 91
Cresson Ct. CH43: Oxton 4B 68
Cresswell Cl. L26: Halew 2A 94
Cresswell St. L6: Liv 3F 53
   (not continuous)
Cresta Dr. WA7: West 1D 122
Cresttor Rd. L25: Woolt 6B 74

Creswell St. WA10: St H 2C 42
Cretan Rd. L15: Wav 2B 72
Crete Towers L5: Kirkd 1E 53
Crewe Grn. CH49: Woodc 1E 85
Cricket Cl. L19: Garst 1H 107
Cricklade Cl. L20: Boot 1B 34
Cringles Dr. L35: Tar G 2A 76
Crispin Rd. L27: N'ley 4G 75
Crispin St. WA10: St H 2C 42
Critchley Rd. L24: Speke 3A 110
Critchley Way L33: Kirkb 5B 14
Croasdale Dr. WA7: Beech 2A 124
Crockett's Wlk. WA10: Eccl 6H 27
Crocus Av. CH41: Birke 2B 68
Crocus Gdns. WA9: Bold 6C 44
Crocus St. L5: Kirkd 6D 34
Croft, The CH49: Grea 1B 84
   L12: W Der 6F 37
   L28: Stockb V 5C 38
   L31: Lyd 2A 6
   L32: Kirkb 4B 24
   WA7: Halt 4B 114
   WA9: St H 4B 44
Croft Av. CH62: Brom 4C 104
Croft Av. E. CH62: Brom 3D 104
Croft Bus. Cen. CH62: Brom 3E 105
Croft Bus. Pk. CH62: Brom 3E 105
Croft Cl. CH43: Noct 5A 68
   CH62: Brom 4D 104
Croft Dr. CH46: More 2C 66
   CH48: Caldy 5C 82
Croft Dr. E. CH48: Caldy 4D 82
Croft Dr. W. CH48: Caldy 4C 82
Croft Edge CH43: Oxton 6D 68
Croft End WA9: St H 4B 44
Crofters, The CH49: Grea 5B 66
Crofters La. L33: Kirkb 4C 14
Croftfield L31: Mag 6D 6
Croft Grn. CH62: Brom 2D 104
Croft La. CH62: Brom 4D 104
   L9: Ain 4B 22
Crofton Cres. L13: Liv 4F 55
Crofton Rd. CH42: Tran 6G 69
   L13: Liv 4F 55
   WA7: Run 4C 112
Croft Retail & Leisure Pk.
   CH62: Brom 2D 104
Croft St. WA8: Wid 5E 97
Croftsway CH60: Hesw 5B 100
Croft Technology Pk. CH62: Brom . . .4F 105
Croft Trade Pk. CH62: Brom 3E 105
Croft Way L23: Thorn 4B 10
Croftwood Gro. L35: Whis 5E 59
Cromarty Rd. CH44: Wall 3B 50
   L13: Liv 4D 54
Cromdale Gro. WA9: St H 3A 44
Cromdale Way WA5: Gt San 3G 81
Cromer Dr. CH45: Wall 2C 50
Cromer Rd. CH47: Hoy 2A 64
   L17: Aig 2C 90
Cromer Way L26: Halew 5H 93
Cromford Rd. L36: Huy 2G 57
Crompton Ct. L3: Liv 3F 53
   (off Haigh St.)
   L18: Moss H 4H 73
Crompton Dr. L12: Crox 2A 38
Cromptons La. L18: Moss H 5H 73
Crompton St. L5: Liv 2D 52
Cromwell Rd. L4: Walt 3F 35
Cromwell St. WA8: Wid 5E 97
Crondall Gro. L15: Wav 2F 73
CRONTON 4A 78
Cronton Av. CH46: Leas 4D 48
   L35: Whis 6C 58
Cronton Farm Ct. WA8: Wid 5C 78
Cronton La. L35: Rainh 6H 59
   WA8: Cron 2H 77
   WA8: Wid 4C 78
Cronton La. M. WA8: Wid 4D 78
Cronton Pk. Av. WA8: Cron 3A 78
Cronton Pk. Cl. WA8: Cron 3A 78
Cronton Rd. L15: Wav 4E 73
   L35: Tar G 2A 76
   WA8: Cron, Wid 4H 77

Cronulla Dr. WA5: Gt San 2F 81
Croome Dr. CH48: W Kir 1C 82
Croppers Hill Ct. WA10: St H 3C 42
(off Prescot Rd.)
Cropper St. L1: Liv 5G 5 (6E 53)
CROSBY 3G 19
Crosby Civic Hall (Theatre) 2G 19
Crosby Cl. CH49: Upton 3D 66
Crosby Coastal Pk. 2E 19
Crosby Grn. L12: W Der 6E 37
Crosby Gro. CH64: Will 6B 120
WA10: St H 4B 42
Crosby Lakeside Adventure Cen. 3F 19
Crosby Leisure Cen. 1D 18
Crosby Rd. Nth. L22: Water 1G 19
Crosby Rd. Sth. L21: Sea 3G 19
L22: Water 3G 19
Crosender Rd. L23: Crosb 6E 9
Crosfield Cl. L7: Liv 6A 54
Crosfield Rd. CH44: Wall 4E 51
L7: Liv 6A 54
L35: Presc 3F 59
Crosfield Wlk. L7: Liv 6A 54
(off Crosfield Cl.)
Crosgrove Rd. L4: Walt 4A 36
Crosland Rd. L32: Kirkb 2C 24
Cross, The CH62: Brom 4E 105
Crossacre Rd. L25: Gate 2D 74
Crossdale Rd. CH62: Brom 1D 120
L23: Crosb 6E 9
Crossdale Way WA11: St H 2F 29
Cross Farm Rd. WA9: St H 4G 43
Crossfield St. WA9: St H 2F 43
Crossford Rd. L14: Knott A 1C 56
Cross Gates WA8: Wid 6B 80
Crosshall St. L1: Liv 3E 5 (5D 52)
Cross Hey L21: Ford 1B 20
L31: Mag .2C 12
Cross Hey Av. CH43: Noct 4H 67
Cross Hillocks La. WA8: Wid 1E 95
Cross La. CH45: Wall 2H 49
CH63: Beb 1H 103
L35: Presc, Whis 3D 58
Crossledge Way L25: Gate 2B 74
Crossley Dr. CH60: Hesw 5B 100
L15: Wav 1E 73
Crossley Rd. WA10: St H 5B 42
Cross Mdw. Ct. WA9: St H 3G 43
(off Appleton Rd.)
Cross Pit La. WA11: Rainf 3F 17
Cross St. CH41: Birke 3H 69
CH62: Port S 6B 88
L22: Water 2F 19
L34: Presc 6E 41
WA7: Run 2E 113
WA8: Wid 2F 97
(not continuous)
WA10: St H 2E 43
Crossvale Rd. L36: Huy 6G 57
Crossway CH43: Bid 1A 68
WA8: Wid 3B 96
Crossway, The CH63: Raby 3E 119
Crossways CH62: Brom 2D 104
L25: Gate 3B 74
Crosswood Cres. L36: Huy 4E 57
Crosthwaite Av. CH62: East 3F 121
Croston Av. L35: Rainh 2H 59
Croston Cl. WA8: Wid 6A 78
Crouch St. L5: Liv 1G 53
WA9: St H 5H 43
Crow La. W.
WA12: Newt W 1H 45
Crowmarsh Cl. CH49: Upton 5D 66
Crown Acres Rd. L25: Woolt 3E 93
Crown Av. WA8: Wid 3H 95
Crown Court
Liverpool 5D 4 (6C 52)
Crown Ga. WA7: Pal F 6B 114
Crown Rd. L12: W Der 6G 37
Crown Sta. Pl. L7: Liv 1G 71
Crown St. L7: Liv 5F 53
(Elizabeth St.)
L7: Liv 1G 71
(Rosemary Cl.)

Crown St. L8: Liv 1G 71
WA9: St H 6B 42
WA12: Newt W 2H 45
Crownway L36: Huy 3F 57
Crow St. L8: Liv 3D 70
Crowther St. WA10: St H 2C 42
CROW WOOD 1H 97
Crow Wood La. WA8: Wid 1H 97
Crow Wood Pl. WA8: Wid 6H 79
Croxdale Rd. L14: Knott A 6C 38
Croxdale Rd. W. L14: Knott A 6B 38
CROXTETH 1G 37
Croxteth Av. CH44: Wall 3D 50
L21: Lith .4A 20
Croxteth Cl. L31: Mag 4D 6
Croxteth Ct. L8: Liv 3H 71
Croxteth Dr. L17: Aig 4A 72
WA11: Rainf 2F 17
Croxteth Ga. L17: Aig 4A 72
Croxteth Gro. L8: Liv 3A 72
Croxteth Hall .4H 37
Croxteth Hall Country Pk. 4A 38
Croxteth Hall La. L11: Crox 2G 37
L12: Crox, W Der 3G 37
Croxteth La. L34: Know 4D 38
CROXTETH PARK 2B 38
Croxteth Rd. L8: Liv 3H 71
L20: Boot 6B 20
Croxteth Vw. L32: Kirkb 4B 24
Croyde Pl. WA9: Sut L 3G 61
Croyde Rd. L24: Speke 2A 110
Croydon Av. L18: Moss H 4D 72
Croylands St. L4: Kirkd 5E 35
Crucian Way L12: Crox 2H 37
Crump St. L1: Liv 2E 71
Crutchley Av. CH41: Birke 1D 68
Crystal Cl. L13: Liv 5E 55
Cubbin Cres. L5: Kirkd 1D 52
Cubert Rd. L11: Crox 1G 37
Cuckoo Cl. L25: Gate 5C 74
Cuckoo La. L25: Gate 4C 74
Cuckoo Way L25: Gate 5C 74
Cuerden St. L3: Liv 2F 5 (5D 52)
CUERDLEY CROSS 1C 98
Cuerdley Grn. WA5: Cuerd 1C 98
Cuerdley Rd. WA5: Penk 6E 81
Culford Cl. WA7: Wind H 4F 115
Cullen Av. L20: Boot 6D 20
Cullen Cl. CH63: East 3D 120
Cullen Dr. L21: Lith 4A 20
Cullen Rd. WA7: West P 6B 112
Cullen St. L8: Liv 2A 72
Culme Rd. L12: W Der 6D 36
Culzean Cl. L12: Crox 2A 38
Cumberland Av. CH43: Pren 1C 86
L17: Liv 3B 72
L30: N'ton 6C 10
WA10: St H 5H 41
Cumberland Cl. L6: Liv 6B 36
Cumberland Cres. WA11: Hay 5C 30
Cumberland Ga. L30: N'ton 5G 11
Cumberland Rd. CH45: New B 6E 33
Cumberland St. L1: Liv 3D 4 (5C 52)
Cumber La. L35: Whis 3F 59
Cumbria Way L12: W Der 4G 37
Cummings St. L1: Liv 1E 71
Cumpsty Rd. L21: Lith 2C 20
Cunard Av. CH44: Wall 2F 51
Cunard Cl. CH43: Bid 3G 67
Cunard Rd. L21: Lith 4B 20
Cunliffe Cl. WA7: Pal F 6C 114
Cunliffe St. L2: Liv 2D 4 (5C 52)
WA5: Gt San 4H 81
Cunningham Cl. WA10: St H 2A 42
Cunningham Dr. CH63: Brom 6C 104
WA7: Run 5C 112
(not continuous)
Cunningham Rd. L13: Liv 5E 55
WA8: Wid 3B 96
Cunscough La. L31: Mag 5H 7
Cuper Cres. L36: Huy 3F 57
Curate Rd. L6: Liv 6A 36
Curlender Cl. CH41: Birke 6A 50

Curlender Way L24: Hale 3E 111
Curlew Av. CH49: Upton 3B 66
Curlew Cl. CH49: Upton 3B 66
Curlew Ct. CH46: More 6A 48
Curlew Gro. L26: Halew 2G 93
Curlew Way L33: Kirkb 4H 13
Curran Way L33: Kirkb 4H 13
Curtana Cres. L11: Crox 2G 37
Curtis Rd. L4: Walt 4A 36
Curwell Cl. CH63: Spit 2B 104
Curzon Av. CH41: Birke 2D 68
CH45: New B 5D 32
Curzon Rd. CH42: Tran 1D 86
CH47: Hoy 2A 64
L22: Water 2G 19
Curzon St. WA7: Run 4D 112
Cusson Rd. L33: Know I 2D 24
Custley Hey L28: Stockb V 5D 38
Custom Ho. Pl. L1: Liv 6D 4 (1C 70)
Cut La. L33: Kirkb 4G 25
Cygnet Ct. L33: Kirkb 1C 24
Cygnet Gdns. WA9: St H 3A 44
Cynthia Rd. WA7: Run 4D 112
Cypress Av. WA8: Wid 6F 79
Cypress Cl. L31: Mell 6E 13
Cypress Cft. CH63: Spit 2B 104
Cypress Gdns. WA9: St H 6A 42
Cypress Gro. WA7: Run 6G 113
Cypress Rd. L36: Huy 1F 75
Cyprian's Way L30: N'ton 6E 11
Cyprus Gro. L8: Liv 5G 71
Cyprus St. L34: Presc 1D 58
Cyprus Ter. CH45: New B 6D 32
Cyril Gro. L17: Aig 1C 90

D

DACRE HILL 3H 87
Dacre's Bri. La. L35: Tar G 2D 76
Dacre St. CH41: Birke 3G 69
L20: Boot 4B 34
Dacy Rd. L5: Liv 2G 53
Daffodil Cl. WA8: Wid 5A 80
Daffodil Gdns. WA9: Bold 6C 44
Daffodil Rd. CH41: Birke 2B 68
L15: Wav .3F 73
Dagnall Rd. L32: Kirkb 2G 23
Dahlia Cl. L9: Walt 1H 35
WA9: Bold 6C 44
Dairy Farm Rd. WA11: Rainf 3B 16
Dairylands Cl. L16: Moss H 3G 73
Daisy Bank Rd. WA5: Penk 5H 81
Daisy Gro. L7: Liv 6H 53
(off Dorothy Dr.)
Daisy M. L21: Lith 5B 20
Daisy Mt. L31: Mag 1C 12
Daisy St. L5: Kirkd 6D 34
Daisy Wlk. CH44: Wall 4D 50
Dakin Wlk. L33: Kirkb 1B 24
Dakota Bus. Pk. L19: Speke 1A 108
Dakota Dr. L24: Speke 2H 107
Dalby Cl. WA11: St H 6G 29
Dalcross Way L11: Crox 1F 37
Dale, The WA5: Gt San, Penk 4H 81
Dale Acre Dr. L30: N'ton 6C 10
Dale Av. CH60: Hesw 4D 100
CH62: Brom 5D 104
Dalebrook Cl. L25: Gate 2D 74
Dale Cl. L31: Mag 5B 6
WA8: Wid 3G 95
Dale Ct. CH60: Hesw 5D 100
Dale Cres. WA9: Sut L 1H 61
Dale End Rd. CH61: Barn 1G 101
Dale Gdns. CH60: Hesw 4B 100
Dalegarth Av. L12: W Der 4B 38
Dale Hall L18: Moss H 1D 90
Dalehead Pl. WA11: St H 7F 29
Dale Hey CH44: Wall 4D 50
CH66: Hoot 5E 121
Dalehurst Cl. CH44: Wall 3F 51
Dale La. L33: Kirkb 4C 14
Dalemeadow Rd. L14: Knott A 4H 55
Dale M. L25: Gate 5D 74

Dale Rd.—Dell La.

Dale Rd. CH62: Brom . . . 1D 120
DALES, THE . . . 5C 100
Dales, The CH46: More . . . 1E 67
Daleside Cl. CH61: Irby . . . 5D 84
Daleside Rd. L33: Kirkb . . . 6B 14
Daleside Wlk. L33: Kirkb . . . 6B 14
Dales Row L36: Huy . . . 5B 58
Dale St. L2: Liv . . . 3D 4 (5C 52)
L19: Garst . . . 6G 91
WA7: Run . . . 4E 113
Dalesway CH60: Hesw . . . 5C 100
Dale Vw. Cl. CH61: Pens . . . 6E 85
Dalewood L12: Crox . . . 2A 38
Dalewood Gdns. L35: Whis . . . 5F 59
Daley Pl. L20: Boot . . . 4E 21
Daley Rd. L21: Lith . . . 2C 20
Dallas Gro. L9: Ain . . . 5G 21
Dallington Ct. L13: Liv . . . 5F 55
Dalmeny St. L17: Aig . . . 6H 71
Dalmorton Rd. CH45: New B . . . 5D 32
Dalry Cres. L32: Kirkb . . . 4B 24
Dalrymple St. L5: Liv . . . 2D 52
Dalry Wlk. L32: Kirkb . . . 4B 24
Dalston Dr. WA11: St H . . . 2F 29
Dalton Cl. L12: W Der . . . 3G 37
Dalton Ct. WA7: Ast . . . 2A 114
Dalton Rd. CH45: New B . . . 6E 33
Dalton St. WA7: Run . . . 3H 113
Daltry Cl. L12: W Der . . . 6E 37
Dalwood Cl. WA7: Murd . . . 6G 115
Damerham M. L25: Gate . . . 2C 74
Damfield La. L31: Mag . . . 6B 6
Damson Gro. WA11: Rainf . . . 2E 17
Damson Gro. Ct. WA11: Rainf . . . 2E 17
Damson Rd. L27: N'ley . . . 3G 75
Damwood Rd. L24: Speke . . . 3E 109
Danby Cl. L5: Liv . . . 2F 53
WA7: Beech . . . 1H 123
Danby Fold L35: Rainh . . . 4H 59
Dane Cl. CH61: Irby . . . 5D 84
Dane Ct. L35: Rainh . . . 4A 60
Danefield Pl. L19: Aller . . . 3H 91
Danefield Rd. CH49: Grea . . . 1A 84
L19: Aller . . . 3H 91
Danefield Ter. *L19: Aller* . . . *4H 91*
(off Mather Av.)
Danehurst Rd. CH45: Wall . . . 6B 32
L9: Ain . . . 4H 21
Danescourt Rd. CH41: Birke . . . 1C 68
L12: W Der . . . 2G 55
Danescroft WA8: Wid . . . 6H 77
Daneshill Cl. L17: Aig . . . 4D 90
Dane St. L4: Walt . . . 4F 35
Daneswell Dr. CH46: More . . . 6D 48
Daneswell Rd. L24: Speke . . . 3A 110
Daneville Rd. L4: Walt . . . 3B 36
Danger La. CH46: More . . . 5D 48
Daniel Cl. L20: Boot . . . 5A 20
Daniel Davies Dr. L8: Liv . . . 2G 71
Daniel Ho. L20: Boot . . . 3C 34
Dannette Hey L28: Stockb V . . . 1E 57
Dansie St. L3: Liv . . . 4H 5 (6F 53)
Dan's Rd. WA8: Wid . . . 1A 98
Dante Cl. L9: Ain . . . 3A 22
Danube St. L8: Liv . . . 2A 72
Dapple Heath Av. L31: Mell . . . 6E 13
Darby Gro. L19: Garst . . . 5F 91
Darby Rd. L19: Gras . . . 3E 91
Darent Rd. WA11: Hay . . . 4D 30
Daresbury Cl. L32: Kirkb . . . 1G 23
Daresbury Ct. WA8: Wid . . . 6H 79
Daresbury Expressway
WA4: Moore, Dares . . . 3B 114
WA7: Run, Ast, Wind H, Nort . . . 3E 113
Daresbury Pk. WA4: Dares . . . 5H 115
(not continuous)
Daresbury Rd. CH44: Wall . . . 3C 50
WA10: Eccl . . . 1H 41
Dark Entry L34: Know P . . . 4G 39
Dark La. L31: Mag . . . 6C 6
Darkstar Laser
St Helens . . . *1E 43*
(off Central St.)
Darley Cl. WA8: Wid . . . 6H 77
Darleydale Dr. CH62: East . . . 2F 121
Darley Dr. L12: W Der . . . 1G 55
Darlington Cl. CH44: Wall . . . 3F 51
Darlington Ct. WA8: Wid . . . 4E 97
Darlington St. CH44: Wall . . . 3F 51
Darmond Rd. L33: Kirkb . . . 6C 14
Darmond's Grn. CH48: W Kir . . . 6B 64
Darmonds Grn. Av. L6: Liv . . . 6B 36
Darnley St. L8: Liv . . . 4E 71
Darrel Dr. L7: Liv . . . 2A 72
Darsefield Rd. L16: Child . . . 2A 74
Dartford Cl. L14: Knott A . . . 1B 56
Dartington Rd. L16: Child . . . 1H 73
Dartmouth Av. L10: Ain . . . 1A 22
Dartmouth Dr. L30: N'ton . . . 5C 10
WA10: Windle . . . 5A 28
Darwall Rd. L19: Aller . . . 3H 91
Darwen St. L5: Liv . . . 2C 52
Darwick Dr. L36: Huy . . . 1H 75
Darwin Gro. WA9: St H . . . 6C 42
Daryl Rd. CH60: Hesw . . . 4E 101
Daulby St. L3: Liv . . . 5F 53
Dauntsey Brow L25: Gate . . . 2D 74
Dauntsey M. L25: Gate . . . 2D 74
Davenham Av. CH43: Oxton . . . 6B 68
Davenham Cl. CH43: Oxton . . . 1B 86
Davenham Ct. L15: Wav . . . 2F 73
Davenhill Pk. L10: Ain . . . 1A 22
Davenport Cl. CH48: Caldy . . . 5C 82
Davenport Gro. L33: Kirkb . . . 5A 14
Davenport Rd. CH60: Hesw . . . 6C 100
Davenport Row WA7: Run . . . 5H 113
Daventree Rd. CH45: Wall . . . 2D 50
Daventry Rd. L17: Aig . . . 1C 90
David Lewis St. L1: Liv . . . 5E 5 (6D 52)
David Lloyd Leisure
Liverpool . . . 2C 24
David Lloyd Racquet & Fitness Club
Speke . . . 1A 108
Davidson Rd. L13: Liv . . . 4D 54
David St. L8: Liv . . . 5F 71
Davids Wlk. L25: Woolt . . . 6E 75
Davies Cl. WA8: Wid . . . 1E 113
Davies St. L1: Liv . . . 3D 4 (5C 52)
L20: Boot . . . 1D 34
WA9: St H . . . 1G 43
Davis Rd. CH46: Leas . . . 4F 49
Davy Cl. WA10: Eccl . . . 6H 27
Davy Rd. WA7: Ast . . . 2A 114
Davy St. L5: Liv . . . 1G 53
Dawber Cl. L6: Liv . . . 3G 53
Dawlish Cl. L25: Hunts X . . . 3E 93
Dawlish Rd. CH44: Wall . . . 3B 50
CH61: Irby . . . 6A 84
Dawn Cl. WA9: St H . . . 6C 42
Dawn Wlk. *L10: Faz* . . . *5F 23*
(off Panton Way)
Dawpool Cotts. CH48: Caldy . . . 5G 83
Dawpool Dr. CH46: More . . . 1C 66
CH62: Brom . . . 6C 104
Dawpool Farm CH61: Thurs . . . 6H 83
Dawson Av. CH41: Birke . . . 1D 68
WA9: St H . . . 6H 43
Dawson Gdns. L31: Mag . . . 5B 6
Dawson Ho. WA5: Gt San . . . 3E 81
Dawson St. L1: Liv . . . 4E 5 (6D 52)
Dawson Way L1: Liv . . . 4F 5
Dawstone Ri. CH60: Hesw . . . 6D 100
Dawstone Rd. CH60: Hesw . . . 6D 100
Days Mdw. CH49: Grea . . . 6A 66
Day St. L13: Liv . . . 4E 55
Deacon Cl. L22: Water . . . 3F 19
Deacon Ct. L22: Water . . . 3F 19
L25: Woolt . . . 1D 92
Deacon Pk. L33: Know I . . . 3D 24
Deacon Rd. WA8: Wid . . . 2F 97
Deacon Trad. Est. WA12: Newt W . . . 3H 45
Deakin St. CH41: Birke . . . 1B 68
Dealcroft L25: Woolt . . . 1B 92
Dean Av. CH45: Wall . . . 1A 50
Dean Cl. WA8: Wid . . . 3F 97
Dean Dillistone Ct. *L1: Liv* . . . *2E 71*
(off Cathedral Ga.)
Deane Rd. L7: Liv . . . 5A 54
Dean Ho. L22: Water . . . 3G 19
Deanland Dr. L24: Speke . . . 1D 108
Dean Patey Ct. L1: Liv . . . 1E 71
Deansburn Rd. L13: Liv . . . 1C 54
Deanscales Rd. L11: Norr G . . . 3D 36
Dean St. L22: Water . . . 3F 19
WA8: Wid . . . 3F 97
Deans Way CH41: Birke . . . 1B 68
Deansway WA8: Wid . . . 3A 96
Deanwood Cl. L35: Whis . . . 5F 59
Dearham Av. WA11: St H . . . 4E 29
Dearne Cl. L12: W Der . . . 2A 56
Dearnford Av. CH62: Brom . . . 1D 120
Dearnford Cl. CH62: Brom . . . 1D 120
Dearnley Av. WA11: St H . . . 6A 30
Deauville Rd. L9: Ain . . . 4A 22
Debra Cl. L31: Mell . . . 5F 13
Decks, The WA7: Run . . . 2E 113
Dee Cl. L33: Kirkb . . . 3B 14
Dee Ct. L25: Gate . . . 6E 75
Dee Ho. L25: Gate . . . 6E 75
Dee La. CH48: W Kir . . . 1A 82
Deeley Cl. L7: Liv . . . 6A 54
Dee Pk. Cl. CH60: Hesw . . . 1F 117
Dee Pk. Rd. CH60: Hesw . . . 1F 117
Deepdale WA8: Wid . . . 6A 78
Deepdale Av. L20: Boot . . . 6A 20
WA11: St H . . . 2G 29
Deepdale Cl. CH43: Bid . . . 3G 67
WA5: Gt San . . . 3H 81
Deepdale Dr. L35: Rainh . . . 4B 60
Deepdale Rd. L25: Gate . . . 2C 74
Deepfield Dr. L36: Huy . . . 1H 75
Deepfield Rd. L15: Wav . . . 3D 72
Deepwood Gro. L35: Whis . . . 5E 59
Deerbarn Dr. L30: N'ton . . . 5H 11
Deerbolt Cl. L32: Kirkb . . . 6G 13
Deerbolt Cres. L32: Kirkb . . . 6G 13
Deerbolt Way L32: Kirkb . . . 6G 13
Deerbourne Cl. L25: Woolt . . . 1B 92
Deerfield Cl. WA9: St H . . . 1A 44
Dee Rd. L35: Rainh . . . 4H 59
Deer Pk. Ct. WA7: Pal F . . . 1A 124
Dee Sailing Club . . . 6D 82
Deeside CH60: Hesw . . . 5A 100
Deeside Cl. CH43: Bid . . . 3F 67
Deeside Ct. CH64: Park . . . 6F 117
Dee Vw. Rd. CH60: Hesw . . . 5D 100
De Grouchy St. CH48: W Kir . . . 6B 64
De Havilland Dr. L24: Speke . . . 1A 108
Deirdre Av. WA8: Wid . . . 2E 97
Dekker Rd. L33: Kirkb . . . 3A 14
Delabole Rd. L11: Crox . . . 6H 23
De Lacy Row WA7: Cas . . . 3C 114
Delagoa Rd. L10: Faz . . . 5D 22
Delamain Rd. L13: Liv . . . 1C 54
Delamere Av. CH62: East . . . 3E 121
WA8: Wid . . . 2A 96
WA9: Sut M . . . 4E 61
Delamere Cl. CH43: Bid . . . 3F 67
CH62: East . . . 3E 121
L12: Crox . . . 2H 37
Delamere Gro. *CH44: Wall* . . . *5G 51*
(off Tudor Av.)
Delamere Pl. WA7: Run . . . 4D 112
Delamore Pl. L4: Kirkd . . . 4E 35
Delamore's Acre CH64: Will . . . 6A 120
Delamore St. L4: Kirkd . . . 4E 35
Delavor Cl. CH60: Hesw . . . 5C 100
Delavor Rd. CH60: Hesw . . . 5B 100
Delaware Cres. L32: Kirkb . . . 6G 13
Delaware Rd. L20: Boot . . . 1C 34
Delfby Cres. L32: Kirkb . . . 2C 24
Delf La. L4: Walt . . . 3G 35
L24: Speke . . . 6D 92
Dell, The CH42: Rock F . . . 2B 88
L12: W Der . . . 5A 38
Della Robbia Ho. *CH41: Birke* . . . *4F 69*
(off Clifton Rd.)
Dell Cl. CH63: Brom . . . 1B 120
Dell Ct. CH43: Pren . . . 2B 86
Dellfield La. L31: Mag . . . 6D 6
Dell Gro. CH42: Rock F . . . 3B 88
Dell La. CH60: Hesw . . . 6F 101

152 A-Z Liverpool

Dellside Gro.—Ditton Rd.

Dellside Gro. WA9: St H . . . 5G 43
Dell St. L7: Liv . . . 5A 54
Delph Ct. L21: Lith . . . 3A 20
WA9: St H . . . 5F 43
Delphfield WA7: Nort . . . 5F 115
Delph Hollow Way
WA9: St H . . . 5F 43
Delph La. L35: Whis . . . 2F 59
WA4: Dares . . . 2H 115
Delph Rd. L23: Lit C . . . 1F 9
Delphwood Dr. WA9: St H . . . 4F 43
Delta Dr. L12: W Der . . . 5A 38
Delta Rd. L21: Lith . . . 4B 20
WA9: St H . . . 1B 44
Delta Rd. E. CH42: Rock F . . . 2B 88
Delta Rd. W. CH42: Rock F . . . 2B 88
Deltic Pl. L33: Know I . . . 2D 24
Deltic Way L30: N'ton . . . 3G 21
L33: Know I . . . 3D 24
Delves Av. CH63: Spit . . . 2H 103
Delyn Cl. CH42: Rock F . . . 2G 87
Demesne St. CH44: Wall . . . 4G 51
Denbigh Av. WA9: St H . . . 6G 43
Denbigh Ct. WA7: Cas . . . 3C 114
Denbigh Rd. CH44: Wall . . . 4F 51
L9: Walt . . . 2F 35
Denbigh St. L5: Liv . . . 2B 52
Dencourt Rd. L11: Norr G . . . 4F 37
Deneacres L25: Woolt . . . 1C 92
Dene Av. WA12: Newt W . . . 1H 45
Denebank Rd. L4: Walt . . . 6H 35
Denecliff L28: Stockb V . . . 5D 38
Dene Ct. L9: Faz . . . 1D 36
Denehurst Cl. WA5: Penk . . . 5H 81
Deneshey Rd. CH47: Meols . . . 1C 64
Denes Way L28: Stockb V . . . 6C 38
Denford Rd. L14: Knott A . . . 2B 56
Denham Cl. CH43: Bid . . . 2G 67
L12: Crox . . . 2B 38
Denise Av. WA5: Penk . . . 4G 81
Denise Rd. L10: Faz . . . 4F 23
Denison Gro. WA9: St H . . . 6C 42
Denison St. L3: Liv . . . 1B 4 (4B 52)
Denman Dr. L6: Liv . . . 3A 54
Denman Gro. *CH44: Wall . . . 5G 51*
(off Tudor Av.)
Denman St. L6: Liv . . . 4H 53
Denman Way L6: Liv . . . 3A 54
Denmark St. L22: Water . . . 2F 19
Dennett Cl. L31: Mag . . . 2B 12
Dennett Rd. L35: Presc . . . 3C 58
Denning Dr. CH61: Irby . . . 4B 84
Dennis Av. WA10: St H . . . 6A 42
Dennis Rd. WA8: Wid . . . 4G 97
Denny Cl. CH49: Upton . . . 5D 66
Denston Cl. CH43: Bid . . . 2F 67
Denstone Av. L10: Ain . . . 1B 22
Denstone Cl. L25: Woolt . . . 3D 92
Dentdale Dr. L5: Liv . . . 3E 53
Denton Dr. CH45: Wall . . . 1E 51
Denton Gro. L6: Liv . . . 2A 54
DENTON'S GREEN . . . 6C 28
Dentons Grn. La. WA10: St H . . . 6B 28
Denton St. L8: Liv . . . 5F 71
WA8: Wid . . . 2G 97
Dentwood St. L8: Liv . . . 5G 71
Denver Pk. L32: Kirkb . . . 2G 23
Denver Rd. L32: Kirkb . . . 2G 23
Depot Rd. L33: Know I . . . 5F 15
Derby Bldgs. *L7: Liv . . . 6H 53*
(off Irvine St.)
Derby Dr. WA11: Rainf . . . 3G 17
Derby Gro. L31: Mag . . . 3B 12
Derby Hall L17: Aig . . . 5C 72
Derby La. L13: Liv . . . 3E 55
Derby Rd. CH42: Tran . . . 6F 69
CH45: Wall . . . 1C 50
L5: Kirkd . . . 1B 52
L20: Boot . . . 2B 34
L36: Huy . . . 5G 57
(not continuous)
WA8: Wid . . . 6E 79
DERBYSHIRE HILL . . . 3C 44
Derbyshire Hill Rd. WA9: St H . . . 2C 44
Derby Sq. L2: Liv . . . 5D 4 (6C 52)
L34: Presc . . . 1E 59
Derby St. L13: Liv . . . 4D 54
L19: Garst . . . 1G 107
L34: Presc . . . 1C 58
L36: Huy . . . 5A 58
Derby Ter. L36: Huy . . . 4G 57
Dereham Av. CH49: Upton . . . 2E 67
Dereham Cres. L10: Faz . . . 4D 22
Dereham Way WA7: Nort . . . 2F 115
Derna Rd. L36: Huy . . . 3F 57
Derringstone Cl. WA10: St H . . . 4B 42
Derwent Av. L34: Presc . . . 1F 59
Derwent Cl. CH63: Hghr B . . . 6F 87
L31: Mag . . . 5E 7
L33: Kirkb . . . 5H 13
L35: Rainh . . . 4H 59
Derwent Ct. L18: Moss H . . . 4H 73
Derwent Dr. CH45: Wall . . . 1C 50
CH61: Pens . . . 1D 100
CH66: Hoot . . . 5H 121
L21: Lith . . . 3D 20
Derwent Rd. CH43: Oxton . . . 5D 68
CH47: Meols . . . 1E 65
CH63: Hghr B . . . 6F 87
L23: Crosb . . . 1H 19
WA8: Wid . . . 2A 96
WA11: St H . . . 4F 29
Derwent Rd. E. L13: Liv . . . 3E 55
Derwent Rd. W. L13: Liv . . . 3D 54
Derwent Sq. L13: Liv . . . 3E 55
Desborough Cres. L12: W Der . . . 6E 37
Desford Av. WA11: St H . . . 5H 29
Desford Cl. CH46: More . . . 6H 47
Desford Rd. L19: Aig . . . 3C 90
De Silva St. L36: Huy . . . 5A 58
Desmond Cl. CH43: Bid . . . 2G 67
Desmond Gro. L23: Crosb . . . 6H 9
Desoto Rd. WA8: Wid . . . 1B 112
Desoto Rd. E. WA8: Wid . . . 5D 96
(not continuous)
Desoto Rd. W. WA8: Wid . . . 5D 96
Deva Cl. L33: Kirkb . . . 2A 14
Deva Rd. CH48: W Kir . . . 1A 82
Deveraux Dr. CH44: Wall . . . 4D 50
Deverell Gro. L15: Wav . . . 6F 55
Deverell Rd. L15: Wav . . . 1E 73
Deverill Rd. CH42: Rock F . . . 2G 87
Devilla Cl. L14: Knott A . . . 2C 56
De Villiers Av. L23: Crosb . . . 4G 9
Devisdale Gro. CH43: Bid . . . 2G 67
Devizes Cl. L25: Gate . . . 2D 74
Devizes Dr. CH61: Irby . . . 4B 84
Devoke Av. WA11: St H . . . 2E 29
Devon Av. CH45: Wall . . . 2E 51
Devon Cl. L23: Blun . . . 5C 8
Devon Ct. *L5: Liv . . . 2G 53*
(off Tynemouth Cl.)
Devondale Rd. L18: Moss H . . . 4E 73
Devon Dr. CH61: Pens . . . 1C 100
Devonfield Rd. L9: Walt . . . 6F 21
Devon Gdns. CH42: Rock F . . . 2H 87
L16: Child . . . 4A 74
Devon Pl. WA8: Wid . . . 6E 79
Devonport St. L8: Liv . . . 4F 71
Devonshire Cl. CH43: Oxton . . . 4D 68
L33: Kirkb . . . 5A 14
Devonshire M. *L8: Liv . . . 4H 71*
(off Devonshire Rd.)
DEVONSHIRE PARK . . . 6E 69
Devonshire Pl. CH43: Oxton . . . 4C 68
L5: Liv . . . 1E 53
(not continuous)
WA7: Run . . . 3E 113
Devonshire Rd. CH43: Oxton . . . 4D 68
CH44: Wall . . . 3D 50
(not continuous)
CH48: W Kir . . . 2C 82
CH49: Upton . . . 4C 66
CH61: Pens . . . 1C 100
L8: Liv . . . 4G 71
L22: Water . . . 1E 19
WA10: St H . . . 6B 28
Devonshire Rd. W. L8: Liv . . . 4G 71
Devon St. L3: Liv . . . 2H 5 (5E 53)
WA10: St H . . . 1B 42
Devonwall Gdns. L8: Liv . . . 4H 71
Devon Way L16: Child . . . 3A 74
L36: Huy . . . 3A 58
(not continuous)
Dewar Ct. WA7: Ast . . . 2A 114
Dewberry Cl. CH42: Tran . . . 5F 69
Dewey Av. L9: Ain . . . 3H 21
Dewlands Rd. L21: Sea . . . 3H 19
Dewsbury Rd. L4: Walt . . . 1H 53
Dexter St. L8: Liv . . . 3E 71
Deycroft Av. L33: Kirkb . . . 5C 14
Deycroft Wlk. L33: Kirkb . . . 5C 14
Deyes Ct. L31: Mag . . . 6D 6
Deyes End L31: Mag . . . 6D 6
Deyes La. L31: Mag . . . 6C 6
Deysbrook La. L12: W Der . . . 1G 55
Deysbrook Side L12: W Der . . . 1G 55
Deysbrook Way L12: W Der . . . 5H 37
Dial Rd. CH42: Tran . . . 6F 69
Dial St. L7: Liv . . . 5A 54
Diamond Bus. Pk. WA11: Rainf . . . 4H 17
Diamond St. L5: Liv . . . 3D 52
Diana Rd. L20: Boot . . . 4D 20
Diana St. L4: Walt . . . 5G 35
Diane Ho. *L8: Liv . . . 2F 71*
(off Birley Ct.)
Dibbinsdale Rd. CH63: Brom . . . 5B 104
Dibbins Grn. CH63: Brom . . . 1B 120
Dibbins Hey CH63: Spit . . . 3A 104
Dibbinview Gro. CH63: Spit . . . 3B 104
Dibb La. L23: Lit C . . . 2E 9
Dicconson St. WA10: St H . . . 1E 43
Dickens Av. CH43: Pren . . . 2B 86
Dickens Cl. CH43: Pren . . . 2B 86
L32: Kirkb . . . 3H 23
Dickenson St. L1: Liv . . . 1D 70
Dickens Rd. WA10: St H . . . 5A 42
Dickens St. L8: Liv . . . 3F 71
Dickinson Cl. WA11: Hay . . . 5C 30
Dickson Cl. WA8: Wid . . . 3F 97
Dickson St. L3: Liv . . . 3B 52
WA8: Wid . . . 3E 97
(not continuous)
Didcot Cl. L25: Hunts X . . . 3F 93
Didsbury Cl. L33: Kirkb . . . 1B 24
Digg La. CH46: More . . . 6B 48
Digital Way L7: Liv . . . 5B 54
Digmoor Rd. L32: Kirkb . . . 4B 24
Digmoor Wlk. L32: Kirkb . . . 4B 24
Dignum Mead L27: N'ley . . . 4G 75
Dilloway St. WA10: St H . . . 1C 42
Dinaro Cl. L25: Gate . . . 5E 75
Dinas La. L36: Huy . . . 3C 56
Dinas La. Pde. L14: Huy . . . 3C 56
Dinesen Rd. L19: Garst . . . 4G 91
DINGLE . . . 6F 71
Dingle Av. WA12: Newt W . . . 3H 45
Dinglebrook Rd. L9: Ain . . . 2A 36
Dingle Brow L8: Liv . . . 6G 71
Dingle Grange *L8: Liv . . . 6G 71*
(off Dingle Brow)
Dingle Gro. L8: Liv . . . 5G 71
Dingle La. L8: Liv . . . 6G 71
Dingle Mt. L8: Liv . . . 6G 71
Dingle Rd. CH42: Tran . . . 5E 69
L8: Liv . . . 6F 71
Dingle Va. L8: Liv . . . 6G 71
Dingley Av. L9: Walt . . . 5F 21
Dingwall Dr. CH49: Grea . . . 6B 66
Dinmore Rd. CH44: Wall . . . 3D 50
Dinnington Ct. WA8: Wid . . . 6C 78
Dinorben Av. WA9: St H . . . 6G 43
Dinorwic Rd. L4: Walt . . . 1G 53
Dinsdale Rd. CH62: Brom . . . 3E 105
Discovery Rd. L19: Garst . . . 1H 107
Ditchfield Pl. WA8: Wid . . . 3H 95
Ditchfield Rd. WA5: Penk . . . 6G 81
WA8: Wid . . . 3G 95
DITTON . . . 4H 95
Ditton Ct. WA8: Hale B . . . 6A 96
Ditton La. CH46: Leas . . . 4B 48
Ditton Rd. WA8: Wid . . . 5A 96

Dixon M. L30: N'ton 5E 11
Dixon Rd. L33: Know I 2D 24
Dobson St. L6: Liv 3G 53
Dobsons Way WA9: St H 5D 42
Dock Rd. CH41: Birke 5C 50
L19: Garst 6F 91
WA8: Wid 6D 96
(not continuous)
Dock Rd. Nth. CH62: Port S 5C 88
Dock Rd. Sth. CH62: Brom 1D 104
Docks Link CH44: Wall 4B 50
Docks Rd. WA7: Run 3C 112
Dock St. WA8: Wid 6E 97
Dodd Av. CH49: Grea 6B 66
WA10: St H 1A 42
Doddridge Rd. L8: Liv 4E 71
Dodd's La. L31: Mag 5B 6
Dodleston Cl. CH43: Noct 5H 67
Dodman Rd. L11: Crox 6H 23
DOE GREEN 6F 81
Doe Pk. Courtyard
L25: Woolt 3D 92
Doe's Mdw. Rd. CH63: Brom ...6B 104
DOG & GUN 2F 37
Dolan Ct. L25: Gate 1B 74
Dolomite Av. L24: Speke 5B 92
Domar Cl. L32: Kirkb 2B 24
Dombey Pl. *L8: Liv* *3F 71*
(off Dombey St.)
Dombey St. L8: Liv 3F 71
Domingo Dr. L33: Kirkb 4H 13
Dominic Cl. L16: Child 1A 74
Dominic Rd. L16: Child 1A 74
Dominion St. L6: Liv 2A 54
Domino Ct. WA7: Manor P 1D 114
Domville L35: Whis 5E 59
Domville Dr. CH49: Woodc 6E 67
Domville Rd. L13: Liv 6F 55
Donaldson Ct. L5: Liv 1G 53
Donaldson St. L5: Liv 1G 53
Donalds Way L17: Aig 2C 90
Doncaster Dr. CH49: Upton 3D 66
Donegal Rd. L13: Liv 4F 55
Donne Av. CH63: Spit 2H 103
Donne Cl. CH63: Spit 2A 104
Donnington Cl. L36: Roby 1F 75
Donsby Rd. L9: Ain 5H 21
Dooley Dr. L30: N'ton 5H 11
Doon Cl. L4: Kirkd 5E 35
Dorans La. L2: Liv 4D 4 (6C 52)
Dorbett Dr. L23: Crosb 1H 19
Dorchester Cl. CH49: Upton 5D 66
Dorchester Dr. L33: Kirkb 4C 14
Dorchester Pk. CH43: Noct 6H 67
WA7: Nort 2F 115
Dorchester Park Local Nature Reserve
...........................2F 115
Dorchester Rd. L25: Gate 3D 74
Dorchester Way CH43: Noct 6H 67
WA5: Burtw 1H 63
Doreen Av. CH46: More 1B 66
Dorgan Cl. L35: Rainh 3H 59
Doric Rd. L13: Liv 3E 55
Doric St. CH42: Rock F 1H 87
L21: Sea 4H 19
Dorien Rd. L13: Liv 5D 54
Dorincourt CH43: Oxton 5C 68
Dorking Gro. L15: Wav 3F 73
Dorney Ct. L12: W Der 6H 37
Dorothea Cl. WA8: Wid 5A 80
Dorothy Dr. L7: Liv 6H 53
Dorothy St. L7: Liv 6H 53
WA9: St H 6C 42
Dorrington Dr. L11: Norr G 3E 37
Dorrington Cl. WA7: Murd 5F 115
Dorrington Wlk. *L5: Liv* *3E 53*
(off Roscommon St.)
Dorrit St. L8: Liv 3F 71
Dorset Av. L15: Wav 2B 72
Dorset Cl. L20: Boot 2D 34
Dorset Ct. L25: Gate 3D 74
Dorset Dr. CH61: Pens 1C 100
Dorset Gdns. CH42: Rock F 2H 87
WA7: Pal F 1C 124

Dorset Rd. CH45: New B 6C 32
CH48: W Kir 6C 64
L6: Liv 1B 54
L36: Huy 4A 58
WA10: St H 4B 42
Doughton Grn. WA8: Wid 6C 78
Douglas Av. WA9: Bold 1D 62
Douglas Cl. L13: Liv 3D 54
WA8: Wid 6B 80
Douglas Dr. CH46: More 1B 66
L31: Mag 5E 7
Douglas Pl. L20: Boot 3B 34
Douglas Rd. CH48: W Kir 6D 64
L4: Walt 1H 53
Douglas St. CH41: Birke 3G 69
WA10: St H 2B 42
Douglas Way L33: Kirkb 3B 14
Doulton Cl. CH43: Bid 1B 86
Doulton Pl. L35: Whis 5C 58
Doulton St. WA10: St H 2D 42
Douro Pl. L13: Liv 5D 54
Douro St. L5: Liv 3E 53
DOVECOT 3B 56
Dovecot Av. L14: Knott A 4B 56
Dovecote Dr. WA11: Hay 4E 31
Dovecot Pl. *L14: Knott A* *3B 56*
(off Dovecot Av.)
Dove Ct. L25: Woolt 6D 74
Dovedale Av. CH62: East 2E 121
L31: Mag 5B 6
Dovedale Cl. CH43: Pren 1B 86
Dovedale Dr. WA8: Wid 6H 77
Dovedale Rd. CH45: Wall 6C 32
CH47: Hoy 1B 64
L18: Moss H 4D 72
Dovepoint Rd. CH47: Meols 6E 47
Dovercliffe Rd. L13: Liv 4F 55
Dover Cl. CH41: Birke 2F 69
WA7: Murd 1G 125
Dovercroft L25: Woolt 1B 92
Dover Dr. CH60: Hesw 1B 74
Dove Rd. L9: Walt 5F 21
Dover Rd. L31: Mag 3A 12
Dover St. L3: Liv 6F 53
WA7: Run 2F 113
Dovesmead Rd. CH60: Hesw 6G 101
Dovestone Cl. L7: Liv 1H 71
Dove St. L8: Liv 2H 71
Dovey St. L8: Liv 4G 71
Doward St. WA8: Wid 1G 97
Dowhills Dr. L23: Blun 4D 8
Dowhills Pk. L23: Blun 3D 8
Dowhills Rd. L23: Blun 3D 8
Downes Grn. CH63: Spit 4A 104
Downgreen Cl. L32: Kirkb 2G 23
Downham Cl. L25: Woolt 4B 74
Downham Dr. CH60: Hesw 5E 101
Downham Grn. L25: Woolt 4B 74
Downham Rd. CH42: Tran 6F 69
Downham Rd. Nth. CH61: Hesw ...3E 101
Downham Rd. Sth. CH60: Hesw ...5E 101
Downham Way L25: Woolt 4B 74
Downing Cl. CH43: Oxton 6D 68
Downing Rd. L20: Boot 3D 34
Downing St. L5: Liv 2G 53
Downlands Rd. L27: N'ley 5H 75
Downland Way WA9: St H 4B 44
Downs, The L23: Blun 6D 8
Downside WA8: Wid 4B 74
Downside Cl. L30: N'ton 5E 11
Downside Dr. L10: Ain 2D 22
Downs Rd. WA7: Run 4E 113
WA10: St H 3B 42
Downway La. WA9: St H 4C 44
Dowsefield La. L18: Aller 6A 74
Dragon Cl. L11: Crox 1G 37
Dragon Cres. L35: Whis 3F 59
Dragon Dr. L35: Whis 4E 59
Dragon La. L35: Whis 5D 58
Dragon Wlk. *L11: Crox* *1G 37*
(off Dragon Cl.)
Dragon Yd. WA8: Wid 5F 79
Drake Cl. L10: Faz 4E 23
L35: Whis 5E 59

Drake Cres. L10: Faz 4D 22
Drakefield Rd. L11: Norr G 2C 36
Drake Gdns. WA9: St H 1C 60
Drake Pl. L10: Faz 4D 22
Drake Rd. CH46: Leas 3F 49
CH64: Nest 6A 118
L10: Faz 4D 22
Drake St. L20: Boot 4B 34
WA10: St H 1B 42
Drake Way L10: Faz 4E 23
Draw Well Rd. L33: Know I 1F 25
Draycott St. L8: Liv 6F 71
Drayton Cl. CH61: Irby 6B 84
WA7: Run 4D 112
Drayton Cres. WA11: St H 5H 29
Drayton Rd. CH44: Wall 4F 51
L4: Walt 3G 35
Dream 5G 61
Drennan Rd. L19: Aller 3A 92
Drewell Rd. L18: Moss H 6D 72
Driffield Rd. L34: Presc 1C 58
Drinkwater Gdns. L3: Liv 4E 53
Drive, The L12: W Der 2F 55
Driveway L35: Whis 4F 59
Droitwich Av. CH49: Grea 5A 66
Dromore Av. L18: Moss H 6E 73
Dronfield Way L25: Gate 2B 74
(not continuous)
Droxford Dr. L25: Gate 2B 74
Druids Cross Gdns. L18: Moss H ...5H 73
Druids Cross Rd. L18: Moss H ...5H 73
Druids Pk. L18: Moss H 5A 74
Druidsville Rd. L18: Moss H 5A 74
Druids Way CH49: Woodc 1E 85
Drum Cl. L14: Knott A 2C 56
Drummond Ct. WA8: Wid 1H 97
Drummond Rd. CH47: Hoy 4A 64
L4: Walt 4A 36
L23: Thorn 4B 10
Drummoyne Ct. L23: Blun 4C 8
Druridge Dr. WA5: Penk 5H 81
Drury La. L2: Liv 4C 4 (6C 52)
Drybeck Gro. WA9: St H 1H 61
Dryburgh Way *L4: Kirkd* *5E 35*
(off Bradwell St.)
Dryden Cl. CH43: Bid 2G 67
L35: Whis 4E 59
Dryden Gro. L36: Huy 6H 57
Dryden Rd. L7: Liv 6C 54
Dryden St. L5: Liv 3D 52
L20: Boot 6A 20
Dryfield Cl. CH49: Grea 5B 66
Dublin St. L3: Liv 3B 52
Ducie St. L8: Liv 3H 71
Duckinfield St. L3: Liv 5H 5 (6F 53)
Duck Pond La. CH42: Tran 1C 86
Duddingston Av. L18: Moss H 4E 73
L23: Crosb 1G 19
Duddon Av. L31: Mag 5E 7
Duddon Cl. CH43: Oxton 6B 68
Dudley Av. WA7: Run 3H 113
Dudley Cl. CH43: Oxton 5D 68
Dudley Cres. CH65: Hoot 4H 121
Dudley Gro. L23: Crosb 1G 19
Dudley Pl. WA9: St H 2H 43
Dudley Rd. CH45: New B 5C 32
L18: Moss H 4D 72
Dudlow Ct. L18: Moss H 4G 73
Dudlow Dr. L18: Moss H 4G 73
Dudlow Gdns. L18: Moss H 4G 73
Dudlow La. L18: Moss H 3F 73
Dudlow Nook Rd. L18: Moss H ...3G 73
Dugdale Cl. L19: Gras 4E 91
Duke Cl. WA7: Run 3D 112
Duke of York Cotts. CH62: Port S ...5A 88
Dukes Rd. L5: Liv 1E 53
Dukes Ter. L1: Liv 6G 5 (1E 71)
Duke St. CH41: Birke 6E 51
CH45: New B 5D 32
L1: Liv 6E 5 (1D 70)
L19: Garst 5G 91
L22: Water 3F 19
L34: Presc 1D 58
WA10: St H 1D 42

Duke St. Bri. CH41: Birke 6E 51
Duke St. La. L1: Liv 6E 5 (1D 70)
Dukes Wharf WA7: Pres B 1G 125
Dulas Grn. L32: Kirkb 2C 24
Dulas Rd. L15: Wav 3F 73
　L32: Kirkb 2C 24
Dulson Way L34: Presc 2A 58
Dulverton Rd. L17: Aig 3C 90
Dumbarton St. L4: Walt 4E 35
Dumbrees Gdns. L12: W Der 5A 38
Dumbrees Rd. L12: W Der 5A 38
Dumbreeze Gro. L34: Know 1F 39
Dumfries Way L33: Kirkb 3H 13
Dunacre Way L26: Halew 4H 93
Dunbabin Rd. L15: Wav 3F 73
　L16: Child 3G 73
Dunbar St. L4: Walt 3F 35
Dunbeath Av. L35: Rainh 6B 60
Dunbeath Cl. L35: Rainh 6B 60
Duncan Av. WA7: Run 4G 113
Duncan Cl. WA10: St H 3C 42
Duncan Dr. CH49: Grea 5B 66
Duncansby Cres. WA5: Gt San 3G 81
Duncansby Dr. CH63: East 3C 120
Duncan St. CH41: Birke 3H 69
　L1: Liv 2E 71
　WA10: St H 2C 42
Dunchurch Rd. L14: Knott A 2B 56
Duncombe Rd. Nth. L19: Gras 4F 91
Duncombe Rd. Sth. L19: Garst 4F 91
Duncote Cl. CH43: Oxton 5C 68
　L35: Whis 2G 59
Dundale Rd. L13: Liv 4F 55
Dundalk La. WA8: Wid 3B 96
Dundalk Rd. WA8: Wid 3B 96
Dundas St. L20: Boot 4B 34
Dundee Gro. CH44: Wall 4C 50
Dundonald Rd. L17: Aig 2C 90
Dundonald St. CH41: Birke 1C 68
Dunedin St. WA9: St H 6C 42
Dunes Way L5: Kirkd 1C 52
Dunfold Cl. L32: Kirkb 2B 24
Dungeon La. L24: Hale 3H 109
Dunham Cl. CH62: East 4F 121
Dunham Rd. L15: Wav 6F 55
Dunkeld Cl. L6: Liv 4G 53
Dunkerron Cl. L27: N'ley 2F 75
Dunlin Cl. L27: N'ley 5G 75
　WA7: Beech 2B 124
Dunlin Ct. L25: Gate 4C 74
Dunlins Ct. CH45: Wall 5A 32
Dunlop Dr. L31: Mell 5F 13
Dunlop Rd. L24: Speke 3E 109
Dunluce St. L4: Walt 4E 35
Dunmail Av. WA11: St H 2G 29
Dunmail Gro. WA7: Beech 3A 124
Dunmore Rd. L13: Liv 4C 54
Dunmow Way L25: Hunts X 3E 93
Dunnerdale Rd. L11: Norr G 3E 37
Dunnett St. L20: Kirkd 4B 34
Dunning Cl. CH49: Upton 4C 66
Dunnings Bri. Rd. L30: N'ton 2E 21
Dunnings Wlk. L30: N'ton 5G 11
Dunnock Cl. L25: Gate 4C 74
Dunraven Rd. CH48: W Kir 1A 82
Dunriding La. WA10: St H 2B 42
Dunscroft WA9: St H 6H 43
Dunsdon Cl. L25: Woolt 5A 74
Dunsdon Rd. L25: Woolt 4A 74
Dunsford WA8: Wid 6A 78
Dunsmore Cl. WA11: Hay 4E 31
Dunsop Av. WA9: Clock F 3H 61
Dunstall Cl. CH46: Leas 4C 48
Dunstan La. L7: Liv 1A 72
Dunstan St. L15: Wav 1C 72
Dunster Gro. CH60: Hesw 6F 101
　WA9: Sut L 3H 61
Durants Cotts. L31: Mag 2C 12
Durban Av. L23: Crosb 4G 9
Durban Rd. CH45: Wall 1D 50
　L13: Liv 5F 55
Durden St. L7: Liv 2A 72
Dures Ct. CH43: Clau 3C 68
Durham Av. L30: N'ton 2F 21

Durham Mews E. L30: N'ton 2G 21
Durham Mews W. L30: N'ton 2G 21
Durham Rd. L21: Sea 4H 19
　WA8: Wid 6F 79
Durham St. L19: Garst 1H 107
Durham Way L30: N'ton 2G 21
　L36: Huy 4A 58
Durley Dr. CH43: Pren 2A 86
Durley Pk. Cl. CH43: Pren 3A 86
Durley Rd. L9: Ain 5H 21
Durlston Cl. WA8: Wid 1A 96
Durning Rd. L7: Liv 6A 54
Durrant Rd. L11: Norr G 5C 36
Dursley L35: Whis 5F 59
Durston Rd. L16: Child 1H 73
Dutton Dr. CH63: Spit 3H 103
Duxbury Cl. L31: Mag 4D 6
　WA11: Rainh 2G 17
Dwerryhouse La. L11: Norr G 3F 37
DW Fitness
　Bromborough 3E 105
　Halton 2G 97
　St Helens 4E 43
Dyke St. L6: Liv 3G 53
Dykin Cl. WA8: Wid 6A 80
Dykin Rd. WA8: Wid 6H 79
Dylan Cl. L4: Walt 6F 35
Dymchurch Rd. L24: Speke 1D 108
Dymoke Rd. L11: Crox 2G 37
Dymoke Wlk. L11: Crox 2G 37
　　　　　　　　　(off Dymoke Rd.)
Dyson Hall Dr. L9: Faz 6B 22
Dyson St. L4: Walt 4F 35

Eagle Cres. WA11: Rainf 3G 17
Eagle Dene L10: Faz 5E 23
Eaglehall Rd. L9: Faz 1D 36
Eaglehurst Rd. L25: Gate 5D 74
Eagles Cl. L32: Kirkb 1A 24
Eaglesfield Cl. WA9: St H 6H 43
Eagles Way WA7: Pal F 1A 124
Ealing Cl. WA7: Nort 4F 115
Ealing Rd. L9: Ain 4H 21
Eanleywood Farm Cl.
　WA7: Nort 6E 115
Eanleywood La. WA7: Nort 6E 115
Eardisley Rd. L18: Moss H 3E 73
Earle Av. L36: Roby 5D 56
Earle Cl. WA12: Newt W 2H 45
Earle Cres. CH64: Nest 6H 117
Earle Dr. CH64: Park 6H 117
Earle Rd. L7: Liv 1A 72
　WA8: Wid 4G 97
Earle St. L3: Liv 2C 4 (5C 52)
　WA12: Newt W 3H 45
Earl Rd. L20: Boot 1D 34
Earl's Cl. L23: Crosb 6F 9
Earlsfield Rd. L15: Wav 3D 72
Earlston Rd. CH45: Wall 1C 50
Earl St. CH62: New F 3B 88
　WA9: St H 1G 43
Earls Way WA7: Pal F 6A 114
Earlswood Cl. CH46: More 1H 65
Earlwood Gdns. L35: Whis 5E 59
Earp St. L19: Garst 5G 91
Easby Cl. WA7: Run 3G 113
Easby Rd. L4: Kirkd 6E 35
　L5: Kirkd 6D 34
Easedale Wlk. L33: Kirkb 4H 13
Easenhall Cl. WA8: Wid 5F 79
Easington Dr. WA9: St H 1B 60
E. Albert Rd. L17: Aig 5H 71
East Bank CH42: Tran 6E 69
Eastbourne M. L9: Ain 4H 21
　　　　　　　　　(off Eastbourne Rd.)
Eastbourne Rd. CH41: Birke 3E 69
　L9: Ain 4H 21
　L22: Water 1D 18
Eastbourne Wlk. L6: Liv 1F 53
Eastbury Cl. WA8: Wid 4G 79
Eastcliffe Rd. L13: Liv 4F 55

East Cl. L34: Eccl P 6G 41
Eastcote Rd. L19: Aller 3G 91
Eastcott Cl. CH49: Grea 6A 66
Eastcroft Rd. CH44: Wall 4E 51
Eastdale Rd. L15: Wav 1D 72
E. Damwood Rd. L24: Speke 3H 109
Eastern Av. CH62: Brom 1D 104
　L24: Speke 3H 109
Eastern Dr. L19: Gras 4E 91
E. Farm M. CH48: Caldy 3F 83
Eastfield Dr. L17: Aig 6A 72
Eastfield Wlk. L32: Kirkb 2F 23
E. Float Quay CH41: Birke 6F 51
East Front L35: Whis 6C 59
Eastgate Rd. WA7: Manor P 6G 99
Eastgate Way WA7: Manor P 1F 115
EASTHAM 2E 121
Eastham Cl. L16: Child 6B 56
Eastham Country Pk. 5G 105
Eastham Cres. WA9: Clock F 3E 61
EASTHAM FERRY 5G 105
Eastham Lodge Golf Course 1G 121
Eastham M. CH62: East 3G 121
Eastham Rake CH62: East 5C 120
Eastham Rake Station (Rail) 4D 120
Eastham Village Rd. CH62: East ...2G 121
Eastlake Av. L5: Liv 2F 53
E. Lancashire Rd.
　L11: Crox, Norr G 2C 36
　L33: Know I 2C 36
　L34: Know 2C 36
　WA10: Eccl, St H, Windle 2C 36
　WA11: Hay, St H 2C 36
East La. WA7: Pal F 6B 114
Eastleigh Dr. CH61: Irby 4B 84
East Mains L24: Speke 2A 110
Eastman Rd. L13: Liv 6C 36
East Meade L31: Mag 5B 6
E. Millwood Rd. L24: Speke 1H 109
East O' Hills Cl. CH60: Hesw 4E 101
Easton Rd. CH62: New F 3B 88
　L36: Huy 5C 56
E. Orchard La. L9: Ain 4B 22
E. Prescot Rd. L14: Knott A 4G 55
East Quay L3: Liv 2C 70
　L24: Halew 6A 94
　L31: Mag 6E 7
East Side WA9: St H 3G 43
Eastside Ind. Est. WA9: St H 3G 43
East St. CH41: Birke 5G 51
　L3: Liv 2C 4 (5C 52)
　L22: Water 1F 19
　L34: Presc 1E 59
　WA8: Wid 2H 97
Eastview Cl. CH43: Noct 5H 67
East Village L1: Liv 6G 5
Eastway CH46: More 6C 48
　CH49: Grea 5C 66
　L31: Mag 5C 6
　　　　　　　　　(not continuous)
　WA7: Pal F 6B 114
　WA8: Wid 2B 96
Eastwood L17: Aig 6G 71
　WA7: Wind H 3E 115
Eastwood Rd. WA5: Burtw 6H 45
Eaton Av. CH44: Wall 3E 51
　L20: Boot 6D 20
　　　　　　　　　(off Aughton Rd.)
　L21: Lith 4B 20
Eaton Cl. L12: W Der 6E 37
　L36: Roby 5F 57
Eaton Gdns. L12: W Der 3H 55
Eaton Grange L12: W Der 2G 55
Eaton Rd. CH43: Oxton 4D 68
　CH48: W Kir 2A 82
　L12: W Der 6F 37
　　　　　　　　　(not continuous)
　L19: Gras 5E 91
　L31: Mag 3B 12
　WA10: St H 5B 28
Eaton Rd. Nth. L12: W Der 6E 37
Eaton St. CH44: Wall 2D 50
　L3: Liv 1C 4 (4C 52)

Eaton St.—Elmbank Rd.

Eaton St. L34: Presc 6D **40**
WA7: Run 3E **113**
Eaves La. WA9: St H 1G **61**
Ebenezer Howard Rd. L21: Ford 1C **20**
Ebenezer St. CH42: Rock F 1A **88**
WA11: Hay 5B **30**
Eberle St. L2: Liv 3D **4** (5C **52**)
Ebony Cl. CH46: More 1H **65**
Ebony Way L33: Kirkb 4A **14**
Ebor La. L5: Liv 3E **53**
Ebrington St. L19: Garst 5G **91**
Ecclesall Av. L21: Lith 3D **20**
Eccles Dr. L25: Gate 2D **74**
Ecclesfield Rd. WA10: Eccl 6G **27**
Eccles Gro. WA9: Clock F 4A **62**
Eccleshall Rd. CH62: Port S 5C **88**
Eccleshill Rd. L13: Liv 2E **55**
ECCLESTON 6A **28**
Eccleston Av. CH62: Brom 4C **104**
Eccleston Cl. CH43: Oxton 6B **68**
Eccleston Dr. WA7: Run 4G **113**
Eccleston Gdns. WA10: St H 4G **41**
ECCLESTON PARK 6G **41**
Eccleston Pk. Dr. L35: Rainh 1H **59**
Eccleston Park Golf Course 1H **59**
Eccleston Park Station (Rail) 1G **59**
Eccleston Pk. Trade Cen.
WA10: St H 5G **41**
Eccleston Rd. L9: Walt 5F **21**
Eccleston St. L34: Presc 1D **58**
WA10: St H 2C **42**
Echo Arena 2C **70**
Echo La. CH48: W Kir 2C **82**
Edale Cl. CH62: East 2E **121**
Edale Rd. L18: Moss H 5F **73**
Eddisbury Rd. CH44: Wall 2E **51**
CH47: Hoy 5A **64**
CH48: W Kir 5A **64**
Eddisbury Way L12: W Der 6E **37**
Eden Av. WA11: Rainf 2E **17**
Eden Cl. L33: Kirkb 3B **14**
L35: Rainh 5H **59**
Edendale WA8: Wid 1H **95**
Eden Dr. Nth. L23: Crosb 6A **10**
Eden Dr. Sth. L23: Crosb 6A **10**
Edenfield Cres. L36: Huy 4H **57**
Edenfield Rd. L15: Wav 3D **72**
Edenhall Dr. L25: Woolt 6E **75**
Edenhurst Av. CH44: Wall 2E **51**
L16: Child 1C **74**
Edenhurst Ct. *L36: Huy* *3D* ***56***
(off Harrington Rd.)
Edenpark Rd. CH42: Tran 6E **69**
Eden Sq. L2: Liv 2D **4**
Eden St. L8: Liv 2H **71**
Eden Va. L30: N'ton 5E **11**
Edgar Ct. CH41: Birke 2F **69**
L21: Lith 2B **20**
Edgar St. L3: Liv 1E **5** (4D **52**)
Edgbaston Cl. L36: Roby 6E **57**
Edgbaston Way CH43: Bid 1G **67**
Edgefield Cl. CH43: Noct 5H **67**
Edgefold Rd. L32: Kirkb 2B **24**
Edge Gro. L7: Liv 5B **54**
EDGE HILL 1H **71**
Edgehill Rd. CH46: More 1A **66**
Edge Hill Station (Rail) 1A **72**
Edge La. L7: Liv 6H **53**
L13: Liv 6H **53**
L23: Thorn 3A **10**
Edge La. Dr. L13: Liv 5E **55**
Edge La. Retail Pk. L13: Liv 5D **54**
Edgeley Gdns. L9: Walt 5F **21**
Edgemoor Cl. CH43: Bid 2F **67**
L12: W Der 2H **55**
L23: Thorn 4B **10**
Edgemoor Dr. CH61: Irby 4A **84**
L10: Faz 4E **23**
L23: Thorn 4A **10**
Edgemoor Rd. L12: W Der 2H **55**
Edge St. WA9: St H 1A **60**
Edgewell Dr. L15: Wav 1F **73**
Edgewood Cl. WA8: Wid 3H **95**
Edgewood Dr. CH62: Brom 2D **120**
Edgewood Rd. CH47: Meols 6D **46**
CH49: Upton 3D **66**
Edgeworth Cl. WA9: St H 5A **44**
Edgeworth St. WA9: St H 6A **44**
Edgworth Rd. L4: Walt 1H **53**
Edinburgh Cl. L30: N'ton 3G **21**
Edinburgh Dr. CH43: Pren 2C **86**
L36: Huy 1A **76**
Edinburgh Rd. CH45: Wall 2D **50**
L7: Liv 5G **53**
(not continuous)
WA8: Wid 3H **95**
Edington St. L15: Wav 1C **72**
Edison Rd. WA7: Ast 2H **113**
Edith Rd. CH44: Wall 4G **51**
L4: Walt 1G **53**
L20: Boot 5D **20**
Edith St. WA7: Run 2D **112**
WA9: St H 6B **44**
Edmondson St. WA9: St H 2B **44**
Edmonton Cl. L5: Kirkd 1D **52**
Edmund Ct. CH62: Brom 2D **104**
Edmund St. L3: Liv 3C **4** (5C **52**)
Edna Av. L10: Faz 4E **23**
Edrich Av. CH43: Bid 1G **67**
Edward Jenner Av. L30: N'ton 6F **11**
Edward Manton Cl. CH63: Hghr B 5E **87**
Edward Pav. L3: Liv 6C **4** (1C **70**)
Edward Rd. CH47: Hoy 3C **64**
L35: Whis 2F **59**
WA5: Gt San 3F **81**
Edward's La. L24: Speke 5D **92**
Edward's La. Ind. Est.
L24: Speke 6D **92**
Edward St. WA8: Wid 2H **97**
WA9: St H 4H **43**
WA11: Hay 5C **30**
Edwards Way WA8: Wid 3A **96**
Edwin St. WA8: Wid 2G **97**
Effingham St. L20: Boot 4B **34**
Egan Ct. *CH41: Birke* *2G* ***69***
(off Lord St.)
Egan Rd. CH43: Bid 1A **68**
Egbert Rd. CH47: Meols 1C **64**
Egdon Cl. WA8: Wid 1A **98**
Egerton Ct. CH41: Birke 2G **69**
Egerton Dr. CH48: W Kir 1B **82**
Egerton Gdns. CH42: Rock F 2G **87**
Egerton Gro. CH45: Wall 2D **50**
Egerton Ho. WA7: Run 2F **113**
Egerton Pk. CH42: Rock F 2G **87**
Egerton Pk. Cl. CH42: Rock F 2G **87**
Egerton Rd. CH43: Clau 3C **68**
CH62: New F 4B **88**
L15: Wav 2B **72**
L34: Presc 6C **40**
Egerton St. CH45: New B 5D **32**
L8: Liv 2F **71**
WA7: Run 2D **112**
WA9: St H 4H **43**
Egerton Wharf CH41: Birke 1G **69**
Eglington Av. L35: Whis 5D **58**
EGREMONT 2F **51**
Egremont Cl. L27: N'ley 5A **76**
Egremont Lawn L27: N'ley 5A **76**
Egremont Prom. CH44: Wall 1F **51**
CH45: Wall 1F **51**
Egypt St. WA8: Wid 4D **96**
Eighth Av. L9: Ain 4B **22**
Eilian Gro. L14: Knott A 5H **55**
Elaine Cl. WA8: Wid 1G **97**
Elaine Norris Sports Cen. 3C **52**
Elaine Price Ct. WA7: Run 4D **112**
Elaine St. L8: Liv 3F **71**
Elderberry Cl. L11: Crox 3G **37**
Elderdale Rd. L4: Walt 6H **35**
Elderflower Rd. WA10: St H 6C **28**
Elder Gdns. L19: Gras 3F **91**
Elder Gro. CH48: W Kir 1B **82**
Eldersfield Rd. L11: Norr G 3F **37**
Elderswood L35: Rainh 3A **60**
Elderwood Rd. CH42: Tran 6G **69**
Eldon Cl. *WA10: St H* *3C* ***42***
(off Eldon St.)
Eldon Gro. *L3: Liv* *3D* ***52***
(off Limekiln La.)
Eldonian Way L3: Liv 3C **52**
Eldon Pl. L3: Liv 3C **52**
Eldon Rd. CH42: Rock F 1H **87**
CH44: Wall 3D **50**
Eldon St. L3: Liv 3C **52**
WA10: St H 3C **42**
Eldred Rd. L16: Child 3G **73**
Eleanor Pk. CH43: Bid 1G **67**
Eleanor Rd. CH43: Bid 6H **49**
CH46: More 6A **48**
L20: Boot 5D **20**
Eleanor St. L20: Kirkd 4B **34**
WA8: Wid 4E **97**
Electric Av. L10: Faz 6F **23**
L11: Crox 6F **23**
Elephant La. WA9: St H 6B **42**
Elfet St. CH41: Birke 1B **68**
Elgar Av. CH62: East 2E **121**
Elgar Rd. L14: Knott A 2B **56**
Elgin Ct. L35: Rainh 5B **60**
Elgin Dr. CH45: Wall 1E **51**
Elgin Way CH41: Birke 2G **69**
Eliot Cl. CH62: New F 4A **88**
Eliot St. L20: Boot 6B **20**
Elizabeth Ct. WA8: Wid 4F **97**
Elizabeth Rd. L10: Faz 4F **23**
L20: Boot 5D **20**
L36: Huy 1H **75**
WA11: Hay 4G **31**
Elizabeth St. L3: Liv 5F **53**
WA9: Clock F 4A **62**
WA9: St H 5A **44**
Elizabeth Ter. WA8: Wid 2B **96**
Eliza St. WA9: St H 6B **44**
Elkan Cl. WA8: Wid 6A **80**
Elkan Rd. WA8: Wid 6H **79**
Elkstone Rd. L11: Norr G 4F **37**
Ellaby Rd. L35: Rainh 3A **60**
Ellamsbridge Rd. WA9: St H 5A **44**
Ellel Gro. L6: Liv 2A **54**
Ellencliffe Dr. L6: Liv 2A **54**
Ellen Gdns. WA9: St H 5A **44**
Ellens Cl. L6: Liv 5G **53**
Ellen's La. CH63: Beb 6B **88**
Ellen St. WA9: St H 6A **44**
Elleray Dr. L8: Liv 5F **71**
Elleray Pk. Rd. CH45: Wall 6C **32**
Ellerby Cl. WA7: Murd 6G **115**
Ellergreen Rd. L11: Norr G 3D **36**
Ellerman Rd. L3: Liv 6E **71**
(not continuous)
Ellerslie Av. L35: Rainh 2H **59**
Ellerslie Rd. L13: Liv 1B **54**
Ellerton Cl. WA8: Wid 6B **78**
Ellerton Way L12: Crox 2A **38**
Ellesmere Dr. L10: Ain 1A **22**
Ellesmere Gro. CH45: Wall 1D **50**
Ellesmere St. WA7: Run 3F **113**
Ellington Way WA9: St H 2D **60**
Elliot Dr. L32: Kirkb 3H **23**
Elliot St. L1: Liv 4F **5** (6D **52**)
WA8: Wid 3F **97**
WA10: St H 2C **42**
Ellis Ashton St. L36: Huy 5A **58**
Ellis La. WA6: Frod 6H **123**
Ellison Dr. WA10: St H 1A **42**
Ellison Gro. L36: Huy 5F **57**
Ellison St. L13: Liv 3D **54**
Ellis Pl. L8: Liv 4F **71**
Ellis St. WA8: Wid 4E **97**
Ellon Av. L35: Rainh 5B **60**
Elloway Rd. L24: Speke 2A **110**
Ellwood Cl. L24: Hale 3E **111**
Elmar Rd. L17: Aig 1C **90**
(not continuous)
Elm Av. CH49: Upton 3B **66**
L23: Crosb 4H **9**
WA8: Wid 1F **97**
Elm Bank *L4: Walt* *6F* ***35***
(off Walton Breck Rd.)
Elmbank Rd. CH62: New F 5B **88**
L18: Moss H 4C **72**

Elmbank St. CH44: Wall 4E **51**
Elm Cl. CH61: Pens 1E **101**
   L12: Crox 2B **38**
Elm Ct. CH63: Hghr B 5F **87**
   L23: Blun 5E **9**
Elmcroft Cl. L9: Ain 5B **22**
Elmdale Rd. L9: Walt 1G **35**
Elmdene Ct. CH49: Grea 1A **84**
Elm Dr. CH49: Grea 6A **66**
   L21: Sea 5H **19**
Elmfield Cl. WA9: St H 5C **42**
Elmfield Rd. L9: Walt 6G **21**
Elm Gdns. *L21: Sea* . . . . *.5A 20*
                (off Elm Rd.)
   WA11: Rainf 3F **17**
Elm Grn. CH64: Will 6H **119**
Elm Gro. CH42: Tran 5F **69**
   CH47: Hoy 2C **64**
   L7: Liv .6G **53**
   L34: Eccl P 6F **41**
   WA8: Wid 2F **97**
Elm Hall Dr. L18: Moss H 4E **73**
Elmham Cres. L10: Faz 4D **22**
Elm Ho. *L22: Water* . . . . *.2G 19*
              (off Lorne Rd.)
   L34: Presc 1C **58**
Elm Ho. M. L25: Gate 5D **74**
Elmhurst CH42: Rock F 3H **87**
Elmhurst Rd. L25: Gate 2C **74**
Elmore Cl. L5: Liv 2F **53**
   WA7: Wind H 4F **115**
ELM PARK 4A **54**
Elm Pk. Rd. CH45: Wall 6C **32**
Elm Rd. CH42: Tran 1D **86**
             (Elm Rd. Nth.)
   CH42: Tran 6F **69**
             (Walker M.)
   CH61: Irby 5D **84**
   CH63: Hghr B 4H **87**
   CH64: Will 6H **119**
   L4: Walt 3G **35**
   L21: Sea 5H **19**
   L32: Kirkb 6H **13**
   WA5: Penk 5H **81**
   WA7: Run 5G **113**
   WA9: St H 5B **42**
   WA10: St H 5B **42**
   WA11: Hay 4G **31**
Elm Rd. Nth. CH42: Tran 1D **86**
Elms, The L8: Liv 5G **71**
   L31: Lyd .4C **6**
   WA7: Run 4D **112**
Elmsdale Rd. L18: Moss H 4E **73**
Elmsett Cl. WA5: Gt San 4G **81**
Elmsfield Cl. L25: Gate 4C **74**
Elmsfield Pk. L39: Augh 1F **7**
Elmsfield Rd. L23: Thorn 3B **10**
Elms Ho. Rd. L13: Liv 4D **54**
Elmsley Ct. L18: Moss H 6E **73**
Elmsley Rd. L18: Moss H 5D **72**
Elms Pk. CH61: Thing 6E **85**
Elms Rd. L31: Mag 3B **12**
Elm St. CH41: Birke 3F **69**
   L36: Huy 5A **58**
Elmswood Av. L35: Rainh 6B **60**
Elmswood Cct. L18: Moss H 6D **72**
Elmswood Gro. L36: Huy 4E **57**
Elmswood Rd. CH42: Tran 5E **69**
   CH44: Wall 3F **51**
   L17: Aig .1B **90**
   L18: Moss H 1C **90**
Elm Ter. CH47: Hoy 2C **64**
   L7: Liv .5A **54**
Elmtree Cl. L12: W Der 6G **37**
Elm Tree Ct. CH47: Hoy 1C **64**
Elmtree Gro. CH43: Bid 1A **68**
Elmure Av. CH63: Hghr B 6F **87**
Elm Va. L6: Liv 3B **54**
Elmway Cl. L13: Liv 5D **54**
Elmwood WA7: Nort 4E **115**
Elmwood Av. L23: Crosb 4A **10**
Elmwood Dr. CH61: Hesw 3D **100**
Elphin Gro. L4: Walt 4G **35**
Elric Wlk. L33: Kirkb 6B **14**

Elsbeck Gro. WA9: St H 1H **61**
Elsie Rd. L4: Walt 1H **53**
Elsmere Av. L17: Aig 6A **72**
Elstead Rd. L9: Faz 1C **36**
   L32: Kirkb 2G **23**
Elstow St. L5: Kirkd 6D **34**
Elstree Cl. WA8: Wid 5H **79**
Elstree Rd. L6: Liv 4B **54**
Elswick St. L8: Liv 6F **71**
Eltham Av. L21: Lith 2B **20**
Eltham Cl. CH49: Woodc 1F **85**
   WA8: Wid 6A **80**
Eltham Grn. CH49: Woodc 1F **85**
Eltham St. L7: Liv 5B **54**
Eltham Wlk. WA8: Wid 6A **80**
Elton Av. L23: Blun 5E **9**
   L30: N'ton 6E **11**
Elton Cl. CH62: East 4E **121**
Elton Dr. CH63: Spit 3A **104**
Elton Head Rd. WA9: St H 2A **60**
Elton St. L4: Walt 3F **35**
Elvington Cl. WA7: Sut W 4B **124**
Elwick Dr. L11: Crox 3G **37**
Elwood Cl. L33: Kirkb 3A **14**
Elworth Av. WA8: Wid 4E **79**
Elworthy Av. L26: Halew 2H **93**
Elwyn Dr. L26: Halew 3H **93**
Elwyn Rd. CH47: Meols 6E **47**
Ely Av. CH46: More 1A **66**
Ely Cl. L30: N'ton 2F **21**
Ely Pk. WA7: Nort 3G **115**
Ember Cres. L6: Liv 3F **53**
Embledon St. L8: Liv 2H **71**
Embleton Gro. WA7: Beech 2H **123**
Emerald Cl. L30: N'ton 6H **11**
Emerald St. L8: Liv 6G **71**
Emerson St. L8: Liv 2F **71**
Emery St. L4: Walt 4F **35**
Emily St. WA8: Wid 4E **97**
   WA9: St H 6A **42**
Emlyn St. WA9: St H 4H **43**
Emmett St. WA9: St H 4G **43**
Empire Rd. L21: Lith 5B **20**
Empress Cl. L31: Mag 6A **6**
   L6: Liv .1A **54**
   L7: Liv .5H **53**
          (not continuous)
Emstrey Wlk. L32: Kirkb 1G **23**
Emborne Rd. L9: Walt 5G **21**
Endbutt La. L23: Crosb 5G **9**
Enderby Av. WA11: St H 5H **29**
Endfield Pk. L19: Gras 3F **91**
Endmoor Rd. L36: Huy 2F **57**
Endsleigh Rd. L13: Liv 4C **54**
   L22: Water 1D **18**
Enerby Cl. CH43: Bid 2G **67**
Enfield Av. L23: Crosb 5G **9**
Enfield Rd. L13: Liv 5F **55**
Enfield St. WA10: St H 3C **42**
Enfield Ter. CH43: Oxton 4D **68**
Enford Dr. WA9: St H 6H **43**
Enid St. L8: Liv 3F **71**
Ennerdale Av. CH62: East 3F **121**
   L31: Mag 5D **6**
   WA11: St H 3F **29**
Ennerdale Cl. L33: Kirkb 4H **13**
Ennerdale Dr. L21: Lith 3D **20**
   WA6: Frod 6G **123**
Ennerdale Rd. CH43: Pren 2A **86**
   CH45: Wall 5B **32**
   L9: Ain .5B **22**
Ennerdale St. L3: Liv 3D **52**
Ennis Cl. L24: Hale 3D **110**
Ennis Ct. L11: Norr G 2F **37**
Ennisdale Dr. CH48: W Kir 6C **64**
Ennismore Rd. L13: Liv 4D **54**
   L23: Crosb 4E **9**
Ennis Rd. L12: W Der 1A **56**
Ensor St. L20: Boot 4B **34**
Enstone Av. L21: Lith 2A **20**
Enstone Rd. L25: Hunts X 5D **92**
Ensworth Rd. L18: Moss H 4F **73**

Enterprise Pk. WA11: Rainf 5H **17**
Enterprise Way L13: Wav 6C **54**
Epping Av. WA9: Sut M 4F **61**
Epping Cl. L35: Rainh 5B **60**
Epping Ct. CH60: Hesw 4E **101**
Epping Gro. L15: Wav 3F **73**
Epsom Cl. L10: Ain 2C **22**
Epsom Gro. L33: Kirkb 3C **14**
Epsom Rd. CH46: Leas 4D **48**
Epsom Way L5: Liv 2D **52**
Epstein Ct. *L6: Liv* . . . . *.4H 53*
          (off Coleridge St.)
Epstein Theatre, The . . . . . .5F **5 (6D 52)**
   WA5: Burtw 1H **63**
Epworth Grange *CH43: Clau* . . . . . . *.3C 68*
           (off Epworth Cl.)
Epworth St. L6: Liv 5F **53**
Eremon Cl. L9: Ain 3B **22**
Erfurt Av. CH63: Beb 1A **104**
Erica Ct. CH60: Hesw 3C **100**
Erica Gro. CH44: Wall 3C **50**
Erica Pk. L27: N'ley 4G **75**
Eric Gro. CH44: Wall 3C **50**
Eric St. WA8: Wid 1G **97**
Eridge St. L8: Liv 5G **71**
Erin Cl. L8: Liv 3E **71**
Erl St. L9: Ain 5G **21**
Ermine Cres. L5: Liv 2F **53**
Errington Cl. L17: Aig 3C **90**
Errington St. L5: Kirkd 1C **52**
Errol St. L17: Aig 6H **71**
Erskine Cl. WA11: St H 5A **30**
Erskine Rd. CH44: Wall 4E **51**
Erskine St. L6: Liv 5F **53**
Erskine St. Ind. Est. *L6: Liv* 5G **53**
           (off Prospect St.)
Erylmore Rd. L18: Moss H 2E **91**
Escolme Dr. CH49: Grea 6B **66**
Escor Rd. L25: Gate 3C **74**
Escort Cl. L25: Hunts X 3E **93**
Esher Cl. CH43: Bid 2G **67**
   CH62: New F 3B **88**
Eshe Rd. L23: Blun 5E **9**
Eshe Rd. Nth. L23: Blun 4D **8**
Esher Rd. CH62: New F 3B **88**
   L6: Liv .4A **54**
Eskburn Rd. L13: Liv 1C **54**
Eskdale Av. CH46: More 6A **48**
   CH62: East 2E **121**
   WA11: St H 3F **29**
Eskdale Cl. WA7: Beech 2H **123**
Eskdale Dr. L31: Mag 5D **6**
Eskdale Rd. L9: Walt 6G **21**
Esk St. L20: Kirkd 5B **34**
Eslington St. L19: Gras 4E **91**
Esmond St. L6: Liv 2H **53**
Esonwood Rd. L35: Whis 4D **58**
Espin St. L4: Walt 4F **35**
Esplanade CH42: Rock F 1B **88**
Esplanade, The CH62: New F 2B **88**
   L20: Boot . . . . *.2C 34*
       (off Strand Shop. Cen.)
   L22: Water 3F **19**
Esplen Av. L23: Crosb 4H **9**
Essex Rd. CH48: W Kir 6C **64**
   L36: Huy 3A **58**
Essex Way L20: Boot 1D **34**
Esthwaite Av. WA11: St H 3G **29**
Estuary Banks L24: Speke 1B **108**
Estuary Banks Bus. Pk.
   L24: Speke 1B **108**
Estuary Blvd. L24: Speke 2B **108**
Estuary Commerce Pk.
   L24: Speke 1B **108**
          (not continuous)
Etal Cl. L11: Norr G 4F **37**
Ethelbert La. CH47: Meols 1C **64**
Ethelbert Rd. CH47: Meols 1C **64**
Ethel Rd. CH44: Wall 4F **51**
Etna St. L13: Liv 4D **54**

Eton Ct. L18: Moss H 4H **73**
Eton Dr. CH63: Thorn H 1B **118**
L10: Ain 1A **22**
Eton Hall Dr. WA9: St H 6G **43**
Eton St. L4: Walt 4F **35**
Etruscan Rd. L13: Liv 3E **55**
Ettington Rd. L4: Walt 6H **35**
Ettrick Cl. L33: Kirkb 3H **13**
Eurolink WA9: St H 3D **60**
Eurolink Bus. Pk. WA9: St H 4D **60**
Europa Blvd. CH41: Birke 3G **69**
Europa Cen., The
   CH41: Birke 3F **69**
Europa Pools 3F **69**
Europa Sq. CH41: Birke 3G **69**
Euston Gro. CH43: Oxton 4D **68**
Euston St. L4: Walt 3F **35**
Evans Cl. WA11: Hay 4H **31**
Evans Rd. CH47: Hoy 2B **64**
   L24: Speke 6D **92**
Evans St. L34: Presc 6D **40**
Evellynne Cl. L32: Kirkb 1H **23**
Evelyn Av. L34: Presc 1E **59**
   WA9: St H 2A **44**
Evelyn Rd. CH44: Wall 4E **51**
Evelyn St. L5: Kirkd 1D **52**
   WA9: St H 2A **44**
Evenson Way L13: Liv 3E **55**
Evenwood WA9: St H 1G **61**
Evenwood Cl. WA7: Manor P 1G **115**
Everdon Wood L33: Kirkb 6B **14**
Evered Av. L9: Walt 1G **35**
Everest Rd. CH42: Tran 1F **87**
   L23: Crosb 5G **9**
Evergreen Cl. CH49: Upton 3C **66**
   L27: N'ley 3G **75**
Evergreen Way WA9: Bold 6C **44**
Everite Rd. WA8: Wid 4H **95**
Everleigh Cl. CH43: Bid 2F **67**
Eversleigh Dr. CH63: Beb 1A **104**
Eversley WA8: Wid 1H **95**
Eversley Pk. CH43: Oxton 6D **68**
Eversley St. L8: Liv 3G **71**
   (not continuous)
EVERTON 2E **53**
Everton Brow L3: Liv 4E **53**
Everton FC 4F **35**
Everton Gro. WA11: St H 6H **29**
Everton Rd. L6: Liv 3F **53**
Everton Valley L4: Walt 6E **35**
Everton Vw. L20: Boot 3B **34**
Everyman Liverpool Playhouse ...6F **53**
Every St. L6: Liv 3H **53**
Evesham Cl. L25: Woolt 1B **92**
Evesham Rd. CH45: Wall 1B **50**
   L4: Walt 4B **36**
Ewanville L36: Huy 6G **57**
Ewart Rd. L16: Child 1C **74**
   L21: Sea 4A **20**
   WA11: St H 5F **29**
Ewden Cl. L16: Child 2A **74**
Exchange Flags L2: Liv 3C **4**
Exchange Pas. E. L2: Liv ...3C **4** (5C **52**)
Exchange Pas. W.
   L2: Liv 3C **4** (5C **52**)
Exchange Pl. L35: Rainh 4A **60**
Exchange St. WA10: St H 2E **43**
Exchange St. E. L2: Liv ...3C **4** (5C **52**)
Exchange St. W.
   L2: Liv 4C **4** (6C **52**)
Exeley L35: Whis 5E **59**
Exeter Cl. L10: Ain 2C **22**
Exeter Rd. CH44: Wall 2E **51**
   L20: Boot 3C **34**
Exeter St. WA10: St H 2B **42**
Exford Rd. L12: W Der 5H **37**
Exmoor Cl. CH61: Pens 6D **84**
Exmouth Cl. CH41: Birke 3F **69**
Exmouth Cres. WA7: Murd 1G **125**
Exmouth Gdns. CH41: Birke 3F **69**
Exmouth St. CH41: Birke 3F **69**
Exmouth Way CH41: Birke 3F **69**
   WA5: Burtw 1H **63**
Express Ind. Est. WA8: Wid 4G **95**

Expressway Bus. Pk. CH42: Tran 6H **69**
Extension Vw. WA9: St H 5H **43**

F

Fab4D 5B **4** (6B **52**)
FACT 6G **5** (1E **71**)
Factory La. WA8: Wid 6F **79**
Factory Row WA10: St H 4C **42**
Fairacre Rd. L19: Gras 4E **91**
Fairacres Rd. CH63: Beb 1A **104**
Fairbairn Rd. L22: Water 2G **19**
Fairbank St. L15: Wav 2C **72**
Fairbeech M. CH43: Bid 2G **67**
Fairbrook Dr. CH41: Birke 6A **50**
Fairburn Cl. WA8: Wid 6A **80**
Fairburn Rd. L13: Liv 1C **54**
Fairclough Cl. L35: Rainh 4H **59**
Fairclough Cres.
   WA11: Hay 5C **30**
Fairclough La. CH43: Oxton 5D **68**
Fairclough Rd. L35: Rainh 4H **59**
   L36: Huy 1E **57**
   WA10: St H 1A **42**
Fairclough St. L1: Liv 5F **5** (6D **52**)
Fairfax Dr. WA7: Run 3H **113**
Fairfax Pl. L11: Norr G 3B **36**
Fairfax Rd. CH41: Tran 5G **69**
   L11: Norr G 3C **36**
FAIRFIELD 4B **54**
Fairfield L23: Crosb 5G **9**
Fairfield Av. L36: Huy 5C **56**
Fairfield Cl. L36: Huy 5C **56**
Fairfield Cres. CH46: More 1B **66**
   L6: Liv 4B **54**
   L36: Huy 5C **56**
Fairfield Dr. CH48: W Kir 6E **65**
Fairfield Gdns. WA11: Crank 1C **28**
Fairfield Rd. CH42: Tran 1G **87**
   WA8: Wid 2F **97**
   WA10: St H 6A **28**
Fairfield St. L7: Liv 4C **54**
Fairford Cres. L14: Knott A 3F **55**
Fairford Rd. L14: Knott A 3F **55**
Fairhaven L33: Kirkb 4A **14**
Fairhaven Cl. CH42: Rock F 1H **87**
Fairhaven Dr. CH63: Brom 2C **120**
Fairhaven Ho. L19: Aig 4D **90**
   (off The Spinnakers)
Fairhaven Rd. WA8: Wid 1G **97**
Fairhaven's Cl. WA8: Wid 3F **97**
Fairholme Av. CH64: Nest 6H **117**
   L34: Eccl P 1F **59**
Fairholme Cl. L12: W Der 5E **37**
Fairholme M. L23: Crosb 5G **9**
   (off Fairholme Rd.)
Fairholme Rd. L23: Crosb 5G **9**
Fairhurst Ter. L34: Presc 1E **59**
   (off Scotchbarn La.)
Fairlawn CH63: Raby M 1A **120**
Fairlawn Cl. CH43: Oxton 4B **68**
Fairlawn Cl. L33: Kirkb 4A **14**
Fairlie Cres. L20: Boot 4D **20**
Fairlie Dr. L35: Rainh 5B **60**
Fairmead Rd. CH46: More 6C **48**
   L11: Norr G 3C **36**
Fair Oak St. WA7: Pres B 4H **125**
Fairoak La. WA7: Pres B 4H **125**
Fairthorn Wlk. L33: Kirkb 6C **14**
Fairview CH41: Tran 5G **69**
Fairview Av. CH45: Wall 2C **50**
Fairview Cl. CH43: Oxton 6D **68**
Fairview Pl. L18: Liv 4G **71**
Fairview Rd. CH43: Oxton 1D **86**
Fairview Way CH61: Pens 2D **100**
Fairway L36: Huy 3G **57**
   WA10: Windle 6A **28**
Fairway, The L12: Knott A 3H **55**
Fairway Cres. CH62: Brom 1D **104**
Fairway Nth. CH62: Brom 1D **104**
Fairways CH42: Tran 3D **86**
   L23: Crosb 4F **9**

Fairways, The CH48: Caldy 5D **82**
   L25: Hunts X 3F **93**
   WN4: Ash M 1G **31**
Fairways Cl. L25: Woolt 3D **92**
Fairway Sth. CH62: Brom 2D **104**
Fairway Trad. Est. WA8: Wid 4C **96**
Falcon Cres. L27: N'ley 5H **75**
Falconer St. L20: Boot 5A **20**
Falcongate Ind. Est. CH44: Wall ..6E **51**
Falconhall Rd. L9: Faz 1D **36**
Falcon Hey L10: Faz 5E **23**
Falcon Rd. CH41: Birke 5E **69**
Falcons Way WA7: Pal F 1A **124**
Falkirk Av. WA8: Wid 6C **78**
Falkland Rd. CH44: Wall 3F **51**
Falklands App. L11: Norr G 3C **36**
Falkland St. CH41: Birke 1C **68**
   L3: Liv 5F **53**
   (not continuous)
Falkner Sq. L7: Liv 1G **71**
   L8: Liv 2F **71**
Falkner St. L7: Liv 1G **71**
   L8: Liv 6H **5** (1F **71**)
   (not continuous)
Falkner Ter. L8: Liv 2G **71**
   (off Up. Parliament St.)
Fallbrook Dr. L12: W Der 5F **37**
Fallow Cl. WA9: Clock F 3G **61**
Fallowfield L33: Kirkb 5A **14**
   WA7: Run 4H **113**
Fallowfield Rd. L15: Wav 3D **72**
Fallows Way L35: Whis 6C **58**
Falls La. L26: Halew 2G **93**
Falmouth Dr. WA5: Penk 6G **81**
Falmouth Pl. WA7: Murd 1G **125**
Falmouth Rd. L11: Crox 6H **23**
Falstaff St. L20: Kirkd 5C **34**
Falstone Dr. WA7: Murd 5G **115**
Faraday Rd. L13: Wav 6C **54**
   L33: Know I 4D **24**
   WA7: Ast 2H **113**
Faraday St. L5: Liv 2G **53**
Fareham Cl. CH49: Upton 3C **66**
Fareham Rd. L7: Liv 5B **54**
Faringdon Cl. L25: Hunts X 5D **92**
Farley Av. CH62: Brom 4C **104**
Farlow Rd. CH42: Rock F 2H **87**
Farmbrook Rd. L25: Gate 2D **74**
Farm Cl. CH49: Grea 5A **66**
   WA9: Clock F 4H **61**
Farmdale Cl. L18: Moss H 1F **91**
Farmdale Dr. L31: Mag 6D **6**
Far Mdw. La. CH61: Irby 5A **84**
Farmer Pl. L20: Boot 4E **21**
Farmers La. WA5: Burtw 1H **63**
Farmfield Dr. CH43: Bid 2G **67**
Far Moss Rd. L23: Blun 3D **8**
Farm Rd. WA9: Clock F 4H **61**
Farmside CH46: Leas 4D **48**
Farm Vw. L21: Ford 1B **20**
Farmview Cl. L27: N'ley 2E **75**
Farnborough Gro. L26: Halew 2H **93**
Farndale WA8: Wid 4E **79**
Farndale Cl. WA5: Gt San 2H **81**
Farndon Av. CH45: Wall 1A **50**
   WA9: Sut M 3F **61**
Farndon Dr. CH48: W Kir 6E **65**
Farndon Way CH43: Oxton 5B **68**
Farnham Cl. L32: Kirkb 2B **24**
Farnhill Cl. WA7: Nort 5F **115**
Farnley Cl. WA7: Wind H 4F **115**
Farnside Ct. L17: Aig 4C **90**
FARNWORTH 6F **79**
Farnworth Av. CH46: Leas 4C **48**
Farnworth Cl. WA8: Wid 5F **79**
Farnworth Gro. L33: Kirkb 4A **14**
Farnworth M. WA8: Wid 6F **79**
Farnworth Rd. WA5: Penk 5D **80**
   WA8: Wid 5F **79**
   WA9: St H 1G **43**
Farrant St. WA8: Wid 3F **97**
Farrar St. L13: Liv 6C **36**
Farrell Cl. L31: Mell 5F **13**

Farr Hall Dr. CH60: Hesw 6C 100
Farr Hall Rd. CH60: Hesw 5C 100
Farrier Rd. L33: Kirkb 1C 24
Farriers Wlk. WA9: Clock F 3G 61
Farriers Way CH48: Frank 1H 83
   L30: N'ton 3F 21
Farringdon Cl. WA9: St H 2D 60
Farthing Cl. L25: Hunts X 4C 92
Farthingstone Cl. L35: Whis 1G 59
Fatherside Dr. L30: N'ton 6C 10
Faversham Rd. L11: Norr G 2C 36
Faversham Way
   CH42: Rock F 1H 87
Fawcett Rd. L31: Lyd 4C 6
Fawley Rd. L18: Moss H 1G 91
   L35: Rainh 6C 60
FAZAKERLEY 4D 22
Fazakerley Cl. L9: Walt 1G 35
Fazakerley Rd. L9: Walt 1G 35
   L35: Presc 3E 59
Fazakerley Sports Cen. 3D 22
Fazakerley Station (Rail) 4B 22
Fazakerley St. L3: Liv 3B 4 (5B 52)
Fearnley Hall CH41: Birke 4F 69
Fearnley Rd. CH41: Birke 4F 69
Fearnside St. L7: Liv 1A 72
Feather La. CH60: Hesw 5D 100
Feathers, The WA10: St H 2B 42
Feeny St. WA9: Sut M 5F 61
Feilden Rd. CH63: Beb 1A 104
Felcroft Way L33: Kirkb 1B 24
Felicity Gro. CH46: More 6B 48
Fell Gro. WA11: St H 3E 29
Fell St. CH44: Wall 5G 51
   L7: Liv 5H 53
Felltor Cl. L25: Woolt 6B 74
Fellwood Gro. L35: Whis 5E 59
Felmersham Av. L11: Norr G 2D 36
Felspar Rd. L32: Kirkb 4B 24
Felstead Av. L25: Woolt 1E 93
Felsted Dr. L10: Ain 2C 22
Felthorpe Cl. CH49: Upton 2F 67
Felton Cl. CH46: More 1A 66
Felton Ct. L17: Aig 6A 72
                                 (off Lark La.)
Felton Gro. L13: Liv 3D 54
Feltwell Rd. L4: Walt 1H 53
Feltwood Cl. L12: W Der 6B 38
Feltwood Mnr. L12: W Der 5B 38
Feltwood Rd. L12: W Der 5B 38
Feltwood Wlk. L12: W Der 6B 38
Fendale Av. CH46: More 6E 49
Fender Cl. CH49: Woodc 2H 85
Fender La. CH43: Bid 6E 49
   CH46: More 6E 49
Fenderside Rd. CH43: Bid 1G 67
Fender Vw. Rd. CH46: More 1E 67
Fender Way CH43: Bid 3F 67
   CH61: Pens 1E 101
Fenham Dr. WA5: Penk 5G 81
Fenton Cl. L24: Speke 2F 109
   L30: N'ton 3H 21
   WA8: Wid 6A 78
   WA10: St H 1D 42
Fenton Grn. L24: Speke 3F 109
Fenwick La. WA7: Run 1H 123
Fenwick St. L2: Liv 4C 4 (6C 52)
Ferguson Av. CH49: Grea 6B 66
Ferguson Rd. L11: Norr G 5C 36
   L21: Lith .2C 20
Fern Bank L31: Mag 6D 6
   WA11: Rainf 2E 17
Fernbank Av. L36: Huy 5F 57
Fernbank Dr. L30: N'ton 5G 11
Fernbank La. CH49: Upton 2D 66
Fern Cl. L27: N'ley 5G 75
   L32: Kirkb 5B 14
Ferndale Av. CH44: Wall 3E 51
   CH48: Frank 2H 83
Ferndale Cl. L9: Walt 4G 21
   WA8: Bold H 2A 80
Ferndale Rd. CH47: Hoy 2B 64
   L15: Wav 3C 72
   L22: Water 1F 19

Fern Gdns. L34: Eccl P 6F 41
Fern Gro. CH43: Noct 5H 67
   L8: Liv 3A 72
   L20: Boot 1C 34
Fern Hey L23: Thorn 4B 10
Fernhill CH45: New B 5D 32
Fernhill Av. L20: Boot 2E 35
Fernhill Cl. L20: Boot 2E 35
                             (not continuous)
Fernhill Dr. L8: Liv 3G 71
Fernhill Gdns. L20: Boot 2E 35
Fernhill Mews E. L20: Boot 2E 35
                            (off Fernhill Rd.)
Fernhill Mews W. L20: Boot 2E 35
Fernhill Rd. L20: Boot 5D 20
Fernhill Wlk. WA9: Clock F 4G 61
Fernhill Way L20: Boot 2E 35
Fernhurst WA7: Run 5H 113
Fernhurst Rd. L32: Kirkb 2G 23
Fernie Cres. L8: Liv 4F 71
Fernlea Av. WA9: St H 6B 42
Fernlea M. CH43: Bid 1G 67
Fernlea Rd. CH60: Hesw 5E 101
Fernleigh Rd. L13: Liv 4F 55
Fern Lodge L8: Liv 3A 72
Ferns Cl. CH60: Hesw 4A 100
Ferns Rd. CH63: Hghr B 6F 87
Fernwood WA7: Nort 4D 114
Fernwood Dr. L26: Halew 3G 93
Fernwood Rd. L17: Aig 1C 90
Ferny Brow Rd.
   CH49: Woodc 6F 67
Ferrey Rd. L10: Faz 4E 23
Ferries Cl. CH42: Rock F 3A 88
Ferry Rd. CH62: East 2G 121
Ferryside CH44: Wall 5G 51
Ferry Vw. Rd. CH44: Wall 5G 51
Ferryview Wlk. WA7: Cas 3B 114
Festival Cl. L11: Norr G 2F 37
Festival Rd. WA11: Rainf 4G 17
Festival Ter. WA7: Run 5G 113
                             (off Festival Way)
Festival Way WA7: Run 5G 113
Ffrancon Dr. CH63: Hghr B 4H 87
FIDDLER'S FERRY 2F 99
Fiddlers Ferry Rd.
   WA8: Wid 3G 97
Fiddler's Ferry Sailing Club 2G 99
Field Av. L21: Lith 3A 20
Field Cl. CH62: New F 3B 88
   WA9: Clock F 4H 61
Fieldfare Cl. L25: Gate 4C 74
Fieldgate WA8: Wid 4H 95
Field Hey La. CH64: Will 6B 120
                             (not continuous)
Field Ho. L12: W Der 6E 37
Fieldhouse Row WA7: Run 6H 113
Fieldings, The L31: Lyd 3A 6
Fielding St. L6: Liv 4G 53
Field La. L10: Faz 5E 23
   L21: Lith .2A 20
Field Rd. CH45: New B 6D 32
Field Way L35: Rainh 2A 60
   WA9: Clock F 4H 61
Field's End L36: Huy 1G 75
Fieldsend Cl. L27: N'ley 5G 75
Fieldside Rd.
   CH42: Rock F 1G 87
Field St. L3: Liv 4E 53
                             (not continuous)
Fieldsway WA7: West 1E 123
Fieldton Rd. L11: Norr G 3F 37
Field Vw. L21: Lith 3A 20
Field Wlk. L23: Thorn 4B 10
Fieldway CH45: Wall 2C 50
   CH47: Meols 1E 64
   CH60: Hesw 4G 101
   CH63: Hghr B 3F 87
   L15: Wav 1G 73
   L31: Mag 2C 12
   L36: Huy .1H 75
   WA8: Wid 1A 98
Fieldway Ct. CH41: Birke 1E 69

Fifth Av. CH43: Bid 2F 67
   L9: Ain 4C 22
                                  (Broadway)
   L9: Ain 4B 22
                                  (Sixth Av.)
   WA7: Pal F 6B 114
Filbert Cl. L33: Kirkb 3B 14
Filby Gdns. WA9: St H 1C 60
Fillmore Gro. WA8: Wid 6D 78
Filton Rd. L14: Knott A 2D 56
Finborough Rd. L4: Walt 3A 36
FINCHAM 2D 56
Fincham Grn. L14: Knott A 2D 56
Fincham Rd. L14: Knott A 2C 56
Fincham Sq. L14: Knott A 2C 56
Finch Av. WA11: Rainf 4G 17
Finch Cl. WA9: Clock F 4H 61
Finch Ct. CH41: Birke 2F 69
Finchdean Cl. CH49: Grea 5A 66
Finch Dene L14: Knott A 1B 56
Finch La. L14: Knott A 1B 56
   L26: Halew 5B 94
Finch Lea Dr. L14: Knott A 2C 56
Finchley Dr. WA11: St H 4G 29
Finchley Rd. L4: Walt 6H 35
Finch Mdw. Cl. L9: Faz 1D 36
Finch Pl. L3: Liv 5F 53
Finch Rd. L14: Knott A 1C 56
Finch Way L14: Knott A 2B 56
Findley Dr. CH46: Leas 4D 48
Findon Rd. L32: Kirkb 3B 24
Fingall Rd. L15: Wav 3F 73
Finger Ho. La. WA8: Bold H 6H 61
Fingland Rd. L15: Wav 2C 72
Finlan Rd. WA8: Wid 4D 96
Finlay Av. WA5: Penk 6G 81
Finlay St. L6: Liv 4A 54
Finlay Ct. L30: N'ton 5F 11
Finney, The CH48: Caldy 5D 82
Finney Gro. WA11: Hay 5G 31
Finsbury Pk. WA8: Wid 4G 79
Finstall Rd. CH63: Spit 3H 103
Finvoy Rd. L13: Liv 6C 36
Fiona Wlk. L10: Faz 4F 23
Fir Av. L26: Halew 3A 94
Firbank Cl. WA7: Wind H 4F 115
Firbrook Ct. CH43: Bid 6G 49
Fir Cl. L26: Halew 3A 94
Fir Cotes L31: Mag 6D 6
Firdale Rd. L9: Walt 1G 35
Firdene Cres. CH43: Noct 5A 68
Fire Station Cl. L23: Crosb 5F 9
Fire Station Rd. L35: Whis 2F 59
Firethorne Rd. L26: Halew 1F 93
Fir Gro. L9: Ain 3A 22
Fir La. L15: Wav 2E 73
Fir Rd. L22: Water 1G 19
Firs, The CH43: Bid 1A 68
Firs Av. CH63: Beb 2H 103
Firscraig L28: Stockb V 6E 39
Firshaw Rd. CH47: Meols 6C 46
First Av. CH43: Bid 3G 67
   L9: Ain 4A 22
                                  (Higher La.)
   L9: Ain 5C 22
                                  (Second Av.)
   L23: Crosb 5F 9
   L35: Rainh 3H 59
Firstone Gro. L32: Kirkb 3A 24
Fir St. WA8: Wid 1G 97
   WA10: St H 5B 42
Firthland Way WA9: St H 3B 44
Fir Tree Dr. Nth. L12: Crox 2H 37
Fir Tree Dr. Sth. L12: Crox 2H 37
Fir Tree La. WA5: Burtw 6H 45
Firway CH60: Hesw 2F 117
Firwood Gro. WN4: Ash M 1H 31
Fisher Av. L35: Whis 5D 58
Fisher Ct. WA7: Run 2F 113
Fisher Pl. L35: Whis 5D 58
Fishers La. CH61: Pens 1C 100
Fisher St. L8: Liv 3D 70
   WA7: Run 2F 113
   WA9: St H 5A 44

Fishguard Cl. L6: Liv 3F 53
Fishwicks Ind. Est. WA9: St H 5G 43
  WA11: Hay 3H 31
Fistral Cl. L10: Faz 5F 23
Fistral Dr. WA10: Windle 5H 27
Fitness First
  Halton Lea 6A 114
Fitzclarence Wlk. L6: Liv 3F 53
  (off Plumpton St.)
Fitzclarence Way L6: Liv 3F 53
Fitzgerald Rd. L13: Liv 4E 55
Fitzpatrick Ct. L3: Liv 3C 52
Fitzroy Way L6: Liv 4G 53
Fitzwilliam Wlk. WA7: Cas 3C 114
Fiveways WA10: Eccl 1G 41
Fiveways Pk. CH64: Nest 4B 118
Flail Cl. CH49: Grea 5A 66
Flambards CH49: Woodc 6F 67
Flander Cl. WA8: Wid 1A 96
Flatfield Way L31: Mag 6D 6
Flatt La. CH43: Oxton 6B 68
Flavian Ct. WA7: Cas 4A 114
Flawn Rd. L11: Norr G 5C 36
Flaxhill CH46: More 6B 48
Flaxman Ct. L7: Liv 5A 54
  (off Botanic Gro.)
Flaxman St. L7: Liv 5A 54
Flaybrick Cl. CH43: Bid 1A 68
Fleck La. CH48: Caldy, W Kir 2D 82
Fleetcroft Rd. CH49: Woodc 1E 85
Fleet La. WA9: St H 2A 44
Fleet La. Ind. Est. WA9: St H 3A 44
Fleet St. L1: Liv 5F 5 (6D 52)
Fleetwood Gdns. L33: Kirkb 4B 14
  (not continuous)
Fleetwood Pl. L25: Woolt 1B 92
  (off Castle St.)
Fleetwoods La. L30: N'ton 5D 10
Fleetwood Wlk. WA7: Murd 6E 115
Fleming Ct. L13: Liv 3C 52
Fleming Rd. L24: Speke 5E 93
Flemington Av. L4: Walt 4B 36
Fleming Way CH46: Leas 5E 49
Fletcher Av. CH42: Rock F 1G 87
  L34: Presc 6E 41
Fletcher Cl. CH49: Woodc 6E 67
Fletcher Dr. L19: Gras 4E 91
Fletchers Row WA7: Halt 4B 114
  (off Spark La.)
Flint Dr. L12: Crox 4H 37
Flintshire Gdns. WA10: St H 3D 42
Flint St. L1: Liv 2D 70
Flixton Gdns. WA9: St H 1C 60
Floral Pavilion Theatre 4E 33
Floral Wood L17: Aig 1F 89
Florence Av. CH60: Hesw 4D 100
Florence Cl. L9: Walt 2F 35
Florence Ct. L9: Walt 2F 35
  (off Buchanan Rd.)
Florence Nightingale Cl. L30: N'ton . . .5F 11
Florence Rd. CH44: Wall 4G 51
Florence St. CH41: Birke 3F 69
  L4: Walt 5F 35
  WA9: St H 6A 42
Florentine Rd. L13: Liv 3E 55
Florida Ct. L19: Gras 3F 91
Florida Way L35: Presc 3D 58
Flowermead Cl. CH47: Meols 6F 47
Fluin La. WA6: Frod 6G 123
Fluker's Brook La. L34: Know 4D 38
  (not continuous)
Focus Building, The L3: Liv 2E 5
  (off Crosshall St.)
Foinavon Cl. L9: Walt 4F 21
Folds, The CH63: Thorn H 1C 118
Folds La. WA11: St H 4E 29
Folds Rd. WA11: Hay 6B 30
Foley Cl. L4: Kirkd 6E 35
Foley St. L4: Kirkd 6E 35
Folkestone Way WA7: Murd 6E 115
Folly La. CH44: Wall 2A 50
  (not continuous)
  WA7: Run 4B 112
Fontenoy St. L3: Liv 1E 5 (5D 52)

Fonthill Cl. L4: Kirkd 6D 34
Fonthill Rd. L4: Kirkd 5D 34
FORD
  CH43 . . . . .3G 67
  L21 . . . . .1B 20
Ford Av. L33: Kirkb 3A 14
Ford Cl. CH49: Upton 5F 67
  L20: Boot 4E 21
  L21: Ford 1B 20
Fordcombe Rd. L25: Gate 5E 75
Ford Dr. CH49: Upton 4F 67
Fordham St. L4: Kirkd 5E 35
Fordhill Vw. CH46: More 1E 67
Ford La. CH49: Upton 4F 67
  L21: Ford 1B 20
Fordlea Rd. L12: W Der 5E 37
Fordlea Way L12: W Der 5E 37
Ford Rd. CH49: Upton 4E 67
  L35: Presc 1F 59
Ford St. L3: Liv 4C 52
Ford Vw. L21: Ford 6B 10
Ford Way WA9: Upton 5E 67
Ford Way M. CH49: Upton 5E 67
Forefield La. L23: Crosb 4H 9
Foreland Cl. WA5: Gt San 2E 81
Forest Cl. CH47: Meols 6D 46
  L34: Eccl P 6F 41
Forest Ct. CH43: Clau 3B 68
Forest Dr. L36: Huy 4E 57
Forest Grn. L12: W Der 5F 37
Forest Gro. L34: Eccl P 6F 41
Forest Lawn L12: W Der 5F 37
Forest Mead WA10: Eccl 2G 41
Forest Rd. CH43: Clau 2C 68
  CH47: Meols 6D 46
  CH60: Hesw 4E 101
  WA9: Sut M 4E 61
Forest Wlk. WA7: Pal F 6B 114
  (off Halton Lea Shop. Cen.)
Forfar Rd. L13: Liv 1B 54
Forge Cl. WA8: Cron 4A 78
Forge Cotts. L17: Aig 5A 72
Forge Rd. WA5: Gt San 4H 81
Forge St. L20: Kirkd 5C 34
Formby Av. WA10: St H 4B 42
Formby Cl. WA5: Penk 5H 81
Formosa Dr. L10: Faz 4D 22
Formosa Rd. L10: Faz 4D 22
Formosa Way L10: Faz 4D 22
Fornalls Grn. La. CH47: Meols 2E 65
Forrester Av. WA9: St H 6A 42
Forrest St. L1: Liv 6E 5 (1D 70)
Forshaw Av. WA10: St H 5A 42
Forshaw's La. WA5: Burtw 5G 45
Forsythia Cl. L9: Walt 2A 36
Forthlin Rd. L18: Aller 2G 91
  (not continuous)
Forth St. L20: Kirkd 4C 34
Forton Lodge Flats L23: Blun 5E 9
  (off Blundellsands Rd. E.)
Fort Perch Rock Marine Radio Mus.
  . . . . .4D 32
Fort St. CH45: New B 6E 33
Forwood Rd. CH62: Brom 5D 104
Foscote Rd. L33: Kirkb 5C 14
Foster Cl. L35: Whis 2G 59
Fosters Gro. WA11: Hay 5B 30
Fosters Rd. WA11: Hay 5B 30
Foster St. L20: Kirkd 6C 34
  WA8: Wid 2F 97
Foundation, The L3: Liv 6F 53
Foundry, The L1: Liv 6F 5
Foundry Ind. Est. WA8: Wid 4F 97
Foundry St. WA10: St H 2E 43
  (not continuous)
Fountain Ct. L23: Blun 4C 8
Fountain Rd. CH45: New B 6D 32
  L34: Know 2F 39
Fountains Av. WA11: Hay 4H 31
Fountains Cl. L4: Walt 6F 35
  WA7: Brook 2E 125
Fountains Ct. L4: Kirkd 6D 34
  (off Stanley Cl.)

Fountains Rd. L4: Kirkd, Walt 6D 34
  (not continuous)
Fountain St. CH42: Tran 6E 69
  WA9: St H 1A 60
Four Acre Dr. L21: Ford 6B 10
Four Acre La. WA9: Clock F 3F 61
Four Acre Pct. WA9: Clock F 3F 61
Fouracres L31: Mag 2H 11
Four Bridges CH41: Birke 6G 51
Fourth Av. CH43: Bid 3F 67
  L9: Ain .4C 22
  (Broadway)
  L9: Ain .4B 22
  (Fifth Av.)
  WA7: Pal F 6B 114
Fowell Rd. CH45: New B 5D 32
Fowler Cl. L7: Liv 6A 54
Fox Bank Cl. WA8: Wid 5D 78
Foxcote WA8: Wid 1H 95
Foxcover Rd. CH60: Hesw 6G 101
Foxcovers Rd. CH63: Beb 2A 104
Fox Covert WA7: Nort 6E 115
Foxdale Cl. CH43: Oxton 4C 68
Foxdale Rd. L15: Wav 3D 72
Foxdell Cl. L13: Liv 5E 55
Foxes, The CH61: Thing 5E 85
Foxes Ct. CH43: Oxton 4D 68
Foxfield Rd. CH47: Meols 1D 64
  WA9: St H 3C 60
Foxglove Av. L26: Halew 2G 93
Foxglove Cl. L9: Faz 1D 36
Foxglove Rd. CH41: Birke 2B 68
Fox Hey Rd. CH44: Wall 4B 50
Foxhill Cl. L8: Liv 3G 71
Foxhill La. L26: Halew 1G 93
Foxhouse La. L31: Mag 1C 12
Foxhunter Dr. L9: Ain 3A 22
Foxleigh L26: Halew 2F 93
Foxleigh Grange
  CH41: Birke 6B 50
Foxley Heath WA8: Wid 3C 96
Fox Pl. WA10: St H 1E 43
Fox's Bank La. L35: Whis 3F 77
  (not continuous)
Foxshaw Cl. L35: Whis 6D 58
Fox St. CH41: Birke 3E 69
  L3: Liv .3E 53
  WA7: Run 4E 113
Foxton Cl. CH46: More 6H 47
  WA11: St H 6H 29
Foxwood L12: W Der 5A 38
  WA9: St H 6A 42
Foxwood Cl. CH48: W Kir 6E 65
Framlington Ct.
  WA7: Cas 3A 114
Frampton Rd. L4: Walt 3B 36
Francine Cl. L3: Liv 2C 52
Francis Av. CH43: Clau 3D 68
  CH46: More 1B 66
Francis Cl. L35: Rainh 3A 60
  WA8: Wid 3A 96
Francis Rd. WA6: Frod 6G 123
Francis St. WA9: St H 6B 44
Francis Way L16: Child 1H 73
FRANKBY 1H 83
Frankby Av. CH44: Wall 3C 50
Frankby Cl. CH49: Grea 6H 65
Frankby Grn. CH48: Frank 1G 83
Frankby Gro. CH49: Upton 4D 66
Frankby Rd. CH47: Meols 1D 64
  CH48: Frank, W Kir 6D 64
  CH49: Grea 6D 64
  L4: Walt 5H 35
Frankby Stiles
  CH48: Frank 6F 65
Franklin Gro. L33: Kirkb 3A 14
Franklin Pl. L6: Liv 2H 53
Franklin Rd. CH46: Leas 3E 49
Frank St. WA8: Wid 2G 97
Franton Wlk. L32: Kirkb 1G 23
Fraser Rd. WA5: Gt San 3F 81
Fraser St. L3: Liv 2G 5 (5E 53)
Freckleton Dr. L33: Kirkb 4C 14
Freckleton Rd. WA10: St H 4H 41

Freda Av. WA9: St H 1G 61
Frederick Banting Cl.
  L30: N'ton 5F 11
Frederick Gro. L15: Wav 1E 73
Frederick Lunt Av. L34: Know 2E 39
Frederick St. WA8: Wid 2F 97
  (not continuous)
  WA9: St H 5B 44
Frederick Ter. WA8: Hale B 1G 111
Frederic Pl. WA7: Run 2F 113
Freedom Cl. L7: Liv 1G 71
Freehold St. L7: Liv 4B 54
Freeland St. L4: Kirkd 6E 35
Freeman St. CH41: Birke 2G 69
  L7: Liv 1A 72
Freemantle Av. WA9: St H 6C 42
Freemason's Row L3: Liv 1D 4 (4C 52)
Freemont Rd. L12: W Der 6E 37
Freeport Gro. L9: Ain 4H 21
Freesia Av. L9: Walt 1H 35
Freme Cl. L11: Norr G 2F 37
Frenchfield St.
  WA9: Clock F 4H 61
French St. WA8: Wid 2H 97
  WA10: St H 4B 42
Frensham Cl. CH63: Spit 3H 103
Freshfield Cl. L36: Huy 4E 57
Freshfield Rd. L15: Wav 3D 72
Freshford WA9: St H 1H 61
Freshwater Cl. WA5: Gt San 2F 81
Friars Av. WA5: Gt San 4G 81
Friars Cl. CH63: Beb 6H 87
Friarsgate Cl. L18: Moss H 4G 73
Friar St. L5: Liv 2F 53
  WA10: St H 5D 28
Friends La. WA5: Gt San 3F 81
Frinsted Rd. L11: Norr G 4E 37
Frith Cl. L35: Rainh 3A 60
  (off Ratcliffe Pl.)
Frobisher Rd. CH46: Leas 3E 49
  CH64: Nest 6A 118
FRODSHAM 6G 123
Frodsham Bus. Cen.
  WA6: Frod 6G 123
Frodsham Dr. WA11: St H 6H 29
Frodsham Pk. Homes
  WA6: Frod 6E 123
Frodsham Station (Rail) 6F 123
Frodsham St. CH41: Tran 5G 69
  (not continuous)
  L4: Walt 4F 35
Frogmore Rd. L13: Liv 4C 54
Frome Cl. CH61: Irby 4B 84
Frome Way L25: Hunts X 3F 93
Frontfield Ct. WA9: St H 3G 43
  (off Appleton Rd.)
Frost Dr. CH61: Irby 5A 84
Frost St. L7: Liv 5A 54
Fryer St. WA7: Run 2E 113
Fry St. WA9: St H 2A 44
  (not continuous)
Fuchsia Wlk. CH49: Grea 1A 84
Fulbeck WA8: Wid 1A 96
Fulbrook Cl. CH63: Spit 3H 103
Fulbrook Rd. CH63: Spit 3H 103
Fulford Cl. L12: W Der 1B 56
Fulford Pk. CH46: More 1C 66
Fullerton Gro. L36: Huy 3G 57
Fulmar Cl. L27: N'ley 4G 75
  WA11: St H 5F 29
Fulmar Gro. L12: Crox 2A 38
Fulshaw Cl. L27: N'ley 3F 75
Fulton Av. CH48: W Kir 6D 64
Fulton St. L5: Liv 2B 52
Fulwood Cl. L17: Aig 1B 90
Fulwood Dr. L17: Aig 1A 90
Fulwood Pk. L17: Aig 2A 90
Fulwood Rd. L17: Aig 1A 90
Fulwood Way L21: Ford 5B 10
Furlong Cl. L9: Ain 3B 22
Furness Av. L12: W Der 4G 37
  WA10: St H 4C 28
Furness Cl. CH49: Upton 3C 66
Furness Ct. WA7: Nort 1H 115

Furness St. L4: Walt 6E 35
Furze Way CH46: More 6C 48

G

Gable Ct. L11: Norr G 2C 36
Gables, The L31: Mag 2C 12
  L34: Eccl P 1F 59
Gable Vw. L11: Norr G 2C 36
Gabriel Cl. CH46: More 1D 66
Gainford Cl. WA8: Wid 6A 78
Gainford Rd. L14: Knott A 1C 56
Gainsborough Av. L31: Mag 1H 11
Gainsborough Cl. L12: W Der 2A 56
Gainsborough Ct. WA8: Wid 2H 95
Gainsborough Rd. CH45: Wall 3A 50
  CH49: Upton 3C 66
  L15: Wav 3C 72
Gaisgill Cl. WA8: Wid 2A 96
Gala Bingo
  Bromborough 2E 105
  Kirkby 1A 24
  Liverpool, E. Lancashire Rd. . . .1E 37
  Liverpool, Wavertree Rd. 6A 54
  Widnes .3F 97
Gala Cl. L14: Knott A 3A 56
Gala Leo Casino 2D 70
Galbraith Cl. L17: Aig 1A 90
Galemeade L11: Norr G 2F 37
Gale Rd. L21: Lith 2C 20
  L33: Know I 3E 25
Galingale Rd. L11: Norr G 4E 37
Galion Way WA8: Wid 5D 78
Gallagher Ind. Est. CH44: Wall 5D 50
Gallopers La. CH61: Thing 5F 85
Galloway Rd. L22: Water 1G 19
Galloway St. L7: Liv 1B 72
Galston Av. L35: Rainh 5B 60
Galston Cl. L33: Kirkb 3H 13
Galsworthy Av. L30: Boot 3D 20
Galsworthy Pl. L30: Boot 3E 21
Galsworthy Wlk. L30: Boot 4E 21
Galton St. L3: Liv 1A 4 (4B 52)
Galtres Ct. CH63: Hghr B 3G 87
Galtres Pk. CH63: Hghr B 3G 87
Galway Av. WA8: Wid 6C 78
Galway Cres. WA11: Hay 4F 31
Gambier Ter. L1: Liv 2F 71
Gamble Av. WA10: St H 5C 28
Gamlin St. CH41: Birke 1B 68
Gamston Wood Cl. L32: Kirkb 2G 23
Ganneys Mdw. Cl. CH49: Woodc . . .6G 67
Ganney's Mdw. Rd. CH49: Woodc . . .1G 85
Gannock St. L7: Liv 5A 54
Ganton Cl. WA8: Wid 5F 79
Ganworth Cl. L24: Speke 3G 109
Ganworth Rd. L24: Speke 3G 109
Garage Rd. L24: Halew 6H 93
Garden Apartments L18: Moss H . . .6D 72
Garden Cotts. L12: W Der 3H 55
Garden Ct. CH42: Tran 2E 87
Gardeners Vw. L33: Kirkb 3C 14
Gardeners Way L35: Rainh 2A 60
Garden Hey Rd. CH46: More 2H 65
  CH47: Meols 1C 64
Gardenia Gro. L17: Aig 1G 89
Garden La. CH46: More 6C 48
  L5: Liv 3F 53
  L9: Ain 3B 22
Garden Lodge Gro. L27: N'ley 4F 75
Gardenside CH46: Leas 3F 49
Gardenside St. L6: Liv 4F 53
Gardens Rd. CH63: Beb 6B 88
Garden St. L25: Woolt 1C 92
Garden Wlk. L34: Presc 2D 58
Gardiner Av. WA11: Hay 5E 31
Gardner Av. L20: Boot 4D 20
Gardner Rd. L13: Liv 2C 54
Gardner's Dr. L6: Liv 3A 54
Gardner's Row L3: Liv 1E 5 (4D 52)
Gareth Av. WA11: St H 5F 29
Garfield Ter. CH49: Upton 4E 67
Garfourth Cl. L19: Garst 4H 91

Garfourth Rd. L19: Garst 4H 91
Garmoyle Cl. L15: Wav 2C 72
Garmoyle Rd. L15: Wav 2C 72
Garnet St. L13: Liv 6D 54
  WA9: St H 6H 43
Garnett Av. L4: Kirkd 5E 35
Garnetts La. L35: Tar G 2D 94
  WA8: Hale B 1G 111
Garrick Av. CH46: More 1A 66
Garrick Rd. CH43: Pren 3B 86
Garrick St. L7: Liv 2A 72
Garrigill Cl. WA8: Wid 4F 79
Garrison Cl. L8: Liv 3H 71
Garrowby Dr. L36: Huy 4E 57
Garsdale Av. L35: Rainh 5B 60
Garsdale Cl. WA5: Gt San 2H 81
Garsfield Rd. L4: Walt 4B 36
GARSTON .5G 91
Garston Ind. Est. L19: Garst 1G 107
Garston Old Rd. L19: Garst, Gras . . .4F 91
Garston Way L19: Garst 5G 91
Garswood Av. WA11: Rainf 2G 17
Garswood Cl. CH46: Leas 3C 48
  L31: Mag 4D 6
Garswood Old Rd. WA11: St H 3G 29
  WN4: Garsw 2B 30
Garswood Rd. WA11: Hay 2D 30
  WN4: Garsw 1E 31
Garswood St. L8: Liv 6F 71
  WA10: St H 1E 43
Garter Cl. L11: Crox 2G 37
Garth, The CH43: Oxton 4A 68
  L36: Huy .4G 57
Garth Blvd. CH63: Hghr B 3G 87
Garth Ct. L22: Water 2G 19
Garthdale Rd. L18: Moss H 5E 73
Garth Dr. L18: Moss H 5E 73
Garthowen Rd. L7: Liv 5B 54
Garth Rd. L32: Kirkb 3C 24
Garth Wlk. L32: Kirkb 3C 24
Gartons La. WA9: Clock F, Sut M 4G 61
Garway L25: Woolt 6E 75
Garway Cl. WA9: St H 2B 44
Gaskell Cl. WA9: St H 2B 44
Gaskell Rake L30: N'ton 4D 10
  (off Higher End Pk.)
Gaskell St. WA9: St H 4H 43
Gaskill Rd. L24: Speke 1F 109
Gatclif Rd. L13: Liv 5C 36
GATEACRE .4D 74
Gateacre Brow L25: Gate 5D 74
Gateacre Ct. L25: Gate 2B 74
  (off Headbourne Cl.)
Gateacre Neighbourhood Cen.
  L25: Gate 3C 74
Gateacre Pk. Dr. L25: Gate 2B 74
Gateacre Ri. L25: Gate 5D 74
Gateacre Va. Rd. L25: Woolt 6D 74
Gateside Cl. L27: N'ley 4G 75
Gates La. L29: Thorn 1B 10
Gateway, The CH62: Brom 4E 105
Gathurst Ct. WA8: Wid 3B 96
Gatley Dr. L31: Mag 2C 12
Gatley Wlk. L24: Speke 1H 109
Gaunts Way WA7: Pal F 1A 124
Gautby Rd. CH41: Birke 6A 50
Gavin Rd. WA8: Wid 4H 95
Gawsworth Cl. CH43: Oxton 6B 68
  WA10: Eccl 2H 41
Gaybeech Cl. CH43: Bid 1F 67
Gayhurst Cres.
  L11: Norr G 3E 37
Gaynor Av. WA11: Hay 4H 31
GAYTON 6F 101
Gayton Av. CH45: New B 5D 32
  CH63: Hghr B 3E 87
Gayton Farm Rd. CH60: Hesw 2E 117
Gayton La. CH60: Hesw 1F 117
Gayton Mill Cl. CH60: Hesw 6F 101
Gayton Parkway CH60: Hesw 2G 117
Gayton Rd. CH60: Hesw 6D 100
Gayton Sands Nature Reserve 5D 116
Gaytree Ct. CH43: Bid 2G 67
Gaywood Av. L32: Kirkb 3B 24

Gaywood Cl. CH43: Bid 2G 67
  L32: Kirkb 3B 24
Gaywood Ct. L23: Blun 6D 8
Gaywood Grn. L32: Kirkb 3B 24
Gellings La. L34: Know 6C 24
Gellings Rd. L34: Know 6C 24
Gelling St. L8: Liv 4F 71
Gemini Cl. L20: Boot 1B 34
Gemini Dr. L14: Knott A 3B 56
Gem St. L5: Liv 2C 52
General Dr. L12: W Der 6H 37
Geneva Cl. L36: Huy 3G 57
                 (off Salerno Dr.)
Geneva Rd. CH44: Wall 5F 51
  L6: Liv .4A 54
Genista Cl. L9: Walt 2G 35
Genoa Cl. L25: Gate 2D 74
Gentwood Pde. L36: Huy 3F 57
Gentwood Rd. L36: Huy 3E 57
George Hale Av. L34: Know P 1G 57
George Harrison Cl. L6: Liv 4H 53
George Moore Ct. L23: Thorn 3B 10
George Rd. CH47: Hoy 3C 64
George's Dock Gates L3: Liv . .4B 4 (6B 52)
Georges Dock Way L3: Liv . . .5C 4 (6B 52)
George's Rd. L6: Liv 2H 53
George St. CH41: Birke 2G 69
  L3: Liv 3C 4 (5C 52)
  WA10: St H 2E 43
Georgia Av. CH62: Brom 2E 105
  L33: Kirkb 3H 13
Georgia Cl. L20: Boot 2C 34
Georgian Cl. L26: Halew 5H 93
  L35: Eccl P 1G 59
Geraint St. L8: Liv 3F 71
Gerald Rd. CH43: Oxton 5C 68
Gerard Av. CH45: Wall 6C 32
Gerard Rd. CH45: Wall 1B 50
  CH48: W Kir 6B 64
GERARD'S BRIDGE 6E 29
Gerards Ct. WA11: St H 3F 29
Gerards La. WA9: St H, Sut L 6H 43
Gerards Pk. WA11: St H 6F 29
Gerard St. L3: Liv 2F 5 (5E 53)
Gerard Way L33: Kirkb 1B 24
Germander Cl. L26: Halew 2G 93
Gerneth Cl. L24: Speke 1E 109
Gerneth Rd. L24: Speke 2D 108
Gerrard's La. L26: Halew 1G 93
Gerrard St. WA8: Wid 3F 97
Gertrude Rd. L4: Walt 1H 53
Gertrude St. CH41: Birke 3H 69
  WA9: St H 6A 42
Geves Gdns. L22: Water 2G 19
Ghyll Gro. WA11: St H 2F 29
Gibbons Av. WA10: St H 2A 42
Gibbon's Rd. WN4: Garsw 1F 31
Gibbs Ct. CH61: Irby 5D 84
Gibfield Rd. WA9: St H 2C 60
Gibraltar Row L3: Liv 2B 4 (5B 52)
Gibson Cl. CH61: Pens 2D 100
  L33: Kirkb 4H 13
Gibson Rd. L8: Liv 2F 71
Gibson Ter. CH44: Wall 2F 51
               (off Royden Av.)
Giddygate La. L31: Mag, Mell 1F 13
Gidlow Rd. L13: Liv 4D 54
Gidlow Rd. Sth. L13: Liv 5D 54
Gilbert Cl. CH63: Spit 3H 103
Gilbert Ho. WA7: Run 2C 112
Gilbert Rd. L35: Whis 2F 59
Gilbert St. L1: Liv 6E 5 (1D 70)
Gildarts Gdns. L3: Liv 3C 52
Gildart St. L3: Liv 2H 5 (5F 53)
Gilead St. L7: Liv 5H 53
Gilescroft Av. L33: Kirkb 5C 14
Gilescroft Wlk. L33: Kirkb 5C 14
Gillan Cl. WA7: Brook 2E 125
GILLAR'S GREEN 3E 41
Gillars Grn. Dr. WA10: Eccl 2F 41
Gillar's La. WA10: Eccl 2E 41
Gillbrook Sq. CH41: Birke 1B 68
Gilleney Gro. L35: Whis 2G 59
GILLMOSS 6H 23

Gillmoss Cl. L11: Crox 1G 37
Gillmoss Ind. Est. L10: Faz 5F 23
Gillmoss La. L11: Crox 6G 23
Gills La. CH61: Barn, Pens 1E 101
Gill St. L3: Liv 3H 5 (5F 53)
Gilman St. L4: Walt 6G 35
Gilmartin Gro. L6: Liv 4G 53
Gilmour Mt. CH43: Oxton 5D 68
Gilpin Av. L31: Mag 5D 6
Gilroy Nature Pk. 5C 64
Gilroy Rd. CH48: W Kir 6C 64
  L6: Liv .4H 53
Giltbrook Cl. WA8: Wid 6D 78
Gilwell Av. CH46: More 2C 66
Gilwell Cl. CH46: More 2C 66
Ginnel, The CH62: Port S 6B 88
Gipsy Gro. L18: Moss H 4A 74
Gipsy La. L18: Moss H 4A 74
Girton Av. L20: Boot 3E 35
Girtrell Cl. CH49: Upton 4B 66
Girtrell Rd. CH49: Upton 4H 99
Givenchy Cl. L16: Child 1A 74
Glacier Bldg. L3: Liv 5E 71
Glade, The CH47: Meols 6D 46
Glade Pk. Ct. L8: Liv 5H 71
Glade Rd. L36: Huy 3G 57
Gladeswood Rd. L33: Know I 2D 24
Gladeville Rd. L17: Aig 1C 90
Gladica Cl. L36: Huy 5B 58
Gladstone Av. L16: Child 1C 74
  L21: Sea 4A 20
           (off Gladstone Rd.)
Gladstone Cl. CH41: Birke 3F 69
Gladstone Ct. L8: Liv 2F 71
          (off Up. Parliament St.)
Gladstone Hall Rd. CH62: Port S . . .1B 104
Gladstone Rd. CH42: Rock F 6H 69
  CH44: Wall 4F 51
  L7: Liv .6H 53
  L9: Walt 2G 35
  L19: Garst 5G 91
  L21: Sea 4H 19
Gladstone St. L3: Liv 1D 4 (4C 52)
  L25: Woolt 1B 92
  WA8: Wid 3F 97
  WA10: St H 2B 42
Gladstone Theatre 1B 104
Gladsville Rd. L27: N'ley 5H 75
Gladstone St. L5: Liv 1G 53
Glamis Cl. CH43: Noct 6H 67
Glamis Gro. WA9: St H 6G 43
Glamis Rd. L13: Liv 1B 54
Glamorgan Cl. WA9: St H 3D 42
Glan Aber Pk. L12: W Der 5A 38
Glasier Rd. CH46: More 6A 48
Glaslyn Way L9: Walt 2G 35
Glastonbury Cl. L6: Liv 6B 36
  WA7: Nort 2H 115
Glasven Rd. L33: Kirkb 6B 14
Glazebrook La. WA8: Wid 3E 79
Gleadmere WA8: Wid 1A 96
Gleaner Cl. WA7: Run 2D 112
Gleaston Cl. CH62: Brom 4D 104
Gleave Cl. WA5: Burtw 1H 63
Gleave Cres. L6: Liv 3G 53
Gleave St. WA10: St H 1E 43
Glebe, The WA7: Run 4A 114
Glebe Bus. Pk. WA8: Wid 5G 79
Glebe Cl. L31: Mag 6A 6
Glebe End L29: Seft 2F 11
Glebe Hey L27: N'ley 4G 75
Glebe Hey Rd. CH49: Woodc 6E 67
Glebelands Rd. CH46: More 1C 66
Glebe La. WA8: Wid 4E 79
Glebe Rd. CH45: Wall 1C 50
Gleggside CH48: W Kir 1C 82
Glegg St. L3: Liv 3B 52
Glegside Rd. L33: Kirkb 1C 24
Glen, The CH63: Spit 2C 104
  L18: Moss H 6G 73
  WA7: Pal F 1B 124
Glenacres L25: Woolt 6C 74
Glenalmond Rd. CH44: Wall 3F 51
Glenathol Rd. L18: Moss H 1G 91

Glenavon Rd. CH43: Pren 2C 86
  L16: Child 1G 73
Glen Bank L22: Water 1E 19
Glenbank Cl. L9: Walt 6G 21
Glenburn Av. CH62: East 3E 121
Glenburn Rd. CH44: Wall 4F 51
Glenby Av. L23: Crosb 1H 19
Glencairn Rd. L13: Liv 4D 54
Glencoe Rd. CH45: Wall 1D 50
Glenconner Rd. L16: Child 6A 56
Glencourse Rd. WA8: Wid 4E 79
Glencroft Cl. L36: Huy 2E 57
Glendale Cl. L8: Liv 6F 71
Glendale Gro. CH63: Spit 3B 104
  L33: Kirkb 4C 14
Glendale Rd. WA11: St H 4E 29
Glendevon Rd. L16: Child 6G 55
  L36: Huy 6G 57
Glendower Rd. L22: Water 2G 19
Glendower St. L20: Boot 4C 34
Glendyke Rd. L18: Moss H 1G 91
Gleneagles Cl. CH61: Pens 1D 100
  L33: Kirkb 3H 13
Gleneagles Dr. WA8: Wid 4E 79
  WA11: Hay 6C 30
Gleneagles Rd. L16: Child 6A 56
Glenfield Cl. CH43: Bid 1G 67
  CH46: More 6H 47
Glenfield Rd. L15: Wav 3E 73
Glengariff St. L13: Liv 6C 36
Glenham Cl. CH47: Meols 1E 65
Glenhead Rd. L19: Aller 3F 91
Glenholm Rd. L31: Mag 2A 12
Glenluce Rd. L19: Aig 3F 91
Glenlyon Rd. L16: Child 1G 73
Glenmarsh Cl. CH63: Hghr B 6F 87
  L12: W Der 1G 55
Glenmaye Cl. L12: Crox 3A 38
Glenmore Av. L18: Moss H 6E 73
Glenmore Rd. CH43: Oxton 5C 68
Glenn Pl. WA8: Wid 2C 96
Glen Pk. Rd. CH45: Wall 6C 32
Glen Rd. L13: Liv 5F 55
Glen Ronald Dr. CH49: Grea 4B 66
Glenrose Rd. L25: Woolt 5C 74
Glenside L18: Aller 1G 91
Glentree Cl. CH49: Grea 4B 66
Glentrees Rd. L12: W Der 5F 37
Glentworth Cl. L31: Mag 2B 12
Glenville Cl. L25: Woolt 5D 74
  WA7: Run 1F 123
Glenvine Cl. L16: Child 1A 74
Glen Way L33: Kirkb 3B 14
Glenway Cl. L12: Crox 1B 38
Glenwood WA7: Nort 4E 115
Glenwood Cl. L35: Whis 5F 59
Glenwood Dr. CH61: Irby 4C 84
Glenwyllin Rd. L22: Water 1G 19
Globe Pl. L20: Boot 1B 34
Globe St. L4: Walt 6E 35
Gloucester Ct. L6: Liv 4G 53
Gloucester Pl. L6: Liv 4G 53
             (off Gilmartin Gro.)
Gloucester Rd. CH45: Wall 1A 50
  L6: Liv .2B 54
  L20: Boot 1D 34
  L36: Huy 4A 58
  WA8: Wid 6F 79
Gloucester Rd. Nth. L6: Liv 1B 54
Gloucester St. WA9: St H 3H 43
Glover Pl. L20: Boot 1B 34
Glover's Brow L32: Kirkb 5G 13
Glovers Ct. L32: Kirkb 6G 13
Glover's La. L30: N'ton 5E 11
Glover St. CH42: Tran 5E 69
  WA10: St H 3D 42
Glyn Av. CH62: Brom 6E 105
Glynne Gro. L16: Child 1C 74
Glynn St. L15: Wav 2D 72
Glyn Rd. CH44: Wall 2D 50
Goddard Rd. WA7: Ast 2A 114
Godetia Cl. L9: Faz 1D 36
Godfrey Pilkington Art Gallery 2E 43
Godshill Cl. WA5: Gt San 2F 81

Godstow WA7: Nort 1G **115**
Goldcrest Cl. L12: Crox 1B **38**
  WA7: Beech 2B **124**
Goldcrest M. L26: Halew 2G **93**
Golden Gro. L4: Walt 4G **35**
Golden Triangle Ind. Est.
  WA8: Hale B 6H **95**
Golders Grn. L7: Liv 1A **72**
Goldfinch Cl. L26: Halew 2G **93**
Goldfinch Farm Rd. L24: Speke 2E **109**
Goldie St. L4: Walt 6F **35**
Goldsmith Rd. CH43: Pren 2B **86**
Goldsmith St. L6: Liv 4H **53**
  L20: Boot 1A **34**
Goldsmith Way CH43: Pren 2B **86**
Goldsworth Fold L35: Rainh 4G **59**
Golf Links Rd. CH42: Tran 2D **86**
Gondover Av. L9: Walt 5F **21**
Gonville Rd. L20: Boot 3D **34**
Goodacre Rd. L9: Ain 4H **21**
Goodakers Ct. CH49: Woodc 1E **85**
  (off Childwall Grn.)
Goodakers Mdw. CH49: Woodc 1E **85**
Goodall Pl. L4: Kirkd 5E **35**
Goodall St. L4: Kirkd 4E **35**
Goodban St. WA9: St H 5A **44**
Goodier Ct. WA7: Run 5G **113**
Goodison Av. L4: Walt 5F **35**
Goodison Park 5F **35**
Goodison Pl. L4: Walt 4F **35**
Goodison Rd. L4: Walt 4F **35**
Goodlass Rd. L24: Speke 5C **92**
Goodleigh Pl. WA9: Sut L 2G **61**
Good Shepherd Cl. L11: Norr G 3F **37**
Goodwood Cl. L36: Roby 6F **57**
Goodwood Ct. WA9: St H 1B **60**
Goodwood Dr. CH46: Leas 4D **48**
Goodwood St. L5: Liv 2D **52**
Gooseberry Hollow WA7: Wind H 4F **115**
Gooseberry La. WA7: Nort 4F **115**
Goose Green, The CH47: Meols 6D **46**
Goostrey Cl. CH63: Spit 4B **104**
Gordale Cl. L8: Liv 5G **71**
  WA5: Gt San 2H **81**
Gordon Av. CH49: Grea 6C **66**
  CH62: Brom 6E **105**
  L22: Water 1E **19**
  L31: Mag .4B **6**
  WA11: Hay 4H **31**
Gordon Ct. CH49: Grea 6C **66**
Gordon Dr. L14: Broad G 4A **56**
  L19: Gras 4E **91**
Gordon Pl. L18: Moss H 6E **73**
Gordon Rd. CH45: New B 6E **33**
  L21: Sea .4H **19**
Gordon St. CH41: Birke 3E **69**
  L15: Wav .2C **72**
Goree L2: Liv 4B **4** (6C **52**)
Goree Piazza L2: Liv 4C **4**
  (off The Strand)
Gores Rd. L33: Know I 2D **24**
Gore St. L8: Liv 3E **71**
Gorleston M. L32: Kirkb 2B **24**
Gorleston Way L32: Kirkb 2B **24**
Gorran Haven WA7: Brook 1E **125**
Gorse Av. L12: W Der 4F **37**
Gorsebank Rd. L18: Moss H 4C **72**
Gorsebank St. CH44: Wall 4E **51**
Gorseburn Rd. L13: Liv 1C **54**
Gorse Cres. CH44: Wall 5E **51**
Gorsedale Pk. CH44: Wall 5E **51**
Gorsedale Rd. CH44: Wall 5D **50**
  L18: Moss H 5E **73**
Gorsefield WA9: St H 6B **42**
Gorsefield Av. CH62: Brom 2D **120**
  L23: Thorn 4A **10**
Gorsefield Cl. CH62: Brom 2D **120**
Gorsefield Rd. CH42: Tran 6E **69**
Gorse Hey Ct. L13: W Der 2E **55**
Gorsehill Rd. CH45: New B 6C **32**
  CH60: Hesw 4E **101**
Gorselands Ct. L17: Aig 1B **90**
Gorse La. CH48: W Kir 2E **83**
Gorse Rd. CH47: Meols 1D **64**

Gorsewood Cl. L25: Gate 4E **75**
  (off Gorsewood Rd.)
Gorsewood Gro. L25: Gate 4D **74**
Gorsewood Rd. L25: Gate 4D **74**
  WA7: Murd 1F **125**
Gorsey Av. L30: N'ton 6C **10**
Gorsey Cop Rd. L25: Gate 3C **74**
Gorsey Cop Way L25: Gate 3C **74**
Gorsey Cft. L34: Eccl P 6F **41**
Gorsey La. CH44: Wall 5D **50**
  L21: Ford 2B **20**
  L30: N'ton 2B **20**
  WA5: Burtw 2D **62**
  WA8: Wid 3A **98**
  WA9: Bold, Clock F 4A **62**
Gorseyville Cres. CH63: Hghr B 6G **87**
Gorseyville Rd. CH63: Hghr B 6G **87**
Gorseywell La. WA7: Pres B 1H **125**
Gorst St. L4: Walt 6F **35**
Gorton Rd. L13: Liv 5F **55**
Gort Rd. L36: Huy 4G **57**
Goschen St. L5: Liv 6F **35**
  L13: Liv .4D **54**
Gosford St. L8: Liv 5F **71**
Gosforth Ct. WA7: Pal F 6A **114**
Goswell St. L15: Wav 1C **72**
Gotham Rd. CH63: Spit 3A **104**
Gothic St. CH42: Rock F 1H **87**
Gough Rd. L13: Liv 6C **36**
Goulders Ct. WA7: Brook 2D **124**
Gourley Grange CH48: W Kir 2D **82**
Gourley Rd. L13: Liv 6F **55**
Gourleys La. CH48: W Kir 2D **82**
Government Rd. CH47: Hoy 2B **64**
Govett Rd. WA9: St H 6A **42**
Gower St. L3: Liv 1C **70**
  L20: Boot 6B **20**
  WA9: St H 4H **43**
Gowrie Gro. L21: Lith 4B **20**
Grace Av. L10: Faz 4E **23**
Grace Cl. CH45: Wall 2D **50**
Grace Rd. L9: Walt 5G **21**
Grace St. L8: Liv 5F **71**
  WA9: St H 5G **43**
Gradwell St. L1: Liv 5E **5** (6D **52**)
Graeme Bryson Ct. L11: Norr G 4D **36**
Grafton Cres. L8: Liv 3E **71**
Grafton Dr. CH49: Upton 5E **67**
Grafton Gro. L8: Liv 5E **71**
Grafton Rd. CH45: New B 6D **32**
Grafton St. CH43: Oxton 4D **68**
  L8: Liv 6F **71**
  (Beresford Rd.)
  L8: Liv 3D **70**
  (Stanhope St., not continuous)
  WA10: St H 2B **42**
Grafton Wlk. CH48: W Kir 1C **82**
Graham Cl. WA8: Wid 2A **96**
Graham Dr. L26: Halew 3A **94**
Graham Rd. CH48: W Kir 6A **64**
  WA8: Wid 3A **96**
Graham's Rd. L36: Huy 5H **57**
Graham St. WA9: St H 1G **43**
Grainger Av. CH43: Pren 1B **86**
  CH48: W Kir 5B **64**
  L20: Boot 6E **21**
Grain Ind. Est. L8: Liv 5E **71**
Graley Cl. L26: Halew 5H **93**
Grammar School La. CH48: W Kir 2D **82**
Grampian Av. CH46: More 1D **66**
Grampian Rd. L7: Liv 5C **54**
Grampian Way CH46: More 1C **66**
  CH62: East 2E **121**
Granams Cft. L30: N'ton 5D **10**
Granard Rd. L15: Wav 3E **73**
Granary Mill WA4: Pres H 1H **125**
Granary Way L3: Liv 3D **70**
Granborne Chase L32: Kirkb 6F **13**
GRANBY 2G **71**
Granby Cl. WA7: Brook 2E **125**
Granby Cres. CH63: Spit 3A **104**
Granby St. L8: Liv 2G **71**
Grand Central L3: Liv 4G **5**
Grandison Rd. L4: Walt 4A **36**

Grand National Av. L9: Ain 2H **21**
GRANGE 1C **82**
Grange, The CH42: Rock F 2H **87**
  CH44: Wall 3E **51**
  L20: Boot 5C **20**
Grange & Pyramids Shop. Cen., The
  CH41: Birke 3F **69**
Grange Av. CH45: Wall 1D **50**
  L12: W Der 2A **56**
  L25: Hunts X 4F **93**
Grange Av. Nth. L12: W Der 2A **56**
Grange Ct. CH43: Oxton 6C **68**
  L15: Wav 2D **72**
  (off Grange Ter.)
  L23: Blun .6E **9**
Grange Cres. CH66: Hoot 6G **121**
Grange Cross Cl. CH48: W Kir 2E **83**
Grange Cross Hey CH48: W Kir 2E **83**
Grange Cross La. CH48: W Kir 2E **83**
Grange Dr. CH60: Hesw 3D **100**
  CH63: Thorn H 6C **102**
  WA5: Penk 5H **81**
  WA8: Wid 3B **96**
  WA10: St H 5H **41**
Grange Farm Cres. CH48: W Kir 6E **65**
Grangehurst Ct. L25: Gate 5D **74**
Grange La. L25: Gate 4C **74**
Grangemeadow Rd. L25: Gate 4C **74**
Grangemoor WA7: Run 5H **113**
Grange Mt. CH43: Oxton 4E **69**
  CH48: W Kir 1D **82**
  CH60: Hesw 4D **100**
Grange Old Rd. CH48: W Kir 1C **82**
GRANGE PARK 5H **41**
Grange Pk. L31: Mag 2C **12**
Grange Pk. Av. WA7: Run 3G **113**
Grange Park Golf Course 4A **42**
Grange Pk. Rd. WA10: St H 4A **42**
Grange Pl. CH41: Birke 3E **69**
Grange Pct. CH41: Birke 3G **69**
Grange Rd. CH41: Birke 3F **69**
  (not continuous)
  CH48: W Kir 1A **82**
  CH60: Hesw 3D **100**
  L30: N'ton 1H **21**
  WA7: Run 3G **113**
  WA11: Hay, Newt W 6F **31**
Grange Rd. E. CH41: Birke 3G **69**
Grange Rd. Nth. WA7: Run 3G **113**
Grange Road Sports Cen. 4D **68**
Grange Rd. W. CH41: Birke 3D **68**
  CH43: Oxton 3D **68**
Grangeside L25: Gate 4C **74**
Grange St. L6: Liv 2B **54**
Grange Ter. L15: Wav 2D **72**
Grange Valley WA11: Hay 5F **31**
Grange Vw. CH43: Oxton 4E **69**
Grange Wlk. CH48: W Kir 2D **82**
Grange Way L25: Gate 4C **74**
Grangeway WA7: Run 5G **113**
Grangeway Ct. WA7: Run 5G **113**
Grange Weint L25: Gate 5C **74**
Grange Wood CH48: W Kir 2D **82**
Grangewood L16: Child 6B **56**
Granite Ter. L14: Knott A 5B **56**
Grant Av. L15: Wav 2E **73**
Grant Cl. L14: Knott A 4C **56**
  WA10: St H 1C **42**
Grant Ct. L20: Boot 2C **34**
  (off Clairville Cl.)
Grantham Cl. CH61: Pens 1C **100**
Grantham Cres. WA11: St H 6G **29**
Grantham Rd. L33: Kirkb 4A **14**
Grantham St. L6: Liv 4H **53**
Grantham Way L30: N'ton 5H **11**
Grantley Rd. L15: Wav 3F **73**
Granton Rd. L5: Liv 1G **53**
Grant Rd. CH46: Leas 4F **49**
  L14: Knott A 4B **56**
Granville Av. L31: Mag 5B **6**
Granville Cl. CH45: Wall 1A **50**
Granville Ct. CH45: Wall 1A **50**
Granville Rd. L15: Wav 2B **72**
  L19: Garst 5G **91**

Granville St. WA7: Run 2E **113**
   WA9: St H 2H **43**
Grappenhall Way CH43: Bid 2G **67**
Grasmere Av. CH43: Noct 4G **67**
   L34: Presc 1F **59**
   WA11: St H 4F **29**
Grasmere Cl. L33: Kirkb 5H **13**
   WA11: St H 4F **29**
Grasmere Ct. *CH41: Birke* *4E 69*
   (off Penrith St.)
   WA11: St H 4F **29**
Grasmere Dr. CH45: Wall 1D **50**
   L21: Lith 2E **21**
   WA7: Beech 2H **123**
Grasmere Fold WA11: St H 4F **29**
Grasmere Gdns. L23: Crosb 6H **9**
Grasmere Ho. *L17: Aig* *1B 90*
   (off Mossley Hill Dr.)
Grasmere Rd. L31: Mag 5C **6**
   WA6: Frod 6G **123**
Grasmere St. L5: Liv 2H **53**
GRASSENDALE 3E **91**
Grassendale Ct. *L19: Gras* *4E 91*
   (off Grassendale Rd.)
Grassendale Esplanade L19: Gras . . .5D **90**
Grassendale La. L19: Gras 4E **91**
Grassendale Rd. L19: Gras 4E **91**
Grassington Cres. L25: Woolt 1E **93**
Grassmoor Cl. CH62: Brom 5E **105**
Grassway Rd. CH49: Woodc 1F **85**
Grasville Rd. CH42: Tran 6G **69**
Gratrix Rd. CH62: Brom 5D **104**
Gray Av. WA11: Hay 5F **31**
Gray Gro. L36: Huy 1H **75**
Graylag Cl. WA7: Beech 2B **124**
Graylands Pl. L4: Walt 4A **36**
Graylands Rd. CH62: Port S 5C **88**
   L4: Walt 4A **36**
Graylaw Ind. Est. L9: Ain 5A **22**
Grayling Dr. L12: Crox 2H **37**
Gray's Av. L35: Presc 1F **59**
Grayson M. *CH41: Birke* *2H 69*
   (off John St.)
Graysons Rd. WA11: Rainf 1F **17**
Grayson St. L1: Liv 1D **70**
Grayston Av. WA9: Sut L 1H **61**
Gray St. L20: Boot 6A **20**
GREASBY 6B **66**
Greasby Hill Rd. CH48: W Kir 2C **82**
Greasby Rd. CH44: Wall 3C **50**
   CH49: Grea 6A **66**
Great Ashfield WA8: Wid 6B **78**
Gt. Charlotte St. L1: Liv 4F **5** (6D **52**)
   (Elliot St.)
   L1: Liv 4F **5** (6D **52**)
   (Roe St.)
GREAT CROSBY 4G **9**
Gt. Crosshall St. L3: Liv 2D **4** (5C **52**)
Great Delph WA11: Hay 4F **31**
Gt. George Pl. L1: Liv 2E **71**
Gt. George Sq. L1: Liv 1E **71**
Gt. George's Rd. L22: Water 3F **19**
Gt. George's Sq. *L1: Liv* *1E 71*
   (off Grenville St. Sth.)
Gt. George St. L1: Liv 1E **71**
Gt. Heath Rd. L4: Kirkd 6D **34**
Great Hey L30: N'ton 4D **10**
Gt. Homer St. L5: Liv 1E **53**
Gt. Homer St. Shop. Cen. L5: Liv 2E **53**
Gt. Howard St. L3: Liv 1B **4** (4B **52**)
   L5: Liv 1B **52**
GREAT MEOLS 6E **47**
Gt. Mersey St. L5: Kirkd 1D **52**
   (not continuous)
Gt. Nelson St. L3: Liv 3D **52**
Gt. Newton St. L3: Liv 3H **5** (5F **53**)
Gt. Orford St. L3: Liv 5H **5** (6F **53**)
Gt. Richmond St. L3: Liv 4E **53**
Great Riding WA7: Nort 6E **115**
GREAT SANKEY 3H **81**
Great Sankey Leisure Cen. 1F **81**
Gt. Western Ho. CH41: Birke 2H **69**
Greaves St. L8: Liv 4F **71**
Grebe Av. WA10: St H 5G **41**

Grecian St. L21: Sea 3H **19**
Grecian Ter. L5: Liv 2F **53**
Gredington St. L8: Liv 5G **71**
Greek St. L3: Liv 3H **5** (5E **53**)
   WA7: Run 2D **112**
Green, The CH48: Caldy 4D **82**
   CH62: Brom 6D **88**
   CH63: Raby 3E **119**
   L13: Liv 5G **55**
   L23: Crosb 5F **9**
   L34: Eccl P 6F **41**
   WA7: Halt 4B **114**
Greenacre Cl. L25: Hunts X 3E **93**
Greenacre Dr. CH63: Brom 6C **104**
Greenacre Rd. L25: Hunts X 3E **93**
Greenacres Cl. CH43: Bid 1G **67**
Greenacres Ct. CH43: Bid 1G **67**
Greenall Av. WA5: Penk 5F **81**
Greenall Ct. L34: Presc 1C **58**
Greenall St. WA10: St H 1C **42**
GREEN BANK 3C **42**
Green Bank CH63: Brim 3C **102**
Greenbank Av. CH45: New B 6D **32**
   L31: Mag 4B **6**
Greenbank Cl. L17: Aig 4C **72**
Greenbank Cres. WA10: St H 2D **42**
Greenbank Dr. CH61: Pens 2D **100**
   L10: Faz 4F **23**
   L17: Aig 5C **72**
Greenbank La. L17: Aig 5C **72**
Greenbank Rd. CH42: Tran 6E **69**
   CH48: W Kir 5B **64**
   L18: Moss H 4C **72**
Greenbank Sports Academy 5C **72**
Greenbridge Cl. WA7: Cas 3C **114**
Greenbridge Rd. WA7: Wind H 3D **114**
Greenburn Av. WA11: St H 2G **29**
Green Coppice WA7: Nort 5E **115**
Greencroft Hey CH63: Spit 3B **104**
Greencroft Rd. CH44: Wall 4E **51**
Greendale Rd. CH62: Port S 5A **88**
   L25: Woolt 5B **74**
Green End La. WA9: St H 5G **43**
Green End Pk. L12: W Der 6E **37**
Greenes Rd. L35: Whis 5D **58**
Greenfield Cl. L18: Aller 2G **91**
Greenfield Dr. L36: Huy 1H **75**
Greenfield Gro. L36: Huy 6H **57**
Greenfield La. CH60: Hesw 3A **100**
   L21: Lith 2A **20**
   WA6: Frod 6F **123**
Greenfield Rd. L13: Liv 4E **55**
   WA10: St H 6B **28**
GREENFIELDS 1G **67**
Greenfields Av. CH62: Brom 6C **104**
Greenfields Cres. CH62: Brom 6C **104**
Greenfield Wlk. L36: Huy 6H **57**
Greenfield Way CH44: Wall 3D **50**
   L18: Aller 2G **91**
Greenfinch Cl. L12: Crox 2B **38**
Greenfinch Gro. L26: Halew 2G **93**
Green Gables L33: Kirkb 5H **13**
Greengables Cl. L8: Liv 4G **71**
Green Gates L36: Huy 1G **57**
Greenham Av. L33: Kirkb 3B **14**
Green Haven CH43: Noct 4H **67**
Greenhaven Cl. L10: Faz 4E **23**
Greenheath Way CH46: Leas 4D **48**
Greenhey Dr. L30: N'ton 1C **20**
Green Heys Dr. L31: Mag 6E **6**
Greenheys Gdns. L8: Liv 3A **72**
Greenheys Rd. CH44: Wall 4D **50**
   CH61: Irby 6A **84**
   L8: Liv .3H **71**
Greenhill Av. L18: Moss H 4G **73**
Greenhill Cl. L18: Moss H 1F **91**
Greenhill Pl. L36: Huy 6G **57**
Greenhill Rd. L18: Aller, Moss H 6F **73**
   L19: Aller 3G **91**
Greenholme Cl. L11: Norr G 2E **37**
Greenhouse Farm Rd. WA7: Pal F . . .1D **124**
Greenhow Av. CH48: W Kir 6B **64**
Green Jones Brow WA5: Burtw 1H **63**

Greenlake Rd. L18: Moss H 1F **91**
Greenlands L36: Huy 6G **57**
Greenland St. L1: Liv 2D **70**
Green La. CH41: Tran 5G **69**
   CH45: Wall 2F **49**
   (not continuous)
   CH62: East 5F **105**
   CH63: Beb 6H **87**
   L3: Liv 5H **5** (6E **53**)
   L13: Liv 2C **54**
   L18: Moss H 5F **73**
   (not continuous)
   L21: Ford 1B **20**
   L21: Sea 4A **20**
   (not continuous)
   L22: Water 1E **19**
   L23: Thorn 3B **10**
   L31: Mag 5A **6**
   WA5: Burtw 6G **45**
   WA8: Wid 2C **96**
   WA10: Eccl 5E **27**
   WA11: Rainf 4G **17**
Green La. Nth. L16: Child 3G **73**
Green Lane Station (Rail) 5H **69**
Green Lawn CH42: Rock F 2H **87**
   L36: Huy 3A **58**
Green Lawn Gro. CH42: Rock F 2H **87**
GREEN LEACH 4E **29**
Green Leach Av. WA11: St H 4F **29**
Green Leach Ct. WA11: St H 4F **29**
Green Leach La. WA11: St H 4F **29**
Greenlea Cl. CH63: Beb 5H **87**
Greenleaf St. L8: Liv 2A **72**
Greenleas Cl. CH45: Wall 1H **49**
Greenleas Rd. CH45: Wall 1H **49**
Greenleigh Rd. L18: Moss H 1F **91**
Green Link L31: Mag 5A **6**
Green Mt. CH49: Upton 4E **67**
Greenoaks Farm Ind. Est.
   WA8: Wid 2G **97**
Green Oaks Path WA8: Wid 3H **97**
Green Oaks Shop. Cen. WA8: Wid . . .2F **97**
   (Deacon Rd.)
   WA8: Wid 3F **97**
   (Green Oaks Way)
Green Oaks Way WA8: Wid 3F **97**
Greenock M. WA8: Wid 6C **78**
Greenock St. L3: Liv 1A **4** (4B **52**)
Greenodd Av. L12: W Der 4G **37**
Greenore Dr. L24: Hale 3D **110**
Greenough Av. L35: Rainh 2A **60**
Greenough St. L25: Woolt 1B **92**
Green Pk. L30: N'ton 4F **11**
Green Pk. Dr. L31: Mag 6A **6**
Green Rd. L34: Presc 1C **58**
Greensbridge La. L26: Halew, Tar G . .2A **94**
   L35: Tar G 2B **94**
Greens Health & Fitness
   Liverpool 6F **71**
Greenside L6: Liv 4F **53**
Greenside Av. L10: Ain 1C **22**
   L15: Wav 1E **73**
Greenside Cl. L33: Kirkb 3C **14**
Green St. L5: Liv 3C **52**
Greens Wlk. *L17: Aig* *6C 72*
   (off Aigburth Va.)
Greenville Cl. CH63: Beb 6H **87**
Greenville Dr. L31: Mag 6B **6**
Greenville Rd. CH63: Beb 6H **87**
Greenway CH49: Grea 5C **66**
   CH61: Pens 1C **100**
   CH62: Brom 2D **104**
   CH64: Park 5F **117**
   L23: Crosb 4A **10**
   L36: Huy 3D **56**
   WA5: Gt San 2G **81**
Greenway, The L12: Knott A 3A **56**
Greenway Cl. L36: Huy 3D **56**
Greenway Rd. CH42: Tran 6F **69**
   L24: Speke 2A **110**
   WA7: Run 3E **113**
   WA8: Wid 1F **97**
Greenways Ct. CH62: Brom 1C **120**
Greenwell Rd. WA11: Hay 5E **31**

Greenwich Av.—Halewood Cl.

Greenwich Av. WA8: Wid 5H **79**
Greenwich Ct. L9: Ain 3H **21**
Greenwich Rd. L9: Ain 3H **21**
Greenwood Cl. L34: Presc 1E **59**
Greenwood Ct. WA9: Clock F 3G **61**
Greenwood Dr. WA7: Manor P 1H **115**
Greenwood La. CH44: Wall 2E **51**
Greenwood Rd. CH47: Meols 1E **65**
CH49: Woodc 6E **67**
L18: Aller 2F **91**
Greetham St. L1: Liv 6E **5** (1D **70**)
Gregory Cl. L16: Child 1A **74**
Gregory Way L16: Child 1A **74**
Gregson Ct. CH45: New B 5E **33**
Gregson Rd. L35: Presc 3D **58**
WA8: Wid 2G **97**
Gregson St. L6: Liv 4F **53**
Grenadier Dr. L12: W Der 6A **38**
Grenfell Cl. CH64: Park 6G **117**
Grenfell Ct. CH64: Park 6G **117**
Grenfell Pk. CH64: Park 6G **117**
Grenfell Rd. L13: Liv 5C **36**
Grenfell St. WA8: Wid 3F **97**
Grennan, The CH45: New B 5D **32**
Grennan Ct. *CH45: New B 5D **32***
(off The Grennan)
Grenville Cres. CH63: Brom 6C **104**
Grenville Dr. CH61: Pens 2C **100**
Grenville Rd. CH42: Tran 6H **69**
CH64: Nest 6A **118**
Grenville St. Sth. L1: Liv 1D **70**
Grenville Way CH42: Tran 6H **69**
Gresford Av. CH43: Pren 1C **86**
CH48: W Kir 6C **64**
L17: Liv 3C **72**
Gresford Cl. L35: Whis 4F **59**
Gresham St. L7: Liv 5C **54**
Gresley Cl. L7: Liv 6A **54**
Gressingham Rd. L18: Moss H 6G **73**
Gretton Rd. L14: Knott A 2D **56**
Greyhound Farm Rd.
L24: Speke 2E **109**
Grey Rd. L9: Walt 1F **35**
Greystoke Cl. CH49: Upton 5D **66**
Greystone Cres. L14: Broad G 4A **56**
Greystone Pl. L10: Faz 4D **22**
Greystone Rd. L10: Faz 4C **22**
L14: Broad G 5A **56**
WA5: Penk 5H **81**
Grey St. L8: Liv 3F **71**
Gribble Rd. L10: Faz 4E **23**
Grierson St. L8: Liv 2H **71**
Grieve Rd. L10: Faz 4E **23**
Griffin Av. CH46: More 1C **66**
Griffin Cl. L11: Crox 1G **37**
WA10: Eccl 1F **41**
Griffin M. WA8: Wid 6F **79**
Griffin St. WA9: St H 6A **44**
Griffiths Cl. CH49: Grea 6A **66**
Griffiths Rd. L36: Huy 5G **57**
Griffiths St. L1: Liv 1E **71**
Grimsby Ct. L19: Garst 5F **91**
Grimshaw St. L20: Boot 3B **34**
WA9: Sut L 1G **61**
Grinfield St. L7: Liv 6G **53**
Grinshill Cl. L8: Liv 3G **71**
Grinton Cres. L36: Roby 5F **57**
Grisedale Cl. WA7: Beech 2A **124**
Grisedale Rd. CH62: Brom 5F **105**
Grizedale WA8: Wid 1H **95**
Grizedale Av. WA11: St H 3F **29**
Groarke Dr. WA5: Penk 4F **81**
Groes Rd. L19: Gras 4F **91**
Grogan Sq. L20: Boot 5D **20**
Gronow Pl. *L20: Boot 5E **21***
(off Hughes Dr.)
Grosmont Rd. L32: Kirkb 3B **24**
Grosmont Way WA8: Wid 5A **80**
Grosvenor Av. CH48: W Kir 1B **82**
L23: Crosb 1G **19**
Grosvenor Cl. L30: N'ton 6F **11**
Grosvenor Ct. CH43: Oxton 4D **68**
CH47: Hoy 3B **64**
L15: Wav 2G **73**
Grosvenor Ct. L18: Moss H 6C **72**
*L34: Presc 1D **58***
(off Grosvenor Rd.)
Grosvenor Dr. CH45: New B 5D **32**
Grosvenor Pl. CH43: Oxton 4C **68**
Grosvenor Rd. CH43: Oxton 3C **68**
CH45: New B 5D **32**
CH47: Hoy 3B **64**
L4: Walt 3F **35**
L15: Wav 1B **72**
L19: Gras 5E **91**
L31: Mag 3A **12**
L34: Presc 1D **58**
WA8: Wid 5F **79**
WA10: St H 3B **42**
WA11: Hay 4D **30**
Grosvenor St. CH44: Wall 2D **50**
L3: Liv 4D **52**
WA7: Run 2F **113**
Grosvenor Ter. *L8: Liv 5H **71***
(off Wellesley Rd.)
Grove, The CH43: Oxton 6D **68**
CH44: Wall 4E **51**
CH63: Beb 6A **88**
L13: Liv 1D **54**
L28: Stockb V 6E **39**
WA5: Penk 5H **81**
WA10: Windle 6A **28**
Grove Av. CH60: Hesw 4D **100**
Grovedale Dr. CH46: More 6E **49**
Grovedale Rd. L18: Moss H 4D **72**
Grovehurst Av. L14: Knott A 3B **56**
Groveland Av. CH45: Wall 1H **49**
CH47: Hoy 2B **64**
Groveland Rd. CH45: Wall 1H **49**
Grovelands *L7: Liv 1G **71***
(off Falkner St.)
Grove Mead L31: Mag 6E **7**
Grove Pk. L8: Liv 3A **72**
Grove Pk. Av. L12: W Der 5F **37**
Grove Pl. CH47: Hoy 2B **64**
Grove Rd. CH42: Rock F 1H **87**
CH45: Wall 1A **50**
CH47: Hoy 2B **64**
L6: Liv 4B **54**
Groves, The CH43: Oxton 4D **68**
*L7: Liv 1G **71***
(off Grove St.)
L32: Kirkb 4A **24**
Groveside CH48: W Kir 1A **82**
L7: Liv 1G **71**
Grove Sq. CH62: New F 4A **88**
Grove St. CH62: New F 4B **88**
L7: Liv 1G **71**
L15: Wav 1D **72**
L20: Boot 1A **34**
WA7: Run 2D **112**
WA10: St H 2D **42**
Grove Ter. CH47: Hoy 2B **64**
Grove Way L7: Liv 1G **71**
Grovewood Ct. CH43: Oxton 6D **68**
Grovewood Gdns. L35: Whis 4E **59**
Grundy Cl. WA8: Wid 6D **78**
Grundy St. L5: Kirkd 1B **52**
Guardian Ct. CH48: W Kir 2B **82**
Guelph Pl. *L7: Liv 5G **53***
(off Guelph St.)
Guelph St. L7: Liv 5G **53**
Guernsey Rd. L13: Liv 3D **54**
WA8: Wid 6A **80**
Guest St. WA8: Wid 4E **97**
Guffitts Cl. CH47: Meols 6E **47**
Guffitt's Rake CH47: Meols 6E **47**
Guildford Av. L30: N'ton 2F **21**
Guildford St. CH44: Wall 3F **51**
Guildhall Rd. L9: Ain 5G **21**
Guild Hey L34: Know 1F **39**
Guillemot Way L26: Halew 2G **93**
Guilsted Rd. L11: Norr G 3E **37**
Guinea Gap CH44: Wall 4G **51**
Guinea Gap Leisure Cen. **4G 51**
Guion Rd. L21: Lith 4B **20**
Guion St. L6: Liv 3H **53**
Gulls Way CH60: Hesw 5B **100**
Gunning Av. WA10: Eccl 6H **27**
Gunning Cl. WA10: Eccl 6H **27**
Gurnall St. L4: Walt 6F **35**
Gutticar Rd. WA8: Wid 2H **95**
Guy Cl. CH41: Tran 5G **69**
Gwendoline Cl. CH61: Thing 6E **85**
Gwendoline St. L8: Liv 3F **71**
Gwenfron Rd. L6: Liv 4H **53**
Gwent Cl. L6: Liv 2H **53**
Gwent St. L8: Liv 3G **71**
Gwladys St. L4: Walt 4F **35**
Gwydir St. L8: Liv 4G **71**
Gwydrin Rd. L18: Moss H 4G **73**
Gym, The
Liverpool **5D 4**
Gym Health & Fitness, The
St Helens **2D 42**

H

Hackett Av. L20: Boot 5D **20**
Hackett Pl. L20: Boot 5D **20**
Hackins Hey L2: Liv 3C **4** (5C **52**)
Hackthorpe St. L5: Liv 6E **35**
Hadassah Gro. L17: Aig 5A **72**
Hadden Cl. L35: Rainh 3G **59**
Haddock St. L20: Kirkd 4B **34**
Haddon Av. L9: Walt 5F **21**
Haddon Dr. CH61: Pens 1D **100**
WA8: Wid 5H **77**
Haddon Rd. CH42: Rock F 1A **88**
Haddon Wlk. L12: Crox 2A **38**
Hadfield Av. CH47: Hoy 2C **64**
Hadfield Cl. WA8: Wid 2A **98**
Hadfield Gro. L25: Woolt 6E **75**
Hadleigh Cl. WA5: Gt San 4F **81**
Hadleigh Gro. WA7: Cas 3B **114**
Hadleigh Rd. L32: Kirkb 2B **24**
Hadley Av. CH62: Brom 4C **104**
Haggerston Rd. L4: Walt 3G **35**
Hahnemann Rd. L4: Walt 3E **35**
Haig Av. CH46: More 1D **66**
Haigh Cl. WA9: St H 2D **60**
Haigh Cres. L31: Lyd 3B **6**
Haigh Rd. L22: Water 2G **19**
Haigh St. L3: Liv 3F **53**
(not continuous)
Haig Rd. WA8: Wid 2E **97**
Haileybury Av. L10: Ain 1B **22**
Haileybury Rd. L25: Woolt 3D **92**
Hailsham Rd. L19: Aig 3D **90**
Halby Rd. L9: Ain 5H **21**
Halcombe Rd. L12: W Der 5H **37**
Halcyon Rd. CH41: Birke 5E **69**
Haldane Av. CH41: Birke 2B **68**
Haldane Rd. L4: Walt 3G **35**
HALE **4D 110**
HALE BANK **6H 95**
Halebank Rd. WA8: Hale B 6E **95**
Hale Bank Ter. WA8: Hale B 1G **111**
Hale Ct. WA8: Hale B 1G **111**
Hale Dr. L24: Speke 3F **109**
Halefield St. WA10: St H 1D **42**
(not continuous)
Hale Ga. Rd. WA8: Hale B 3F **111**
Hale Gro. WA5: Gt San 3H **81**
HALE HEATH **3A 110**
Hale M. WA8: Wid 4A **96**
Hale Rd. CH45: Wall 1E **51**
L4: Walt 4E **35**
L24: Speke 2D **108**
(not continuous)
WA8: Hale B, Wid 1H **111**
WA8: Wid 4A **96**
Hale Rd. Ind. Est. WA8: Hale B 6H **95**
Hale St. L2: Liv 3D **4** (5C **52**)
Hale Vw. WA7: Run 5C **112**
Hale Vw. Rd. L36: Huy 5A **58**
HALEWOOD **4H 93**
Halewood Caravan Pk.
L26: Halew 3C **94**
Halewood Centre, The L26: Halew 4H **93**
Halewood Cl. L25: Gate 5D **74**

A-Z Liverpool 165

Halewood Dr. L25: Woolt 1D 92	HALTON LODGE 5G 113	Hanlon Av. L20: Boot 5D 20
(Kings Dr.)	Halton Lodge Av. WA7: Run 6H 113	(off Ainsdale Rd.)
L25: Woolt 1E 93	Halton Miniature Railway 6D 114	Hanmer Rd. L32: Kirkb 1F 23
(Layton Rd.)	Halton Rd. CH45: Wall 1C 50	Hannah Cl. CH61: Pens 2C 100
HALEWOOD GREEN 1G 93	L31: Lyd 4C 6	Hannan Rd. L6: Liv 4A 54
Halewood Leisure Cen. 4A 94	WA5: Gt San 3H 81	Hanns Hall Rd. CH64: Nest, Will ...6F 119
Halewood Pl. L25: Woolt 6E 75	WA7: Run 3F 113	Hanover Cl. CH43: Clau 3B 68
Halewood Rd. L25: Gate, Woolt ...5D 74	Halton Sta. Rd. WA7: Sut W 4B 124	Hanover Ct. WA7: Brook 1D 124
Halewood Station (Rail) 3H 93	Halton St. WA11: Hay 5G 31	Hanover St. L1: Liv 6E 5 (6D 52)
Halewood Triangle Country Pk. ...3F 93	HALTON VIEW 2H 97	Hansard St. WA9: St H 6B 42
Halewood Triangle Vis. Cen. 3F 93	Halton Vw. Rd. WA8: Wid 2G 97	Hansby Dr. L24: Speke 6D 92
Halewood Way L25: Woolt 1E 93	HALTON VILLAGE 5B 114	Hanson Pk. CH43: Oxton 4A 68
Haley Rd. Nth. WA5: Burtw 1G 63	Halton Wlk. L25: Gate 3C 74	Hanson Rd. L9: Ain 6A 22
Haley Rd. Sth. WA5: Burtw 2G 63	(off Hartsbourne Av.)	Hanson Rd. Bus. Pk. L9: Ain 6A 22
Half Crown St. L5: Kirkd 1C 52	Halton Wood L32: Kirkb 6F 13	Hans Rd. L4: Walt 4G 35
Halfpenny Cl. L19: Gras 4F 91	Hambledon Dr. CH49: Grea 5A 66	Hanwell St. L6: Liv 1H 53
Half-Tide Wharf L3: Liv 2C 70	Hamble Dr. WA5: Penk 6H 81	Hanworth Cl. L12: Crox 2A 38
Halidon Ct. L20: Boot 1A 34	Hambleton Cl. L11: Crox 1F 37	Hapsford Rd. L21: Lith 5B 20
Halifax Cres. L23: Thorn 3B 10	WA8: Wid 6A 78	Hapton St. L5: Liv 1E 53
Halkirk Rd. L18: Aller 2G 91	Hamblett Cres. WA11: St H 5F 29	Harbern Cl. L12: W Der 1H 55
Halkyn Av. L17: Liv 3B 72	Hamer St. WA10: St H 1D 42	Harbord Rd. L22: Water 2E 19
Halkyn Dr. L5: Liv 2G 53	Hamer St. Sth. WA10: St H 2D 42	Harbord St. L7: Liv 6H 53
Hallam Wlk. L7: Liv 6A 54	(off Nth. John St.)	Harbord Ter. L22: Water 2E 19
(off Crosfield Rd.)	Hamil Cl. CH47: Meols 6E 47	Harborne Dr. CH63: Spit 3H 103
Hall Av. WA8: Wid 2G 95	Hamilton Cl. CH64: Park 5F 117	Harbour Cl. WA7: Murd 1F 125
Hall Dr. CH49: Grea 6A 66	Hamilton Ct. L23: Blun 5D 8	Harbour Dr. L19: Garst 1G 107
L32: Kirkb 6A 14	Hamilton Ho. L3: Liv 2D 4	Harbreck Gro. L9: Ain 2B 36
Hall La. L7: Liv 5G 53	Hamilton La. CH41: Birke 2G 69	Harcourt Av. CH44: Wall 4G 51
L9: Ain 4H 21	Hamilton Plaza CH41: Birke 3H 69	Harcourt St. CH41: Birke 2E 69
L31: Mag 2A 12	(off Duncan St.)	L4: Kirkd 6D 34
L32: Kirkb 1H 23	Hamilton Rd. CH45: New B 5C 32	Hardie Av. CH46: More 6A 48
L33: Sim 2B 14	L5: Liv 2F 53	Hardie Cl. WA9: Sut M 4E 61
L34: Presc 2D 58	WA10: Windle 5A 28	Hardie Rd. L36: Huy 4A 58
L35: Cron, Rainh 1A 78	Hamilton Sq. CH41: Birke 2H 69	Harding Av. CH63: Beb 1H 103
L36: Huy 5H 57	Hamilton Square Station (Rail) 2H 69	Harding Cl. L5: Liv 2G 53
WA5: Burtw 6H 45	Hamilton St. CH41: Birke 3G 69	Hardinge Rd. L19: Aller 3G 91
WA8: Cron 2A 78	(not continuous)	Hardknott Rd. CH62: Brom 4E 105
WA9: Bold 4B 62	Hamlet Ct. L17: Aig 6A 72	Hard La. WA10: St H 5B 28
Hall Nook WA5: Penk 5H 81	Hamlet Rd. CH45: Wall 1B 50	Hardman St. L1: Liv 6H 5 (1E 71)
Hall Pk. L23: Blun 5D 8	Hamlin Cl. WA7: West 1E 123	Hardshaw Cen. WA10: St H 2E 43
Hall Rd. WA11: Hay 4G 31	Hamlin Rd. L19: Garst 5H 91	Hardshaw St. WA10: St H 2E 43
Hall Rd. E. L23: Blun 3D 8	Hammersley Av. WA9: Clock F 4G 61	Hardwick Rd. WA7: Ast 2H 113
Hall Road Station (Rail) 3C 8	Hammersley St. WA9: Clock F 4G 61	Hardy St. L1: Liv 2E 71
Hall Rd. W. L23: Blun 3C 8	Hammersmith Way WA8: Wid 5H 79	L19: Garst 1H 107
Hallsands Rd. L32: Kirkb 3A 24	Hammill Av. WA10: St H 5C 28	Harebell Cl. WA8: Wid 5C 78
Hallside Cl. L19: Aig 3E 91	Hammill St. WA10: St H 6B 28	Harebell St. L5: Kirkd 6D 34
Hall St. WA9: Clock F 4H 61	Hammond Rd. L33: Know I 6E 15	Hare Cft. L28: Stockb V 5B 38
WA10: St H 2E 43	Hammond St. WA9: St H 3H 43	Harefield Grn. L24: Speke 2F 109
Hall Ter. WA5: Gt San 2G 81	Hamnett Rd. L34: Presc 6E 41	Harefield Rd. L24: Speke 3F 109
Halltine Cl. L23: Blun 4C 8	Hampden Gro. CH42: Tran 5G 69	HARESFINCH 4F 29
Hallville Rd. CH44: Wall 4E 51	Hampden Rd. CH42: Tran 5F 69	Haresfinch Cl. L26: Halew 2A 94
L18: Moss H 4E 73	Hampden St. L4: Walt 3F 35	Haresfinch Rd. WA11: St H 5F 29
Hall Wood Av. WA11: Hay 3H 31	Hampshire Av. L30: N'ton 6C 10	Haresfinch Vw. WA11: St H 5F 29
Hallwood Cl. WA7: Run 1F 123	Hampshire Gdns. WA10: St H 3D 42	Harewell Rd. L11: Norr G 4E 37
Hallwood Link Rd. WA7: Pal F 1B 124	Hampson Cl. L6: Liv 2A 54	Harewood Cl. L36: Huy 4G 57
HALLWOOD PARK 1A 124	Hampson St. L6: Liv 4A 54	Harewood Rd. CH45: New B 6C 32
Hallwood Pk. Av. WA7: Pal F 1A 124	Hampstead Rd. CH44: Wall 4E 51	Harewood St. L6: Liv 3G 53
Halsall Cl. L23: Crosb 4G 9	L6: Liv 4A 54	Harford Cl. WA5: Penk 5H 81
WA7: Brook 2E 125	Hampton Chase CH43: Noct 4H 67	Hargate Rd. L33: Kirkb 1B 24
Halsall Grn. CH63: Spit 4B 104	Hampton Ct. WA8: Wid 6A 80	Hargate Wlk. L33: Kirkb 1B 24
Halsall Rd. L20: Boot 5C 20	Hampton Ct. WA7: Manor P 1E 115	Hargrave Av. CH43: Oxton 6A 68
Halsall St. L34: Presc 6D 40	Hampton Ct. Rd. L12: W Der 2H 55	Hargrave Cl. CH43: Oxton 6A 68
Halsbury Rd. CH45: Wall 1D 50	Hampton Ct. Way WA8: Wid 5H 79	Hargrave La. CH64: Will 2H 119
L6: Liv 4A 54	Hampton Dr. WA8: Cron 4A 78	Hargreaves Ct. WA8: Wid 2H 97
Halsey Av. L12: W Der 6D 36	Hampton Pl. WA11: St H 5F 29	Hargreaves Ho. WA8: Wid 2H 97
Halsey Cres. L12: W Der 6D 36	Hampton St. L8: Liv 2F 71	(off Hargreaves Ct.)
Halsnead Av. L35: Whis 6C 58	Hanbury Rd. L4: Walt 5B 36	Hargreaves Rd. L17: Aig 6A 72
Halsnead Caravan Est. L35: Whis ...6E 59	Handel Ct. L8: Liv 3H 71	Hargreaves St. WA9: St H 1A 44
Halsnead Cl. L15: Wav 6E 55	Handel Rd. L27: N'ley 3E 75	Harkbridge Dr. L7: Liv 1H 71
Halstead Rd. CH44: Wall 4E 51	Handfield Pl. L5: Liv 2G 53	Harker St. L3: Liv 1G 5 (4E 53)
WA5: Penk 5F 21	Handfield Rd. L22: Water 2F 19	Harland Grn. L24: Speke 2H 109
Halstead Wlk. L32: Kirkb 2G 23	Handfield St. L5: Liv 2G 53	Harland Rd. CH42: Tran 5F 69
(off Downgreen Cl.)	Handford Av. CH62: East 2F 121	Harlech Ct. CH63: Beb 1H 103
HALTON 6B 114	Handforth La. WA7: Run 1H 123	Harlech Gro. WA7: Cas 3B 114
HALTON BROOK 5A 114	Handley Ct. L19: Aig 3D 90	Harlech Rd. L23: Blun 6E 9
Halton Brook Av. WA7: Run 5H 113	Handley St. WA7: Run 2D 112	Harlech St. CH44: Wall 5G 51
Halton Brow WA7: Halt 4A 114	Hands St. L21: Lith 5B 20	L4: Kirkd, Walt 4E 35
Halton Castle 4B 114	Hanford Av. L9: Walt 5F 21	Harleston Rd. L33: Kirkb 6C 14
Halton Ct. WA7: Run 3H 113	Hanging Birches WA8: Wid 4D 78	Harleston Wlk. L33: Kirkb 6C 14
Halton Cres. CH49: Grea 6H 65	Hankey Dr. L20: Boot 6E 21	Harley Av. CH63: Hghr B 3E 87
Halton Hey L35: Whis 6D 58	Hankey St. WA7: Run 3D 112	Harley St. L9: Walt 5G 21
HALTON LEA 6B 114	Hankinson St. L13: Liv 6E 55	Harlian Av. CH46: More 2B 66
Halton Lea Shop. Cen. WA7: Pal F ..6B 114	Hanley Cl. WA8: Wid 2A 96	Harlow Cl. WA9: St H 6D 42
Halton Link Rd. WA7: Pal F 5A 114	Hanley Rd. WA8: Wid 2A 96	Harlow St. L8: Liv 5E 71

Harlyn Cl. L26: Halew 5G 93
Harlyn Gdns. WA5: Penk 6F 81
Harmony Way L13: Liv 6E 55
Haroldene Gro. L34: Presc 2H 57
Harold Newgrass Dr.
   L19: Garst .6F 91
Harold Rd. WA11: Hay 4H 31
Harper Rd. L9: Walt 1G 35
Harpers Pond La. L15: Wav 1E 73
Harper St. L6: Liv 5G 53
Harps Cft. L30: N'ton 6C 10
Harptree Cl. L35: Whis 4E 59
Harradon Rd. L9: Ain 4H 21
Harrier Dr. L26: Halew 2G 93
Harringay Av. L18: Moss H 4D 72
Harrington Av. CH47: Hoy 2C 64
Harrington Rd. L3: Liv 5E 71
   L21: Lith .2D 20
   L23: Crosb 5F 9
   L36: Huy .3D 56
Harrington St. L2: Liv 4D 4 (6C 52)
Harrington Vw. CH44: Wall 2F 51
   (off Greenwood La.)
Harris Cl. CH63: Spit 3A 104
Harris Dr. L30: Boot 5C 20
   L30: Boot .4D 20
Harris Gdns. WA9: St H 4F 43
Harrismith Rd. L10: Faz 4D 22
Harrison Dr. CH45: Wall 6A 32
   L20: Boot .2E 35
   WA11: Hay 5C 30
   WA11: Rainf 1F 17
Harrison Hey L36: Huy 6G 57
Harrison St. WA8: Hale B 5H 95
Harrison's Yd. CH62: East 1F 121
Harrison Way L3: Liv 5E 71
   WA10: St H 1C 42
Harrocks Cl. L30: N'ton 4D 10
Harrock Wood Cl. CH61: Irby 5C 84
Harrogate Cl. CH62: East 3D 120
Harrogate Dr. L5: Liv 2F 53
Harrogate Rd. CH42: Rock F 3A 88
   CH62: East 3D 120
Harrogate Wlk. CH42: Rock F 3A 88
Harron Cl. L32: Kirkb 1G 23
Harrop Rd. WA7: Run 4F 113
Harrops Cft. L30: N'ton 5E 11
Harrowby Cl. L8: Liv 2G 71
Harrowby Rd. CH42: Tran 5E 69
   CH44: Wall 3G 51
   L21: Sea .4H 19
Harrowby Rd. Sth. CH42: Tran 5E 69
Harrowby St. L8: Liv 2G 71
   (Granby St.)
   L8: Liv 2G 71
   (Park Way)
Harrow Cl. CH44: Wall 2B 50
   L30: N'ton 1F 21
Harrow Dr. L10: Ain 1B 22
   WA7: Run 3A 114
Harrow Gro. CH62: Brom 5E 105
Harrow Rd. CH44: Wall 2B 50
   L4: Walt 1H 53
Hartdale Rd. L18: Moss H 5E 73
   L23: Thorn 3A 10
Hartford Cl. CH43: Oxton 6B 68
Harthill Av. L18: Moss H 5F 73
Harthill M. CH43: Bid 6G 49
Harthill Rd. L18: Moss H 4G 73
Hartington Av. CH41: Birke 3D 68
Hartington Rd. CH44: Wall 3D 50
   L8: Liv 3A 72
   L12: W Der 1G 55
   L19: Garst 5G 91
   WA10: St H 6A 28
Hartington Ter. L19: Garst 5F 91
   (off St Mary's Rd.)
Hartismere Rd. CH44: Wall 4F 51
Hartland Cl. WA8: Wid 4E 79
Hartland Gdns. WA9: St H 1B 60
Hartland Rd. L11: Norr G 3C 36
Hartley Av. L9: Ain 6H 21
Hartley Cl. L4: Walt 6F 35

Hartley Gro. L33: Kirkb 4B 14
   WA10: St H 5A 42
Hartley Quay L3: Liv 6C 4 (1C 70)
HARTLEY'S VILLAGE 6H 21
Hartley's Village L9: Ain 6H 21
Hartnup St. L5: Liv 1G 53
   (Adkins St.)
   L5: Liv 1F 53
   (Mycroft Cl.)
Hartnup Way CH43: Bid 2G 67
Harton Cl. WA8: Wid 6C 78
Hartopp Rd. L25: Gate 3C 74
Hartopp Wlk. L25: Gate 2C 74
   (off Hartopp Rd.)
Hartor Cl. L5: Liv 1E 53
   (not continuous)
Hartsbourne Av. L25: Gate 1B 74
   (not continuous)
Hartsbourne Cl. L25: Gate 2B 74
Hartsbourne Wlk. L25: Gate 2C 74
Hart St. L3: Liv 3H 5 (5E 53)
Hartwell St. L21: Lith 5B 20
Hartwood Cl. L32: Kirkb 4B 24
Hartwood Rd. L32: Kirkb 4B 24
Hartwood Sq. L32: Kirkb 4B 24
Harty Rd. WA11: Hay 6C 30
Harvard Cl. WA7: Wind H 3F 115
Harvard Gro. L34: Presc 6E 41
Harvest Ct. CH46: More 6C 48
Harvester Way CH49: Grea 5A 66
   L30: N'ton 5G 11
Harvest La. CH46: More 6B 48
Harvest Way WA9: Clock F 3G 61
Harvey Av. CH49: Grea 6B 66
   WA12: Newt W 2H 45
Harvey Rd. CH45: Wall 1C 50
   CH46: Leas 5E 49
Harwich Gro. L16: Child 1B 74
Harwood Rd. L19: Garst 5H 91
Harworth Rd. WA9: St H 2C 60
Haselbeech Cl. L11: Norr G 2D 36
Haselbeech Cres.
   L11: Norr G 2D 36
Hasfield Rd. L11: Norr G 3F 37
Haslemere L35: Whis 4F 59
Haslemere Dr. WA5: Penk 5F 81
Haslemere Rd. L25: Gate 3D 74
Haslemere Way L25: Gate 2C 74
Haslingden Cl. L13: Liv 1F 55
Haslington Gro. L26: Halew 5A 94
Hassal Rd. CH42: Rock F 3A 88
Hastie Cl. L27: N'ley 4G 75
Hastings Dr. L36: Huy 1A 76
Hastings Rd. L22: Water 1D 18
Haswell Dr. L28: Stockb V 5C 38
Hatchmere Cl. CH43: Oxton 6B 68
Hatfield Cl. L12: Crox 2B 38
   WA9: St H 6D 42
Hatfield Gdns. L36: Huy 6H 57
Hatfield Rd. L20: Boot 2E 35
Hathaway Cl. L25: Gate 3C 74
Hathaway Cl. L25: Gate 3C 74
Hathaway Rd. L25: Gate 3C 74
Hatherley Av. L23: Crosb 1G 19
Hatherley Cl. L8: Liv 2G 71
   (not continuous)
Hatherley St. CH44: Wall 5G 51
   L8: Liv 2G 71
Hathersage Rd. L36: Huy 2G 57
Hatherton Gro. L26: Halew 5A 94
Hatton Av. CH62: East 4E 121
Hatton Cl. CH60: Hesw 4B 100
Hatton Gdn. L3: Liv 2D 4 (5C 52)
Hatton Gdn. Ind. Est.
   L3: Liv 2E 5
Hatton Hill Rd. L21: Lith 2A 20
Hattons La. L16: Child 3G 73
Hauxwell Gro. WA11: St H 5G 29
Havannah La. WA9: St H 2D 44
Havelock Cl. WA10: St H 2D 42
Havelock Rd. L20: Boot 5C 20
Haven Rd. L10: Faz 3D 22
Haven Wlk. L31: Lyd 3B 6
Havergal St. WA7: Run 4D 112

Haverstock Rd. L6: Liv 4B 54
Haverton Wlk. L12: Crox 2A 38
   (not continuous)
Hawarden Av. CH43: Oxton 3E 69
   CH44: Wall 3E 51
   L17: Liv 3C 72
Hawarden Ct. CH63: Beb 1H 103
Hawarden Gro. L21: Sea 5A 20
Hawdon Ct. L7: Liv 1A 72
Hawes Av. WA11: St H 3G 29
Haweswater Av. WA11: Hay 5C 30
Haweswater Cl. L33: Kirkb 4H 13
   WA7: Beech 2C 124
Haweswater Gro. L31: Mag 5E 7
Hawgreen Rd. L32: Kirkb 1F 23
Hawick Cl. L33: Kirkb 3H 13
Hawke Grn. L35: Tar G 2A 76
Hawke St. L3: Liv 4G 5 (6E 53)
Hawkesworth St. L4: Walt 1G 53
Hawkhurst Cl. L8: Liv 5F 71
Hawkhurst Dr. CH42: Rock F 2A 88
Hawkins Rd. CH64: Nest 6A 118
Hawkins St. L6: Liv 4H 53
Hawks Ct. WA7: Pal F 1A 124
Hawkshead Av. L12: W Der 4G 37
Hawkshead Cl. L31: Mag 5D 6
   WA7: Beech 2C 124
Hawkshead Dr. L21: Lith 3D 20
Hawkshead Rd. CH62: Brom 4E 105
   WA5: Burtw 1G 63
Hawksmoor Cl. L10: Faz 4E 23
Hawksmoor Rd. L10: Faz 5E 23
Hawkstone Ct. CH49: Upton 3B 66
Hawkstone St. L8: Liv 4G 71
   (not continuous)
Hawkstone Wlk. L8: Liv 5G 71
   (off Hawkstone St.)
Hawks Way CH60: Hesw 5C 100
Haworth Dr. L20: Boot 4D 20
Hawthorn Av. WA7: Run 4E 113
   WA8: Wid 1F 97
Hawthorn Cl. WA11: Hay 6C 30
Hawthorn Dr. CH48: W Kir 1E 83
   CH61: Hesw 2D 100
   WA10: Eccl 1H 41
Hawthorne Av. L26: Halew 5G 93
   WA5: Gt San 3H 81
Hawthorne Ct. L21: Lith 3B 20
   (off Sefton Rd.)
Hawthorne Dr. CH64: Will 6B 120
   L33: Kirkb 6B 14
Hawthorne Gro. CH44: Wall 5G 51
Hawthorne Rd. CH42: Tran 6F 69
   L20: Boot 6D 20
   L21: Lith .3B 20
   WA6: Frod 6F 123
   WA9: Sut L 1H 61
Hawthornes, The CH42: Rock F 2A 88
Hawthorn Gro. L12: W Der 1F 55
Hawthorn La. CH62: Brom 5D 104
Hawthorn Rd. CH64: Park 5F 117
   L34: Presc 1E 59
   L36: Roby 5E 57
Haxted Gdns. L19: Garst 5H 91
Haydn Rd. L14: Knott A 1B 56
HAYDOCK 5E 31
Haydock Cross WA11: Hay 2H 31
Haydock Ind. Est. WA11: Hay 3G 31
Haydock La. WA11: Hay 5E 31
   (not continuous)
Haydock La. Ind. Est. WA11: Hay . . .3H 31
Haydock Leisure Cen. 5D 30
Haydock Pk. Rd. L10: Ain 6C 12
Haydock Rd. CH45: Wall 6E 33
Haydock St. WA10: St H 2E 43
   WA12: Newt W 1H 45
Hayes Av. L35: Presc 2E 59
Hayes Cres. WA6: Frod 6G 123
Hayes Dr. L31: Mell 6F 13
Hayes St. WA10: St H 5A 42
Hayfield Cl. L26: Halew 2A 94
Hayfield Pl. CH46: More 1E 67
Hayfield St. L4: Walt 6F 35
Hayfield Way WA9: Clock F 3G 61

Hayles Cl. L25: Gate 3C 74
Hayles Grn. L25: Gate 3C 74
Hayles Gro. L25: Gate 3C 74
Hayling Ho. L19: Aig 4D 90
Haylock Cl. L8: Liv 5F 71
Haymans Cl. L12: W Der 6E 37
Haymans Grn. L12: W Der 6E 37
    L31: Mag 6D 6
Haymans Gro. L12: W Der 6E 37
Haywood Cres.
    WA7: Wind H 3F 115
Haywood Gdns. WA10: St H 3B 42
Haywood Rd. L28: Stockb V 5D 38
Hazel Av. L32: Kirkb 6G 13
    L35: Whis .4E 59
    WA7: Run 5C 112
Hazel Bus. Pk. WA11: Rainf 5H 17
Hazel Ct. L8: Liv 5G 71
    (off Byles St.)
    L20: Boot .3C 34
Hazeldale Rd. L9: Walt 1G 35
Hazeldene Av. CH45: Wall 2C 50
    CH61: Thing 5F 85
Hazeldene Way
    CH61: Thing 5F 85
Hazelfield Ct. WA9: Clock F 3G 61
Hazel Gro. CH61: Irby 4B 84
    CH63: Hghr B 1G 103
    L9: Ain 5H 21
    L23: Crosb .6H 9
    L32: Kirkb 3B 24
    WA10: St H 2A 42
Hazelhurst Rd. L4: Walt 6H 35
Hazelmere Ho. L17: Aig 1B 90
    (off Mossley Hill Dr.)
Hazel M. L31: Mell 6F 13
Hazel Rd. CH41: Birke 4F 69
    CH47: Hoy 2C 64
    L36: Huy .2H 57
Hazelslack Rd. L11: Norr G 3E 37
Hazelwood CH49: Grea 4B 66
Hazelwood Cl. WA8: Wid 3G 95
    WA9: Sut M 4F 61
Hazelwood Gro. L26: Halew 1F 93
Hazleton Rd. L14: Knott A 4G 55
Headbolt La. L33: Kirkb 5A 14
Headbourne Cl. L25: Gate 2B 74
Headbourne Ct. L25: Gate 2B 74
    (off Headbourne Cl.)
Head Farm Ct. WA12: Newt W 2H 45
Headingley Cl. L36: Roby 1E 75
    WA9: St H 1G 61
Headington Rd. CH49: Upton 4B 66
Headland Cl. CH48: W Kir 3B 82
Headley Cl. WA10: St H 2D 42
Head St. L8: Liv 3E 71
Heald St. L19: Garst 5G 91
    WA12: Newt W 2H 45
Healy Cl. L27: N'ley 5A 76
Hearne Rd. WA10: St H 1B 42
Hearts Health Club
    Great Crosby 4F 9
Hearts Ladies Health Club
    Wallasey .3C 50
Heartwood Cl. L9: Walt 4G 21
    CH61: Irby 4A 84
Heathbank Av. CH44: Wall 4C 50
    CH61: Irby 4A 84
Heathbank Rd. CH42: Tran 6F 69
Heath Business & Technical Park, The
    WA7: West 6E 113
Heath Cl. CH48: W Kir 3B 82
    L25: Woolt 4B 74
    L32: Kirkb .6F 41
Heathcote Cl. L7: Liv 1A 72
Heathcote Gdns. CH63: Beb 6H 87
Heathcote Rd. L4: Walt 3F 35
Heathdale CH63: Beb 2H 103
Heath Dr. CH49: Upton 4E 67
    CH60: Hesw 4D 100
    WA7: West 6E 113
Heather Bank CH63: Hghr B 5F 87
Heather Brae L34: Presc 2A 58
    WA12: Newt W 1H 45
Heather Brow CH43: Clau 2B 68

Heather Cl. CH46: More 6A 48
    L4: Walt 5F 35
    L33: Kirkb .5A 14
    (off Heathfield Dr.)
    WA7: Beech 3A 124
Heather Ct. L4: Walt 5F 35
    (off Tetlow St.)
Heatherdale Cl. CH42: Tran 5E 69
Heatherdale Rd. L18: Moss H 5E 73
Heather Dene CH62: Brom 2D 104
Heatherdene Rd. CH48: W Kir 6B 64
Heatherfield Ct. CH42: Tran 5E 69
    (off Victoria Flds.)
Heathergreen Ct. L4: Walt 4H 35
Heatherleigh CH48: Caldy 5D 82
    WA9: St H 1A 60
Heatherleigh Cl. L9: Walt 4G 21
Heather Rd. CH60: Hesw 4E 101
    CH63: Hghr B 1F 103
Heathers Cft. L30: N'ton 6E 11
Heather Way L23: Thorn 3B 10
Heathfield CH62: Brom 3D 104
Heathfield Av. WA9: St H 5C 42
Heathfield Cl. L21: Lith 5C 20
Heathfield Dr. L20: Boot 5C 20
    L33: Kirkb .5A 14
Heathfield Gdns. WA7: Run 5E 113
Heathfield Ho. CH61: Thing 5E 85
Heathfield Pk. WA8: Wid 6B 78
Heathfield Rd. CH43: Oxton 5E 69
    CH63: Beb 6H 87
    L15: Wav 3E 73
    L22: Water 1E 19
    L31: Mag .1D 12
Heathfield St. L1: Liv 5G 5 (6E 53)
    (not continuous)
Heathgate Av. L24: Speke 3H 109
Heath Hey L25: Woolt 4B 74
Heathland Rd. WA9: Clock F 3G 61
Heath La. CH64: Will 6C 120
Heathmoor Rd. CH46: More 6B 48
Heath Pk. Gro. WA7: Run 5D 112
Heath Rd. CH63: Beb, Hghr B 6G 87
    L19: Aller .3G 91
    L36: Huy 2E 57
    WA5: Penk 4H 81
    WA7: Run 5E 113
    WA8: Wid .1B 96
Heath Rd. Cres. WA7: Run 5F 113
Heath Rd. Sth. WA7: Run, West 2D 122
Heathside CH60: Hesw 4A 100
Heath Vw. L21: Ford 6B 10
Heathview Cl. WA8: Hale B 6G 95
Heathview Rd. WA8: Hale B 1G 111
Heathwaite Cres. L11: Norr G 4E 37
Heathway CH60: Hesw 6F 101
Heathwood L12: W Der 2F 55
Heatley Cl. CH43: Bid 2C 67
Heaton Cl. L24: Speke 2H 109
Hebburn Way L12: Crox 2C 38
Hebden Pde. L11: Norr G 2G 37
Hebden Rd. L11: Norr G 2F 37
Hedgebank Cl. L9: Ain 3B 22
Hedgecote L32: Kirkb 4A 24
Hedgecroft L23: Thorn 3C 10
Hedgefield Rd. L25: Gate 4D 74
Hedgehey Wall WA7: Cas 4C 114
Hedgerows, The WA11: Hay 4H 31
Hedges Cres. L11: Norr G 6C 36
Hedingham Cl. L26: Halew 2A 94
Hedworth Gdns. WA9: St H 1B 60
Heigham Gdns. WA9: St H 1C 60
Helena Rd. WA9: St H 6B 44
Helena St. CH41: Birke 4G 69
    L7: Liv 6H 53
    L9: Walt 2F 35
Helen Bank Dr. WA11: Rainf 1F 17
Helen Ho. L8: Liv 2A 72
    (off Birley Ct.)

Helmingham Gro. CH41: Tran 5G 69
Helmsley Rd. L26: Halew 4H 93
Helsby Av. CH62: East 4F 121
Helsby Ct. L34: Presc 2D 58
Helsby Rd. L9: Ain 4H 21
Helsby St. L7: Liv 6G 53
    WA9: St H 4A 44
Helston Av. L26: Halew 2H 93
    WA11: St H 4H 29
Helston Cl. WA5: Penk 4G 81
    WA7: Brook 2D 124
Helston Grn. L36: Huy 4B 58
Helston Rd. L11: Crox 6H 23
Helton Cl. CH43: Noct 6A 68
Hemans St. L20: Boot 1A 34
Hemer Ter. L20: Boot 6A 20
Hemingford St. CH41: Birke 3F 69
Hemlock Cl. L12: Crox 2H 37
Hemmingsway L35: Rainh 4G 59
Hempstead Cl. WA9: St H 6D 42
Henbury Pl. WA7: Run 1F 123
Henderson Cl. CH49: Upton 3B 66
    WA5: Gt San 3F 81
Henderson Dr. WA11: Rainf 1G 17
Henderson Rd. L36: Huy 4A 58
    WA8: Wid .3D 96
Hendon Rd. L6: Liv 3B 54
Hendon Wlk. CH49: Grea 6A 66
Hengest Cl. L33: Kirkb 3A 14
Henglers Cl. L6: Liv 4G 53
Henley Av. L21: Lith 3A 20
Henley Cl. CH63: Spit 3A 104
Henley Ct. WA7: Run 3H 113
    WA10: St H 4B 42
Henley Ho. L19: Aig 4D 90
Henley Rd. L18: Moss H 4F 73
Henllan Gdns. WA9: St H 6B 44
Henlow Av. L32: Kirkb 3B 24
Henna Way L11: Norr G 4E 37
Hennawood Cl. L6: Liv 2H 53
Henrietta Gro. L34: Presc 2H 57
Henry Edward St. L3: Liv 1E 5 (4D 52)
Henry Hickman Cl. L30: N'ton 5F 11
Henry St. CH41: Birke 3G 69
    L1: Liv 6E 5 (1D 70)
    L13: Liv 5D 54
    WA8: Wid .2G 97
    WA10: St H 1D 42
Henthorne Rd. CH62: New F 3B 88
Henthorne St. CH43: Oxton 4E 69
Herald Av. L24: Speke 5B 92
Herald Cl. L11: Crox 2G 37
Heralds Cl. WA8: Wid 3H 95
Herbarth Cl. L9: Walt 2F 35
Herberts La. CH60: Hesw 5D 100
Herbert St. WA5: Burtw 1G 63
    WA9: St H 6A 44
Herbert Taylor Cl. L6: Liv 2A 54
Herbie Higgins Cl. L8: Liv 3G 71
Herculaneum Ct. L8: Liv 6F 71
Herculaneum Rd. L8: Liv 5E 71
Hercules Dr. L24: Speke 2B 108
Herdman Cl. L25: Gate 4D 74
Hereford Av. CH49: Upton 3C 66
Hereford Cl. WA10: St H 3D 42
Hereford Dr. L30: N'ton 2F 21
Hereford Rd. L15: Wav 3E 73
    L21: Sea 4G 19
Heriot St. L5: Kirkd 1D 52
    (not continuous)
Hermes Cl. L30: Boot 3E 21
    (off Atlantic Way)
Hermes Rd. L11: Crox 5F 23
Hermitage, The CH60: Hesw 6D 100
    (off School Hill)
Hermitage Gro. L20: Boot 4D 20
Herm Rd. L5: Liv 2C 52
Heron Bus. Pk. WA8: Wid 3H 97
Heron Cl. WA7: Nort 5F 115
Heron Ct. L26: Halew 2G 93
Herondale Rd. L18: Moss H 5E 73
Heron Gro. WA11: Rainf 4H 17
Heronhall Rd. L9: Faz 1D 36
Heronpark Way CH63: Spit 3B 104

Heron Rd. CH47: Meols 2F **65**
 CH48: W Kir 2F **65**
Herons Cl. L31: Lyd 3A **6**
Herons Way WA7: Nort 1H **115**
Hero St. L20: Boot 3D **34**
Herrick St. L13: Liv 4D **54**
Herschell St. L15: Liv 1G **53**
Hertford Cl. L26: Halew 4H **93**
Hertford Dr. CH45: Wall 1E **51**
Hertford Rd. L20: Boot 3C **34**
Hertford St. WA9: St H 3H **43**
Hesketh Av. CH42: Rock F 2F **87**
Hesketh Cl. WA5: Penk 5H **81**
Hesketh Ct. WA11: Rainf 5G **17**
Hesketh Dr. CH60: Hesw 4E **101**
 L31: Mag 6E **7**
Hesketh Rd. L24: Hale 4E **111**
Hesketh St. L17: Aig 5A **72**
Hesketh Wlk. CH62: Brom 2C **104**
Hesketh Way CH62: Brom 2C **104**
Heskin Cl. L31: Lyd 3C **6**
 L32: Kirkb 4A **24**
 L35: Rainh 4H **59**
Heskin Rd. L32: Kirkb 4A **24**
Heskin Wlk. L32: Kirkb 4A **24**
Hessle Dr. CH60: Hesw 6D **100**
Hesslewell Ct. CH60: Hesw 4E **101**
HESWALL 5E **101**
Heswall Av. CH63: Hghr B 3E **87**
 WA9: Clock F 3F **61**
Heswall Dales Local Nature Reserve
 . . . . .4C **100**
Heswall Golf Course 2E **117**
Heswall Mt. CH61: Thing 6E **85**
Heswall Point CH60: Hesw 5E **101**
Heswall Rd. L9: Ain 4H **21**
Heswall Station (Rail) 5H **101**
Hever Dr. L26: Halew 2H **93**
Heward Av. WA9: St H 1G **61**
Hewitson Av. L13: Liv 1D **54**
Hewitson Rd. L13: Liv 1D **54**
Hewitt Av. WA10: St H 1A **42**
Hewitt's La. L33: Kirkb 5F **25**
 L34: Know 5F **25**
Hewitts Pl. L2: Liv 3D **4**
      (off Vernon St.)
Hexagon, The L20: Boot 2C **34**
    (off Strand Shop. Cen.)
Hexham Cl. L30: N'ton 2G **21**
 WA9: St H 1B **60**
Heyburn Rd. L13: Liv 1C **54**
Heydale Rd. L18: Moss H 5E **73**
Heydean Rd. L18: Aller 2G **91**
Heydean Wlk. L18: Aller 2G **91**
     (off Heydean Rd.)
Heydon Av. L32: Kirkb 2G **23**
Heydon Cl. L26: Halew 4A **94**
Heyes, The L25: Woolt 1D **92**
Heyes Av. WA11: Hay 6F **31**
 WA11: Rainf 3G **17**
Heyes Dr. CH45: Wall 3G **49**
Heyes Gro. WA11: Rainf 3G **17**
Heyesmere Ct. L17: Aig 4D **90**
Heyes Mt. L35: Rainh 5A **60**
Heyes Rd. WA8: Wid 3A **96**
Heyes St. L5: Liv 2G **53**
Heyeswood WA11: Hay 5F **31**
Heygarth Dr. CH49: Grea 5B **66**
Heygarth Rd. CH62: East 2E **121**
Hey Grn. Rd. L15: Wav 1C **72**
Hey Pk. L36: Huy 5H **57**
Hey Rd. L36: Huy 5H **57**
Heys, The CH62: East 2F **121**
 WA7: Run 4A **114**
Heys Av. CH62: Brom 5D **104**
Heyscroft Rd. L25: Woolt 1D **92**
Heysham Cl. WA7: Murd 1F **125**
Heysham Lawn L27: N'ley 6A **76**
Heysham Rd. L30: N'ton 1G **21**
Heysmoor Hgts. L8: Liv 3H **71**
Heythrop Dr. CH60: Hesw 5G **101**
Heyville Rd. CH63: Hghr B 5G **87**
Heywood Blvd. CH61: Thing 5E **85**
Heywood Cl. CH61: Thing 5E **85**

Heywood Ct. L15: Wav 6G **55**
Heywood Gdns. L35: Whis 5E **59**
Heywood Rd. L15: Wav 1G **73**
Heyworth St. L5: Liv 2F **53**
Hickling Gdns. WA9: St H 1C **60**
Hickmans Rd. CH41: Birke 6D **50**
Hickory Gro. L31: Mell 1E **23**
Hickson Av. L31: Mag 4B **6**
Hicks Rd. L21: Sea 4A **20**
 L22: Water 1G **19**
Highacre Rd. CH45: New B 6C **32**
Higham Av. WA10: Eccl 2F **41**
Higham Sq. L5: Liv 3E **53**
High Bank Cl. CH43: Noct 4H **67**
Highbank Dr. L19: Garst 5H **91**
Highbanks L31: Lyd 4B **6**
High Beeches L16: Child 6B **56**
High Carrs L36: Roby 5D **56**
Highclere Cres. L36: Huy 2G **57**
Highcroft, The CH63: Beb 6A **88**
Highcroft Av. CH63: Beb 6A **88**
Highcroft Grn. CH63: Beb 6A **88**
Highcross WA11: Rainf 2F **17**
      (off Victoria St.)
Higher Ashton WA8: Wid 6D **78**
HIGHER BEBINGTON 4F **87**
Higher Bebington Rd. CH63: Hghr B . . .5F **87**
Higher End Pk. L30: N'ton 4D **10**
Higher La. L9: Ain, Faz 4A **22**
      (not continuous)
Higher Parr St. WA9: St H 2G **43**
Higher Rd. L25: Hunts X 4F **93**
 L26: Halew 5B **94**
 WA8: Hale B 5B **94**
HIGHER RUNCORN 4D **112**
Highfield L33: Kirkb 4A **14**
Highfield Av. WA5: Gt San 4H **81**
Highfield Cl. CH44: Wall 4C **50**
Highfield Cres. CH42: Rock F 2H **87**
 WA8: Wid 1E **97**
Highfield Dr. CH49: Grea 5B **66**
Highfield Gdns. CH43: Clau 3B **68**
Highfield Gro. CH42: Rock F 2H **87**
 L23: Crosb 4H **9**
Highfield Pk. L31: Mag 6E **7**
Highfield Rd. CH42: Rock F 1H **87**
 L9: Walt 1F **35**
 L13: Liv .3E **55**
 L21: Lith 3A **20**
 L36: Huy 1F **57**
 WA8: Wid 2D **96**
Highfields CH60: Hesw 4D **100**
 L34: Presc 1C **58**
Highfield Sth. CH42: Rock F 4H **87**
Highfield Sq. L13: Liv 3E **55**
Highfield St. L3: Liv 1C **4** (4C **52**)
      (not continuous)
 WA9: St H 5H **43**
Highfield Vw. L13: Liv 3E **55**
Highgate Cl. CH60: Hesw 3D **100**
 WA7: Nort 4F **115**
Highgate Ct. L7: Liv 6H **53**
      (off Grinfield St.)
Highgate Rd. L31: Lyd 4C **6**
Highgate St. L7: Liv 6G **53**
Highgreen Rd. CH42: Tran 6E **69**
Highgrove Pk. L19: Gras 3E **91**
Highlands Rd. WA7: Run 4D **112**
High Legh WA10: Eccl 2H **41**
High Mt. CH60: Hesw 5D **100**
Highoaks Rd. L25: Woolt 2D **92**
Highpark Rd. CH42: Tran 6E **69**
High Pk. St. L8: Liv 4F **71**
Highsted Gro. L33: Kirkb 4A **14**
High St. CH62: Brom 4H **87**
 L2: Liv 3C **4** (5C **52**)
 L15: Wav 1D **72**
 L24: Hale 4D **110**
 L25: Woolt 1C **92**
 L34: Presc 1D **58**
 WA6: Frod 6F **123**
 WA7: Run 3D **112**

Hightor Rd. L25: Woolt 6B **74**
Highville Rd. L16: Child 3H **73**
Highwood Cl. L33: Kirkb 5B **14**
Hignett Av. WA9: St H 3C **44**
Higson Ct. L8: Liv 6G **71**
Hilary Av. L14: Broad G 5A **56**
Hilary Cl. L4: Walt 5A **36**
 L34: Eccl P 6E **41**
 WA5: Gt San 3F **81**
 WA8: Wid 6A **80**
Hilary Dr. CH49: Upton 3E **67**
Hilary Mans. CH44: Wall 3C **50**
      (off Colville Rd.)
Hilary Rd. L4: Walt 5A **36**
Hilberry Av. L13: Liv 2C **54**
Hilbre Av. CH44: Wall 3C **50**
 CH60: Hesw 1C **116**
Hilbre Ct. CH48: W Kir 2A **82**
Hilbre Rd. CH48: W Kir 2B **82**
Hilbre St. CH41: Birke 1F **69**
 L3: Liv 4G **5** (6E **53**)
Hilbre Vw. CH48: W Kir 1C **82**
Hilda Rd. L12: W Der 2A **56**
Hildebrand Cl. L4: Walt 5A **36**
Hildebrand Rd. L4: Walt 5A **36**
Hillaby Cl. L8: Liv 3G **71**
Hillam Rd. CH45: Wall 1H **49**
Hillary Cres. L31: Mag 6C **6**
Hillary Dr. L23: Crosb 5A **10**
Hillary Rd. CH62: East 2D **120**
Hillary Wlk. L23: Crosb 5A **10**
Hill Bark Rd. CH48: Frank 1G **83**
Hillbrae Av. WA11: St H 3E **29**
Hillbrook Dr. L9: Ain 2B **36**
Hillburn Dr. CH41: Birke 6A **50**
Hill Crest L20: Boot 3E **35**
Hillcrest L31: Mag 6E **7**
 WA7: Run 4H **113**
Hillcrest Av. L36: Huy 5A **58**
Hillcrest Ct. CH44: Wall 4C **50**
Hillcrest Dr. CH49: Grea 6A **66**
Hillcrest Pde. L36: Huy 5A **58**
Hillcrest Rd. L4: Walt 4B **36**
 L23: Crosb 5A **10**
Hillcroft Rd. CH44: Wall 4E **51**
 L25: Woolt 5B **74**
Hillerton Cl. L12: W Der 3F **37**
Hillfield WA7: Nort 5F **115**
Hillfield Dr. CH61: Hesw 3D **100**
Hillfoot Av. L25: Hunts X 5D **92**
Hillfoot Cl. CH43: Bid 1G **67**
Hillfoot Grn. L25: Woolt 4C **92**
Hillfoot Rd.
 L25: Hunts X, Woolt 2B **92**
Hill Gro. CH46: More 2C **66**
Hillhead Rd. L20: Boot 3E **35**
Hillingden Av. L26: Halew 4H **93**
Hillingdon Av. CH61: Hesw 3D **100**
Hillingdon Rd. L15: Wav 3F **73**
Hill Ridge CH43: Noct 4H **67**
Hill Rd. CH43: Clau 2A **68**
Hill School Rd. WA10: St H 5G **41**
Hillside Av. L36: Huy 1E **57**
 WA7: Run 5C **112**
 WA10: St H 5C **28**
 WA12: Newt W 3H **45**
Hillside Cl. CH41: Tran 5G **69**
 L20: Boot 3E **35**
Hillside Ct. CH41: Tran 5G **69**
 L25: Woolt 6C **74**
Hillside Cres. L36: Huy 1E **57**
Hillside Dr. L25: Woolt 6D **74**
Hillside Gro. WA5: Penk 5H **81**
Hillside Rd. CH41: Tran 5G **69**
 CH43: Bid 1H **67**
 CH44: Wall 3A **50**
 CH48: W Kir 1D **82**
 CH60: Hesw 6E **101**
 L18: Moss H 4F **73**
 L36: Huy 2G **57**
Hillside St. L6: Liv 4F **53**
Hillside Vw. CH43: Oxton 6C **68**
Hillsmore Way L5: Liv 1F **53**
Hills Pl. L15: Wav 2E **73**

Hill St. L8: Liv 3D **70**
    (not continuous)
  L34: Presc 1D **58**
  WA7: Run 3E **113**
  WA10: St H 6E **29**
Hill St. Bus. Cen. L8: Liv 3D **70**
    (off Hill St.)
Hilltop WA7: Nort 6E **115**
Hilltop La. CH60: Hesw 5F **101**
Hill Top Rd. WA4: Pres H 1H **125**
  WA11: Rainf 1H **27**
Hilltop Rd. L16: Child 2H **73**
Hill Vw. WA8: Wid 4D **78**
Hillview L17: Aig 1C **90**
Hillview Av. CH48: W Kir 6B **64**
Hillview Ct. CH43: Bid 6G **49**
Hill Vw. Dr. CH49: Upton 3E **67**
Hillview Gdns. L25: Woolt 6B **74**
Hillview Rd. CH61: Irby 4A **84**
Hillwood Cl. CH63: Spit 4A **104**
Hilton Cl. CH41: Birke 3E **69**
Hilton Ct. L30: N'ton 5D **10**
Hilton Gro. CH48: W Kir 6A **64**
Hinchley Grn. L31: Mag 6A **6**
Hinckley Rd. WA11: St H 6G **29**
Hindburn Av. L31: Mag 5E **7**
HINDERTON 6D **118**
Hinderton Cl. CH41: Birke 5G **69**
Hinderton Dr. CH48: W Kir 2E **83**
  CH60: Hesw 1D **116**
Hinderton La. CH64: Nest 6C **118**
Hinderton Rd. CH41: Birke 4G **69**
  CH64: Nest 6C **118**
Hindley Beech L31: Mag 5B **6**
Hindley Wlk. L24: Speke 3F **109**
Hindlip St. L8: Liv 6G **71**
Hind St. CH41: Birke 4G **69**
Hinson St. CH41: Birke 3G **69**
Hinton Rd. WA7: Run 5E **113**
Hinton St. L6: Liv 4A **54**
  L21: Lith 5B **20**
Hitchens Cl. WA7: Murd 6F **115**
HMP Altcourse L9: Faz 5B **22**
HMP Kennet L31: Mag 5H **7**
HMP Liverpool L9: Walt 6F **21**
Hobart Dr. L33: Kirkb 3A **14**
Hobart St. WA9: St H 5C **42**
Hobby Ct. WA7: Pal F 1A **124**
Hobhouse Ct. CH43: Clau 3D **68**
Hoblyn Rd. CH43: Bid 1A **68**
Hockenhall All. L2: Liv 3D **4** (5C **52**)
Hockenhull Ct. CH63: Spit 3A **104**
Hodder Av. L31: Mag 5E **7**
Hodder Cl. WA11: St H 4F **29**
Hodder Rd. L5: Liv 1F **53**
Hodder St. L5: Liv 1F **53**
Hodson Pl. L6: Liv 3G **53**
Hogarth Dr. CH43: Noct 6H **67**
Hogarth St. L21: Sea 5A **20**
    (off Seaforth Va. Nth.)
Hogarth Wlk. L4: Kirkd 5D **34**
Hoghton Cl. WA9: St H 5B **44**
Hoghton La. WA9: St H 5B **44**
    (not continuous)
Hoghton Rd. L24: Hale 3E **111**
  WA9: St H 5B **44**
Hoghton Twr. Ct. L24: Hale 3C **110**
Holbeck WA7: Nort 6E **115**
Holbeck St. L4: Walt 1H **53**
Holborn Ct. WA8: Wid 6D **78**
Holborn Hill CH41: Tran 5G **69**
Holborn Sq. CH41: Tran 5G **69**
Holborn Sq. Ind. Est. CH41: Tran . .5G **69**
Holborn St. L6: Liv 5G **53**
Holbrook Cl. WA5: Gt San 3G **81**
  WA9: St H 1G **61**
Holcombe Cl. CH49: Grea 5B **66**
Holden Gro. L22: Water 1E **19**
Holden Rd. L22: Water 1D **18**
  L35: Presc 3C **58**
Holden Rd. E. L22: Water 1E **19**
Holden St. L8: Liv 1H **71**
Holden Ter. L22: Water 1E **19**
Holdsworth Dr. L7: Liv 5H **53**

Holford Moss WA7: Nort 2F **115**
Holgate L23: Thorn 1B **10**
Holgate Pk. L23: Thorn 2B **10**
HOLIDAY MOSS 3H **17**
Holingsworth Cl. WA10: St H 1F **43**
Holkham Cl. WA8: Wid 2D **96**
Holkham Gdns. WA9: St H 1B **60**
Holland Cl. L30: N'ton 5D **10**
Holland Gro. CH60: Hesw 4D **100**
Holland Pl. L7: Liv 6H **53**
Holland Rd. CH45: Wall 6E **33**
  L24: Speke 3G **109**
  L26: Halew 5G **93**
Holland St. L7: Liv 4B **54**
Holland Way L26: Halew 5G **93**
Holley Ct. L35: Rainh 4A **60**
    (off Rainhill Rd.)
Holliers Cl. L31: Mag 6C **6**
Hollies, The L25: Woolt 6A **74**
  WA7: Run 5H **113**
Hollies Rd. L26: Halew 4H **93**
Hollingbourne Pl. L11: Norr G 2E **37**
Hollingbourne Rd.
  L11: Norr G 2E **37**
Hollinghurst Rd. L33: Kirkb 4B **14**
Hollingwood Cl. WN4: Ash M 1H **31**
Hollingworth Cl. L9: Walt 2G **35**
Hollinhey Cl. L30: N'ton 4G **11**
Hollins Cl. L15: Wav 1E **73**
Hollins Way WA8: Hale B 6H **95**
Hollocombe Rd. L12: W Der 3F **37**
Holloway WA7: Run 4D **112**
Hollow Cft. L28: Stockb V 4C **38**
Holly Av. CH63: Beb 2H **103**
Hollybank Ct. CH41: Birke 4F **69**
  WA8: Wid 1D **96**
Hollybank Grange L26: Halew 3H **93**
Holly Bank Gro. WA9: St H 1G **43**
Hollybank Rd. CH41: Birke 4F **69**
  L18: Moss H 4C **72**
  WA7: Halt 5B **114**
Holly Bank St. WA9: St H 1G **43**
Holly Cl. L24: Hale 3D **110**
  WA10: Eccl 1H **41**
Holly Ct. L20: Boot 6B **20**
Holly Cres. WA11: Rainf 3G **17**
Hollydale Rd. L18: Moss H 4E **73**
Holly Farm Ct. WA8: Wid 5D **78**
Holly Farm Rd. L19: Garst 5H **91**
Hollyfield Rd. L9: Walt 6F **21**
Holly Gro. CH42: Tran 5G **69**
  L21: Sea 5H **19**
  L36: Roby 5D **56**
Holly Hey L35: Whis 6D **58**
Hollyhurst Cl. L8: Liv 4G **71**
Hollymead Cl. L25: Gate 5D **74**
Holly M. L23: Crosb 4H **9**
Holly Mt. L12: W Der 1E **55**
  WA10: St H 3B **42**
Holly Pl. CH46: More 2D **66**
Holly Rd. L7: Liv 5B **54**
  WA5: Penk 4G **81**
  WA11: Hay 6B **30**
Hollyrood L34: Presc 2A **58**
Holly St. L20: Boot 1C **34**
Holly Ter. WA5: Penk 5H **81**
Hollytree Rd. L25: Woolt 6D **74**
Hollywood Bowl
  Liverpool 5D **54**
Hollywood Rd. L17: Aig 6C **72**
Holman Rd. L19: Garst 5H **91**
Holm Cotts. CH43: Oxton 1B **86**
Holme Cl. L34: Eccl P 6G **41**
Holmefield Av. L19: Aig 2E **91**
Holmefield Rd. L19: Aig 3D **90**
Holme Rd. WA10: St H 3H **41**
Holmes Ct. CH42: Tran 6E **69**
Holmes La. L21: Lith 4A **20**
    (off Bridge Rd.)
Holmes St. L8: Liv 2A **72**
Holme St. L5: Kirkd 1C **52**
Holmesway CH61: Pens 1D **100**
Holmfield CH43: Oxton 1B **86**
Holmfield Av. WA7: Run 3G **113**

Holmfield Gro. L31: Mag 6B **6**
  L36: Huy 1H **75**
Holm Hey Rd. CH43: Pren 1B **86**
Holm Hill CH48: W Kir 2C **82**
Holmlands Cres. CH43: Oxton 1A **86**
Holmlands Dr. CH43: Oxton 1A **86**
Holmlands Way CH43: Oxton 1B **86**
Holm La. CH43: Oxton 1B **86**
Holmleigh Rd. L25: Gate 3C **74**
Holmrook Rd. L11: Norr G 3E **37**
Holmside Cl. CH46: More 1D **66**
Holmside La. CH43: Oxton 1B **86**
Holm Vw. Cl. CH43: Oxton 6C **68**
Holmville Rd. CH63: Hghr B 6G **87**
Holmway CH63: Hghr B 6H **87**
Holmwood Av. CH61: Thing 6G **85**
Holmwood Dr. CH61: Thing 6G **85**
Holmwood Gdns. CH48: W Kir 2E **83**
HOLT 3G **59**
Holt Av. CH46: More 1C **66**
HOLT GREEN 1F **7**
Holt Hill CH41: Birke 5G **69**
Holt Hill Ter. CH42: Tran 4G **69**
Holt La. L27: N'ley 2G **75**
    (not continuous)
  L35: Rainh 3G **59**
  WA7: Halt 5B **114**
Holt Rd. CH41: Tran 5G **69**
  L7: Liv 5A **54**
Holt Way L32: Kirkb 1H **23**
Holy Cross Cl. L3: Liv 1E **5** (4D **52**)
Holyrood L23: Blun 5C **8**
Holyrood Av. WA8: Wid 5E **79**
Holywell Cl. CH64: Park 6F **117**
  WA9: St H 1H **61**
Homedove Ho. L23: Blun 5E **9**
Home Farm 4H **37**
Home Farm Cl. CH49: Woodc 1G **85**
Home Farm Rd. CH49: Woodc 1F **85**
  L34: Know 3E **39**
Homer Rd. L34: Know 2E **39**
Homerton Rd. L6: Liv 4B **54**
Homestall Rd. L11: Norr G 3E **37**
Homestead Av. L30: N'ton 6H **11**
  WA11: Hay 4G **31**
Homestead Cl. L36: Huy 4A **58**
Homestead M. CH48: W Kir 1B **82**
Honeybourne Dr. L35: Whis 1G **59**
Honey Hall Rd. L26: Halew 5G **93**
Honeys Grn. Cl. L12: W Der 2H **55**
Honeys Grn. La. L12: W Der 2H **55**
Honeys Grn. Pct. L12: W Der 2H **55**
Honey Spot Gro. WA8: Wid 5A **80**
Honey St. WA9: St H 6A **42**
Honeysuckle Cl. L26: Halew 1F **93**
  WA8: Wid 5F **79**
Honeysuckle Dr. L9: Walt 2H **35**
Honey Way WA11: St H 3G **29**
Honister Gro. WA7: Beech 2A **124**
Honister Wlk. L27: N'ley 6A **76**
Honiston Av. L35: Rainh 3H **59**
Honiton Rd. L17: Aig 2C **90**
Honiton Way WA5: Penk 5G **81**
Hood Rd. WA8: Wid 2D **96**
Hood St. CH44: Wall 4F **51**
  L1: Liv 3E **5** (5D **52**)
  L20: Boot 6A **20**
Hoole Rd. CH49: Woodc 6F **67**
Hoose Ct. CH47: Hoy 2C **64**
HOOTON 6G **121**
Hooton Grn. CH66: Hoot 5G **121**
Hooton La. CH66: Hoot 6H **121**
Hooton Pk. La. CH65: Hoot 6H **121**
Hooton Park Outdoor Karting Circuit
  . . . . .3H **121**
Hooton Rd. CH64: Will 6A **120**
  CH66: Hoot 6A **120**
  L9: Ain 4H **21**
Hooton Station (Rail) 6D **120**
Hooton Way CH66: Hoot 5F **121**
Hooton Works Trad. Est.
  CH66: Hoot 5E **121**
Hope Cl. WA10: St H 1C **42**
Hope Pk. L16: Child 4H **73**

Hope Pl. L1: Liv 6H **5** (1E **71**)
Hope St. CH41: Birke 2F **69**
    CH45: New B 5D **32**
    L1: Liv 6H **5** (1F **71**)
    L34: Presc 1D **58**
Hope Way L8: Liv 1F **71**
Hopfield Rd. CH46: More 1D **66**
Hopkins Cl. WA10: St H 1B **42**
Hopwood Cres. WA11: Rainf 4G **17**
Hopwood St. L5: Liv 2D **52**
Horace St. WA10: St H 1B **42**
Horatio St. CH41: Birke 3F **69**
Hornbeam Cl. CH46: More 1H **65**
    WA7: Wind H 4E **115**
    WA11: Hay 6B **30**
Hornbeam Rd. L9: Walt 2A **36**
    L26: Halew 4A **94**
Hornby Av. CH62: Brom 4C **104**
    L20: Boot 6B **20**
Hornby Blvd. L20: Boot 5B **20**
    L21: Lith 5B **20**
Hornby Chase L31: Mag 2B **12**
Hornby Cl. L9: Walt 1F **35**
Hornby Ct. CH62: Brom 4D **104**
    L9: Walt 6G **21**
Hornby Cres. WA9: Clock F 3H **61**
Hornby Flats *L21: Lith* *5B* **20**
    (off Linacre Rd.)
Hornby La. L18: Moss H 4H **73**
Hornby Pk. L18: Moss H 4H **73**
Hornby Pl. L9: Walt 6G **21**
Hornby Rd. CH62: Brom 4C **104**
    L9: Walt 1F **35**
    L20: Boot 6B **20**
    (Hornby Av.)
    L20: Boot 1C **34**
    (Roby St.)
Hornby St. CH41: Birke 3H **69**
    L21: Sea 5A **20**
    L23: Crosb 5G **9**
Hornby Wlk. L5: Liv 3C **52**
Horne St. L6: Liv 3H **53**
Hornet Cl. L6: Liv 2G **53**
Hornhouse La. L33: Know I 3D **24**
Hornsey Rd. L4: Walt 1H **53**
Hornsmill Av. WA8: Wid 4E **79**
Hornspit La. L12: W Der 5E **37**
Horringford Rd. L19: Aig 3D **90**
Horrocks Av. L19: Garst 5H **91**
Horrocks Cl. L36: Huy 3F **57**
Horrocks Rd. L36: Huy 4F **57**
Horseman Pl. CH44: Wall 5G **51**
Horseshoe Cl. WA9: St H 2C **44**
Horseshoe Dr. L10: Faz 4F **23**
Horsey Mere Gdns. WA9: St H 1C **60**
Horsfall Gro. L8: Liv 5E **71**
Horsfall St. L8: Liv 5E **71**
Horton Cl. L33: Kirkb 3A **14**
Horwood Av. L35: Rainh 3H **59**
Horwood Cl. L12: W Der 3G **37**
Hoscar Ct. WA8: Wid 4B **96**
Hoscote Pk. CH48: W Kir 1A **82**
Hose Side Rd. CH45: Wall 6C **32**
Hospital St. WA10: St H 1F **43**
Hospital Way WA7: Pal F 6B **114**
Hosta Cl. L33: Kirkb 4H **13**
Hostock Cl. L35: Whis 5D **58**
Hotham St. L3: Liv 3G **5** (5E **53**)
Hothfield Rd. CH44: Wall 4F **51**
Hotspur St. L20: Boot 5C **34**
HOUGH GREEN 2G **95**
Hough Grn. Rd. WA8: Wid 1G **95**
Hough Green Station (Rail) 2H **95**
Houghton Cl. WA8: Wid 1G **97**
Houghton Cft. WA8: Cron 4A **78**
Houghton La. L1: Liv 4F **5** (6D **52**)
Houghton Rd. CH49: Woodc 5F **67**
    L24: Hale 3E **111**
Houghton's La. WA10: Eccl 5F **27**
Houghton St. L1: Liv 4F **5** (6D **52**)
    L34: Presc 1D **58**
    L35: Rainh 4A **60**
    WA8: Wid 1H **97**
Houghton Way L1: Liv 4F **5**

Hougoumont Av. L22: Water 2G **19**
Hougoumont Gro. L22: Water 2G **19**
Houlding St. L4: Walt 1C **53**
Houlgrave Rd. L5: Liv 2C **52**
Houlston Rd. L32: Kirkb 1F **23**
Houlston Wlk. L32: Kirkb 1F **23**
House La. WA8: Wid 4D **96**
Hove, The WA7: Murd 1F **125**
    (not continuous)
Hoveton Gdns. WA9: St H 1B **60**
Howard Av. CH62: Brom 5E **105**
Howard Cl. L21: Ford 1C **20**
    (not continuous)
    L31: Mag 6E **7**
Howard Ct. CH64: Nest 6B **118**
Howard Dr. L19: Gras 4E **91**
Howard Florey Av. L30: N'ton 5F **11**
Howard's La. WA10: Eccl 1E **41**
Howards Rd. CH61: Thing 5F **85**
Howard St. WA10: St H 5B **42**
Howarth Ct. WA7: Run 3F **113**
Howbeck Cl. CH43: Clau 3B **68**
Howbeck Ct. CH43: Oxton 4B **68**
Howbeck Dr. CH43: Clau 3B **68**
Howbeck Rd. CH43: Oxton 4B **68**
Howden Dr. L36: Huy 4C **56**
Howell Dr. CH49: Grea 1B **84**
Howell Rd. CH62: New F 4A **88**
Howells Cl. L31: Mag 5C **6**
Howison St. L20: Boot 4B **34**
Howson St. CH42: Rock F 1H **87**
HOYLAKE .3B **64**
Hoylake Cl. WA7: Murd 1E **125**
    (not continuous)
Hoylake Gro. WA9: Clock F 3G **61**
Hoylake Golf Course 3B **64**
Hoylake Lifeboat Mus. 2A **64**
Hoylake Rd. CH41: Birke 5H **49**
    CH46: More 2H **65**
Hoylake Station (Rail) 3B **64**
Hoyle Ct. CH47: Hoy 1B **64**
Hoyle Rd. CH47: Hoy 1B **64**
Huddleston Cl. CH49: Woodc 6F **67**
Huddleston Rd. L15: Wav 6F **55**
Hudson Pl. CH49: Upton 3C **66**
Hudson Rd. CH46: Leas 3E **49**
    L31: Mag 2B **12**
Hudson St. L30: N'ton 2H **21**
Hughenden Rd. L13: Liv 2D **54**
Hughes Av. L35: Presc 6D **58**
Hughes Cl. L7: Liv 6A **54**
Hughes Dr. L20: Boot 5E **21**
Hughes La. CH43: Oxton 6D **68**
Hughes St. L6: Liv 3G **53**
    (not continuous)
    L19: Garst 6G **91**
    WA9: St H 5H **43**
Hughestead Gro. L19: Garst 5F **91**
Hughson St. L8: Liv 4E **71**
Hull Cl. L19: Garst 5F **91**
Hulme Cl. CH62: Brom 1C **104**
Hulme Wlk. CH62: Brom 1C **104**
Hulmewood CH63: Beb 4A **88**
Hulton Av. L35: Whis 3F **59**
Humber Cl. L4: Kirkd 5E **35**
    WA8: Wid 6B **80**
Humber Cres. WA9: Sut L 1G **61**
Humber St. CH41: Birke 6B **50**
Hume Ct. CH47: Meols 1C **64**
Humphrey's Cl. WA7: Murd 6F **115**
Humphreys Hey L23: Thorn 4B **10**
Huncote Av. WA11: St H 5H **29**
Hunslet Rd. L9: Ain 5H **21**
Hunstanton Cl. CH49: Upton 2E **67**
Hunter Ct. L34: Presc 1E **59**
Hunters Ct. WA7: Pal F 1A **124**
Hunters La. L15: Wav 2E **73**
Hunter St. L3: Liv 2F **5** (5D **52**)
    WA9: St H 3G **43**
Huntingdon Gro. L31: Lyd 3B **6**
Huntington Cl. CH46: More 1H **65**
Huntley Av. WA9: St H 6G **43**
Huntley Gro. WA9: St H 6G **43**

Huntley Rd. L6: Liv 4A **54**
Hunt Rd. L31: Mag 5C **6**
    WA11: Hay 5G **31**
HUNTS CROSS 4D **92**
Hunts Cross L25: Hunts X 4E **93**
Hunts Cross Av. L25: Woolt 6D **74**
    (not continuous)
Hunts Cross Shop. Pk.
    L24: Hunts X 5C **92**
Hunt's Cross Station (Rail) 4E **93**
Huntsman Cl. L25: Hunts X 2F **93**
Huntsman Wood L12: W Der 5A **38**
Hurlingham Rd. L4: Walt 3A **36**
Hurrell Rd. CH41: Birke 6H **49**
Hurricane Dr. L24: Speke 2B **108**
Hursley Rd. L9: Faz 1C **36**
Hurst Bank CH42: Rock F 3H **87**
Hurstlyn Rd. L18: Aller 2G **91**
Hurst Pk. Cl. L36: Huy 3A **58**
Hurst Pk. Dr. L36: Huy 3A **58**
Hurst Rd. L31: Mag 2C **12**
Hurst St. L1: Liv 1D **70**
    WA8: Wid 1E **113**
Huskisson St. L8: Liv 2F **71**
Hutchinson Cl. CH43: Bid 3F **67**
Hutchinson St. L6: Liv 4G **53**
    WA8: Wid 5D **96**
Hutchinson Wlk. L6: Liv 4G **53**
Hutfield Rd. L24: Speke 1A **110**
Huxley Cl. CH46: More 1H **65**
Huxley St. L13: Liv 6B **36**
HUYTON 5G **57**
Huyton & Prescot Golf Course 3A **58**
Huyton Av. WA10: St H 5C **28**
Huyton Brook L36: Huy 1H **75**
Huyton Bus. Pk. L35: Whis 6C **58**
    L36: Huy 6A **58**
    (Brickfields)
    L36: Huy 6H **57**
    (Octavia Ct.)
    L36: Huy 1B **76**
    (Stretton Way)
Huyton Chu. Rd. L36: Huy 5G **57**
Huyton Gallery 5G **57**
Huyton Hall Cres. L36: Huy 5G **57**
Huyton Hey Rd. L36: Huy 5G **57**
Huyton Ho. Rd. L36: Huy 3D **56**
Huyton La. L34: Presc 4G **57**
    L36: Huy 4G **57**
Huyton Lane Wetland Pk. 4H **57**
Huyton Station (Rail) 5G **57**
HUYTON-WITH-ROBY 4E **57**
Hyacinth Av. L33: Kirkb 4H **13**
Hyacinth Cl. WA11: Hay 5H **31**
Hyacinth Gro. CH46: More 5E **49**
Hyde Cl. WA7: Beech 1H **123**
Hyde Rd. L22: Water 2F **19**
Hyde's Brow WA11: Rainf 1G **17**
Hydrangea Way WA9: Bold 6C **44**
Hydro Av. CH48: W Kir 2B **82**
Hygeia St. L6: Liv 3G **53**
Hylton Av. CH44: Wall 3C **50**
Hylton Rd. L19: Aller 3H **91**
Hyslop St. L8: Liv 3E **71**
Hythe Av. L21: Lith 3C **20**
Hythedale Cl. L17: Aig 1A **90**

I

Ibbotson's La. L17: Aig 5C **72**
Iberis Gdns. WA9: Bold 6C **44**
Ibstock Rd. L20: Boot 6B **20**
Iffley Cl. CH49: Upton 4B **66**
Ikin Cl. CH43: Bid 6G **49**
Ilchester Rd. CH41: Birke 6B **50**
    CH44: Wall 4F **51**
    L16: Child 6A **56**
Ilford Av. CH44: Wall 5D **50**
    L23: Crosb 4F **9**
Ilford St. L3: Liv 2H **5** (5F **53**)
Ilfracombe Rd. WA9: Sut L 2G **61**
Iliad St. L5: Liv 3E **53**
Ilkley Wlk. L24: Speke 1F **109**

Ilsley Cl. CH49: Upton 5D 66
Image Bus. Pk. L33: Know I 1F 25
Imber Rd. L32: Kirkb 3B 24
Imison St. L9: Walt 2F 35
Imison Way L9: Walt 2E 35
Immingham Dr. L19: Garst 5F 91
Imperial Av. CH45: Wall 1E 51
Imperial Chambers L1: Liv 3D 4
Imperial Ct. L2: Liv 3C 4
Imrie St. L4: Walt 3F 35
Ince Av. CH62: East 4E 121
    L4: Walt 5H 35
    L21: Lith 4B 20
    L23: Crosb 4E 9
Ince Cl. CH43: Oxton 5B 68
Ince Gro. CH43: Oxton 5B 68
Ince La. L23: Thorn 1A 10
Incemore Rd. L18: Moss H 2F 91
Ince Rd. L23: Thorn 2A 10
Inchcape Rd. CH45: Wall 2H 49
    L16: Child 6A 56
Index St. L4: Walt 4F 35
Ingestre Ct. CH43: Oxton 6C 68
Ingestre Rd. CH43: Oxton 6C 68
Ingham Rd. WA8: Wid 5D 78
Ingleborough Rd. CH42: Tran 1F 87
Ingleby Rd. CH44: Wall 4C 50
    CH62: New F 3B 88
Ingledene Rd. L18: Moss H 4H 73
Inglefield Ct. CH42: Rock F 2A 88
    (off The Hawthornes)
Ingle Grn. L23: Blun 4C 8
Inglegreen CH60: Hesw 5F 101
Ingleholme Gdns.
    L34: Eccl P 6G 41
Ingleholme Rd. L19: Aig 2E 91
Inglemere Rd. CH42: Rock F 1G 87
Inglemoss Dr. WA11: Rainf 2H 27
Inglenook Rd. WA5: Penk 5H 81
Ingleside Ct. L23: Blun 6E 9
Ingleton Cl. CH49: Grea 5B 66
Ingleton Dr. WA11: St H 2F 29
Ingleton Grn. L32: Kirkb 3B 24
Ingleton Rd. L18: Moss H 4D 72
    L32: Kirkb 3B 24
Inglewood L12: Crox 3C 38
Inglewood Av. CH46: More 2B 66
Inglewood Rd. WA11: Rainf 2A 28
Inglis Rd. L9: Ain 4H 21
Ingoe Cl. L32: Kirkb 2F 23
Ingoe La. L32: Kirkb 2F 23
    (not continuous)
Ingrave Rd. L4: Walt 3A 36
Ingrow Rd. L6: Liv 4H 53
Inigo Rd. L13: Liv 3F 55
Inley Cl. CH63: Spit 3A 104
Inley Rd. CH63: Spit 3H 103
Inman Av. WA9: St H 3D 44
Inman Rd. CH49: Upton 3C 66
    L21: Lith 4B 20
Inner Central Rd. L24: Halew 6H 93
Inner Forum L11: Norr G 2C 36
Inner South Rd. L24: Halew 1G 109
Inner West Rd. L24: Halew 6G 93
Innovation Blvd. L7: Liv 6B 54
Insall Rd. L13: Liv 6F 55
Interchange Motorway Ind. Est.
    L36: Huy 6A 58
International Slavery Mus. 6C 4 (1C 70)
Inveresk Cl. CH43: Noct 3A 68
Invergarry Rd. L11: Crox 1F 37
Invincible Cl. L30: Boot 3E 21
Invincible Way L11: Crox 5G 23
Inwood Rd. L19: Garst 4H 91
Iona Cl. L12: Crox 2C 38
Iona Cres. WA8: Wid 3D 78
Iona Gdns. WA9: St H 6H 43
Ionic Rd. L13: Liv 3E 55
Ionic St. CH42: Rock F 1H 87
    L21: Sea 4H 19
Ipswich Cl. L19: Garst 5F 91
IRBY 5B 84
Irby Av. CH44: Wall 3C 50

IRBY HEATH 5A 84
IRBY HILL 3A 84
Irby Rd. CH61: Hesw, Irby, Pens ...6B 84
    L4: Walt 5H 35
Irbyside Rd. CH48: Frank 2H 83
Ireland Rd. L24: Hale 3E 111
    (not continuous)
    WA11: Hay 5E 31
Ireland St. WA8: Wid 2H 97
Irene Av. WA11: St H 4G 29
Irene Rd. L16: Child 3G 73
Ireton St. L4: Walt 3F 35
Iris Av. CH41: Birke 1B 68
Iris Gro. L33: Kirkb 4H 13
Iris Pk. Wlk. L31: Mell 6E 13
Irlam Dr. L32: Kirkb 1A 24
Irlam Ho. L20: Boot 2B 34
Irlam Pl. L20: Boot 1B 34
Irlam Rd. L20: Boot 1B 34
Ironbridge Vw. L8: Liv 5F 71
Ironside Rd. L36: Huy 3F 57
Irvine St. L7: Liv 6G 53
Irvine St. W. L7: Liv 6G 53
Irvine Ter. CH62: New F 3C 88
Irving Cl. L9: Ain 3A 22
Irwell Chambers L3: Liv 3C 4
Irwell Cl. L17: Aig 6C 72
Irwell Ho. L17: Aig 6C 72
Irwell La. L17: Aig 6C 72
    WA7: Run 2F 113
Irwell St. WA8: Wid 1E 113
    WA9: St H 6G 43
Isaac St. L8: Liv 5F 71
Isabel Gro. L13: Liv 6C 36
Island Pl. L19: Garst 5G 91
Island Rd. L19: Garst 5G 91
    L21: Lith 4A 20
Island Rd. Sth. L19: Garst 5H 91
Islands Brow WA11: St H 5F 29
Isla Sq. L5: Liv 1F 53
Isleham Cl. L19: Aller 3G 91
Islington L3: Liv 2C 5 (5E 53)
    L23: Crosb 5F 9
Islington Grn. WA8: Wid 5H 79
Islington Sq. L3: Liv 4F 53
Islip Cl. CH61: Irby 4B 84
Ismay Dr. CH44: Wall 2F 51
Ismay Rd. L21: Lith 4B 20
Ismay St. L4: Walt 4F 35
Ivanhoe Rd. L17: Aig 5A 72
    L23: Blun 5E 9
Ivatt Way L7: Liv 6A 54
Iveagh Cl. WA7: Pal F 6C 114
Iver Cl. WA8: Cron 3A 78
Ivernia Rd. L4: Walt 3H 35
Ivor Rd. CH44: Wall 2E 51
Ivory Dr. L33: Kirkb 4A 14
Ivy Av. CH63: Hghr B 6G 87
    L19: Gras 4F 91
    L35: Whis 3G 59
Ivychurch M. WA7: Run 3H 113
Ivy Farm Ct. L24: Hale 4D 110
Ivy Farm Rd. L35: Rainh 3H 59
Ivyhurst Cl. L19: Aig 3D 90
Ivy La. CH46: More 5C 48
Ivy Leigh L13: Liv 2C 54
Ivy St. CH41: Birke 3H 69
    WA7: Run 4E 113

J

Jack McBane Ct. L3: Liv 3C 52
Jack's Brow L34: Know P 2G 39
Jacksfield Way L19: Gras 4D 90
Jackson Cl. CH63: Hghr B 3H 87
    L35: Rainh 6B 60
Jacksons Pond Dr. L25: Gate 2B 74

Jackson St. CH41: Birke 4G 69
    L19: Garst 5G 91
    WA5: Burtw 1G 63
    WA9: St H 2G 43
    WA11: Hay 4C 30
Jackson St. Ind. Est.
    WA9: St H 3G 43
Jacobs Cl. L21: Lith 5B 20
Jacob St. L8: Liv 5F 71
Jacqueline Ct. L36: Roby 5E 57
Jacqueline Dr. L36: Huy 3A 58
Jade Cl. L33: Kirkb 6C 14
Jade Rd. L6: Liv 3H 53
Jamaica St. L1: Liv 2D 70
Jamesbrook Cl. CH41: Birke 1C 68
James Clarke St. L5: Liv 3C 52
James Cl. WA8: Wid 1E 113
James Ct. L25: Woolt 1D 92
James Ct. Apartments
    L25: Woolt 1C 92
James Dixon Ct. L30: N'ton 4D 10
James Dunne Av. L5: Liv 2C 52
James Gro. WA10: St H 3C 42
James Holt Av. L32: Kirkb 2G 23
James Hopkins Way L4: Kirkd 6D 34
James Horrigan Ct.
    L30: N'ton 6C 10
James Larkin Way L4: Kirkd 6D 34
James Rd. L25: Woolt 1D 92
    WA11: Hay 4H 31
James Simpson Way L30: N'ton 5F 11
    (off Alexander Fleming Av.)
James St. CH43: Oxton 5E 69
    CH44: Wall 5G 51
    L2: Liv 5C 4 (6C 52)
    L19: Garst 5G 91
    WA9: Clock F 4H 61
James Street Station (Rail) ..5C 4 (6C 52)
Jamieson Av. L23: Crosb 5A 10
Jamieson Rd. L15: Wav 2C 72
Jane St. WA9: St H 6B 44
Janet St. L7: Liv 6H 53
Japonica Gdns. WA9: Bold 6C 44
Jardin M. L17: Aig 5H 71
    (off Parkfield M.)
Jarrett Rd. L33: Kirkb 5C 14
Jarrett Wlk. L33: Kirkb 5C 14
Jarrow Cl. CH43: Oxton 5D 68
Jasmine Cl. CH49: Upton 2B 66
    L5: Liv 3F 53
Jasmine Ct. L36: Huy 2H 57
Jasmine Gdns. WA9: Bold 6C 44
Jasmine Gro. WA8: Wid 3B 96
Jasmine M. L17: Aig 6G 71
Jason St. L5: Liv 1E 53
Jason Wlk. L5: Liv 1E 53
Java Rd. L4: Walt 3B 36
Jay's Cl. WA7: Murd 6G 115
Jean Wlk. L10: Faz 5F 23
Jedburgh Dr. L33: Kirkb 3H 13
Jefferys Cres. L36: Huy 5D 56
Jefferys Dr. L36: Huy 4C 56
Jefferson Gdns. WA8: Wid 6D 78
Jeffreys Dr. CH49: Grea 4B 66
Jellicoe Cl. CH48: Caldy 5D 82
Jenkinson St. L3: Liv 4E 53
Jenner Dr. CH46: Leas 5E 49
Jensen Ct. WA7: Ast 2G 113
Jericho Cl. L17: Aig 1B 90
Jericho Ct. L17: Aig 1B 90
Jericho Farm Cl. L17: Aig 2B 90
Jericho Farm Wlk.
    L17: Aig 2B 90
Jericho La. L17: Aig 2B 90
Jermyn St. L8: Liv 3G 71
Jerningham Rd. L11: Norr G 2B 36
Jersey Av. L21: Lith 2B 20
Jersey Cl. L20: Boot 2C 34
Jersey St. L20: Boot 2C 34
    WA7: Clock F 4G 61
Jesmond St. L15: Wav 1B 72
Jessamine Rd. CH42: Tran 6G 69
Jessop Ho. WA7: Run 2C 112
Jet Cl. L6: Liv 3H 53

Jeudwine Cl. L25: Woolt 2D **92**
Joan Av. CH46: More 1B **66**
  CH49: Grea 5C **66**
Jocelyn Cl. CH63: Spit 2A **104**
Jockey's Brow La. WA9: St H 5D **42**
John Bagot Cl. L5: Liv 2E **53**
John Hunter Way L30: N'ton 6F **11**
John Lennon Dr. L6: Liv 4H **53**
John Lennon Statue 4D **4**
  (above The Cavern Club)
John Middleton Cl. L24: Hale 3D **110**
John Moores Cl. L7: Liv 1G **71**
Johns Av. WA7: Run 5D **112**
  WA11: Hay 4G **31**
Johnson Av. L35: Presc 3D **58**
Johnson Gro. L12: W Der 2A **56**
Johnson Rd. CH43: Pren 2B **86**
Johnson's La. WA8: Wid 2A **98**
Johnson St. L3: Liv 2E **5** (5D **52**)
  WA9: St H 1G **43**
Johnson Wlk. L7: Liv 6A **54**
  (off Claughton Cl.)
Johnston Av. L20: Boot 5E **21**
John St. CH41: Birke 2H **69**
  L3: Liv 1H **5** (4E **53**)
John Willis Ho.
  CH42: Rock F 1A **88**
Jones Farm Rd. L25: Gate 4E **75**
Jonson Rd. CH64: Nest 6A **118**
Jonville Rd. L9: Ain 4A **22**
Jordan St. L1: Liv 2D **70**
Joseph Gardner Way
  L20: Boot 6B **20**
Josephine Butler Sq. L6: Liv 4F **53**
  (off Shaw St.)
Joseph Lister Cl. L30: N'ton 6F **11**
Joseph St. WA8: Wid 1G **97**
  WA9: St H 6A **44**
Joshua Cl. L5: Liv 1E **53**
Joyce Wlk. L10: Faz 4G **23**
Joy La. WA5: Burtw 3F **63**
  WA8: Clock F 5A **62**
  WA9: Clock F 5A **62**
Joy Wlk. WA9: Clock F 4A **62**
Jubilee Av. L14: Broad G 6H **55**
  WA5: Penk 5G **81**
Jubilee Ct. WA11: Hay 4D **30**
Jubilee Cres. CH62: Port S 6B **88**
  WA11: Hay 4H **31**
Jubilee Dr. CH48: W Kir 5A **64**
  L7: Liv .5H **53**
  L30: N'ton 2G **21**
  L35: Whis 5D **58**
Jubilee Rd. L21: Lith 4B **20**
  L23: Crosb 6E **9**
Jubilee Sports Bank 5H **53**
Jubilee Way WA8: Wid 2C **96**
Jubits La. WA8: Bold H 1E **79**
  WA9: Sut M 1E **79**
Juddfield St. WA11: Hay 5C **30**
Judges Dr. L6: Liv 3A **54**
Judges Way L6: Liv 3A **54**
Jugglers Yd. L3: Liv 1D **4**
  (off Marlborough St.)
Julian Way WA8: Wid 5D **78**
Julie Gro. L12: W Der 2B **56**
Juliet Av. CH63: Hghr B 4G **87**
July Rd. L6: Liv 2B **54**
July St. L20: Boot 6C **20**
Junction La. WA9: St H 6A **44**
  WA12: Newt W 3H **45**
Junction One Retail Pk.
  CH44: Wall 4H **49**
Junction Rd. WA11: Rainf 1E **17**
June Av. CH62: Brom 5E **105**
June Rd. L6: Liv 2B **54**
June St. L20: Boot 1C **34**
Juniper Cl. CH49: Grea 1A **84**
  L28: Stockb V 6D **38**
  WA10: St H 1B **42**
Juniper Gdns. L23: Thorn 3B **10**
Juniper Gro. WA7: Murd 6F **115**
Juniper St. L20: Kirkd 5C **34**
Justan Way L35: Rainh 2H **59**

Juvenal Pl. L3: Liv 3E **53**
Juvenal St. L3: Liv 4D **52**

K

Kaber Ct. L8: Liv 5E **71**
Kaigh Av. L23: Crosb 4F **9**
Kale Cl. CH48: W Kir 2B **82**
Kale Gro. L33: Kirkb 4C **14**
Kamala Way L11: Norr G 4E **37**
Kara Cl. L20: Boot 2C **34**
Karan Way L31: Mell 6F **13**
Karen Cl. WA5: Burtw 1H **63**
Karonga Rd. L10: Faz 4C **22**
Karonga Way L10: Faz 4D **22**
Karslake Rd. CH44: Wall 4F **51**
  L18: Moss H 4D **72**
Katherine Wlk. L10: Faz 4G **23**
Kearsley Cl. L4: Walt 6E **35**
Kearsley St. L4: Walt 6E **35**
Keats Av. L35: Whis 4F **59**
Keats Cl. WA8: Wid 3D **96**
Keats Gro. L36: Huy 6H **57**
Keats St. L20: Boot 6B **20**
Keble Dr. CH45: Wall 1H **49**
  L10: Ain 6A **12**
Keble Gro. L20: Boot 4C **34**
Keble St. L6: Liv 4G **53**
  WA8: Wid 4F **97**
KECKWICK 1H **115**
Keckwick La. WA4: Dares 1H **115**
Kedleston St. L8: Liv 5G **71**
Keegan Dr. CH44: Wall 5G **49**
Keele Cl. CH43: Bid 5G **49**
Keel Hey CH64: Will 6B **120**
Keel Wharf L3: Liv 2C **70**
Keenan Dr. L20: Boot 6E **21**
Keene Cl. L30: N'ton 5D **10**
Keepers La. CH63: Store 6D **86**
Keepers Wlk. WA7: Cas 3B **114**
Keighley Av. CH45: Wall 2A **50**
Keightley St. CH41: Birke 2F **69**
Keir Hardie Av. L20: Boot 6E **21**
Keith Av. L4: Walt 3F **35**
  WA5: Gt San 3F **81**
Keith Dr. CH63: East 2C **120**
Keithley Wlk. L24: Speke 1G **109**
Kelbrook Cl. WA9: St H 1H **61**
Kelburn Gro. L12: W Der 5H **37**
Kelby Cl. L8: Liv 5G **71**
Kelda Cl. L25: Gate 3C **74**
Kelday Cl. L33: Kirkb 1A **24**
Kelk Beck Cl. L31: Mag 5E **7**
Kellet's Pl. CH42: Rock F 6H **69**
Kellett Rd. CH46: Leas 4F **49**
Kellitt Rd. L15: Wav 2C **72**
Kelly Dr. L20: Boot 6E **21**
Kelly St. L34: Presc 1E **59**
Kelmscott Dr. CH44: Wall 3A **50**
Kelsall Av. CH62: East 4E **121**
  WA9: Sut M 5H **43**
Kelsall Cl. CH43: Oxton 6B **68**
  CH62: East 4E **121**
  WA8: Wid 2B **96**
Kelsey Cl. WA10: St H 1B **42**
Kelso Cl. L33: Kirkb 3H **13**
Kelso Rd. L6: Liv 4A **54**
Kelton Gro. L17: Aig 1C **90**
Kelvin Cl. CH44: Wall 6G **51**
Kelvin Gro. L8: Liv 3G **71**
Kelvington Cl. L10: Faz 4D **22**
Kelvin Pk. CH41: Tran 6G **51**
Kelvin Rd. CH41: Tran 5G **69**
  CH44: Wall 6G **51**
Kelvinside CH44: Wall 6F **51**
  L23: Crosb 1H **19**
Kemberton Dr. WA8: Wid 4E **79**
Kemble St. L6: Liv 4H **53**
  L34: Presc 1E **59**
Kemlyn Rd. L4: Walt 6G **35**
Kemp Av. L5: Liv 1F **53**
Kempsell Wlk. L26: Halew 4A **94**
Kempsell Way L26: Halew 4A **94**

Kempsey Gro. WA9: St H 6C **42**
Kempson Ter. CH63: Beb 1H **103**
Kempston St. L3: Liv 2H **5** (5E **53**)
Kempton Cl. L36: Roby 6E **57**
  WA7: Run 1G **123**
Kempton Pk. Rd. L10: Ain 6C **12**
Kempton Rd. CH62: New F 3B **88**
  L15: Wav 1B **72**
Kemsley Rd. L14: Knott A 4B **56**
Kenbury Cl. L33: Kirkb 5C **14**
Kenbury Rd. L33: Kirkb 5C **14**
Kendal Cl. CH63: Beb 5H **87**
Kendal Dr. L31: Mag 5C **6**
  L35: Rainh 4G **59**
  WA11: St H 3F **29**
Kendal M. L33: Kirkb 5H **13**
  (off Windermere Dr.)
Kendal Pk. L12: W Der 1H **55**
Kendal Ri. WA7: Beech 2H **123**
Kendal Rd. CH44: Wall 5C **50**
  L16: Child 2A **74**
  L33: Kirkb 5H **13**
  WA8: Wid 2A **96**
Kendal St. CH41: Birke 3G **69**
Kendricks Fold L35: Rainh 4H **59**
Kenilworth Av. WA7: Run 5F **113**
Kenilworth Cl. L25: Woolt 6A **74**
Kenilworth Dr. CH61: Pens 6C **84**
Kenilworth Gdns. CH49: Upton 3C **66**
Kenilworth Rd. CH44: Wall 4F **51**
  L16: Child 2H **73**
  L23: Blun 5E **9**
Kenilworth St. L20: Boot 2B **34**
Kenilworth Way L25: Woolt 6A **74**
Kenley Av. WA8: Cron 4B **78**
Kenmare Rd. L15: Wav 3C **72**
Kenmay Wlk. L33: Kirkb 6C **14**
Ken M. L20: Boot 5C **20**
Kennedy Rd. CH43: Pren 2A **86**
Kennelwood Av. L33: Kirkb 6B **14**
Kennessee Cl. L31: Mag 1C **12**
KENNESSEE GREEN 1B **12**
Kenneth Cl. L30: N'ton 6E **11**
  L34: Presc 2D **58**
Kenneth Rd. WA8: Wid 4A **96**
Kennet Rd. CH63: Hghr B 6F **87**
  WA11: Hay 5E **31**
Kennford Rd. L11: Crox 6G **23**
Kennington Pk. WA8: Wid 6C **78**
KENSINGTON 5H **53**
Kensington L7: Liv 5G **53**
Kensington Av. WA9: St H 6G **43**
Kensington Cl. WA8: Wid 5H **79**
Kensington Dr. L34: Presc 2A **58**
Kensington Gdns. CH46: More 1C **66**
Kensington St. L6: Liv 5G **53**
Kent Av. L21: Lith 3C **20**
Kent Cl. CH63: Brom 5B **104**
  L20: Boot 1D **34**
  (off Brookhill Rd.)
Kent Gro. WA7: Run 4F **113**
Kentmere Av. WA11: St H 3G **29**
Kentmere Dr. CH61: Pens 2D **100**
Kent M. CH43: Oxton 5D **68**
  (off Kent St.)
Kenton Cl. L25: Gate 2D **74**
Kenton Rd. L26: Halew 4H **93**
Kent Rd. CH44: Wall 4C **50**
  WA9: St H 5G **43**
Kents Bank L12: W Der 4G **37**
Kent St. CH43: Oxton 5D **68**
  L1: Liv 6F **5** (1D **70**)
  WA8: Wid 2F **97**
Kentwell Gro. L12: W Der 6H **37**
Kenview Cl. WA8: Hale B 1G **111**
Kenway WA11: Rainf 3G **17**
Kenwood Cl. L27: N'ley 4H **75**
Kenwright Cres. WA9: St H 5G **43**
Kenwyn Rd. CH45: Wall 2D **50**
Kenyon Av. WA5: Penk 4G **81**
Kenyon Cl. L33: Kirkb 3B **14**
Kenyon Ct. L8: Liv 3F **71**
  (off Park Rd.)
Kenyon Rd. L15: Wav 4E **73**

Kenyons La. L31: Lyd, Mag 3C 6
Kenyons La. Nth. WA11: Hay 3H 31
Kenyons La. Sth. WA11: Hay 4H 31
Kenyons Lodge L31: Mag 4D 6
Kenyons Pl. L31: Lyd 4C 6
Kenyon Ter. CH43: Oxton 4D 68
Kepler St. L21: Sea 5A 20
Keppel St. L20: Boot 4B 34
Kerman Cl. L12: W Der 4F 37
Kerr Cl. L33: Kirkb 3A 14
Kerr Gro. WA9: St H 2A 44
Kerris Cl. L17: Aig 1A 90
Kerrysdale Cl. WA9: St H 6H 43
Kersey Rd. L32: Kirkb 3B 24
Kersey Wlk. L27: N'ley 3B 24
Kershaw Av. L23: Crosb 6H 9
Kershaw St. WA8: Wid 2B 96
Kerswell Cl. WA9: St H 1H 61
Keston Wlk. L26: Halew 5H 93
Kestrel Av. CH49: Upton 3B 66
Kestrel Cl. CH49: Upton 3B 66
    WA11: St H 5F 29
Kestrel Ct. L23: Blun 6C 8
Kestrel Dene L10: Faz 5E 23
Kestrel Gro. L26: Halew 2F 93
Kestrel Rd. CH46: More 6A 48
    CH60: Hesw 6G 101
Kestrels Way WA7: Pal F 1B 124
Keswick Av. CH63: East 2C 120
Keswick Cl. L31: Mag 5D 6
    WA8: Wid 2A 96
Keswick Dr. L21: Lith 3D 20
Keswick Gdns. CH63: Brom 2C 120
Keswick Pl. CH43: Bid 6H 49
Keswick Rd. CH45: Wall 6A 32
    L18: Aller 1G 91
    WA10: St H 6C 28
Keswick Vs. L16: Child 1C 74
                             (off Buttermere Rd.)
Keswick Way L16: Child 1C 74
Ketterer Cl. WA9: St H 3G 43
Kevelioc Cl. CH63: Spit 2H 103
Kew Gdns. Cl. WA8: Wid 5H 79
Kew St. L5: Liv 2D 52
Keybank Rd. L12: W Der 5E 37
Keys Ct. L1: Liv 5E 5 (6D 52)
Keystone Cl. L7: Liv 1H 71
Kiddman St. L9: Walt 2F 35
Kidstone Cl. WA9: St H 6H 43
Kilbuck La. WA11: Hay . . . . . .3H 31 & 2H 31
Kilburn Av. CH62: East 1E 121
Kilburn Gro. WA9: St H 6C 42
Kilburn St. L21: Lith 5B 20
Kildale Cl. L31: Mag 5B 6
Kildare Cl. L24: Hale 3D 110
Kildonan Rd. L17: Aig 1B 90
Kilgraston Gdns. L17: Aig 2D 90
Killarney Gro. CH44: Wall 4C 50
Killarney Rd. L13: Liv 4F 55
Killester Rd. L25: Gate 5D 74
Killington Way L4: Kirkd 5E 35
Kilmalcolm Cl. CH43: Oxton 5B 68
Kilmore Cl. L9: Ain 3A 22
Kilmory Av. L25: Woolt 1E 93
Kiln Cl. WA10: Eccl 6A 28
Kilncroft WA7: Brook 2D 124
                                   (not continuous)
Kiln Hey L12: W Der 2G 55
Kiln La. WA10: Eccl, Windle 6H 27
Kiln Rd. CH49: Woodc 6E 67
Kilnyard Rd. L23: Crosb 5F 9
Kilrea Cl. L11: Norr G 5D 36
Kilrea Lodge L11: Norr G 5D 36
Kilrea Rd. L11: Norr G 5C 36
Kilsail Rd. L32: Kirkb 4C 24
Kilsby Dr. WA8: Wid 1A 98
Kilshaw Rd. WA5: Burtw 1H 63
Kilshaw St. L6: Liv 3G 53
                                   (not continuous)
Kimberley Av. L23: Crosb 6F 9
    WA9: St H 6C 42
Kimberley Cl. L8: Liv 2G 71
Kimberley Dr. L23: Crosb 6F 9

Kimberley Rd. CH45: Wall 1D 50
Kindale Rd. CH43: Pren 2A 86
Kinder St. L6: Liv 4F 53
King Arthurs Wlk. WA7: Cas 4C 114
King Av. L20: Boot 5E 21
King Edward Cl. L35: Rainh 3H 59
King Edward Dr. CH62: Port S 5B 88
King Edward Ind. Est. L3: Liv 2A 4
King Edward Pde. L3: Liv 2B 4
King Edward Rd. L35: Rainh 3H 59
    WA10: St H 5B 28
Kingfield Rd. L9: Walt 6F 21
Kingfisher Bus. Pk. L20: Boot 4C 20
    WA8: Wid 3H 97
Kingfisher Cl. L27: N'ley 4H 75
    L33: Kirkb 3A 14
    WA7: Beech 2B 124
Kingfisher Ct. L31: Lyd 3A 6
Kingfisher Dr. WA11: St H 5F 29
Kingfisher Gro. L12: W Der 4B 38
Kingfisher Ho. CH41: Birke 3A 70
    L13: Liv .6E 55
Kingfisher Way CH49: Upton 3B 66
King George V Sports Complex 3H 57
King George Dr. CH44: Wall 1F 51
King George Rd. WA11: Hay 4H 31
King George's Dr. CH62: Port S 5B 88
King George's Way CH43: Bid 2A 68
Kingham Cl. CH46: Leas 4F 49
    L25: Woolt 1E 93
    WA8: Wid 2H 97
Kingham M. L25: Woolt 1E 93
King James Ct. WA7: Pal F 1A 124
Kinglake Rd. CH44: Wall 3F 51
Kinglake St. L7: Liv 6H 53
Kinglass Rd. CH63: Spit 2B 104
King Oswald Cres. WA8: Wid 3D 78
King's Av. CH47: Meols 1D 64
Kingsbrook Way CH63: Hghr B 3F 87
King's Brow CH63: Hghr B 5F 87
Kingsbury CH48: W Kir 6D 64
Kingsbury Rd. WA8: Wid 5H 79
King's Bus. Pk. L34: Presc 2A 58
Kings Cl. CH63: Hghr B 4F 87
    L17: Aig .1A 90
Kings Ct. CH43: Oxton 5D 68
    CH47: Hoy 2A 64
    CH63: Hghr B 4F 87
    L21: Sea 4H 19
    WA7: Manor P 1F 115
Kingscourt Rd. L12: W Der 2G 55
Kingsdale Av. CH42: Tran 1F 87
    L35: Rainh 4B 60
Kingsdale Rd. L18: Moss H 4E 73
    WA5: Gt San 1H 81
Kings Dock St. L1: Liv 2D 70
Kingsdown Rd. L11: Norr G 4E 37
Kingsdown St. CH41: Tran 5G 69
Kings Dr. CH48: Caldy 4C 82
    CH61: Pens 6D 84
    L25: Gate 5E 75
    L25: Woolt 1D 92
    L34: Presc 2A 58
King's Dr. Nth. CH48: W Kir 2D 82
Kingsfield Rd. L31: Mag 2A 12
King's Gap, The CH47: Hoy 2A 64
Kingshead Cl. WA7: Cas 3C 114
Kingsheath Av. L14: Knott A 3A 56
Kingsland Cres. L11: Norr G 2C 36
Kingsland Rd. CH42: Tran 5E 69
    L11: Norr G 2C 36
King's La. CH63: Hghr B 4F 87
Kingsley Av. CH62: East 4E 121
Kingsley Cl. CH61: Pens 2E 101
    L31: Lyd .2B 6
Kingsley Cres. WA7: Run 4E 113
Kingsley Rd. CH44: Wall 4D 50
    L8: Liv 2H 71
    WA7: Run 4E 113
    WA10: St H 2H 43
Kingsley St. CH41: Birke 1C 68
Kings Lynn Dr. L19: Garst 5F 91
Kingsmead Dr. L25: Hunts X 4D 92

Kingsmead Gro. CH43: Oxton 4B 68
Kings Mdw. WA7: Nort 5E 115
Kingsmead Rd. CH43: Oxton 4B 68
    CH46: More 5D 48
Kingsmead Rd. Nth. CH43: Oxton 4B 68
Kingsmead Rd. Sth. CH43: Oxton 4B 68
Kings Mt. CH43: Oxton 5D 68
Kingsnorth L35: Whis 5F 59
Kings Pde. CH45: New B 4C 32
    CH45: Wall, New B 5A 32
    L3: Liv 2C 70
Kings Pk. L21: Sea 4H 19
Kings Rd. CH63: Hghr B 3F 87
    L20: Boot 3C 34
    L23: Crosb 5F 9
    WA10: St H 3A 42
Kings Sq. CH41: Birke 3H 69
Kings Ter. L20: Boot 4C 34
Kingsthorne Pk. L25: Hunts X 5E 93
Kingsthorne Rd. L25: Hunts X 5E 93
Kingston Av. WA5: Gt San 3G 81
Kingston Cl. CH46: More 1C 66
    L12: W Der 2A 56
    WA7: Run 3A 114
King St. CH42: Rock F 2A 88
    CH44: Wall 2F 51
    L19: Garst 1G 107
    L22: Water 2F 19
    WA7: Run 2E 113
    WA10: St H 2D 42
Kingsville Rd. CH63: Hghr B 6G 87
Kings Wlk. CH42: Rock F 2A 88
    CH48: W Kir 1C 82
KINGSWAY 3E 97
Kingsway CH45: Wall 1C 50
    CH60: Hesw 1G 117
    CH63: Hghr B 4F 87
    L3: Liv 4C 52
    L22: Water 1G 19
    L35: Presc 2D 58
    L36: Huy, Roby 3F 57
    WA8: Wid 4E 97
    WA11: St H 3E 29
Kingsway Ct. L3: Liv 3D 52
Kingsway Ho. WA8: Wid 4E 97
Kingsway Leisure Cen. 3E 97
Kingsway Pde. L36: Huy 3E 57
                                       (off Kingsway)
Kingsway Pk. L3: Liv 3D 52
Kingsway Tunnel App. CH44: Wall 4A 50
Kingswell Cl. L7: Liv 1H 71
Kings Wharf CH41: Birke 6H 51
Kingswood L36: Huy 4E 57
Kingswood Av. L9: Ain 4H 21
    L22: Water 1H 19
Kingswood Blvd. CH63: Hghr B 3G 87
Kingswood Ct. L33: Kirkb 5B 14
Kingswood Dr. L23: Crosb 6F 9
Kingswood Rd. CH44: Wall 2E 51
Kington Rd. CH48: W Kir 6A 64
Kinley Gdns. L20: Boot 6E 21
                                 (off Wheatley Av.)
Kinloch Cl. L26: Halew 4A 94
Kinloss Rd. CH49: Grea 6A 66
Kinmel Cl. CH41: Birke 2F 69
    L4: Walt .3E 35
Kinmel St. L8: Liv 4G 71
    WA9: St H 5G 43
Kinnaird Rd. CH45: Wall 1C 50
Kinnaird St. L8: Liv 6G 71
Kinnerton Cl. CH46: More 1H 65
Kinnock Pk. WA5: Burtw 1G 63
Kinross Rd. CH45: Wall 1H 49
    L10: Faz .4D 22
    L22: Water 3G 19
Kinsale Dr. L19: Aller 4H 91
Kinsman Ho. L19: Grea 4D 90
Kintore Cl. CH63: East 3C 120
Kintore Dr. WA5: Gt San 3F 81
Kintore Rd. L19: Gras 4F 91
Kipling Av. CH42: Rock F 2H 87
    L36: Huy .6A 58
Kipling Cres. WA8: Wid 3D 96
Kipling Gro. WA9: Sut M 4E 61

Kipling St.—Lancelyn Pct.

Kipling St. L20: Boot 6A **20**
Kirby Cl. CH48: W Kir 2C **82**
Kirby Mt. CH48: W Kir 3C **82**
Kirby Pk. CH48: W Kir 2C **82**
Kirby Pk. Mans. CH48: W Kir 2B **82**
Kirby Rd. L20: Boot 5D **20**
Kirkbride Cl. L27: N'ley 5A **76**
Kirkbride Lawn *L27: N'ley 5A **76***
(off Kirkbride Cl.)
Kirkbride Wlk. *L27: N'ley 5A **76***
(off Kirkbride Cl.)
Kirkburn Cl. L8: Liv 5F **71**
KIRKBY 1A **24**
Kirkby Bank Rd. L33: Know I 1D **24**
Kirkby Gallery 1A **24**
Kirkby Leisure Cen. 2A **24**
KIRKBY PARK 6G **13**
Kirkby Row L32: Kirkb 6G **13**
Kirkby Station (Rail) 6G **13**
Kirkcaldy Av. WA5: Gt San 3F **81**
Kirk Cotts. CH45: Wall 6D **32**
KIRKDALE 5E **35**
Kirkdale Rd. L5: Kirkd 1D **52**
Kirkdale Station (Rail) 4D **34**
Kirkdale Va. L4: Walt 6E **35**
Kirket Cl. CH63: Beb 1A **104**
Kirket La. CH63: Beb 1H **103**
Kirkfield Gro. CH42: Rock F 2A **88**
Kirkham Rd. WA8: Wid 1G **97**
Kirkland Av. CH42: Tran 1F **87**
Kirkland Cl. L9: Walt 4F **21**
Kirkland Rd. CH45: New B 5E **33**
Kirklands, The CH48: W Kir 2C **82**
Kirkland St. WA10: St H 1D **42**
Kirkmaiden Rd. L19: Aller 3F **91**
Kirkman Fold L35: Rainh 4H **59**
Kirkmore Rd. L18: Moss H 1E **91**
Kirkmount CH49: Upton 4E **67**
Kirk Rd. L21: Lith 5C **20**
Kirkside Cl. L12: Crox 2H **37**
Kirkstead Wlk. L31: Mell 6F **13**
Kirkstone Av. WA11: St H 3G **29**
Kirkstone Cres. WA7: Beech 3C **124**
Kirkstone Rd. Nth. L21: Lith 2C **20**
Kirkstone Rd. Sth. L21: Lith 3D **20**
Kirkstone Rd. W. L21: Ford, Lith 1B **20**
Kirk St. L5: Liv 1E **53**
Kirkwall Dr. WA5: Penk 6H **81**
Kirkway CH45: Wall 6D **32**
CH49: Grea 5C **66**
CH49: Upton 4D **66**
CH63: Hghr B 4F **87**
Kitchener Dr. L9: Walt 5F **21**
Kitchener St. WA10: St H 1B **42**
Kitchen St. L1: Liv 2D **70**
Kitling Rd. L34: Know 6D **24**
Kiverley Cl. L18: Aller 6A **74**
Klick Fitness
Aintree 2H **21**
Knap, The CH60: Hesw 1E **117**
Knaresborough Rd. CH44: Wall 3B **50**
Knavesmire Way L19: Aller 4H **91**
Knebworth Cl. L12: W Der 6H **37**
Knighton Rd. L4: Walt 4B **36**
Knight Rd. WA5: Burtw 1H **63**
Knightsbridge Cl. WA8: Wid 5H **79**
Knightsbridge Ct. CH43: Noct 6H **67**
Knightsbridge Wlk. L33: Kirkb 3H **13**
Knights Cl. WA8: Wid 5A **80**
Knights Grange WA9: St H 1G **43**
Knight St. L1: Liv 6G **5** (1E **71**)
Knightsway L22: Water 1H **19**
Knightswood Ct. L18: Aller 3G **91**
Knoclaid Rd. L13: Liv 6C **36**
Knoll, The CH43: Oxton 6C **68**
WA7: Pal F 6B **114**
KNOTTY ASH 4G **55**
Knotty M. L25: Woolt 6E **75**
Knowe, The CH64: Will 6A **120**
Knowle Cl. L12: W Der 3G **37**
Knowles, The L23: Blun 6D **8**
Knowles Ho. Av. WA10: Eccl 2F **41**
Knowles St. CH41: Birke 2E **69**
WA8: Wid 1G **97**
Knowl Hey Rd. L26: Halew 5A **94**
KNOWSLEY 1F **39**
Knowsley Bus. Pk. L34: Know 5C **24**
(School La., not continuous)
L34: Know 5E **25**
(Villiers Rd.)
Knowsley Cl. CH42: Rock F 2A **88**
Knowsley Ct. CH42: Rock F 2A **88**
Knowsley Ent. Workshops
L33: Know I 2D **24**
Knowsley Expressway L35: Tar G 3D **76**
WA8: Wid 1E **95**
Knowsley Hall 5H **39**
Knowsley Hgts. L36: Huy 2G **57**
Knowsley Ind. Pk. L33: Know I 4D **24**
(Faraday Rd.)
L33: Know I 1E **25**
(Manor Complex)
Knowsley La. L34: Know P 5E **39**
L34: Know, Know P 4E **39**
L36: Huy 5E **39**
Knowsley Leisure & Culture Pk. 4A **58**
KNOWSLEY PARK 6H **25**
Knowsley Pk. La. L34: Presc 6C **40**
Knowsley Rd. CH42: Rock F 2A **88**
CH45: Wall 1C **50**
L19: Gras 5E **91**
L20: Boot 6A **20**
L35: Rainh 5B **60**
WA10: St H 2A **42**
Knowsley Safari Pk. 6C **40**
Knowsley St. L4: Walt 3F **35**
Knowsley Vw. WA11: Rainf 1E **17**
Knox Cl. CH62: Port S 5B **88**
Knox St. CH41: Birke 3H **69**
Knutsford Cl. WA10: Eccl 3H **41**
Knutsford Grn. CH46: More 6D **48**
Knutsford Rd. CH46: More 6C **48**
Knutsford Wlk. L31: Lyd 3C **6**
Kramar Wlk. L33: Kirkb 1B **24**
Kremlin Dr. L13: Liv 2D **54**
Kylemore Av. L18: Moss H 6D **72**
Kylemore Cl. CH61: Pens 2C **100**
Kylemore Ct. L26: Halew 4G **93**
Kylemore Dr. CH61: Pens 2C **100**
Kylemore Rd. CH43: Oxton 5C **68**
Kylemore Way CH61: Pens 2C **100**
L26: Halew 4F **93**
Kynance Rd. L11: Crox 6H **23**

L

Laburnham Ter. *L19: Garst 5G **91***
(off Chapel Rd.)
Laburnum Av. L36: Huy 1G **75**
WA11: St H 4H **29**
Laburnum Ct. *L8: Liv 5G **71***
(off Weller Way)
Laburnum Cres. L32: Kirkb 6H **13**
Laburnum Gro. CH61: Irby 5B **84**
*L15: Wav 1E **73***
(off Chestnut Gro.)
L31: Mag 6E **7**
WA7: Run 5F **113**
Laburnum La. WA5: Gt San 3E **81**
Laburnum Pl. L20: Boot 2D **34**
Laburnum Rd. CH43: Oxton 5E **69**
CH45: New B 6D **32**
L7: Liv 4B **54**
Lace St. L3: Liv 2E **5** (5D **52**)
Lacey Ct. WA8: Wid 4F **97**
Lacey Rd. L34: Presc 2E **59**
Lacey St. WA8: Wid 4E **97**
WA10: St H 5B **42**
Laddock Cl. L4: Walt 6A **36**
Ladies' Wlk. WA9: Bold 4C **62**
Ladybower Cl. CH49: Upton 3C **66**
L7: Liv 1H **71**
Lady Chapel Cl. L1: Liv 2E **71**
Lady Chapel Sq. *L1: Liv 2E **71***
(off Lady Chapel Cl.)
Ladyewood Rd. CH44: Wall 4E **51**
Ladyfield CH43: Bid 2G **67**
Ladyfields L12: W Der 2F **55**
Lady Lever Art Gallery 5B **88**
Lady Mountford Ho. L18: Moss H 6D **72**
Ladypool L24: Hale 4C **110**
Lady Richeld Cl. WA7: Nort 2F **115**
Ladysmith Rd. L10: Faz 4D **22**
LAFFAK 4H **29**
Laffak Rd. WA11: St H 4G **29**
LA Fitness
Mossley Hill 6E **73**
Lagan Ho. CH46: Leas 3C **48**
Laggan St. L7: Liv 5H **53**
Lagrange Arc. WA10: St H 2E **43**
Laird Cl. CH41: Birke 1B **68**
Lairds Pl. L3: Liv 3D **52**
Laird St. CH41: Birke 1B **68**
Laithwaite Cl. WA9: Sut M 4F **61**
Lake Ent. Pk. CH62: Brom 3E **105**
Lakeland Cl. L1: Liv 6E **5** (1D **70**)
Lakemoor Cl. WA9: St H 6H **43**
Lakenheath Rd. L26: Halew 5G **93**
Lake Pl. CH47: Hoy 2B **64**
Lake Rd. CH47: Hoy 2B **64**
L15: Wav 2E **73**
Lakeside Cl. WA8: Wid 4G **95**
Lakeside Ct. CH45: New B 5E **33**
WA11: Rainf 3G **17**
Lakeside Gdns. L23: Thorn 3B **10**
WA11: Rainf 3G **17**
Lakeside Lawn L27: N'ley 5A **76**
Lakeside Vw. L22: Water 3F **19**
Lakes Rd. L9: Ain 4B **22**
Lake St. L4: Walt 6G **35**
Lake Vw. L35: Whis 1E **77**
Lake Vw. Ct. L4: Walt 3G **35**
Laleston Cl. WA8: Wid 3C **96**
Lambert St. L3: Liv 2H **5** (5E **53**)
(Kempston St.)
L3: Liv 2H **5**
(Lambert Way)
Lambert Way L3: Liv 2H **5** (5E **53**)
Lambeth Ct. CH47: Hoy 2A **64**
Lambeth Rd. L4: Kirkd 6D **34**
L5: Kirkd 6D **34**
Lambourn Av. WA8: Cron 4A **78**
Lambourne Gro. WA9: St H 2C **44**
Lambourne Rd. L4: Walt 4B **36**
Lambrigg Row L5: Liv 6F **35**
Lambshear La. L31: Lyd 3B **6**
Lambsickle Cl. WA7: West 1D **122**
Lambsickle La. WA7: Run, West 1D **122**
Lambton Rd. L17: Aig 6H **71**
Lamerton Cl. WA5: Penk 5F **81**
Lammermoor Rd. L18: Moss H 1E **91**
Lampeter Rd. L6: Liv 1A **54**
Lamport Cl. WA8: Wid 6A **80**
Lamport St. L8: Liv 3E **71**
Lanark Cl. WA10: St H 3D **42**
Lanark Gdns. WA8: Wid 6C **78**
Lancashire Gdns. WA10: St H 3D **42**
Lancaster Av. CH45: Wall 2D **50**
L17: Liv 3B **72**
L23: Crosb 6F **9**
L35: Whis 4D **58**
WA7: Run 5C **112**
WA8: Wid 1G **95**
Lancaster Cl. CH62: Port S 5B **88**
L5: Kirkd 1D **52**
L31: Mag 6E **7**
WA12: Newt W 1H **45**
Lancaster Rd. L36: Huy 3A **58**
WA8: Wid 6E **79**
Lancaster St. L5: Kirkd 1D **52**
L9: Walt 2F **35**
Lancaster Wlk. *L36: Huy 3A **58***
(off Lancaster Rd.)
Lance Cl. L5: Liv 2F **53**
Lancefield Rd. L9: Walt 6F **21**
Lance Gro. L15: Wav 2E **73**
Lance La. L15: Wav 2E **73**
Lancelots Hey L3: Liv 3B **4**
Lancelyn Ct. CH63: Spit 2A **104**
Lancelyn Pct. *CH63: Spit 2A **104***
(off Spital Rd.)

Lancelyn Ter. CH63: Beb 1H **103**
Lancer Ct. WA7: Ast 2A **114**
Lancer Way L12: W Der 6A **38**
Lancing Cl. L25: Hunts X 2F **93**
Lancing Dr. L10: Ain 1B **22**
Lancing Rd. L25: Hunts X 2F **93**
Lancing Way L25: Hunts X 2F **93**
Lancots La. WA9: St H 5H **43**
Land End L31: Mag 6H **7**
Lander Rd. L21: Lith 5B **20**
Landford Av. L9: Faz 1C **36**
Landford Pl. L9: Faz 1C **36**
LANDICAN 3G **85**
Landican Cemetery & Crematorium
    CH49: Woodc 2F **85**
Landican La. CH49: Woodc 3G **85**
    CH63: Store 5A **86**
Landican Rd. CH49: Woodc 4F **85**
Landor Cl. L5: Liv 2C **52**
Landsdowne Ho. CH41: Birke 3A **70**
Landseer Rd. L5: Liv 2F **53**
LANE ENDS 5E **95**
Lanfranc Cl. L16: Child 1A **74**
Lanfranc Way L16: Child 1A **74**
Langbar L35: Whis 5E **59**
Langdale Av. CH61: Pens 1D **100**
Langdale Cl. L32: Kirkb 2B **24**
    WA8: Wid 3A **96**
Langdale Ct. CH41: Birke 1D **68**
Langdale Dr. L31: Mag 5D **6**
Langdale Gro. WA11: St H 4F **29**
Langdale Rd. CH45: Wall 6B **32**
    CH63: Beb 1G **103**
    L15: Wav 3C **72**
    WA7: Run 4F **113**
Langdale St. L20: Boot 2D **34**
Langdale Way WA6: Frod 6G **123**
Langfield Gro. CH62: Brom 2D **120**
Langford L24: Hale 3C **110**
Langford Rd. L19: Aig 3D **90**
Langham Av. L17: Aig 6A **72**
Langham Ct. L4: Walt 5F **35**
Langham St. L4: Walt 5F **35**
Langham St. Ind. Est. *L4: Walt* *5F **35***
    (off Langham St.)
Langland Cl. L4: Walt 5B **36**
Lang La. CH48: W Kir 6B **64**
Lang La. Sth. CH48: W Kir 6C **64**
Langley Beck WA8: Wid 5G **79**
Langley Cl. CH63: Spit 3A **104**
    L12: Crox 2B **38**
Langley Cl. Shop. Cen. L12: Crox . . .2B **38**
Langley Rd. CH63: Spit 3A **104**
Langley St. L8: Liv 3E **71**
Langrove St. L5: Liv 2E **53**
Langsdale St. L3: Liv 1H **5** (4E **53**)
    (not continuous)
Langshaw Lea L27: N'ley 5H **75**
Langstone Av. CH49: Grea 6A **66**
Langton Cl. WA8: Wid 6H **77**
Langton Rd. L15: Wav 2B **72**
    L33: Kirkb 4B **14**
Langtree Park 3F **43**
Langtree St. WA9: St H 2G **43**
Langtry Cl. L4: Kirkd 5D **34**
Langtry Rd. L4: Kirkd 5D **34**
Lansbury Av. WA9: St H 3A **44**
Lansbury Rd. L36: Huy 5A **58**
Lansdown L12: W Der 1E **55**
Lansdowne Cl. CH41: Birke 1C **68**
Lansdowne Ct. CH43: Bid 1B **68**
    WA9: St H 6H **43**
Lansdowne Pl. CH43: Bid 1B **68**
    L5: Liv 1F **53**
Lansdowne Rd. CH41: Birke 1B **68**
    CH43: Bid 1B **68**
    CH45: Wall 5B **32**
Lansdowne Way L36: Huy 5G **57**
Lanville Rd. L19: Aig 2F **91**
Lanyork Rd. L3: Liv 1B **4** (4B **52**)
Lapford Cres. L33: Kirkb 5C **14**
Lapford Wlk. L33: Kirkb 5C **14**
Lapwing Cl. L12: W Der 4A **38**
Lapwing Ct. L26: Halew 2G **93**

Lapwing Gro. WA7: Pal F 1C **124**
Lapwing La. WA4: Moore 4H **99**
Lapwing Rd. CH60: Hesw 1D **116**
Lapworth Cl. CH46: More 1H **65**
Lapworth St. L5: Kirkd 1D **52**
Larch Av. WA5: Penk 4G **81**
    WA8: Wid 1F **97**
Larch Cl. L19: Gras 4D **90**
    WA7: Run 6G **113**
Larch Ct. *L8: Liv* *5G **71***
    (off Weller Way)
Larchdale Gro. L9: Walt 1H **35**
Larchfield Rd. L23: Thorn 4A **10**
Larch Gro. CH43: Bid 1A **68**
    L15: Wav 6E **55**
Larch Ho. *L7: Liv* *1F **71***
    (off Mulberry St.)
Larch Lea L6: Liv 2H **53**
    (not continuous)
Larch Rd. CH42: Tran 4E **69**
    L36: Roby 5E **57**
    WA7: Run 6G **113**
    WA11: Hay 4G **31**
Larchtree M. L12: W Der 5A **38**
Larchwood Av. L31: Mag 2A **12**
Larchwood Cl. CH61: Pens 2D **100**
    L25: Gate 4D **74**
Larchwood Dr. CH63: Hghr B 4H **87**
Larcombe Av. CH49: Upton 4D **66**
Larkfield Cl. L17: Aig 1A **90**
Larkfield Ct. WA11: St H 3D **28**
Larkfield Gro. L17: Aig 1A **90**
Larkfield Rd. L17: Aig 1A **90**
Larkfield Vw. L15: Wav 1C **72**
Larkhill Av. CH49: Upton 2E **67**
Larkhill Cl. L13: Liv 6C **36**
Larkhill La. L13: Liv 6C **36**
Larkhill Pl. L13: Liv 6D **36**
Larkhill Vw. L13: Liv 6D **36**
Larkhill Way CH49: Upton 2E **67**
Larkin Cl. CH62: New F 4A **88**
Lark La. L17: Aig 6A **72**
Larkspur Cl. WA7: Beech 3B **124**
Larkspur Ct. L31: Mell 6E **13**
Larksway CH60: Hesw 5F **101**
Lark Way L17: Aig 6A **72**
Larne Ct. WA8: Wid 1C **96**
Larton Farm Cl. CH48: W Kir 1E **83**
Larton Rd. CH48: W Kir 6E **65**
Lartonwood CH48: W Kir 6E **65**
Lascelles Rd. L19: Aller 4H **91**
Lascelles St. WA9: St H 2G **43**
Latchford Rd. CH60: Hesw 1F **117**
Late Moffatt Rd. W. *L9: Ain* *4H **21***
    (off Moffatt Rd.)
Latham Av. WA7: Run 4F **113**
Latham Cl. L7: Liv 5B **54**
Latham St. L5: Kirkd 1D **52**
    (not continuous)
Latham Way CH63: Spit 3B **104**
Lathbury La. L17: Aig 4C **72**
Lathom Av. CH44: Wall 3D **50**
    L21: Sea *5H **19***
    (off Chatham Cl.)
Lathom Cl. *L21: Sea* *5H **19***
    (off Chatham Cl.)
    L36: Huy 1A **58**
Lathom Ct. L36: Huy 1A **58**
Lathom Dr. L31: Mag 4D **6**
    WA11: Rainf 2F **17**
Lathom Rd. L20: Boot 6C **20**
    L36: Huy 4G **57**
Lathum Cl. L35: Presc 2E **59**
Latimer Cl. WA8: Wid 5G **79**
Latimer St. L5: Liv 1D **52**
Latrigg Rd. L17: Aig 1C **90**
Lauder Cl. L33: Kirkb 3H **13**
Launceston Cl. WA7: Brook 1E **125**
Launceston Dr. WA5: Penk 6G **81**
Laund, The CH45: Wall 2B **50**
Laurel Av. CH60: Hesw 4D **100**
    CH63: Hghr B 1G **103**
Laurel Bank WA8: Wid 6E **79**
Laurelbanks CH60: Hesw 4C **100**

Laurel Ct. *L7: Liv* *4B **54***
    (off Laurel Rd.)
    WA11: St H 4F **29**
Laurel Dr. CH64: Will 6B **120**
    WA10: Eccl 1F **41**
Laurel Gro. L8: Liv 3A **72**
    L22: Water 1F **19**
    L36: Huy 1G **75**
Laurelhurst Av. CH61: Pens 1E **101**
Laurel Rd. CH42: Tran 5F **69**
    L7: Liv 4B **54**
    L34: Presc 1E **59**
    WA10: St H 3B **42**
    WA11: Hay 6B **30**
Laurels, The CH46: Leas 4C **48**
Laurel Way WA10: St H 3B **42**
Laurence Deacon Ct. CH41: Birke . . .2F **69**
Lauren Cl. L36: Huy 5B **58**
Lauriston Rd. L4: Walt 4A **36**
Laurus Cl. L27: N'ley 4H **75**
Lavan Cl. L6: Liv 4G **53**
Lavan St. L6: Liv 4G **53**
Lavender Cl. WA7: Run 4G **113**
Lavender Cres. L34: Presc 1E **59**
Lavender Gdns. L23: Thorn 4B **10**
    WA9: Bold 6C **44**
Lavender Way L9: Walt 1H **35**
Lavrock Bank L8: Liv 5E **71**
Lawford Dr. CH60: Hesw 5G **101**
Lawler Gro. L34: Presc 6E **41**
Lawler St. L21: Lith 5B **20**
Lawnhurst Gro. L17: Aig 3C **90**
Lawns, The CH43: Bid 2H **67**
Lawns Av. CH63: Raby M 1B **120**
Lawnside Cl. CH42: Rock F 2H **87**
Lawnswood Cl. CH42: Rock F 3A **88**
Lawrence Cl. L19: Gras 4E **91**
Lawrence Ct. CH42: Rock F 3A **88**
Lawrence Gro. L15: Wav 2C **72**
Lawrence Rd. L15: Wav 2B **72**
    WA10: Windle 5A **28**
Lawrenson St. WA10: St H 2C **42**
Lawson Ho. WA7: Run 5E **113**
Lawson Rd. WA7: Run 5E **113**
Lawson Wlk. L12: Crox 2H **37**
Lawton Av. L20: Boot 6E **21**
Lawton Rd. L22: Water 1F **19**
    L35: Rainh 5B **60**
    L36: Roby 6E **57**
Lawton St. L1: Liv 5G **5** (6E **53**)
Laxey St. L8: Liv 3E **71**
Laxton Rd. L25: Hunts X 4E **93**
Layford Rd. L36: Huy 2F **57**
Layton Av. CH43: Pren 1B **86**
Layton Cl. L25: Woolt 1E **93**
Layton Rd. L25: Woolt 1E **93**
Layton Way L34: Presc 2D **58**
Lazonby Cl. CH43: Bid 1G **67**
Leach Cft. L28: Stockb V 6C **38**
Leach La. WA9: Sut L 3H **61**
Leach St. WA10: St H 1D **42**
Leach Vw. WA11: St H 4F **29**
Leach Way CH61: Irby 5A **84**
Lea Cl. CH43: Noct 5A **68**
Lea Cross Gro. WA8: Wid 6A **78**
Leadenhall Cl. L5: Liv 1F **53**
Leafield Cl. CH61: Irby 5D **84**
Leafield Rd. L25: Hunts X 5D **92**
Leagate L10: Faz 3D **22**
LEA GREEN 2D **60**
Lea Grn. Bus. Pk. WA9: St H 3D **60**
Lea Grn. Ind. Est. WA9: St H 4E **61**
Lea Grn. Rd. WA9: St H 4D **60**
Lea Green Station (Rail) 4D **60**
Leamington Cl. WA5: Gt San 1H **81**
Leamington Rd. L11: Norr G 3B **36**
Leamoore Cl. L12: Knott A 1B **56**
Leander Rd. CH45: Wall 2C **50**
Lea Rd. CH44: Wall 2E **51**
Leas, The CH45: Wall 6A **32**
    CH61: Thing 5F **85**
Leaside WA7: Run 4H **113**
    WA9: St H 2D **60**
LEASOWE .3F **49**
Leasowe (Park & Ride) 5E **49**

Leasowe Av. CH45: Wall 1A 50
Leasowe Gdns. CH46: Leas 4C 48
Leasowe Golf Course 3D 48
Leasowe Lighthouse 4A 48
Leasowe Recreation Cen. 4E 49
Leasowe Rd. CH44: Wall 3D 48
    CH45: Wall 3D 48
    CH46: Leas 4B 48
    L9: Ain 4H 21
Leasoweside CH46: Leas 3E 49
Leasowe Station (Rail) 5D 48
Leas Pk. CH47: Hoy 5A 64
Leatherbarrows La.
    L31: Mag, Mell 2D 12
Leather La. L2: Liv 3D 4
Leather's La. L26: Halew 5H 93
Leathwood L31: Mag 1C 12
Leaway CH49: Grea 5B 66
Leawood Gro. CH46: More 1D 66
L E C Complex L15: Wav 1B 72
Leckwith Rd. L30: N'ton 1H 21
Leda Gro. L17: Aig 54 72
                                (off Hesketh St.)
Ledbury Cl. CH43: Oxton 1A 86
    L12: Crox 1B 38
    WA10: Eccl .2H 41
Ledger Rd. WA11: Hay 6C 30
Ledsham Cl. CH43: Noct 5A 68
Ledsham Rd. L32: Kirkb 1G 23
Ledsham Wlk. L32: Kirkb 1G 23
Ledson Pk. L33: Kirkb 3B 14
Ledsons Gro. L31: Mell 6E 13
Ledston Cl. WA7: Wind H 4F 115
Leece St. L1: Liv 6H 5 (1E 71)
Lee Cl. L35: Rainh 6B 60
Lee Ct. CH47: Hoy 2C 64
Leecourt Cl. L12: W Der 2H 55
Leeds St. L3: Liv 1B 4 (4B 52)
Lee Hall Rd. L25: Gate 4E 75
Leeming Dr. L19: Garst 6G 91
Lee Pk. Av. L25: Gate 4E 75
Lee Park Golf Course 5F 75
Lee Rd. CH47: Hoy 2C 64
Lees Av. CH42: Rock F 1H 87
Leeside Av. L32: Kirkb 3A 24
Leeside Cl. L32: Kirkb 2B 24
Lees La. L12: W Der 6H 37
Lees Rd. L33: Know I 2D 24
Lee St. WA9: St H 5A 44
Leeswood L22: Water 2G 19
Leeswood Rd. CH49: Woodc 6E 67
Lee Vale Rd. L25: Gate 5E 75
Lee Valley Millennium Cen. 3E 75
Leeward Dr. L24: Speke 1C 108
Legh Rd. CH62: New F 4B 88
    WA11: Hay .5C 30
Legh St. WA12: Newt W 1H 45
                                (not continuous)
Legion La. CH62: Brom 4D 104
Legion Rd. WA10: St H 5B 42
Leicester Av. L22: Water 1F 19
Leicester Rd. L20: Boot 1D 34
Leicester St. WA9: St H 5B 42
Leigh Av. WA8: Wid 2D 96
Leigh Bri. Way L5: Liv 2C 52
                          (off New Hedley Gro.)
Leigh Grn. Cl. WA8: Wid 3A 96
Leigh Pl. L1: Liv 4F 5
Leigh Rd. CH48: W Kir 6B 64
Leighs Hey Cres. L32: Kirkb 1B 24
Leigh St. L1: Liv 4E 5 (6D 52)
                                (not continuous)
    L7: Liv 6B 54
Leighton Av. CH47: Meols 1E 65
    L31: Mag 5C 6
Leighton Chase CH64: Nest 6H 117
Leighton Dr. WA9: Sut H 6G 43
Leighton Rd. CH41: Tran 5G 69
    CH64: Nest 4G 117
Leighton St. L4: Kirkd 4E 35
Leinster Gdns. WA7: Run 2D 112
Leinster Rd. L13: Liv 4F 55
Leinster St. WA7: Run 2D 112
Leiria Way WA7: Run 3E 113

Leison St. L4: Kirkd 6D 34
    L5: Kirkd 1D 52
Leiston Cl. CH61: Irby 4C 84
Lemon Cl. L7: Liv 6A 54
Lemon Gro. L8: Liv 3A 72
Lemon St. L5: Kirkd 1D 52
Lemon Tree Wlk. WA10: St H 4B 42
Lenfield Dr. WA11: Hay 5B 30
Lenham Way L24: Speke 1D 108
Lennox Av. CH45: New B 6D 32
Lennox La. CH43: Bid 6G 49
Lennox Way L7: Liv 5H 53
Lenthall St. L4: Walt 3F 35
Lenton Rd. L25: Gate 4E 75
Lentworth Ct. L17: Aig 4D 90
Leo Cl. L14: Knott A 3B 56
Leominster Rd. CH44: Wall 3D 50
Leonard Cheshire Dr. L30: N'ton 6F 11
Leonard Ho. CH41: Birke 5H 51
Leonards Cl. L36: Huy 1F 57
Leonard St. WA7: West P 6B 112
    WA9: St H 6B 44
Leon Cl. WA5: Gt San 2F 81
Leonora St. L8: Liv 5G 71
Leopold Gro. WA9: Sut L 2G 61
Leopold Rd. L7: Liv 5H 53
                                (not continuous)
    L22: Water .1E 19
Leopold St. CH44: Wall 4G 51
Leslie Av. CH49: Grea 6B 66
Leslie Rd. WA10: St H 5A 42
Lesseps Rd. L8: Liv 2A 72
Lessingham Rd. WA8: Wid 6D 78
Lester Cl. L4: Kirkd 6E 35
Lester Dr. CH61: Irby 4A 84
    WA10: Eccl .6G 27
Lester Gro. L36: Huy 3H 57
Lestock St. L8: Liv 2E 71
Leta St. L4: Walt 4F 35
                                (not continuous)
Letchworth St. L6: Liv 2A 54
Lethbridge Cl. L5: Kirkd 1C 52
Letitia St. L8: Liv 4F 71
Levens Hey CH46: More 1B 66
Leven St. L4: Kirkd 5E 35
Levens Way WA8: Wid 3A 96
Lever Av. CH44: Wall 5G 51
Lever C'way. CH63: Hghr B, Store 6C 86
Leveret Rd. L24: Speke 2A 110
Leverhulme Ct. CH63: Beb 1A 104
Lever St. WA9: Clock F 4H 61
Lever Ter. CH42: Tran 6G 69
                          (off Summerford Cl.)
Leveson Rd. L13: Liv 6F 55
Lewis Cres. WA8: Wid 4E 97
Lewis Gro. WA8: Wid 2B 96
Lewisham Rd. CH62: Port S 5C 88
    L11: Norr G .3D 36
Lewis St. WA10: St H 2C 42
Lexham Rd. L14: Knott A 4G 55
Lexington Way L33: Kirkb 3A 14
Leybourne Cl. L25: Gate 3C 74
Leybourne Grn. L25: Gate 4C 74
Leybourne Gro. L25: Gate 4C 74
Leybourne Rd. L25: Gate 3C 74
Leyburn Cl. L32: Kirkb 4A 24
                                (not continuous)
Leyburn Rd. CH45: Wall 1B 50
Ley Cl. WA9: Clock F 3G 61
Leyfield Cl. L12: W Der 1H 55
Leyfield Ct. L12: W Der 1H 55
Leyfield Rd. L12: W Der 1G 55
Leyfield Wlk. L12: W Der 1H 55
Leyland Gro. WA11: Hay 5D 30
Leyland Rd. WA11: Rainf 3F 17
Leyland St. L34: Presc 1D 58
Leyton Cl. WA7: Run 1F 123
Liberton Ct. L5: Liv 1G 53
                          (off St Domingo Va.)
Liberty Pl. WA10: St H 2B 42
Liberty St. L15: Wav 2C 72
Libra Cl. L14: Knott A 2C 56

Library St. WA10: St H 2E 43
Librex Cl. L20: Boot 5C 20
Lichfield Av. L22: Water 6F 9
Lichfield Cl. L30: N'ton 2G 21
Lichfield Rd. L15: Wav 3E 73
    L26: Halew .5G 93
Lichfield St. CH45: New B 6E 33
Lickers La. L35: Whis 5D 58
Liddell Av. L31: Mell 5F 13
Liddell Ct. CH45: Wall 2H 49
Liddell Rd. L12: W Der 6D 36
Lidderdale Ct. L15: Wav 3C 72
                          (off Lidderdale Rd.)
Lidderdale Rd. L15: Wav 3C 72
Lidgate Cl. L33: Kirkb 4A 14
Liebig St. WA8: Wid 3F 97
Liege Ho. CH49: Upton 3D 66
                          (off Manorside Cl.)
Lifestyles
    Alsop 3F 35
    Croxteth 1G 37
    Everton 1E 53
    Garston 4G 91
    Liverpool - Millennium 3E 5
    Liverpool - Peter Lloyd 1D 54
    Mill Yard - Cardinal Heenan 2H 55
    Norris Green - Ellergreen 3E 37
    Speke - Austin Rawlinson 2G 109
    Toxteth - Park Road 4F 71
    Toxteth Sports Cen. 3F 71
    Walton 3H 35
    Wavertree - Tennis Cen. 2D 72
Liffey Ct. L3: Liv 5F 53
                                (off London Rd.)
Liffey St. L8: Liv 2H 71
Lifton Rd. L33: Kirkb 1C 24
Lightbody St. L5: Liv 2B 52
Lightburn St. WA7: Run 4D 112
Light Cinema, The 4D 32
Lightfoot Cl. CH60: Hesw 6F 101
Lightfoot La. CH60: Hesw 6F 101
Lighthouse Rd. CH47: Hoy 3B 64
    L24: Hale 6E 111
Lightoaks Dr. L26: Halew 2B 94
Lightstream Dr. L24: Speke 5D 92
Lightwood Dr. L7: Liv 1A 72
Lightwood St. L7: Liv 1A 72
Lilac Av. WA8: Wid 1F 97
Lilac Cres. WA7: Run 5G 113
Lilac Gro. L36: Huy 1F 75
    WA11: Hay .6B 30
Lilford Av. L9: Walt 5F 21
Lilford Dr. WA5: Gt San 3H 81
Lilley Rd. L7: Liv 4B 54
Lillian Rd. L4: Walt 1H 53
Lillie Cl. CH43: Bid 1G 67
Lillyfield CH60: Hesw 1D 116
Lilly Grn. L4: Walt 4H 35
                                (off Lilly Gro.)
Lilly Gro. L4: Walt 4H 35
                                (not continuous)
Lilly Va. L7: Liv .4B 54
Lily Gro L7: Liv .6H 53
                          (off Dorothy Dr.)
Lily Rd. L21: Lith 5B 20
Limbo La. CH61: Irby 3B 84
Lime Av. CH63: Hghr B 1F 103
    WA8: Wid 1F 97
Lime Cl. L13: Liv 3E 55
Limedale Rd. L18: Moss H 4E 73
Lime Gro. L8: Liv 3A 72
    L21: Sea 5A 20
    WA7: Run .5G 113
    WA11: Rainf 3F 17
Limehurst Gro. CH62: Brom 1D 120
Limekiln La. CH44: Wall 5C 50
    L3: Liv 3D 52
                                (not continuous)
    L5: Liv 2D 52
    WA5: Burtw 4G 63
Limekiln Row WA7: Cas 5C 114
Limerick Cl. WA8: Wid 6C 78
Limes, The CH49: Upton 4D 66
Lime St. L1: Liv 3F 5 (5D 52)

Lime St. Chambers L1: Liv 3G 5
Lime Street Station (Rail) 3G 5 (6E 53)
Limetree Cl. L9: Walt 1H 35
Lime Tree Gro. CH60: Hesw 5G 101
Lime Va. Rd. WN5: Bil 1G 29
Linacre Ho. L20: Boot 3C 34
Linacre La. L20: Boot 6C 20
    WA8: Wid 4C 78
Linacre Rd. L21: Lith 4B 20
Linby Way WA9: St H 3C 60
Lincoln Cl. L6: Liv 3H 53
    L36: Huy 4B 58
    WA7: Run 1G 123
Lincoln Cres. L20: Boot 3C 34
    WA11: St H 5F 29
Lincoln Dr. CH45: Wall 1E 51
    L10: Ain 6B 12
Lincoln Grn. L21: Lith 1H 11
Lincoln Rd. WA10: St H 3B 42
Lincoln Sq. WA8: Wid 1F 97
Lincoln St. CH41: Birke 6C 50
    L19: Garst 1G 107
Lincoln Way L35: Rainh 6B 60
    L36: Huy 4B 58
        (off Lincoln Cl.)
Lincombe Rd. L36: Huy 3D 56
Lindale Cl. CH46: More 6E 49
Lindale Dr. WA9: Clock F 3G 61
Lindale Rd. L7: Liv 4C 54
Lindby Cl. L32: Kirkb 3C 24
Lindby Rd. L32: Kirkb 3C 24
Linden Av. L23: Blun 5E 9
    L30: N'ton 1F 21
Linden Ct. WA8: Wid 5D 78
Linden Dr. CH43: Pren 2A 86
    L36: Huy 1G 75
Linden Gro. CH45: Wall 6D 32
Linden Rd. L27: N'ley 4G 75
Lindens, The CH43: Oxton 4E 69
    L31: Mag 2A 12
Linden Way WA8: Wid 5D 78
    WA10: Eccl 1H 41
Lindenwood L32: Kirkb 3B 24
Lindeth Av. CH44: Wall 5D 50
Lindfield Cl. L8: Liv 5F 71
Lindisfarne Cl. WA8: Wid 3D 78
Lindisfarne Dr. L12: Crox 2B 38
Lindley Cl. L7: Liv 1A 72
Lindley St. L7: Liv 1A 72
Lindrick Cl. L35: Rainh 3G 59
Lindsay Rd. L4: Walt 5B 36
Lindsay St. WA9: Clock F 4H 61
Lind St. L4: Walt 4F 35
Lindwall Cl. CH43: Bid 6G 49
Linear Pk. CH46: More 6A 48
Lineside Cl. L25: Gate 4D 74
Linford Gro. WA11: St H 6G 29
Lingdale Av. CH43: Clau 3B 68
Lingdale Ct. CH43: Clau 2B 68
    CH48: W Kir 1A 82
Lingdale Rd. CH43: Clau 2B 68
    CH48: W Kir 1A 82
Lingdale Rd. Nth. CH41: Birke 2B 68
Lingfield Cl. L30: N'ton 2G 21
    L36: Roby 6E 57
Lingfield Gro. L14: Broad G 5H 55
Lingfield Rd. L14: Broad G 5G 55
    WA7: Run 4C 112
Lingford Cl. L27: N'ley 5H 75
Lingham Cl. CH46: More 5B 48
Lingham La. CH46: More 4A 48
        (not continuous)
Lingholme Rd. WA10: St H 1C 42
Lingley Ct. WA5: Gt San 3F 81
LINGLEY GREEN 2F 81
Lingley Grn. Av. WA5: Gt San 3E 81
LINGLEY MERE 6F 63
Lingley Mere Bus. Pk. WA5: Gt San . .6F 63
Lingley Rd. WA5: Gt San 3F 81
Lingmell Av. WA11: St H 7F 29
Lingmell Rd. L12: W Der 5F 37
Ling St. L7: Liv 5H 53
Lingtree Rd. L32: Kirkb 1F 23
Lingwell Av. WA8: Wid 1B 96

Lingwell Pk. WA8: Wid 1B 96
Lingwood Rd. WA5: Gt San 3H 81
Linhope Way L17: Aig 6A 72
Link Av. L23: Thorn 4A 10
    WA11: St H 5A 30
Linkfield Cl. L27: N'ley 3F 75
Link Rd. L36: Huy 6B 58
Links, The CH43: Oxton 4B 68
Links Cl. CH45: Wall 6B 32
    CH48: W Kir 2D 82
    CH63: Raby M 1B 120
Links Hey Rd. CH48: Caldy 5E 83
Linkside CH63: Hghr B 4F 87
Linkside Cl. L23: Blun 4C 8
Linkside Rd. L25: Woolt 2E 93
Links Rd. L32: Kirkb 3C 24
Linkstor Rd. L25: Woolt 1B 92
Links Vw. CH43: Oxton 4A 68
    CH45: Wall 5B 32
Linksview L25: Woolt 1B 92
Linksway CH45: Wall 6B 32
Linkway WA7: Run 5G 113
    WA10: Windle 5H 27
Linkway E. WA9: St H 3F 43
Linkway W. WA9: St H 2D 42
    WA10: St H 2D 42
Linner Rd. L24: Speke 3E 109
Linnet Cl. L17: Aig 4A 72
Linnet Ct. L17: Aig 5A 72
Linnet Ho. L17: Aig 4A 72
Linnet La. L17: Aig 4H 71
Linnets Pk. WA7: Run 2F 113
Linnets Way CH60: Hesw 5C 100
Linnet Way L33: Kirkb 2A 14
Linslade Cl. L33: Kirkb 5B 14
Linslade Cres. L33: Kirkb 5B 14
Linton Pl. L32: Kirkb 6G 13
Linton St. L4: Walt 4F 35
Linum Gdns. WA9: Bold 6D 44
Linville Av. L23: Blun 5D 8
Linwood Cl. WA7: Brook 2E 125
Linwood Gro. L35: Whis 5E 59
Linwood Rd. CH42: Tran 6G 69
Lionel St. WA9: St H 6B 44
Lions Cl. CH43: Clau 3B 68
Lipton Cl. L20: Boot 3C 34
Lisburn La. L13: Liv 6C 36
Lisburn Rd. L17: Aig 1C 90
LISCARD 2D 50
Liscard Cres. CH44: Wall 3D 50
Liscard Gro. CH44: Wall 3C 50
Liscard Rd. CH44: Wall 3D 50
Liscard Rd. CH44: Wall 3D 50
        (not continuous)
    L15: Wav 2B 72
Liscard Village CH45: Wall 2D 50
Liscard Way CH44: Wall 3D 50
Liskeard Cl. WA7: Brook 1D 124
Lisleholme Cl. L12: W Der 1G 55
Lisleholme Cres. L12: W Der 1G 55
Lisleholme Rd. L12: W Der 1G 55
Lismore Cl. L23: Blun 5E 9
Lismore Rd. L18: Moss H 1E 91
Lister Av. CH46: Leas 5E 49
Lister Cres. L7: Liv 5A 54
Lister Dr. L6: Liv 3C 54
    L13: Liv 3C 54
Lister Rd. L7: Liv 4A 54
    WA7: Ast 2G 113
Liston St. L4: Walt 3F 35
Litcham Cl. CH49: Upton 2E 67
Litchborough Gro. L35: Whis 1G 59
LITHERLAND 2B 20
Litherland Av. CH46: More 6B 48
Litherland Cres. WA11: St H 4G 29
Litherland Pk. L21: Lith 3B 20
Litherland Rd. L20: Boot 1D 34
Litherland Rd. L20: Boot 5C 20
Litherland Sports Pk. 2D 20
Lithou Cl. L5: Liv 2D 52
Little Acre L31: Mag 1C 12
Lit. Barn Hey L30: N'ton 5D 10
LITTLE BONGS 3H 55
Littlebourne WA7: Murd 6G 115

Lit. Brook La. L32: Kirkb 3H 23
Lit. Canning St. L8: Liv 2F 71
Lit. Catharine St. L8: Liv 2F 71
Littlecote Cl. WA9: Clock F 3G 61
Little Cl. L3: Liv 3C 52
Little Cft. L35: Whis 4D 58
LITTLE CROSBY 1F 9
Lit. Crosby Rd. L23: Crosb, Lit C 1F 9
Littledale L14: Knott A 4H 55
Littledale Rd. CH44: Wall 4F 51
    WA5: Gt San 2H 81
Littlegate WA7: Run 5A 114
Little Delph WA11: Hay 4E 31
Lit. Hardman St. L1: Liv 6H 5 (1E 71)
Lit. Heath Rd. L24: Speke 3G 109
Lit. Heyes St. L5: Liv 1G 53
Lit. Howard St. L3: Liv 3B 52
Lit. Huskisson St. L8: Liv 2F 71
Little La. CH64: Park 6G 117
Littlemore Cl. CH49: Upton 4B 66
Lit. Moss Hey L28: Stockb V 6D 38
Lit. Parkfield Rd. L17: Aig 5H 71
Littler Rd. WA11: Hay 6C 30
Little St Bride St. L8: Liv 1F 71
Littlestone Cl. WA8: Wid 5E 79
Lit. Storeton La. CH63: Store 5C 86
Little St. WA9: St H 4A 44
Littleton Cl. CH43: Noct 5A 68
Littlewood Cl. L35: Whis 4E 59
Lit. Woolton St. L7: Liv 6G 53
Littondale Av. L35: Rainh 5B 60
Liver Ind. Est. L9: Ain 1A 36
Livermore Ct. L8: Liv 3A 72
LIVERPOOL 5D 4 (6C 52)
Liverpool Aquatics Cen. 2D 72
Liverpool Arts Village L1: Liv 6E 5
Liverpool Cathedral Church of Christ
    . . . . .2E 71
Liverpool Cruise Terminal 4A 4 (6B 52)
Liverpool Empire Theatre 3G 5 (5E 53)
Liverpool FC 6G 35
Liverpool Innovation Pk. L7: Liv 5B 54
Liverpool Intermodal Freeport Terminal
    L20: Boot 1A 34
Liverpool International Bus. Pk.
    L24: Speke 2B 108
LIVERPOOL JOHN LENNON AIRPORT
    . . . . .4E 109
Liverpool John Moores University
    City Campus -
        Byrom St. 1F 5 (4D 52)
        Tithebarn St. 2D 4 (5C 52)
        Webster St. 2E 5
        William Brown St. 2F 5 (5D 52)
    IM Marsh Campus 2D 90
    Mount Pleasant Campus 5H 5 (6E 53)
    Myrtle St. 1F 71
Liverpool Metropolitan Cathedral of
    Christ the King (RC) 6F 53
Liverpool Municipal Golf Course . . .3F 23
Liverpool One L1: Liv 5D 4 (6C 52)
Liverpool Parish Church 4B 4
Liverpool Pl. WA8: Wid 2A 96
Liverpool Playhouse 4F 5 (6D 52)
Liverpool Rd. CH64: Nest 6A 118
        (not continuous)
    L14: Huy 3D 56
    L23: Crosb 4G 9
    L31: Lyd 4B 6
    L34: Presc 1B 58
    L36: Huy 3D 56
        (not continuous)
    WA5: Gt San 3E 81
    WA8: Wid 2H 95
    WA10: St H 2D 42
    WA11: Hay 4C 30
        (not continuous)
    WN4: Ash M, Garsw 3C 30
Liverpool Rd. Nth. L31: Mag 4B 6
Liverpool Rd. Sth. L31: Mag 6B 6
Liverpool Sailing Club 3A 108
Liverpool Science Pk. ic1 L3: Liv . . .6F 53
Liverpool Science Pk. ic2 L3: Liv . . .6F 53
        (off Brownlow Hill)

Liverpool South Parkway Station (Rail)
.............................5H 91
Liverpool St. WA10: St H 2D 42
LIVERPOOL WATERS 2A 52
Liverpool Watersports Cen. 3D 70
Liverpool Way, The L33: Kirkb 2C 24
Liverside Rd. CH42: Tran 5F 69
Liver St. L1: Liv 6D 4 (1C 70)
Livingston Av. L15: Aig 5A 72
Livingston Ct. L17: Aig 5A 72
        (not continuous)
Livingston Dr. L17: Aig 6A 72
Livingston Dr. Nth. L17: Aig 6A 72
Livingston Dr. Sth. L17: Aig 6A 72
Livingstone Gdns. CH41: Birke 2E 69
Livingstone Rd. CH46: Leas 3E 49
Livingstone St. CH41: Birke 2E 69
Llanrwst Cl. L8: Liv 4E 71
Lloyd Av. CH41: Birke 2D 68
Lloyd Cl. L6: Liv 3F 53
Lloyd Cres. WA12: Newt W 2H 45
Lloyd Dr. CH49: Grea 6A 66
Lloyd Rd. L34: Presc 6E 41
Lloyd St. WA11: Hay 5B 30
Lobelia Av. L9: Walt 1H 35
Lobelia Gro. WA7: Beech 2B 124
Local Cen. WA7: Run 6A 114
Lochinvar St. L9: Walt 2F 35
Lochmore Rd. L18: Moss H 2F 91
Lochryan Rd. L19: Aller 3F 91
Loch St. WA7: Run 2E 113
        (not continuous)
Lockerby Rd. L7: Liv 4B 54
Locker Pk. CH49: Grea 5A 66
Locke St. L19: Garst 1G 107
Lockett Rd. WA8: Wid 1E 97
Lockfield WA7: Run 3C 112
Lockfields Vw. WA11: Rainf 2C 52
Lockgate E. WA7: Wind H 3E 115
Lockgate W. WA7: Wind H 3D 114
Lockington Cl. L8: Liv 5G 71
Lock Rd. CH62: East 5G 105
Lock St. WA9: St H 6G 29
Lockton Rd. L34: Know 6D 24
Lockwood Vw. WA7: Pres B 2H 125
Loddon Cl. CH49: Upton 2F 67
Lodge, The CH43: Noct 3H 67
Lodge La. CH62: Port S 5B 88
    L8: Liv 2H 71
    WA7: Halt 5A 114
    WA8: Cron 5G 77
Lodge Rd. WA8: Wid 3H 95
Lodge Works L33: Know I 6E 15
Lodwick St. L20: Kirkd 4B 34
Lofthouse Ga. WA8: Wid 6D 78
Logan Rd. CH41: Birke 6D 50
Logfield Dr. L19: Garst 6H 91
Lognor Rd. L32: Kirkb 1G 23
Lognor Wlk. L32: Kirkb 1G 23
Logwood Rd. L36: Huy 1A 76
Lois Ct. CH45: Wall 1E 51
Lombard Rd. CH46: More 5D 48
Lombardy Av. CH49: Grea 1H 83
Lomond Gro. CH46: More 1D 66
Lomond Rd. L7: Liv 4C 54
Londonderry Rd. L13: Liv 6B 36
London Rd. L3: Liv 3G 5 (5E 53)
Longacre Cl. CH45: Wall 2H 49
Longacre Rd. CH64: Nest 5A 118
Long Acres CH49: Grea 4B 66
Long Av. L9: Ain 5H 21
Longbenton Way WA7: Manor P ...1D 114
Longborough Rd. L34: Know 2E 39
Longcroft Av. L19: Aller 4H 91
Longcroft Sq. L19: Aller 4H 91
Longdale La. L29: Seft 2D 15
Longdown Rd. L10: Faz 5F 23
Longfellow Cl. L32: Kirkb 3H 23
Longfellow Dr. CH62: New F 4A 88
Longfellow St. L8: Liv 2A 72
        (not continuous)
    L20: Boot 6A 20
Longfield Av. L23: Crosb 3G 9
Longfield Cl. CH49: Grea 5B 66

Longfield Pk. WA9: Clock F 3H 61
Longfield Rd. L21: Lith 5B 20
Longfield Wlk. L23: Crosb 3G 9
Longfold L31: Mag 6D 6
Longford Dr. WA8: Wid 1C 96
Longford St. L8: Liv 6G 71
Long Hey L35: Whis 5D 58
Long Hey Rd. CH48: Caldy 4E 83
Longland Rd. CH45: Wall 1D 50
Long La. L9: Ain, Faz 5H 21
    L15: Wav 1D 72
    L19: Garst 4G 91
    L29: Thorn 1A 10
Long Meadow CH60: Hesw 1D 116
    WA10: Eccl 1H 41
Longmeadow Rd. L34: Know 1F 39
Longmoor Cl. L10: Faz 4C 22
Longmoor Gro. L9: Ain 5H 21
Longmoor La. L9: Ain 5H 21
Long Moss L30: N'ton 6C 10
Longreach Rd. L14: Knott A 3B 56
Longridge Av. CH49: Upton 3C 66
    WA11: St H 6H 29
Longridge Wlk. L4: Kirkd 5E 35
Long Spinney WA7: Nort 5E 115
Longstone Wlk. L7: Liv 1H 71
Longton La. L35: Rainh 2H 59
LONGVIEW 2H 57
Longview Av. CH45: Wall 2C 50
    L35: Rainh 3G 59
Longview Cres. L36: Huy 4H 57
Longview Dr. L36: Huy 3H 57
Longview La. L36: Huy 2H 57
Longview Rd. L35: Rainh 3G 59
    L36: Huy 4H 57
Longville St. L8: Liv 4E 71
Longworth Way L25: Woolt 6C 74
Lonie Gro. WA10: St H 5A 42
Lonsboro Rd. CH44: Wall 4E 51
Lonsdale Av. CH45: Wall 1C 50
    WA10: St H 6H 41
Lonsdale Cl. L21: Ford 1B 20
    WA5: Gt San 1G 81
    WA8: Wid 3A 96
Lonsdale M. L21: Ford 1B 20
Lonsdale Rd. L21: Ford 1B 20
    L26: Halew 5G 93
Lonsdale Vs. CH45: Wall 1C 50
        (off Seaview Rd.)
Looe Cl. WA8: Wid 1C 96
Looe Rd. L11: Crox 6H 23
Looms, The CH64: Park 5F 117
Loomsway CH61: Irby 3E 85
Lopwell Dr. L6: Liv 3G 53
Loraine St. L5: Liv 2F 53
Lordens Cl. L14: Knott A 2C 56
Lordens Rd. L14: Knott A 2C 56
        (not continuous)
Lord Nelson St. L1: Liv 3G 5 (5E 53)
    ....3G 5 (5E 53)
Lords Av. CH43: Bid 1G 67
Lords Fold WA11: Rainf 2E 17
Lord St. CH41: Birke 2G 69
    L2: Liv 4D 4 (6C 52)
    L19: Garst 1H 107
    WA7: Run 2D 112
    WA10: St H 6D 28
        (not continuous)
Loreburn Rd. L15: Wav 3E 73
Lorenzo Dr. L11: Norr G 4C 36
Loretto Dr. CH49: Upton 3E 67
Loretto Rd. CH44: Wall 2B 50
Lorn Ct. CH41: Birke 3G 69
Lorne Ct. CH43: Oxton 5D 68
Lorne Rd. CH43: Oxton 5C 68
    L22: Water 2F 19
Lorne St. L7: Liv 4C 54
    CH41: Birke 3G 69
Lorton Av. WA11: St H 3E 29
Lorton St. L8: Liv 2H 71
Lothair Rd. L4: Walt 6G 35
Lothian St. L8: Liv 3G 71

Lotus Gdns. WA9: Bold 6C 44
Loudon Gro. L8: Liv 3G 71
Lough Grn. CH63: Spit 3A 104
Loughlin Dr. L33: Kirkb 4B 14
Loughrigg Av. WA11: St H 2F 29
Louis Braille Cl. L30: N'ton 5F 11
Louis Pasteur Av. L30: N'ton 5F 11
Lovelace Rd. L19: Gras 4F 91
Love La. CH44: Wall 4C 50
    L3: Liv 3C 52
Lovel Rd. L24: Speke 3F 109
Lovel Ter. WA8: Hale B 6H 95
Lovel Way L24: Speke 2F 109
Lovett Dr. L35: Presc 2E 59
Lowbridge Ct. L19: Garst 5H 91
Lowden Av. L21: Lith 2B 20
Lowell St. L4: Walt 4F 35
Lwr. Appleton Rd. WA8: Wid 2F 97
Lwr. Bank Vw. L20: Kirkd 4B 34
LOWER BEBINGTON 6A 88
Lwr. Breck Rd. L6: Liv 1A 54
Lowerbrook Way L4: Kirkd 6D 34
Lwr. Castle St. L2: Liv 4C 4 (6C 52)
Lwr. Church St. WA8: Wid 6E 97
Lower Cl. L26: Halew 3A 94
Lwr. Farm Rd. L25: Gate 2C 74
Lwr. Flaybrick Rd. CH43: Bid 1A 68
Lwr. Gill St. L3: Liv 5F 53
Lower Grn. CH49: Woodc 6E 67
Lwr. Hall St. WA10: St H 1F 43
Lower Hey L23: Thorn 4B 10
LOWER HOUSE 3C 96
Lower Ho. La. L11: Norr G 1E 37
    WA8: Wid 4D 96
Lower La. L9: Faz 4C 22
Lwr. Mersey Vw. L20: Kirkd 4B 34
Lwr. New Hall Pl. L3: Liv 3B 4
Lower Rd. CH62: Port S 5B 88
    L26: Halew 3B 94
    WA8: Hale B 3B 94
Lower Sandfield L25: Gate 5D 74
Lowerson Cres. L11: Norr G 5C 36
Lowerson Rd. L11: Norr G 5C 36
Lwr. Thingwall La. CH61: Thing 5G 85
Lowestoft St. L19: Garst 5F 91
Lowe St. WA10: St H 1D 42
Lowe St. Sth. WA10: St H 2D 42
Loweswater Cres. WA11: Hay 5C 30
Loweswater Way L33: Kirkb 4H 13
Lowfield Ind. Est. WA9: St H 2D 60
Lowfield La. WA9: St H 1D 60
Lowfield Rd. L14: Knott A 4G 55
Lowfields Av. CH62: East 4D 120
Lowfields Cl. CH62: East 4E 121
Low Hill L6: Liv 4G 53
    L7: Liv 5G 53
Lowlands Rd. WA7: Run 3D 112
Lowndes Rd. L6: Liv 1B 54
Lowry Bank CH44: Wall 4G 51
Lowry Cl. L33: Kirkb 3A 14
Lowther Av. L10: Ain 1B 22
    L31: Mag 5D 6
Lowther Cres. WA10: St H 5H 41
Lowther Dr. L35: Rainh 4H 59
Lowther St. L8: Liv 2G 71
Low Wood Gro. CH61: Barn 1G 101
Lowwood Gro. CH41: Birke 4F 69
Lowwood Rd. CH41: Birke 4F 69
Low Wood St. L6: Liv 4G 53
Loxdale Cl. L8: Liv 5G 71
Loxwood Cl. L25: Gate 2D 74
Loyola Hey L35: Rainh 1C 78
Lucan Rd. L17: Aig 1C 90
Lucas Ct. L35: Rainh 3A 60
        (off Ratcliffe Pl.)
Lucerne Rd. CH44: Wall 5F 51
Lucerne St. L17: Aig 6A 72
Lucius Cl. L9: Walt 4F 21
Lucknow St. L17: Aig 5A 72
Ludlow Cl. CH48: W Kir 2B 82
Ludlow Cres. WA7: Run 5F 113
Ludlow Dr. CH48: W Kir 2B 82
Ludlow Gro. CH62: Brom 4D 104
Ludlow St. L4: Kirkd 4F 35

Ludwig Rd. L4: Walt 1H **53**
Lugard Rd. L17: Aig 1C **90**
LUGSDALE 4G **97**
Lugsdale Rd. WA8: Wid 4E **97**
Lugsmore La. WA10: St H 4B **42**
Luke St. CH44: Wall 5G **51**
   L8: Liv .3F **71**
Lulworth Av. L22: Water 1E **19**
Lulworth Rd. L25: Gate 4E **75**
Lumber La. WA5: Burtw 5G **45**
Lumina CH62: Brom 3E **105**
Lumley Rd. CH44: Wall 4F **51**
Lumley St. L19: Garst 4F **91**
Lumley Wlk. L24: Hale 4E **111**
Lunar Dr. L30: N'ton 4F **11**
Lunar Rd. L9: Ain 5H **21**
Lunesdale Av. L9: Ain 4H **21**
Lune St. L23: Crosb 5G **9**
Lune Way WA8: Wid 2A **96**
Lunsford Rd. L14: Knott A 3B **56**
LUNT 1D **10**
Lunt Av. L30: N'ton 1G **21**
   L35: Whis 4E **59**
Lunt La. L29: Seft 1D **10**
Lunt Rd. L20: Boot 5C **20**
   L29: Seft, Thorn 1C **10**
LUNTS HEATH 5F **79**
Lunt's Heath Rd. WA8: Wid 4E **79**
Lupin Dr. WA11: Hay 5H **31**
Lupton Dr. L23: Crosb 5A **10**
Luscombe Cl. L26: Halew 3A **94**
Lusitania Rd. L4: Walt 3G **35**
Luther Gro. WA9: St H 3D **44**
Luton Gro. L4: Walt 5F **35**
Luton St. L5: Kirkd 1B **52**
   WA8: Wid 4E **97**
Lutyens Cl. L4: Walt 5F **35**
Luxmore Rd. L4: Walt 4G **35**
Lybro Way L7: Liv 6H **53**
Lycett Rd. CH44: Wall 2A **50**
   L4: Walt 6A **36**
Lyceum Pl. L1: Liv 5F **5**
Lycroft Cl. WA7: Run 1F **123**
Lydbrook Cl. CH42: Rock F 6H **69**
Lydbury Cres. L32: Kirkb 3B **24**
Lydford Rd. L12: W Der 5F **37**
Lydia Ann St. L1: Liv 6E **5** (1D **70**)
LYDIATE .2A **6**
Lydiate, The CH60: Hesw 6D **100**
Lydiate La. CH64: Will 6G **119**
   L23: Seft, Thorn 3B **10**
   L25: Woolt 1E **93**
   L26: Halew 1F **93**
   L29: Thorn 3B **10**
   WA7: West P 6B **112**
Lydiate Pk. L23: Thorn 3B **10**
Lydiate Rd. L20: Boot 6C **20**
Lydia Wlk. L10: Faz 4F **23**
Lydieth Lea L27: N'ley 3G **75**
Lydney Rd. L36: Huy 3D **56**
Lyelake Cl. L32: Kirkb 2B **24**
Lyelake Gdns. *L32: Kirkb* *2B **24***
             (off Lyelake Rd.)
Lyelake Rd. L32: Kirkb 2B **24**
Lyle St. L5: Liv 2D **52**
Lyme Cl. L36: Huy 1A **58**
Lymecroft L25: Woolt 1B **92**
Lyme Cross Rd. L36: Huy 1G **57**
Lyme Gro. L36: Huy 2G **57**
Lyme St. WA11: Hay 5G **31**
   WA12: Newt W 1G **45**
Lyme Tree Ct. WA8: Cron 3A **78**
Lymewood Ct. WA11: Hay 4G **31**
Lymington Gro. L30: N'ton 6F **11**
Lymington Rd. CH44: Wall 3B **50**
Lymm Rd. CH43: Bid 2H **67**
Lynas Gdns. L19: Gras 3F **91**
Lynas St. CH41: Birke 1F **69**
Lyncot Rd. L9: Ain 3H **21**
Lyncroft Rd. CH44: Wall 5E **51**
Lyndale WA7: Run 5G **113**
Lyndale Av. CH62: East 3E **121**
Lyndene Rd. L25: Gate 3C **74**

Lyndhurst L31: Mag 6C **6**
Lyndhurst Av. CH61: Pens 2E **101**
   L18: Moss H 6D **72**
Lyndhurst Cl. CH61: Thing 6E **85**
Lyndhurst Rd. CH45: Wall 1B **50**
   CH47: Meols 6E **47**
   CH61: Irby 6A **84**
   L18: Moss H 5D **72**
   L23: Crosb 5A **10**
Lyndhurst Way L36: Huy 5G **57**
Lyndon Dr. L18: Moss H 5F **73**
Lyndon Gro. WA7: Run 5F **113**
Lyndor Cl. L25: Woolt 2D **92**
Lyndor Rd. L25: Woolt 2D **92**
Lyneham L35: Whis 5F **59**
Lynholme Rd. L4: Walt 6H **35**
Lynmouth Rd. L17: Aig 3C **90**
Lynnbank CH43: Oxton 5D **68**
Lynnbank Rd. L18: Moss H 4H **73**
Lynn Cl. WA7: Run 6G **113**
   WA10: St H 1A **42**
Lynscott Pl. L16: Child 1H **73**
Lynsted Rd. L14: Knott A 3B **56**
Lynton Cl. CH60: Hesw 1F **117**
   L19: Aller 3F **91**
   WA5: Penk 5G **81**
Lynton Ct. L23: Blun 5D **8**
Lynton Cres. WA8: Wid 1C **96**
Lynton Dr. CH63: Beb 2A **104**
Lynton Grn. L25: Woolt 5B **74**
Lynton Gro. WA9: Sut L 2G **61**
Lynton Rd. CH45: Wall 1A **50**
   L36: Huy 4B **58**
Lynton Way WA10: Windle 5H **27**
Lynwood Av. CH44: Wall 4C **50**
Lynwood Dr. CH61: Irby 5C **84**
Lynwood Gdns. L9: Walt 6F **21**
Lynwood Rd. L9: Walt 6F **21**
Lynxway, The L12: Knott A 3H **55**
Lyon Cl. WA10: St H 2D **42**
Lyon Ind. Est. WA9: St H 1A **62**
Lyon Rd. L4: Walt 1H **53**
Lyons Cl. CH46: More 6C **48**
Lyons Rd. L25: Hunts X 3F **93**
Lyons Rd. CH46: More 6C **48**
   WA5: Penk 5H **81**
Lyon St. L19: Garst 1G **107**
   WA10: St H 2C **42**
Lyra Rd. L22: Water 2F **19**
Lysander Cl. L6: Liv 3G **53**
Lyster Rd. L20: Boot 2A **34**
Lytham Cl. L10: Faz 2D **22**
Lytham Ct. L32: Kirkb 5G **13**
Lytham Rd. WA8: Wid 1F **97**
Lytham Way L12: W Der 1B **56**
Lyttelton Rd. L17: Aig 1C **90**
Lytton Av. CH42: Rock F 2H **87**
Lytton Gro. *L21: Sea* *5A **20***
             (off Ash Gro.)
Lytton St. L6: Liv 4F **53**

M

Maberley Vw. L15: Wav 6E **55**
Mab La. L12: W Der 5B **38**
McAllester Lodge
   CH43: Oxton *1B **68***
            (off Bidston Rd.)
Macalpine Cl. CH49: Upton 3E **67**
Macbeth St. L20: Kirkd 4C **34**
McBride St. L19: Garst 5G **91**
McClellan Pl. WA8: Wid 2F **97**
McCormack Av. WA9: St H 1A **44**
McCulloch St. WA9: St H 2G **43**
Macdermott Rd. WA8: Wid 6D **96**
Macdona Dr. CH48: W Kir 3B **82**
Macdonald Av. WA11: St H 6A **30**
Macdonald Dr. CH49: Grea 6B **66**
Macdonald Rd. CH46: More 1A **66**
Macdonald St. L15: Wav 1C **72**
Mace Rd. L11: Crox 2G **37**
McFarlane Av. WA10: St H 1A **42**
Macfarren St. L13: Liv 4E **55**

McGill Ct. *CH41: Birke* *2F **69***
            (off Cathcart St.)
McGough Cl. WA9: Sut M 4E **61**
McKeagney Gdns. WA8: Wid 4B **96**
Mackenzie Rd. CH46: Leas 4F **49**
McKeown Cl. L5: Liv 2D **52**
Mackets Cl. L25: Woolt 2E **93**
Macket's La. L25: Woolt 1E **93**
Mack Gro. L30: N'ton 1D **20**
McKinley Way WA8: Wid 6D **78**
McMinnis Av. WA9: St H 3C **44**
McNair Hall L18: Moss H 6D **72**
Macqueen St. L13: Liv 5E **55**
McVinnie Rd. L35: Presc 1F **59**
Maddock Rd. CH44: Wall 2F **51**
Maddocks St. L13: Liv 5E **55**
Maddock St. CH41: Birke 1E **69**
Maddrell St. L3: Liv 3B **52**
Madeira Dr. L25: Gate 3D **74**
Madelaine St. L8: Liv 3G **71**
Madeleine McKenna Ct. WA8: Wid . .6H **77**
Madeley Cl. CH48: W Kir 2B **82**
Madeley Dr. CH48: W Kir 2B **82**
Madeley St. L6: Liv 4A **54**
Madison Sq. L1: Liv 6G **5** (1E **71**)
Madryn Av. L33: Kirkb 1C **24**
Madryn St. L8: Liv 4G **71**
Maelor Cl. CH63: Brom 1C **120**
Mafeking Cl. L15: Wav 6D **54**
Magazine Av. CH45: New B 6D **32**
Magazine Brow CH45: New B 6E **33**
Magazine La. CH45: New B 6D **32**
Magazine Rd. CH62: Brom 2D **104**
Magazines Prom. CH45: New B 5E **33**
Magazine Wlk. CH62: Brom 2D **104**
Magdala St. L8: Liv 2A **72**
Magdalen Ho. L20: Boot 3C **34**
Magdalen Sq. L30: N'ton 5F **11**
Maggots Nook Rd. WA11: Rainf 1G **17**
MAGHULL 5C **6**
Maghull La. L31: Mag 6G **7**
Maghull Smallholdings Est.
   L31: Mag 4F **7**
Maghull Station (Rail) 2C **12**
Magistrates' Court
   Liverpool *3E **5***
            (off Victoria St.)
   Liverpool & Knowsley 3E **5**
            (Dale St.)
   Runcorn (Halton) 5B **114**
   St Helens 1E **43**
   South Sefton 2C **34**
   Wirral 3H **69**
Magnolia Cl. L26: Halew 1F **93**
   WA11: Hay 6B **30**
Magnolia Dr. WA7: Beech 3B **124**
Magnolia Wlk. CH49: Grea 1A **84**
Magnus Cl. L13: Liv 2D **54**
Maguire Av. L20: Boot 1E **35**
Mahon Av. L20: Boot 5D **20**
Mahon Ct. *L8: Liv* *2F **71***
            (off Morpeth St.)
Maiden La. L13: Liv 6B **36**
Maidford Rd. L14: Knott A 2B **56**
Maidstone Cl. L25: Hunts X 3E **93**
Maidstone Dr. L12: W Der 2B **56**
Main Av. WA10: St H 5A **42**
Main Cl. WA11: Hay 5C **30**
Main Dr. L35: Whis 6D **58**
Main Front L35: Whis 1E **77**
Main Rd. CH62: Port S 1B **104**
Mainsail Cl. L3: Liv 3C **52**
Mainside Rd. L32: Kirkb 2B **24**
Main St. WA6: Frod 6F **123**
   WA7: Halt 4B **114**
Maintree Cres. L24: Speke 1A **110**
Mainwaring Rd. CH44: Wall 4F **51**
   CH62: Brom 5D **104**
Maisemore Flds. WA8: Wid 6C **78**
Maitland Cl. L8: Liv 2H **71**
Maitland Rd. CH45: New B 5E **33**
Maitland St. L8: Liv 2H **71**
Majestic Cl. L11: Crox 2G **37**
Major Cross St. WA8: Wid 4E **97**

Major St. L5: Kirkd 1D 52
Makepeace Wlk. L8: Liv 3F 71
(off Thackeray Cl.)
Makin St. L4: Walt 3F 35
Malahide Ct. WA8: Wid 1C 96
Malcolm Cres. CH63: Brom 1C 120
Malcolm Gro. L20: Kirkd 4D 34
Malcolm Pl. L15: Wav 6D 54
Malcolm St. WA7: Run 3F 113
Malden Rd. L6: Liv 4A 54
Maldon Cl. L26: Halew 5H 93
Maldwyn Rd. CH44: Wall 2D 50
Maley Cl. L8: Liv 5G 71
Malham Cl. WA5: Gt San 1G 81
Malhamdale Av. L35: Rainh 5B 60
Malin Cl. L24: Hale 3D 110
Mall, The L5: Liv 2G 53
Mallaby Ct. CH41: Birke 1C 68
(off Mallaby St.)
Mallaby St. CH41: Birke 1C 68
Mallard Cl. L12: Crox 2B 38
L26: Halew 2G 93
WA7: Beech 2B 124
Mallard Gdns. WA9: St H 1C 60
Mallard Ho. L31: Lyd 3A 6
Mallard Way CH46: More 6A 48
WA11: St H 5F 29
Malleson Rd. L13: Liv 6C 36
Mallins Cl. L8: Liv 5G 71
Mallory Av. L31: Lyd 3A 6
Mallory Gro. WA11: St H 5H 29
Mallory Rd. CH42: Tran 1F 87
Mallowdale Cl. CH62: East 2F 121
Mallow Rd. L6: Liv 4A 54
Mallow Way L36: Huy 1H 75
Malmesbury Cl. CH49: Grea 5A 66
Malmesbury Pk. WA7: Nort 2F 115
Malmesbury Rd. L11: Norr G 3C 36
Malpas Av. CH43: Pren 1C 86
Malpas Dr. CH63: Hghr B 4G 87
Malpas Gro. CH45: Wall 1C 50
Malpas Rd. CH45: Wall 1B 50
L11: Crox 6H 23
WA7: Run 1F 123
Malta Cl. L36: Huy 4F 57
Malta St. L8: Liv 4F 71
Malta Wlk. L8: Liv 4F 71
Maltby Cl. WA9: St H 2C 60
Malt Ho. Ct. WA10: Windle 5A 28
Malton Cl. WA8: Cron 4A 78
Malton Rd. L25: Woolt 2D 92
Malt St. L7: Liv 1H 71
Malvern Av. L14: Broad G 5B 56
Malvern Cl. L32: Kirkb 5G 13
WA5: Gt San 1H 81
Malvern Cres. L14: Broad G 5B 56
L10: Ain 1A 22
Malvern Gro. CH42: Tran 1F 87
Malvern Rd. CH45: Wall 2H 49
L6: Liv 4A 54
L20: Boot 6C 20
WA9: St H 2B 44
Malwood St. L8: Liv 5F 71
Manchester Rd. L34: Presc 1B 58
Mandela Ct. L8: Liv 4H 71
Manderston Dr. L12: W Der 6H 37
Mandeville St. L4: Walt 3F 35
Manesty's La. L1: Liv 5E 5 (6D 52)
Manfred St. L6: Liv 5G 53
Manica Cres. L10: Faz 4D 22
Manion Av. L31: Lyd 2A 6
Manion Cl. L31: Lyd 2A 6
Manley Cl. CH43: Oxton 6B 68
Manley Pl. WA9: St H 6C 42
Manley Rd. L22: Water 1E 19
L36: Huy 1A 76
Mannering Ct. L17: Aig 5A 72
(off Mannering Rd.)
Mannering Rd. L17: Aig 5H 71
Manners La. CH60: Hesw 1C 116
Manningham Rd. L4: Walt 1H 53
Manning St. WA10: St H 2D 42
Mannington Cl. CH47: Meols 1E 65
Mann Island L3: Liv 5B 4 (6C 52)

Mann Island Apartments
L3: Liv 5C 4 (6B 52)
Mann St. L8: Liv 3E 71
Manor Av. L23: Crosb 4F 9
L35: Rainh 5A 60
WA12: Newt W 1H 45
Manorbier Cres. L9: Walt 2G 35
Manor Cl. L20: Boot 3E 35
Manor Complex L33: Know I 1E 25
Manor Ct. CH48: W Kir 6A 64
(off Bridge Rd.)
CH49: Grea 6A 66
CH61: Irby 5B 84
WA9: Sut L 2G 63
Manor Cres. L25: Woolt 2D 92
Manor Dr. CH49: Upton 2D 66
L23: Crosb 4F 9
L30: N'ton 6H 11
Mnr. Farm Ct. WA6: Frod 6G 123
Mnr. Farm M. WA7: Manor P 1F 115
Mnr. Farm Rd. L36: Huy 6H 57
WA7: Manor P 1E 115
Manor Fell WA7: Pal F 6D 114
MANOR GREEN 2G 67
Manor Gro. L32: Kirkb 1F 23
Manor Hill CH43: Clau, Oxton 3C 68
Manor Ho. CH62: Brom 5D 104
L17: Aig 6H 71
L31: Mag 6A 6
Manor House, The CH49: Upton 2D 66
Manor Ho. Cl. L31: Mag 6B 6
WA11: St H 2E 29
Manor La. CH42: Rock F 1A 88
CH45: Wall 2E 51
Manor M. CH45: Wall 2E 51
MANOR PARK 1E 115
Manor Pk. Av. WA7: Manor P 1E 115
Manor Pk. Bus. Pk.
WA7: Manor P 1D 114
Manor Pk. Cl. CH61: Thing 5E 85
Manor Pk. Ct. WA7: Manor P 1E 115
Manor Pl. CH62: Brom 6D 88
WA8: Wid 2H 95
Manor Rd. CH44: Wall 2D 50
CH45: Wall 2D 50
CH47: Hoy 1C 64
CH61: Irby 5B 84
CH62: East 1D 120
CH63: Thorn H 4B 102
L23: Blun, Crosb 3E 9
L25: Woolt 2D 92
WA6: Frod 6G 123
WA7: Run 3H 113
WA8: Wid 2H 95
WA11: Hay 4H 31
Manor Road Station (Rail) 2C 64
Manorside Cl. CH49: Upton 3D 66
Manor St. WA9: St H 3G 43
Manor Vw. L12: W Der 4B 38
Manor Way CH43: Bid 2G 67
L25: Woolt 2D 92
(not continuous)
Manorwood Dr. L35: Whis 5E 59
Mansell Cl. WA8: Wid 4G 79
Mansell Dr. L26: Halew 5G 93
Mansell Rd. L6: Liv 4H 53
Mansfield Rd. L20: Boot 3C 34
Mansfield St. L3: Liv 1G 5 (4E 53)
Mansion Dr. L11: Crox 1F 37
Manston Rd. WA5: Penk 6H 81
Manton Rd. L6: Liv 4A 54
Manton Way WA9: St H 3C 60
Manvers Rd. L16: Child 1A 74
Manville Rd. CH45: New B 6D 32
Manville St. WA9: St H 4G 43
Maple Av. WA7: Run 5G 113
WA7: Sut W 3C 124
WA8: Wid 2F 97
WA11: Hay 4D 30
Maple Cl. L12: Crox 2H 37
L21: Sea 5A 20
L35: Whis 4E 59
Maple Ct. L21: Lith 3B 20
L34: Know 1E 39

Maple Cres. L36: Roby 5F 57
WA5: Penk 5H 81
Mapledale Rd. L18: Moss H 4F 73
Maple Gro. CH62: Brom 5C 104
L8: Liv 3A 72
L35: Presc 2E 59
WA10: St H 2A 42
Maple Leaf Dr. L36: Huy 1F 57
Maples Ct. CH43: Oxton 6C 68
Maple St. CH41: Birke 4F 69
Mapleton Cl. CH43: Pren 2A 86
Mapleton Dr. WA7: Sut W 4B 124
Maple Tree Gro. CH60: Hesw 5G 101
Maplewood L32: Kirkb 3B 24
Maplewood Cl. L27: N'ley 4G 75
WA8: Wid 4G 95
Maplewood Gro. CH43: Bid 1A 68
Marathon Cl. L6: Liv 3F 53
Marbury Rd. L32: Kirkb 1G 23
Marc Av. L31: Mell 5F 13
Marcham Way L11: Norr G 4F 37
Marchfield Rd. L9: Walt 6F 21
March Rd. L6: Liv 2B 54
Marchwood Way L25: Gate 2C 74
Marcien Way WA8: Wid 6D 78
Marcot Rd. L6: Liv 3B 54
Marcus Cl. L36: Huy 3A 58
(off Mosscroft Cl.)
Marcus St. CH41: Birke 2G 69
(not continuous)
Mardale Av. WA11: St H 3F 29
Mardale Cl. L27: N'ley 6A 76
Mardale Lawn L27: N'ley 6A 76
Mardale Rd. L36: Huy 2E 57
Mardale Wlk. L27: N'ley 6A 76
(off Mardale Cl.)
L36: Huy 2E 57
Mareth Cl. L18: Moss H 1E 91
Marford Rd. L12: W Der 6F 37
Marfords Av. CH63: Brom 6C 104
Margaret Av. L20: Boot 5C 20
WA9: St H 5G 43
Margaret Ct. WA8: Wid 4F 97
WA10: St H 4B 42
Margaret Rd. L4: Walt 3E 35
L23: Blun 4C 8
Margaret St. L6: Liv 3G 53
WA9: Clock F 4A 62
Margery Rd. WA10: St H 4A 42
Margreen Rd. L4: Kirkd 6D 34
Marian Av. WA12: Newt W 2H 45
Marian Cl. L35: Rainh 5A 60
L35: Rainh 5H 59
Marian Dr. CH46: More 1C 66
Marian Rd. WA11: Hay 4G 31
Marian Sq. L30: N'ton 6F 11
Marian Way, The L30: N'ton 6E 11
Maria Rd. L9: Walt 2F 35
Marie Curie Av. L30: N'ton 5F 11
(not continuous)
Marigold Way L11: Bold 6C 44
Marina Av. L21: Lith 4B 20
WA9: St H 6G 43
Marina Cres. L30: N'ton 2G 21
L36: Huy 6F 57
Marina Gro. WA7: Run 3F 113
Marina La. WA7: Murd 6G 115
Marina Village WA7: Pres B 6G 115
Marine AFC .6E 9
Marine Cres. L22: Water 2F 19
Marine Dr. CH60: Hesw 6B 100
Marine Pk. CH48: W Kir 5B 64
Marine Pk. Mans. CH45: New B 4D 32
Marine Point CH45: New B 4D 32
Marine Point Health & Fitness 4C 32
Marine Prom. CH45: New B 4D 32
Mariner Cl. WA7: Murd 1F 125
Mariner Rd. CH47: Hoy 2A 64
Mariners Ho. L1: Liv 2D 70
(off Queens Dock Commercial Cen.)
Mariners Pk. CH45: Wall 1F 51
Mariners Rd. CH45: New B 6E 33
L23: Blun 1D 18

Mariners Way L20: Boot 2C **34**
　　　　　　(off Strand Shop. Cen.)
Mariners Wharf L3: Liv 3C **70**
Marine Ter. CH45: Wall 6E **33**
　　L22: Water 3F **19**
Marion Dr. WA7: West 1D **122**
Marion Gro. L18: Moss H 1G **91**
Marion Rd. L20: Boot 5D **20**
Marion St. CH41: Birke 3G **69**
　　CH41: Tran 5H **69**
Maritime Bus. Pk. CH41: Birke 6F **51**
Maritime Cen. L21: Sea 4G **19**
Maritime Ct. CH49: Woodc 2F **85**
　　　　　　(off Childwall Grn.)
　　L12: W Der 5E **37**
　　L30: N'ton 4F **11**
Maritime Ent. Pk. L20: Boot 2B **34**
Maritime Grange CH44: Wall 5G **51**
Maritime Gro. CH43: Oxton 4D **68**
Maritime Lodge L5: Liv 1F **53**
　　　　　　(off Towson St.)
Maritime Pk. CH43: Oxton 4E **69**
Maritime Pl. L3: Liv 1H **5** (4E **53**)
Maritime Vw. CH42: Tran 6F **69**
Maritime Way L1: Liv 6E **5** (1D **70**)
Marius Cl. L4: Walt 5F **35**
Markden M. L8: Liv 2F **71**
Market Pl. L34: Presc 1D **58**
　　WA8: Wid 4E **97**
Market Pl. Sth. CH41: Birke 3H **69**
Market Sq. L1: Liv 4F **5**
　　L32: Kirkb 1A **24**
Market St. CH41: Birke 3G **69**
　　CH47: Hoy 3B **64**
　　WA8: Wid 4E **97**
　　WA10: St H 2E **43**
　　WA12: Newt W 1H **45**
Market Way L1: Liv 4F **5**
Markfield Cres. L25: Woolt 2E **93**
　　WA11: St H 6G **29**
Markfield Rd. L20: Boot 6B **20**
Markham Gro. CH43: Bid 1B **68**
Mark Rake CH62: Brom 4D **104**
Mark St. CH44: Wall 5G **51**
　　L5: Liv .6E **35**
Marksway CH61: Pens 1E **101**
Marlborough Av. L30: N'ton 1G **21**
　　L31: Lyd .4C **6**
Marlborough Ct. L17: Aig 1C **90**
　　　　　　(off Aigburth Va.)
Marlborough Cres. WA8: Wid 4E **79**
Marlborough Gro. CH43: Oxton 5E **69**
Marlborough Pl. L3: Liv 1D **4** (4C **52**)
Marlborough Rd. CH45: New B 6E **33**
　　L13: Liv .1B **54**
　　L22: Water 3G **19**
　　L23: Crosb 6F **9**
　　L34: Presc 6E **41**
Marlborough St. L3: Liv 1D **4** (4C **52**)
Marlborough Way WA11: Hay 3G **31**
Marlbrook Rd. L25: Gate 3D **74**
Marlcroft Dr. L17: Aig 3C **90**
Marldon Av. L23: Crosb 1G **19**
Marldon Rd. L12: W Der 5E **37**
Marled Hey L28: Stockb V 5C **38**
Marley Cl. L35: Rainh 6C **60**
Marlfield La. CH61: Pens 1E **101**
Marlfield Rd. L12: W Der 1F **55**
Marline Av. CH63: Brom 1C **120**
Marling Pk. WA8: Wid 2H **95**
Marlowe Cl. WA8: Wid 2D **96**
Marlowe Dr. L12: W Der 1E **55**
Marlowe Rd. CH44: Wall 3C **50**
　　CH64: Nest 6A **118**
Marl Rd. L30: N'ton 6H **11**
　　L33: Know I 6E **15**
Marlsford St. L6: Liv 4A **54**
Marlston Av. CH61: Irby 5D **84**
Marlston Pl. WA7: Run 1F **123**
Marlwood Av. CH45: Wall 2A **50**
Marmaduke St. L7: Liv 6H **53**
Marmion Av. L20: Boot 4E **21**
Marmion Rd. CH47: Hoy 2B **64**
　　L17: Aig .5A **72**

Marmonde St. L4: Walt 5E **35**
Marnell Cl. L5: Liv 2C **52**
Marnwood Rd. L32: Kirkb 2H **23**
Marnwood Wlk. L32: Kirkb 2G **23**
Marple Cl. CH43: Oxton 6A **68**
Marquis St. CH41: Tran 5G **69**
　　CH62: New F 4B **88**
　　L3: Liv 3H **5** (5E **53**)
Marram Cl. CH46: More 5E **49**
Marsden Av. WA10: St H 1B **42**
Marsden Cl. CH44: Wall 2F **51**
　　CH45: New B 6D **32**
　　WA8: Wid 5C **78**
Marsden Rd. L26: Halew 5H **93**
Marsden St. L6: Liv 4G **53**
Marsden Way L6: Liv 4G **53**
MARSH, THE 6C **96**
Marshall Av. WA9: St H 5G **43**
Marshall Cl. L33: Kirkb 4B **14**
Marshall Pl. L3: Liv 3C **52**
Marshall's Cl. L31: Lyd 3B **6**
MARSHALL'S CROSS 2F **61**
Marshalls Cross (Park & Ride) 1F **61**
Marshalls Cross Rd. WA9: St H 1F **61**
Marshall St. CH41: Birke 1E **69**
Marsham Cl. CH49: Upton 2E **67**
Marsham Rd. L25: Gate 4E **75**
Marsh Av. L20: Boot 5E **21**
Marsh Brook Rd. WA8: Wid 4F **79**
Marshfield Rd. L36: Huy 4H **57**
Marshfield Ct. CH46: Leas 4C **48**
Marshfield Rd. L11: Norr G 4F **37**
　　　　　　(not continuous)
Marshgate WA8: Wid 4H **95**
Marshgate Pl. WA6: Frod 5H **123**
Marshgate Rd. L12: W Der 3F **37**
Marsh Hall Pad WA8: Wid 5F **79**
Marsh Hall Rd. WA8: Wid 5F **79**
Marshlands Rd. CH45: Wall 1A **50**
Marsh La. CH63: Hghr B 4E **87**
　　L20: Boot 1A **34**
　　WA5: Cuerd 1E **99**
　　WA7: Ast 2B **114**
Marshside Cl. L8: Liv 4F **71**
Marsh St. L20: Kirkd 4D **34**
　　WA8: Wid 5E **97**
　　WA9: St H 2G **43**
Marsland Gro. WA9: St H 5A **44**
Marston Cl. CH43: Oxton 6B **68**
　　CH62: East 4E **121**
Marsworth Dr. L6: Liv 3F **53**
Marten Av. CH63: Brom 6C **104**
Martensen St. L7: Liv 6H **53**
Martham Gdns. WA9: St H 1C **60**
Martial Arts Studio, The 1E **43**
　　　　　　(off Tolver St.)
Martin Av. WA10: St H 5D **28**
Martin Cl. CH61: Irby 5A **84**
　　L18: Moss H 2E **91**
　　L35: Rainh 3G **59**
　　WA7: Pal F 6C **114**
Martindale Gro. WA7: Beech 2H **123**
Martindale Rd. CH62: Brom 4E **105**
　　L18: Moss H 4H **73**
　　WA11: St H 1F **29**
Martine Cl. L31: Mell 5F **13**
Martin Gro. L35: Presc 2E **59**
Martinhall Rd. L9: Faz 1D **36**
Martin Rd. L18: Moss H 2E **91**
Martin's La. CH44: Wall 3E **51**
Martland Av. L10: Ain 6C **12**
Martland Rd. L25: Gate 5E **75**
Martlesham Cres. WA9: Grea 6H **65**
Martlett Rd. L12: W Der 2H **55**
Martock L35: Whis 5F **59**
Marton Cl. L24: Speke 3F **109**
Marton Grn. L24: Speke 3F **109**
Marton Rd. L36: Huy 1G **57**
Marvin St. L6: Liv 4G **53**
Marwood Towers L5: Liv 1E **53**
　　　　　　(off Boundary St. E.)
Marybone L3: Liv 2D **4** (5D **52**)
Marybone Apartments L3: Liv 1E **5**
　　　　　　(off Marybone)

Marybone Student Village L3: Liv 2E **5**
　　　　　　(off Marybone)
Maryhill Rd. WA7: Run 5E **113**
Maryland Ho. L20: Boot 2C **34**
　　　　　　(off Georgia Cl.)
Maryland La. CH46: More 6B **48**
Maryland St. L1: Liv 6H **5** (1E **71**)
Marylebone Av. WA9: St H 1D **60**
Marymount Cl. CH44: Wall 4D **50**
Maryport Cl. L5: Liv 1F **53**
Mary Rd. L20: Boot 5D **20**
Mary Stockton Ct. L21: Sea 5A **20**
　　　　　　(off Seaforth Va. W.)
Mary St. WA8: Wid 4H **97**
　　WA9: Clock F 4A **62**
Maryton Grange L18: Aller 1H **91**
Maryville Rd. L34: Presc 1E **59**
Marywell Cl. WA9: St H 6H **43**
Marzhan Way WA8: Wid 2G **97**
Masefield Av. WA8: Wid 3D **96**
Masefield Cl. CH62: New F 4A **88**
Masefield Cres. L30: Boot 3D **20**
Masefield Gro. L16: Child 1B **74**
　　WA10: St H 6B **28**
Masefield Pl. L30: Boot 3E **21**
Masefield Rd. L23: Thorn 3C **10**
Maskell Rd. L13: Liv 4D **54**
Mason Av. WA8: Wid 5F **79**
Mason St. CH45: New B 5D **32**
　　L7: Liv 6G **53**
　　L22: Water 2F **19**
　　L25: Woolt 1C **92**
　　WA7: Run 2G **113**
Massam Cl. WA11: Rainf 3G **17**
Masseyfield Rd. WA7: Brook 2C **124**
Massey Pk. CH45: Wall 2C **50**
Massey St. CH41: Birke 1F **69**
　　WA9: St H 5G **43**
Master's Way L19: Garst 1H **107**
Matchwood Cl. L19: Garst 6H **91**
Matchworks, The L19: Garst 6A **92**
Mater Cl. L9: Ain 2B **36**
Mather Av. L18: Aller, Moss H 5F **73**
　　L19: Aller 1G **91**
　　WA7: West P 6B **112**
　　WA9: St H 2A **44**
Mather Ct. CH43: Oxton 4D **68**
Mather Rd. CH43: Oxton 4D **68**
Matheson St. L2: Liv 4D **4** (6C **52**)
Mathieson Rd. WA8: Wid 6C **96**
Matlock Av. L9: Walt 5G **21**
Matlock Cl. WA5: Gt San 6H **63**
Matthew Cl. CH44: Wall 5G **51**
Matthew St. CH44: Wall 5G **51**
　　L2: Liv 3C **5**
Maud Roberts Ct. L21: Lith 3A **20**
Maud St. L8: Liv 3G **71**
Maunders Ct. L23: Crosb 4H **9**
Maureen Wlk. L10: Faz 4F **23**
Mauretania Rd. L4: Walt 3G **35**
Maurice Jones Ct.
　　CH46: More 6C **48**
Mavis Dr. CH49: Woodc 6E **67**
Max Rd. L14: Knott A 2B **56**
Maxton Rd. L6: Liv 4A **54**
Maxwell Cl. CH49: Upton 3E **67**
Maxwell Ct. CH42: Tran 6E **69**
Maxwell Pl. L13: Liv 1D **54**
Maxwell Rd. L13: Liv 1D **54**
Maxwell St. WA10: St H 2C **42**
May Av. CH44: Wall 5F **51**
Maybank Gro. L17: Aig 2D **90**
Maybank Rd. CH42: Tran 5F **69**
Maybury Way L17: Aig 1A **90**
May Cl. L21: Lith 5B **20**
Mayer Av. CH63: Beb 1H **103**
Mayew Rd. CH61: Irby 5D **84**
Mayfair Av. L14: Broad G 5B **56**
　　L23: Crosb 4G **9**
Mayfair Cl. L6: Liv 3H **53**
　　WA5: Gt San 2F **81**
Mayfair Ct. CH43: Oxton 6D **68**
　　　　　　(off The Grove)
Mayfair Gro. WA8: Wid 2B **96**
Mayfayre Av. L31: Lyd 2A **6**

Mayfield Av. WA8: Wid	.2H **95**	
WA9: St H	.5C **42**	
Mayfield Cl. L12: W Der	.1G **55**	
Mayfield Ct. WA8: Wid	.1E **97**	
Mayfield Dr. CH62: East	.1H **121**	
Mayfield Gdns. CH64: Nest	.6A **118**	
L19: Gras	.4E **91**	
Mayfield Rd. CH45: Wall	.2B **50**	
CH63: Beb	.2A **104**	
L19: Gras	.4E **91**	
Mayfields L4: Kirkd	.5E **35**	
Mayfields Ho. *CH62: New F*	*.4B **88***	
(off Mayfields Nth.)		
Mayfields Nth. CH62: New F	.4B **88**	
Mayfields Sth. CH62: New F	.4B **88**	
Mayflower Av. L24: Speke	.5C **92**	
Mayford Cl. L25: Gate	.3E **75**	
Mayhall Cl. L31: Mag	.5C **6**	
May Pl. L13: Liv	.5E **55**	
Maypole Ct. L30: N'ton	.4D **10**	
Maypole Farm Ct. L34: Know	.6E **25**	
May Rd. CH60: Hesw	.5E **101**	
May St. L3: Liv	.5H **5** (6E **53**)	
L20: Boot	.6C **20**	
Maytree Cl. L27: N'ley	.3E **75**	
Mayville Rd. L18: Moss H	.4F **73**	
Mazenod Ct. L3: Liv	.1E **5**	
Mazzini Cl. L5: Liv	.2E **53**	
Mead Av. L21: Lith	.3C **20**	
Meade Cl. L35: Rainh	.6B **60**	
Meade Rd. L13: Liv	.1C **54**	
Meadfoot Rd. CH46: More	.6B **48**	
Meadow, The CH49: Woodc	.6F **67**	
(not continuous)		
Meadow Av. WA9: Clock F	.4H **61**	
Meadow Bank L31: Mag	.5A **6**	
L32: Kirkb	.5G **13**	
Meadowbank Cl. L12: W Der	.2A **56**	
Meadowbarn Cl. L32: Kirkb	.2A **24**	
Meadow Brook Cl. L10: Faz	.4F **23**	
Meadowbrook Rd. CH46: More	.2B **66**	
Meadow Cl. CH64: Will	.6H **119**	
WA8: Wid	.6B **78**	
WA12: Newt W	.2H **45**	
Meadow Ct. L11: Norr G	.2F **37**	
L25: Woolt	.6D **74**	
Meadow Cres. CH49: Woodc	.1E **85**	
Meadow Cft. CH64: Will	.6G **119**	
Meadowcroft CH60: Hesw	.4G **101**	
WA9: St H	.1G **61**	
Meadowcroft Ct. WA7: Cas	.5C **114**	
Meadowcroft Pk. L12: W Der	.3H **55**	
Meadowcroft Rd. CH47: Meols	.6E **47**	
Meadow Dr. L36: Huy	.1H **75**	
Meadowfield Cl. CH42: Rock F	.1H **87**	
L9: Walt	.4G **21**	
Meadowgate CH48: Caldy	.6D **82**	
Meadow Hey L20: Boot	.6A **20**	
Meadow Hey Cl. L25: Woolt	.6D **74**	
Meadow La. CH42: Rock F	.1H **87**	
CH64: Will	.6G **119**	
L12: W Der	.4F **37**	
L31: Mag	.6D **6**	
WA9: St H	.3B **44**	
Meadow Oak Dr. L25: Gate	.5C **74**	
Meadow Pk. CH42: Rock F	.1H **87**	
Meadow Rd. CH48: W Kir	.6F **65**	
Meadow Row WA7: Cas	.4C **114**	
Meadows, The *CH41: Birke*	*.2F **69***	
(off Conway St.)		
CH62: Brom	.6D **104**	
L31: Mag	.6C **6**	
L35: Rainh	.4A **60**	
Meadowside CH46: Leas	.3F **49**	
Meadowside Dr. L33: Kirkb	.1E **23**	
Meadowside Rd. CH62: Brom	.6D **104**	
Meadows Leisure Cen.	.1A **12**	
Meadow St. CH45: New B	.5C **32**	
Meadowsweet Rd. L32: Kirkb	.5B **14**	
Meadow Vw. L21: Ford	.1A **20**	
Meadow Wlk. CH61: Pens	.2C **100**	
WA7: Pal F	*.1B **114***	
(off Halton Lea Shop. Cen.)		
Meadow Way L12: W Der	.4F **37**	

Meads, The L34: Eccl P	.6G **41**	
Meadway CH45: Wall	.2C **50**	
CH49: Upton	.3F **67**	
CH60: Hesw	.1D **116**	
CH62: Spit	.3C **104**	
L15: Wav	.1G **73**	
L30: N'ton	.1G **21**	
L31: Mag	.2H **11**	
L35: Whis	.3F **59**	
WA7: Run	.4A **114**	
WA8: Wid	.2G **95**	
Mealor's Weint CH64: Park	.6F **117**	
Meander, The L12: W Der	.4A **38**	
Measham Cl. WA11: St H	.6G **29**	
Measham Way L12: Crox	.2A **38**	
Mecca Bingo		
Birkenhead	.3F **69**	
Liverpool	.3A **56**	
St Helens	.1D **42**	
Medbourne Ct. L32: Kirkb	.3B **24**	
Medbourne Cres. L32: Kirkb	.3B **24**	
Meddowcroft Rd. CH45: Wall	.1B **50**	
Medea Cl. L5: Liv	.1E **53**	
Medlock Ct. CH43: Oxton	.4C **68**	
Medlock St. L4: Kirkd	.5E **35**	
Medway L20: Boot	*.2C **34***	
(off Strand Shop. Cen.)		
Medway Ct. WA9: St H	.2B **44**	
Medway Rd. CH42: Rock F	.1A **88**	
Meerbrook Gro. *L33: Kirkb*	*.4B **14***	
(off Langton Rd.)		
Meeting La. WA5: Penk	.4F **81**	
Melbourne Cl. L24: Speke	.1D **108**	
Melbourne St. CH45: New B	.5C **32**	
WA9: St H	.6C **42**	
Melbreck Rd. L18: Aller	.2F **91**	
Melbury Rd. L14: Knott A	.1D **56**	
Melda Cl. L6: Liv	.4F **53**	
Meldon Cl. L12: W Der	.3G **37**	
Meldrum Rd. L15: Wav	.3F **73**	
Melford Dr. CH43: Oxton	.2A **86**	
WA7: Run	.4G **113**	
Melford Gro. L6: Liv	.1B **54**	
Meliden Gdns. WA9: St H	.6B **44**	
Melksham Dr. CH61: Irby	.4B **84**	
MELLING	.4D **12**	
Melling Av. L9: Ain	.4H **21**	
Melling Ct. CH45: New B	.6E **33**	
Melling Dr. L32: Kirkb	.6A **14**	
Melling La. L31: Mag	.2C **12**	
MELLING MOUNT	.2G **13**	
Melling Rd. CH45: New B	.6E **33**	
L9: Ain	.3H **21**	
L20: Boot	.6C **20**	
Melling Way L32: Kirkb	.6A **14**	
Melloncroft Dr. CH48: Caldy	.3B **82**	
Melloncroft Dr. W. CH48: Caldy	.4C **82**	
Mellor Cl. L35: Tar G	.2A **76**	
WA7: Wind N	.5F **115**	
Mellor Rd. CH42: Tran	.1E **87**	
Melly Rd. L17: Aig	.6H **71**	
Melrose CH46: More	.6E **49**	
Melrose Av. CH47: Hoy	.2B **64**	
L23: Crosb	.6G **9**	
WA5: Burtw	.6H **45**	
WA10: Eccl	.6H **27**	
Melrose Gdns. CH43: Pren	.3B **86**	
Melrose Pk. *L22: Water*	*.3G **19***	
(off Melrose Rd.)		
Melrose Rd. L4: Kirkd	.5D **34**	
L22: Water	.3G **19**	
L33: Kirkb	.3H **13**	
Melton Cl. CH49: Upton	.4C **66**	
Melton Rd. WA7: Run	.1G **123**	
Melverley Rd. L32: Kirkb	.1F **23**	
Melville CH62: New F	.2B **88**	
Melville Av. CH42: Rock F	.2A **88**	
Melville Cl. WA8: Wid	.2H **97**	
WA10: St H	.1B **42**	
Melville Pl. L7: Liv	.1G **71**	
Melville Rd. CH63: Hghr B	.6G **87**	
L20: Boot	.4C **20**	
Melville St. L8: Liv	.4G **71**	
Melwood Dr. L12: W Der	.6G **37**	

Melwood (Liverpool FC Training Ground)		
	.6G **37**	
Menai M. *L34: Presc*	*.1E **59***	
(off St James' Rd.)		
Menai Rd. L20: Boot	.5D **20**	
Menai St. CH41: Birke	.3E **69**	
Mendell Cl. CH62: Brom	.5E **105**	
Mendell Ct. CH62: Brom	.5E **105**	
Mendip Cl. CH42: Tran	.2C **87**	
L26: Halew	.4G **93**	
Mendip Gro. WA9: St H	.2B **44**	
Mendip Rd. CH42: Tran	.2C **87**	
L15: Wav	.3E **73**	
Mendips		
(Childhood Home of John Lennon)		
	.6A **74**	
Menlo Av. CH61: Irby	.5D **84**	
Menlo Cl. CH43: Oxton	.5A **68**	
Menlove Av. L18: Aller, Moss H	.4F **73**	
L25: Woolt	.5H **73**	
Menlove Ct. L18: Moss H	.4G **73**	
Menlove Gdns. Nth. L18: Moss H	.4F **73**	
Menlove Gdns. Sth. L18: Moss H	.4F **73**	
Menlove Gdns. W. L18: Moss H	.4F **73**	
Menlove Mans. L18: Moss H	.3G **73**	
Menstone Rd. L13: Liv	.3D **54**	
Mentmore Cres. L11: Norr G	.4F **37**	
Mentmore Rd. L18: Moss H	.1E **91**	
MEOLS	.1E **65**	
Meol's Cl. L24: Hale	.3E **111**	
Meols Ct. CH47: Hoy	.3A **64**	
Meols Dr. CH47: Hoy	.6A **64**	
CH48: W Kir	.6A **64**	
Meols Pde. CH47: Meols	.1B **64**	
Meols Station (Rail)	.1E **65**	
Mercer Av. L32: Kirkb	.1G **23**	
Mercer Ct. L12: W Der	.1A **56**	
L20: Boot	*.2C **34***	
(off Clairville Cl.)		
Mercer Dr. L4: Kirkd	.6E **35**	
Mercer Rd. CH43: Bid	.1A **68**	
WA11: Hay	.5F **31**	
Mercer St. L19: Garst	.6G **91**	
WA5: Burtw	.1G **63**	
Merchant Cl. L30: N'ton	.3H **21**	
Merchants Ct. L1: Liv	.5D **4**	
L15: Wav	.1C **72**	
Mercury Ct. L2: Liv	.2C **4** (5C **52**)	
Mere Av. CH63: Raby M	.1B **120**	
Mere Bank L17: Aig	.5C **72**	
Merebank CH43: Oxton	.5A **68**	
Merecroft Av. CH44: Wall	.5E **51**	
Meredale Rd. L18: Moss H	.5E **73**	
Meredith St. L19: Garst	.6A **92**	
Mere Farm Gro. CH43: Oxton	.5B **68**	
Mere Farm Rd. CH43: Oxton	.5A **68**	
Mere Grn. L4: Walt	.4G **35**	
Mere Gro. WA11: St H	.2F **29**	
Mereheath CH46: Leas	.4C **48**	
Mereheath Gdns. *CH46: Leas*	*.4C **48***	
(off Mereheath)		
Mere Hey WA10: Eccl	.2G **41**	
Mereland Way WA9: St H	.3B **44**	
Mere La. CH45: Wall	.6A **32**	
CH60: Hesw	.3C **100**	
L5: Liv	.2F **53**	
Mere Pk. L23: Blun	.5E **9**	
Mere Rd. WA9: Grea	.6A **66**	
Meres Rd. L9: Ain	.4C **22**	
Merevale Cl. WA7: Beech	.1A **124**	
Mereview Cres. L12: Crox	.2H **37**	
Merewood L32: Kirkb	.3B **24**	
Mereworth CH48: Caldy	.5D **82**	
Meribel Cl. L23: Crosb	.4A **10**	
Meribel Sq. L34: Presc	.1D **58**	
Meriden Av. CH63: Spit	.4A **104**	
Meriden Cl. WA11: St H	.5H **29**	
Meriden Rd. L25: Gate	.3D **74**	
Meridian Bus. Village L24: Speke	.5E **93**	
Merlin Av. CH49: Upton	.3B **66**	
Merlin Cl. CH49: Upton	.3B **66**	
WA7: Cas	.4C **114**	
WA11: St H	.5F **29**	

Merlin Ct. L26: Halew 2F **93**
Merlin Rd. CH42: Tran 6E **69**
Merlin St. L8: Liv 3F **71**
Merrills La. CH49: Upton 4E **67**
Merrilocks Grn. L23: Blun 4C **8**
Merrilocks Rd. L23: Blun 4C **8**
Merrilox Av. L31: Lyd 4C **6**
Merrion Cl. L25: Woolt 6B **74**
Merritt Av. CH41: Birke 1D **68**
Merrivale Rd. L25: Woolt 1E **93**
Merrydale Dr. L11: Crox 2G **37**
Mersey Av. L19: Aig 3D **90**
 L31: Mag 5E **7**
Merseybank Ho. CH62: New F 3B **88**
 (off New Ferry Rd.)
Merseybank Cl. CH62: New F 3B **88**
Mersey Cotts. L19: Garst 6H **91**
Mersey Ct. CH44: Wall 5G **51**
 (off Borough Rd. E.)
 L23: Crosb 6E **9**
Mersey Ho. L20: Boot 1B **34**
Mersey La. Sth. CH42: Rock F 1A **88**
Mersey Multimodal Gateway
 WA8: Wid 6D **96**
Mersey Rd. CH42: Rock F 1A **88**
 L17: Aig 4C **90**
 L23: Blun, Crosb 6E **9**
 WA7: Run 2D **112**
 (not continuous)
 WA8: Wid 1E **113**
Merseyside Maritime Mus. 6C **4** (1C **70**)
Merseyside Youth Challenge Trust ...2B **92**
Mersey St. CH44: Wall 5G **51**
 WA9: St H 2C **44**
Mersey Tunnel - Toll L3: Liv ...6A **4** (4H **51**)
 (not continuous)
Mersey Valley Golf Course 2B **80**
Mersey Vw. CH41: Tran 5G **69**
 (off Marquis St.)
 CH63: Hghr B 5F **87**
 L22: Water 1E **19**
 WA7: West P 6B **112**
Mersey Vw. Cotts. WA7: West 1D **122**
Mersey Vw. Rd. WA8: Hale B 1H **111**
Mersey Wlk. CH42: Tran 6G **69**
Mersey Wave 1A **110**
Mersham Ct. WA8: Wid 5D **78**
Merstone Cl. L26: Halew 4H **93**
Merthyr Gro. L16: Child 6A **56**
Merton Bank Rd. WA9: St H 6G **29**
Merton Cl. L36: Huy 5D **56**
Merton Cres. L36: Huy 5D **56**
Merton Dr. CH49: Woodc 6E **67**
 L36: Huy 5C **56**
Merton Gro. L20: Boot 2C **34**
 L23: Blun 6E **9**
Merton Ho. L20: Boot 2C **34**
Merton Pl. CH43: Oxton 3E **69**
Merton Rd. CH45: Wall 2C **50**
 CH65: Hoot 4H **121**
 L20: Boot 2C **34**
Merton St. WA9: St H 6G **29**
Merton Towers L20: Boot 2D **34**
Mesham Cl. CH49: Upton 4C **66**
Metcalf Cl. L33: Kirkb 3H **13**
Methuen St. CH41: Birke 1C **68**
 L15: Wav 1C **72**
Metquarter L1: Liv 4E **5** (6D **52**)
Mevagissey Rd. WA7: Brook 2E **125**
Mews, The L17: Aig 2D **90**
 L23: Crosb 6G **9**
 L28: Stockb V 6E **39**
 WA5: Burtw 1G **63**
Meyrick Ct. WA12: Newt W 2H **45**
Meyrick Rd. L11: Norr G 3C **36**
Micawber Cl. L8: Liv 4F **71**
Michael Dragonette Ct. L3: Liv ...3C **52**
Michigan Cl. L27: N'ley 4G **75**
Mickering La. L39: Augh 1G **7**
Micklefield Rd. L15: Wav 3D **72**
Micklegate WA7: Murd 6F **115**
Micklehead Bus. Village WA9: St H ...4E **61**
MICKLEHEAD GREEN 4E **61**
Micklehead Grn. WA9: St H 4D **60**

Middlefield Rd. L18: Aller 6A **74**
Middleham Cl. L32: Kirkb 2G **23**
Middlehey Av. L34: Know 1F **39**
Middlehurst Av. WA10: St H 1D **42**
Middlehurst Cl. WA8: Eccl P 6G **41**
Middlemass Hey L27: N'ley 4G **75**
Middle Rd. L24: Halew 6H **93**
 (not continuous)
Middlesex Rd. L20: Boot 1D **34**
Middleton Ct. L24: Speke 3G **109**
Middleton Rd. L7: Liv 5C **54**
 L22: Water 1H **19**
Middle Way L11: Crox 1H **37**
Middlewood L32: Kirkb 3B **24**
Midghall St. L3: Liv 1D **4** (4C **52**)
Midhurst Rd. L12: Crox 2B **38**
Midland St. CH43: Oxton 4E **69**
 WA8: Wid 2F **97**
Midland Ter. L22: Water 2F **19**
Midlothian Dr. L23: Blun 6E **9**
Midway Rd. L36: Huy 3G **57**
Midwood St. WA8: Wid 3F **97**
Milbrook Cres. L32: Kirkb 6A **14**
Milbrook Dr. L32: Kirkb 6A **14**
Mildenhall Rd. L25: Gate 3C **74**
Mildenhall Way L25: Gate 3D **74**
 (off Mildenhall Rd.)
Mildmay Rd. L11: Norr G 3C **36**
 L20: Boot 6B **20**
Mile End L5: Liv 3D **52**
Miles Cl. CH49: Grea 6A **66**
Miles La. CH49: Grea 1A **84**
Miles St. L8: Liv 5G **71**
Milestone Hey L28: Stockb V 5D **38**
Milestone Rd. L32: Kirkb 1G **23**
Milford Dr. L12: Crox 2A **38**
Milford St. L5: Kirkd 1C **52**
Milk St. WA10: St H 2E **43**
Millachip Ct. L6: Liv 3H **53**
 (off White Rock St.)
Millar Cl. L11: Crox 2G **37**
Millar Cres. WA8: Wid 4E **97**
Millar Rd. WA5: Gt San 2G **81**
Mill Bank L13: Liv 1D **54**
Millbank Cotts. L31: Mag 4D **6**
Millbank Ct. L9: Ain 3B **22**
Millbank La. L31: Augh, Mag 4E **7**
 L39: Augh 4E **7**
Millbank Linnets Stadium 2E **125**
Millbank Rd. CH44: Wall 4C **50**
Millbeck Cl. L32: Kirkb 5A **14**
Millbeck Gro. WA11: St H 1F **29**
Mill Brook Bus. Pk.
 WA11: Rainf 6H **17**
Millbrook Cl. L34: Know 6E **25**
Millbrook La. WA10: Eccl 1H **41**
Millbrook Rd. CH41: Birke 5D **50**
Mill Brow CH63: Hghr B 5F **87**
 WA8: Wid 1G **97**
 WA9: Sut L 2H **61**
 WA10: Eccl 1H **41**
Mill Brow Cl. WA9: Sut L 2H **61**
Millbutt Cl. CH63: Hghr B 5F **87**
Mill Cl. CH42: Tran 5F **69**
 L23: Crosb 3G **9**
Mill Ct. L30: N'ton 4D **10**
Mill Cft. CH64: Nest 6A **118**
Millcroft L23: Crosb 4A **10**
Millcroft Pk. CH49: Grea 6H **65**
Millcroft Rd. L25: Woolt 2E **93**
Millennium Ct. CH64: Nest 6A **118**
Millennium Rd. CH64: Nest 6A **118**
Miller Av. L23: Crosb 4F **9**
Miller Rd. L20: Boot 3B **34**
Millers Bri. L20: Boot 3B **34**
Millers Bri. Ind. Est. L20: Boot ...3B **34**
Millers Cl. CH46: More 6H **49**
Millerscroft L32: Kirkb 6G **13**
Millersdale WA9: Clock F 3G **61**
Millersdale Av. L9: Ain 4H **21**
Millersdale Cl. CH62: East 2F **121**
Millersdale Gro. WA7: Beech 1A **124**
Millersdale Rd. L18: Moss H 5E **73**
Millers Fold WA10: Eccl 1H **41**

Millers Way CH46: More 1A **66**
Millfield CH64: Nest 6A **118**
Millfield Bus. Pk. WA11: Hay 3G **31**
Millfield Cl. CH63: Hghr B 6F **87**
 L13: W Der 1E **55**
Millfield La. WA11: Hay 1G **31**
 WN4: Ash M 1G **31**
Millfield Rd. WA8: Wid 1G **97**
Millfields WA10: Eccl 2G **41**
Mill Grn. CH64: Will 6H **119**
Millgreen Cl. L12: Crox 2A **38**
Mill Grn. La. WA8: Wid 4H **79**
Mill Gro. L21: Lith 3B **20**
Mill Hey L35: Rainh 6C **60**
Mill Hey Rd. CH48: Caldy 5D **82**
Mill Hill CH43: Oxton 6C **68**
Mill Hill Rd. CH61: Irby 3A **84**
Millhouse Cl. CH46: More 6H **47**
Millhouse Ct. L12: W Der 1E **55**
Millhouse La. CH46: More 6H **47**
Millington Cl. CH43: Pren 2A **86**
 WA7: Sut W 3B **124**
 WA8: Wid 3D **96**
Mill La. CH44: Wall 4C **50**
 CH49: Grea 6A **66**
 CH60: Hesw 5F **101**
 CH64: Will 6G **119**
 L3: Liv 2F **5** (5D **52**)
 L12: W Der 1E **55**
 L13: Liv 5E **55**
 L15: Wav 5E **55**
 L20: Boot 2D **34**
 L32: Kirkb 5G **13**
 L34: Know 6F **25**
 L35: Rainh 5A **60**
 WA6: Frod 5A **124**
 WA8: Cron 4B **78**
 WA8: Wid, Bold H 4H **79**
 WA9: Sut L 2G **61**
 WA11: Rainf 1H **27**
Millom Av. L35: Rainh 3H **59**
Millom Gro. L12: W Der 4G **37**
 WA10: St H 5A **42**
Mill Pk. Dr. CH62: East 4E **121**
Mill Rd. CH61: Thing 5E **85**
 CH62: Brom 2D **104**
 CH63: Hghr B 4F **87**
 L6: Liv 3F **53**
 (not continuous)
Mill Spring Ct. L20: Boot 2D **34**
Mill Sq. L10: Ain 1C **22**
Millstead Rd. L15: Wav 1E **73**
Millstead Wlk. L15: Wav 1E **73**
 (off Millstead Rd.)
Mill Stile L25: Woolt 1C **92**
Mill Stream Cl. L29: Seft 2F **11**
Millstream Way L4: Kirkd 6D **34**
Mill St. CH42: Tran 5F **69**
 L8: Liv 3E **71**
 L25: Woolt 1C **92**
 L34: Presc 1D **58**
 WA10: St H 1D **42**
Mill Ter. CH63: Hghr B 6F **87**
Millthwaite Ct. CH44: Wall 3B **50**
Millthwaite Rd. CH44: Wall 3B **50**
Millvale St. L6: Liv 4A **54**
Mill Vw. L8: Liv 4E **71**
Millview L32: Kirkb 5G **13**
Mill Vw. Dr. CH63: Hghr B 5E **87**
Millway Rd. L24: Speke 1A **110**
Mill Weir Gdns. L29: Seft 2F **11**
Millwood CH63: Hghr B 5F **87**
 WA7: Nort 4E **115**
Millwood Av. WA10: Eccl 2F **41**
Millwood Ct. L24: Speke 1A **110**
Millwood Gdns. L35: Whis 5F **59**
Millwood Rd. L24: Speke 2G **109**
MILL YARD 3H **55**
Mill Yd. CH61: Thing 5F **85**
Milman Cl. CH49: Upton 5D **66**
Milman Ct. L25: Woolt 6A **74**
Milman Rd. L4: Walt 4F **35**
Milner Cop CH60: Hesw 5E **101**
Milne Rd. L13: Liv 5C **36**

Milner Rd. CH60: Hesw 5E **101**
  L17: Aig .2C **90**
Milner St. CH41: Birke 1C **68**
Milnthorpe Cl. L4: Kirkd 5E **35**
Milnthorpe Rd. WA5: Burtw 1G **63**
Milnthorpe St. L19: Garst 5G **91**
Milroy Way L7: Liv 2C **90**
Milton Av. L14: Broad G 5A **56**
  L35: Whis 4E **59**
  WA8: Wid 3D **96**
Milton Cl. L35: Whis 4E **59**
Milton Cres. CH60: Hesw 4E **101**
Milton Grn. CH61: Thing 5F **85**
Milton Pavement CH41: Birke 3F **69**
Milton Rd. CH42: Tran 5F **69**
  CH44: Wall 5F **51**
  CH48: W Kir 6A **64**
  L4: Walt 3E **35**
  L7: Liv .5C **54**
  L22: Water 1G **19**
  WA8: Wid 3D **96**
Milton Rd. E. CH42: Tran 5F **69**
Milton St. L20: Boot 1B **34**
  WA8: Wid 6E **97**
  WA9: Sut M 5E **61**
Milton Way L31: Mag 6A **6**
Milverny Way WA9: St H 4E **43**
Milverton St. L6: Liv 3A **54**
Mimosa Rd. L15: Wav 2F **73**
Mindale Rd. L15: Wav 1D **72**
Minehead Gro. WA9: Sut L 2H **61**
Minehead Rd. L17: Aig 2C **90**
Miners Way L24: Speke 2A **110**
  WA8: Wid 4E **97**
Mines Av. L17: Aig 4D **90**
  L34: Presc 1E **59**
Mine Way WA11: Hay 4H **31**
Minstead Av. L33: Kirkb 1B **24**
Minster Ct. L7: Liv 1G **71**
  WA7: Run 5C **112**
Minto Cl. L7: Liv 5A **54**
Minton Cl. L12: Crox 2B **38**
Minton Way WA8: Wid 4F **79**
Mintor Rd. L33: Kirkb 1C **24**
Minver Rd. L12: W Der 6H **37**
Miranda Av. CH63: Hghr B 4G **87**
Miranda Pl. L20: Kirkd 4D **34**
Miranda Rd. L20: Boot 4D **34**
Miranda Rd. Sth. L20: Kirkd 4D **34**
Mirfield Cl. L26: Halew 5H **93**
Mirfield St. L6: Liv 4H **53**
Miriam Pl. CH41: Birke 1B **68**
Miriam Rd. L4: Walt 1G **53**
Miskelly St. L20: Kirkd 5C **34**
Missouri Dr. WA5: Gt San 2H **81**
Missouri Rd. L13: Liv 6B **36**
Mistle Thrush Way L12: Crox 2B **38**
Miston St. L20: Kirkd 5C **34**
Misty Cl. WA8: Wid 1A **96**
Mitchell Av. WA5: Burtw 2G **63**
Mitchell Ct. CH41: Birke 4F **69**
Mitchell Cres. L21: Lith 3B **20**
Mitchell Pl. L1: Liv 4G **5** (6D **52**)
Mitchell Rd. L34: Presc 1C **58**
  WA10: St H 4A **42**
Mithril Cl. WA8: Wid 6A **80**
Mitre Cl. L35: Whis 6D **58**
Mitylene St. L5: Liv 1E **53**
Mobberley Cl. CH63: Spit 2A **104**
Mobberley Way CH63: Spit 2A **104**
Mockbeggar Dr. CH45: Wall 6A **32**
Mockbeggar Wharf
  CH45: Wall 6A **32**
Modred St. L8: Liv 4F **71**
Moel Famau Vw. L17: Aig 1H **89**
Moffatdale Rd. L4: Walt 5A **36**
Moffatt Rd. L9: Ain 4A **22**
Moira Sephton Ct. CH43: Noct 5H **67**
     (off Sandalwood Dr.)
Molesworth Gro. L16: Child 6B **56**
Molineux Av. L14: Broad G 6H **55**
Molland Cl. L12: W Der 4H **55**
Mollington Av. L11: Norr G 3D **36**
Mollington Link CH41: Birke 4G **69**

Mollington Rd. CH44: Wall 4E **51**
  L32: Kirkb 1G **23**
Mollington St. CH41: Birke 4G **69**
Molly's La. L33: Kirkb 4F **25**
Molton Rd. L16: Child 1G **73**
Molyneux Cl. CH49: Upton 4D **66**
  L35: Presc 3D **58**
  L36: Huy 5H **57**
Molyneux Ct. L11: Norr G 2F **37**
  L14: Broad G 6H 55
     (off Molineux Av.)
Molyneux Dr. CH45: New B 5D **32**
  L35: Presc 3D **58**
Molyneux Rd. L6: Liv 4H **53**
  L18: Moss H 5D **72**
  L22: Water 1G **19**
  L31: Mag 2D **12**
Molyneux Way L10: Ain 6A **12**
Monaghan Cl. L9: Walt 4G **21**
Monarchs Quay L3: Liv 2C **70**
Monash Cl. L33: Kirkb 3A **14**
Monash Rd. L11: Norr G 5D **36**
Monastery La. WA9: St H 6H **43**
Monastery Rd. L6: Liv 1A **54**
  WA9: St H 6A **44**
Mona St. CH41: Birke 2B **68**
  L20: Boot 5D **20**
  WA10: St H 3B **42**
Mond Rd. L10: Faz 4E **23**
  WA8: Wid 3E **97**
Monfa Rd. L20: Boot 5C **20**
Monica Dr. WA8: Wid 4E **79**
Monica Rd. L25: Woolt 2D **92**
Monkfield Way L19: Garst 1H **107**
Monk Rd. CH44: Wall 3D **50**
Monksdown Rd. L11: Norr G 4E **37**
Monks Ferry CH41: Birke 3H **69**
Monksferry Wlk. L19: Gras 4D **90**
Monk St. *CH41: Birke 3H 69*
     (off Cross St.)
  L5: Liv .1F **53**
Monks Way CH48: W Kir 1B **82**
  CH63: Beb 1H **103**
  L25: Woolt 1D **92**
  WA7: Pres B 2G **125**
Monkswell Dr. L15: Wav 1E **73**
Monkswell St. L8: Liv 6G **71**
Monmouth Cl. L10: Ain 2D **22**
Monmouth Gro. WA9: St H 3H **43**
Monmouth Rd. CH44: Wall 3B **50**
Monro Cl. L8: Liv 5F **71**
Monro St. L8: Liv 5F **71**
Mons Sq. *L20: Boot 2C 34*
     (off Strand Shop. Cen.)
Montague Rd. L13: Liv 5E **55**
  WA8: Wid 5G **95**
Montclair Dr. L18: Moss H 3F **73**
Monterey Rd. L13: Liv 5F **55**
Montfort Dr. L19: Gras 4E **91**
Montgomery Cl. L35: Whis 5D **58**
  WA5: Gt San 1H **81**
Montgomery Hill CH48: Caldy, Frank . .3F **83**
Montgomery Rd. L9: Walt 5G **21**
  L36: Huy 3F **57**
  WA8: Wid 3B **96**
Montgomery Way L6: Liv 3H **53**
Montpelier Av. WA7: West 1D **122**
Montpelier Dr. L8: Liv 5F **71**
Montpelier Ct. *CH45: New B 5C 32*
     (off Montpellier Cres.)
Montpellier Cres. CH45: New B 5C **32**
Montpellier Ho. CH45: New B 5C **32**
Montreal Rd. L27: N'ley 4G **75**
Montrose Av. CH44: Wall 6G **51**
Montrose Bus. Pk. *L7: Liv 6B 54*
     (off Tattersall Way)
Montrose Ct. CH47: Hoy 3B **64**
  L12: W Der 6B **38**
Montrose Pl. L26: Halew 5H **93**
Montrose Rd. L13: Liv 1B **54**
Montrose Way L13: Liv 5D **54**
Montrovia Cres. L10: Faz 4G **22**
Monument Pl. L3: Liv 3H **5** (5F **53**)
Monville Rd. L9: Ain 4A **22**

Moorbridge Cl. L30: N'ton 5G **11**
Moor Cl. L23: Crosb 4H **9**
Moor Coppice L23: Crosb 4H **9**
Moor Ct. L10: Faz 4E **23**
Moorcroft Rd. CH45: Wall 2H **49**
  L18: Aller 2G **91**
Moorditch La. WA6: Frod 6D **122**
Moor Dr. L23: Crosb 4G **9**
Moore Av. CH42: Rock F 1G **87**
  WA9: St H 2D **44**
Moore Cl. WA8: Wid 1H **97**
Moor Dr. WA11: Hay 4H **31**
Moore's Ho. L4: Walt 3F **35**
Moore St. L20: Boot 6B **20**
Mooreway L35: Rainh 6C **60**
Moorfield L33: Kirkb 4B **14**
Moorfield Cen. L33: Kirkb 3B **14**
Moorfield Dr. CH64: Park 5G **117**
Moorfield Rd. L23: Crosb 4A **10**
  WA8: Wid 5H **79**
  WA10: St H 6A **28**
Moorfields L2: Liv 3D **4** (5C **52**)
Moorfields Av. CH43: Noct 5H **67**
Moorfields Station (Rail) . . .3D **4** (5C **52**)
Moorfoot Rd. WA9: St H 2B **44**
Moorfoot Rd. Ind. Est. WA9: St H 1B **44**
Moorfoot Way L33: Kirkb 3H **13**
Moorgate Av. L23: Crosb 6H **9**
Moorgate La. L32: Kirkb 3C **24**
Moorgate Point L33: Know I 4C **24**
Moorgate Rd. L33: Kirkb 5B **24**
Moorgate Rd. Sth. L34: Know 5B **24**
Moorgate St. L7: Liv 6H **53**
Moorhead Cl. L21: Lith 4A **20**
Moorhey Rd. L31: Mag 2B **12**
Moor Ho. L23: Crosb 4G **9**
Mooring Cl. WA7: Murd 1F **125**
Moorings, The CH41: Birke 4F **69**
  CH60: Hesw 5A **100**
  L31: Lyd .3A **6**
Moorings Cl. CH64: Park 6F **117**
Moorland Av. L23: Crosb 4G **9**
Moorland Cl. CH60: Hesw 6E **101**
Moorland Dr. WA7: Murd 6G **115**
Moorland Pk. CH60: Hesw 6E **101**
Moorland Rd. CH42: Tran 6G **69**
  L31: Mag 3A **12**
Moorlands Rd. L23: Thorn 3B **10**
Moor La. CH60: Hesw 5D **100**
  L4: Walt 2G **35**
  L10: Faz 4E **23**
  L23: Crosb 4G **9**
  L23: Crosb, Thorn 4G **9**
  L29: Seft 1D **10**
  L32: Kirkb 3F **23**
  WA6: Frod 6F **123**
  WA8: Wid 4D **96**
     (not continuous)
Moor La. Bus. Cen. WA8: Wid 4E **97**
Moor La. Sth. WA8: Wid 4D **96**
MOOR PARK 3G **9**
Moor Pl. L3: Liv 3H **5** (5E **53**)
Moorside Cl. L23: Crosb 5H **9**
Moorside Ct. WA8: Wid 4D **96**
Moorside Rd. L23: Crosb 5H **9**
Moor St. L2: Liv 4C **4** (6C **52**)
Moorway CH60: Hesw 5F **101**
Moorwood Cres. WA9: Clock F 3G **61**
Moray Cl. WA10: St H 6C **28**
Morcott La. L24: Hale 3D **110**
Morcroft Rd. L36: Huy 5C **58**
Morden St. L6: Liv 4A **54**
Morecambe St. L6: Liv 2A **54**
Morecroft Rd. CH42: Rock F 2A **88**
Morella Rd. L4: Walt 5A **36**
Morello Cl. WA10: St H 6D **28**
Morello Dr. CH63: Spit 3B **104**
Moresby Cl. WA7: Murd 6G **115**
Moret Cl. L23: Crosb 4A **10**
MORETON 1C **66**
Moreton Av. WA9: Clock F 3G **61**
MORETON COMMON 3B **48**
Moreton Gro. CH45: Wall 1A **50**
Moreton Hills Golf Cen. 5B **48**

Moreton Rd. CH49: Upton 2D **66**
Moreton Station (Rail) 5C **48**
Morgan M. L30: N'ton 6D **10**
Morgan St. WA9: St H 3H **43**
Morland Av. CH62: Brom 1D **120**
Morley Av. CH41: Birke 1D **68**
Morley Ct. L14: Knott A 3A **56**
Morley Rd. CH44: Wall 4C **50**
 WA7: Run 4E **113**
Morley St. L4: Walt 6E **35**
 WA10: St H 6D **28**
 (not continuous)
Morley Way WA10: St H 1D **42**
Morningside L23: Crosb 6H **9**
Morningside Pl. L11: Norr G 4D **36**
Morningside Rd. L11: Norr G 4D **36**
Morningside Vw. L11: Norr G 5D **36**
Morningside Way L11: Norr G 5D **36**
Mornington Av. L23: Crosb 1G **19**
Mornington Rd. CH45: New B 1D **50**
Mornington St. L8: Liv 4E **71**
Morpeth Cl. CH46: More 1H **65**
Morpeth Rd. CH47: Hoy 4A **64**
Morpeth St. L8: Liv 2F **71**
Morpeth Walkway CH41: Birke 1G **69**
Morpeth Wharf CH41: Birke 1G **69**
Morris Cl. WA11: Hay 6C **30**
Morris Ct. CH43: Oxton 4B **68**
Morrison Cl. WA5: Gt San 4H **81**
Morrison M. WA8: Wid 1B **96**
Morrissey Cl. WA10: St H 1B **42**
Morris St. WA9: St H 4A **44**
Morston Av. L32: Kirkb 3A **24**
Morston Cres. L32: Kirkb 3A **24**
Morston Wlk. L32: Kirkb 3A **24**
Mortar Mill Quay CH41: Birke 6F **51**
Mortimer St. CH41: Birke 3H **69**
Mortlake Cl. WA8: Wid 6A **78**
Morton Ho. L18: Moss H 6D **72**
Morton Rd. WA7: Nort 5F **115**
Morton St. L8: Liv 4F **71**
 (not continuous)
Mortuary Rd. CH45: Wall 1D **50**
Morvah Cl. L12: W Der 3G **37**
Morval Cres. L4: Walt 3E **35**
 WA7: Run 4H **113**
Moscow Dr. L13: Liv 2D **54**
Mosedale Av. WA11: St H 2F **29**
Mosedale Gro. WA7: Beech 2A **124**
Mosedale Rd. CH62: Brom 3E **105**
 L9: Walt 6G **21**
Moseley Av. CH45: Wall 3C **50**
Moseley Rd. CH63: Spit 4A **104**
Moses St. L8: Liv 5F **71**
MOSS BANK
 WA8 . . . . .4H **97**
 WA11 .3E **29**
Moss Bank Pk. L21: Lith 3A **20**
Moss Bank Rd. WA8: Wid 4H **97**
 WA11: St H 3D **28**
Mossborough Hall La. WA11: Raint . .6B **16**
Mossborough Rd. WA11: Raint 1D **26**
Moss Brow WA11: Raint 2F **17**
Mossbrow Rd. L36: Huy 3G **57**
Mosscraig L28: Stockb V 6E **39**
Mosscroft Cl. L36: Huy 3A **58**
Mossdale Cl. WA5: Gt San 2H **81**
Mossdale Dr. L35: Rainh 4B **60**
Mossdale Rd. L33: Kirkb 4B **14**
Mossdene Rd. CH44: Wall 3B **50**
Moss End Way L33: Know I 6F **15**
Mossfield Rd. L9: Walt 5F **21**
Moss Ga. Gro. L14: Knott A 4C **56**
Moss Ga. Rd. L14: Knott A 4C **56**
Moss Grn. Cl. L36: Huy 3D **56**
Moss Grn. Way WA9: St H 4C **44**
Moss Gro. CH42: Tran 1D **86**
 L8: Liv 3A **72**
Mosshey Ct. CH63: Spit 2A **104**
Mosshill Cl. L31: Mag 4B **6**
Mosslake Way L4: Kirkd 6D **34**
Mosslands WA10: Eccl 1G **41**
Mosslands Dr. CH44: Wall 2A **50**
 CH45: Wall 2A **50**

Moss La. CH42: Tran 1D **86**
 L9: Walt 5F **21**
 L20: Boot 5E **21**
 L21: Lith 3B **20**
 L23: Lit C 1F **9**
 L31: Lyd 2A **6**
 L31: Mag 5D **6**
 L33: Kirkb 6D **14**
 L33: Sim 1B **14**
 WA9: St H 3C **44**
 WA11: Windle 4F **27**
Mosslawn Rd. L32: Kirkb 2C **24**
Mosslea Pk. L18: Moss H 5D **72**
Mossley Av. CH62: Brom 5D **104**
 L18: Moss H 4D **72**
 L18: Moss H 6E **73**
MOSSLEY HILL 6D **72**
Mossley Hill Dr. L17: Aig 4B **72**
 (not continuous)
Mossley Hill Rd. L18: Moss H 1D **90**
 L19: Aig 1D **90**
Mossley Hill Station (Rail) 6E **73**
Mossley Rd. CH42: Tran 6G **69**
MOSS NOOK 4B **44**
Moss Nook La. L31: Mag, Mell 1E **13**
 WA11: Rainf 3E **17**
 (not continuous)
Mossock Hall Golf Course 4H **7**
Moss Pits Cl. L10: Faz 4D **22**
Moss Pits La. L10: Faz 4C **22**
 L15: Wav 3F **73**
MOSS SIDE
 L31 . . . . .5D **6**
 WA4 .4H **99**
Moss Side L14: Knott A 4C **56**
Moss Side La. WA4: Moore 4G **99**
Moss St. L6: Liv 5F **53**
 L19: Garst 5G **91**
 L34: Presc 6D **40**
 WA8: Wid 4H **97**
Moss Vw. L21: Lith 3C **20**
 L31: Mag 6E **7**
Mossville Cl. L18: Moss H 1E **91**
Mossville Rd. L18: Moss H 1F **91**
Moss Way L11: Crox 6G **23**
Mossy Bank Rd. CH44: Wall 3F **51**
Mostyn Av. CH48: W Kir 5A **82**
 CH60: Hesw 5A **100**
 L10: Ain 6A **12**
 L19: Aller 3H **91**
Mostyn Cl. L4: Kirkd 6E **35**
Mostyn Gdns. CH64: Park 6F **117**
Mostyn Sq. CH64: Park 6F **117**
Mostyn St. CH44: Wall 4D **50**
Motherwell Cl. WA8: Wid 6C **78**
Mottershead Cl. WA8: Wid 3E **97**
Mottershead Rd. WA8: Wid 3E **97**
Moughland La. WA7: Run 4D **112**
Mould St. L5: Liv 1D **52**
Moulton Cl. WA7: Sut W 3B **124**
Mounsey Rd. CH42: Tran 4F **69**
Mount, The CH44: Wall 3E **51**
 CH60: Hesw 5D **100**
Mount Av. CH60: Hesw 5D **100**
 CH63: Hghr B 4F **87**
 L20: Boot 4D **20**
Mount Cl. L32: Kirkb 5G **13**
Mount Ct. CH45: Wall 5C **32**
 CH60: Hesw 5D **100**
Mount Cres. L32: Kirkb 5G **13**
Mount Dr. CH63: Hghr B 4F **87**
Mount Gro. CH41: Birke 4E **69**
Mount Gro. Pl. CH41: Birke 4E **69**
 (off Mount Gro.)
Mt. Haven Cl. CH49: Upton 5A **66**
Mount Olive CH43: Oxton 6C **68**
Mount Pk. CH63: Hghr B 4F **87**
 L25: Woolt 6C **74**
Mount Pk. Ct. L25: Woolt 6C **74**
Mt. Pleasant CH43: Oxton 6D **68**
 L3: Liv 5G **5** (6E **53**)
 L22: Water 2F **19**
 WA8: Wid 1F **97**

Mt. Pleasant Av. WA9: St H 2C **44**
Mt. Pleasant Cl. CH45: New B 6D **32**
Mt. Pleasant Rd.
 CH45: New B, Wall 1C **50**
Mount Rd. CH42: Tran 2E **87**
 CH45: Wall 5C **32**
 CH48: W Kir 2C **82**
 CH49: Upton 4E **67**
 CH63: Hghr B, Spit 3G **103**
 L32: Kirkb 6F **13**
 (not continuous)
 WA7: Halt 1E **127**
Mount St. L1: Liv 6H **5** (1E **71**)
 L22: Water 2F **19**
 L25: Woolt 1C **92**
 WA8: Wid 1F **97**
Mount Vernon L7: Liv 6G **53**
Mt. Vernon Grn. L7: Liv 5G **53**
Mt. Vernon Rd. L7: Liv 5G **53**
Mt. Vernon St. L7: Liv 5G **53**
Mountview Cl. L8: Liv 4G **71**
Mount Way CH63: Hghr B 4F **87**
Mountwood Rd. CH42: Tran 3E **87**
Mowbray Av. WA11: St H 6G **29**
Mowbray Ct. L20: Kirkd 4C **34**
Mowbray Gro. L13: Liv 6E **55**
Mowcroft La. WA5: Cuerd 6C **80**
Moxon St. WA10: St H 3A **42**
Moyles Cl. WA8: Wid 1B **96**
Mozart Cl. L8: Liv 3H **71**
Mr Hardman's Photographic Studio . . .1E **71**
Muirfield Cl. L12: W Der 1A **56**
Muirfield Rd. L36: Roby 6E **57**
Muirhead Av. L6: Liv 3A **54**
 L13: Liv, W Der 1C **54**
 L13: W Der 6D **36**
 (not continuous)
Muirhead Av. E. L11: Norr G 5E **37**
Muir Rd. L9: Ain 5B **22**
Mulberry Av. WA8: Wid 4G **97**
 WA10: St H 2A **42**
Mulberry Cl. CH42: Rock F 1H **87**
 L33: Kirkb 3B **14**
Mulberry Ct. L7: Liv 1F **71**
 (off Mulberry St.)
Mulberry Gro. CH44: Wall 4F **51**
Mulberry Pl. L7: Liv 1F **71**
Mulberry Rd. CH42: Rock F 1H **87**
Mulberry St. L7: Liv 1F **71**
Mulcrow Cl. WA9: St H 1H **43**
Mulgrave St. L8: Liv 2G **71**
Mulliner St. L7: Liv 2A **72**
Mullion Cl. L26: Halew 3G **93**
 WA7: Brook 1D **124**
Mullion Rd. L11: Crox 6G **23**
Mullion Wlk. L11: Crox 6G **23**
Mullrea Cl. L27: N'ley 3E **75**
Mullwood Cl. L12: Crox 2B **38**
Mulrankin Ct. L13: Liv 5F **55**
Mulveton Rd. CH63: Spit 3H **103**
Mumfords Gro. CH47: Meols 6E **47**
Mumfords La. CH47: Meols 6D **46**
 (not continuous)
Muncaster Cl. CH62: Brom 4D **104**
Muncaster Dr. WA7: Cas 3B **114**
Muncaster Dr. WA11: Rainf 2G **17**
Munster Rd. L13: Liv 4F **55**
Murat Gro. L22: Water 2E **19**
Murat St. L22: Water 2E **19**
Murcote Rd. L14: Knott A 2B **56**
MURDISHAW 1F **125**
Murdishaw Av. WA7: Brook, Murd . . .2E **125**
Murdock Way L10: Faz 5F **23**
Muriel Cl. WA5: Gt San 3F **81**
Muriel St. L4: Walt 5G **35**
Murphy Gro. WA9: St H 1A **44**
Murrayfield Dr. CH46: Leas 3D **48**
Murrayfield Rd. L25: Gate 3D **74**
Murrayfield Wlk. L25: Gate 2D **74**
 (off Murrayfield Rd.)
Murray Gro. CH48: W Kir 6A **64**
Museum of Liverpool 5B **4** (6B **52**)
Musker Dr. L30: N'ton 6C **10**
Musker Gdns. L23: Crosb 6H **9**

Musker St. L23: Crosb 6H 9
Muspratt Rd. L21: Sea 6A 20
Muttocks Rake L30: N'ton 4D 10
(off Great Hey)
Mycroft Cl. L5: Liv 1F 53
Myers Av. L35: Whis 2G 59
Myerscough Av. L20: Boot 6E 21
Myers Ct. L23: Crosb 1H 19
Myers Rd. E. L23: Crosb 6G 9
Myers Rd. W. L23: Crosb 6F 9
Mylia Cl. L14: Knott A 4C 56
Mynsule Rd. CH63: Spit 2H 103
Myrtle Av. WA11: Hay 4D 30
Myrtle Cl. L7: Liv 1G 71
L8: Liv 1G 71
Myrtle Gro. CH44: Wall 4G 51
L22: Water 1F 19
WA8: Wid 3B 96
Myrtle Pde. L7: Liv 1F 71
Myrtle St. L7: Liv 1F 71
Myrtle Way CH49: Woodc 5F 67
Mystery Cl. L15: Wav 2C 72

N

Naburn Gro. CH46: More 2C 66
Nairn Cl. CH63: East 3D 120
Nansen Gro. L4: Walt 4G 35
Nant Pk. Ct. CH45: New B 5E 33
Nantwich Cl. CH49: Woodc 1E 85
Napier Cl. WA10: St H 2C 42
Napier Dr. CH46: More 1D 66
Napier Rd. CH62: New F 3B 88
Napier St. L20: Boot 4B 34
WA10: St H 2C 42
Naples Rd. CH44: Wall 4F 51
Napps Cl. L25: Gate 2B 74
Napps Wlk. L25: Gate 2B 74
(off Napps Cl.)
Napps Way CH61: Hesw 3E 101
L25: Gate 1B 74
Naseby Cl. CH43: Noct 5G 67
Naseby St. L4: Walt 3F 35
Natal Rd. L9: Ain 5H 21
Nathan Dr. WA11: Hay 5G 31
Nathan Gro. L33: Kirkb 5B 14
National Museum & Galleries,
Merseyside Conservation Cen.
. . . . .3E 5 (5D 52)
National Wildflower Cen. 6B 56
Naughton Lea WA8: Wid 6B 78
Naughton Rd. WA8: Wid 3E 97
Navigation Cl. L30: N'ton 5G 11
WA7: Murd 1F 125
Navigation Rd. WA9: St H 1G 43
Navigation Wharf L3: Liv 3D 70
Naylor Rd. CH43: Bid 1A 68
WA8: Wid 2H 97
Naylorsfield Dr. L27: N'ley 3E 75
Naylor's Rd. L25: Gate 4F 75
L27: N'ley 2E 75
Naylor St. L3: Liv 1D 4 (4C 52)
Nazareth Ho. La. WA8: Wid 4A 96
Nazeby Av. L23: Crosb 6A 10
Neale Dr. CH49: Grea 6C 66
Neasham Cl. L26: Halew 3H 93
Nedens Gro. L31: Lyd 4B 6
Nedens La. L31: Lyd 4B 6
Needham Cl. WA7: Run 3H 113
Needham Cres. CH43: Noct 5H 67
Needham Rd. L7: Liv 5A 54
Needwood Dr. CH63: Beb 2H 103
Neills Rd. WA9: Bold 2D 62
Neilson Rd. L17: Aig 6H 71
Neilson St. L17: Aig 6H 71
Neil St. WA8: Wid 1G 97
Nell's La. L39: Augh 2E 7
Nelson Av. L35: Whis 5E 59
Nelson Ct. CH42: Rock F 2A 88
CH45: New B 4D 32
Nelson Dr. CH61: Pens 1C 100
WA7: West 1D 122
Nelson Ho. CH42: Rock F 2A 88

Nelson Memorial 3C 4
(off Exchange Pas. E.)
Nelson Pl. L35: Whis 5E 59
Nelson Rd. CH42: Rock F 2A 88
L1: Liv 6H 53
L21: Lith 4B 20
(off Bridge Rd.)
Nelson's Cft. CH63: Beb 2A 104
Nelson St. CH45: New B 6E 33
L1: Liv 2D 70
(not continuous)
L15: Wav 1C 72
L20: Boot 3B 34
WA7: Run 3E 113
WA8: Wid 5E 97
WA12: Newt W 2H 45
(not continuous)
Nelville Rd. L9: Ain 4A 22
Neptune Cl. WA7: Murd 6F 115
Neptune St. CH41: Birke 1F 69
Ness Gro. L32: Kirkb 1G 23
NESTON 6A 118
Neston Av. WA9: Clock F 3F 61
Neston Gdns. CH41: Birke 1D 68
(off Churchview Rd.)
Neston Recreation Cen. 6B 118
Neston Rd. CH63: Thorn H 3B 118
CH64: Nest 3B 118
Neston St. L4: Walt 4F 35
Netherby St. L8: Liv 6F 71
Netherfield WA8: Wid 3B 96
Netherfield Cl. CH43: Noct 5G 67
Netherfield Rd. Nth. L5: Liv 1E 53
Netherfield Rd. Sth. L5: Liv 3E 53
NETHERLEY 4G 75
Netherley Rd. L27: N'ley 4H 75
L35: Tar G 4H 75
WA8: Wid 6C 76
NETHERTON 6F 11
Netherton Activity Cen. 5E 11
Netherton Grange L30: N'ton 6H 11
Netherton Grn. L30: N'ton 4F 11
Netherton Ind. Est. L30: N'ton 3F 21
Netherton La. L30: N'ton 4E 11
(not continuous)
Netherton Pk. Rd. L21: Lith 3D 20
Netherton Rd. CH46: More 1C 66
L18: Moss H 2E 91
L20: Boot 5D 20
Netherton Way L30: Boot 3E 21
(off Captain's La.)
L30: N'ton 2E 21
Netherwood Rd. L11: Norr G 3C 36
Netley St. L4: Kirkd 5E 35
Nettle Hill CH48: W Kir 6A 64
Nettlestead Rd. L11: Norr G 5E 37
Neva Av. CH46: More 1B 66
Nevada Bobs Driving Range 6H 17
Neville Av. WA9: St H 3D 44
Neville Cl. CH43: Noct 5G 67
Neville Cres. WA5: Penk 6H 81
Neville Rd. CH44: Wall 3C 50
CH62: Brom 6E 105
L22: Water 2G 19
Neville St. WA12: Newt W 1H 45
Nevin St. L6: Liv 4G 53
Nevison St. L7: Liv 6H 53
Nevitte Cl. L28: Stockb V 5C 38
New Acres Cl. CH43: Bid 1G 67
New Albert Ter. WA7: Run 2F 113
(off Frederic Pl.)
Newark Cl. CH43: Noct 5G 67
L30: N'ton 4H 11
L36: Huy 1F 57
Newark St. L4: Walt 4F 35
New Bank Pl. WA8: Wid 2H 95
New Bank Rd. WA8: Wid 2H 95
New Barnet WA8: Wid 6D 78
New Bird St. L1: Liv 2D 70
New Bold Cl. WA9: Bold 6C 44
Newbold Cres. CH48: W Kir 6E 65
Newbold Gro. L12: Crox 3B 38
Newborough Av. L18: Moss H 4D 72
L23: Crosb 5A 10

NEW BOSTON 5G 31
Newbridge Cl. CH49: Woodc 5F 67
WA7: Brook 1E 125
Newbridge Farm Caravan Pk.
L33: Sim 2G 15
NEW BRIGHTON 4D 32
New Brighton Station (Rail) 5C 32
Newburgh Cl. WA7: Wind N 4F 115
Newburn CH43: Oxton 4D 68
Newburns La. CH43: Oxton 6D 68
Newburn St. L4: Walt 3F 35
Newbury Cl. L36: Roby 6F 57
WA8: Wid 6E 79
Newbury Way CH46: Leas 4D 48
L12: W Der 2A 56
Newby Av. L35: Rainh 3G 59
Newby Dr. L36: Huy 4E 57
Newby Gro. L12: W Der 3G 37
Newby Pl. WA11: St H 3E 29
Newby St. L4: Walt 5F 35
Newcastle Rd. L15: Wav 3E 73
New Chester Rd. CH41: Birke, Tran . . .4H 69
CH42: Rock F, Tran 5H 69
CH62: Brom, East, New F, Port S
. . . . .1A 88
CH66: Hoot 5G 121
Newchurch Cl. L27: N'ley 5H 75
Newcombe St. L6: Liv 2H 53
Newcroft Rd. L25: Woolt 5B 74
New Cross St. L34: Presc 6D 40
WA10: St H 1D 42
(Henry St.)
WA10: St H 2D 42
(Westfield St.)
New Cross St. Sth. WA10: St H 2D 42
(off Nth. John St.)
New Cut La. L33: Kirkb, Rainf 4A 26
WA11: Rainf 2B 26
Newdales Cl. CH43: Bid 1G 67
Newdown Rd. L11: Crox 6H 23
Newdown Wlk. L11: Crox 6H 23
Newell Rd. CH44: Wall 2D 50
Newenham Cres. L14: Knott A 3A 56
NEW FERRY 4B 88
New Ferry By-Pass
CH62: New F, Port S 3B 88
New Ferry Rd. CH62: New F 4B 88
Newfield Cl. L23: Thorn 3C 10
Newfields WA10: St H 1A 42
New Fort Way L20: Boot 5A 20
New Glade Hill WA11: St H 5H 29
New Grey Rock Cl. L6: Liv 3H 53
New Hall L10: Faz 3D 22
New Hall La. CH47: Hoy 3B 64
L11: Norr G 5C 36
New Hall Mnr. CH64: Nest 1A 118
New Hall Pl. L3: Liv 3B 4 (5B 52)
Newhall St. L1: Liv 2D 70
Newhaven Rd. CH45: New B 6E 33
New Hawthorne Gdns. L18: Moss H . . .6D 72
New Hedley Gro. L5: Liv 2C 52
New Henderson St. L8: Liv 3E 71
New Hey L12: W Der 2E 55
New Heyes CH64: Nest 6A 118
New Hey Rd. CH49: Woodc 5F 67
New Heys Dr. L18: Aller 2H 91
Newholme Cl. L12: Crox 2A 38
Newhope Rd. CH41: Birke 2E 69
Newhouse Rd. L15: Wav 2B 72
New Hutte La. L26: Halew 5G 93
Newick Pk. L32: Kirkb 2G 23
Newick Rd. L32: Kirkb 2G 23
Newington L1: Liv 5G 5 (6E 53)
Newington Way WA8: Wid 6D 78
New Islington L3: Liv 2G 5 (5E 53)
Newland Cl. WA8: Wid 6A 78
Newland Ct. L17: Aig 6A 72
Newland Dr. CH44: Wall 3C 50
Newlands Rd. CH63: Beb 1B 104
WA11: St H 4G 29
Newling St. CH41: Birke 2E 69
Newlove Av. WA10: St H 2A 42
Newlyn Av. L21: Lith 2A 20
L31: Mag 6D 6

Newlyn Cl. CH47: Meols 6E 47
 WA7: Brook 1D 124
Newlyn Gdns. WA5: Penk 6F 81
Newlyn Rd. CH47: Meols 6E 47
 L11: Crox .6H 23
Newlyn Wlk. L11: Crox 6H 23
Newman St. L4: Kirkd 6D 34
New Mkt. Cl. L21: Lith 4B 20
Newmarket Gdns. WA9: St H 1A 60
New Mkt. Hall WA7: Run 2E 113
 (off Granville St.)
New Mersey Retail Pk. L24: Speke 6B 92
New Mersey Shop. Pk. L24: Speke 6B 92
New Mill Stile L25: Woolt 6C 74
Newmoore La. WA7: Nort 2G 115
Newmorn Ct. L17: Aig 1A 90
New Palace Amusement Pk. 4D 32
Newport Av. CH45: Wall 6A 32
Newport Cl. CH43: Noct 5G 67
Newport St. L5: Liv 2C 52
New Quay L3: Liv 3B 4 (5B 52)
Newquay Cl. WA7: Brook 1D 124
New Quay Ter. L3: Liv 3B 4
New Red Rock Vw. L6: Liv 3H 53
New Rd. L13: Liv 2C 54
 L34: Eccl P 6E 41
New Rd. Ct. L13: Liv 2C 54
 (off Oak Leigh)
New School La. CH66: Chil T 6H 121
Newsham Cl. WA8: Wid 5H 77
Newsham Dr. L6: Liv 3A 54
 (not continuous)
Newsham Rd. L36: Huy 1A 76
Newsham St. L5: Liv 2D 52
News La. WA11: Rainf 1G 17
Newstead Av. L23: Blun 6D 8
Newstead Rd. L8: Liv 2A 72
 WA8: Wid 5F 95
Newstet Rd. L33: Know I 1D 24
New St. CH44: Wall 5G 51
 WA7: Run 3E 113
 WA8: Wid 3F 97
 WA9: St H, Sut L 2G 61
NEWTON 1E 83
Newton Cl. L12: W Der 5F 37
NEWTON COMMON 2G 45
Newton Ct. CH42: Rock F 2A 88
 (off New Chester Rd.)
 L13: Wav 6C 54
Newton Cross La. CH48: W Kir 1E 83
Newton Dr. CH48: W Kir 1E 83
NEWTON-LE-WILLOWS 2H 45
Newton Pk. Rd. CH48: W Kir 1E 83
Newton Rd. CH44: Wall 3C 50
 CH47: Hoy 2C 64
 L13: Liv .3C 54
 WA9: St H 2C 44
Newton St. CH41: Birke 2F 69
Newton Wlk. L20: Boot 1B 34
 (off Capricorn Way)
Newton Way CH49: Upton 4D 66
 L3: Liv 4H 5 (6F 53)
New Tower Ct. CH45: New B 5E 33
NEWTOWN .6H 123
Newtown Gdns. L32: Kirkb 1A 24
Newway L14: Knott A 2C 56
New Way Bus. Cen. CH44: Wall 5F 51
Nicander Rd. L18: Moss H 4D 72
Nicholas Ho. L23: Blun 5D 8
Nicholas Rd. L23: Blun 5D 8
 WA8: Wid 3A 96
Nicholas St. L3: Liv 4D 52
Nicholl Rd. WA10: Eccl 5G 27
Nicholls Dr. CH61: Pens 1D 100
Nichols Gro. L18: Aller 2G 91
Nicholson St. WA9: St H 1A 44
Nickleby Cl. L8: Liv 4F 71
Nickleford Hall Dr. WA8: Wid 3D 78
Nicola Cl. CH45: Wall 1E 51
Nidderdale Av. L35: Rainh 4B 60
Nigella Dr. L11: Norr G 4E 37
Nigel Rd. CH60: Hesw 5G 101
Nigel Wlk. WA7: Cas 3C 114

Nightingale Cl. L27: N'ley 4H 75
 L32: Kirkb 6F 13
 WA7: Beech 2B 124
Nightingale Rd. L12: Crox 2B 38
Nimrod St. L4: Walt 4F 35
Ninth Av. L9: Ain 4B 22
Nithsdale Rd. L15: Wav 3C 72
Nixon St. L4: Walt 3F 35
NOCTORUM .5H 67
Noctorum Av. CH43: Noct 4G 67
Noctorum Dell CH43: Noct 5H 67
Noctorum La. CH43: Noct, Oxton 3H 67
Noctorum Rd. CH43: Noct 4H 67
Noctorum Way CH43: Noct 5H 67
Noel St. L8: Liv 2A 72
Nook, The CH43: Oxton 3D 68
 CH48: Frank 1H 83
 L25: Gate 6D 74
 WA10: Windle 5H 27
Nook La. WA9: St H 4B 44
Nook Ri. L15: Wav 1F 73
Noonan Cl. L9: Walt 1F 35
Norbreck Av. L14: Broad G 5B 56
Norbury Av. CH63: Hghr B 6G 87
 L18: Moss H 4D 72
Norbury Cl. CH63: Hghr B 6H 87
 L32: Kirkb 1H 23
 WA8: Wid 2H 97
Norbury Fold L35: Rainh 6C 60
Norbury Rd. L32: Kirkb 1H 23
Norbury Wlk. L32: Kirkb 1H 23
Norcliffe Rd. L35: Rainh 3H 59
Norcott Dr. WA5: Burtw 1H 63
Norfolk Cl. CH43: Noct 5G 67
 L20: Boot 1D 34
 (off Brookhill Rd.)
Norfolk Dr. CH48: W Kir 2C 82
 WA5: Gt San 3G 81
Norfolk Pl. L21: Sea 4A 20
 WA8: Wid 3A 96
Norfolk Rd. L31: Mag 2A 12
 WA10: St H 4B 42
Norfolk St. L1: Liv 2D 70
 WA7: Run 2F 113
Norgate St. L4: Walt 6F 35
Norgrove Cl. WA7: Murd 5F 115
Norlands Ct. CH42: Rock F 2G 87
Norland's La. L35: Rainh 1C 78
 WA8: Cron, Wid 1C 78
Norlands Pk. WA8: Wid 3D 78
Norland St. WA8: Wid 2H 97
Norleane Cres. WA7: Run 5F 113
Norley Av. CH62: East 4E 121
Norley Dr. WA10: Eccl 2G 41
Norley Pl. L26: Halew 5G 93
Norman Av. WA11: Hay 4H 31
Normandale Rd. L4: Walt 4B 36
Normandy Rd. L36: Huy 4F 57
Norman Rd. CH44: Wall 5G 51
 L20: Boot 4C 20
 L23: Crosb 6F 9
Norman Salisbury Ct. WA10: St H 6E 29
Normans Rd. WA9: St H 6B 44
Normanston Cl. CH43: Oxton 5D 68
Normanston Rd. CH43: Oxton 5D 68
Norman St. CH41: Birke 1B 68
 L3: Liv 5F 53
 (off London Rd.)
Normanton Av. L17: Aig 6A 72
Norma Rd. L22: Water 2G 19
Normington Cl. L31: Lyd 3B 6
Norris Cl. CH43: Noct 5G 67
NORRIS GREEN 3D 36
Norris Grn. Cres. L11: Norr G 4E 37
Norris Grn. Rd. L12: W Der 1F 55
Norris Gro. WA8: Hale B 6A 96
Norris Rd. L34: Presc 1C 58
Norseman Cl. L12: W Der 5F 37
North Av. L10: Ain 1C 22
 L24: Speke 5C 92

Nth. Barcombe Rd. L16: Child 2H 73
Northbrook Cl. L8: Liv 2G 71
Nth. Brooke Way CH49: Woodc 6E 67
Northbrook Rd. CH44: Wall 4F 51
Northbrook St. L8: Liv 2G 71
 (Granby St.)
 L8: Liv 2G 71
 (Rosebery St.)
Nth. Cantril Av. L12: W Der 5A 38
Nth. Cheshire Trad. Est.
 CH43: Pren 3A 86
North Cl. CH62: Brom 3C 104
Northcote Cl. L5: Liv 3F 53
Northcote Rd. CH45: Wall 1H 49
 L9: Walt 2F 35
Northdale Rd. L15: Wav 1D 72
North Dingle L4: Kirkd 5D 34
 (not continuous)
North Dr. CH45: Wall 5B 32
 CH60: Hesw 6E 101
 L12: W Der 2E 55
 L15: Wav 1D 72
NORTH END .6G 75
North End La. L26: Halew 6G 75
Northern La. WA8: Wid 6G 75
Northern Perimeter Rd. L30: N'ton 4E 11
Northern Rd., The L23: Crosb 4G 9
Northfield Cl. L33: Kirkb 5C 14
 WA9: Clock F 4H 61
Northfield Rd. L9: Walt 5E 21
 L20: Boot 5E 21
NORTH FLORIDA 3F 31
Nth. Florida Rd. WA11: Hay 3F 31
North Front L35: Whis 6E 59
Northgate Rd. L13: Liv 2E 55
North Gro. L18: Aller 2G 91
North Hill St. L8: Liv 4F 71
Nth. John St. L2: Liv 3D 4 (6C 52)
 WA10: St H 2D 42
 (not continuous)
Nth. Linkside Rd. L25: Woolt 2E 93
Nth. Manor Way L25: Woolt 2E 93
North Meade L31: Mag 5B 6
Northmead Rd. L19: Aller 4A 92
Nth. Mersey Bus. Cen. L33: Know I 5E 15
Nth. Mossley Hill Rd. L18: Moss H 5D 72
Nth. Mount Rd. L32: Kirkb 5F 13
Northop Rd. CH45: Wall 1B 50
North Pde. CH47: Hoy 2A 64
 CH64: Park 5F 117
 L24: Speke 2G 109
 L32: Kirkb 1A 24
North Pk. Ct. CH44: Wall 4G 51
 (off Demesne St.)
North Pk. Rd. L32: Kirkb 5F 13
Nth. Parkside Wlk. L12: W Der 5E 37
 (off Parkside Dr.)
Nth. Perimeter Rd. L33: Know I 5D 14
North Quay L3: Liv 2C 70
Northridge Rd. CH61: Pens 6E 85
North Rd. CH42: Tran 6E 69
 CH48: W Kir 4A 82
 CH65: Ell P 3H 121
 L14: Broad G 5G 55
 L19: Gras 5D 90
 L24: Halew 6G 93
 WA10: St H 6D 28
North St. L3: Liv 2E 5 (5D 52)
 WA11: Hay 5G 31
 WA12: Newt W 1H 45
Nth. Sudley Rd. L17: Aig 1C 90
Nth. Ter. CH47: Meols 6D 46
Northumberland Gro. L8: Liv 4D 70
Northumberland St. L8: Liv 4E 71
Northumberland Ter. L5: Liv 1E 53
Northumberland Way L30: N'ton 6C 10
North Vw. L7: Liv 6G 53
 L36: Huy .5A 58
 WA5: Gt San 2G 81
Nth. Wallasey App. CH45: Wall 1G 49
Northway CH60: Hesw 4H 101
 L15: Wav 6F 55
 L31: Augh, Lyd, Mag 2A 12
 (not continuous)

Northway L39: Augh 2E 7
  WA7: Pal F 5B 114
  WA8: Wid 2B 96
Northways CH62: Brom 2D 104
North West Museum of Road Transport
  . . . . .1E 43
Northwich Cl. L23: Thorn 3B 10
Northwich Rd. WA4: Dutt 3F 125
  WA7: Brook 2D 124
  WA7: Dutt, Pres B 3F 125
Nth. William St. WA44: Wall 5G 51
North Wirral Coastal Pk. 5F 47
NORTHWOOD 1B 24
Northwood Rd. CH43: Pren 1B 86
  L36: Huy 3H 57
  WA7: Run 3A 114
NORTON 5F 115
Norton Av. WA5: Penk 4G 81
Norton Ct. CH44: Wall 4G 51
              (off Borough Rd.)
Norton Dr. CH61: Irby 4A 84
Norton Ga. WA7: Nort 5E 115
Norton Gro. L31: Mag 3B 12
  WA9: St H 6B 42
Norton Hill WA7: Wind H 4E 115
Norton La. WA7: Halt, Nort 5C 114
             (not continuous)
  WA7: Nort 4F 115
Norton Priory Gdns. 2D 114
Norton Priory Mus. 2D 114
Norton Rd. CH48: W Kir 6A 64
Norton Sta. Rd. WA7: Murd, Nort . . .5F 115
Norton St. L3: Liv 2C 5 (5E 53)
  L20: Boot 6B 20
Norton Vw. WA7: Halt 5C 114
Norton Village WA7: Nort 5F 115
Norton Village Gdns.
  WA7: Nort 5F 115
Nortonwood La. WA7: Wind H 5E 115
Norville Rd. L14: Broad G 5G 55
Norwich Dr. CH49: Upton 2E 67
Norwich Rd. L15: Wav 3E 73
Norwich Way L32: Kirkb 1A 24
Norwood Av. L21: Lith 2B 20
Norwood Ct. CH49: Grea 6B 66
Norwood Gro. L6: Liv 3H 53
  WA11: Rainf 3G 17
Norwood Rd. WA44: Wall 5D 50
  CH49: Grea 5B 66
Norwyn Rd. L11: Norr G 3C 36
Nottingham Cl. L35: Rainh 2A 60
Nottingham Rd. L36: Roby 6E 57
Nowshera Av. CH61: Pens 6D 84
Nuffield Cl. CH49: Upton 5D 66
Nuffield Rd. L20: Boot 3C 34
Nun Cl. CH43: Oxton 6D 68
Nunn St. WA9: St H 2H 43
Nunsford Cl. L21: Lith 1D 20
Nunthorpe Av. L34: Know 6D 24
Nurse Rd. CH61: Thing 5F 85
Nursery Cl. CH43: Oxton 6D 68
  L25: Hunts X 3E 93
  WA8: Wid 6H 79
Nursery La. L19: Garst 4G 91
Nursery Rd. L31: Lyd 3B 6
  WA9: St H 6B 42
NUT GROVE 1A 60
Nutgrove Av. WA9: St H 6B 42
Nutgrove Hall Dr. WA9: St H 6B 42
Nutgrove Rd. WA9: St H 1A 60
Nut St. WA9: St H 6B 42
Nuttall Way L7: Liv 6A 54
Nyland Rd. L36: Huy 2F 57

O

Oak Av. CH49: Upton 3B 66
  L9: Ain 5H 21
  WA11: Hay 4G 31
Oak Bank CH41: Birke 4E 69
Oakbank Rd. L18: Moss H 4C 72
Oakbank St. CH44: Wall 4E 51
Oakbourne Cl. L17: Aig 1A 90

Oak Cl. CH46: More 2B 66
  L12: W Der 4B 38
  L35: Whis 4E 59
Oak Ct. L8: Liv 5G 71
            (off Weller Way)
  WA7: Cas 3C 114
Oakcross Gdns. L25: Woolt 1E 93
Oakdale Av. CH44: Wall 5F 51
Oakdale Cl. L32: Kirkb 2G 23
Oakdale Dr. CH49: Grea 1A 84
Oakdale Rd. CH44: Wall 5F 51
  L18: Moss H 4E 73
  L22: Water 1F 19
Oakdale Row L32: Kirkb 3B 24
Oakdene Cl. CH62: Brom 2D 120
Oakdene Ct. L35: Rainh 5B 60
Oakdene Rd. CH42: Tran 6E 69
  L4: Walt 6H 35
Oak Dr. WA7: Run 6G 113
Oakenholt Rd.
  CH46: More 6C 48
Oakes St. L3: Liv 5F 53
Oakfield L4: Walt 1H 53
Oakfield Av. L25: Gate 5C 74
Oakfield Cl. WA9: St H 6B 42
Oakfield Dr. L36: Huy 1H 75
  WA8: Wid 3G 95
Oakfield Gro. L36: Huy 1H 75
Oakfield Rd. CH62: Brom 5C 104
  L4: Walt 1G 53
Oak Gdns. WA5: Penk 5F 81
Oakgate Cl. L11: Norr G 2F 37
Oak Grange L26: Halew 3H 93
Oakham Dr. CH46: More 6H 47
  L10: Ain 2D 22
Oakham St. L8: Liv 3D 70
Oakhill Cl. L12: Crox 2H 37
  L31: Mag 5C 6
Oakhill Cott. La. L31: Lyd 3C 6
  L31: Lyd 3C 6
OAK HILL PARK 5F 55
Oakhill Pk. L13: Liv 5F 55
Oakhill Rd. L13: Liv 5F 55
  L31: Mag 5C 6
Oakhouse Pk. L9: Walt 2F 35
Oakhurst Cl. L25: Gate 4D 74
Oakland Cl. L21: Lith 5C 20
Oakland Dr. CH49: Upton 3E 67
Oakland Rd. L19: Aig 3D 90
Oaklands CH62: Brom 1D 120
  L35: Rainh 4A 60
Oaklands Av. L23: Crosb 4G 9
Oaklands Ct. WA9: Clock F 3G 61
Oaklands Dr. CH61: Hesw 4E 101
  CH63: Beb 5A 88
Oaklands Office Pk.
  CH66: Hoot 5E 121
Oaklands Ter. CH61: Hesw 3E 101
Oakland St. WA8: Wid 1E 113
Oakland Va. CH45: New B 5E 33
Oak La. L12: W Der 4G 37
Oak La. Nth. L12: Crox 3G 37
Oakleaf M. CH43: Noct 4H 67
Oaklea Rd. CH61: Irby 5D 84
Oaklee Gro. L33: Kirkb 5C 14
Oakleigh L31: Liv 2C 54
Oakleigh Gro. CH63: Beb 5H 87
Oakley Cl. L12: Crox 2A 38
Oak Mdws. Ct. L35: Rainh 6C 60
Oakmere Cl. CH46: Leas 3C 48
  L9: Walt 4G 21
Oakmere Dr. CH49: Grea 5A 66
  WA5: Penk 6H 81
Oakmere St. WA7: Run 3E 113
Oakmoore WA7: Nort 1H 115
Oakridge Cl. CH62: Spit 3C 104
Oakridge Rd. CH62: Spit 3C 104
Oak Rd. CH63: Hghr B 4H 87
  CH66: Hoot 6E 121
  L35: Whis 4E 59
  L36: Huy 1F 75
  WA5: Penk 6H 81
Oaks, The CH62: Brom 5C 104
  L12: Crox 2B 38

Oaks, The WA8: Wid 5H 79
        (off Hampton Ct. Way)
  WA9: Sut L 3H 61
Oaks La. CH9: Clock F 4H 61
Oaks La. CH61: Pens 1E 101
Oaksmeade Cl. L12: Crox 3B 38
Oaks Pl. WA8: Wid 4E 97
Oakston Av. L35: Rainh 5B 60
Oak St. L20: Boot 1C 34
              (off Holly St.)
  WA9: St H 5A 44
Oaksway CH60: Hesw 1F 117
Oak Ter. L7: Liv 5A 54
Oakthorn Gro. WA11: Hay 5E 31
Oaktree Gdns. L9: Faz 1D 36
          (off Ternhall Way)
Oaktree Pl. CH42: Rock F 6H 69
Oak Tree Rd. WA10: Eccl 6G 27
Oak Vale L13: Liv 5F 55
OAK VALE PARK 5F 55
Oak Vw. L24: Speke 2A 110
Oakwood Cl. L25: Gate 4D 74
Oakwood Dr. CH43: Bid 1A 68
  L36: Huy 6H 57
Oakwood Pk. CH43: Bid 1A 68
  CH62: Brom 2D 120
Oakwood Rd. L26: Halew 4G 93
Oakworth Cl. L33: Kirkb 5A 14
Oakworth Dr. CH62: New F 4C 88
  L35: Tar G 2A 76
Oarside Dr. CH45: Wall 1C 50
Oasis Health & Fitness
  Eccleston 6B 28
Oatfield La. L21: Ford 1B 20
Oatlands, The CH48: W Kir 2C 82
Oatlands Rd. L32: Kirkb 1G 23
Oban Dr. CH60: Hesw 5E 101
Oban Rd. L4: Walt 1H 53
Oberon St. L20: Boot 4C 34
O'Brien Gro. WA9: St H 1A 44
Observatory Rd. CH43: Bid 1A 68
Oceanic Rd. L13: Liv 5D 54
Ocean Pk. CH41: Wall 6F 51
Ocean Rd. L21: Lith 4B 20
O'Connell Cl. WA11: Hay 5E 31
O'Connell Rd. L3: Liv 3D 52
O'Connor Gro. L33: Kirkb 3A 14
Octavia Cl. L36: Huy 6H 57
Octavia Hill Rd. L21: Ford 2C 20
October Dr. L6: Liv 1B 54
Oddfellows Arms Yd. L25: Woolt 1C 92
         (off Allerton Rd.)
Odeon Cinema
  Bootle 6G 11
  Bromborough 2E 105
  Liverpool 5D 4 (6C 52)
Odsey St. L7: Liv 5A 54
Odyssey Cen. CH41: Birke 1E 69
Ogden Cl. L13: W Der 5E 37
Ogle Cl. L35: Presc 2E 59
OGLET 5G 109
Oglet La. L24: Hale 5F 109
  L24: Speke 3E 109
Ogle Way L36: Huy 2G 57
Oil St. L3: Liv 3B 52
O'Keeffe Rd. WA9: St H 1G 43
Okehampton Rd. L16: Child 1H 73
Okell Dr. L26: Halew 1F 93
Okell St. WA7: Run 3E 113
Old Albert Ter. WA7: Run 2F 113
          (off Thomas St.)
Old Barn Rd. CH44: Wall 4C 50
  L4: Walt 1H 53
Old Bidston Rd. CH41: Birke 1D 68
OLD BOSTON 4H 31
Oldbridge Rd. L24: Speke 3H 109
Old Chester Rd. CH41: Tran 5G 69
  CH42: Rock F, Tran 5G 69
  CH63: Beb, Hghr B 2H 87
Old Church Cl. L9: Ain 4H 21
Old Churchyard L2: Liv 4C 4 (6B 52)
Old Clatterbridge Rd. CH63: Spit . . .3G 103
Old Coach Rd. WA7: Run 2D 112
Old College Pl. L7: Liv 6A 54

Old Colliery Rd. L35: Whis 4D 58
Old Court Ho. CH62: Brom 6D 88
Old Distillery Rd. L24: Speke 6E 93
Old Dover Rd. L36: Roby 1E 75
Old Eccleston La. WA10: St H 2A 42
Old Elton Head Rd. WA9: St H 2F 61
Old Farm Rd. L23: Crosb 5H 9
    L32: Kirkb 5B 24
Oldfield L35: Whis 3F 59
Oldfield Cl. CH60: Hesw 3C 100
Oldfield Dr. CH60: Hesw 3B 100
Oldfield Gdns. CH60: Hesw 4B 100
Oldfield La. CH48: W Kir 5G 65
Oldfield Rd. L45: Wall 1B 50
    CH60: Hesw 3B 100
    L19: Aig .3E 91
Oldfield St. WA10: St H 6D 28
Oldfield Way CH60: Hesw 3B 100
Old Forge Row L31: Mag 4B 6
Oldgate WA8: Wid 4A 96
Old Gorsey La. CH44: Wall 5D 50
Old Greasby Rd. CH49: Upton 4D 66
Old Hall L35: Whis 1E 77
Old Hall Cl. L31: Mag 2B 12
Old Hall Dr. WN4: Ash M 1H 31
Old Hall Gdns. WA11: Rainf 2G 17
Old Hall La. L32: Kirkb 1H 23
    L31: Mag 1B 12
Old Hall Rd. CH62: Brom 4E 105
Old Hall St. L3: Liv 2B 4 (5B 52)
Oldham Pl. L1: Liv 5H 5 (6E 53)
Oldham St. L1: Liv 6G 5 (1E 71)
Old Haymarket L1: Liv 3E 5 (5D 52)
    (not continuous)
Old Higher Rd. WA8: Hale B 6D 94
Old Hutte La. L24: Halew 6A 94
    L26: Halew 6A 94
Old Kennel Cl. L12: W Der 5B 38
Old La. CH60: Hesw 5H 101
    L31: Lyd 3D 6
    L34: Eccl P 6E 41
    L35: Eccl P 6E 41
    L35: Rainh 4H 59
    WA8: Wid 4B 96
    WA11: Rainf 2F 17
Old Leeds St. L3: Liv 2B 4 (5B 52)
Old Lodge Cl. L12: W Der 5F 37
Old Maryland La. CH46: More 6C 48
Old Meadow L34: Know 1F 39
Old Meadow Rd. CH61: Pens 1C 100
Old Mill Av. WA9: Sut L 2H 61
Old Mill Cl. CH60: Hesw 6F 101
    L15: Wav 1E 73
Old Mill La. L15: Wav 1E 73
    L34: Know 1G 39
Old Nook La. WA11: St H 5A 30
Old Orchard L35: Whis 6E 59
Old Post Office Pl. L1: Liv 5E 5
Old Prescot Cl. L31: Mag 5H 7
Old Pump La. CH49: Grea 6A 66
Old Quarry, The L25: Woolt 1C 92
Old Quay St. WA7: Run 2F 113
Old Racecourse Rd. L31: Mag 1H 11
Old Rectory Grn. L29: Seft 2E 11
Old Riding L14: Knott A 2B 56
Old Roan Station (Rail) 6A 12
Old Ropery L2: Liv 4C 4
Old Rough La. L33: Kirkb 6A 14
Old School Ho., The CH43: Oxton 4C 68
    (off Beresford Rd.)
Old School Way CH41: Birke 2A 68
Old Stableyard, The L7: Liv 6G 53
OLD SWAN .4E 55
Old Thomas La. L14: Broad G 6H 55
Old Upton La. WA8: Wid 5C 78
Old Whint Rd. WA11: Hay 5C 30
    (Edward St.)
    WA11: Hay 1C 44
    (Harty Rd.)
Old Wood La. L27: N'ley 5H 75
Old Wood Rd. CH61: Pens 1D 100
Oleander Dr. WA10: St H 1A 42
Olga Rd. WA9: St H 6G 43
Olinda St. CH62: New F 4B 88

Olive Cl. L31: Mell 1E 23
Olive Cres. CH41: Tran 5G 69
Olivedale Rd. L18: Moss H 4D 72
Olive Gro. L15: Wav 6E 55
    L30: N'ton 2G 21
    L36: Roby 5F 57
Olive La. L15: Wav 6E 55
Olive Mt. CH41: Tran 6G 69
Olive Mt. Hgts. L15: Wav 1F 73
Olive Mt. Rd. L15: Wav 1E 73
Olive Mt. Vs. L15: Wav 6E 55
Olive Mt. Wlk. L15: Wav 1F 73
    (off Olive Mt. Rd.)
Oliver La. CH41: Birke 3G 69
Oliver Lyme Ho. L34: Presc 1E 59
    (off Oliver Lyme Rd.)
Oliver Lyme Rd. L34: Presc 1E 59
Olive Rd. L22: Water 3G 19
Oliver Rd. WA10: St H 4A 42
Oliver St. CH41: Birke 3F 69
Oliver St. E. CH41: Birke 3F 69
Olivetree Rd. L15: Wav 1F 73
Olive Va. L15: Wav 1D 72
Olivia Cl. CH43: Noct 5G 67
Olivia M. CH43: Noct 5G 67
Olivia St. L20: Boot 4D 34
Olivia Way L36: Huy 5B 58
Ollerton Cl. CH43: Noct 5G 67
Ollerton Pk. WA5: Burtw 6G 45
Ollery Grn. L30: N'ton 5H 11
Ollier St. WA8: Wid 4E 97
Olney St. L4: Walt 3F 35
Olton St. L15: Wav 1C 72
Olympia St. L6: Liv 4G 53
Olympic Way L30: N'ton 3H 21
Omega Blvd. WA5: Gt San 6F 63
O'Neill St. L20: Boot 1B 34
One Park W. L1: Liv 5D 4 (6C 52)
Onslow Rd. CH45: New B 5D 32
    CH62: New F 3B 88
    L6: Liv .4A 54
Ontario Cl. L27: N'ley 4G 75
Ontario Way L36: Huy 1F 57
Opal Cl. L12: Liv 3H 53
    L21: Lith 3C 20
Opal Ct. L3: Liv 5F 53
    (off London Rd.)
Opco Complex L24: Speke 6D 92
Open Eye Gallery 5C 4 (6C 52)
Openfields Cl. L26: Halew 1G 93
Oppenheim Av. WA10: St H 5A 42
Orange Gro. L8: Liv 3A 72
Orange Tree Cl. L28: Stockb V 5D 38
Oran Way L36: Huy 4F 57
Orb Cl. L11: Crox 2G 37
Orb Wlk. L11: Crox 2G 37
    (off Sceptre Rd.)
Orchard, The CH45: Wall 6C 32
    L17: Aig 2D 90
    L35: Rainh 2A 60
    L36: Huy 5G 57
Orchard Av. L14: Broad G 6H 55
Orchard Cl. L34: Eccl P 6G 41
    L35: Whis 6E 59
    WA11: St H 4H 29
Orchard Ct. CH41: Tran 6H 69
    L31: Mag 6E 7
Orchard Dale L23: Crosb 5H 9
Orchard Dene L35: Rainh 4A 60
Orchard Gdns. L35: Whis 1E 77
Orchard Grange L46: More 2A 66
Orchard Hey L30: N'ton 5H 11
    L31: Mag 1D 12
    WA10: Eccl 2G 41
Orchard Pl. CH62: Spit 3B 104
Orchard Rd. CH46: More 6C 48
Orchard Wlk. WA7: Pal F 6B 114
    (off Halton Lea Shop. Cen.)
Orchard Way CH63: Hghr B 5F 87
    WA8: Wid 6G 77
Orchid Gro. L17: Aig 6D 72
Orchid Way L9: Bold 6D 44
O'Reilly Ct. L3: Liv 3C 52
Orford Cl. L24: Hale 3E 111

Orford St. L15: Wav 1D 72
Oriel Cl. L2: Liv 4C 4
    L10: Ain 6B 12
Oriel Ct. CH42: Tran 2D 86
Oriel Cres. L20: Kirkd 4C 34
Oriel Dr. L10: Ain 6A 12
Oriel Lodge L20: Boot 3C 34
Oriel Rd. CH42: Tran 6G 69
    L20: Boot 2B 34
    L20: Kirkd 4C 34
Oriel St. L3: Liv 1D 4 (4C 52)
Orient Dr. L25: Woolt 6D 74
Origen Rd. L16: Child 6H 55
Oriole Cl. WA10: St H 6H 41
Orion Blvd. WA5: Gt San 6G 63
Orith Av. WA10: Eccl 2F 41
Orkney Cl. WA8: Wid 6A 80
    WA11: St H 4H 29
Orlando Cl. CH43: Noct 5G 67
Orlando St. L20: Boot 4C 34
Orleans Rd. L13: Liv 4E 55
Ormande St. WA9: St H 4F 43
Ormerod Cl. CH63: Beb 6A 88
Ormesby Gdns. WA9: St H 1C 60
Ormesby Gro. CH63: Raby M 1B 120
Ormiston Rd. CH45: New B 6D 32
Ormond Cl. WA8: Wid 1A 96
Ormonde Av. L31: Mag 2A 12
Ormonde Cres. L33: Kirkb 1C 24
Ormonde Dr. L31: Mag 1A 12
Ormond M. CH43: Noct 5G 67
Ormond St. CH45: Wall 2D 50
    L3: Liv 3C 4 (5C 52)
Ormond Way CH43: Noct 5G 67
Ormsby St. L15: Wav 2C 72
Ormside Gro. WA9: St H 6H 43
Ormskirk Rd. L9: Ain 3H 21
    L10: Ain 5H 11
    L34: Know 5F 25
    WA11: Rainf 1D 16
Ormskirk St. WA10: St H 1E 43
Orphan Dr. L6: Liv 2B 54
    (not continuous)
Orphan St. L7: Liv 1G 71
ORRELL 4D 20
Orrell Cl. WA5: Gt San 3H 81
Orrell Hey L20: Boot 4D 20
Orrell La. L9: Walt 5G 21
    L20: Boot 4E 21
Orrell Lodge L20: Boot 5E 21
Orrell Mt. L20: Boot 4C 20
Orrell Mt. Ind. Est. L20: Boot 4C 20
ORRELL PARK 5F 21
Orrell Park Station (Rail) 5G 21
Orrell Rd. CH45: New B 6E 33
    L20: Boot 3C 20
    L21: Lith 3C 20
Orrell St. WA9: St H 2G 43
Orret's Mdw. Rd.
    CH49: Woodc 6F 67
Orrysdale Rd. CH48: W Kir 6A 64
Orry St. L5: Liv 2D 52
Orsett Rd. L32: Kirkb 3B 24
Orston Cres. CH63: Spit 3A 104
Ortega Cl. CH62: New F 4C 88
Orthes St. L3: Liv 6F 53
Orton Rd. L16: Child 1G 73
Orville St. WA9: St H 6B 44
Orwell Cl. WA9: Sut M 4E 61
Orwell Rd. L4: Kirkd 5D 34
Osbert Rd. L23: Blun 5D 8
Osborne Av. CH45: New B 6D 32
Osborne Ct. CH43: Oxton 3D 68
    (off Osborne Rd.)
    CH62: Port S 5B 88
    WA10: St H 5A 42
Osborne Gro. CH45: New B 1D 50
    L34: Presc 2A 58
Osborne Rd. CH43: Oxton 4D 68
    CH45: New B 6E 33
    L13: Liv 1C 54
    L21: Lith 2C 20
    (not continuous)
    WA10: Eccl 6G 27

Osborne Va. CH45: New B 6D **32**
Osborne Wood L17: Aig 2B **90**
Osbourne Cl. CH62: Brom 6E **105**
Osmaston Rd. CH42: Tran 1C **86**
Osprey Cl. L27: N'ley 4G **75**
  WA7: Beech 2B **124**
Ossett Cl. CH43: Noct 5G **67**
  WA7: Nort 5F **115**
Osterley Gdns. L9: Walt 5F **21**
O'Sullivan Cres.
  WA11: St H 6A **30**
Oswald Cl. L33: Kirkb 3A **14**
Oteley Av. CH62: Brom 5D **104**
Othello Cl. L20: Kirkd 4C **34**
Otterburn Cl. CH46: More 1H **65**
Otterburn St. WA7: Nort 2G **115**
OTTERSPOOL 2A **90**
Otterspool Dr. L17: Aig 3B **90**
Otterspool Rd. L17: Aig 2B **90**
Otterton Rd. L11: Crox 6G **23**
Ottley St. L6: Liv 4A **54**
Otway St. L19: Garst 6G **91**
Oulton Cl. CH43: Oxton 6A **68**
  L31: Lyd 3A **6**
Oulton Gdns. WA9: St H 1C **60**
Oulton La. L36: Roby 1F **75**
Oulton Rd. L16: Child 3H **73**
Oulton Way CH43: Oxton 1A **86**
Oundle Cl. L10: Ain 6A **12**
Oundle Pl. L25: Hunts X 4D **92**
Oundle Rd. CH46: More 6C **48**
Outer Central Rd. L24: Halew 6G **93**
Outer Forum L11: Norr G 2C **36**
Out La. L25: Woolt 1C **92**
Outlet La. L31: Bic, Mell 1A **14**
Oval, The CH45: Wall 1B **50**
Oval Leisure Centre, The 4H **87**
Overbrook Ho. L34: Know 6E **25**
Overbrook La. L34: Know 6D **24**
Overbury St. L7: Liv 6H **53**
Overchurch Rd. CH49: Upton 3C **66**
Overdale Av. CH61: Barn 6H **85**
Overdale Rd. CH64: Will 6A **120**
Overdene Wlk. L32: Kirkb 2B **24**
Overgreen Gro. CH46: More 6B **48**
Overstrand CH48: W Kir 1A **82**
Overton Av. L21: Lith 2B **20**
Overton Cl. CH43: Oxton 6B **68**
  L32: Kirkb 2H **23**
  WA6: Frod 6G **123**
Overton Grn. WA6: Frod 6H **123**
Overton Rd. CH44: Wall 3D **50**
Overton St. L7: Liv 6H **53**
Overton Way CH43: Oxton 6B **68**
Ovington Cl. WA7: Sut W 4B **124**
Ovolo Rd. L13: Liv 3E **55**
Owen Cl. WA10: St H 4B **42**
Owen Dr. L24: Speke 2D **108**
Owen Rd. L4: Kirkd 5D **34**
  L33: Know I 4E **25**
  L35: Rainh 5A **60**
Owen St. WA10: St H 4B **42**
Oxborough Cl. WA8: Wid 5D **78**
Oxbow Rd. L12: W Der 5A **38**
Oxendale Cl. L8: Liv 2H **71**
Oxenholme Cres. L11: Norr G 4E **37**
Oxford Av. L20: Boot 2E **35**
  L21: Lith 3B **20**
Oxford Cl. L17: Aig 1A **90**
Oxford Cl. L22: Water 1E **19**
Oxford Dr. CH63: Thorn H 1B **118**
  L22: Water 1E **19**
  L26: Halew 3H **93**
Oxford Ho. *L20: Boot* *2E* **35**
  (off Fernhill Rd.)
Oxford Rd. CH44: Wall 3E **51**
  L9: Ain 3H **21**
  L20: Boot 2D **34**
  L22: Water 1E **19**
  L36: Huy 3A **58**
  WA7: Run 4E **113**
Oxford St. L7: Liv 6F **53**
  (not continuous)
  WA8: Wid 3F **97**

Oxford St. WA10: St H 1D **42**
  (Cooper St.)
  WA10: St H 6D **28**
  (Rutland St.)
Oxford St. E. L7: Liv 6G **53**
Oxheys WA7: Nort 5E **115**
Ox La. L35: Tar G 5B **76**
Oxley Av. CH46: Leas 4F **49**
Oxley St. WA9: St H 6H **43**
Oxmoor Cl. WA7: Brook 2C **124**
Oxmoor Local Nature Reserve 6F **99**
OXTON 5B **68**
Oxton Cl. L17: Aig 1A **90**
  L32: Kirkb 3F **23**
  WA8: Wid 5A **78**
Oxton Ct. CH43: Oxton 5D **68**
Oxton Rd. CH41: Birke 4E **69**
  CH44: Wall 4D **50**
Oxton St. L4: Walt 5F **35**

P

Pacific Rd. CH41: Birke 2H **69**
  L20: Boot 2B **34**
  (Atlantic Rd.)
  L20: Boot 1B **34**
  (Globe Rd.)
Packenham Rd. L13: Liv 1D **54**
Padbury St. L8: Liv 4G **71**
Paddington L7: Liv 6G **53**
  (not continuous)
Paddock, The CH46: More 2A **66**
  CH49: Upton 4F **67**
  CH60: Hesw 5G **101**
  L25: Gate 5D **74**
  L32: Kirkb 4H **23**
  L34: Eccl P 6G **41**
Paddock Cl. L23: Blun 3D **8**
Paddock Dr. CH64: Park 5H **117**
Paddock Gro. WA9: Clock F 4H **61**
Paddock Ri. WA7: Beech 3A **124**
Paddock Rd. L34: Presc 1A **58**
Padeswood Cl. WA9: St H 1G **61**
Padstow Cl. L26: Halew 2G **93**
  WA5: Penk 6G **81**
Padstow Dr. WA10: Windle 5H **27**
Padstow Rd. CH49: Grea 6A **66**
  L16: Child 1H **73**
Padstow Sq. WA7: Brook 2D **124**
Pagebank Rd. L14: Knott A 4C **56**
Pagefield Rd. L15: Wav 3E **73**
Page Grn. L36: Huy 4E **57**
Page La. WA8: Wid 2G **97**
PAGE MOSS 4D **56**
Page Moss Av. L36: Huy 3D **56**
Page Moss La. L14: Knott A 4C **56**
Page Moss Pde. L36: Huy 3D **56**
Page Wlk. L3: Liv 1H **5** (4E **53**)
  (not continuous)
Pagewood Cl. CH43: Noct 5G **67**
Paignton Cl. L36: Huy 4B **58**
  WA5: Penk 5G **81**
Paignton Rd. CH45: Wall 1B **50**
  L16: Child 1H **73**
Paisley Av. CH62: East 3E **121**
  WA11: St H 4H **29**
Paisley Ct. L14: Knott A 4C **56**
Paisley St. L3: Liv 1A **4** (4B **52**)
PALACE FIELDS 1C **124**
Palacefields Av. WA7: Pal F 1B **124**
Palacefields Local Cen.
  WA7: Pal F 1C **124**
Palace Rd. L9: Ain 5G **21**
Palatine, The L20: Boot 2C **34**
Palatine Arc. WA10: St H 2E **43**
Palatine Rd. CH44: Wall 5F **51**
  CH62: Brom 4C **104**
Palermo Cl. CH44: Wall 5F **51**
Paley Cl. L4: Walt 6F **35**
Palin Dr. WA5: Gt San 3H **81**
Palladio Rd. L13: Liv 3F **55**
Pall Mall L3: Liv 1C **4** (4C **52**)
Palmarsh Rd. WA8: Hale B 6H **95**

Palm Cl. L9: Walt 2A **36**
Palm Ct. *L8: Liv* *5G* **71**
  (off Weller Way)
Palmer Cl. CH43: Noct 6H **67**
  WA10: St H 1D **42**
Palmerston Av. L21: Lith 4A **20**
Palmerston Cl. L18: Moss H 6D **72**
Palmerston Ct. L18: Moss H 6E **73**
Palmerston Cres. L19: Garst 5G **91**
Palmerston Dr. L21: Lith 4B **20**
  L25: Hunts X 4F **93**
Palmerston Rd. CH44: Wall 3B **50**
  L18: Moss H 6D **72**
  L19: Garst 5G **91**
Palmerston St. CH42: Rock F 1H **87**
Palmer Vs. CH42: Rock F 2G **87**
Palm Gro. CH43: Oxton 3D **68**
  L25: Woolt 2D **92**
Palm Hill CH43: Oxton 5D **68**
Palmwood Av. L35: Rainh 5B **60**
Palmwood Cl. CH43: Pren 2A **86**
Palomar Cl. L8: Liv 2H **71**
Paltridge Way CH61: Pens 1D **100**
Pamela Cl. L10: Faz 5F **23**
Pampas Gro. L9: Walt 1H **35**
Panama Av. L30: N'ton 2F **21**
Pankhurst Rd. L21: Ford 1C **20**
Pansy St. L5: Kirkd 6D **34**
Panton Way L10: Faz 5F **23**
Papillon Dr. L9: Ain 3B **22**
Parade, The CH64: Park 5F **117**
  L15: Wav 6F **55**
  L26: Halew 4G **93**
Parade Cres. L24: Speke 3G **109**
Parade St. WA10: St H 1E **43**
Paradise Gdns. L15: Wav 2D **72**
Paradise Island Bingo 4E **35**
Paradise La. L35: Whis 5D **58**
Paradise Pl. L1: Liv 5E **5**
Paradise St. L1: Liv 6E **5** (1D **70**)
Paragon Cl. WA8: Wid 4F **79**
Parbold Av. WA11: St H 6H **29**
Parbold Cl. WA8: Wid 3B **96**
Parbold Ct. L36: Huy 1F **57**
Parbrook Cl. L36: Huy 1F **57**
Parbrook Rd. L36: Huy 1F **57**
Parish L14: Knott A 3A **56**
Park, The L36: Huy 6G **57**
  WA5: Penk 6F **81**
  (not continuous)
Park & Ride
  Leasowe 5E **49**
  Marshalls Cross 1F **61**
Park Av. CH44: Wall 4F **51**
  L9: Ain 4B **22**
  L18: Moss H 6C **72**
  L23: Crosb 4G **9**
  L31: Lyd 4C **6**
  L34: Eccl P 6F **41**
  L35: Rainh 3A **60**
  WA8: Wid 1F **97**
  WA11: Hay 5C **30**
Parkbourn L31: Mag 5F **7**
Parkbourn Dr. L31: Mag 5F **7**
Parkbourn Nth. L31: Mag 5F **7**
Parkbourn Sq. L31: Mag 5F **7**
Parkbridge Rd. CH42: Tran 6E **69**
Park Brow Dr. L32: Kirkb 3B **24**
Parkbury Ct. CH43: Oxton 6C **68**
Park Cl. CH41: Birke 3E **69**
  L32: Kirkb 5F **13**
Park Ct. CH48: W Kir 1A **82**
  L22: Water 3G **19**
  L32: Kirkb 6G **13**
  WA7: Run 5E **113**
  WA9: St H 5F **43**
Parkdale CH48: Caldy 5D **82**
Parkdale Av. L9: Walt 4G **21**
Park Dr. CH41: Birke 2C **68**
  (not continuous)
  CH43: Clau 2C **68**
  L23: Blun 4C **8**
  L23: Thorn 2A **10**
Parkend Rd. CH42: Tran 6E **69**
Parker Av. L21: Sea 4H **19**

Parker Cl. L30: N'ton 2H 21
Parkers Ct. WA7: Pal F 1A 124
Parker St. L1: Liv 4F 5 (6D 52)
WA7: Run 2F 113
Parkfield Av. CH41: Birke 3F 69
L30: N'ton 3G 21
Parkfield Dr. CH44: Wall 3D 50
Parkfield Gro. L31: Mag 6B 6
Parkfield M. L17: Aig 5H 71
Parkfield Pl. CH41: Birke 3F 69
Parkfield Rd. CH63: Beb 2A 104
L17: Aig 5H 71
L22: Water 1G 19
PARKGATE 5F 117
Parkgate Cl. L17: Aig 2C 90
Parkgate Ho. CH64: Park 5F 117
(off Greenway)
Parkgate Ho. Ct. CH64: Park 6F 117
Parkgate La. CH64: Nest 2A 118
Parkgate Way WA7: Murd 6E 115
Park Gro. CH41: Birke 4F 69
Parkhill Ct. L8: Liv 5F 71
(off Park Hill Rd.)
Park Hill Rd. L8: Liv 5F 71
Parkhill Rd. CH42: Tran 6E 69
Parkholme L22: Water 2G 19
Parkhurst Rd. CH42: Tran 1E 87
Park Ind. Est. WN4: Ash M 1G 31
Parkinson Rd. L9: Walt 1G 35
Parkland Cl. L8: Liv 4G 71
Parkland Ct. CH43: Bid 1G 67
CH49: Woodc 1E 85
(off Childwall Grn.)
Parklands L34: Know 2F 39
WA8: Wid 6A 78
WA11: Raint 2F 17
Parklands Dr. CH60: Hesw 1F 117
Parklands Way L22: Water 2G 19
Park La. CH47: Meols 6F 47
L1: Liv 6E 5 (1D 70)
L20: Boot 4D 20
L30: N'ton 1F 21
L31: Mag 4E 7
Park La. Dr. L31: Mag 5F 7
Park Lane Holiday Homes
CH47: Meols 5G 47
Park La. W. L30: N'ton 6F 11
Park Pl. L8: Liv 3E 71
L20: Boot 2C 34
Park Rd. CH42: Tran 6G 69
CH44: Wall 4E 51
CH47: Meols 6E 47
CH48: W Kir 1A 82
CH60: Hesw 4F 101
CH62: East 1F 121
CH62: Port S 6B 88
CH64: Will 6B 120
L8: Liv 3F 71
L22: Water 2G 19
L32: Kirkb 6F 13
(not continuous)
L34: Presc 6C 40
WA5: Gt San 2E 81
WA7: Run 5D 112
WA8: Wid 2F 97
WA9: St H 2G 43
WA11: St H 2G 43
Park Rd. E. CH41: Birke 3E 69
Park Rd. Nth. CH41: Birke 2C 68
Park Rd. Sth. CH43: Clau 3D 68
Park Rd. W. CH43: Clau 2C 68
Parkside CH44: Wall 4E 51
L20: Boot 1C 34
(off Strand Shop. Cen.)
Parkside Av. WA9: Sut M 4F 61
Parkside Cl. CH63: Beb 5A 88
L27: N'ley 5G 75
Parkside Ct. WA8: Wid 1E 97
Parkside Dr. L12: W Der 5E 37
Parkside Mans. L36: Huy 5B 58
Parkside Rd. CH42: Tran 6G 69
CH63: Beb 5A 88
Parkside St. L6: Liv 4F 53
Parkstile L11: Crox 1G 37

Parkstone Rd. CH42: Tran 6E 69
Park St. CH41: Birke 3F 69
(not continuous)
CH44: Wall 3E 51
L8: Liv 4E 71
(not continuous)
L20: Boot 2C 34
WA9: St H 1G 43
WA11: Hay 5B 30
Park Ter. L22: Water 3G 19
Parkvale Av. CH43: Pren 3A 86
Park Va. Rd. L9: Walt 5G 21
Park Vw. CH62: Brom 5C 104
CH62: New F 3B 88
L6: Liv 2B 54
L9: Walt 1G 35
(off Brook Rd.)
L17: Aig 4C 72
L22: Water 1F 19
L23: Thorn 2B 10
L36: Huy 3E 57
Parkview Cl. CH49: Woodc 2E 85
Parkview Cl. CH41: Birke 2E 69
Parkview Cl. CH60: Hesw 5D 100
Parkview Dr. L27: N'ley 5G 75
Park Vw. Flats L21: Lith 3A 20
Parkview Rd. L11: Crox 5H 23
Park Wall Rd.
L29: Ince B, Thorn 1A 10
Park Way L8: Liv 2F 71
(not continuous)
L36: Huy 6F 39
Parkway CH45: Wall 6A 32
CH47: Meols 1E 65
CH61: Irby 4D 84
L23: Crosb 1H 19
L30: N'ton 4F 11
Parkway Cl. CH61: Irby 4D 84
Parkway East L32: Kirkb 6F 13
Parkway West L32: Kirkb 6F 13
Park West CH60: Hesw 6B 100
Parkwood Cl. CH62: Brom 4E 105
Parkwood Rd. L25: Woolt 5C 74
L35: Whis 1F 59
Parlane WA9: St H 1G 43
(not continuous)
Parle Ct. L6: Liv 2H 53
Parliament Bus. Pk. L8: Liv 2H 71
(off Commerce Way)
Parliament Cl. L1: Liv 2E 71
Parliament Pl. L8: Liv 2F 71
Parliament St. L8: Liv 2D 70
WA9: St H 6B 42
Parlington Cl. WA8: Wid 4A 96
Parlow Rd. L11: Norr G 5C 36
Parnell Rd. CH63: Spit 3A 104
PARR 2A 44
Parren Av. L35: Whis 6C 58
Parr Gro. CH49: Grea 5A 66
WA11: Hay 5C 30
Parr Ind. Est. WA9: St H 3A 44
Parr Mt. Ct. WA9: St H 2G 43
Parr Mt. St. WA9: St H 2G 43
Parrs Cnr. Trad. Est. L20: Boot 1C 34
(off Stanley Rd.)
Parr's Rd. CH43: Oxton 6D 68
PARR STOCKS 3H 43
Parr Stocks Rd. WA9: St H 2H 43
Parr St. L1: Liv 6F 5 (1D 70)
WA8: Wid 2G 97
WA9: St H 2F 43
Parr Swimming & Fitness Cen. 1H 43
Parry's La. WA7: Run 4E 113
Parry St. CH44: Wall 5F 51
Parsonage Rd. WA8: Wid 1D 112
Parsonage Way WA5: Gt San 4H 81
Parson's Brow WA11: Rainf 3E 17
Parthenon Dr. L11: Norr G 2B 36
Partington Av. L20: Boot 1E 35
Partington Sq. WA7: Nort 1H 115
Parton St. L6: Liv 4A 54
Partridge Cl. L12: Crox 2B 38
Partridge Rd. L23: Blun 5D 8
L32: Kirkb 6F 13

Pass Way WA11: St H 3G 29
(off Honister Av.)
Pasture Av. CH46: More 5C 48
Pasture Cl. L25: Woolt 2D 92
WA9: Clock F 3G 61
Pasture Cres. CH46: More 6C 48
Pasture La. WA11: Rainf 5G 17
Pasture Rd. CH46: More 4B 48
Pastures, The CH48: W Kir 1F 83
WA9: Bold 6C 44
Pateley Cl. L32: Kirkb 2G 23
Pateley Wlk. L24: Speke 1H 109
Paterson St. CH41: Birke 3E 69
Patmos Cl. L5: Liv 1E 53
Paton Cl. CH48: W Kir 6D 64
Patricia Av. CH41: Birke 6B 50
Patricia Cl. WA10: St H 1D 42
(off Albion St.)
Patricia Gro. L20: Boot 5D 20
Patrick Av. L20: Boot 4D 20
Pattens Cl. L30: N'ton 5D 10
Patten St. CH41: Birke 1D 68
Patten's Wlk. L34: Know P 4E 25
Patterdale Cres. L31: Mag 5D 6
Patterdale Dr. WA10: St H 5H 41
Patterdale Rd. CH63: Beb 2H 103
L15: Wav 3D 72
Paul Cl. WA5: Gt San 3F 81
Pauldings La. L21: Lith 3A 20
Pauline Wlk. L10: Faz 4F 23
Paul McCartney Way L6: Liv 4H 53
Paul Orr Ct. L3: Liv 3C 52
Paulsfield Dr. CH46: More 2C 66
Paul St. L3: Liv 4C 52
Paulton Cl. L8: Liv 5F 71
Paveley Bank L27: N'ley 3F 75
Pavilion Bingo Club 2H 71
(off Lodge La.)
Pavilion Cl. L8: Liv 2H 71
Pavilion Ct. WA12: Newt W 2H 45
Pavilions, The CH43: Oxton 5C 68
Paxton Rd. L36: Huy 3G 57
Peacehaven Cl. L16: Child 1B 74
Peach Gro. L31: Mell 5F 13
WA11: Hay 4G 31
Peach St. L7: Liv 6F 53
Peach Tree Cl. L24: Hale 3E 111
Pearce Cl. L25: Woolt 3B 74
Pear Gro. L6: Liv 4H 53
Pearl Way L6: Liv 3H 53
Pearson Ct. L15: Wav 3E 73
Pearson Dr. L20: Boot 4E 21
Pearson Rd. CH42: Tran 4G 69
Pearson St. L15: Wav 2D 72
Pear Tree Av. WA7: Run 6G 113
Peartree Av. L12: W Der 4B 38
Pear Tree Cl. CH60: Hesw 4G 101
L24: Hale 4E 111
WA6: Frod 6H 123
Pear Tree Rd. L36: Huy 1G 75
Peasefield Rd. L14: Knott A 3C 56
PEASLEY CROSS 4G 43
Peasley Cross La. WA9: St H 2F 43
Peatwood Av. L32: Kirkb 4B 24
Peckers Hill Rd. WA9: St H 6A 44
Peckfield Cl. WA7: Brook 2C 124
Peckforton Cl. L13: Liv 1C 54
Peckforton Dr. WA7: Sut W 3B 124
Peckmill Grn. L27: N'ley 5H 75
Pecksniff Cl. L8: Liv 4F 71
Peebles Av. WA11: St H 4H 29
Peebles Cl. L33: Kirkb 3H 13
Peel Av. CH42: Tran 6H 69
Peel Cl. L35: Whis 4E 59
Peel Ho. L21: Sea 5A 20
Peel Ho. La. WA8: Wid 6F 79
Peel Pl. L8: Liv 2F 71
WA10: St H 6E 29
Peel Rd. L20: Boot 6A 20
Peel St. L8: Liv 5G 71
WA7: Run 2D 112
Peel Wlk. L31: Mag 5A 6
Peet Av. WA10: St H 1A 42

Peet St. L7: Liv 6H 53
Pelham Dr. L30: N'ton 3E 21
Pelham Gro. L17: Aig 5A 72
Pelham Rd. CH44: Wall 4C 50
Pelwood Ct. CH44: Wall 6F 67
Pemberton Rd. CH49: Woodc 6F 67
    L13: Liv 4E 55
Pembertons Ct. L34: Presc 1E 59
    (off Scotchbarn La.)
Pemberton St. WA10: St H 2C 42
Pembrey Way L25: Hunts X 3F 93
Pembroke Av. CH46: More 2C 66
Pembroke Cl. WA10: St H 3C 42
Pembroke Ct. CH41: Tran 5H 69
    WA7: Manor P 6E 99
Pembroke Gdns. L3: Liv 5F 53
Pembroke Ho. L6: Liv 3A 54
Pembroke Pl. L3: Liv 3H 5 (5E 53)
Pembroke Rd. L20: Boot 2C 34
Pembroke St. L3: Liv 5F 53
Pembury Cl. L12: Crox 2A 38
Penare WA7: Brook 2E 125
Penarth Cl. L7: Liv 1H 71
Pencombe Rd. L36: Huy 3D 56
Penda Dr. L33: Kirkb 3A 14
Pendennis WA7: Cas 3B 114
Pendennis Rd. CH44: Wall 4E 51
Pendennis St. L6: Liv 1H 53
Pendine Cl. L6: Liv 3A 54
Pendle Av. WA11: St H 6H 29
Pendlebury St. WA9: Clock F 4G 61
Pendle Cl. CH49: Upton 3C 66
Pendle Dr. L21: Ford 5C 10
Pendleton Ct. L34: Presc 2D 58
Pendleton Grn. L26: Halew 4G 93
Pendleton Rd. L4: Walt 3G 35
Pendle Vw. L21: Ford 5C 10
Pendle Vs. L21: Ford 6C 10
Penfold L31: Mag 6D 6
Penfold Cl. L18: Moss H 4H 73
Penfolds WA7: Run 4H 113
Pengwern Gro. L15: Wav 1B 72
Pengwern St. L8: Liv 4G 71
Pengwern Ter. CH45: Wall 6E 33
    (off Holland Rd.)
Penhale Cl. L17: Aig 1H 89
Penhurst Way WA9: St H 6H 43
Peninsula Bus. Pk. CH46: Leas 5E 49
Peninsula Cl. CH45: Wall 5A 32
PENKETH 5H 81
Penketh St. WA5: Penk 5F 81
    WA7: Run 3F 113
Penketh Dr. L24: Speke 1G 109
Penketh Parish Swimming Pool 5G 81
Penketh Rd. L24: Speke 2G 109
Penketh's La. WA7: Run 2E 113
Penkett Ct. CH45: Wall 1E 51
Penkett Gdns. CH45: Wall 1E 51
Penkett Gro. CH45: Wall 1E 51
Penkett Rd. CH45: Wall 1D 50
Penkford La. WA5: Coll G 4F 45
Penkford St. WA12: Newt W 2G 45
Penlake La. WA9: St H 6B 44
Penley Cres. L32: Kirkb 1F 23
Penlinken Dr. L6: Liv 3H 53
Penmann Cl. L26: Halew 3H 93
Penmann Cres. L26: Halew 3H 93
Penmon Dr. CH61: Pens 2D 100
Pennant Av. L12: W Der 4G 37
Pennard Av. L36: Huy 2F 57
    (not continuous)
Pennine Cl. WA9: St H 2A 44
Pennine Dr. WA9: St H 2B 44
Pennine Rd. CH42: Tran 2E 87
    CH44: Wall 3B 50
Pennine Way L32: Kirkb 5G 13
Pennington Av. L20: Boot 4E 21
Pennington Cl. WA6: Frod 5H 123
Pennington Gdns. L34: Presc 1D 58
    (off Houghton St.)
Pennington La. WA9: Coll G, St H 2E 45
Pennington Lodge WA9: St H 5D 42
Pennington Rd. L21: Lith 5C 20
Pennington St. L4: Walt 3F 35

Penn La. WA7: Run 3D 112
Pennsylvania Rd. L13: Liv 6B 36
Pennycress Dr. L11: Norr G 3D 36
Pennyford Dr. L18: Moss H 6C 72
Penny La. L18: Moss H 5D 72
    WA5: Coll G 5F 45
    WA8: Cron 3G 77
    WA11: Hay 4H 31
Penny La. Neighbourhood Cen.
    L15: Wav 3E 73
Pennystone Cl. CH49: Upton 3B 66
Pennywood Dr. L35: Whis 5E 59
Penpoll Cl. L20: Boot 5C 20
Penrhos Rd. CH47: Hoy 3A 64
Penrhyd Rd. CH61: Irby 6B 84
Penrhyn Av. CH61: Thing 5E 85
    L21: Lith 4B 20
Penrhyn Cres. WA7: Run 6F 113
Penrhyn Rd. L34: Know 6D 24
Penrhyn St. L5: Liv 2D 52
Penrith Cl. WA6: Frod 6H 123
Penrith Cres. L31: Mag 5D 6
Penrith Rd. WA10: St H 5H 41
Penrith St. CH41: Birke 4E 69
Penrose Av. E. L14: Broad G 5B 56
Penrose Av. W. L14: Broad G 5A 56
Penrose Gdns. WA5: Penk 6F 81
Penrose St. L5: Liv 1F 53
Penryn Av. WA11: St H 4H 29
Penryn Cl. WA5: Penk 6G 81
Pensall Dr. CH61: Hesw 3D 100
Pensarn Rd. L13: Liv 5D 54
PENSBY 1E 101
Pensby Cl. CH61: Thing 6E 85
Pensby Hall La. CH61: Hesw 3D 100
Pensby Rd. CH60: Hesw 4E 101
    CH61: Hesw, Irby, Pens 4E 101
Pensby St. CH41: Birke 1E 69
Penshaw Cl. L14: Knott A 1C 56
Penshaw Ct. WA7: Pal F 6A 114
Pentire Av. WA10: Windle 5H 27
Pentire Cl. L10: Faz 5F 23
Pentland Av. L4: Walt 4G 35
    WA9: St H 2B 44
Pentland Rd. L33: Kirkb 5C 14
Penuel Rd. L4: Walt 3F 35
Penvalley Cres. L6: Liv 3A 54
Peony Gdns. WA9: Bold 6D 44
Peover St. L3: Liv 1F 5 (4D 52)
Peploe Rd. L4: Walt 3B 36
Peplow Rd. L32: Kirkb 1F 23
Pepper St. L24: Hale 4D 110
Pera Cl. L6: Liv 4G 53
Percival Ct. WA7: Run 4B 112
Percival La. WA7: Run 4B 112
Percival Way WA10: St H 6A 28
Percy Rd. CH44: Wall 5G 51
Percy St. L8: Liv 2F 71
    L20: Boot 6B 20
    WA9: St H 5B 44
Percy Vs. L9: Walt 1G 35
    (off Cedardale Rd.)
Perilla Dr. L11: Norr G 3E 37
Perimeter Rd. L33: Know I 3F 25
Perriam Rd. L19: Aller 3H 91
Perrin Av. WA7: Run 5C 112
Perrin Rd. CH45: Wall 2A 50
Perrins Rd. WA5: Burtw 1H 63
Perrygate Cl. L7: Liv 1H 71
Perry St. L8: Liv 3D 70
    WA7: Run 3F 113
Pershore Ho. CH42: Tran 2D 86
Pershore Rd. L32: Kirkb 3A 24
Perth Av. WA9: St H 6C 42
Perth Cl. L33: Kirkb 3H 13
Perth St. L6: Liv 4G 53
Peter Best Dr. L12: W Der 1F 55
Peterborough Dr. L30: N'ton 5E 11
Peterborough Rd. L15: Wav 3E 73
Peter Ho. L3: Liv 2D 4
Peterhouse M. L20: Boot 2D 34
Peterlee Cl. WA9: St H 6D 42
Peterlee Way L30: N'ton 2G 21
Peter Mahon Way L20: Boot 1B 34

Peter Price's La. CH63: Hghr B 1G 103
Peter Rd. L4: Walt 3E 35
    (not continuous)
Peters Arc. L1: Liv 5E 5
Petersfield Cl. L30: N'ton 2F 21
Petersgate WA7: Murd 6F 115
Peter's La. L1: Liv 5E 5 (6D 52)
Peter St. CH44: Wall 5G 51
    L1: Liv 3E 5 (5D 52)
    WA10: St H 1C 42
Peterwood CH42: Rock F 2A 88
Petham Ct. WA8: Wid 5C 78
Petherick Rd. L11: Crox 6G 23
Petra Ct. L4: Walt 6A 36
Petunia Cl. L14: Knott A 3C 56
    WA9: Bold 6C 44
Petworth Cl. L24: Speke 1D 108
Peveril St. L9: Walt 2F 35
PEWFALL 2E 31
PEX HILL 3C 78
Pex Hill Ct. WA8: Wid 4C 78
Pharmacy Rd. L24: Speke 1E 109
Pheasant Fld. L24: Hale 3C 110
Pheasant Gro. L26: Halew 2G 93
Philbeach Rd. L4: Walt 3B 36
    L11: Norr G 3B 36
Philharmonic Ct. L8: Liv 1F 71
    (off Catharine St.)
Philip Gro. WA9: St H 6G 43
Philip Leverhulme Lodge
    CH62: Port S 5B 88
Philip Rd. WA8: Wid 3H 95
Phillimore Rd. L6: Liv 4A 54
Phillips Cl. L23: Thorn 3B 10
Phillips Dr. WA5: Gt San 3G 81
Phillips St. L3: Liv 1D 4 (4C 52)
Phillips Way CH60: Hesw 5C 100
Phipps La. WA5: Burtw 5G 45
Phoenix Brow WA9: St H 2F 43
Phoenix Dr. L14: Knott A 3C 56
Phoenix Pk. L24: Speke 6C 92
Physics Rd. L24: Speke 6E 93
Phythian Cl. L6: Liv 4H 53
Phythian Cres. WA5: Penk 5H 81
Phythian St. L6: Liv 4G 53
    WA11: Hay 5B 30
Pickerill Rd. CH49: Grea 6B 66
Pickering Rake L30: N'ton 4D 10
    (off Red Lomes)
Pickering Cl. WA7: Run 1G 123
Pickerings Pasture Local Nature Reserve
    . . . . .1G 111
Pickerings Pasture Vis. Cen. 1H 111
Pickerings Rd. WA8: Hale B 6H 95
Pickering St. L6: Liv 2G 53
Pickmere Dr. CH62: East 4F 121
    (not continuous)
    WA7: Brook 2E 125
Pickop St. L3: Liv 1D 4 (4C 52)
Pickwick St. L8: Liv 3F 71
Pickworth Way L31: Mell 1F 23
Picow Farm Rd.
    WA7: Run, West P 4C 112
Picow St. WA7: Run 4D 112
Picton Av. WA7: Run 4F 113
Picton Cl. CH43: Oxton 5B 68
    CH62: East 4D 120
Picton Cres. L15: Wav 1C 72
Picton Gro. L15: Wav 1B 72
    L22: Water 2F 19
Piele Rd. WA11: Hay 4F 31
Pier Head L3: Liv 5A 4 (6B 52)
Pier Ho. CH45: New B 4E 33
Pighue La. L7: Liv 6C 54
    L13: Liv .6E 55
Pigot St. WA10: St H 2C 42
Pigott's Rake L30: N'ton 4D 10
    (off Higher End Pk.)
Pike Ho. Rd. WA10: Eccl 6G 27
Pike Pl. WA10: Eccl 1H 41
Pikes Bri. Fold WA10: Eccl 1G 41

Pikes Hey Rd. CH48: Caldy 4F 83
Pilch Bank Rd. L14: Knott A 3A 56
Pilch La. L14: Knott A 3A 56
Pilch La. E. L36: Huy, Roby 5C 56
Pilgrim St. CH41: Birke 3H 69
  L1: Liv 6H 5 (1E 71)
Pilgrims Way WA7: Nort 2F 115
Pilkington Ct. L34: Presc 2D 58
Pilkington Sailing Club 2G 41
Pilkington St. WA11: Rainf 3F 17
Pilling La. L31: Lyd 2A 6
Pilot Gro. L15: Wav 1B 72
Pimblett Rd. WA11: Hay 4G 31
Pimbley Gro. E. L31: Mag 3A 12
Pimbley Gro. W. L31: Mag 3A 12
Pimhill Cl. L8: Liv 3G 71
Pimlico Rd. WA7: Run 3C 112
Pincroft Way L4: Kirkd 6D 34
  (off Fountains Rd.)
Pine Av. CH63: Beb 2H 103
  WA8: Wid 1F 97
  WA10: St H 5D 28
Pine Cl. L32: Kirkb 6G 13
  L35: Whis 4E 59
  L36: Huy .3F 57
  WA11: Hay 5E 31
Pine Ct. CH41: Birke 3F 69
  L8: Liv 5G 71
  (off Byles St.)
Pine Dale WA11: Rainf 2E 17
Pinedale Cl. CH43: Noct 5H 67
Pinefield Cl. L5: Liv 1F 53
Pine Gro. L20: Boot 1D 34
  L22: Water 1F 19
Pine Hey CH64: Nest 6H 117
Pinehurst Av. L4: Walt 6H 35
  L22: Water 6E 9
Pinehurst Rd. L4: Walt 6H 35
Pinellas WA7: Run 2F 113
Pine Lodge L4: Walt 5A 36
Pine M. L1: Liv 2E 71
Pinemore Rd. L18: Moss H 1E 91
Pineridge Cl. CH62: Spit 2C 104
Pine Rd. CH60: Hesw 4G 101
  WA7: Run 6G 113
Pines, The CH63: Spit 2B 104
  L12: Crox .1B 38
  WA8: Wid .5H 79
  (off Hampton Ct. Way)
Pinetop Cl. L6: Liv 3A 54
Pine Tree Av. CH43: Noct 5G 67
Pinetree Cl. CH46: More 1D 66
  L30: N'ton .6F 11
Pinetree Ct. WA4: Wall 2B 50
Pinetree Dr. CH48: W Kir 2D 82
Pinetree Gro. CH46: More 1D 66
Pinetree Rd. L36: Huy 1F 75
Pine Vw. Dr. CH61: Hesw 3D 100
Pine Walks CH42: Tran 2D 86
  CH48: W Kir 2D 82
Pinewalks Ridge CH42: Tran 3E 87
Pine Way CH60: Hesw 3C 100
Pinewood WN4: Ash M 1H 31
Pinewood Av. L12: Crox 2H 37
Pinewood Cl. L27: N'ley 3G 75
Pinewood Dr. CH60: Hesw 5F 101
Pinewood Gdns. L33: Kirkb 4A 14
Pinewood Rd. WA5: Burtw 6H 45
Pinfold Cl. L30: N'ton 4D 10
Pinfold Cottage Woodland Pk. 4E 11
Pinfold Ct. CH48: W Kir 5A 64
  L23: Crosb .4F 9
Pinfold Cres. L32: Kirkb 3C 24
Pinfold Dr. WA10: Eccl 2G 41
Pinfold La. CH48: W Kir 5A 64
  L34: Know .2D 38
Pinfold Rd. L25: Hunts X 4E 93
Pingwood La. L33: Kirkb 3C 14
Pinners Fold WA7: Nort 4D 114
Pinnington Pl. L36: Huy 5F 57
Pinnington Rd. L35: Whis 4E 59
Pintail Cl. WA11: St H 5F 29
Pipers, The CH60: Hesw 4B 100
Piper's Cl. CH60: Hesw 5B 100

Piper's End CH60: Hesw 5B 100
Pipers La. CH60: Hesw 3A 100
  (not continuous)
Pipistrelle Ri. CH43: Noct 5H 67
Pipit Cl. L26: Halew 1G 93
Pippits Row WA7: Beech 3A 124
Pirrie Rd. L9: Ain 2B 36
Pit La. WA8: Wid 5E 79
Pit Pl. L25: Woolt 1C 92
Pitsford Way L6: Liv 3G 53
Pitsmead Rd. L32: Kirkb 2A 24
Pitts Heath La. WA7: Nort 2F 115
Pitt St. L1: Liv 1D 70
  WA8: Wid .6E 97
  WA9: St H .2G 43
Pitville Av. L18: Moss H 6E 73
Pitville Cl. L18: Moss H 1E 91
Pitville Gro. L18: Moss H 6F 73
Pitville Rd. L18: Moss H 6E 73
Pitville Ter. WA8: Wid 4A 96
Plaistow Ct. WA7: Pal F 6A 114
Plane Cl. L9: Walt 2A 36
Planet Ice
  Widnes .4F 97
Plane Tree Gro. WA11: Hay 4H 31
Plane Tree Rd. CH63: Hghr B 1G 103
Planetree Rd. L12: W Der 6B 38
Plantation Bus. Pk. CH62: Brom 3F 105
Plantation Cl. WA7: Cas 4C 114
Plantation Ct. CH62: Brom 3F 105
Plantation Rd. CH62: Brom 4F 105
Planters, The CH49: Grea 5A 66
  L30: N'ton .5G 11
  (off Harvester Way)
Platinum Ct. L33: Know I 4D 24
Platt Gro. CH42: Rock F 3A 88
Platts St. WA11: Hay 5C 30
Plattsville Rd. L18: Moss H 4E 73
Playfield Rd. L12: W Der 6B 38
Playfield Wlk. L12: W Der 6B 38
Plaza Blvd. L8: Liv 3D 70
Plaza Cinema
  Waterloo 2G 19
Pleasant Hill St. L8: Liv 3D 70
Pleasant St. CH45: New B 6D 32
  L3: Liv 5H 5 (6E 53)
  L20: Boot .3B 34
Pleasant Vw. L20: Boot 3B 34
Pleasington Cl. CH43: Noct 5A 68
Pleasington Dr. CH43: Noct 5A 68
Plemont Rd. L13: Liv 2E 55
Plover Dr. WA7: Nort 5F 115
Pluckington Rd. L36: Huy 4B 58
Plumbers Way L36: Huy 5H 57
Plumer St. CH41: Birke 1C 68
  L15: Wav 2C 72
Plumley Gdns. WA8: Wid 1G 95
Plumpstons La. WA6: Frod 6F 123
Plumpton M. WA8: Wid 2G 97
Plumpton St. L6: Liv 3F 53
Plum Tree Cl. L28: Stockb V 5D 38
Plumtree Cl. L35: Eccl P 1G 59
Plymouth Cl. L19: Garst 6F 91
  WA7: Murd 1G 125
  (not continuous)
Plymyard Av. CH62: Brom, East 1D 120
Plymyard Cl. CH62: Brom 2D 120
Plymyard Copse CH62: Brom 2D 120
Plymyard Ct. CH62: Brom 1C 120
  (off Plymyard Av.)
Pochard Ri. WA7: Nort 5F 115
POCKET NOOK 2G 43
Pocket Nook St. WA9: St H 1G 43
Podium Rd. L13: Liv 3E 55
Poets Cnr. CH62: Port S 6B 88
Poets Grn. L35: Whis 4F 59
  (not continuous)
Poleacre Dr. WA8: Wid 1B 96
Polinda Gdns. WA10: St H 5A 42
Pollard Rd. L15: Wav 6E 55
POLL HILL 3D 100
Poll Hill Rd. CH60: Hesw 4D 100
Pollitt Cres. WA9: Clock F 4G 61

Pollitt Sq. CH62: New F 3C 88
Pollitt St. WA9: Clock F 4G 61
Polperro Cl. L11: Crox 6H 23
  WA5: Penk .6G 81
Pomfret St. L8: Liv 3F 71
Pomona St. L3: Liv 5H 5 (6E 53)
Pond Cl. L6: Liv 3A 54
Pond Grn. Way WA9: St H 4B 44
Pond Vw. Cl. CH60: Hesw 5G 101
Pond Wlk. WA9: St H 4C 44
Pondwater Cl. L32: Kirkb 2A 24
Ponsonby Rd. CH45: Wall 2A 50
Pool Bank CH62: Port S 4B 88
Poolbank Rd. CH62: New F 4B 88
Pool End WA9: St H 3B 44
Poole Rd. CH44: Wall 2F 51
Pool Hey L28: Stockb V 5D 38
  (not continuous)
Pool Hollow WA7: Run 4F 113
Pool La. CH49: Woodc 1E 85
  CH62: Brom 6C 88
  WA7: Run .2F 113
Poolside Rd. WA7: Run 4F 113
Pool St. CH41: Birke 2F 69
  WA8: Wid 4F 97
Poolwood Rd.
  CH49: Woodc 5F 67
Pope St. L20: Boot 6B 20
Poplar Av. CH49: Upton 4D 66
  L23: Crosb .4H 9
  WA5: Penk .5G 81
  WA7: Run .6G 113
  WA10: Eccl 1G 41
Poplar Bank L36: Huy 5G 57
Poplar Cl. L26: Halew 2A 94
  WA7: Run .6G 113
Poplar Ct. L8: Liv 5G 71
  (off Byles St.)
Poplar Dr. CH63: Beb 1B 104
  L5: Liv 2G 53
  L32: Kirkb .6H 13
Poplar Farm Cl. CH46: More 3A 66
Poplar Gro. CH42: Tran 5F 69
  (off Ash Rd.)
  L21: Sea 5H 19
  L35: Presc .2E 59
  WA10: St H .2A 42
  WA11: Hay .5E 31
Poplar Rd. CH43: Oxton 5D 68
  L25: Woolt .6C 74
  WA11: Hay .5E 31
Poplar Ter. CH45: New B 6D 32
Poplar Way L4: Kirkd 5D 34
Poppleford Cl. L25: Gate 5F 75
Poppy Cl. CH46: More 5E 49
Poppy Pl. L22: Water 2G 19
Poppy Rd. L23: Thorn 4B 10
Porchester Rd.
  L11: Norr G 4D 36
Porchfield Cl. L11: Norr G 2F 37
Porlock Av. L16: Child 4A 74
  WA9: Sut L .2G 61
Porlock Cl. CH60: Hesw 1F 117
  WA5: Penk .5G 81
Portal M. CH61: Pens 2D 100
Portal Rd. CH61: Pens 2D 100
Portal Way L11: Crox 4G 23
Portbury Cl. CH62: Port S 5C 88
Portbury Wlk. CH62: Port S 5B 88
Portbury Way CH62: Port S 5C 88
Port C'way. CH62: Brom 1C 104
Portelet Rd. L13: Liv 3D 54
Porter Cl. L35: Rainh 6B 60
Porter St. L3: Liv 3B 52
  WA7: Run .3G 113
Portgate Cl. L12: W Der 3G 37
Porthcawl Cl. WA8: Wid 6A 78
Porthleven Rd. WA7: Brook 2D 124
Portia Av. CH63: Hghr B 4G 87
Portia St. L20: Kirkd 4C 34
PORTICO 6H 41
Portico Av. L35: Eccl P 1G 59
Portico Ct. L35: Eccl P 1G 59
  (off Portico La.)

Portico La. L34: Eccl P 6G 41
L35: Eccl P 1G 59
L35: Presc, Eccl P 1F 59
Portland Av. L22: Water 1E 19
Portland Ct. CH45: New B 4C 32
Portland Gdns. L5: Liv 3C 52
(off Green St.)
Portland Gate CH62: Port S 5C 88
(off Portbury Cl.)
Portland Pl. L5: Liv 3E 53
Portland Rd. WA5: Gt San 1H 81
Portland St. CH41: Birke 1C 68
CH45: New B 4C 32
L5: Liv 3C 52
WA7: Run 2D 112
WA12: Newt W 1H 45
Portland Way WA9: St H 4B 44
Portlemouth Rd. L11: Crox 6G 23
Portloe Av. L26: Halew 2H 93
Portman Rd. L15: Wav 2B 72
Porto Hey Rd. CH61: Irby 6B 84
Porton Rd. L32: Kirkb 2G 23
Portreath Way WA10: Windle 5H 27
Portree Av. CH63: East 2D 120
Portree Cl. L9: Walt 1F 35
Portrush Cl. WA8: Wid 6C 78
Portrush St. L13: Liv 1C 54
Portside WA7: Pres B 6G 115
Portsmouth Pl. WA7: Murd 1G 125
PORT SUNLIGHT 5B 88
Port Sunlight Golf Cen. (Driving Range)
. . . . .6C 88
Port Sunlight Mus. 5B 88
Port Sunlight Station (Rail) 6B 88
Port Talbot Cl. L19: Garst 5F 91
Portway L25: Hunts X 4E 93
Portwood Cl. L7: Liv 1H 71
Post Office La. WA7: West P 6B 112
Potters La. L18: Moss H 4G 73
WA8: Hale B 1F 111
Pottery, The L31: Mell 1E 23
Pottery Cl. L35: Whis 4C 58
Pottery Flds. L34: Presc 1D 58
Pottery La. L35: Whis 4C 58
L36: Huy 4B 58
Poulevara Ho. L13: Liv 5F 55
(off W. Oakhill Pk.)
Poulsom Dr. L30: N'ton 1C 20
Poulter Rd. L9: Ain 4H 21
POULTON
CH44 . . . . .5C 50
CH63 . . . . .3A 104
Poulton Bri. Rd. CH41: Birke 5B 50
CH44: Wall 4C 50
Poulton Cl. L26: Halew 5F 93
Poulton Dr. WA8: Wid 4B 96
Poulton Grn. Cl. CH63: Spit 4H 103
Poulton Hall Rd. CH44: Wall 4C 50
CH63: Raby M 6A 104
Poulton Rd. CH44: Wall 5C 50
CH63: Spit 2A 104
Poulton Royd Dr. CH63: Spit 3H 103
Poulton Vale CH44: Wall 5C 50
Poverty La. L31: Mag 1C 12
Powder Works La. L31: Mag 4H 7
Powell St. WA9: St H 6A 44
Powerhouse L8: Liv 2H 71
(off Commerce Way)
Powerleague
Liverpool 6E 35
Power Rd. CH42: Rock F 3A 88
CH62: Brom 4F 105
Powis St. L8: Liv 4G 71
Pownall Sq. L3: Liv 2D 4 (5C 52)
Pownall St. L1: Liv 6D 4 (1C 70)
Poynter St. WA9: St H 6C 42
Pratt Rd. L34: Presc 1C 58
Precincts, The L23: Crosb 5G 9
Preece Cl. WA8: Wid 6B 78
Preesall Way L11: Crox 6G 23
(not continuous)
Premier St. L5: Liv 2F 53
(not continuous)
Prentice Rd. CH42: Rock F 2G 87

PRENTON .2B 86
Prenton Av. WA9: Clock F 3G 61
Prenton Dell Av. CH43: Pren 3C 86
Prenton Dell Rd. CH43: Pren 2A 86
Prenton Farm Rd. CH43: Pren 3C 86
Prenton Golf Course 3D 86
Prenton Grn. L24: Speke 2G 109
Prenton Hall Rd. CH43: Pren 2B 86
Prenton La. CH42: Tran 2D 86
Prenton Park 1E 87
Prenton Pk. Rd. CH42: Tran 6E 69
Prenton Rd. E. CH42: Tran 1E 87
Prenton Rd. W. CH42: Tran 1E 87
Prenton Village Rd. CH43: Pren 2B 86
Prenton Way CH43: Pren 2H 85
Prenton Way Bus. Units CH43: Pren . .2H 85
Prentonwood Ct. CH42: Tran 2E 87
PRESCOT .1D 58
Prescot Bus. Pk. L34: Presc 2C 58
Prescot By-Pass L34: Presc 1B 58
Prescot Cables FC 6D 40
Prescot Cen. L34: Presc 1D 58
Prescot Ct. L7: Liv 5A 54
Prescot Dr. L6: Liv 4B 54
Prescot Mus. 1D 58
Prescot Rd. L7: Liv 4B 54
L13: Liv 4B 54
L31: Mag, Mell 1G 13
L39: Augh 4H 7
WA8: Cron 5F 77
WA8: Wid 6B 78
WA10: St H 5G 41
Prescot Station (Rail) 2E 59
Prescot St. CH45: New B 5C 32
L7: Liv 5F 53
Prescot Trade Cen. L34: Presc 1E 59
Preseland Rd. L23: Crosb 6G 9
Prestbury Av. CH43: Oxton 1A 86
Prestbury Cl. CH43: Oxton 1A 86
WA8: Wid 3C 96
Prestbury Dr. WA10: Eccl 3H 41
Prestbury Rd. L11: Norr G 1D 36
Preston Av. L34: Presc 2C 58
PRESTON BROOK 1H 125
Preston Gro. L6: Liv 2A 54
PRESTON ON THE HILL 1H 125
Preston St. L1: Liv 3E 5 (6D 52)
WA8: Sut M 5E 61
Preston Way L23: Crosb 5A 10
Prestwick Cl. WA8: Wid 6D 78
WA9: St H 3C 60
Prestwick Dr. L23: Blun 3E 9
Prestwood Cres. L14: Knott A 3B 56
Prestwood Rd. L14: Knott A 3B 56
Pretoria Rd. L9: Ain 5H 21
Price Gro. WA9: St H 3C 44
Price's La. CH43: Oxton 5D 68
Price St. CH41: Birke 1D 68
L1: Liv 6E 5 (1C 70)
Price St. Bus. Cen. CH41: Birke 1E 69
Pride Centre, The 2C 24
Primary Av. L30: N'ton 5H 11
Primrose Cl. WA7: Cas 5C 114
WA8: Wid 2C 96
Primrose Ct. CH45: New B 5D 32
(off Egerton St.)
L36: Huy 1G 57
Primrose Dr. L36: Huy 2G 57
Primrose Gro. CH44: Wall 5G 51
WA11: Hay 4G 31
Primrose Hill CH62: Port S 5D 88
L3: Liv 2E 5 (5D 52)
Primrose Rd. CH41: Birke 2B 68
L18: Moss H 4G 73
Primrose St. L4: Kirkd 6D 34
Primula Cl. WA9: Bold 6C 44
Primula Dr. L9: Walt 1H 35
Prince Albert St. WA9: St H 4B 44
Prince Albert M. L1: Liv 2E 71
(off Up. Frederick St.)
Prince Alfred Rd. L15: Wav 2E 73
Prince Andrew's Gro. WA10: Windle 5A 28
Prince Edward St. CH41: Birke 2E 69
Prince Edwin St. L5: Liv 3E 53

Prince Rupert's Tower 3F 53
Princes Av. CH48: W Kir 1B 82
CH62: East 1E 121
L8: Liv 2F 71
L23: Crosb 5F 9
Princes Blvd. CH63: Hghr B 3F 87
Prince's Cl. WA7: Cas 4B 114
Princes Ct. L8: Liv 3H 71
Princes Gdns. L3: Liv 1C 4 (4C 52)
Princes Ga. E. L8: Liv 3H 71
Princes Ga. Ho. L8: Liv 3H 71
(off Kingsley Rd.)
Princes Ga. W. L8: Liv 3H 71
Princes Pde. L3: Liv 2A 4 (5B 52)
PRINCES PARK 3H 71
Princes Pk. Mans. L8: Liv 4H 71
Princes Pavement CH41: Birke 3G 69
Princes Pl. WA8: Wid 2C 96
Princes Rd. L8: Liv 2F 71
WA10: St H 4A 42
Princess Av. WA5: Gt San 2G 81
WA10: St H 6C 28
WA11: Hay 4H 31
Princess Dr. L12: W Der 5A 38
L14: Knott A 5A 38
Princess Rd. CH45: New B 6D 32
WA5: St H 2E 113
Princess Ter. CH43: Oxton 4E 69
Princes St. L2: Liv 3D 4 (5C 52)
L20: Boot 4B 34
WA8: Wid 3E 97
Princess Way L21: Lith, Sea 5H 19
Prince St. L22: Water 3G 19
Princess Way WA11: St H 3E 29
Princesway CH45: Wall 1C 50
Prince William St. L8: Liv 3H 71
Priors Cl. L25: Woolt 1D 92
Priorsfield CH46: More 1C 66
Priorsfield Rd. L25: Woolt 1D 92
Prior St. L20: Boot 5A 20
Priory, The CH64: Nest 6H 117
L15: Wav 6D 54
L35: Rainh 4A 60
Priory Cl. CH63: Beb 2A 104
L17: Aig 1H 89
L35: Whis 6C 58
WA7: Halt 4C 114
Priory Ct. L36: Huy 5F 57
WA7: Pres B 2G 125
Priory Farm Cl. L19: Gras 4E 91
Priory Gdns. WA10: St H 4D 28
Priory M. CH41: Birke 3H 69
Priory Rd. CH44: Wall 4G 51
CH48: W Kir 1C 82
L4: Walt 5G 35
WA7: Wind H 3E 115
Priory St. CH41: Birke 3H 69
L19: Garst 1H 107
Priory Wharf CH41: Birke 3H 69
Priory Way L25: Woolt 1D 92
Pritchard Av. L21: Sea 4H 19
Pritt St. L3: Liv 1G 5 (4E 53)
Private Dr. CH61: Barn 6H 85
Prizett Rd. L19: Gras 4F 91
Probyn Rd. CH45: Wall 2A 50
Procter Rd. CH42: Rock F 2A 88
Proctor Ct. L30: N'ton 5D 10
Proctor Rd. CH47: Hoy 3C 64
Proctors Cl. WA8: Wid 1G 97
Progress Pl. L1: Liv 3D 4
Promenade, The L17: Aig 2H 89
L19: Aig 4B 90
Promenade Gdns. L17: Aig 6F 71
Prophet Wlk. L8: Liv 4F 71
Prospect Cl. L6: Liv 4B 54
(off Prospect Va.)
Prospect Point L6: Liv 5F 53
Prospect Rd. CH42: Tran 2D 86
WA9: St H 1H 43
Prospect Row WA7: West 6D 112
Prospect St. L6: Liv 5G 53
Prospect Va. CH45: Wall 2B 50
L6: Liv 3B 54
Prospect Way L30: N'ton 6H 11

Proto Cl.—Rainhill Trials Exhibition

Proto Cl. L24: Speke 2G **109**
Proudman Dr. CH43: Bid 2G **67**
Providence Ct. WA10: St H 1E **43**
Providence Cres. L8: Liv 3E **71**
Provident St. WA9: St H 2C **44**
Province Pl. L20: Boot 5D **20**
Province Rd. L20: Boot 5D **20**
Prussia St. L3: Liv 2C **4** (5C **52**)
(not continuous)
Public Hall St. WA7: Run 2E **113**
Pudsey St. L1: Liv 3G **5** (5E **53**)
Pugin St. L4: Walt 6E **35**
Pulford Av. CH43: Pren 1C **86**
Pulford Cl. WA7: Beech 1A **124**
Pulford Rd. CH63: Beb 6H **87**
Pulford St. L4: Walt 6F **35**
Pullman Cl. CH60: Hesw 5H **101**
Puma Ct. L34: Presc 2A **58**
Pumpfields Rd. L3: Liv 1C **4** (4C **52**)
Pump La. CH49: Grea 4H **65**
WA7: Halt 5B **114**
Purbeck Dr. CH61: Irby 4B **84**
Purley Gro. L18: Moss H 1E **91**
Purley Rd. L22: Water 1E **19**
Purser Gro. L15: Wav 1B **72**
Putney Ct. WA7: Pal F 6A **114**
Pyecroft Cl. WA5: Gt San 3F **81**
Pyecroft Rd. WA5: Gt San 3F **81**
Pye Rd. CH60: Hesw 5D **100**
Pyes Gdns. WA11: St H 4F **29**
Pyes La. L36: Huy 6E **39**
Pye St. L15: Wav 2E **73**
PYGON'S HILL 1C **6**
Pygon's Hill La. L31: Lyd 1C **6**
Pym St. L4: Walt 3F **35**

Q

Quadrangle, The L18: Moss H 5F **73**
Quadrant, The CH47: Hoy 3B **64**
Quadrant Cl. WA7: Murd 1F **125**
Quaker La. CH60: Hesw 4C **100**
Quakers All. L2: Liv 3D **4**
Quakers Mdw. L34: Know 1F **39**
Quarry Av. CH63: Beb 1H **103**
Quarry Bank CH41: Birke 4F **69**
L33: Kirkb 6B **14**
Quarry Bank Flats *CH41: Birke 4F* ***69***
(off Quarry Bank)
Quarrybank St. CH41: Birke 4E **69**
Quarrybank Workshops *CH41: Birke . . . 4E* ***69***
(off Quarrybank St.)
Quarry Cl. CH61: Hesw 3D **100**
L13: Liv 2E **55**
L33: Kirkb 6B **14**
WA7: Run 4H **113**
Quarry Ct. WA8: Wid 2A **96**
Quarry Dale L33: Kirkb 6B **14**
Quarry Grn. L33: Kirkb 6B **14**
Quarry Grn. Flats L33: Kirkb 6B **14**
Quarry Hey L33: Kirkb 6B **14**
Quarry La. CH61: Thing 5E **85**
Quarry Pk. *L35: Rainh 6B* ***60***
(off Lincoln Way)
Quarry Pl. *L25: Woolt 1B* ***92***
(off Quarry St.)
Quarry Rd. CH64: Nest 6D **118**
L13: Liv 2D **54**
L20: Boot 3D **34**
L23: Thorn 3A **10**
Quarry Rd. E. CH60: Hesw 4C **100**
CH61: Hesw 4C **100**
CH63: Beb 1A **104**
Quarry Rd. W. CH60: Hesw 4C **100**
Quarryside Dr. L33: Kirkb 6C **14**
Quarry St. L25: Woolt 6B **74**
Quarry St. Sth. L25: Woolt 1C **92**
Quarry Way L36: Huy 5A **58**
Quartz Way L21: Lith 3C **20**
Quay, The WA6: Frod 5H **123**
Quayle Cl. WA11: Hay 5E **31**
Quay Pl. WA7: Pres B 6G **115**
Quay Side WA6: Frod 5H **123**
Quebec Quay L3: Liv 3C **70**
Queen Anne Pde. L3: Liv 3B **4**
Queen Anne St. L3: Liv 1G **5** (4E **53**)
Queen Av. L2: Liv 4D **4**
Queen Elizabeth Ct. L21: Lith 3A **20**
Queen Mary's Dr. CH62: Port S 5B **88**
Queen's Av. CH47: Meols 1D **64**
WA8: Wid 3H **95**
Queensberry St. L8: Liv 4F **71**
Queensbury CH48: W Kir 6D **64**
Queensbury Av. CH62: Brom 4E **105**
Queensbury Way WA8: Wid 6B **78**
Queens Cl. L19: Garst 5G **91**
WA7: Run 4D **112**
Queens Ct. CH47: Hoy 2B **64**
L6: Liv 2G **53**
L15: Wav 6G **55**
Queenscourt Rd. L12: W Der 2G **55**
Queensdale Rd. L18: Moss H 4E **73**
Queens Dock Commercial Cen.
L1: Liv 2D **70**
Queens Dr. CH43: Pren 2C **86**
CH60: Hesw 5C **100**
L12: W Der 3F **55**
WA10: Windle 5A **28**
Queens Dr. Mossley Hill
L18: Moss H 5C **72**
Queens Dr. Stoneycroft L13: Liv 2E **55**
Queens Dr. Walton L4: Walt 3G **35**
Queens Dr. Wavertree L15: Wav 6G **55**
Queens Dr. W. Derby L13: W Der 5C **36**
Queensland Av. WA9: St H 6C **42**
Queensland Pl. WA9: St H 6C **42**
Queensland St. L7: Liv 6H **53**
Queens M. L6: Liv 3G **53**
Queens Park Leisure Cen. 1C **42**
Queen Sq. L1: Liv 3F **5** (5D **52**)
Queens Rd. CH42: Rock F 2A **88**
CH44: Wall 3G **51**
CH47: Hoy 2A **64**
L6: Liv 2G **53**
L20: Boot 3C **34**
L23: Crosb 5G **9**
L34: Presc 1E **59**
WA7: Run 4D **112**
WA10: St H 4A **42**
WA11: Hay 4H **31**
Queen St. CH41: Tran 5G **69**
CH45: Wall 2D **50**
L19: Garst 6G **91**
L22: Water 3F **19**
WA7: Run 2E **113**
WA10: St H 6D **28**
Queen's Wlk. *L1: Liv 2E* ***71***
(off Lady Chapel Cl.)
Queensway CH41: Birke 5A **4** (1A **70**)
CH45: Wall 1C **50**
CH60: Hesw 1G **117**
L22: Water 1H **19**
WA7: Run 2D **112**
WA8: Wid 5D **96**
WA11: Rainf 4G **17**
WA11: St H 3E **29**
Queensway Trad. Est. WA8: Wid 6E **97**
Queens Wharf L3: Liv 2C **70**
Queenswood Av. CH63: Hghr B 3G **87**
Quernmore Rd. L33: Kirkb 6C **14**
Quernmore Wlk. L33: Kirkb 6C **14**
Quickswood Cl. L25: Woolt 4B **74**
Quickswood Dr. L25: Woolt 4B **74**
Quickswood Grn. L25: Woolt 4B **74**
Quickthorn Cres. L28: Stockb V 6D **38**
Quigley Av. L30: N'ton 2G **21**
Quigley St. CH41: Tran 5H **69**
Quinesway CH49: Upton 4D **66**
Quinn St. WA8: Wid 4F **97**
Quintbridge Cl. L26: Halew 4G **93**
Quorn St. L7: Liv 5H **53**

R

RABY 3E **119**
Raby Av. CH63: Raby M 1B **120**
Raby Cl. CH60: Hesw 6D **100**
CH63: Raby M 6A **104**
WA8: Wid 1A **98**
Raby Dell CH63: Raby M 1B **120**
Raby Dr. CH46: More 2B **66**
CH63: Raby M 6A **104**
Raby Gro. CH63: Hghr B 3F **87**
Raby Hall Rd.
CH63: Brom, Raby M 2G **119**
RABY MERE 6A **104**
Raby Mere Rd.
CH63: Raby, Raby M 3E **119**
(not continuous)
Raby Pk. Rd. CH64: Nest 6A **118**
Raby Rd. CH63: Raby, Thorn H 1D **118**
Racecourse Retail Pk. L9: Ain 1H **21**
Rachel St. L5: Liv 3D **52**
Radburn Cl. L23: Thorn 4B **10**
Radburn Rd. L23: Thorn 4B **10**
Radford Av. CH63: Spit 3B **104**
Radford Cl. WA8: Wid 4A **96**
Radlett Cl. WA5: Penk 6G **81**
Radley Dr. CH63: Thorn H 1B **118**
L10: Ain 6A **12**
Radley Rd. CH44: Wall 2B **50**
Radleys Ct. *L8: Liv 3F* ***71***
(off Up. Warwick St.)
Radley St. WA9: St H 6C **42**
Radmore Rd. L14: Knott A 4H **55**
Radnor Av. CH60: Hesw 4D **100**
Radnor Cl. L26: Halew 5G **93**
Radnor Dr. CH45: Wall 1E **51**
L20: Boot 2E **35**
WA8: Wid 1B **96**
Radnor Pl. CH43: Oxton 3E **69**
L6: Liv 2B **54**
Radshaw Nook L32: Kirkb 5A **24**
Radstock Gro. WA9: Sut L 2H **61**
Radstock Rd. CH44: Wall 2A **50**
L6: Liv 4A **54**
Radstock Wlk. *L26: Halew 5H* ***93***
(off Romford Way)
Radway Rd. L36: Huy 2H **57**
Raeburn Av. CH48: W Kir 6C **64**
CH62: East 1D **120**
Raffles Rd. CH42: Tran 4E **69**
Raffles St. L1: Liv 2E **71**
Rafter Av. L20: Boot 5E **21**
(not continuous)
Raglan Cl. L19: Garst 6G **91**
Railbrook Hey L13: Liv 6E **55**
Railside Ct. L5: Liv 2C **52**
Railton Av. L35: Rainh 5B **60**
Railton Cl. L35: Rainh 6B **60**
Railton Rd. L11: Norr G 3C **36**
Railway Cotts. CH66: Hoot 6D **120**
L25: Hunts X 4E **93**
Railway St. L19: Garst 6G **91**
WA10: St H 1F **43**
Railway Vw. L32: Kirkb 6G **13**
Railyard, The L7: Liv 1G **71**
Rainbow Cl. WA8: Wid 6A **78**
Rainbow Dr. L26: Halew 3G **93**
L31: Mell 5F **13**
Raines Cl. CH49: Grea 5C **66**
RAINFORD 2G **17**
Rainford Av. L20: Boot 6E **21**
Rainford By-Pass
WA11: Rainf, Windle 1D **16**
Rainford Gdns. L2: Liv 4E **5**
Rainford Hall Cotts. WA11: Crank 1D **28**
Rainford Ind. Est. WA11: Rainf 5H **17**
(not continuous)
Rainford Rd. WA10: St H, Windle 4A **28**
WA11: Windle 4A **28**
(not continuous)
Rainford Sq. L2: Liv 4D **4** (6C **52**)
Rainham Cl. L19: Aller 3G **91**
RAINHILL 4A **60**
Rainhill Rd. L35: Rainh 3A **60**
WA9: St H 3A **60**
Rainhill Station (Rail) 4A **60**
RAINHILL STOOPS 6C **60**
Rainhill Trials Exhibition 4A **60**

Rake, The CH62: Brom 5C **104**
Rake Cl. CH49: Upton 5E **67**
Rake Hey CH46: More 1H **65**
Rake Hey Cl. CH46: More 1A **66**
Rake La. CH45: New B, Wall 6D **32**
   CH49: Upton 5E **67**
Rake M. CH49: Upton 5E **67**
Rakersfield Ct. CH45: New B 5E **33**
Rakersfield Rd. CH45: New B 5E **33**
Raleigh Av. L35: Whis 5D **58**
Raleigh Rd. CH46: Leas 3E **49**
   CH64: Nest 6B **118**
Raleigh St. L20: Boot 4B **34**
Rambaldi Sq. WA8: Wid 2F **97**
         (off Cross St.)
Rame Cl. L10: Faz 5F **23**
Ramford St. WA9: St H 3H **43**
Ramilies Rd. L18: Moss H 4D **72**
Ramleh Pk. L23: Blun 6C **8**
Rampit Cl. WA11: Hay 4H **31**
Ramsbrook Cl. L24: Speke 1E **109**
Ramsbrook La. L24: Hale 6C **94**
   WA8: Hale B 6C **94**
Ramsbrook Rd. L24: Speke 1E **109**
Ramsbury Dr. L24: Speke 1D **108**
Ramsey Cl. L19: Aller 3H **91**
   L35: Whis 4E **59**
   WA8: Wid 6A **80**
Ramsey Ct. CH48: W Kir 3B **82**
Ramsey Rd. L19: Aller 3H **91**
Ramsfield Rd. L24: Speke 1A **110**
Ramsons Cl. L26: Halew 2G **93**
Randall Dr. L30: N'ton 1C **20**
Randle Av. WA11: Rainf 1E **17**
Randle Brook Ct. WA11: Rainf .. .1E **17**
Randle Cl. CH63: Spit 3A **104**
Randle Hgts. L11: Crox 6A **24**
Randle M. WA8: Wid 2F **97**
Randles Rd. L34: Know 6C **24**
Randolph St. L4: Walt 6F **35**
Randon Gro. WA10: St H 1D **42**
Ranelagh Av. L21: Lith 3A **20**
Ranelagh Dr. Nth. L19: Gras 3E **91**
Ranelagh Dr. Sth. L19: Gras 3E **91**
Ranelagh Ho. L1: Liv 5G **5**
Ranelagh Pl. L3: Liv 4G **5** (6E **53**)
Ranelagh St. L1: Liv 5F **5** (6D **52**)
Ranfurly Rd. L19: Gras 4F **91**
Rangemore Rd. L18: Moss H 2E **91**
Rankin Hall L18: Moss H 1C **90**
Rankin St. CH44: Wall 5C **50**
Rankin Way CH62: Brom 4E **105**
Ranworth Cl. L11: Norr G 2C **36**
Ranworth Gdns. WA9: St H 1B **60**
Ranworth Pl. L11: Norr G 2C **36**
Ranworth Rd. WA5: Gt San 3G **81**
Ranworth Sq. L11: Norr G 2D **36**
Ranworth Way L11: Norr G 2D **36**
Rappart Rd. CH44: Wall 4F **51**
Rashid Mufti Ct. L8: Liv 3G **71**
Ratcliffe Pl. L35: Rainh 3H **59**
Rathbone Hall L17: Aig 5C **72**
Rathbone Rd. L13: Liv, Wav 1D **72**
   L15: Wav 1D **72**
Rathlin Cl. WA8: Wid 6A **80**
Rathmore Av. L18: Moss H 6E **73**
Rathmore Cl. CH43: Oxton 6C **68**
Rathmore Dr. CH43: Oxton 5C **68**
Rathmore Rd. CH43: Oxton 5C **68**
Raven Cl. L6: Liv 4G **53**
Ravendale Cl. CH43: Noct 5H **67**
Ravenfield Cl. L26: Halew 3G **93**
Ravenfield Dr. WA8: Wid 6A **78**
Ravenglass Av. L31: Mag 5C **6**
RAVENHEAD 3C **42**
Ravenhead Av. L32: Kirkb 4A **24**
Ravenhead Ind. Pk. WA10: St H .. .4D **42**
Ravenhead Pk. WA9: St H 4E **43**
Ravenhead Rd. WA10: St H 4C **42**
Ravenhead Row WA10: St H 4C **42**
Ravenhill Cres. CH46: Leas 3D **48**
Ravenhurst Way L35: Whis 6D **58**
Ravenna Rd. L19: Aller 3H **91**
Ravens Ct. L26: Halew 4H **93**

Ravenscroft Rd. CH43: Oxton 4E **69**
Ravensthorpe Grn. L11: Norr G .. .2D **36**
Ravenstone Cl. CH49: Upton 2D **66**
Ravenstone Dr. WA9: St H 6H **43**
Ravenstone Rd. L19: Aller 3F **91**
Ravenswood Av. CH42: Rock F .. .3H **87**
Ravenswood Rd. CH61: Hesw 3E **101**
   L13: Liv 4E **55**
Raven Way L20: Boot 2C **34**
     (off Strand Shop. Cen.)
Rawcliffe Cl. WA8: Wid 5D **78**
Rawcliffe Rd. CH42: Tran 4F **69**
   L9: Walt 1F **35**
Rawdon Cl. WA7: Pal F 6C **114**
Rawlinson Cres. L26: Halew 3B **94**
Rawlinson Rd. L13: Liv 4D **54**
Rawlins St. L7: Liv 4B **54**
Rawson Cl. L21: Sea 4H **19**
Rawson Rd. L21: Sea 3H **19**
Raydale Cl. L9: Walt 2G **35**
Raymond Av. L30: N'ton 2G **21**
Raymond Pl. L5: Liv 3D **52**
Raymond Rd. CH44: Wall 4E **51**
Raynham Rd. L13: Liv 5D **54**
Rayrig Fold WA11: Rainf 3F **17**
Reach, The L3: Liv 1E **5** (4D **52**)
Reade Cl. CH63: Spit 4A **104**
Reading Cl. L5: Kirkd 6D **34**
Reading St. L5: Kirkd 6D **34**
Reads Ct. L5: Walt 5F **21**
Reapers Way L30: N'ton 5G **11**
Rear Comn. Pas. L6: Liv 4B **54**
Reay Ct. CH44: Wall 4G **51**
Reay St. WA8: Wid 1G **97**
Rebecca Gdns. WA9: St H 6G **43**
Recreation St. WA9: St H 1G **43**
Rector Rd. L6: Liv 6A **36**
Rectory Cl. CH42: Tran 5F **69**
   CH60: Hesw 6D **100**
Rectory Dr. L26: Halew 2H **93**
Rectory Gdns. WA9: St H 1G **61**
Rectory La. CH60: Hesw 6C **100**
Rectory Rd. CH48: W Kir 2B **82**
Redacre Cl. WA4: Dutt 4H **125**
Redbourne Av. L26: Halew 5H **93**
Redbourne Dr. WA8: Wid 5H **77**
Redbourn St. L6: Liv 1A **54**
Redbrook Cl. CH62: Brom 1D **120**
Redbrook St. L6: Liv 1A **54**
Red Brow La. WA4: Dares 5G **115**
   WA7: Murd 5G **115**
Redbrow Way L33: Kirkb 5A **14**
Redburn Cl. L8: Liv 5G **71**
Redcap Cl. CH45: Wall 5A **32**
Redcar Dr. CH62: East 2D **120**
Redcar M. L6: Liv 1H **53**
Redcar Rd. CH45: Wall 1H **49**
Redcar St. L6: Liv 1A **54**
Redcote Ct. CH48: W Kir 2A **82**
Redcroft CH49: Grea 5A **66**
Red Cross St. L1: Liv 5C **4** (6C **52**)
Red Cut La. L33: Kirkb 3G **25**
Redditch Cl. CH49: Grea 5A **66**
Redfern St. L20: Kirkd 5C **34**
Redfield Cl. CH44: Wall 3F **51**
Redford Cl. CH49: Grea 5A **66**
Redford St. L6: Liv 1A **54**
Redgate Av. L23: Crosb 5A **10**
Redgate Dr. WA9: St H 2H **43**
Redgrave Ct. L20: Boot 3C **34**
Redgrave St. L7: Liv 5A **54**
Redhill Av. L32: Kirkb 3B **24**
Red Hill Rd. CH63: Store 6D **86**
Redhouse Bank CH48: W Kir 6A **64**
Redhouse La. CH48: W Kir 6A **64**
Redington Rd. L19: Aller 3H **91**
Redland Rd. L9: Ain 3H **21**
       (off Lyncot Rd.)
Red Lion Cl. L31: Mag 6B **6**
Red Lion Dene. L31: Mag 6B **6**
Red Lomes L30: N'ton 4D **10**
Redmain Way L12: Crox 3B **38**
Redmere Dr. CH60: Hesw 5H **101**
Redmires Cl. L7: Liv 1H **71**

Redmont St. CH41: Tran 5G **69**
Redmoor Cres. L33: Kirkb 4A **14**
Redoaks Way L26: Halew 2B **94**
Redpoll Gro. L26: Halew 1G **93**
Red Rocks Marsh Nature Reserve .. .5A **64**
Red Rock St. L6: Liv 3H **53**
Red Rum Cl. L9: Ain 3B **22**
Redruth Av. WA11: St H 4H **29**
Redruth Cl. WA7: Brook 1E **125**
Redruth Rd. L11: Crox 6H **23**
Redstone Cl. CH47: Meols 1D **64**
Redstone Dr. CH60: Hesw 4A **100**
Redstone M. CH47: Meols 1D **64**
Redstone Pk. CH45: Wall 1G **32**
Redstone Ri. CH43: Noct 3H **67**
Redstone Way L35: Whis 2G **59**
Redtail Cl. WA7: Run 2D **112**
Redvers Av. CH66: Hoot 5G **121**
Redvers Dr. L9: Walt 5F **21**
Redwald Cl. L33: Kirkb 3B **14**
Redwing La. L25: Gate 5C **74**
Redwing Way L26: Halew 1F **93**
Redwood Av. L31: Lyd 4B **6**
Redwood Cl. CH43: Oxton 1B **86**
   L25: Gate 4E **75**
Redwood Ct. L8: Liv 5G **71**
         (off Byles St.)
Redwood Dr. WA11: Hay 6B **30**
Redwood Gro. L20: Boot 1C **34**
      (off Strand Shop. Cen.)
Redwood Rd. L25: Gate 4D **74**
Redwood Way L33: Kirkb 3A **14**
Reedale Cl. L18: Moss H 5E **73**
Reedale Rd. L18: Moss H 5E **73**
Reedmace Rd. L5: Liv 1F **53**
Reeds Av. E. CH46: Leas 4D **48**
Reeds Av. W. CH46: Leas 4D **48**
Reeds Brow WA11: Rainf 1H **31**
Reeds La. CH46: Leas, More 3D **48**
   WA11: Rainf 5E **17**
Reeds Rd. L36: Huy 3G **57**
Reedville CH43: Oxton 4A **68**
Reedville Gro. CH46: Leas 5D **48**
Reedville Rd. CH63: Beb 6H **87**
Reel Cinema
   Widnes 4F **97**
Reeve Ct. Village WA9: St H 1A **60**
Reeves Av. L20: Boot 6E **21**
Reeves St. WA9: St H 2A **44**
Reflection Ct. WA10: St H 2D **42**
Regal Cres. WA8: Wid 3H **95**
Regal Dr. WA10: Windle 6A **28**
Regal Rd. L11: Crox 2G **37**
Regal Wlk. L4: Walt 6F **35**
Regency Ct. CH42: Rock F 2A **88**
      (off Rock La. W.)
Regency Pk. WA8: Wid 6C **78**
Regent Av. L14: Broad G 5A **56**
   L30: N'ton 6F **11**
   WA11: Hay 4D **30**
Regent Pk. L36: Huy 5G **57**
Regent Rd. CH45: Wall 1H **49**
   L3: Liv 1B **52**
   L5: Kirkd, Liv 1B **52**
   L20: Boot, Kirkd 6H **19**
   L23: Crosb 5F **9**
   WA8: Wid 2F **97**
Regents Cl. CH61: Thing 5F **85**
Regents Way WA10: St H 3A **42**
Regent St. L3: Liv 3B **52**
   WA7: Run 2E **113**
   WA12: Newt W 2H **45**
Regina Av. L22: Water 1E **19**
Regiment Way L12: W Der 6H **37**
Reginald Rd. WA9: St H 1A **62**
Regina Rd. L9: Walt 5G **21**
Reigate Cl. L25: Woolt 6E **75**
Reins Cft. CH64: Nest 6A **118**
Remington Pl. WA4: Dutt 4H **125**
Renaissance Way L24: Halew 6F **93**
Rendal Cl. L5: Liv 2G **53**
Rendcombe Grn. L11: Norr G 2D **36**
Rendlesham Cl. CH49: Upton 4C **66**

Rendel St.—Rivington Av.

Rendel St. CH41: Birke 2F **69**
Renfrew Av. CH62: East 2E **121**
WA11: St H 4H **29**
Renfrew St. L7: Liv 5G **53**
Renlake Ind. Est. WA9: St H 1B **62**
Rennell Rd. L14: Knott A 4G **55**
Rennie Av. WA10: St H 1A **42**
Renown Way L24: Speke 5C **92**
Renshaw St. L1: Liv 5G **5** (6E **53**)
Renton Av. WA7: Run 3H **113**
Renville Rd. L14: Broad G 5G **55**
Renwick Av. L35: Rainh 3G **59**
Renwick Rd. L9: Walt 6G **21**
Repton Gro. L10: Ain 1A **22**
Repton Rd. L16: Child 1H **73**
Reservoir Rd. CH42: Tran 2D **86**
L25: Woolt 6B **74**
Reservoir Rd. Nth.
CH42: Tran 1D **86**
Reservoir St. L6: Liv 3G **53**
WA9: St H 6A **42**
Rest Hill Rd. CH63: Store 6D **86**
Retford Rd. L33: Kirkb 1B **24**
Retford Wlk. L33: Kirkb 1B **24**
Reva Rd. L14: Broad G 4B **56**
Revesby Cl. WA8: Wid 1B **96**
Rex Cohen Ct. L17: Aig 4C **72**
Rexmore Rd. L18: Moss H 1E **91**
Rexmore Way L15: Wav 2C **72**
Reynolds Av. WA9: St H 3D **44**
Reynolds Cl. L6: Liv 3G **53**
Reynolds Way L25: Woolt 1C **92**
Rhiwlas St. L8: Liv 4G **71**
Rhodesia Rd. L9: Ain 5H **21**
Rhodesway CH60: Hesw 6F **101**
Rhona Cl. CH63: East 3C **120**
Rhona Dr. WA5: Gt San 3G **81**
Rhosesmor Cl. L32: Kirkb 4B **24**
Rhosesmor Rd. L32: Kirkb 5B **24**
Rhuddlan Cl. L13: Liv 5D **54**
Rhyl St. L8: Liv 4F **71**
WA8: Wid 4D **96**
Rialto Cl. L8: Liv 2F **71**
Ribble Av. L31: Mag 5D **6**
L35: Rainh 4A **60**
Ribble Cl. WA8: Wid 6B **80**
Ribbledale Rd.
L18: Moss H 5E **73**
Ribble Ho. L25: Gate 5E **75**
Ribble Rd. L25: Gate 6E **75**
Ribblers La. L32: Kirkb 4H **23**
L34: Know 5B **24**
Ribblesdale Av. L9: Ain 4H **21**
Ribblesdale Cl. CH62: East 2F **121**
Ribble St. CH41: Birke 6B **50**
Ribchester Way L35: Tar G 2A **76**
Rice Hey Rd. CH44: Wall 2E **51**
Rice La. CH44: Wall 2E **51**
(not continuous)
L9: Walt 2F **35**
Rice Lane City Farm **1F 35**
Rice Lane Station (Rail) **6G 21**
Rice St. L1: Liv 6H **5** (1E **71**)
Richard Allen Way *L5: Liv* *3F **53***
(off Netherfield Rd. Sth.)
Richard Chubb Dr. CH44: Wall 1F **51**
Richard Cl. WA7: Cas 4C **114**
Richard Gro. L12: W Der 2A **56**
Richard Hesketh Dr.
L32: Kirkb 1G **23**
Richard Kelly Cl. L4: Walt 5B **36**
Richard Kelly Dr. L4: Walt 3B **36**
Richard Kelly Pl. L4: Walt 5B **36**
Richard Martin Rd. L21: Ford 2C **20**
Richard Rd. L23: Blun 4C **8**
Richards Gro. WA9: St H 1A **44**
Richardson Rd. CH42: Rock F 2G **87**
Richardson St. L7: Liv 2A **72**
Richland Rd. L13: Liv 2D **54**
Richmond Av. L21: Lith 3A **20**
WA7: Run 3A **114**
WA11: Hay 4D **30**
Richmond Cl. CH63: Beb 5A **88**
WA10: Eccl 1G **41**
Richmond Ct. *L6: Liv* *2G **53***
(off Richmond Ter.)
L21: Lith *4B **20***
(off Delta Rd.)
WA8: Wid 5H **79**
Richmond Cres. L30: N'ton 6F **11**
Richmond Gro. L31: Lyd 4D **6**
Richmond Pk. L6: Liv 1H **53**
Richmond Rd. CH63: Beb 5H **87**
L23: Crosb 4G **9**
Richmond Row L3: Liv 1G **5** (4E **53**)
Richmond St. CH45: New B 4D **32**
L1: Liv 4E **5** (6D **52**)
WA8: Wid 2G **97**
Richmond Ter. L6: Liv 2H **53**
Richmond Way CH61: Hesw 3D **100**
CH61: Thing 4E **85**
L35: Tar G 2A **76**
Rich Vw. CH43: Oxton 6D **68**
Rickaby Cl. CH63: Brom 5C **104**
Rickman St. L4: Kirkd 6D **34**
Rickman Way L36: Huy 1H **75**
Ridding La. WA7: Brook 2D **124**
Riddock Rd. L21: Lith 6B **20**
Rides, The WA11: Hay 5F **31**
Ridge, The CH60: Hesw 3B **100**
Ridgefield Rd. CH61: Pens 6D **84**
Ridgemere Rd. CH61: Pens 6D **84**
Ridgetor Rd. L25: Woolt 6B **74**
Ridgeview Rd. CH43: Noct 4H **67**
Ridgeway, The CH47: Meols 2E **65**
CH60: Hesw 6F **101**
CH63: Hghr B 3F **87**
L25: Woolt 6C **74**
WA7: Murd 1F **125**
WA8: Cron 3A **78**
Ridgeway Dr. L31: Lyd 3C **6**
Ridgewell Cl. L21: Lith 4A **20**
Ridgewood Dr. CH61: Pens 1C **100**
WA9: St H 1G **61**
Ridgewood Way L9: Walt 4G **21**
Ridgmont Av. L11: Norr G 3D **36**
Riding Cl. WA9: Clock F 3G **61**
Ridingfold L26: Halew 1F **93**
Riding Hill Rd. L34: Know 3F **39**
Riding Hill Wlk. L34: Know 3F **39**
Ridings, The CH43: Noct 4H **67**
Ridings Hey CH43: Noct 5H **67**
Riding St. L3: Liv 3H **5** (5F **53**)
Ridley Gro. CH48: W Kir 6A **64**
Ridley La. L31: Mag 6C **6**
Ridley Rd. L6: Liv 4A **54**
Ridley St. CH43: Oxton 4E **69**
Ridsdale WA8: Wid 3A **96**
Ridsdale Lawn L27: N'ley 6A **76**
Riesling Dr. L33: Kirkb 4H **13**
Rigby Dr. CH49: Grea 1B **84**
Rigby Rd. L31: Mag 4A **6**
Rigby St. L3: Liv 2B **4** (5B **52**)
WA10: St H 2D **42**
(Clock Twr. St.)
WA10: St H 1D **42**
(Henry St.)
Rigby St. Sth. *WA10: St H* *2D **42***
(off Nth. John St.)
Riley Av. L20: Boot 6D **20**
Riley Dr. WA7: Run 5E **113**
Rimmer Av. L16: Child 6C **56**
Rimmerbrook Rd. L25: Gate 2D **74**
Rimmer Cl. L21: Lith 4B **20**
Rimmer Gro. WA9: St H 2A **44**
Rimmer St. L3: Liv 2H **5** (5E **53**)
Rimmington Rd. L17: Aig 1C **90**
Rimrose Bus. Pk. L20: Boot 1A **34**
Rimrose Rd. L20: Boot 6A **20**
Rimrose Valley Country Pk. **5B 10**
Rimrose Valley Rd. L23: Crosb 6A **10**
Rimsdale Cl. L17: Aig 4C **90**
Ringcroft Rd. L13: Liv 4F **55**
Ringo Starr Dr. L6: Liv 4H **53**
Ringsfield Rd. L24: Speke 3A **110**
Ringway CH64: Nest 5A **118**
Ringway Rd. L25: Gate 5E **75**
WA7: Run 3H **113**
Ringways CH62: Brom 2D **104**
Ringwood CH43: Oxton 6C **68**
Ringwood Av. L14: Broad G 5B **56**
Rio Ct. L34: Presc 6D **40**
Ripley Av. L21: Lith 2B **20**
Ripley Cl. L31: Mag 6D **6**
Ripley Way WA9: St H 3D **60**
Ripon Cl. L30: N'ton 2F **21**
L36: Huy 4A **58**
Ripon Rd. CH45: Wall 1A **50**
Ripon Row WA7: Run 1H **123**
Ripon St. CH41: Tran 5G **69**
L4: Walt 4F **35**
Risbury Rd. L11: Norr G 3D **36**
Rishton Cl. L5: Liv 2G **53**
Rishton St. *L5: Liv* *2G **53***
(off Tynemouth Cl.)
Ritchie Av. L9: Ain 5A **22**
Ritherup La. L35: Rainh 3A **60**
Ritson St. L8: Liv 3H **71**
Rivacre Rd. CH62: East 2G **121**
CH66: Ell P, Hoot 5H **121**
Riva La. CH60: Hesw 3C **100**
Rivenhall Sq. L24: Speke 1D **108**
Rivenmill Cl. WA8: Wid 4G **79**
Riveracre Rd. CH65: Hoot 5H **121**
River Avon St. L8: Liv 2A **72**
(not continuous)
Riverbank Cl. CH60: Hesw 1D **116**
Riverbank Rd. CH60: Hesw 1C **116**
CH62: Brom 1E **105**
L19: Gras 4E **91**
River Gro. CH62: New F 3B **88**
Riverpark Gdns. *L8: Liv* *3E **71***
(off Hyslop St.)
Riversdale WA6: Frod 6G **123**
Riversdale Cl. L33: Kirkb 5B **14**
Riversdale Ct. L19: Aig 3D **90**
Riversdale M. L19: Aig 3D **90**
Riversdale Rd. CH44: Wall 3F **51**
CH48: W Kir 1A **82**
L19: Aig 4D **90**
L21: Sea 4H **19**
WA7: Halt 4A **114**
Riverside CH48: W Kir 3B **82**
CH62: Port S 6B **88**
L12: W Der 4A **38**
Riverside Bowl **4D 32**
Riverside Cl. L20: Boot 6A **20**
Riverside Ct. CH62: New F 2B **88**
Riverside Dr. L3: Liv 6E **71**
L17: Aig 1G **89**
Riverside Gro. WA9: St H 6H **43**
Riverside Ho. CH41: Birke 6H **51**
Riverside M. L36: Huy 1E **57**
Riverside Trad. Est.
WA5: Penk 2F **99**
Riverside Vw. L17: Aig 2A **90**
Riverside Wlk. L3: Liv 4D **70**
(Atlantic Way)
L3: Liv 6B **4** (1B **70**)
(The Colonnades)
Riverslea Rd. L23: Blun 1D **18**
River St. CH41: Birke 3F **69**
River Vw. *CH41: Tran* *5G **69***
(off Marquis St.)
CH62: New F 3C **88**
L22: Water 1E **19**
Riverview CH49: Woodc 2E **85**
Riverview Gdns. CH42: Rock F 1H **87**
River Vw. Residential Caravan Pk.
WA8: Wid 3G **97**
Riverview Rd. CH44: Wall 4G **51**
CH62: Brom 2F **105**
Riverview Wlk. *L8: Liv* *5F **71***
(off Cockburn St.)
River Wlk. *WA7: Pal F* *6B **114***
(off Halton Lea Shop. Cen.)
River Way L25: Gate 6E **75**
Riverwood Rd. CH62: Brom 4F **105**
Riviera Dr. CH42: Rock F 2F **87**
L11: Crox 1G **37**
Rivington Av. CH43: Noct 5A **68**
WA10: St H 5C **28**

Rivington Rd. CH44: Wall 4F 51
  WA7: Pres B 4H 125
  WA10: St H 2B 42
Rivington St. WA10: St H 3B 42
Roadwater Cl. CH25: Gate 2D 74
Robarts Rd. L4: Walt 1H 53
ROBBINS BRIDGE 2D 6
Robbins Bri. L31: Lyd 2D 6
Robeck Rd. L13: Liv 6F 55
Robert Dr. CH49: Grea 6C 66
Robert Gro. L12: W Der 2A 56
Roberts Av. WA11: Hay 6C 30
Roberts Ct. WA7: Pal F 1B 124
Roberts Dr. L20: Boot 4E 21
Roberts St. L3: Liv 1A 4 (4B 52)
Robert St. CH41: Birke 2F 69
  WA7: Run 3G 113
  WA8: Wid 2F 97
Robina Rd. WA9: St H 5H 43
Robin Cl. WA7: Murd 6F 115
Robins La. WA9: St H 5G 43
Robinson Pl. WA9: St H 2H 43
Robinson Rd. L21: Lith 2C 20
Robin Way CH45: Woodc 1F 85
Robsart St. L5: Liv 2E 53
Robson St. L5: Liv 6B 36
  L13: Liv 6E 55
ROBY 5E 57
Roby Cl. L35: Rainh 3A 60
Roby Ct. L36: Roby 6F 57
Roby Gro. WA5: Gt San 3H 81
Roby Mt. Av. L36: Roby 5F 57
Roby Rd. L14: Broad G 6B 56
  L36: Roby 5C 56
             (not continuous)
Roby Station (Rail) 5E 57
Roby St. L15: Wav 2C 72
  L20: Boot 1C 34
  WA10: St H 4B 42
Rocastle Cl. L6: Liv 4G 53
Rochester Av. L30: N'ton 2F 21
Rochester Gdns. WA10: St H 4B 42
Rochester Rd. CH42: Rock F 1A 88
Rock Av. CH60: Hesw 4D 100
Rock Bank CH49: Upton 4E 67
Rockbank Rd. L13: Liv 2D 54
Rockbourne Av. L25: Woolt 4B 74
Rockbourne Grn. L25: Woolt 4B 74
Rockbourne Way L25: Woolt 4B 74
Rock Cl. CH42: Rock F 1H 87
Rock Ct. WA6: Frod 6F 123
Rock Dr. WA6: Frod 6G 123
Rocket Trad. Cen. L14: Broad G 6G 55
ROCK FERRY 2A 88
Rock Ferry By-Pass
  CH42: Rock F 6A 70
Rock Ferry Station (Rail) 1H 87
Rockfield Cl. WA8: Wid 1B 96
Rockfield Gdns. L31: Mag 5B 6
            (off East Meade)
Rockfield Rd. L4: Walt 6F 35
Rockford Av. L32: Kirkb 4A 24
Rockford Cl. L32: Kirkb 4A 24
Rockford Gdns. WA5: Gt San 1H 81
Rockford Wlk. L32: Kirkb 4A 24
Rock Gro. L13: Liv 4E 55
Rockhill Rd. L25: Woolt 1D 92
Rockhouse St. L6: Liv 2A 54
Rockingham Ct. L33: Kirkb 5B 14
Rockland Rd. CH45: Wall 6B 32
  L22: Water 1G 19
Rocklands, The CH43: Noct 3H 67
Rocklands Av. CH63: Beb 4A 88
Rocklands La. CH63: Thorn H 5E 103
Rock La. L31: Mell 3D 12
  WA8: Wid 5D 78
Rock La. E. CH42: Rock F 2A 88
            (not continuous)
Rock La. W. CH42: Rock F 2H 87
Rockley St. L4: Kirkd, Walt 5E 35
            (not continuous)
Rockmount Cl. L25: Woolt 6B 74
Rockmount Pk. L25: Woolt 6B 74

Rockmount Rd. L17: Aig 2D 90
Rock Pk. CH42: Rock F 1A 88
            (not continuous)
Rock Pk. Rd. CH42: Rock F 2B 88
Rockpoint Av. CH45: New B 6E 33
Rock Retail Pk. CH41: Birke 4G 69
ROCKSAVAGE 2G 123
Rocksavage Expressway
  WA7: Clftn 2H 123
Rocksavage Way WA7: Run 2E 123
Rockside Rd. L18: Moss H 2E 91
Rock St. L13: Liv 4E 55
  WA10: St H 5A 42
Rock Vw. L31: Mell 5E 13
Rockville Rd. L14: Broad G 6G 55
Rockville St. CH42: Rock F 1H 87
Rockwell Cl. L12: W Der 5H 37
Rockwell Rd. L12: W Der 5H 37
Rocky Bank Rd.
  CH42: Tran 6F 69
Rocky La. CH60: Hesw 5D 100
  L6: Liv .2A 54
  L16: Child 1G 73
Rocky La. Sth. CH60: Hesw 5E 101
Rococo Sq. CH45: New B 4E 33
Roderick Rd. L4: Walt 3G 35
Roderick St. L3: Liv 1H 5 (4E 52)
Rodgers Cl. WA6: Frod 6F 123
Rodick St. L25: Woolt 1B 92
Rodmell Rd. L9: Ain 5H 21
Rodney St. CH41: Birke 4F 69
  L1: Liv 6H 5 (1E 71)
  WA10: St H 2C 42
Roe All. L1: Liv 5F 5
Roeburn Way WA5: Penk 6F 81
Roedean Cl. L25: Woolt 2D 92
  L31: Mag 5C 6
Roehampton Dr. L23: Blun 3E 9
  WA7: Pal F 6A 114
Roemarsh Cl. L12: W Der 3F 37
Roemarsh Ct. WA7: Pal F 1A 124
Roe St. L1: Liv 4F 5 (6D 52)
Roften Works Ind. Est.
  CH66: Hoot 6D 120
Roger Arden Ct. L20: Boot 1D 34
Rogers Av. L20: Boot 6E 21
Rogersons Grn. L26: Halew 1G 93
Rokeby Cl. L3: Liv 4E 53
  L20: Boot 4E 21
Rokeby Ct. WA7: Manor P 6F 99
Rokeby St. L3: Liv 4E 53
Roker Av. CH44: Wall 4C 50
Rokesmith Av. L7: Liv 1A 72
Roklis Bldg. CH44: Wall 3F 51
            (off Liscard Rd.)
Roklis Ct. CH49: Upton 5E 67
            (off Rake La.)
Roland Av. CH63: Hghr B 5F 87
  WA7: Run 3D 112
Rolands Wlk. WA7: Cas 4B 114
Roleton Cl. L30: N'ton 5H 11
Rollesby Gdns. WA9: St H 1C 60
Rolleston Dr. CH45: Wall 6B 32
  CH63: Beb 1A 104
Rolling Mill La. WA9: St H 5B 44
Roman Cl. WA7: Cas 3A 114
Roman Rd. CH43: Pren 3C 86
  CH47: Meols 6D 46
  CH63: Store 3C 86
Roman Way L33: Kirkb 6C 14
Rome Cl. L36: Huy 4F 57
Romer Rd. L6: Liv 4A 54
Romford Way L26: Halew 5H 93
            (not continuous)
Romilly St. L6: Liv 4H 53
Romley St. L4: Walt 4F 35
Romney Cl. WA8: Wid 1A 98
Romulus St. L7: Liv 5B 54
Ronald Cl. L22: Water 2H 19
Ronald Rd. L22: Water 2H 19
Ronald Ross Av. L30: N'ton 6F 11
Ronald St. L13: Liv 4D 54

Ronaldsway CH49: Upton 3D 66
  CH60: Hesw 1D 116
  L10: Faz 4E 23
  L23: Thorn 3A 10
  L26: Halew 3A 94
Ronan Cl. L20: Boot 1A 34
Ronan Rd. WA8: Wid 6C 96
            (not continuous)
Rone Cl. CH46: More 1B 66
Rookery Dr. L19: Aig 3D 90
  WA11: Rainf 3G 17
Rookery La. WA11: Rainf 4G 17
Rookley Cl. L27: N'ley 5H 75
Rooks Way CH60: Hesw 5C 100
Rooseyelt Dr. L9: Ain 3H 21
Roper's Bri. Cl. L35: Whis 5D 58
Ropers Ct. L34: Presc 2D 58
Roper St. L8: Liv 4F 71
  WA9: St H 1G 43
Ropewalk, The CH64: Park 6G 117
Ropewalks Sq. L1: Liv 6G 5
Ropeworks Cl. L20: Boot 6D 20
Rosalind Av. CH63: Hghr B 4G 87
Rosalind Way L20: Kirkd 4D 34
Rosam Ct. WA7: Pal F 1A 124
Roscoe & Gladstone Hall L17: Aig . . .5C 72
Roscoe Cl. L35: Tar G 2A 76
Roscoe Cres. WA7: West P 6C 112
Roscoe La. L1: Liv 6G 5
Roscoe Pl. L1: Liv 6G 5 (1E 71)
Roscoe St. L1: Liv 6H 5 (1E 71)
  WA10: St H 2B 42
Roscommon St. L5: Liv 3E 53
Roscommon Way WA8: Wid 6C 78
Roscote, The CH60: Hesw 6D 100
Roscote Cl. CH60: Hesw 6D 100
Roseacre CH48: W Kir 6A 64
Roseate Ct. CH45: Wall 5A 32
Rose Av. L20: Boot 4C 20
  WA9: St H 6G 43
  WA11: Hay 5G 31
Rose Bailey Cl. L11: Norr G 1F 37
Rose Bank Rd. L16: Child 2H 73
Rosebank Rd. L36: Huy 2E 57
Rosebank Way L36: Huy 2E 57
Rosebery Av. CH44: Wall 3E 51
  L22: Water 1E 19
Rosebery Gro. CH42: Tran 1D 86
Rosebery Rd. WA10: St H 6B 28
Rosebery St. L8: Liv 2G 71
Rosebourne Cl. L17: Aig 1A 90
Rose Brae L18: Moss H 5F 73
Rosebrae Ct. CH41: Birke 2H 69
  CH60: Hesw 4E 101
Rosebrae Wlk. CH41: Birke 2A 70
Rosebrow St. L25: Woolt 5C 74
Rose Cl. L26: Halew 4A 94
  WA7: Murd 2F 125
Rose Ct. CH41: Birke 3F 69
  L15: Wav 2C 72
Rose Cres. WA8: Wid 4D 96
Rosecroft CH62: Brom 1C 120
Rosecroft Cl. CH47: Hoy 3A 64
Rosedale Av. L23: Crosb 5G 9
Rosedale Cl. L9: Walt 1H 35
Rosedale Rd. CH42: Tran 6G 69
  L18: Moss H 5F 73
Rose Dr. WA11: Rainf 4G 17
Rosefield Av. CH63: Hghr B 4G 87
Rosefield Rd. L25: Woolt 2E 93
Rosegarth Grn. L13: Liv 3F 55
          (off Black Horse La.)
Roseheath Dr. L26: Halew 4H 93
Rose Hill L3: Liv 4D 52
Rosehill Av. WA9: Bold 2D 62
Rosehill Ct. L25: Woolt 5C 74
Roseland Cl. L31: Lyd 3A 6
Roselands Ct. CH42: Rock F 2G 87
Rose La. L18: Moss H 6D 72
Rose Lea Cl. WA8: Wid 5E 79
Roselee Cl. CH42: Rock F 2A 88
Rosemary Av. WA7: Beech 3B 124

Rosemary Cl. CH43: Bid 1A 68
  L7: Liv 1G 71
Rosemead Av. CH61: Pens 1D 100
Rosemoor Rd. L17: Aig 1D 90
Rosemoor Dr. L23: Crosb 4A 10
Rosemoor Gdns. L11: Norr G 3E 37
Rose Mt. CH43: Oxton 6D 68
Rosemount Cl. CH43: Oxton 6C 68
Rose Mt. Dr. CH45: Wall 1C 50
Rosemount Pk. CH43: Oxton 5C 68
Rose Pl. CH42: Tran 5F 69
  L3: Liv 4D 52
      (not continuous)
  WA11: Rainf 4G 17
Roseside Dr. L27: N'ley 3H 75
Rose St. L1: Liv 3F 5 (6D 52)
  L25: Woolt 1B 92
  WA8: Wid 4D 96
Rose Ter. L18: Moss H 5E 73
Rose Va. L5: Liv 3E 53
      (not continuous)
Rose Vw. Av. WA8: Wid 1E 97
Rose Vs. L15: Wav 2D 72
Rosewarne Cl. L17: Aig 1H 89
Rosewood Cl. L27: N'ley 4G 75
  L28: Stockb V 6D 38
Rosewood Dr. CH46: More 1H 65
Rosewood Farm Ct. WA8: Wid ...5C 78
Rosewood Gdns. L11: Norr G 4F 37
Rosewood Gro. WA8: Wid 3H 95
Roseworth Av. L9: Walt 4G 21
Roskell Rd. L25: Hunts X 4E 93
Roslin Ct. CH43: Oxton 5D 68
Roslin Rd. CH43: Oxton 5D 68
  CH61: Irby 5B 84
Roslyn St. CH41: Tran 6H 69
  CH42: Tran 6H 69
Rossall Av. L10: Ain 6B 12
Rossall Cl. L24: Hale 3E 111
Rossall Ct. CH46: Leas 5D 48
Rossall Rd. CH46: More 6D 48
  L13: Liv 5F 55
  WA8: Wid 1H 97
Ross Av. CH46: Leas 3G 49
Ross Cl. L34: Know 2F 39
Rosscourt Vw. CH42: Rock F ...1B 88
Rossendale Cl. CH43: Noct 5H 67
Rossett Av. L17: Liv 3C 72
Rossett Rd. L23: Crosb 6E 9
Rossett St. L6: Liv 2A 54
Rossington Gdns. WA9: St H 2D 60
Rossini St. L21: Sea 5A 20
Rossiter Dr. CH43: Bid 3G 67
Rosslyn Av. L31: Mag 1H 11
Rosslyn Cres. CH46: More 1C 66
Rosslyn Dr. CH46: More 1C 66
Rosslyn Pk. CH46: More 2C 66
Rosslyn St. L17: Aig 6H 71
Rossmore Gdns. L4: Walt 5A 36
Ross St. WA8: Wid 2F 97
Rostherne Av. CH44: Wall 4C 50
Rostherne Cres. WA8: Wid 1B 96
Rosthwaite Dr. WA11: St H 2F 29
Rosthwaite Rd. L12: W Der 1G 55
Roswell Ct. L28: Stockb V 1D 56
Rothay Dr. WA5: Penk 6F 81
Rothbury Cl. CH46: More 1A 66
  WA7: Beech 1A 124
Rothbury Ct. WA9: Sut M 5F 61
Rothbury Rd. L14: Knott A 1B 56
Rotherham Cl. L36: Huy 3H 57
Rotherwood Cl. CH43: Noct 4H 67
Rotherwood Cl. CH63: Hghr B ...5F 87
Rothesay Cl. WA7: Cas 3B 114
  WA11: St H 4A 30
Rothesay Ct. CH63: Beb 1H 103
Rothesay Dr. CH62: East 3E 121
  L23: Crosb 6G 9
Rothesay Gdns. CH43: Pren 2B 86
Rothsay Cl. L5: Liv 3F 53
Rothwells La. L23: Thorn 3B 10
Rothwell St. L6: Liv 3G 53
Rotunda St. L5: Liv 2D 52

Roughdale Av. L32: Kirkb 4B 24
  WA9: Sut M 3F 61
Roughdale Cl. L32: Kirkb 4B 24
Roughley Ho. CH41: Birke 2H 69
      (off Bridge St.)
Roughsedge Ho. L28: Stockb V ..5D 38
Roughwood Dr. L33: Kirkb 6B 14
Roundabout, The WA8: Cron 3B 78
Round Hey L28: Stockb V 5C 38
Round Meade, The L31: Mag 5A 6
Roundwood Dr. WA9: St H 4F 43
Routledge St. WA8: Wid 2F 97
Row, The CH47: Hoy 2B 64
Rowan Av. L12: W Der 4B 38
Rowan Cl. WA5: Gt San 3H 81
  WA7: Run 6G 113
  WA11: Hay 6B 30
  WA11: St H 4H 29
Rowan Ct. CH49: Grea 1H 83
  CH63: Hghr B 5F 87
Rowan Dr. L32: Kirkb 6G 13
Rowan Gro. CH63: Hghr B 1G 103
  L36: Huy 1F 75
Rowans, The L39: Augh 1F 7
  WA8: Wid 4B 78
     (off Hampton Ct. Way)
Rowan Tree Cl. CH49: Grea 6H 65
Rowena Cl. L23: Crosb 5H 9
Rowen Ct. L17: Aig 1C 90
Rowlings Way L32: Kirkb 3B 24
     (off Park Brow Dr.)
Rowsley Gro. L9: Ain 4H 21
Rowson Ct. CH45: New B 5D 32
     (off Pickering Rd.)
Rowson St. CH45: New B 4D 32
  L34: Presc 6D 40
Rowthorn Cl. WA8: Wid 3C 96
Roxborough Cl. WA5: Burtw 1H 63
Roxborough Wlk. L25: Woolt ...6E 75
Roxburgh Av. CH42: Tran 1F 87
  L17: Aig 6A 72
Roxburgh St. L4: Kirkd 3E 35
  L20: Boot 3E 35
Royal, The CH47: Hoy 3A 64
Royal Av. WA8: Wid 3H 95
Royal Cl. CH42: Rock F 2A 88
     (off Rock La. W.)
Royal Court Theatre 3F 5 (6D 52)
Royal Cft. L12: W Der 3F 55
Royal Gro. WA10: St H 4B 42
Royal Liverpool Golf Course 4A 64
Royal Liverpool Philharmonic Hall
..................6H 5 (1F 71)
Royal Mail St. L3: Liv 4G 5 (6E 53)
Royal Mersey Yacht Club 1A 88
Royal Pl. WA8: Wid 3H 95
Royal Quay L3: Liv 1C 70
Royal Standard Way CH42: Tran ..6H 69
Royal St. L4: Walt 6E 35
Royden Av. CH44: Wall 2F 51
  WA7: Run 5D 112
Royden Rd. CH49: Upton 3C 66
Royden Way L3: Liv 6E 71
Roysten Gdns. WA9: St H 3H 43
Royston St. L7: Liv 6H 53
Royton Cl. L26: Halew 5H 93
Royton Rd. L22: Water 1H 19
Rubbing Stone CH48: Caldy 5D 82
Ruby Cl. L21: Lith 3C 20
Ruby St. L8: Liv 6F 71
      (not continuous)
Rudd Av. WA9: St H 3D 44
Rudd St. CH47: Hoy 2B 64
Rudgate L35: Whis 5E 59
Rudgrave M. CH44: Wall 2F 51
Rudgrave Pl. CH44: Wall 2F 51
Rudgrave Sq. CH44: Wall 2F 51
Rudheath La. WA7: Nort 2F 115
Rudley Wlk. L24: Speke 3H 109
Rudston Rd. L16: Child 1G 73
Rudyard Cl. L14: Knott A 4G 55
Rudyard Rd. L14: Knott A 4G 55
Rufford Av. L31: Mag 4D 6

Rufford Cl. L10: Faz 2D 22
  L35: Presc 2F 59
  WA8: Wid 1A 96
Rufford Rd. CH44: Wall 4E 51
  L6: Liv 4A 54
  L20: Boot 6C 20
  WA11: Rainf 2F 17
Rufford Wlk. WA11: St H 5A 30
Rugby Dr. L10: Ain 2C 22
Rugby Rd. CH44: Wall 2B 50
  L9: Ain 3H 21
Ruislip Cl. L25: Woolt 1E 93
Rullerton Rd. CH44: Wall 3C 50
Rumford Pl.
  L3: Liv 3B 4 (5C 52)
Rumford St. L2: Liv 3C 4 (5C 52)
Rumney Pl. L4: Kirkd 5E 35
      (not continuous)
Rumney Rd. L4: Kirkd 5E 35
Rumney Rd. W. L4: Kirkd 5D 34
RUNCORN 2E 113
Runcorn WA7: Run 3C 112
Runcorn East Station (Rail) 6F 115
Runcorn Golf Course 6E 113
Runcorn Hill Local Nature Reserve
..............................5D 112
Runcorn Hill Vis. Cen. 5D 112
Runcorn Linnets FC 2E 125
Runcorn Rd.
  WA4: Dares, Moore 1H 115
Runcorn Ski & Snowboard Cen. ..6D 114
Runcorn Spur Rd. WA7: Run 3F 113
Runcorn Station (Rail) 3D 112
Runcorn Swimming Pool 2F 113
Rundle Rd. L17: Aig 1C 90
Rundle St. CH41: Birke 1C 68
Runic St. L13: Liv 5D 54
Runnell, The CH64: Nest 4H 117
Runnell's La. L23: Thorn 4C 10
Runnymede L36: Huy 3F 57
Runnymede Cl. L25: Woolt 5C 74
Runnymede Ct. WA8: Wid 2G 97
     (off William St.)
Runnymede Dr. WA11: Hay 5C 30
Runnymede Gdns. WA8: Wid 2G 97
      (off Cliffe St.)
Runnymede Wlk. WA8: Wid 1G 97
     (off William St.)
Runton Rd. L25: Gate 4E 75
Rupert Dr. L6: Liv 3G 53
Rupert Rd. L36: Huy 4E 57
Rupert Row WA7: Cas 5C 114
Ruscar Cl. L26: Halew 1G 93
Ruscolm Cl. WA5: Gt San 2F 81
Ruscombe Rd. L14: Knott A 2B 56
Rushbury Cl. L15: Wav 1D 72
Rushden Rd. L32: Kirkb 2C 24
Rushey Hey Rd. L32: Kirkb 1A 24
Rushfield Cres. WA7: Brook ...2D 124
Rushgreen Cl. CH43: Bid 2G 67
Rushlake Dr. L27: N'ley 4F 75
Rushmere Rd. L11: Norr G 4E 37
Rushmore Dr. WA8: Wid 6D 78
Rusholme Cl. L26: Halew 5A 94
Rushton Cl. WA5: Burtw 6H 45
  WA8: Wid 6D 78
Rushton Pl. L25: Woolt 1C 92
Rushton's Wlk. L30: N'ton 4D 10
Rushy Vw. WA12: Newt W 1H 45
Ruskin Av. CH42: Rock F 2H 87
  CH44: Wall 4C 50
Ruskin Cl. L20: Boot 2C 34
Ruskin Dr. WA10: St H 1B 42
Ruskin St. L4: Kirkd 4E 35
Ruskin Way CH43: Noct 6H 67
  L36: Huy 6F 57
Rusland Av. CH61: Pens 1D 100
Rusland Rd. L32: Kirkb 3B 24
Russell Ct. WA8: Wid 5F 79
Russell Pl. L19: Garst 5G 91
Russell Rd. CH42: Rock F 6H 69
      (not continuous)
  CH44: Wall 2A 50
  L18: Moss H 4D 72

Russell Rd. L19: Garst 5G **91**
  L36: Huy 5B **58**
  WA7: Run 4C **112**
Russell St. CH41: Birke 2G **69**
  L3: Liv 3H **5** (6E **53**)
Russet Cl. L27: N'ley 4G **75**
  WA10: St H 6D **28**
Russian Av. L13: Liv 2D **54**
Russian Dr. L13: Liv 2D **54**
Rutherford Cl. L13: Wav 6C **54**
Rutherford Rd. L18: Moss H 3F **73**
  L31: Mag 2C **12**
  WA10: Windle 5A **28**
Rutherglen Av. L23: Crosb 1H **19**
Ruth Evans Ct. L35: Rainh 3G **59**
Ruthin Cl. WA7: Cas 3C **114**
Ruthven Ct. L21: Lith 4A **20**
Ruthven Rd. L13: Liv 6F **55**
  L21: Lith 4A **20**
Rutland Av. L17: Liv 3B **72**
  L26: Halew 3H **93**
Rutland Cl. L5: Liv 2G **53**
Rutland Ho. L17: Aig 4B **72**
  L23: Blun 6D **8**
Rutland St. L20: Boot 1D **34**
  WA7: Run 3D **112**
  WA10: St H 6D **28**
Rutland Way L36: Huy 4B **58**
Rutter St. L8: Liv 4E **71**
Rycot Rd. L24: Speke 1D **108**
Rycroft Rd. CH44: Wall 4E **51**
  CH47: Meols 1E **65**
  L10: Faz 3C **22**
Rydal Av. CH43: Noct 4G **67**
  L23: Crosb 1H **19**
  L34: Presc 1F **59**
Rydal Bank CH44: Wall 3E **51**
  CH63: Beb 4A **88**
Rydal Cl. CH61: Pens 1D **100**
  L10: Ain 1D **22**
  L33: Kirkb 5H **13**
Rydal Gro. WA7: Run 5F **113**
  WA11: St H 4E **29**
Rydal Rd. L36: Huy 6G **57**
Rydal St. L5: Liv 1G **53**
Rydal Way WA8: Wid 2A **96**
Rydecroft L25: Woolt 1B **92**
Ryder Cl. L35: Rainh 3G **59**
Ryder Ct. L35: Rainh 1H **59**
Ryder Rd. WA8: Wid 5F **79**
Rye Cl. WA9: Clock F 3G **61**
Ryecote L32: Kirkb 4A **24**
Ryecroft L21: Ford 6B **10**
Ryecroft Rd. CH60: Hesw 6G **101**
Ryedale Cl. L8: Liv 2H **71**
Ryefield La. L21: Ford 6B **10**
Ryegate Rd. L19: Gras 3F **91**
Rye Gro. L12: W Der 1A **56**
Rye Hey Rd. L32: Kirkb 1A **24**
Ryland Pk. CH61: Thing 6E **85**
Rylands Hey CH49: Grea 5B **66**
Rylands St. WA8: Wid 3F **97**
Ryleys Gdns. L2: Liv 3D **4**
Rymer Gro. L4: Walt 4G **35**

S

Sabre Cl. WA7: Murd 6F **115**
Sackville Rd. WA10: Windle 5A **28**
Saddle Cl. L9: Ain 3B **22**
Saddlers Ri. WA7: Nort 5E **115**
Saddlestone Gro. L8: Liv 4E **71**
Sadler's La. WA11: Windle 4E **27**
Sadler St. WA8: Wid 2G **97**
Saffron Gdns. WA9: St H 3H **43**
Saffron M. L23: Thorn 3B **10**
Sage Dr. L11: Norr G 4E **37**
St Agnes Rd. L4: Kirkd 5D **34**
  L36: Huy 5G **57**
St Aidans Ct. CH43: Clau 3B **68**
  WA9: Clock F 4A **62**
St Aidans Dr. WA8: Wid 3D **78**
St Aidan's Gro. L36: Huy 6E **39**

St Aidan's Ter. CH43: Clau 3B **68**
St Aidan's Way L30: N'ton 6D **10**
St Alban Rd. WA5: Penk 4G **81**
St Albans L6: Liv 2H **53**
St Albans Cl. WA11: Hay 4H **31**
St Albans Ct. L5: Liv 2C **52**
St Albans Rd. CH43: Clau 2C **68**
  CH44: Wall 3D **50**
  L20: Boot 2C **34**
St Alban's Sq. L20: Boot 3C **34**
St Alexander Cl. L20: Kirkd 4D **34**
St Ambrose Cft. L30: N'ton 5E **11**
St Ambrose Gro. L4: Walt 1H **53**
St Ambrose Rd. WA8: Wid 2G **97**
St Ambrose Way L5: Liv 3E **53**
        (off Everton Brow)
St Andrew Rd. L4: Walt 1H **53**
St Andrews Av. L12: W Der 1A **56**
St Andrews Ct. CH43: Noct 3H **67**
  L22: Water 3G **19**
St Andrews Dr. L23: Blun 3E **9**
  L36: Huy 6E **39**
St Andrews Gdns. L3: Liv 3H **5**
St Andrews Gro. L30: N'ton 6C **10**
  WA11: St H 5F **29**
St Andrews Pl. L17: Aig 6A **72**
        (off Normanton Av.)
St Andrews Rd. CH43: Oxton 3D **68**
  CH63: Beb 1A **104**
  L20: Boot 5C **20**
  L23: Blun 3D **8**
St Andrew St. L3: Liv 4H **5** (6F **53**)
St Andrews Vw. L33: Kirkb 3A **14**
St Annes Cl. CH41: Birke 2F **69**
St Anne's Cotts. L14: Knott A 4G **55**
        (off Rudyard Cl.)
St Annes Ct. L3: Liv 4E **53**
        (off St Anne St.)
  L13: Liv 4D **54**
  L17: Aig 2C **90**
St Annes Gdns. L17: Aig 2D **90**
St Annes Gro. CH41: Birke 1E **69**
  L17: Aig 2C **90**
St Anne's Ho. L20: Boot 3D **34**
        (off University Rd.)
St Anne's Pl. CH41: Birke 1E **69**
St Annes Rd. L17: Aig 2D **90**
  L36: Huy 6G **57**
  WA8: Wid 1F **97**
St Annes Ter. CH41: Birke 1E **69**
St Anne St. CH41: Birke 2E **69**
        (Livingstone Gdns.)
  CH41: Birke 2F **69**
        (Robert St.)
  CH41: Birke 1E **69**
        (St Anne's Pl.)
  L3: Liv 1G **5** (3E **53**)
St Annes Way CH41: Birke 2F **69**
St Ann Pl. L35: Rainh 3A **60**
ST ANNS .3B **42**
St Ann's Rd. WA10: St H 2A **42**
St Anthony's Cl. L36: Huy 6E **39**
St Anthony's Gro. L30: N'ton 6D **10**
St Anthony's Rd. L23: Blun 4D **8**
St Anthony's Shop. Cen. L5: Liv 2E **53**
St Asaph Gro. L30: N'ton 2F **21**
St Augustine St. L5: Liv 2D **52**
St Augustine's Way L30: N'ton 5D **10**
St Austell Cl. CH46: More 6H **47**
  WA5: Penk 6G **81**
  WA7: Brook 1D **124**
St Austells Rd. L4: Walt 3E **35**
St Bartholomew Rd. L3: Liv . .1E **5** (4D **52**)
St Bartholomews Ct. L36: Huy 5E **57**
St Bedes Vw. WA8: Wid 2E **97**
St Benedict's Gro. L36: Huy 6E **39**
St Benet's Way L30: N'ton 6E **11**
St Bernards Cl. L8: Liv 2H **71**
  L30: N'ton 6D **10**
St Bernard's Dr. L30: N'ton 6D **10**
St Brendan's Cl. L36: Huy 6E **39**
St Brides Cl. WA5: Penk 6G **81**
St Bride's Rd. CH44: Wall 2F **51**
St Bride St. L8: Liv 1F **71**

St Bridgets Cl. WA8: Wid 6E **97**
St Bridget's Gro. L30: N'ton 6D **10**
St Bridget's La. CH48: W Kir 2B **82**
St Brigid's Cres. L5: Liv 2C **52**
        (off Silvester St.)
St Catherine's Cl. L36: Huy 6G **57**
St Catherines Gdns. CH42: Tran 5F **69**
St Catherine's Rd. L20: Boot 2C **34**
St Chad's Dr. L32: Kirkb 1A **24**
St Chads Pde. L32: Kirkb 1A **24**
St Christopher Dr. L36: Huy 6E **39**
St Christopher's Av. L30: N'ton 5D **10**
St Columba's Cl. CH44: Wall 2F **51**
St Cuthberts Cl. L12: Crox 2A **38**
St Cyrils Cl. L27: N'ley 3E **75**
St Cyril's Ct. L27: N'ley 3E **75**
St Damian's Cft. L30: N'ton 6E **11**
St David Rd. CH43: Clau 3C **68**
  CH62: East 1G **121**
St David's Cl. L35: Rainh 3A **60**
St David's Gro. L30: N'ton 1D **20**
St Davids La. CH43: Noct 4H **67**
St Davids Rd. L4: Walt 1H **53**
  L14: Knott A 2D **56**
St Domingo Gro. L5: Liv 1G **53**
St Domingo Rd. L5: Liv 6E **35**
St Domingo Va. L5: Liv 1F **53**
St Dunstan's Gro. L30: N'ton 6D **10**
St Edmond's Rd. L20: Boot 3C **34**
St Edmund's Rd. CH63: Beb 6H **87**
St Edwards Cl. CH41: Birke 1D **68**
St Edwards M. CH41: Birke 1D **68**
        (off Old Bidston Rd.)
St Elmo Rd. CH44: Wall 2F **51**
St Gabriel's Av. L36: Huy 5A **58**
St George's Av. CH42: Tran 1F **87**
  WA10: Windle 6A **28**
St Georges Ct. L31: Mag 1B **12**
  WA8: Wid 3B **96**
St George's Gro. CH46: More 1B **66**
  L30: N'ton 1D **20**
St George's Hall 3F **5** (5D **52**)
St George's Hill L5: Liv 2F **53**
St George's Mt. CH45: New B 5D **32**
St George's Pk. CH45: New B 5D **32**
St George's Pl. L1: Liv 3F **5** (5D **52**)
St Georges Rd. CH45: Wall 1A **50**
  L36: Huy 2G **57**
  WA10: St H 3B **42**
St George's Way CH63: Thorn H 1C **118**
  L1: Liv 4F **5**
St Gerard Cl. L5: Liv 1D **52**
St Gregory's Cft. L30: N'ton 5E **11**
ST HELENS 2E **43**
St Helens Central Station (Rail) 2F **43**
St Helens Cl. CH43: Clau 3D **68**
St Helens Crematorium
  WA10: Windle 4A **28**
St Helens Junction Station (Rail) 6B **44**
St Helens Linkway L35: Rainh 6D **60**
  WA9: St H 3E **43**
St Helens Retail Pk. WA9: St H 2F **43**
St Helens RLFC 3F **43**
St Helens Rd. L34: Presc, Eccl P 6D **40**
  WA11: Rainf 1H **27**
St Helens Theatre Royal 2E **43**
St Hilary Brow CH44: Wall 3B **50**
St Hilary Dr. CH45: Wall 2B **50**
St Hilda's Dr. WA6: Frod 6G **123**
St Hilda St. L4: Walt 5E **35**
St Hugh's Cl. CH43: Clau 3D **68**
St Hugh's Ho. L20: Boot 3C **34**
St Ives Cl. CH43: Clau 2C **68**
St Ives Gro. L13: Liv 4D **54**
St Ives Rd. CH43: Clau 3C **68**
St Ives Way L26: Halew 3H **93**
St James Cen. CH41: Birke 1B **68**
        (off Laird St.)
St James Cl. CH49: Grea 5B **66**
  L12: W Der 1E **55**
  WA6: Frod 6G **123**
St James Ct. CH45: New B 5D **32**
        (off Victoria Rd.)
St James Dr. L20: Boot 1B **34**

St James M. L20: Boot 1B **34**
St James Mt. L35: Rainh 5A **60**
St James Pl. L8: Liv 2E **71**
St James Rd. CH41: Birke 1B **68**
  CH45: New B 5D **32**
  L1: Liv .2E **71**
  L34: Eccl P, Presc 6E **41**
  L35: Rainh 5A **60**
  L36: Huy 6G **57**
St James St. L1: Liv 2D **70**
St James Way L30: N'ton 5D **10**
           (off St Nicholas' Dr.)
St Jerome's Way L30: N'ton 5E **11**
St Johns Av. L9: Walt 6G **21**
St Johns Brow WA7: Run 2F **113**
St John's Cen. L1: Liv 4F **5** (6D **52**)
St John's Cl. CH47: Meols 1D **64**
St John's Ct. L22: Water 2F **19**
St John's Ho. L20: Boot 2D **34**
St John's La. L1: Liv 3F **5** (5D **52**)
St John's Pavement CH41: Birke 3F **69**
St John's Pl. L22: Water 2F **19**
St John's Rd. CH45: Wall 2A **50**
  CH62: East 2G **121**
  L20: Boot 3B **34**
  L22: Water 2F **19**
  L36: Huy 6H **57**
St John's Sq. CH41: Birke 3F **69**
  L1: Liv 4F **5**
St John's Ter. L20: Boot 4B **34**
            (off St John's Rd.)
St John St. CH41: Birke 3F **69**
  WA7: Run 2F **113**
  WA10: St H 5B **42**
  WA12: Newt W 2H **45**
St Johns Vs. WA8: Wid 1B **96**
St John's Way L1: Liv 4F **5**
St Josephs Cl. L36: Huy 6E **39**
  WA5: Penk 4G **81**
  WA9: St H 4G **43**
            (off Cleveland St.)
St Josephs Cres. L3: Liv 1G **5** (4E **53**)
St Jude's Cl. L36: Huy 6E **39**
St Kevin's Dr. L32: Kirkb 5A **14**
St Kilda's Rd. CH46: More 2C **66**
St Laurence Cl. CH41: Birke 2F **69**
St Laurence Ct. CH41: Birke 2F **69**
St Laurence Gro. L32: Kirkb 3B **24**
St Lawrence Cl. L8: Liv 5G **71**
St Leonard's Cl. L30: N'ton 5D **10**
St Lucia Rd. CH44: Wall 2F **51**
St Lukes Cl. L14: Knott A 1B **56**
St Luke's Cl. L4: Walt 3G **35**
St Luke's Cres. WA8: Wid 5F **79**
St Luke's Gro. L30: N'ton 5D **10**
            (off Dartmouth Dr.)
St Lukes Pl. L1: Liv 6G **5** (1E **71**)
St Luke's Rd. L23: Crosb 5F **9**
  WA10: St H 2B **42**
St Luke's Way L36: Huy 6E **39**
  WA6: Frod 6F **123**
St Margaret's Gro. L30: N'ton 1C **20**
St Margaret's Rd. CH47: Hoy 3A **64**
St Marks Ct. CH43: Oxton 4D **68**
St Mark's Gro. L30: N'ton 5C **10**
St Mark's Rd. L36: Huy 6H **57**
St Mark's St. WA11: Hay 5C **30**
St Martins Gro. L32: Kirkb 4B **24**
St Martin's Ho. L20: Boot 2C **34**
St Martin's La. WA7: Murd 6F **115**
St Martins M. L5: Liv 3E **53**
St Mary's Arc. WA10: St H 2E **43**
       (within St Mary's Mkt.)
St Mary's Av. CH44: Wall 3D **50**
  L4: Walt .3G **35**
St Mary's Cl. L13: Liv 6D **54**
  L20: Boot 2B **34**
  L24: Hale 3D **110**
St Marys Ct. CH49: Upton 5E **67**
  L25: Woolt 1C **92**
St Mary's Ga. CH41: Birke 3H **69**
St Mary's Gro. L4: Walt 3G **35**
  L30: N'ton 6C **10**
St Mary's La. L4: Walt 3G **35**

St Mary's Mkt. WA10: St H 2E **43**
St Mary's Pl. L4: Walt 3G **35**
St Marys Rd. L19: Garst, Gras 4F **91**
  L22: Water 2H **19**
  L36: Huy 5G **57**
  WA5: Gt San, Penk 4H **81**
  WA7: Halt 4B **114**
  WA8: Wid 1E **113**
St Mary's St. CH44: Wall 3D **50**
  L25: Woolt 1C **92**
St Mary's Tower 3H **69**
St Mathews Cl. L4: Walt 3B **36**
  L36: Huy 4H **57**
St Matthew's Av. L21: Lith 3C **20**
St Matthews Gro. WA10: St H 5A **42**
St Mawes Cl. WA8: Wid 1C **96**
St Mawes Way WA10: Windle 5H **27**
St Michael Rd. L39: Augh 1E **7**
St Michael's Chu. Rd. L17: Aig 6H **71**
St Michaels Cl. L17: Aig 1A **90**
  WA8: Wid 4A **96**
St Michaels Ct. L36: Huy 4G **57**
St Michael's Golf Course 4C **96**
St Michaels Gro. CH46: More 1B **66**
  L6: Liv 3H **53**
  L30: N'ton 6C **10**
St Michael's Hall L17: Aig 1H **89**
ST MICHAEL'S HAMLET 1H **89**
St Michael's Ind. Est. WA8: Wid 4A **96**
St Michaels Pk. CH62: Port S 5B **88**
St Michaels Rd. L17: Aig 1H **89**
  L23: Blun, Crosb 4D **8**
  WA8: Wid 4A **96**
  WA9: St H 4E **61**
St Michael's Station (Rail) 1H **89**
St Michael's Vw. WA8: Wid 4B **96**
St Monica's Dr. L30: N'ton 5D **10**
St Nicholas' Dr. L30: N'ton 5D **10**
St Nicholas Gro. WA9: St H 6H **43**
St Nicholas Pl. L3: Liv 4A **4** (6B **52**)
            (not continuous)
St Nicholas Rd. CH45: Wall 2H **49**
  L35: Whis 6D **58**
St Oswald's Av. CH43: Bid 6G **49**
St Oswald's Ct. L30: N'ton 6F **11**
St Oswald's La. L30: N'ton 6F **11**
St Oswald's M. CH43: Bid 6G **49**
St Oswald's St. L13: Liv 5E **55**
St Paschal Baylon Blvd. L16: Child . . .1B **74**
St Patricks Cl. L33: Kirkb 4A **14**
  WA8: Wid 6E **97**
St Patrick's Dr. L30: N'ton 5D **10**
St Paul's Av. CH44: Wall 5G **51**
St Pauls Ct. CH42: Rock F 1G **87**
  L33: Kirkb 4H **13**
St Pauls Pl. L20: Boot 3D **34**
St Paul's Rd. CH42: Rock F 1H **87**
  CH44: Wall 5F **51**
  WA8: Wid 4E **97**
St Paul's Sq. L3: Liv 2B **4** (5B **52**)
            (not continuous)
St Paul St. WA10: St H 2C **42**
St Paul's Vs. CH42: Rock F 1H **87**
St Peters Cl. CH60: Hesw 6D **100**
  L33: Kirkb 4H **13**
St Peter's Ct. CH42: Rock F 2A **88**
  L17: Aig .5H **71**
St Peter's Ho. L20: Boot 3D **34**
St Peter's M. CH42: Rock F 2B **88**
St Peter's Rd. CH42: Rock F 2A **88**
  L9: Ain 4A **22**
St Peters Row L31: Mag 3B **12**
St Peter's Sq. L1: Liv 6G **5**
St Peter's Way CH43: Noct 5G **67**
St Philip's Av. L21: Lith 3C **20**
St Richards Cl. L20: Kirkd 4D **34**
Saints Cl. L13: Liv 5F **55**
St Seiriol Gro. CH43: Clau 3C **68**
St Stephen Rd.
  WA5: Gt San, Penk 4H **81**
St Stephens Cl. CH60: Hesw 1G **117**
  L25: Gate 4E **75**
St Stephen's Ct. CH42: Tran 2D **86**
St Stephen's Gro. L30: N'ton 6D **10**

St Stephen's Pl. L3: Liv 1E **5** (4D **52**)
St Stephen's Rd. CH42: Tran 1D **86**
St Teresa's Cl. L11: Norr G 3D **36**
St Teresa's Rd. WA10: St H 1B **42**
St Thomas Cl. WA8: Wid 2B **96**
St Thomas Ct. WA8: Wid 5B **28**
St Thomas's Dr. L30: N'ton 6D **10**
St Vincent Rd. CH43: Clau 3C **68**
  CH44: Wall 2F **51**
  WA5: Penk 4H **81**
St Vincents Cl. L12: W Der 1A **56**
St Vincent St. L3: Liv 3H **5** (5E **53**)
St Vincent Way L3: Liv 3H **5**
St Werburgh's Sq. CH41: Birke 3G **69**
St Wilfreds Rd. WA8: Wid 5A **80**
St William Rd. L23: Thorn 4B **10**
St William Way L23: Thorn 3B **10**
St Winifred Rd.
  CH45: New B 6D **32**
  L35: Rainh 2H **59**
Saker St. L4: Walt 6F **35**
Salacre Cl. CH49: Upton 5F **67**
Salacre Cres. CH49: Upton 5E **67**
Salacre La. CH49: Upton 4E **67**
Salacre Ter. CH49: Upton 4E **67**
            (off Salacre La.)
Salcombe Dr. L25: Hunts X 4D **92**
Salem Vw. CH43: Oxton 6D **68**
Salerno Dr. L36: Huy 3F **57**
Saleswood Av. WA10: Eccl 2G **41**
Salhouse Gdns. WA9: St H 1B **60**
Saline Cl. L14: Knott A 1C **56**
Salisbury Av. CH48: W Kir 1A **82**
  L30: N'ton 2G **21**
Salisbury Ct. CH42: Rock F 2G **87**
Salisbury Dr. CH62: New F 4B **88**
Salisbury Hall L18: Moss H 1D **90**
Salisbury Ho. L20: Boot 1B **34**
Salisbury Pk. L16: Child 4H **73**
Salisbury Rd. CH45: New B 5C **32**
  L5: Liv 1G **53**
  L15: Wav 2B **72**
  L19: Gras 5E **91**
  L20: Boot 1B **34**
  WA11: Hay 3G **31**
Salisbury St. CH41: Birke 4F **69**
  L3: Liv 1H **5** (3F **53**)
  L34: Presc 1D **58**
  WA7: Run 4E **113**
  WA8: Wid 3F **97**
  WA10: St H 2E **43**
Salisbury Ter. L15: Wav 1D **72**
Salop St. L4: Walt 5F **35**
Saltash Cl. L26: Halew 3G **93**
  WA7: Brook 1D **124**
Saltburn Rd. CH45: Wall 2H **49**
Saltergate Rd. L8: Liv 5G **71**
Salthouse Quay L3: Liv 6C **4** (1C **70**)
Saltney St. L3: Liv 3B **52**
Saltpit La. L31: Mag 6D **6**
Saltwood Dr. WA7: Brook 2E **125**
Saltworks Cl. WA6: Frod 5H **123**
Salvia Way L33: Kirkb 4H **13**
Samaria Av. CH62: New F 4C **88**
Samphire Gdns. WA9: Bold 6D **44**
Samuel St. WA9: St H 6B **42**
Sanbec Gdns. WA8: Cron 4B **78**
Sandalwood L23: Crosb 5F **9**
  WA7: Nort 4D **114**
Sandalwood Cl. L6: Liv 2H **53**
Sandalwood Dr. CH43: Noct 5H **67**
Sandalwood Gdns. WA9: St H 6G **43**
Sandbanks CH47: Hoy 2A **64**
Sandbeck St. L8: Liv 6F **71**
Sandbrook Ct. CH46: More 1C **66**
Sandbrook La. CH46: More 1C **66**
Sandbrook Rd. L25: Gate 1C **74**
Sandcliffe Rd. CH45: Wall 5A **32**
Sandeman Rd. L4: Walt 5B **36**
Sanderling Rd. L33: Kirkb 6C **14**
Sanders Hey Cl. WA7: Brook 2C **124**
Sanderson Cl. WA5: Gt San 3F **81**
Sandfield L36: Huy 5F **57**
Sandfield Av. CH47: Meols 6D **46**

Sandfield Cl. CH63: Hghr B 5F **87**
L12: W Der 2G **55**
Sandfield Ct. WA6: Frod 6F **123**
Sandfield Cres. L35: Whis 2G **59**
WA10: St H 2D **42**
(off Liverpool Rd.)
Sandfield Hey L12: W Der 1G **55**
(off Sandfield Pk. E.)
SANDFIELD PARK 2F **55**
Sandfield Pk. CH60: Hesw 5B **100**
Sandfield Pk. E. L12: W Der 1G **55**
Sandfield Pl. L20: Boot 1B **34**
Sandfield Rd.
CH45: New B 6D **32**
CH49: Woodc 1F **85**
CH63: Hghr B 5F **87**
L20: Boot 3D **34**
L25: Gate 5D **74**
WA10: Eccl 6G **27**
Sandfield Ter. CH45: New B 6D **32**
Sandfield Wlk. L13: W Der 3F **55**
Sandford Dr. L31: Mag 5C **6**
Sandford St. CH41: Birke 2G **69**
Sandforth Cl. L12: W Der 1E **55**
Sandforth Ct. L13: W Der 2E **55**
Sandforth Rd. L12: W Der 2E **55**
Sandgate Cl. L24: Speke 1D **108**
Sandham Gro. CH60: Hesw 5G **101**
Sandham Rd. L24: Speke 1A **110**
Sandhead St. L7: Liv 1B **72**
Sandhey Rd. CH47: Meols 1C **64**
Sandheys CH64: Park 6G **117**
Sandheys Av. L22: Water 2E **19**
Sandheys Cl. L4: Walt 6E **35**
Sandheys Gro. L22: Water 1F **19**
Sandheys Rd. CH45: New B 6D **32**
Sandheys Ter. L22: Water 2E **19**
Sandhills CH46: Leas 4C **48**
Sandhills Bus. Est.
L5: Kirkd 1C **52**
Sandhills Bus. Pk. L5: Kirkd 6C **34**
Sandhills La. L5: Kirkd 6B **34**
Sandhills Station (Rail) 1C **52**
Sandhills Vw. CH45: Wall 2H **49**
Sandhurst L23: Blun 5E **9**
Sandhurst Cl. L21: Sea 4H **19**
Sandhurst Dr. L10: Ain 1C **22**
Sandhurst Rd. L26: Halew 5A **94**
L35: Rainh 2G **59**
Sandhurst St. L17: Aig 6H **71**
Sandhurst Way L31: Lyd 2A **6**
Sandicroft Rd. L12: Crox 3B **38**
Sandino St. L8: Liv 3F **71**
Sandiway CH47: Meols 6D **46**
CH63: Brom 1C **120**
L35: Whis 5D **58**
L36: Huy 6H **57**
Sandiway Av. WA8: Wid 2G **95**
Sandiways L31: Mag 6D **6**
Sandiways Av. L30: N'ton 1G **21**
Sandiways Rd. CH45: Wall 1A **50**
Sandlea Pk. CH48: W Kir 1A **82**
Sandlewood Gro. L33: Kirkb 5B **14**
Sandon Cl. L35: Rainh 3H **59**
Sandon Ct. L22: Water 2F **19**
(off Sandon St.)
Sandon Gro. WA11: Rainf 3G **17**
Sandon Ind. Est. L5: Kirkd 1B **52**
Sandon Lodge L21: Sea 5A **20**
(off Seaforth Rd.)
Sandon Pl. WA8: Wid 2H **97**
Sandon Prom. CH44: Wall 3G **51**
Sandon Rd. CH44: Wall 3G **51**
Sandon St. L8: Liv 1F **71**
L22: Water 2F **19**
Sandon Way L5: Kirkd 1B **52**
Sandown Cl. WA7: Run 1G **123**
Sandown Ct. L15: Wav 1D **72**
Sandown La. L15: Wav 1D **72**
SANDOWN PARK 6D **54**
Sandown Pk. Rd. L10: Ain 6C **12**
Sandown Rd. L15: Wav 6D **54**
L21: Sea 4H **19**
Sandpiper Cl. CH49: Upton 3B **66**

Sandpiper Gro. L26: Halew 2G **93**
Sandpipers Ct. CH47: Hoy 2B **64**
L22: Water 1E **19**
(off Bridge Rd.)
Sandridge Rd. CH45: New B 6D **32**
CH61: Pens 6D **84**
Sandringham Av. CH47: Meols 1C **64**
L22: Water 3G **19**
Sandringham Cl. CH47: Meols 2C **64**
CH62: New F 4A **88**
L33: Kirkb 4A **14**
Sandringham Dr. CH45: New B 5C **32**
L17: Aig 5H **71**
WA9: St H 1G **61**
Sandringham M. CH47: Meols 2C **64**
Sandringham Rd. L13: Liv 1C **54**
L22: Water 3G **19**
L31: Mag 1A **12**
WA8: Wid 5E **79**
Sandrock Cl. CH45: New B 6D **32**
Sandrock Rd. CH45: New B 6D **32**
Sands Rd. L18: Moss H 5D **72**
Sandstone CH45: Wall 2E **51**
Sandstone Cl. L35: Rainh 6A **60**
Sandstone Dr. CH48: W Kir 1E **83**
L35: Whis 2G **59**
Sandstone M. WA8: Wid 5C **78**
Sandstone Rd. E. L13: Liv 3E **55**
Sandstone Rd. W. L13: Liv 3D **54**
Sandstone Wlk. CH60: Hesw 6E **101**
Sandwash Cl. WA11: Rainf 5H **17**
Sandway Cres. L11: Norr G 3E **37**
Sandy Brow La. L33: Kirkb 4G **25**
Sandy Grn. L9: Ain 5A **22**
Sandy Gro. L13: Liv 1D **54**
Sandy Ho. L21: Sea 4H **19**
Sandy Knowe L15: Wav 6E **55**
Sandy La. CH45: Wall 1A **50**
CH48: W Kir 3B **82**
CH60: Hesw 4E **101**
CH61: Irby 4A **84**
L9: Ain 5H **21**
L13: Liv 1D **54**
L21: Sea 4A **20**
(not continuous)
L31: Lyd 1A **6**
L31: Mell 4E **13**
L39: Augh 1G **7**
WA5: Penk 4H **81**
WA7: Pres B 1H **125**
WA7: Run, West P 6B **112**
WA8: Cron, Wid 4B **78**
WA8: Wid 3C **80**
WA11: St H 2C **28**
Sandy La. Nth. CH61: Irby 4A **84**
SANDYMOOR 2F **115**
(Kings Ct.)
Sandymoor La. WA7: Nort 1F **115**
WA7: Nort 2F **115**
(Lady Richeld Cl.)
Sandymount Dr. CH45: Wall 6C **32**
CH63: Beb 1H **103**
Sandy Rd. L21: Sea 3H **19**
Sandyville Gro. L4: Walt 5C **36**
Sandyville Rd. L4: Walt 5B **36**
Sandy Way CH43: Oxton 4C **68**
Sankey (for Penketh) Station (Rail)
. . . . .3H **81**
Sankey Mnr. WA5: Gt San 3H **81**
Sankey Rd. L31: Mag 2B **12**
WA11: Hay 6B **30**
Sankey St. L1: Liv 1E **71**
WA8: Wid 5E **97**
WA9: St H 3H **43**
Sankey Valley Country Pk. 1C **44**
Sankey Valley Country Pk. Vis. Cen.
. . . . .5A **30**
Santon Av. L13: Liv 2C **54**
Sapphire Dr. L33: Kirkb 4A **14**
Sapphire St. L13: Liv 6D **54**
Sarah's Cft. L30: N'ton 6E **11**
Sark Rd. L13: Liv 3D **54**
Sartfield Cl. L16: Child 1A **74**
Sarum Rd. L25: Gate 2C **74**

Sarus Ct. WA7: Manor P 1D **114**
Satinwood Cl. WN4: Ash M 1H **31**
Satinwood Cres. L31: Mell 6E **13**
SAUGHALL MASSIE 3A **66**
Saughall Massie La. CH48: Upton 4C **66**
Saughall Massie Rd. CH48: W Kir 6D **64**
CH49: Grea, Upton 6D **64**
Saughall Rd. CH46: More 2A **66**
L31: Upton 2A **66**
Saunby Cl. L19: Garst 6G **91**
Saunders Av. L35: Presc 3D **58**
Saunderton Cl. WA11: Hay 4E **31**
Saville Rd. L13: Liv 5F **55**
L31: Lyd 4B **6**
Savoylands Cl. L17: Aig 1A **90**
Sawley Cl. WA7: Murd 6G **115**
Sawpit La. L36: Huy 5H **57**
Saxby Rd. L14: Knott A 2C **56**
Saxon Cl. L6: Liv 3H **53**
Saxon Ct. WA10: St H 6C **28**
Saxonia Rd. L4: Walt 3H **35**
Saxon Rd. CH46: More 6D **48**
CH47: Meols 1C **64**
L23: Crosb 6F **9**
WA7: Run 3F **113**
Saxon Ter. WA8: Wid 2F **97**
Saxon Way L33: Kirkb 3A **14**
Saxony Rd. L7: Liv 5G **53**
(not continuous)
Sayce St. WA8: Wid 2F **97**
Scafell Cl. CH62: East 4D **120**
Scafell Lawn L27: N'ley 6A **76**
Scafell Rd. WA11: St H 3D **28**
Scafell Wlk. L27: N'ley 5A **76**
(not continuous)
Scape La. L23: Crosb 4G **9**
Scargreen Av. L11: Norr G 2D **36**
Scarisbrick Av. L21: Lith 4B **20**
Scarisbrick Cl. L31: Mag 4D **6**
Scarisbrick Cres. L11: Norr G 2B **36**
Scarisbrick Dr. L11: Norr G 2B **36**
Scarisbrick Pl. L11: Norr G 3B **36**
Scarisbrick Rd. L11: Norr G 3B **36**
WA11: Rainf 2F **17**
Scarsdale Rd. L11: Norr G 4D **36**
Sceptre Cl. WA12: Newt W 2H **45**
Sceptre Rd. L11: Crox 1G **37**
Sceptre Wlk. L11: Crox 2G **37**
Scholar St. L7: Liv 2A **72**
Scholes, The WA10: St H 6H **41**
Scholes La. WA9: St H 6H **41**
WA10: St H 6H **41**
Scholes Pk. WA10: St H 6H **41**
Schomberg St. L6: Liv 4G **53**
School Cl. CH46: More 6D **48**
L27: N'ley 2E **75**
Schoolfield Cl. CH49: Woodc 1F **85**
Schoolfield Rd. CH49: Woodc 1F **85**
School Hill CH60: Hesw 6D **100**
School La. CH43: Bid 6G **49**
CH44: Wall 2A **50**
CH45: Wall 3A **50**
CH47: Hoy 2B **64**
(not continuous)
CH47: Meols 6D **46**
CH61: Thurs 5H **83**
CH62: New F 4B **88**
CH63: Hghr B 5F **87**
CH64: Nest 5D **118**
CH64: Park 6F **117**
CH66: Chil T 6F **121**
L1: Liv 5E **5** (6D **52**)
L10: Ain 1B **22**
L21: Lith 3B **20**
L21: Sea 4A **20**
L25: Woolt 4C **92**
L31: Mag 5F **7**
L31: Mell 4E **13**
L34: Know 5C **24**
L35: Rainh 6C **60**
(not continuous)
L36: Huy 5A **58**
WA7: Halt 5B **114**
WA8: Bold H 2A **80**

School St.—Shadwell St.

School St. WA11: Hay . . . 5B **30**
School Way L24: Speke . . . 2D **108**
WA8: Wid . . . 6H **79**
Schooner Cl. WA7: Murd . . . 1F **125**
Science Rd. L24: Speke . . . 1E **109**
Scone Cl. L11: Crox . . . 2G **37**
Score, The WA9: St H . . . 1E **61**
(not continuous)
Scorecross WA9: St H . . . 5F **43**
Score La. L16: Child . . . 6G **55**
Scoresby Rd. CH46: Leas . . . 4F **49**
Scorpio Cl. L14: Knott A . . . 2C **56**
Scorton St. L6: Liv . . . 2A **54**
Scotchbarn La. L34: Presc . . . 1E **59**
L35: Presc . . . 1E **59**
Scoter Rd. L33: Kirkb . . . 1B **24**
Scotia Av. CH62: New F . . . 4C **88**
L30: N'ton . . . 2E **21**
Scotia Rd. L13: Liv . . . 3E **55**
Scotland Rd. L3: Liv . . . 1F **5** (4D **52**)
L5: Liv . . . 4D **52**
Scott Av. L35: Whis . . . 4F **59**
L36: Huy . . . 6A **58**
WA8: Wid . . . 3D **96**
WA9: Sut M . . . 4E **61**
Scott Cl. L4: Walt . . . 6F **35**
L31: Mag . . . 6C **6**
Scotts Pl. CH41: Birke . . . 2B **68**
Scotts Quays CH41: Birke . . . 6G **51**
Scott St. CH45: Wall . . . 2D **50**
L20: Boot . . . 6B **20**
Sculthorpe Cl. WA10: St H . . . 2A **42**
Scythes, The CH49: Grea . . . 5A **66**
L30: N'ton . . . 5H **11**
Scythia Cl. CH62: New F . . . 3C **88**
Seabank Av. CH44: Wall . . . 2E **51**
Seabank Cott. CH47: Meols . . . 5E **47**
Seabank Ct. CH48: W Kir . . . 2A **82**
Seabank Rd. CH44: Wall . . . 5D **32**
CH45: New B, Wall . . . 5D **32**
CH60: Hesw . . . 1C **116**
Seacole Cl. L8: Liv . . . 3H **71**
SEACOMBE . . . 6F **51**
Seacombe Prom. CH44: Wall . . . 3G **51**
(not continuous)
Seacombe Vw. CH44: Wall . . . 5G **51**
Sea Ct. CH45: Wall . . . 6B **32**
Seacroft Cl. L14: Knott A . . . 1C **56**
Seacroft Rd. L14: Knott A . . . 1C **56**
Seafarers Dr. L25: Gate . . . 5C **74**
Seafield Av. CH60: Hesw . . . 1C **116**
L23: Crosb . . . 6G **9**
Seafield Dr. CH45: Wall . . . 6C **32**
Seafield Rd. CH62: New F . . . 3B **88**
L9: Walt . . . 6F **21**
*L20: Boot . . . 1B **34***
(off Cleary St.)
Seaford Cl. WA7: Wind H . . . 4F **115**
Seafore Cl. L31: Lyd . . . 3A **6**
SEAFORTH . . . 4H **19**
Seaforth & Litherland Station (Rail) . . . 4A **20**
Seaforth Nature Reserve . . . 4E **19**
Seaforth Dr. CH46: More . . . 2C **66**
Seaforth Rd. L21: Sea . . . 6A **20**
Seaforth Va. Nth. L21: Sea . . . 5A **20**
Seaforth Va. W. L21: Sea . . . 5A **20**
Seagram Cl. L9: Ain . . . 3A **22**
Sea La. WA7: Run . . . 3H **113**
Sealy Cl. CH63: Spit . . . 4A **104**
Seaman Rd. L15: Wav . . . 2C **72**
Seaport St. L8: Liv . . . 3H **71**
Sea Rd. CH45: Wall . . . 5B **32**
Seascale Av. WA10: St H . . . 5H **41**
Seasons, The WA7: Run . . . 4D **112**
Seath Av. WA9: St H . . . 1A **44**
Seathwaite Cl. L23: Blun . . . 6D **8**
WA7: Beech . . . 2A **124**
Seathwaite Cres. L33: Kirkb . . . 5H **13**
Seaton Cl. L12: Crox . . . 2C **38**
Seaton Gro. WA9: St H . . . 1B **60**
Seaton Pk. WA7: Nort . . . 2G **115**
Seaton Rd. CH42: Tran . . . 5E **69**
CH45: Wall . . . 1C **50**
Seaview CH47: Hoy . . . 2B **64**
Seaview Av. CH45: Wall . . . 2C **50**
CH61: Irby . . . 5B **84**
CH62: East . . . 1H **121**
Seaview La. CH61: Irby . . . 5B **84**
Sea Vw. Rd. L20: Boot . . . 1A **34**
Seaview Rd. CH45: Wall . . . 1C **50**
Seaview Ter. L22: Water . . . 2E **19**
Seawood Gro. CH46: More . . . 2B **66**
Second Av. CH43: Bid . . . 3F **67**
L9: Ain . . . 5C **22**
(First Av.)
L9: Ain . . . 4B **22**
(Third Av.)
L23: Crosb . . . 5F **9**
L35: Rainh . . . 3H **59**
WA7: Pal F . . . 5B **114**
Sedbergh Av. L10: Ain . . . 6A **12**
Sedbergh Gro. WA7: Beech . . . 2A **124**
Sedbergh Rd. CH44: Wall . . . 2B **50**
Sedburgh Gro. L36: Huy . . . 4E **57**
Sedburn Rd. L32: Kirkb . . . 4C **24**
Seddon Cl. WA10: Eccl . . . 2F **41**
Seddon Rd. L19: Garst . . . 5G **91**
WA10: St H . . . 5H **41**
Seddons Ct. L34: Presc . . . 1D **58**
Seddon St. L1: Liv . . . 6E **5** (1D **70**)
WA10: St H . . . 4D **28**
Sedgefield Cl. CH46: More . . . 1E **67**
Sedgefield Rd. CH46: More . . . 1E **67**
Sedgeley Wlk. L36: Huy . . . 2H **57**
Sedgemoor Rd. L11: Norr G . . . 2C **36**
Sedgewick Cres. WA5: Burtw . . . 1G **63**
Sedley St. L6: Liv . . . 1H **53**
Sedum Gro. L33: Kirkb . . . 4H **13**
Seeds La. L9: Ain . . . 3A **22**
Seeley Av. CH41: Birke . . . 2C **68**
Seel Rd. L36: Huy . . . 5H **57**
Seel St. L1: Liv . . . 5F **5** (6D **52**)
SEFTON . . . 2F **11**
Sefton Av. L21: Lith . . . 4B **20**
WA8: Wid . . . 6E **79**
Sefton Bus. Pk. L30: N'ton . . . 3G **21**
(not continuous)
Sefton Cl. L32: Kirkb . . . 6G **13**
Sefton Dr. L8: Liv . . . 4A **72**
L10: Ain . . . 1C **22**
L23: Thorn . . . 2A **10**
L31: Mag . . . 1H **11**
L32: Kirkb . . . 6G **13**
Sefton Gro. L17: Aig . . . 5A **72**
Sefton Ho. L9: Ain . . . 4H **21**
Sefton La. L31: Mag . . . 1G **11**
Sefton La. Ind. Est.
L31: Mag . . . 1G **11**
Sefton Mill Ct. L29: Seft . . . 2F **11**
Sefton Mill La. L29: Seft . . . 2F **11**
Sefton Mills L29: Seft . . . 2F **11**
Sefton Moss La. L30: N'ton . . . 6D **10**
Sefton Moss Vs. L21: Lith . . . 3B **20**
SEFTON PARK . . . 5C **72**
Sefton Pk. Ct. *L17: Aig . . . 1C **90***
(off Aigburth Va.)
Sefton Park Palm House . . . 5B **72**
Sefton Pk. Rd. L8: Liv . . . 3H **71**
Sefton Rd. CH42: Rock F . . . 2A **88**
CH45: New B . . . 6D **32**
CH62: New F . . . 3A **88**
L9: Ain . . . 4B **22**
L9: Walt . . . 1G **35**
L20: Boot . . . 6D **20**
L21: Lith . . . 3B **20**
Sefton St. L3: Liv . . . 3D **70**
L8: Liv . . . 3D **70**
L21: Lith . . . 3B **20**
(not continuous)
WA12: Newt W . . . 2H **45**
SEFTON TOWN . . . 5D **10**
Sefton Vw. L21: Lith . . . 3B **20**
L23: Crosb . . . 5A **10**
Seiont Ho. L8: Liv . . . 4F **71**
Selborne L35: Whis . . . 5F **59**
Selborne Cl. L8: Liv . . . 2G **71**
Selborne St. L8: Liv . . . 2F **71**
Selbourne Cl. CH49: Woodc . . . 6G **67**
Selby Cl. WA7: Nort . . . 1G **115**
WA10: St H . . . 3B **42**
Selby Gro. L36: Huy . . . 4B **58**
Selby Rd. L9: Walt . . . 5G **21**
Selby St. CH45: Wall . . . 2D **50**
Seldon St. L6: Liv . . . 4H **53**
Selina Rd. L4: Walt . . . 3F **35**
Selkirk Av. CH62: East . . . 3E **121**
Selkirk Dr. WA10: Eccl . . . 6H **27**
Selkirk Rd. L13: Liv . . . 4D **54**
Sellar St. L4: Kirkd . . . 6E **35**
Selsdon Rd. L22: Water . . . 1E **19**
Selsey Cl. L7: Liv . . . 1H **71**
Selside Lawn *L27: N'ley . . . 5A **76***
(off Selside Wlk.)
Selside Wlk. L27: N'ley . . . 6A **76**
Selston Cl. CH63: Spit . . . 3A **104**
Selworthy Grn. L16: Child . . . 3H **73**
Selwyn Cl. WA8: Wid . . . 6A **80**
Selwyn St. L4: Kirkd . . . 4E **35**
Senator Point L33: Know I . . . 3E **25**
Senator Rd. WA9: St H . . . 6B **42**
Seneschal Ct. WA7: Pal F . . . 1A **124**
Sennen Cl. WA7: Brook . . . 2D **124**
Sennen Rd. L32: Kirkb . . . 3B **24**
Sentinel Way L30: N'ton . . . 3G **21**
September Rd. L6: Liv . . . 2A **54**
Serenade Rd. L33: Kirkb . . . 3B **14**
Sergeant Rd. L12: W Der . . . 6A **38**
Sergrim Rd. L36: Huy . . . 4E **57**
Serpentine, The L19: Gras . . . 3E **91**
L23: Blun . . . 5C **8**
Serpentine Nth., The
L23: Blun . . . 4C **8**
Serpentine Rd. CH44: Wall . . . 2E **51**
Serpentine Sth., The L23: Blun . . . 5D **8**
Servia Rd. L21: Lith . . . 4B **20**
Servite Cl. L22: Water . . . 1E **19**
Servite Ct. L25: Woolt . . . 3E **93**
Servite Ho. L17: Aig . . . 5H **71**
Sessions Rd. L4: Kirkd . . . 5E **35**
Seth Powell Way L36: Huy . . . 1E **57**
Seven Acre Rd. L23: Thorn . . . 4B **10**
Seven Acres La. CH61: Thing . . . 5E **85**
Sevenoak Gro. L35: Tar G . . . 2B **76**
Sevenoaks Cl. L5: Liv . . . 2E **53**
Seventh Av. L9: Ain . . . 4B **22**
(Lakes Rd.)
L9: Ain . . . 4B **22**
(Sixth Av.)
Severn Cl. WA8: Wid . . . 6B **80**
WA9: Sut L . . . 2G **61**
Severn Rd. L33: Kirkb . . . 3B **14**
L35: Rainh . . . 4H **59**
Severn St. CH41: Birke . . . 6C **50**
L5: Liv . . . 1F **53**
Severs St. L6: Liv . . . 3H **53**
Sewell St. L34: Presc . . . 1D **58**
WA7: Run . . . 3F **113**
(Perry St.)
WA7: Run . . . 3F **113**
(Union St.)
Sextant Cl. WA7: Murd . . . 1F **125**
Sexton Av. WA9: St H . . . 3D **44**
Sexton Way L14: Broad G . . . 5B **56**
Seymour Ct. CH42: Tran . . . 5G **69**
L14: Broad G . . . 6H **55**
WA7: Manor P . . . 2E **115**
Seymour Dr. L31: Mag . . . 4D **6**
Seymour Pl. E. CH45: New B . . . 5E **33**
Seymour Pl. W. CH45: New B . . . 5D **32**
Seymour Rd. L14: Broad G . . . 5H **55**
*L21: Lith . . . 4B **20***
(off Bridge Rd.)
Seymour St. CH42: Tran . . . 5G **69**
CH45: New B . . . 5D **32**
L3: Liv . . . 3H **5** (5E **53**)
L20: Boot . . . 3B **34**
Seymour Ter. L3: Liv . . . 3H **5**
Shacklady Rd. L33: Kirkb . . . 5C **14**
Shackleton Av. WA8: Wid . . . 5G **79**
Shackleton Rd. CH46: Leas . . . 3F **49**
Shadowbrook Dr. L24: Speke . . . 5E **93**
Shadwell St. L5: Liv . . . 2B **52**

Shaftesbury Av. L33: Kirkb 4A **14**
  WA5: Penk 1G **99**
Shaftesbury Rd. L23: Crosb 5F **9**
Shaftesbury St. L8: Liv 3E **71**
Shaftesbury Ter. L13: Liv 4E **55**
Shaftesbury Way WA5: Burtw 6H **45**
Shaftway Cl. WA11: Hay 4H **31**
Shakespeare Av. CH42: Rock F 2H **87**
  L32: Kirkb 3H **23**
Shakespeare Cl. L6: Liv 3G **53**
Shakespeare Rd. CH44: Wall 5F **51**
  CH64: Nest 6A **118**
  WA8: Wid 2E **97**
  WA9: Sut M 4E **61**
Shakespeare St. L20: Boot 6A **20**
Shalcombe Cl. L26: Halew 4A **94**
Shaldon Cl. L32: Kirkb 3C **24**
Shaldon Gro. L32: Kirkb 3C **24**
Shaldon Rd. L32: Kirkb 4C **24**
Shaldon Wlk. L32: Kirkb 3C **24**
Shalem Ct. CH63: Hghr B 5F **87**
Shalford Gro. CH48: W Kir 1D **82**
Shallcross Cl. *L6: Liv* *3G* **53**
     (off Shallcross Pl.)
Shallcross Pl. L6: Liv 3G **53**
Shallmarsh Cl. CH63: Hghr B 6F **87**
Shallmarsh Rd. CH63: Hghr B 6F **87**
Shalom Ct. L17: Aig 4C **72**
Shamrock Cl. CH41: Birke 2B **68**
Shand St. L19: Garst 1G **107**
Shanklin Cl. WA5: Gt San 3E **81**
Shanklin Rd. L15: Wav 6D **54**
Shannon Gro. WA8: Wid 1C **96**
Shannon Ho. CH46: Leas 3C **48**
Shannons La. L34: Know 4E **39**
Shannon St. CH41: Birke 6B **50**
Shard Cl. L11: Crox 6F **23**
Shard St. WA9: St H 6A **44**
Sharpeville Cl. L4: Kirkd 6D **34**
Sharples Cres. L23: Crosb 5H **9**
Sharp St. WA8: Wid 3E **97**
Sharwood Rd. L27: N'ley 5H **75**
Shavington Av. CH43: Oxton 6B **68**
Shawbury Av. CH63: Hghr B 4F **87**
Shawell Cl. WA8: Wid 1A **98**
Shaw Entry L35: Whis 1F **77**
Shaw Hill St. L1: Liv 3E **5** (5D **52**)
Shaw La. CH49: Grea 1A **84**
  L35: Presc, Whis 3D **58**
Shaw Rd. L24: Speke 6E **93**
Shaws All. L1: Liv 1D **70**
Shaws Dr. CH47: Meols 1D **64**
Shaw St. CH41: Birke 4F **69**
  CH47: Hoy 2B **64**
  L6: Liv 3F **53**
  WA7: Run 3D **112**
     (not continuous)
  WA10: St H 2F **43**
  WA11: Hay 5G **31**
Shawton Rd. L16: Child 1H **73**
Shearman Cl. CH61: Pens 1E **101**
Shearman Rd. CH61: Pens 1E **101**
Shearwater Cl. L27: N'ley 5H **75**
Sheen Rd. CH45: New B 6E **33**
Sheila Wlk. L10: Faz 5F **23**
Sheil Pl. L6: Liv 4A **54**
Sheil Rd. L6: Liv 3A **54**
Shelagh Av. WA8: Wid 2E **97**
Sheldon Cl. CH63: Spit 4A **104**
Sheldon Rd. L12: W Der 5H **37**
Shelley Cl. L36: Huy 6H **57**
Shelley Ct. L32: Kirkb 3H **23**
Shelley Pl. L35: Whis 4F **59**
Shelley Rd. WA8: Wid 2E **97**
Shelley St. L20: Boot 1B **34**
     (not continuous)
  WA9: Sut M 5F **61**
Shelley Way CH48: W Kir 3B **82**
SHELL GREEN 2A **98**
Shell Grn. WA8: Wid 2A **98**
Shell Grn. Est., The WA8: Wid 3A **98**
Shell Grn. Ho. WA8: Wid 3A **98**
Shellingford Rd. L14: Knott A 3C **56**
Shelmore Dr. L8: Liv 5F **71**

Shelton Cl. L13: Liv 5E **55**
  WA8: Wid 6B **80**
Shelton Rd. CH45: Wall 1C **50**
Shenley Cl. CH63: Beb 5H **87**
Shenley Rd. L15: Wav 1G **73**
Shenstone St. L7: Liv 6H **53**
Shenton Av. WA11: St H 5H **29**
Shepherd Cl. CH49: Grea 5A **66**
Shepherds Fold Cl. L8: Liv 3G **71**
Shepherds Row WA7: Cas 3B **114**
Shepherd St. L6: Liv 5F **53**
Sheppard Av. L16: Child 1C **74**
Shepston Av. L4: Walt 4G **35**
Sherborne Av. L25: Hunts X 3F **93**
  L30: N'ton 5E **11**
Sherborne Cl. WA7: Nort 2H **115**
Sherborne Rd. CH44: Wall 2B **50**
Sherborne Sq. L36: Huy 5G **57**
Sherbourne Way WA5: Burtw 1H **63**
Sherbrooke Cl. L14: Knott A 3A **56**
Sherdley Av. L9: Ain 3B **22**
Sherdley Bus. Pk. WA9: St H 4F **43**
Sherdley Ct. L35: Rainh 3A **60**
Sherdley Park 6F **43**
Sherdley Pk. Dr. WA9: St H 6G **43**
Sherdley Park Municipal Golf Course
      ....6E **43**
Sherdley Rd. WA9: St H 1D **60**
     (not continuous)
Sherdley Rd. Caravan Site
  WA9: St H 5E **43**
Sherdley Rd. Ind. Est. WA9: St H ..4F **43**
Sherford Cl. L27: N'ley 5H **75**
Sheridan Way WA7: Nort 3F **115**
Sheriff Cl. L5: Liv 3E **53**
Sheringham Cl. CH49: Upton 2E **67**
  WA9: St H 2H **43**
Sheringham Rd. WA5: Gt San 3G **81**
Sherlock Av. WA11: Hay 4G **31**
Sherlock La. CH44: Wall 5C **50**
     (not continuous)
Sherman Dr. L35: Rainh 6B **60**
Sherry Cl. L17: Aig 4C **72**
Sherry La. CH49: Woodc 1E **85**
Sherwell Cl. L15: Wav 6E **55**
Sherwood Av. CH61: Irby 4A **84**
  L23: Crosb 4F **9**
Sherwood Cl. L35: Rainh 2H **59**
  WA8: Wid 2A **96**
Sherwood Ct. L12: Crox 2B **38**
  L36: Huy 5H **57**
Sherwood Cres. WA5: Burtw 1G **63**
Sherwood Dr. CH63: Hghr B 4G **87**
  L35: Whis 5F **59**
Sherwood Gro. CH47: Meols 1F **65**
Sherwood Rd. CH44: Wall 4E **51**
  CH47: Meols 1F **65**
  L23: Crosb 4E **9**
Sherwood Row *L26: Halew* *5G* **93**
     (off Honey Hall Rd.)
Sherwood's La. L10: Faz 3D **22**
Sherwood St. L3: Liv 3B **52**
Sherwyn Rd. L4: Walt 5A **36**
Shetland Cl. WA8: Wid 6A **80**
Shetland Dr. CH62: Brom 5E **105**
Shevington Cl. WA8: Wid 6A **80**
  WA9: St H 6G **43**
Shevington's La. L33: Kirkb 4H **13**
Shevington Wlk. WA8: Wid 6A **80**
Shewell Cl. CH42: Tran 5F **69**
Shiel Rd. CH45: New B 6D **32**
Shimmin St. L7: Liv 6G **53**
Shipley Wlk. L24: Speke 1F **109**
Ship St. WA6: Frod 6F **123**
Shipton Cl. CH43: Pren 2A **86**
  L19: Aller 3F **91**
  WA8: Wid 6B **78**
Shirdley Av. L32: Kirkb 4B **24**
Shirdley Wlk. L32: Kirkb 4B **24**
Shirebourne Av. WA11: St H 4F **29**
Shiregreen WA9: St H 1G **61**
Shires, The WA10: St H 3C **42**
Shirley Rd. L19: Aller 3G **91**
Shirley St. CH44: Wall 4G **51**

Shirwell Gro. WA9: Sut L 3G **61**
Shobdon Cl. L12: Crox 1B **38**
Shop La. L31: Mag 6B **6**
Shop Rd. L34: Know 1E **39**
Shore Bank CH62: New F 3C **88**
Shore Dr. CH62: Port S 5C **88**
Shorefields CH62: New F 3C **88**
Shorefields Ho. CH62: New F 4C **88**
Shorefields Village L8: Liv 6F **71**
Shoreham Dr. WA5: Penk 6H **81**
Shore La. CH48: Caldy 4C **82**
Shore Rd. CH41: Birke 2H **69**
  CH48: Caldy 4C **82**
  L20: Boot 6H **19**
Shore Road Pumping Station 2H **69**
Short Cl. WA12: Newt W 2G **45**
Shortfield Rd. CH49: Upton 5E **67**
Shortfield Way CH49: Upton 5E **67**
Short St. WA8: Wid 6E **97**
  WA11: Hay 5G **31**
  WA12: Newt W 2G **45**
Shortwood Rd. L14: Knott A 4B **56**
Shorwell Cl. WA5: Gt San 2E **81**
Shottesbrook Grn. L11: Norr G 2D **36**
Showcase Cinema
  Liverpool 1E **37**
Shrewsbury Av. L10: Ain 6A **12**
  L22: Water 6F **9**
Shrewsbury Cl. CH43: Clau 3B **68**
Shrewsbury Dr. CH49: Upton 3E **67**
Shrewsbury Pl. *L19: Garst* *5G* **91**
     (off Shrewsbury Rd.)
Shrewsbury Rd. CH43: Clau, Oxton ..2B **68**
  CH44: Wall 2B **50**
  CH48: W Kir 2A **82**
  CH60: Hesw 4E **101**
  L19: Garst 5G **91**
Shrewton Rd. L25: Gate 2C **74**
Shropshire Cl. L30: N'ton 5G **11**
Shropshire Gdns. WA10: St H 3D **42**
Sibford Rd. L12: W Der 2H **55**
Siddeley Dr. WA12: Newt W 2H **45**
Siddeley St. L17: Aig 6A **72**
Sidgreave St. WA10: St H 2C **42**
Siding Cl. WA8: Wid 4E **97**
Siding La. L33: Sim 3E **15**
  WA11: Rainf 1C **16**
Sidings, The *L7: Liv* *1G* **71**
     (off Crown St.)
Sidlaw Av. WA9: St H 2B **44**
Sidmouth Cl. WA5: Penk 5G **81**
  WA10: Windle 5A **28**
Sidney Av. CH45: New B 5C **32**
Sidney Cl. CH64: Nest 6B **118**
Sidney Ct. CH42: Tran 6G **69**
Sidney Pl. L7: Liv 6G **53**
Sidney Powell Av. L32: Kirkb 1G **23**
Sidney Rd. CH42: Tran 5G **69**
  CH64: Nest 6B **118**
  L20: Boot 3D **34**
Sidney St. CH41: Birke 2G **69**
  WA10: St H 1B **42**
Sidney Ter. CH42: Tran 6G **69**
Sidwell St. L19: Garst 5G **91**
Sienna Cl. L27: N'ley 3E **75**
Signal Works Rd. L9: Ain, Faz 3C **22**
Silcroft Rd. L32: Kirkb 3A **24**
Silkhouse Ct. L2: Liv 3C **4**
Silkhouse La. L3: Liv 3C **4**
Silkstone Cl. L7: Liv 1H **71**
  WA10: St H 2B **42**
Silkstone Cres. WA7: Pal F 6D **114**
Silkstone Wlk. WA10: St H 2B **42**
     (not continuous)
Silver Av. WA11: Hay 6C **30**
Silverbeech Av. L18: Moss H 5F **73**
Silverbeech Rd. CH44: Wall 4E **51**
Silverbirch Gdns. CH44: Wall 2A **50**
Silver Birch Way L31: Lyd 2A **6**
Silverbrook Rd. L27: N'ley 2F **75**
Silverburn Av. CH46: More 6C **48**
Silverdale Av. L13: Liv 2C **54**
Silverdale Cl. L36: Huy 1G **75**
Silverdale Dr. L21: Lith 3D **20**

Silverdale Gro. WA11: St H 3E 29
Silverdale Rd. CH43: Oxton 5C 68
  CH63: Hghr B 4H 87
Silverlake Cl. L4: Walt 2G 35
Silverlea Av. CH45: Wall 2D 50
Silver Leigh L17: Aig 2B 90
Silverlime Gdns. WA9: St H 6A 42
Silverstone Dr. L36: Roby 1F 75
Silverstone Gro. L31: Lyd 2A 6
Silverton Rd. L17: Aig 3C 90
Silverwell Rd. L11: Crox 6H 23
Silverwell Wlk. L11: Crox 6H 23
Silverwing Ho. L19: Aig 4D 90
Silvester St. L5: Liv 2C 52
Simms Av. WA9: St H 2A 44
SIMM'S CROSS 3F 97
Simm's Rd. L6: Liv 1B 54
Simnel Cl. L25: Gate 3D 74
Simon Ct. CH48: W Kir 1A 82
Simonsbridge CH48: Caldy 5D 82
Simons Cl. L35: Whis 1D 76
Simon's Cft. L30: N'ton 6C 10
Simonside WA8: Wid 1A 96
Simonstone Gro. WA9: St H 6H 43
SIMONSWOOD 3C 14
Simonswood Ind. Pk.
  L33: Sim 3D 14
Simonswood La. L33: Kirkb 2C 24
Simonswood Wlk. L33: Kirkb 1C 24
Simpson St. CH41: Birke 3F 69
  L1: Liv .2D 70
Sim St. L3: Liv 1H 5 (4E 53)
Sinclair Av. L35: Presc 2F 59
  WA8: Wid 3D 96
Sinclair Cl. L35: Presc 1F 59
Sinclair Dr. L18: Moss H 3F 73
Sinclair St. L19: Garst 6G 91
Sinclair Way L34: Presc 2C 58
Sineacre La. L33: Sim 1G 15
  L39: Bic 1G 15
Singleton Av. CH42: Tran 6E 69
  WA11: St H 6H 29
Singleton Dr. L34: Know 2F 39
Sirdar Cl. L7: Liv 1H 71
Sir Howard St. L8: Liv 1F 71
Sir Howard Way L8: Liv 1F 71
     (off Sir Howard St.)
Sir Thomas St. L1: Liv 3D 4 (5D 52)
Siskin Grn. L25: Gate 5C 74
Sisters Way CH41: Birke 3F 69
Six Acre La. WA4: Moore 6H 99
Sixth Av. L9: Ain 4C 22
     (Broadway)
  L9: Ain .4B 22
     (Seventh Av.)
Skeffington L35: Whis 5E 59
Skelhorne St. L3: Liv 4G 5 (6E 53)
Skelton Cl. WA11: St H 4F 29
Skerries Rd. L4: Walt 1G 53
Skiddaw Cl. WA7: Beech 3C 124
Skiddaw Rd. CH62: Brom 3E 105
Skipton Cl. WA7: Cas 4B 114
Skipton Rd. L4: Walt 6H 35
  L36: Huy 4B 58
Skirving Pl. L5: Liv 1D 52
Skirving St. L5: Liv 1E 53
Skye Cl. WA8: Wid 6A 80
Skyhawk Av. L19: Speke 1A 108
Sky Lark Ri. WA9: St H 2C 44
Sky Pk. Ind. Est. L24: Speke 2D 108
Slade La. CH63: Thorn H 6D 102
Slag La. WA11: Hay 3D 30
     (not continuous)
Slater Pl. L1: Liv 6F 5 (1D 70)
Slater St. L1: Liv 6F 5 (1D 70)
Slatey Rd. CH43: Oxton 3D 68
Sleaford Rd. L14: Knott A 2D 56
Sleepers Hill L4: Walt 6F 35
Slessor Av. CH48: W Kir 6D 64
Slim Rd. L36: Huy 4G 57
Slingsby Dr. CH49: Upton 5E 67
Smallholdings, The L31: Mag 4E 7
Smallridge Cl. CH61: Pens 1C 100
Smallwood M. CH60: Hesw 3C 100

Smeaton St. L4: Kirkd 4E 35
     (not continuous)
Smethick Wlk. L30: N'ton 5G 11
Smilie Av. CH46: More 6A 48
Smith Av. CH41: Birke 1D 68
Smithdown Gro. L7: Liv 1G 71
Smithdown La. L7: Liv 6G 53
     (Elm Gro.)
  L7: Liv 1H 71
     (Malt St.)
Smithdown Pl. L15: Wav 4E 73
Smithdown Rd. L7: Liv 2A 72
  L15: Wav 2A 72
Smith Dr. L20: Boot 4H 35
Smithfield St. L3: Liv 2D 4 (5C 52)
  WA9: St H 3H 43
Smithford Wlk. L35: Tar G 2B 76
Smith Pl. L5: Kirkd 1D 52
Smith Rd. WA8: Wid 4D 96
Smith St. L5: Kirkd 6E 35
  L34: Presc 1E 59
  WA9: St H 6A 44
Smithy Cl. WA8: Cron 4A 78
Smithy Heritage Cen. 6H 27
Smithy Hey CH48: W Kir 1C 82
Smithy Hill CH63: Thorn H 1C 118
Smithy La. L39: Augh 1E 7
  WA8: Cron 3A 78
Smithystone Cl. L15: Wav 2E 73
SMM Bus. Pk. CH41: Birke 6E 51
Smollett St. L6: Liv 4H 53
  L20: Boot 5B 20
Smugglers Way CH45: Wall 5A 32
Smyth Rd. WA8: Wid 1H 97
Snaefell Av. L13: Liv 2C 54
Snaefell Gro. L13: Liv 2C 54
Snave Cl. L21: Lith 6B 20
Snowberry Cl. WA8: Wid 5A 80
Snowberry Rd. L14: Knott A 1C 56
Snowden Rd. CH46: More 1A 66
Snowdon Cl. WA5: Gt San 3G 81
Snowdon Gro. WA9: St H 6G 43
Snowdon La. L5: Liv 2C 52
Snowdon Rd. CH42: Tran 1F 87
Snowdrop Av. CH41: Birke 5H 51
Snowdrop Cl. WA7: Beech 3B 124
Snowdrop M. L21: Lith 5B 20
Snowdrop St. L5: Kirkd 6D 34
Soho Pl. L3: Liv 1H 5 (4E 53)
Soho St. L3: Liv 1H 5 (4E 53)
     (not continuous)
Solar Rd. L9: Ain 5H 21
Solly Av. CH42: Rock F 1G 87
Solomon St. L7: Liv 5H 53
Solway Gro. WA7: Beech 2H 123
Solway St. CH41: Birke 6C 50
Solway St. E. L8: Liv 2H 71
Solway St. W. L8: Liv 2H 71
Soma Av. L21: Lith 3C 20
Somerford Ho. L23: Blun 6D 8
Somerford Rd. L14: Knott A 3C 56
Somerford Wlk. WA8: Wid 6A 80
Somerley Cl. L12: W Der 5H 37
Somerset Pl. L6: Liv 2B 54
Somerset Rd. CH45: Wall 2A 50
  CH48: W Kir 6C 64
  CH61: Pens 1C 100
  L20: Boot 1D 34
  L22: Water 1E 19
Somerset St. WA9: St H 3H 43
Somerton St. L15: Wav 1C 72
Somerville Cl. CH63: Brom 1B 120
Somerville Gro. L22: Water 1F 19
Somerville Rd. L22: Water 1F 19
  WA8: Wid 3B 96
Sommer Av. L12: W Der 6E 37
Sonning Av. L21: Lith 2A 20
Sonning Rd. L4: Walt 3B 36
Sorany Cl. L23: Thorn 3A 10
Sorogold Cl. WA9: St H 2G 43
Sorogold St. WA9: St H 2G 43
Sorrel Cl. CH43: Noct 4H 67
Sorrel Way WA9: Clock F 4H 61
Sth. Albert Rd. L17: Aig 5H 71

Southampton Dr. L19: Garst 5F 91
Southampton Way WA7: Murd 1G 125
Sth. Atlantic Av. L30: N'ton 2F 21
South Av. L34: Presc 1B 58
South Bank CH43: Oxton 6D 68
Sth. Bank Rd. L7: Liv 5B 54
  L19: Gras 4F 91
Sth. Bank Ter. WA7: Run 2D 112
Sth. Barcombe Rd. L16: Child 2A 74
Sth. Boundary Rd. L33: Know I 3D 24
Southbourne Rd. CH45: Wall 2H 49
Southbrook Rd. L27: N'ley 3E 75
Southbrook Way L27: N'ley 3E 75
Sth. Cantril Av. L12: W Der 6B 38
Sth. Chester St. L8: Liv 3F 71
Southcroft L33: Kirkb 5A 14
Southcroft Rd. CH45: Wall 2H 49
South Dale WA5: Penk 4H 81
Southdale Rd. CH42: Rock F 1G 87
  L15: Wav 1D 72
Southdean Rd. L14: Knott A 1D 56
SOUTHDENE 3B 24
South Dr. CH49: Upton 4E 67
  CH60: Hesw 6E 101
  CH61: Irby 6A 84
  L12: W Der 2E 55
  L15: Wav 1D 72
Southern Cres. L8: Liv 4E 71
Southern Gateway L24: Speke 6E 93
Southern Rd. L24: Speke 3G 109
Southern's La. WA11: Rainf 3G 17
Southey Cl. WA8: Wid 3D 96
Southey Gro. L31: Mag 3B 12
Southey Rd. WA10: St H 5A 42
Southey St. L15: Wav 2C 72
  L20: Boot 1B 34
     (not continuous)
Sth. Ferry Quay L3: Liv 3D 70
Southfield Rd. L9: Walt 5F 21
Southfields Av. WA5: Gt San 4H 81
South Front L35: Whis 6E 59
Southgate Cl. L12: Crox 2A 38
Southgate Rd. L13: Liv 4F 55
South Gro. L8: Liv 5G 71
  L18: Aller 2G 91
South Hey CH61: Irby 6B 84
Sth. Highville Rd. L16: Child 3H 73
South Hill Gro. CH43: Oxton 6D 68
  L8: Liv .5G 71
South Hill Rd. CH43: Oxton 5E 69
  L8: Liv .5G 71
Sth. Hunter St. L1: Liv 6H 5 (1F 71)
Sth. John St. L1: Liv 5D 4 (6C 52)
  WA9: St H 2G 43
Southlands Av. WA5: Penk 6H 81
Southlands Ct. WA7: Run 5D 112
     (off Southlands M.)
Southlands M. WA7: Run 5D 112
South La. WA8: Wid 5A 80
South La. Entry WA8: Wid 5B 80
South Mnr. Way L25: Woolt 2E 93
South Meade L31: Mag 6A 6
Southmead Gdns. L19: Aller 4A 92
Southmead Rd. L19: Aller 4A 92
Sth. Mossley Hill Rd. L19: Aig, Gras . .2E 91
Southney Cl. L31: Mell 6F 13
South Pde. CH48: W Kir 1A 82
  L23: Crosb 6H 9
  L24: Speke 2G 109
  L32: Kirkb 1A 24
  WA7: West P 6B 112
South Pk. Ct. CH44: Wall 4G 51
     (off Demesne St.)
  L32: Kirkb 6G 13
South Pk. Rd. L32: Kirkb 6F 13
Sth. Parkside Dr. L12: W Der 6G 37
Sth. Parkside Wlk. L12: W Der 5F 37
     (off Parkside Dr.)
South Pk. Way L20: Boot 3D 34
Southport Rd. L20: Boot 5E 21
  L23: Thorn 2A 10
  L31: Lyd 1A 6
Southport St. WA9: St H 2C 44
South Quay L3: Liv 2C 70

Southridge Rd. CH61: Pens 6E 85
South Rd. CH42: Tran 6E 69
  CH48: W Kir 2A 82
  CH65: Hoot 4H 121
  L9: Ain 5B 22
  L14: Broad G 4H 55
  L19: Gras 5E 91
  L22: Water .3F 19
  L24: Halew 1G 109
  WA7: West P 6B 112
Sth. Sefton Bus. Cen. L20: Boot 2B 34
South Sta. Rd. L25: Gate 4D 74
South St. L8: Liv 4G 71
  WA8: Wid .3F 97
  WA9: St H .6B 42
Sth. Sudley Rd. L19: Aig 2E 91
South Vw. CH62: Brom 6D 88
  L8: Liv 5G 71
  (off Dentwood St.)
  L22: Water .3G 19
  L36: Huy 5B 58
South Vw. Ct. L22: Water 3G 19
South Vw. Ter. WA5: Cuerd 1C 98
Southwark Gro. L30: N'ton 2F 21
Southway L15: Wav 1F 73
  WA7: Pal F 6B 114
  (not continuous)
  WA8: Wid 3B 96
Southwell Pl. L8: Liv 4E 71
Southwell St. L8: Liv 4E 71
Southwick Rd. CH42: Tran 6G 69
Southwold Cres. WA5: Gt San 3F 81
Southwood Av. WA7: Wind H 3C 114
Southwood Cl. L32: Kirkb 3D 24
Southwood Rd. CH62: Brom 4F 105
  L17: Aig 1H 89
Sovereign Cl. WA7: Murd 6F 115
Sovereign Hey L11: Crox 2G 37
Sovereign Rd. L11: Crox 2G 37
Sovereign Way CH41: Birke 6F 51
  L11: Crox 2G 37
Spaceport 5H 51
Spark La. WA7: Halt 4B 114
Sparks Cft. CH62: Port S 5C 88
Sparks La. CH61: Thing 5E 85
Sparling St. L1: Liv 2D 70
  (not continuous)
SPARROW HALL 1D 36
Sparrow Hall Cl. L9: Faz 1C 36
Sparrow Hall Rd. L9: Faz 1D 36
Sparrowhawk Cl. L26: Halew 2G 93
  WA7: Pal F 6C 114
Speakman Rd. WA10: St H 5B 28
Speakman St. WA7: Run 2D 112
Speakman Way L34: Presc 2D 58
Speedwell Cl. WA10: St H 5B 28
Speedwell Cl. CH60: Hesw 5G 101
Speedwell Dr. CH60: Hesw 5G 101
Speedwell Rd. CH41: Birke 2B 68
SPEKE 3G 109
Speke Blvd. L24: Speke 1D 108
Speke Chu. Rd. L24: Speke 2D 108
Speke Hall Av. L24: Speke 2C 108
Speke Hall Garden & Estate 3B 108
Speke Hall Ind. Est. L24: Speke 2C 108
Speke Hall Rd. L24: Speke 6C 92
  L25: Hunts X 6C 92
Speke Ho. L24: Speke 3A 110
Spekeland Rd. L7: Liv 1A 72
Speke Rd. L19: Garst 6G 91
  L24: Speke .6H 91
  L25: Hunts X, Woolt 1D 92
  L26: Halew .5C 94
  WA8: Wid 5C 94
Speke Town La. L24: Speke 1D 108
Spellow La. L4: Walt 5F 35
Spellow Pl. L3: Liv 3B 4
Spence Av. L20: Boot 6D 20
Spencer Av. CH46: More 6E 49
Spencer Cl. L36: Huy 1H 75
Spencer Gdns. WA9: St H 5H 43
Spencer Pl. L20: Boot 4D 20
Spencer's La. L31: Mell 1C 22
Spencer St. L6: Liv 3F 53

Spenders La. WA7: Aston 6F 125
Spennymoor Ct. WA7: Pal F 6A 114
Spenser Av. CH42: Rock F 2H 87
Spenser Rd. CH42: Rock F 2H 87
Spenser Cl. WA8: Wid 2D 96
Spenser Rd. CH64: Nest 6A 118
Spenser St. L20: Boot 1B 34
Spicer Gro. L32: Kirkb 1A 24
Spice St. L9: Ain 5H 21
Spike Island Vis. Cen. 6E 97
Spindle Cl. L6: Liv 3F 53
Spindrift Ct. CH48: W Kir 2A 82
Spindus Rd. L24: Speke 2C 108
Spinnaker Cl. WA7: Murd 1F 125
Spinnakers, The L19: Aig 4D 90
Spinners Dr. WA9: St H 5B 44
Spinney, The CH48: W Kir 1E 83
  CH49: Upton 3E 67
  CH60: Hesw 2G 117
  CH63: Spit .2B 104
  CH64: Park 6H 117
  L28: Stockb V 6D 38
  L34: Presc .6C 40
  WA11: Rainf 2F 17
Spinney Av. WA8: Wid 2G 95
Spinney Cl. L33: Know I 3E 25
  WA9: Clock F 3G 61
Spinney Cres. L23: Blun 3D 8
Spinney Grn. WA10: Eccl 2G 41
Spinney Rd. L33: Know I 3F 25
Spinney Vw. L33: Know I 3F 25
Spinney Wlk. WA7: Cas 4C 114
Spinney Way L36: Huy 4E 57
Spire Grn. L9: Walt 5G 21
Spires, The WA10: Eccl 1G 41
SPITAL 2B 104
Spital Heyes CH63: Spit 2B 104
Spital Rd. CH62: Brom, Spit 2A 104
  CH63: Spit 2A 104
Spital Station (Rail) 2B 104
Spitfire Rd. L24: Speke 5B 92
Spofforth Rd. L7: Liv 1B 72
Spooner Av. L21: Lith 4C 20
Sprainger St. L3: Liv 3B 52
Sprakeling Pl. L20: Boot 4E 21
Spray St. WA10: St H 1C 42
Spreyton Cl. L12: W Der 3G 37
Sprig Cl. L9: Ain 3B 22
Springbank Cl. WA7: Run 1F 123
Springbank Rd. L4: Walt 2H 53
Springbourne Rd. L17: Aig 1H 89
Springbrook Cl. WA10: Eccl 1G 41
Spring Cl. L33: Kirkb 4C 14
Spring Ct. WA7: Run 3F 113
Springcroft CH64: Park 6G 117
Springdale Cl. CH46: More 6E 49
  L12: W Der 6G 37
Springfield L3: Liv 1G 5 (4E 53)
  (not continuous)
Springfield Av. CH48: W Kir 6E 65
  L21: Lith 3C 20
Springfield Cl. CH49: Woodc 1G 85
  WA10: St H 5A 42
Springfield Cres. L36: Huy 1E 57
Springfield La. WA10: Eccl 6G 27
Springfield Pk. WA11: Hay 4E 31
Springfield Pl. CH44: Wall 3F 51
Springfield Rd. L39: Augh 2E 7
  WA8: Wid 3G 95
  WA10: St H 5A 42
Springfield Sq. L4: Walt 5F 35
Springfield Way L12: W Der 5A 38
Spring Gdns. L31: Mag 1C 12
Spring Gro. L12: W Der 1G 55
Springhill Av. CH62: Brom 1D 120
Springhill Ct. L15: Wav 3E 73
Springmeadow Rd. L25: Gate 4C 74
Springpool WA9: St H 6H 43
Springs Cl. L20: Boot 1D 34
  (off Davies St.)
Springside Cl. L36: Huy 1E 57
Spring St. CH42: Tran 6H 69
  WA8: Wid 5E 97
SPRINGVALE 1G 17
Spring Vale CH45: Wall 6A 32

Springvale Cl. L32: Kirkb 2H 23
Springville Rd. L9: Ain 4A 22
Springwood Av. L20: Boot 4C 20
Springwood Av. L19: Aller 3H 91
  L25: Woolt .3H 91
Springwood Ct. L19: Aller 4H 91
  (off Brocklebank La.)
Springwood Crematorium L25: Aller . . .3B 92
Springwood Gro. L32: Kirkb 4B 24
Springwood Way CH62: New F 3A 88
Spruce Ct. CH42: Tran 5F 69
Spruce Gro. L28: Stockb V 6D 38
Sprucewood Cl. L6: Liv 2H 53
Spur, The CH23: Crosb 6F 9
Spur Cl. L11: Crox 2G 37
Spurgeon Cl. L5: Liv 2F 53
Spurling Rd. WA5: Burtw 1H 63
Spurriers La. L31: Mell 1G 13
Spurstow Cl. CH43: Oxton 6B 68
Squibb Dr. CH46: Leas 5E 49
Squires Av. WA8: Wid 2D 96
Squires Cl. WA11: Hay 5D 30
Squires St. L7: Liv 6G 53
Stable Cl. CH49: Grea 5B 66
Stables, The L23: Crosb 4A 10
Stables Bus. Cen., The L13: Liv 6C 36
  (off Larkhill La.)
Stables Ct. WA9: St H 3G 43
  (off Appleton Rd.)
Stableyard Cotts. WA11: Crank 1C 28
Stackfield, The CH48: W Kir 6F 65
Stadium Cl. CH62: Brom 3F 105
Stadium Rd. CH62: Brom 2E 105
Stadt Moers Pk. .5B 58
Stadt Moers Vis. Cen. 5C 58
Stafford Cl. L36: Huy 3A 58
Stafford Gro. CH62: Brom 6B 6
Stafford Moreton Way L31: Mag 6B 6
Stafford Rd. WA10: St H 4B 42
Staffordshire Cl. L5: Liv 1E 53
Stafford St. L3: Liv 2H 5 (5E 53)
Stag Rd. L24: Speke 5A 92
Stainburn Av. L11: Norr G 2D 36
Stainer Cl. L14: Knott A 2B 56
Stainton Cl. L26: Halew 5A 93
  WA11: St H 3F 29
Stairhaven Rd. L19: Aller 2F 91
Stakes, The CH46: Leas 4C 48
Stalbridge Av. L18: Moss H 4D 72
Stalbridge Dr. WA7: Nort 1H 115
Staley Av. L23: Crosb 6H 9
Stalisfield Av. L11: Norr G 3E 37
Stalisfield Pl. L11: Norr G 3E 37
Stalmine Rd. L9: Walt 1G 35
Stamford Cl. L20: Boot 2D 34
Stamfordham Dr. L19: Aller 3G 91
Stamfordham Gro. L19: Aller 4H 91
Stamfordham Pl. L19: Aller 4H 91
Stamford St. L7: Liv 5A 54
Stanbury Av. CH63: Beb 5A 88
Standale Rd. L15: Wav 1D 72
Standard Rd. L11: Crox 1G 37
Standedge Way L14: Knott A 1C 56
Standen Cl. WA10: St H 1C 42
Stand Farm Rd. L12: Crox 2B 38
Standish Ct. WA8: Wid 3B 96
Standish St. L3: Liv 1E 5 (5D 52)
Standish Dr. WA11: Rainf 2G 17
Standish St. L3: Liv 1E 5 (5D 52)
  WA10: St H 1E 43
Stanbury Av. CH63: Beb 2H 103
Stanford Av. CH45: New B 6D 32
Stanford Cres. L25: Hunts X 2F 93
Stangate L31: Mag 5A 6
Stanhope Dr. CH62: Brom 4D 104
  L36: Huy 4E 57
Stanhope St. L8: Liv 3D 70
  (not continuous)
  WA10: St H 6D 28
Stanier Way L7: Liv 6A 54

Staniforth Pl. L16: Child 6H 55
STANLEY 5C 54
Stanley Av. CH45: Wall 1H 49
  CH63: Hghr B 3D 86
  WA5: Gt San 2F 81
  WA11: Rainf 2E 17
Stanley Bank Rd. WA11: Hay 4C 30
Stanley Bank Way WA11: Hay 5B 30
Stanley Bungs. L34: Know 2E 39
Stanley Cl. CH44: Wall 5G 51
  L4: Kirkd .6D 34
  WA8: Wid .1G 97
Stanley Ct. CH42: Tran 6H 69
Stanley Cres. L34: Presc 1C 58
Stanley Gdns. L9: Walt 6F 21
Stanley Ho. L20: Boot 1B 34
Stanley La. CH62: East 3F 121
STANLEY PARK 2C 20
Stanley Pk. 5G 35
Stanley Pk. L21: Lith 3A 20
Stanley Pk. Av. Nth. L4: Walt 4H 35
            (not continuous)
Stanley Pk. Av. Sth. L4: Walt 5H 35
Stanley Pct. L20: Boot 2C 34
Stanley Rd. CH41: Birke 6B 50
  CH47: Hoy 3A 64
  CH62: New F 3A 88
  L5: Kirkd .5D 34
  L20: Boot, Kirkd 5C 20
  L20: Kirkd 4D 34
  L22: Water 3G 19
  L31: Mag .3A 12
  L36: Huy .5G 57
Stanley St. CH44: Wall 5G 51
  L1: Liv 3D 4 (5C 52)
  L7: Liv 4C 54
  L19: Garst 1H 107
  WA7: Run 2F 113
Stanley Ter. CH45: New B 6D 32
  L8: Liv 2F 71
        (off Up. Parliament St.)
  L18: Moss H 6E 73
Stanley Theatre 6F 53
Stanley Vs. WA7: Run 4D 112
Stanlowe Vw. L19: Gras 5D 90
Stanmore Pk. CH49: Grea 6H 65
Stanmore Rd. L15: Wav 3F 73
  WA7: Run 3H 113
Stanney Cl. CH62: East 4E 121
Stannyfield Cl. L23: Thorn 3B 10
Stannyfield Dr. L23: Thorn 3B 10
Stansfield Av. L31: Mag 6E 7
Stanstead Av. WA5: Penk 6H 81
Stanton Av. L21: Lith 2A 20
Stanton Cl. L30: N'ton 4D 10
  WA11: Hay 5E 31
Stanton Cres. L32: Kirkb 1G 23
Stanton Rd. CH63: Beb 2G 103
  L18: Moss H 4D 72
Stanwood Cl. WA10: Eccl 2F 41
Stanwood Gdns. L35: Whis 4E 59
Stanza Cl. L5: Liv 2E 53
Stapehill Cl. L13: Liv 5F 55
Stapeley Gdns. L26: Halew 5A 94
Staplands Rd. L14: Broad G 5H 55
Stapleford Rd. L25: Gate 3E 75
Staplehurst Cl. L12: Crox 2A 38
Staplehurst Dr. CH42: Rock F 2H 87
Stapleton Av. CH49: Grea 5B 66
  L24: Speke 2F 109
  L35: Rainh 3A 60
Stapleton Cl. L25: Gate 2D 74
  L35: Rainh 3A 60
Stapleton Rd. L35: Rainh 2H 59
Stapleton Way WA8: Hale B 6H 95
Stapley Cl. WA7: Run 4D 112
Starling Cl. WA7: Murd 6F 115
Starling Gro. L12: W Der 4B 38
Starling Way L30: Boot 3D 20
Star St. L8: Liv 3E 71
Starworth Dr. CH62: New F 4C 88
Statham Rd. CH43: Bid 1G 67
Station App. CH46: More 5C 48
  CH47: Meols 1E 65

Station Cl. L25: Hunts X 4E 93
Station M. L32: Kirkb 6G 13
Station Pas. L9: Walt 1G 35
            (off Walton Pk.)
Station Rd. CH41: Birke 6B 50
  CH44: Wall 3C 50
  CH47: Hoy 3B 64
  CH60: Hesw 1D 116
  CH61: Barn 6H 85
  CH61: Thurs 6G 83
  CH63: Store 6H 85
  CH64: Park 6G 117
  L25: Gate .4C 74
  L31: Lyd 1A 6
  L31: Mag .1C 12
  L31: Mell .6E 13
  L34: Presc 1D 58
            (not continuous)
  L35: Rainh 4A 60
  L36: Roby .5E 57
  WA5: Gt San 4H 81
  WA5: Penk 6G 81
  WA7: Run 3D 112
  WA7: Sut W 3D 124
  WA8: Wid .5G 79
  WA9: St H 6A 44
  WA11: Hay 5E 31
Station St. L35: Rainh 4A 60
Statton Rd. L13: Liv 6F 55
Staveley Rd. L19: Gras 3F 91
Stavert Cl. L11: Norr G 2F 37
Staverton Pk. L32: Kirkb 2G 23
Stavordale Rd. CH46: More 6D 48
Steble St. L8: Liv 4F 71
Steel Av. CH45: Wall 1E 51
Steel Cl. L5: Liv 2C 52
Steeple, The CH48: Caldy 5D 82
Steeplechase Cl. L9: Ain 3A 22
Steeple Vw. L33: Kirkb 4A 14
Steers Cft. L28: Stockb V 5B 38
Steetley Dr. WA9: St H 3C 60
Steinberg Ct. L3: Liv 3C 52
Steley Way L34: Presc 2D 58
Stella Nova L20: Boot 2C 34
Stella Pct. L21: Sea 5A 20
Stenhills Cres. WA7: Run 3G 113
Stephens La. L2: Liv 3D 4
Stephenson Cl. L7: Liv 6A 54
            (off Crosfield Rd.)
Stephenson Ho. L7: Liv 1G 71
Stephenson Rd. L13: Liv 5E 55
Stephenson's Sankey Viaduct 3H 45
Stephenson Way L13: Wav 6C 54
Stephen Way L35: Rainh 2H 59
Stepney Gro. L4: Walt 4G 35
Sterling Way L5: Kirkd 1C 52
Sterndale Cl. L7: Liv 1H 71
Sterrix Av. L30: N'ton 1C 20
Sterrix Grn. L21: Lith 1C 20
Sterrix La. L21: Lith 1C 20
  L30: N'ton 1C 20
Steve Biko Cl. L8: Liv 2H 71
Stevenage Cl. WA9: St H 6D 42
Stevenson Cres. WA10: St H 1B 42
Stevenson Dr. CH63: Spit 2H 103
Stevenson St. L15: Wav 1D 72
Stevens Rd. CH60: Hesw 6G 101
Stevens St. WA9: St H 5B 42
Steventon WA7: Nort 1G 115
Steward Ct. L35: Presc 2F 59
Stewards Av. WA8: Wid 3D 96
Stewart Av. L20: Boot 1E 35
Stewart Cl. CH61: Pens 2D 100
Stile Hey L23: Thorn 4B 10
Stiles Rd. L33: Kirkb 3B 14
Stillington Rd. L8: Liv 5G 71
Stirling Av. L23: Crosb 6G 9
Stirling Cres. WA9: St H 1F 61
Stirling La. L25: Hunts X 4F 93
Stirling Rd. L24: Speke 2D 108
Stirling St. CH44: Wall 5D 50
Stobart Stadium, The 3G 97
Stockbridge La. L36: Huy 2D 56
            (not continuous)

Stockbridge Pl. L5: Liv 2G 53
Stockbridge St. L5: Liv 2G 53
STOCKBRIDGE VILLAGE 5C 38
Stockdale Cl. L3: Liv 1D 4 (4C 52)
Stockdale Cl. WA5: Gt San 2G 81
Stockdale Dr. WA5: Gt San 2G 81
Stockham Cl. WA7: Halt 5C 114
Stockham La.
  WA7: Brook, Halt, Murd, Pal F 5C 114
            (not continuous)
Stockmoor Rd. L11: Norr G 2D 36
Stockpit Rd. L33: Know I 1E 25
Stocks Av. WA9: St H 2A 44
Stocks La. WA5: Gt San, Penk 4F 81
Stockswell Farm Ct. WA8: Wid 5C 78
Stockswell Rd. WA8: Wid 5F 77
Stockton Cres. L33: Kirkb 3H 13
Stockton Gro. WA9: St H 1B 60
Stockton Wood Rd.
  L24: Speke 2E 109
Stockville Rd. L18: Moss H 5A 74
Stoddart Rd. L4: Walt 3G 35
Stoke Cl. CH62: East 4E 121
Stoker Way L9: Walt 6G 21
Stokesay CH43: Noct 3H 67
Stokes Cl. L26: Halew 2A 94
Stokesley Av. L32: Kirkb 1G 23
Stoke St. CH41: Birke 1D 68
Stonebarn Dr. L31: Mag 4B 6
Stone Barn La. WA7: Pal F 1C 124
Stonebridge La. L11: Crox 6F 23
Stoneby Dr. CH45: Wall 6C 32
Stonechat Cl. L27: N'ley 5G 75
  WA7: Beech 2A 124
Stone Ct. WA11: Hay 5D 30
Stonecrop L18: Moss H 4A 74
Stonecrop Cl. WA7: Beech 3B 124
Stone Cross Dr. WA8: Wid 4C 78
Stonecross Ct. L35: Rainh 6B 60
Stonedale Cres. L11: Crox 1F 37
Stonedale Pk. L11: Crox 1E 37
Stonefield Rd. L14: Knott A 3B 56
Stonefont Cl. L9: Walt 2G 35
Stonegate Dr. L8: Liv 5F 71
Stonehaven Cl. L16: Child 1B 74
Stone Hey L35: Whis 6D 58
Stonehey Dr. CH48: W Kir 2C 82
Stonehey Rd. L32: Kirkb 3A 24
Stonehey Wlk. L32: Kirkb 3A 24
Stonehill Av. CH63: Beb 5A 88
  L4: Walt 1H 53
          (off Stonehill St.)
Stonehills Ct. WA7: Run 3G 113
Stonehills La. WA7: Run 3G 113
Stonehill St. L4: Walt 1H 53
Stonehouse M. L18: Aller 6H 73
Stonehouse Rd. CH44: Wall 2A 50
Stonelea WA7: Wind N 4D 114
Stoneleigh Gro. CH42: Rock F 3H 87
Stonemasons Ct. L25: Woolt 6C 74
         (off Clay Cross Rd.)
Stoneridge Ct. CH43: Bid 1G 67
Stone Sq. L20: Boot 6E 21
Stone St. L3: Liv 3B 52
  L34: Presc 1D 58
Stoneville Rd. L13: Liv 3E 55
Stoneway Ct. CH60: Hesw 4D 100
STONEYCROFT 3E 55
Stoneycroft L12: W Der 3F 55
  L13: Liv 5G 55
  L15: Wav .5G 55
Stoneycroft Cl. L13: Liv 2E 55
Stoneycroft Cres. L13: Liv 2E 55
Stoney Hey Rd. CH45: New B 6C 32
Stoneyhurst Av. L10: Ain 6A 12
Stoney La. L35: Rainh, Whis 3F 59
Stoney La. Ind. Est.
  L35: Rainh 4G 59
Stoney Vw. L35: Rainh 4H 59
Stonham Cl. CH49: Upton 4C 66
Stonyfield L30: N'ton 4E 11
Stony Holt WA7: Nort 5E 115
Stonyhurst Av. WA11: St H 4F 29
Stonyhurst Rd. L25: Woolt 2D 92

Stopford St. L8: Liv 5F **71**
Stopgate La. L9: Ain, Faz 1B **36**
  L33: Sim 3C **14**
Store St. L20: Kirkd 4D **34**
STORETON .6C **86**
STORETON BRICKFIELDS 6A **86**
Storeton Cl. CH43: Oxton 6D **68**
Storeton La. CH61: Barn 2G **101**
Storeton Rd. CH42: Tran 6D **68**
  CH43: Oxton 6D **68**
Stormont Rd. L19: Garst 4F **91**
Storrington Av. L11: Norr G 2F **37**
Storrsdale Rd. L18: Moss H 6F **73**
Stour Av. L35: Rainh 4A **60**
Stourcliffe Rd. CH44: Wall 3C **50**
Stourport Cl. CH49: Grea 5A **66**
Stourton Rd. L32: Kirkb 3A **24**
Stourton St. CH44: Wall 5E **51**
Stourvale Rd. L26: Halew 4H **93**
Stowe Av. L10: Ain 1C **22**
Stowe Cl. L25: Hunts X 4C **92**
Stowell St. L7: Liv 1F **71**
Stowford Cl. L12: W Der 3G **37**
Strada Way L3: Liv 1H **5** (4F **53**)
Strafford Dr. L20: Boot 1E **35**
Strand, The L2: Liv 4C **4** (6C **52**)
Strand Rd. CH47: Hoy 2B **64**
  L20: Boot 2A **34**
                 (not continuous)
Strand Shop. Cen. L20: Boot 2C **34**
Strand St. L1: Liv 5C **4** (6C **52**)
Strand Vw. L20: Boot 2A **34**
Stratford Rd. L19: Aig 3D **90**
Strathallan Cl. CH60: Hesw 3C **100**
Strathcona Rd. CH45: Wall 1D **50**
  L15: Wav 2C **72**
Strathearn Rd. CH60: Hesw 1D **116**
Strathlorne Cl. CH42: Tran 6H **69**
Strathmore Dr. L23: Crosb 6G **9**
Strathmore Gro. WA9: St H 1G **61**
Strathmore Rd. L6: Liv 3A **54**
Stratton Cl. CH45: Wall 1E **51**
  L18: Aller 1A **92**
  WA7: Brook 1D **124**
Stratton Dr. WA9: St H 1B **60**
Stratton Pk. WA8: Wid 4D **78**
Stratton Rd. L32: Kirkb 2G **23**
Stratton Wlk. L32: Kirkb 2G **23**
Strauss Cl. L8: Liv 3H **71**
Strawberry Field 6A **74**
Strawberry Rd. L11: Norr G 3C **36**
Streatham Av. L18: Moss H 4D **72**
Street Hey La. CH64: Will 5B **120**
Stretford Cl. L33: Kirkb 4A **14**
Stretton Av. CH44: Wall 3C **50**
  WA9: St H 2B **44**
Stretton Cl. CH43: Oxton 6A **68**
  CH62: East 4E **121**
  L12: Crox 2C **38**
Stretton Way L36: Huy 1B **76**
Strickland St. WA10: St H 6F **29**
Stringhey Rd. CH44: Wall 2E **51**
Stroma Rd. L18: Aller 2F **91**
Stromford Cl. WA8: Wid 3E **79**
Stroud Cl. CH49: Grea 6A **66**
Stuart Av. CH46: More 6D **48**
  L25: Hunts X 4E **93**
Stuart Cl. CH46: More 1E **67**
Stuart Dr. L14: Broad G 4A **56**
Stuart Gro. L20: Kirkd 4D **34**
Stuart Rd. CH42: Tran 6F **69**
  L4: Walt .3E **35**
  L22: Water 1G **19**
  L23: Crosb 1G **19**
  L31: Mell .6F **13**
  WA7: Manor P 1D **114**
  WA10: Windle 5A **28**
Stuart Rd. Nth. L20: Boot 2E **35**
Stubbs La. CH43: Noct 6A **68**
Studholme St. L20: Kirkd 6C **34**
Studland Rd. L9: Faz 1C **36**
Studley Rd. CH45: Wall 1A **50**
Sturdee Rd. L13: Liv 6F **55**
Sturgess St. WA12: Newt W 2H **45**

Suburban Rd. L6: Liv 1A **54**
Sudbury Cl. L25: Woolt 1F **93**
Sudbury Gdns. WA9: St H 1A **60**
Sudbury Rd. L22: Water 1D **18**
Sudell Av. L31: Mag 5E **7**
Sudell La. L31: Lyd 1C **6**
  L39: Augh 1C **6**
Sudley Grange L17: Aig 2C **90**
Sudley House 1D **90**
Sudworth Rd. CH45: New B 6C **32**
Suffield Rd. L4: Kirkd 5D **34**
Suffolk Pl. WA8: Wid 4A **96**
Suffolk St. L1: Liv 6F **5** (1D **70**)
  L20: Boot 1D **34**
  WA7: Run 2D **112**
Suffton Pk. L32: Kirkb 2G **23**
Sugarbrook La. L10: Faz 6D **22**
Sugar La. L34: Know 2E **39**
Sugar St. L9: Ain 6H **21**
Sugnall St. L7: Liv 1F **71**
                 (not continuous)
Sulby Av. L13: Liv 2C **54**
Sulgrave Cl. L16: Child 6G **55**
Sullington Dr. L27: N'ley 3G **75**
                 (not continuous)
Sullivan Av. CH49: Upton 5D **66**
Sullivan Rd. WA8: Wid 4H **97**
Sullivans Way WA9: St H 5F **43**
Sumley St. WA11: St H 6H **29**
Summer Cl. WA7: Halt 4B **114**
Summerfield CH62: Brom 3D **104**
Summerfield Av. WA10: Eccl 2F **41**
Summerford Cl. CH42: Tran 6G **69**
Summerhill Dr. L31: Mag 2D **12**
Summer La. WA4: Dares, Pres H 1H **125**
  WA7: Halt 4B **114**
Summer Rd. L20: Boot 6C **20**
Summers Av. L20: Boot 1E **35**
Summer Seat L3: Liv 3D **52**
  L20: Boot 2A **34**
Summers Rd. L3: Liv 4D **70**
Summertrees Av. CH49: Grea 5B **66**
Summertrees Cl. CH49: Grea 5B **66**
Summerwood CH61: Irby 4B **84**
Summit, The CH44: Wall 2E **51**
Summit Way L25: Woolt 6B **74**
Sumner Cl. L25: Liv 2C **52**
  L35: Rainh 6B **60**
Sumner Gro. *L33: Kirkb* *3B* **14**
             (off Mossdale Rd.)
Sumner Rd. CH43: Bid 1B **68**
Sumners Farm Ct. WA4: Pres H 1H **125**
Sumner St. WA11: Hay 5C **30**
Sunbeam Cl. WA7: Run 2D **112**
Sunbeam Rd. L13: Liv 4E **55**
Sunbourne Rd. L17: Aig 1H **89**
Sunbury Rd. CH44: Wall 4E **51**
  L4: Walt .6H **35**
Sunbury St. WA10: St H 5A **42**
Suncroft Rd. CH60: Hesw 6G **101**
Sundale Av. L35: Presc 1F **59**
Sundene Lodge L22: Water 4G **19**
Sundew Cl. L9: Walt 4F **21**
Sundridge St. L8: Liv 5G **71**
Sunfield Rd. CH46: More 5D **48**
Sunflower Cl. WA9: Bold 6C **44**
Sunlight Lodge CH62: Port S 5B **88**
Sunlight St. L6: Liv 2A **54**
Sunloch Cl. L9: Ain 3B **22**
Sunningdale CH46: More 1E **67**
Sunningdale Av. WA8: Wid 2H **95**
Sunningdale Cl. L36: Roby 6E **57**
  WA5: Burtw 6H **45**
Sunningdale Dr. CH61: Thing 6E **85**
  CH63: Brom 1B **120**
  L23: Blun .3E **9**
Sunningdale Rd. CH45: Wall 5B **32**
  L15: Wav 1D **72**
Sunniside La. WA7: Run 1G **115**
Sunny Bank CH63: Hghr B 5F **87**
Sunnybank CH49: Upton 3D **66**
Sunnybank Av. CH43: Noct 5H **67**
Sunny Bank Rd. L16: Child 2H **73**
Sunnydale L35: Rainh 4B **60**

Sunnygate Rd. L19: Gras 3E **91**
Sunnymede Dr. L31: Lyd 4C **6**
Sunnyside CH46: More 5B **48**
  L8: Liv 4H **71**
  WA5: Gt San 3G **81**
Sunnyside Rd. L23: Crosb 6E **9**
Sunrise Cl. L19: Gras 4F **91**
Sunsdale Rd. L18: Moss H 4E **73**
Sunset Cl. *L33: Kirkb* *4C* **14**
           (off Freckleton Dr.)
Superbowl
  Widnes .4F **97**
Superior Cl. L27: N'ley 4G **75**
Surby Cl. L16: Child 1A **74**
Surlingham Gdns. WA9: St H 1C **60**
Surrey Av. CH49: Upton 4C **66**
Surrey Dr. CH48: W Kir 3C **82**
Surrey St. CH44: Wall 4C **50**
  L1: Liv 6E **5** (1D **70**)
  L20: Boot 1D **34**
  WA7: Run 3E **113**
  WA9: St H 2H **43**
Susan Dr. WA5: Penk 4F **81**
Susan Gro. CH46: More 1B **66**
Susan St. WA8: Wid 1G **97**
Susan Wlk. L35: Whis 2F **59**
Sussex Cl. CH61: Pens 1C **100**
  L20: Boot 1D **34**
Sussex Gro. WA9: St H 3H **43**
Sussex Rd. CH48: W Kir 6C **64**
  L31: Mag 2B **12**
Sussex St. L20: Boot 1D **34**
  L22: Water 1E **19**
  WA8: Wid 2H **97**
Sutcliffe St. L6: Liv 4H **53**
Sutherland Cl. WA7: Nun 3F **113**
Sutherland Dr. CH62: East 3D **120**
Sutherland Rd. L34: Presc 1E **59**
SUTTON 5B **44**
Sutton C'way. WA6: Frod 5A **124**
Sutton Cl. CH62: East 4E **121**
Sutton Fields Golf Driving Range . . .3E **125**
Sutton Fold WA9: St H 5H **43**
Sutton Fold Ind. Pk. WA9: St H 5H **43**
Sutton Hall Golf Course 4C **124**
SUTTON HEATH 6D **42**
Sutton Heath Rd. WA9: St H 1C **60**
SUTTON LEACH 2H **61**
Sutton Leisure Cen. 1F **61**
SUTTON MANOR 5F **61**
Sutton Moss Rd. WA9: St H 5B **44**
Sutton Oak Dr. WA9: St H 4H **43**
Sutton Pk. WA9: St H 6G **43**
Sutton Quays Bus. Pk.
  WA7: Sut W 4A **124**
Sutton Rd. CH45: New B 6D **32**
  WA9: St H 4G **43**
Suttons La. WA8: Wid 4F **97**
Sutton St. L13: Liv 2C **54**
  WA7: Run 3F **113**
Suttons Way *L26: Halew* *2G* **93**
             (off Betony Cl.)
SUTTON WEAVER 4D **124**
Sutton Wood Rd. L24: Speke 2E **109**
Suzanne Boardman Ho. L6: Liv 2A **54**
Swainson Rd. L10: Faz 4D **22**
Swale Av. L35: Rainh 4A **60**
Swaledale Av. L35: Rainh 4B **60**
Swaledale Cl. CH62: East 2E **121**
  WA5: Gt San 2H **81**
Swalegate L31: Mag 5B **6**
Swallow Cl. L12: Crox 2B **38**
  L27: N'ley 4H **75**
  L33: Kirkb 2A **14**
Swallow Flds. L9: Faz 1D **36**
Swallowhurst Cres. L11: Norr G 3E **37**
Swan Av. WA9: St H 3C **44**
Swan Ct. CH43: Pren 1B **86**
Swan Cres. L15: Wav 1F **73**
Swan Gdns. WA9: St H 1C **60**
Swan Hey L31: Mag 2C **12**
Swan La. L39: Augh 1D **6**
Swan Rd. WA12: Newt W 1F **45**

Swansea Cl. L19: Garst 5F **91**
SWANSIDE .4A **56**
Swanside Av. L14: Broad G 4A **56**
Swanside Pde. L14: Knott A 4A **56**
Swanside Rd. L14: Broad G 4A **56**
Swanston Av. L4: Walt 4G **35**
Swan St. L13: Liv 4D **54**
Swan Wlk. L31: Mag 2C **12**
Sweden Gro. L22: Water 2F **19**
Sweet Briar Ct. WA9: Clock F 5H **61**
Sweeting St. L2: Liv 4D **4** (6C **52**)
Swift Gro. L12: Crox 1B **38**
Swift's Cl. L30: N'ton 5D **10**
Swifts La. L30: N'ton 5D **10**
Swift St. WA10: St H 6E **29**
Swift's Weint CH64: Park 6F **117**
           (off Coastguard La.)
Swinbrook Grn. L11: Norr G 2D **36**
Swinburne Cl. L16: Child 1B **74**
Swinburne Rd. WA10: St H 6B **28**
Swindale Cl. L8: Liv 2H **71**
Swinden Cl. WA7: Wind H 3F **115**
Swinderby Dr. L31: Mell 6F **13**
Swindon Cl. CH49: Grea 5A **66**
  L5: Kirkd 6D **34**
Swindon St. L5: Kirkd 6D **34**
Swinford Av. WA8: Wid 1A **98**
Swisspine Gdns. WA9: St H 6A **42**
Swiss Rd. L6: Liv 4A **54**
Switch Island L30: N'ton 4H **11**
Switch Island Leisure Pk.
  L30: N'ton 6G **11**
Sword Cl. L11: Crox 2G **37**
Sword Wlk. L11: Crox 2G **37**
Swynnerton Way WA8: Wid 4F **79**
Sybil Rd. L4: Walt 6G **35**
Sycamore Av. CH49: Upton 2B **66**
  L23: Crosb 3H **9**
  L26: Halew 5H **93**
  WA8: Wid 1F **97**
  WA11: Hay 6C **30**
Sycamore Cl. CH49: Upton 2B **66**
  L9: Walt 2A **36**
  WA10: Eccl 1H **41**
Sycamore Ct. L8: Liv 5G **71**
           (off Weller Way)
  WA7: Manor P 1F **115**
Sycamore Dr. L33: Kirkb 6B **14**
  WA7: Sut W 3C **124**
Sycamore Gdns. WA10: St H 5C **28**
Sycamore Pk. L18: Aller 1H **91**
Sycamore Ri. CH49: Grea 1A **84**
Sycamore Rd. CH42: Tran 5F **69**
  L22: Water 1G **19**
  L36: Huy 1G **75**
  WA7: Run 5G **113**
Syddall St. WA10: St H 4D **28**
Sydenham Av. L17: Liv 4A **72**
Sydenham Ho. L17: Aig 4B **72**
Syder's Gro. L34: Know 2E **39**
Sydney St. L9: Ain 5G **21**
  WA7: West P 6B **112**
Sylvan Cl. L25: Woolt 2D **92**
Sylvandale Gro. CH62: Brom 3D **104**
Sylvania Rd. L4: Walt 3G **35**
Sylvia Cl. L10: Faz 5F **23**
Syren St. L20: Kirkd 5C **34**
Syston Av. WA11: St H 5G **29**

T

Tabley Av. WA8: Wid 1A **96**
Tabley Cl. CH43: Oxton 1B **86**
Tabley Gdns. WA9: St H 1B **60**
Tabley Rd. L15: Wav 2B **72**
Tabley St. L1: Liv 1D **70**
Tace Cl. L8: Liv 2F **71**
Taggart Av. L16: Child 3H **73**
Tagus Cl. L8: Liv 3H **71**
Tagus St. L8: Liv 3H **71**
Tailor's La. L31: Mag 1C **12**
Talbot Av. CH63: Brim 4C **102**
Talbot Cl. WA10: St H 1D **42**

Talbot Ct. CH43: Oxton 5C **68**
  L36: Huy 6G **57**
Talbot Rd. CH43: Oxton 5C **68**
Talbotville Rd. L13: Liv 6G **55**
Talgarth Way L25: Gate 2C **74**
Taliesin St. L5: Liv 2D **52**
Talisman Cl. WA7: Murd 6G **115**
Talisman Way L20: Boot 1A **34**
Talland Cl. L26: Halew 2G **93**
Tallarn Rd. L32: Kirkb 1F **23**
Tall Trees WA9: St H 5F **43**
Talton Rd. L15: Wav 2B **72**
Tamar Cl. L6: Liv 3G **53**
Tamar Gro. CH46: More 1B **66**
Tamarisk Gdns. WA9: St H 6A **42**
Tamar Rd. WA11: Hay 5E **31**
Tame Ct. WA8: Wid 4E **79**
Tamerton Cl. L18: Aller 1A **92**
Tam O'Shanter Urban Farm 2A **68**
Tamworth St. L8: Liv 4E **71**
  WA10: St H 1C **42**
Tanar Cl. CH63: Spit 2B **104**
Tanat Dr. L18: Moss H 5F **73**
Tancred Rd. CH45: Wall 2C **50**
  L4: Walt 6G **35**
Tanhouse WA7: Halt 4A **114**
Tan Ho. La. WA5: Burtw 3H **63**
  WA8: Wid 3G **97**
Tanhouse Rd. L23: Thorn 4B **10**
Tannery La. WA5: Penk 6E **81**
Tansley Cl. CH48: W Kir 1E **83**
Tanworth Gro. CH46: More 6H **47**
Tapestry Gdns. CH41: Birke 6B **50**
Tapley Pl. L13: Liv 5D **54**
Taplow St. L6: Liv 1H **53**
Tapton Way L13: Wav 6D **54**
Tara Pk. Caravan Site L3: Liv 4B **52**
TARBOCK GREEN 5C **76**
Tarbock Interchange L35: Whis 1C **76**
Tarbock Rd. L24: Speke 1F **109**
  L36: Huy 6F **57**
Tarbot Hey CH46: More 1A **66**
Tarbrock Ct. L30: N'ton 4D **10**
           (off Great Hey)
Target Rd. CH60: Hesw 5A **100**
Tariff St. L5: Liv 2D **52**
Tarleton Cl. L26: Halew 4G **93**
Tarleton St. L1: Liv 4E **5** (6D **52**)
Tarlton Cl. L35: Rainh 2G **59**
Tarnbeck WA7: Nort 6E **115**
Tarncliff L28: Stockb V 5E **39**
Tarn Gro. WA11: St H 3F **29**
Tarnmere Cl. L4: Walt 2G **35**
Tarporley Cl. CH43: Oxton 6B **68**
  WA10: Eccl 2H **41**
Tarragon Cl. L23: Thorn 4B **10**
Tarran Dr. CH46: More 5B **48**
Tarran Rd. CH46: More 5B **48**
Tarran Way E. CH46: More 5B **48**
Tarran Way Nth. CH46: More 5B **48**
Tarran Way Sth. CH46: More 5B **48**
Tarran Way W. CH46: More 4B **48**
Tarves Wlk. L33: Kirkb 1B **24**
Tarvin Cl. WA7: Run 1G **123**
  WA9: Sut M 3F **61**
Tarvin Rd. CH62: East 3F **121**
Tasker Ter. L35: Rainh 3A **60**
Tasman Gro. WA9: St H 6C **42**
Tate Cl. WA8: Wid 1B **96**
Tate Liverpool 6B **4** (1B **70**)
Tate St. L4: Walt 5F **35**
Tatlock St. L5: Liv 3C **52**
Tattersall Pl. L20: Boot 3B **34**
Tattersall Rd. L21: Lith 4A **20**
Tattersall Way L7: Liv 5C **54**
Tatton Rd. CH42: Tran 4F **69**
  L9: Walt 5G **21**
Taunton Av. WA9: Sut L 2H **61**
Taunton Dr. L10: Ain 1C **22**
Taunton Rd. CH45: Wall 1A **50**
  L36: Huy 5B **58**
Taurus Rd. L14: Knott A 3C **56**
Tavener Cl. CH63: Brom 2C **120**

Tavington Rd. L26: Halew 2A **94**
Tavistock Rd. CH45: Wall 1A **50**
  WA5: Penk 5G **81**
Tavy Rd. L6: Liv 3G **53**
Tawd St. L4: Kirkd 5E **35**
Tawny Ct. WA7: Pal F 6A **114**
Taylforth Cl. L9: Walt 6G **21**
Taylor Cl. WA9: St H 5A **44**
Taylor Rd. WA11: Hay 5G **31**
Taylors Cl. L9: Walt 2E **35**
Taylors La. L9: Walt 2E **35**
  WA5: Cuerd 1C **98**
Taylors Row WA7: Run 3G **113**
Taylor St. CH41: Birke 2G **69**
  L5: Liv .2D **52**
  WA8: Wid 2G **97**
  WA9: St H 5A **44**
Taylor St. Ind. Est. L5: Liv 2E **53**
Teakwood Cl. L6: Liv 2H **53**
Teal Bus. Pk. WA8: Wid 3G **97**
Teal Cl. WA11: St H 5F **29**
Teal Gro. L26: Halew 2G **93**
Teals Way CH60: Hesw 5B **100**
Teasville Rd. L18: Moss H 5A **74**
Tebay Cl. L31: Mag 5E **7**
Tebay Rd. CH62: East 5E **105**
Teck St. L7: Liv 5G **53**
Tedburn Cl. L25: Gate 5E **75**
Tedbury Cl. L32: Kirkb 3A **24**
Tedbury Wlk. L32: Kirkb 3A **24**
Tedder Sq. WA8: Wid 3B **96**
Teehey Cl. CH63: Hghr B 5F **87**
Teehey Gdns. CH63: Hghr B 5F **87**
Teehey La. CH63: Hghr B 5F **87**
Tees Cl. L4: Kirkd 4E **35**
Teesdale Cl. WA5: Gt San 2H **81**
Teesdale Rd. CH63: Beb 1G **103**
  WA11: Hay 4E **31**
Teesdale Way L35: Rainh 2A **60**
Tees Pl. L4: Kirkd 4E **35**
Tees St. CH41: Birke 6B **50**
  L4: Kirkd 4D **34**
Teign Cl. L6: Liv 3G **53**
Teignmouth Cl. L19: Garst 5F **91**
Teilo St. L8: Liv 4G **71**
Telary Cl. L5: Liv 2C **52**
Telegraph Ho. L23: Crosb 4G **9**
Telegraph La. CH45: Wall 2G **49**
Telegraph Rd. CH48: Caldy 4F **83**
  CH60: Hesw 1A **100**
  CH61: Thurs 4F **83**
Telegraph Way L32: Kirkb 1A **24**
Telford Cl. CH43: Oxton 5D **68**
  WA8: Wid 5B **78**
Telford Ct. L7: Liv 6H **53**
Telford Dr. WA9: St H 6B **44**
Tempest Hey L2: Liv 3C **4** (5C **52**)
Temple Ct. L2: Liv 4D **4** (6C **52**)
Temple La. L2: Liv 3D **4** (5C **52**)
Templemore Av. L18: Moss H 6E **73**
Templemore Rd.
  CH43: Oxton 5C **68**
Temple St. L2: Liv 3D **4** (5C **52**)
Templeton Cres. L12: W Der 4F **37**
Tenbury Cl. WA5: Gt San 1H **81**
Tenby Av. L21: Lith 2A **20**
Tenby Dr. CH46: More 1D **66**
  WA7: Run 3H **113**
Tenby St. L5: Liv 1G **53**
Tennis St. WA10: St H 6C **28**
Tennis St. Nth. WA10: St H 6C **28**
Tennyson Av. CH42: Rock F 2H **87**
Tennyson Rd. L36: Huy 1A **76**
  WA8: Wid 2E **97**
Tennyson St. L20: Boot 6B **20**
  WA9: Sut M 5E **61**
Tennyson Way L32: Kirkb 2H **23**
Tenpin
  Bootle .6G **11**
Tensing Rd. L31: Mag 6C **6**
Tenterden St. L5: Liv 3D **52**
Tenth Av. L9: Ain 4B **22**
Terence Rd. L16: Child 3H **73**

Terminus Rd.—Tobin St.

Terminus Rd. CH62: Brom 2D **104**
L36: Huy 2D **56**
Tern Cl. L33: Kirkb 2A **14**
WA8: Wid 5F **79**
Ternhall Rd. L9: Faz 1D **36**
Ternhall Way L9: Faz 1D **36**
Tern Way CH46: More 6H **47**
WA10: St H 6G **41**
Terrace Rd. WA8: Wid 6E **97**
Terret Cft. L28: Stockb V 6D **38**
Tetbury St. CH41: Birke 4E **69**
Tetchill Cl. WA7: Nort 5F **115**
Tetlow St. L4: Walt 5F **35**
Tetlow Way L4: Walt 5F **35**
Teulon Cl. L4: Walt 5F **35**
Tewit Hall Cl. L24: Speke 2E **109**
Tewit Hall Rd. L24: Speke 2E **109**
Tewkesbury Cl. L12: Crox 1B **38**
L25: Woolt 1F **93**
Teynham Av. L34: Know 1F **39**
Teynham Cres. L11: Norr G 3D **36**
Thackeray Cl. L8: Liv 3F **71**
Thackeray Ct. *L8: Liv* *3F* ***71***
(off Pomfret St.)
Thackeray Gdns. L30: Boot 3D **20**
Thackray Rd. WA10: St H 5B **42**
Thames Rd. WA9: Sut L 1G **61**
Thames St. L8: Liv 3H **71**
Thatchers Mt. WA5: Coll G 4F **45**
THATTO HEATH **5C 42**
Thatto Heath Rd. WA9: St H 5B **42**
WA10: St H 5B **42**
Thatto Heath Station (Rail) **5B 42**
The ....
Names prefixed with 'The' for example 'The Aerodrome' are indexed under the main name such as 'Aerodrome, The'
Thermal Rd. CH62: Brom 1D **104**
Thermopylae Ct. CH43: Noct 3H **67**
Thermopylae Pas. CH43: Noct 3H **67**
Thetford Rd. WA5: Gt San 3G **81**
Thickwood Moss La. WA11: Rainf 4F **17**
THINGWALL **5E 85**
Thingwall Av. L14: Knott A 5H **55**
Thingwall Dr. CH61: Irby 5E **85**
Thingwall Grange CH61: Thing 5F **85**
Thingwall Hall Dr. L14: Broad G 5H **55**
Thingwall La. L14: Knott A 4H **55**
Thingwall Recreation Cen. **5F 85**
Thingwall Rd. CH61: Irby 5B **84**
L15: Wav 2F **73**
Thingwall Rd. E. CH61: Thing 5E **85**
Third Av. CH43: Bid 3F **67**
L9: Ain 4B **22**
(Fourth Av.)
L9: Ain 4C **22**
(Meres Rd.)
L23: Crosb 5F **9**
WA7: Pal F 5B **114**
Thirlmere Av. CH43: Noct 3G **67**
L21: Lith 3D **20**
WA11: St H 3E **29**
Thirlmere Cl. L31: Mag 5D **6**
WA6: Frod 6H **123**
Thirlmere Ct. *L5: Liv* *2G* ***53***
(off Harding Cl.)
Thirlmere Dr. CH45: Wall 2D **50**
L21: Lith 3D **20**
Thirlmere Grn. L5: Liv 2G **53**
Thirlmere Rd. L5: Liv 2G **53**
Thirlmere Wlk. L33: Kirkb 5H **13**
Thirlmere Way WA8: Wid 3A **96**
Thirlstane St. L17: Aig 6H **71**
Thirsk Cl. WA7: Run 1G **123**
Thistledown Cl. L17: Aig 6G **71**
Thistleton Av. CH41: Birke 1B **68**
Thistleton Cl. WA9: St H 1A **44**
Thistlewood Rd. L7: Liv 5C **54**
Thistley Hey Rd. L32: Kirkb 1B **24**
Thomas Cl. L19: Garst 6G **91**
Thomas Ct. CH43: Oxton 4E **69**
WA7: Pal F 6B **114**
Thomas Dr. L14: Broad G 5G **55**
L35: Presc 3C **58**
Thomas Jones Way WA7: Run 3E **113**
Thomas La. L14: Broad G, Knott A 3H **55**
Thomas Steers Way L1: Liv 6D **4** (6C **52**)
Thomas St. CH41: Birke 4G **69**
WA7: Run 2F **113**
WA8: Wid 4E **97**
Thomaston St. L5: Liv 1E **53**
(not continuous)
Thomas Winder Ct. *L5: Kirkd* *1D* ***52***
(off Sterling Way)
Thompson St. CH41: Tran 5G **69**
WA10: St H 4B **42**
Thomson Rd. L21: Sea 4H **19**
(not continuous)
Thomson St. L6: Liv 3H **53**
Thorburn Cl. CH62: New F 3B **88**
Thorburn Ct. CH62: New F 2B **88**
Thorburn Cres. CH62: New F 3B **88**
Thorburn Dr. L7: Liv 6H **53**
Thorburn Lodge CH62: New F 2B **88**
Thorburn Rd. CH62: New F 3B **88**
Thorley Cl. L15: Wav 6E **55**
Thornaby Gro. WA9: St H 1B **60**
Thornbeck Cl. L12: Crox 2B **38**
Thornbridge Av. L21: Lith 3D **20**
Thornbrook Cl. L12: W Der 6H **37**
Thornbury Rd. L4: Walt 6A **36**
Thorncliffe Rd. CH44: Wall 4C **50**
Thorn Cl. WA5: Penk 6H **81**
WA7: Run 6G **113**
Thorncroft Dr. CH61: Barn 1F **101**
Thorndale Rd. L22: Water 1F **19**
Thorndyke Cl. L35: Rainh 6C **60**
Thorne La. CH44: Wall 2B **50**
Thornes Rd. L6: Liv 4H **53**
Thorness Cl. CH49: Grea 1A **84**
Thorneycroft St. CH41: Birke 1C **68**
Thornfield Hey CH63: Spit 3A **104**
Thornfield Rd. L9: Walt 6F **21**
L23: Thorn 3A **10**
Thornham Av. WA9: St H 5G **43**
Thornham Cl. CH49: Upton 2E **67**
Thornhead La. L12: W Der 1H **55**
Thornhill Rd. L15: Wav 2E **73**
Thornholme Cres. L11: Norr G 4E **37**
Thornhurst L32: Kirkb 4A **24**
Thornleigh Av. CH62: East 4F **121**
Thornley Rd. CH46: More 2A **66**
Thornridge CH46: More 1E **67**
Thorn Rd. WA7: Run 6G **113**
WA10: St H 2A **42**
Thorns, The L31: Mag 5A **6**
Thorns Dr. CH49: Grea 1A **84**
Thornside Wlk. L25: Gate 5D **74**
THORNTON **3A 10**
Thornton WA8: Wid 3C **96**
Thornton Av. CH63: Hghr B 3F **87**
L20: Boot 4D **20**
Thornton Comn. Rd.
CH63: Raby M, Thorn H 6D **102**
Thornton Crematorium L23: Thorn 3C **10**
Thornton Cres. CH60: Hesw 1F **117**
Thorntondale Dr. WA5: Gt San 2G **81**
Thornton Gro. CH63: Hghr B 3F **87**
THORNTON HOUGH **1D 118**
Thornton Rd. CH45: Wall 1C **50**
CH63: Hghr B 3F **87**
L16: Child 6A **56**
L20: Boot 6C **20**
(not continuous)
Thornton St. CH41: Birke 1C **68**
L21: Lith 5B **20**
Thorn Tree Cl. L24: Hale 4E **111**
Thorntree Cl. L17: Aig 6G **71**
Thornwood Cl. L6: Liv 2H **53**
Thornycroft Rd. L15: Wav 2B **72**
Thorpe Bank CH42: Rock F 3H **87**
Thorstone Dr. CH61: Irby 4A **84**
Thorsway CH42: Rock F 1H **87**
CH48: Caldy 3D **82**
Threadneedle Ct. WA9: St H 5B **44**
Three Acres Cl. L25: Woolt 6A **74**
Three Butt La. L12: W Der 1D **54**
THREE LANES END **4H 65**
Threlfall St. L8: Liv 5G **71**
Thresher Av. CH49: Grea 5A **66**
Threshers, The *L30: N'ton* *5H* ***11***
(off Reapers Way)
Throne Rd. L11: Crox 2G **37**
Throne Wlk. *L11: Crox* *1G* ***37***
(off Throne Rd.)
Thurne Way L25: Gate 3C **74**
Thurnham St. L6: Liv 2A **54**
Thursby Cl. L32: Kirkb 3B **24**
Thursby Cres. L32: Kirkb 2B **24**
Thursby Dr. L32: Kirkb 2B **24**
Thursby Rd. CH62: Brom 3E **105**
Thursby Wlk. L32: Kirkb 3B **24**
THURSTASTON **6H 83**
Thurstaston Common Local Nature Reserve
3G 83
Thurstaston Rd. CH60: Hesw 4C **100**
CH61: Irby, Thurs 6H **83**
Thurston Billiard & Snooker Mus.
1G 5 (4E 53)
Thurston Rd. L4: Walt 1H **53**
Tibb's Cross La. WA8: Bold H 1H **79**
Tiber St. L8: Liv 3H **71**
Tichbourne Way L6: Liv 4F **53**
Tickford Bank WA8: Wid 1C **96**
Tickle Av. WA9: St H 2H **43**
Tideswell Cl. L7: Liv 1H **71**
Tide Way CH45: Wall 5A **32**
Tiger Ct. L34: Presc 2A **58**
Tilbey Dr. WA6: Frod 6E **123**
Tilbrook Dr. WA9: St H 1H **61**
Tilbury Pl. WA7: Murd 1G **125**
Tildsley Cres. WA7: West 1D **122**
Tilia Rd. L5: Liv 1G **53**
Tillotson Cl. L8: Liv 4E **71**
Tilney St. L9: Walt 5G **21**
Tilstock Av. CH62: New F 3B **88**
Tilstock Cl. L26: Halew 1A **94**
Tilstock Cres. CH43: Pren 2B **86**
Tilston Cl. L9: Faz 2B **36**
Tilston Rd. CH45: Wall 1C **50**
L9: Faz 1B **36**
L32: Kirkb 1G **23**
Timberland Cl. L25: Gate 2C **74**
Time Pk. L35: Whis 2F **59**
Timmis Cres. WA8: Wid 2E **97**
Timon Av. L20: Boot 1E **35**
Timor Av. WA9: St H 5C **42**
Timperley Ct. *WA8: Wid* *3F* ***97***
(off Alfred Cl.)
Timpron St. L7: Liv 1A **72**
Timway Dr. L12: W Der 5A **38**
Tinas Way CH49: Upton 4E **67**
Tinling Cl. L34: Presc 1E **59**
Tinsley Cl. L26: Halew 1G **93**
Tinsley St. L4: Walt 6G **35**
Tintagel Cl. WA7: Brook 1E **125**
Tintagel Rd. L11: Crox 6H **23**
Tintern Dr. CH46: More 1C **66**
Tiptree Cl. L12: Crox 1B **38**
Titchfield St. L3: Liv 3C **52**
L5: Liv 3C **52**
Tithebarn Cl. CH60: Hesw 6D **100**
Tithebarn Dr. CH64: Park 5F **117**
Tithebarn Gro. L15: Wav 2E **73**
Tithebarn La. L31: Mell 4E **13**
L32: Kirkb 2H **23**
Tithebarn Rd. L23: Crosb 5H **9**
L34: Know 1E **39**
WN4: Garsw 1E **31**
Tithebarn St. L2: Liv 3C **4** (5C **52**)
Titherington Way L15: Wav 3B **72**
Tithings, The WA7: Run 4A **114**
Tiverton Av. CH44: Wall 3C **50**
Tiverton Cl. L36: Huy 4B **58**
WA8: Wid 6A **78**
Tiverton Rd. L26: Halew 5G **93**
Tiverton Sq. WA5: Penk 5G **81**
Tiverton St. L15: Wav 1C **72**
TMAS Health & Fitness **2F 29**
Tobermory Cl. WA11: Hay 6C **30**
Tobin Cl. L5: Liv 3C **52**
Tobin St. CH44: Wall 3F **51**

Tobruk Rd. L36: Huy 3F 57
Todd Rd. WA9: St H 2F 43
Toft Cl. WA8: Wid 2D 96
Toft St. L7: Liv 5A 54
Toftwood Av. L35: Rainh 6B 60
Toftwood Gdns. L35: Rainh 6B 60
Tokenspire Pk. L33: Know I 4D 24
Toleman Av. CH63: Beb 6A 88
Tollemache Rd. CH41: Birke 2B 68
   CH43: Bid 2A 68
   CH43: Clau 2B 68
Tollemache St. CH45: New B 5E 33
Tollerton Rd. L12: W Der 1D 54
Tolpuddle Rd. L25: Woolt 6B 74
Tolpuddle Way L4: Kirkd 5D 34
Tolver Ho. WA10: St H 1E 43
                        (off Tolver St.)
Tolver St. WA10: St H 1E 43
Tom Mann Cl. L3: Liv 2F 5 (5D 52)
Tommy Gent Way L31: Mag 1B 12
Tonbridge Cl. L24: Speke 1D 108
Tonbridge Dr. L10: Ain 6B 12
Topaz Cl. L4: Walt 3E 35
Topcliffe Gro. L12: Crox 2C 38
Topgate Cl. CH60: Hesw 5F 101
Topham Dr. L9: Ain 1H 21
Topham Ter. L9: Ain 3H 21
Topsham Cl. L25: Gate 5E 75
Torcross Way L25: Gate 5E 75
   L26: Halew 2G 93
Tordelow Cl. L6: Liv 3G 53
Toronto Cl. L36: Huy 6F 39
Toronto St. CH44: Wall 4G 51
Torpoint Cl. L14: Knott A 1C 56
Torr Dr. CH62: East 6G 105
Torrington Dr. CH61: Thing 5F 85
   L26: Halew 4G 93
Torrington Gdns. CH61: Thing 4F 85
Torrington Rd. CH44: Wall 3C 50
   L19: Gras 4F 91
Torrisholme Rd. L9: Ain 2B 36
Torus Rd. L13: Liv 3E 55
Tor Vw. L15: Wav 3E 73
Torwood CH43: Noct 2H 67
Total Fitness
   Bootle 5H 11
   Prenton .3H 85
Totland Cl. L27: N'ley 5H 75
   WA5: Gt San 2E 81
Totnes Av. L26: Halew 2H 93
Totnes Rd. L11: Crox 6G 23
Tourist Info. Cen.
   Liverpool John Lennon Airport
                              . . . . . . .3E 109
   Runcorn 2E 113
   St Helens 2E 43
Towcester St. L21: Lith 5B 20
Tower Gdns. L3: Liv 4C 4 (6C 52)
TOWER HILL 3B 14
Tower Hill CH42: Tran 6F 69
Towerlands St. L7: Liv 6H 53
Tower La. WA7: Nort 6E 115
Tower Prom. CH45: New B 4E 33
Tower Quays CH41: Birke 1G 69
Tower Rd. CH41: Birke 1G 69
                        (Reservoir Rd.)
   CH42: Tran 2D 86
                        (Reservoir Rd.)
   CH42: Tran 6F 69
                        (Tower Hill)
Tower Rd. Nth. CH60: Hesw 3C 100
Tower Rd. Sth. CH60: Hesw 4D 100
Towers, The CH42: Tran 1G 87
Towers Av. L31: Mag 5C 6
Towers Rd. L16: Child 3G 73
Tower St. L3: Liv 4D 70
Tower Way L25: Woolt 6C 74
Tower Wharf CH41: Birke 1G 69
Towneley Ct. WA8: Wid 2E 97
TOWN END 3A 78
Townfield Cen. CH43: Oxton 6A 68
Townfield Cl. CH43: Oxton 6A 68
Townfield Gdns. CH63: Hghr B 4H 87
Townfield La. CH43: Oxton 6A 68
   CH63: Beb 4H 87

Townfield La. CH63: Beb, Hghr B 4H 87
   WA6: Frod 6H 123
Townfield Rd. CH48: W Kir 1B 82
   WA7: Wind H 3E 115
Town Flds. CH47: Hoy 1A 50
Townfield Vw. WA7: Wind H 3E 115
Townfield Way CH44: Wall 3D 50
Towngate Bus. Cen. WA8: Wid 4H 95
Town Hall Dr. WA7: Run 4F 113
Town La. CH63: Hghr B 5F 87
   L24: Hale 4D 110
Townley Ct. CH47: Hoy 2B 64
                        (off Seaview)
Town Mdw. La. CH46: More 1H 65
Town Rd. CH42: Tran 6F 69
Town Row L12: W Der 6F 37
Townsend Av. L11: Norr G 5C 36
   L13: Liv .5C 36
Townsend La. L4: Walt 1H 53
   L6: Liv .1A 54
   L13: Liv .1A 54
Townsend St. CH41: Birke 6A 50
   L5: Kirkd 1C 52
Townsend Vw. L11: Norr G 5C 36
   L21: Ford 1B 20
Townshend Av. CH61: Irby 6B 84
Town Sq. WA7: Pal F 2B 114
                    (off Halton Lea Shop. Cen.)
Town Vw. CH43: Oxton 4E 69
Town Vw. M. CH43: Oxton 4E 69
Town Wlk. WA7: Pal F 6B 114
                    (off Halton Lea Shop. Cen.)
Towson St. L5: Liv 1F 53
                        (Adam St.)
   L5: Liv .1G 53
                        (Hartnup St.)
TOXTETH 5F 71
Toxteth Gro. L8: Liv 5G 71
Toxteth St. L8: Liv 4F 71
                        (not continuous)
Tradewind Sq. L1: Liv 1E 71
                        (off Kent St.)
TRAFALGAR 1A 104
Trafalgar Av. CH44: Wall 2F 51
Trafalgar Ct. WA8: Wid 5E 97
Trafalgar Dr. CH63: Beb 1A 104
Trafalgar Rd. CH44: Wall 2E 51
Trafalgar St. WA10: St H 1C 42
Trafalgar Way L6: Liv 4F 53
Trafford Cres. WA7: Run 1G 123
Tragan Dr. WA5: Penk 4E 81
Tramway Rd. L17: Aig 6A 72
TRANMERE 6H 69
Tranmere Ct. CH42: Tran 5F 69
Tranmere Recreation Cen. 1E 87
Tranmere Rovers FC 1E 87
Trapwood Cl. WA10: Eccl 2H 41
Travanson Cl. L10: Faz 5F 23
Travers' Entry WA9: Bold 6C 44
Traverse St. WA9: St H 2G 43
Travis Dr. L33: Kirkb 4B 14
Travis St. WA8: Wid 1F 111
Trawden Way L21: Ford 5C 10
Traynor Ct. CH43: Oxton 4C 68
                        (off Beresford Rd.)
Treborth St. L8: Liv 4G 71
Trecastle Rd. L33: Kirkb 5C 14
Tree Bank Cl. WA7: Run 5E 113
Treetop Ct. L6: Liv 3A 54
Treetops Dr. CH41: Birke 6H 49
Trefoil Cl. L8: Liv 3F 71
Treforris Rd. CH45: Wall 6B 32
Trefula Pk. L12: W Der 1E 55
Trelawney Cl. L25: Gate 3D 74
Tremore Cl. L12: W Der 4F 37
Trenance Cl. WA7: Brook 2E 125
Trendeal Rd. L11: Crox 6H 23
Trent Av. L14: Broad G 4B 56
   L31: Mag 5E 7
Trent Cl. L12: Crox 2H 37
   L35: Rainh 4H 59
   WA8: Wid 5F 79
   WA9: Sut L 2G 61

Trentham Av. L18: Moss H 4D 72
Trentham Cl. WA8: Wid 5F 79
   WA9: St H 2D 60
Trentham Rd. CH44: Wall 4E 51
   L32: Kirkb 2G 23
Trentham St. WA7: Run 2D 112
Trentham Wlk. L32: Kirkb 2G 23
Trent Pl. L35: Rainh 4H 59
Trent Rd. L35: Rainh 4H 59
Trent St. CH41: Birke 6B 50
   L5: Kirkd 1C 52
Trent Way CH60: Hesw 1F 117
   L21: Lith 2A 20
Tressel Dr. WA9: Sut M 4E 61
Tressell St. L9: Walt 2F 35
Trevelyan St. L9: Walt 2F 35
Treviot Cl. L33: Kirkb 3H 13
Trevor Dr. L23: Crosb 6H 9
Trevor Rd. L9: Walt 5G 21
Triad, The L20: Boot 1C 34
Trident Pk. WA7: Pal F 6A 114
Trimley Cl. CH49: Upton 4C 66
Tring Cl. CH49: Upton 2E 67
Trinity Cl. CH47: Hoy 2B 64
Trinity Gdns. CH43: Oxton 4B 68
   CH47: Hoy 2B 64
   WA6: Frod 6G 123
Trinity Gro. L23: Blun 1D 18
Trinity Ho. WA6: Frod 6G 123
Trinity La. CH41: Birke 2G 69
Trinity Pl. L20: Boot 2D 34
   WA8: Wid 4F 97
Trinity Rd. CH44: Wall 2D 50
   CH47: Hoy 2B 64
   L20: Boot 3C 34
Trinity St. CH41: Birke 2E 69
   WA7: Run 2F 113
   WA9: St H 1G 43
Trinity Wlk. L3: Liv 1H 5
Trispen Cl. L26: Halew 3G 93
Trispen Rd. L11: Crox 1H 37
Trispen Wlk. L11: Crox 1H 37
                        (off Trispen Rd.)
Tristram's Cft. L30: N'ton 6D 10
Triumph Trading Pk., The
   L24: Speke 5B 92
Triumph Way
   L24: Hunts X, Speke 5B 92
Troon Cl. CH63: Brom 2C 120
   L12: W Der 1A 56
   WA11: Hay 6C 30
Trooper Cl. L12: W Der 6A 38
Trotwood Cl. L9: Ain 3B 22
Troutbeck Av. L31: Mag 5D 6
   WA12: Newt W 1G 45
Troutbeck Cl. CH49: Woodc 1E 85
   WA7: Beech 2C 124
Troutbeck Gro. WA11: St H 1F 29
Troutbeck Rd. L18: Moss H 4H 73
Trouville Rd. L4: Walt 6A 36
Trowbridge St. L3: Liv 4H 5 (6E 53)
Trueman Cl. CH43: Bid 1A 68
Trueman St. L3: Liv 2E 5 (5D 52)
Truman Cl. WA8: Wid 6D 78
Truro Av. L30: N'ton 5F 11
Truro Cl. WA7: Brook 1E 125
   WA11: St H 4H 29
Truro Rd. L15: Wav 3E 73
Tudor Av. CH44: Wall 5G 51
   CH63: Beb 2A 104
   L14: Knott A 2D 56
Tudor Cl. L7: Liv 6F 53
   WA11: Rainf 1E 17
Tudor Ct. L19: Gras 4E 91
                        (off Dugdale Cl.)
Tudor Grange CH49: Grea 6B 66
Tudor Rd. CH42: Tran 6G 69
   L23: Crosb 6F 9
   L25: Hunts X 4E 93
   WA7: Manor P 2D 114
Tudor St. Nth. L6: Liv 4H 53
Tudor St. Sth. L6: Liv 4H 53
Tudor Vw. L33: Kirkb 4A 14
                        (not continuous)

Tudorville Rd. CH63: Beb 6H 87
Tudor Way CH60: Hesw 5F 101
TUE BROOK .1C 54
Tue La. WA8: Cron 3H 77
Tuffins Cnr. L27: N'ley 4F 75
Tulip Av. CH41: Birke 1B 68
Tulip Rd. L15: Wav 2F 73
   WA11: Hay 5H 31
Tullimore Rd. L18: Moss H 2E 91
Tullis St. WA10: St H 3C 42
Tulloch St. L6: Liv 4H 53
Tully Av. WA12: Newt W 2G 45
Tumilty Av. L20: Boot 1E 35
Tunbridge Cl. WA5: Gt San 1H 81
Tundra Cl. L4: Walt 3G 35
Tunnage Sq. L1: Liv 6F 5
Tunnel End WA4: Dutt 3H 125
Tunnel Rd. CH41: Birke 4H 69
   L7: Liv 1H 71
Tunnel Top Nth. WA4: Dutt 1H 125
   WA7: Pres B 1H 125
Tunstall Cl. CH49: Upton 4C 66
Tunstall St. L7: Liv 2A 72
Tunstalls Way WA9: Clock F 3H 61
Tupelo Cl. L12: Crox 1B 38
Tupman St. L8: Liv 4F 71
Turmar Av. CH61: Thing 5F 85
Turnacre L14: Broad G 4A 56
Turnall Rd. WA8: Wid 4H 95
Turnberry Cl. CH46: More 6H 47
   L12: W Der 1B 56
   L36: Roby 6E 57
Turnbridge Rd. L31: Mag 4B 6
Turner Av. L20: Boot 4E 21
Turner Cl. L8: Liv 6G 71
   WA8: Wid 6B 78
Turner Gro. L33: Kirkb 3A 14
Turner Home, The L8: Liv 5H 71
Turners Ct. L25: Gate 6E 75
Turner St. CH41: Birke 4E 69
Turners Vw. CH64: Nest 5H 117
Turney Rd. CH44: Wall 3C 50
Turnstone Bus. Pk.
   WA8: Wid 4G 97
Turnstone Cl. L12: Crox 2A 38
Turnstone Dr. L26: Halew 2G 93
Turret Rd. CH45: Wall 1C 50
Turriff Dr. CH63: East 3C 120
Turriff Rd. L14: Knott A 2C 56
Turton Cl. L24: Hale 4D 110
Turton St. L5: Kirkd 1D 52
Tuscan Cl. WA8: Wid 4F 79
Tuson Dr. WA8: Wid 5D 78
Tweed Cl. L6: Liv 3A 54
Tweed St. CH41: Birke 6C 50
Twickenham Dr. CH46: Leas 4D 48
   L36: Roby 6E 57
Twickenham St. L6: Liv 1H 53
Twigden Cl. L10: Faz 3D 22
Twig La. L31: Mag 6D 6
   L36: Huy 4E 57
Two Butt La. L35: Whis, Rainh 2G 59
Twomey Cl. L5: Liv 3C 52
Twyford Av. L21: Lith 2B 20
Twyford Cl. L31: Mag 6D 6
   WA8: Wid 5F 79
Twyford La. WA8: Wid 2G 79
Twyford Pl. WA9: St H 2G 43
Twyford St. L6: Liv 1H 53
Tyberton Pl. L25: Hunts X 5E 93
Tyburn Cl. CH63: Spit 3H 103
Tyburn Rd. CH63: Spit 3H 103
Tyle St. L20: Kirkd 6B 34
Tyndall Av. L22: Water 3H 19
Tyne Cl. L4: Kirkd 5E 35
   WA9: St H 1B 60
Tynemouth Cl. L5: Liv 2G 53
Tynemouth Rd. WA7: Murd 1E 125
Tyne St. CH41: Birke 6B 50
Tynron Gro. CH43: Noct 5H 67
Tynville Rd. L9: Ain 4A 22
Tynwald Cl. L13: Liv 2D 54
Tynwald Cres. WA8: Wid 4D 78
Tynwald Hill L13: Liv 3D 54

Tynwald Pl. L13: Liv 3D 54
Tynwald Rd. CH48: W Kir 1A 82
Tyrer Gro. L34: Presc 6E 41
Tyrers Av. L31: Lyd 2A 6
Tyrer St. CH41: Birke 6B 50
   L1: Liv 4F 5 (6D 52)

U

U-boat Story .2A 70
Uldale Cl. L11: Norr G 3E 37
Uldale Way L11: Norr G 3E 37
Ullet Rd. L8: Liv 5H 71
   L17: Aig .5H 71
Ullet Wlk. L17: Aig 4B 72
Ullswater Av. CH43: Noct 3H 67
   WA11: St H 3E 29
Ullswater Cl. L33: Kirkb 5H 13
Ullswater Gro. WA7: Beech 2H 123
Ullswater Ho. L17: Aig 1B 90
Ullswater St. L5: Liv 1G 53
Ulster Rd. L13: Liv 4F 55
Ulverscroft CH43: Oxton 5B 68
Ulverston Cl. L31: Mag 5D 6
   WA11: Hay 5C 30
Ulverston Lawn L27: N'ley 5H 75
Undercliffe Rd. L13: Liv 3E 55
Underhill Rd. WA10: St H 3B 42
Underley St. L7: Liv 2A 72
Underley Ter. CH62: New F 4B 88
Underwater Street Discovery Cen.
   . . . . .4B 4 (6B 52)
Underway, The WA7: Halt 5B 114
Unicorn Rd. L11: Crox 1G 37
Unicorn Way CH41: Tran 4H 69
Union Bank La.
   WA8: Bold H 6F 61
Union Ct. L2: Liv 4D 4 (6C 52)
Union St. CH42: Tran 6H 69
   CH44: Wall 3F 51
   L3: Liv 3B 4 (5B 52)
   WA7: Run 3F 113
   WA10: St H 6E 29
Union Ter. CH45: New B 4D 32
Unity Bldg. L3: Liv 3B 4
Unity Gro. L34: Know 6C 24
Unity Theatre 6H 5
University of Liverpool
   Cambridge St. 1F 71
   Central Campus 6F 53
   North Campus 6F 53
   Peach St. 6G 53
University of Liverpool Library 1G 71
   (off Chatham St.)
University of Liverpool Sports Cen. . . .6F 53
University Rd. L20: Boot 3D 34
Upavon Av. CH49: Grea 6H 65
Upchurch Cl. L8: Liv 5F 71
Upland Cl. WA10: St H 5H 41
Upland Rd. CH49: Upton 3D 66
   WA10: St H 5H 41
Uplands, The CH43: Oxton 5A 68
   WA7: Pal F 6B 114
Uplands Rd. CH62: Brom 4C 104
Up. Baker St. L6: Liv 4G 53
Up. Beau St. L5: Liv 3E 53
Up. Beckwith St. CH41: Birke 1D 68
UPPER BIDSTON VILLAGE 6G 49
Up. Brassey St. CH41: Birke 1B 68
Upperbrook Way L4: Kirkd 6D 34
Up. Bute St. L5: Liv 3E 53
Up. Duke St. L1: Liv 1E 71
Up. Essex St. L8: Liv 4F 71
Up. Flaybrick Rd.
   CH41: Birke 2A 68
Up. Frederick St. L1: Liv 6E 5 (1D 70)
   (not continuous)
Up. Hampton St. L8: Liv 2F 71
Up. Harrington St. L8: Liv 3E 71
Up. Hill St. L8: Liv 3E 71
   (not continuous)
Up. Hope Pl. L7: Liv 6H 5 (1F 71)
Up. Huskisson St. L8: Liv 2G 71

Up. Mann St. L8: Liv 3E 71
   (not continuous)
Up. Mason St. L7: Liv 6G 53
Up. Mersey Rd. WA8: Wid 6E 97
Upper Newington L1: Liv 5G 5 (6E 53)
Up. Park St. L8: Liv 4F 71
Up. Parliament St. L8: Liv 2E 71
Up. Pitt St. L1: Liv 1D 70
   (not continuous)
Up. Pownall St. L1: Liv 1D 70
Up. Raby Rd. CH63: Raby 5C 118
   CH64: Nest 5C 118
Up. Rice La. CH44: Wall 2E 51
Up. Stanhope St. L8: Liv 2E 71
   (not continuous)
Up. Warwick St. L8: Liv 3F 71
Up. William St. L3: Liv 3B 52
Uppingham Av. L10: Ain 1C 22
Uppingham Rd. CH44: Wall 2B 50
   L13: Liv .2D 54
UPTON
   CH49 . . . . .4E 67
   WA8 . . . . .6H 77
Upton Barn L31: Mag 5B 6
Upton Bridle Path WA8: Wid 5D 78
Upton By-Pass CH49: Upton 3C 66
Upton Cl. CH49: Upton 4D 66
   L24: Speke 2G 109
Upton Ct. CH49: Upton 3E 67
Upton Dr. WA5: Penk 4H 81
Upton Grange WA8: Wid 6B 78
Upton Grn. L24: Speke 2G 109
Upton La. WA8: Wid 5C 78
Upton Mdw. CH49: Upton 5D 66
Upton Pk. Dr. CH49: Upton 3E 67
Upton Rd. CH41: Birke 4G 67
   CH43: Bid, Noct 4G 67
   CH46: More 1C 66
UPTON ROCKS 6D 78
Upton Rocks Av. WA8: Wid 5C 78
Upton Rocks M. WA8: Wid 5C 78
Upton Station (Rail) 4G 67
Urmson Rd. CH45: Wall 2D 50
Ursula St. L20: Boot 4D 34
Utkinton Cl. CH43: Oxton 6B 68
Utting Av. L4: Walt 6H 35
Utting Av. E. L11: Norr G 4C 36
UVECO Bus. Cen.
   CH41: Birke 6D 50
Uxbridge St. L7: Liv 6H 53
   (not continuous)

V

Vahler Ter. WA7: Run 3G 113
Vale Ct. *L21: Sea* *5A 20*
   (off Seaforth Va. Nth.)
Vale Dr. CH45: New B 6E 33
Vale Gro. L32: Kirkb 2C 24
Vale Lodge L9: Walt 1F 35
Valencia Gro. L34: Eccl P 6G 41
Valencia Rd. L15: Wav 1E 73
Valentia Rd. CH47: Hoy 3A 64
Valentine Gro. L10: Ain 2C 22
Valentine Rd.
   WA12: Newt W 2H 45
Valentines Bldg. L9: Ain 2A 22
Valentines Way L9: Ain 1A 22
Valerian Rd. CH41: Birke 2B 68
Valerie Cl. L10: Faz 5F 23
Valerie Park .6D 40
Vale Rd. L23: Crosb 5F 9
   L25: Woolt 6A 74
Valescourt Rd. L12: W Der 2G 55
Valiant Cl. L12: Crox 3C 38
Valiant Ho. CH41: Birke 3H 69
Valiant Way CH41: Tran 5H 69
Valkyrie Rd. CH45: Wall 2C 50
Vallance Rd. L4: Walt 6A 36
Valleybrook Gro. CH63: Spit 3B 104
Valley Cl. L10: Ain 2D 22
   L23: Crosb 5B 10
Valley Community Theatre 4F 75

Valley Rd. CH41: Birke 5H **49**
   CH62: Brom 5D **104**
   L4: Walt 1G **53**
   L32: Faz, Kirkb 4E **23**
Valley Rd. Bus. Pk. CH41: Birke . . .6A **50**
Vanbrugh Cres. L4: Walt 6A **36**
Vanbrugh Rd. L4: Walt 5A **36**
Vancouver Rd. L27: N'ley 4G **75**
Vanderbilt Av. L9: Ain 3H **21**
Vanderbyl Av. CH62: Spit 3C **104**
Vandries St. L3: Liv 3B **52**
Vandyke St. L8: Liv 2A **72**
Vanguard St. L5: Liv 1F **53**
Vanguard Way CH41: Tran 6H **69**
Vardon St. CH41: Birke 1F **69**
Varley Rd. L19: Aig 2E **91**
   WA9: St H 1G **43**
Varthen St. L5: Liv 1G **53**
Vaughan Rd. CH45: New B 5E **33**
Vaughan St. CH41: Birke 1B **68**
Vaux Cres. L20: Boot 6D **20**
VAUXHALL .3C **52**
Vauxhall Bus. Cen. L3: Liv 1C **4**
Vauxhall Cl. WA5: Penk 5H **81**
Vauxhall Rd. L3: Liv 1D **4** (4C **52**)
   L5: Liv 4C **52**
Vaux Pl. L20: Boot 6D **20**
Venables Cl. CH63: Spit 4B **104**
Venables Dr. CH63: Spit 3A **104**
Venice St. L5: Liv 1F **53**
Venmore St. L5: Liv 1F **53**
          (not continuous)
Ventnor Cl. WA5: Gt San 2E **81**
Ventnor Rd. L15: Wav 1D **72**
Venture Ct. CH41: Birke 4G **69**
Venture Flds. WA8: Wid 4F **97**
Venture Point W. L24: Speke 6D **92**
Venture Works L33: Know I 2E **25**
Verbena Cl. WA7: Beech 3B **124**
Verbena Dr. L11: Norr G 3E **37**
Verdala Pk. L18: Moss H 1G **91**
Verdi Av. L21: Sea 5A **20**
Verdi St. L21: Sea 5H **19**
Verdi Ter. L21: Sea 6H **19**
Vere St. L8: Liv 4E **71**
Vermont Av. L23: Crosb 5F **9**
Vermont Cl. L33: Kirkb 2H **13**
Vermont Rd. L23: Crosb 5F **9**
Vermont Way L20: Boot 1C **34**
Verney Cres. L19: Aller 3G **91**
Verney Cres. Sth. L19: Aller 3G **91**
Vernon Av. CH44: Wall 5F **51**
   CH66: Hoot 5G **121**
Vernon St. L2: Liv 3D **4** (5C **52**)
   WA9: St H 1G **43**
Verona St. L5: Liv 1F **53**
Veronica Cl. L12: Crox 2A **38**
Veronica M. WA8: Wid 2B **96**
Verulam Cl. L8: Liv 2G **71**
Verwood Cl. CH61: Irby 4B **84**
Verwood Dr. L12: Crox 2C **38**
Veryan Cl. L26: Halew 2H **93**
Vescock St. L5: Liv 3D **52**
Vesta Rd. L19: Garst 1H **107**
Vesty Bus. Pk. L30: N'ton 3G **21**
Vesty Rd. L30: N'ton 3G **21**
Vesuvian Dr. L19: Garst 1H **107**
Vesuvius Pl. L5: Kirkd 1D **52**
Vesuvius St. L5: Kirkd 1D **52**
Viaduct St. WA12: Newt W 2H **45**
Vicarage Cl. CH42: Tran 2D **86**
   L18: Moss H 1F **91**
   L24: Hale 4E **111**
Vicarage Dr. WA11: Hay 4C **30**
Vicarage Gro. CH44: Wall 2E **51**
Vicarage Lawn L25: Gate 4E **75**
Vicarage Pl. L34: Presc 1C **58**
Vicarage Rd. WA8: Wid 4E **97**
   WA11: Hay 4C **30**
Vicar Rd. L6: Liv 6A **36**
Viceroy St. L5: Liv 1F **53**
Victoria Av. CH60: Hesw 1D **116**
   L14: Broad G 5H **55**
   L15: Wav 1D **72**

Victoria Av. L23: Blun 5E **9**
   WA5: Gt San 3F **81**
   WA8: Wid 6E **79**
   WA11: St H 3E **29**
Victoria Cl. L17: Aig 6C **72**
Victoria Ct. CH42: Rock F 2A **88**
   L15: Wav 1E **73**
   L17: Aig 5H **71**
       (off Lit. Parkfield Rd.)
Victoria Dr. CH42: Rock F 2A **88**
   CH48: W Kir 1A **82**
   L9: Walt 5F **21**
Victoria Falls Rd. L27: N'ley 5H **75**
Victoria Flds. CH42: Tran 5E **69**
Victoria Gallery & Museum 6F **53**
Victoria Gdns. CH43: Oxton 5D **68**
Victoria Gro. WA8: Wid 6E **79**
Victoria Hall L2: Liv 2D **4**
Victoria Hall Wlk.
   CH63: Hghr B 5F **87**
Victoria Ho. L34: Presc 1D **58**
Victoria La. CH43: Oxton 5D **68**
Victoria Mt. CH43: Oxton 5D **68**
Victoria Pde. CH45: New B 4E **33**
VICTORIA PARK
   L15 .1E **73**
   L20 .4E **21**
Victoria Park 5D **28**
Victoria Park Glasshouses 2E **97**
Victoria Pk. Rd. CH42: Tran 1F **87**
Victoria Pl. CH44: Wall 5H **51**
   L35: Rainh 4A **60**
Victoria Prom. WA8: Wid 1E **113**
Victoria Rd. CH42: Tran 5E **69**
   CH45: New B 5C **32**
   CH48: W Kir 2A **82**
   CH63: Hghr B 5F **87**
   L13: Liv 1C **54**
   L17: Aig 1C **90**
   L22: Water 3G **19**
   L23: Crosb 5F **9**
   L36: Huy 5H **57**
   WA5: Penk 5F **81**
   WA7: Run 3E **113**
          (not continuous)
   WA8: Wid 4E **97**
Victoria Rd. W. L23: Blun 5E **9**
Victoria Sq. WA8: Wid 4E **97**
   WA10: St H 1E **43**
Victoria St. CH62: Port S 6B **88**
   L1: Liv 4D **4** (6C **52**)
   L2: Liv 4D **4** (6C **52**)
   L35: Rainh 4A **60**
   WA8: Wid 4F **97**
   WA10: St H 6E **29**
   WA11: Rainf 2F **17**
Victoria Ter. *L15: Wav* 3E **73**
       (off Prince Alfred Rd.)
   L35: Rainh 4A **60**
Victoria Trad. Est. *L35: Rainh* 4A **60**
       (off Victoria St.)
   WA8: Wid 5E **97**
Victoria Vs. L35: Rainh 4A **60**
Victor St. L15: Wav 1B **72**
Victory Cl. L30: Boot 3E **21**
Vienna St. L5: Liv 1F **53**
Viennese Rd. L25: Gate 3D **74**
View 146 L5: Liv 2E **53**
Viewpark Cl. L16: Child 2B **74**
View Rd. L35: Rainh 5A **60**
Viking Cl. L21: Lith 4A **20**
Viking Ct. *WA8: Wid* 4E **97**
        (off Vine St.)
Village, The CH63: Beb 5A **88**
Village Cl. CH45: Wall 1A **50**
   WA7: Cas 5C **114**
Village Ct. CH43: Oxton 5C **68**
   CH61: Irby 5B **84**
   L17: Aig 1A **90**
Village Courts L30: N'ton 4F **11**
Village Grn. Ct. CH43: Bid 1G **67**
Village M. CH45: Wall 1A **50**
   CH63: Hghr B 5F **87**
Village Nook L10: Ain 1C **22**

Village Rd. CH43: Oxton 5C **68**
   CH48: W Kir 2B **82**
   CH60: Hesw 6D **100**
   CH63: Hghr B 5F **87**
Village Square, The WA7: Cas 3C **114**
Village St. L6: Liv 3F **53**
   WA7: Nort 3G **115**
Village Way CH45: Wall 2A **50**
Villa Gloria Cl. L19: Aig 3E **91**
Villas Rd. L31: Mag 6G **7**
Villiers Ct. L34: Know 6D **24**
Villiers Cres. WA10: Eccl 6F **27**
Villiers Rd. L34: Know 5D **24**
Vincent Cl. L1: Liv 6F **5** (1D **70**)
Vincent Naughton Ct. CH41: Birke . . .4G **69**
Vincent Rd. L21: Lith 2C **20**
   L35: Rainh 3H **59**
Vincent St. CH41: Birke 3F **69**
   L13: Liv 6E **55**
   WA8: Wid 1E **43**
Vine Cres. WA5: Gt San 3H **81**
Vine Ho. L21: Sea 5A **20**
Vineries, The L25: Woolt 6A **74**
Vineside Rd. L12: W Der 2H **55**
Vine St. L7: Liv 1G **71**
   WA7: Run 3E **113**
   WA8: Wid 4E **97**
Vine Ter. WA8: Wid 1G **95**
Vineyard St. L19: Garst 6A **92**
Vining Rd. L35: Presc 1F **59**
Vining St. L8: Liv 3F **71**
Viola Cl. L33: Kirkb 4H **13**
Viola St. L20: Boot 4C **34**
Violet Cft. CH63: Beb 1H **103**
Violet Rd. CH41: Birke 2B **68**
   L21: Lith 5B **20**
Violet St. WA8: Wid 4E **97**
Virgil St. L5: Liv 3E **53**
   WA10: St H 1C **42**
Virginia Av. L31: Lyd 4C **6**
Virginia Gro. L31: Lyd 4B **6**
Virginia Rd. CH45: New B 4D **32**
Virgin's La. L23: Thorn 2H **9**
Viscount Cen. L24: Speke 6F **93**
Viscount Dr. L24: Hale 3G **109**
Vista Rd. WA7: Run 5E **113**
   WA11: Hay 4H **31**
   WA12: Newt W 1H **45**
Vista Way WA12: Newt W 1H **45**
Vitesse Rd. L24: Speke 5B **92**
Vittoria Cl. CH41: Birke 2F **69**
Vittoria Ct. CH41: Birke 2F **69**
Vittoria St. CH41: Birke 2E **69**
Vivian Av. CH44: Wall 5G **51**
Vixen Gro. WA8: Wid 5D **78**
Voelas St. L8: Liv 3G **71**
Vogan Av. L23: Crosb 6A **10**
Volunteer St. WA6: Frod 6H **123**
   WA10: St H 1D **42**
Vronhill Cl. L8: Liv 3G **71**
Vue Cinema
   Birkenhead 3G **69**
Vulcan Cl. CH41: Birke 1B **68**
   L19: Garst 1G **107**
Vulcan St. CH41: Birke 1B **68**
   L3: Liv 3B **52**
   L20: Boot 1A **34**
Vyner Cl. CH43: Noct 3A **68**
Vyner Ct. CH43: Noct 3A **68**
Vyner Cft. CH43: Clau 3A **68**
Vyner Pk. CH43: Noct 3A **68**
Vyner Rd. CH45: Wall 2B **50**
Vyner Rd. Nth. CH43: Bid 2H **67**
   L25: Gate 4C **74**
Vyner Rd. Sth. CH43: Bid, Noct 3H **67**
   L25: Gate 4D **74**
Vyrnwy St. L5: Liv 1G **53**

W

WADDICAR 5E **13**
Waddicar La. L31: Mell 6E **13**
Wadebridge Rd. L10: Faz 5F **23**

Wadeson Rd. L4: Walt 3B 36
Wadham Pk. L20: Boot 3D 34
Wadham Rd. L20: Boot 4C 34
Wagon La. WA11: Hay 1D 44
Waine Gro. L35: Whis 2G 59
Waine St. WA9: St H 1H 43
WA11: Hay 5B 30
Wainwright Cl. L7: Liv 1A 72
Wainwright Gro.
L19: Garst 5G 91
Wakefield Dr. CH46: Leas 3D 48
Wakefield Rd. L30: N'ton 1G 21
Wakefield St.
L3: Liv 1G 5 (4E 53)
Walby Cl. CH49: Woodc 1G 85
Walden Rd. L14: Knott A 4G 55
Waldgrave Pl. L15: Wav 6F 55
Waldgrave Rd. L15: Wav 6E 55
Waldron Cl. L3: Liv 1D 4 (4C 52)
Walford Cl. CH63: Spit 3H 103
Walk, The L24: Speke 3B 108
L28: Stockb V 6E 39
(off Dannette Hey)
Walker Art Gallery 2F 5 (5D 52)
Walker Av. WA9: Sut M 4F 61
Walker Dr. L20: Boot 4C 20
Walker Hgts. CH42: Tran 6F 69
(off Walker St.)
Walker M. CH42: Tran 6F 69
Walker Pl. CH42: Tran 6F 69
Walker Rd. L21: Lith 4A 20
Walker's Cft. CH45: Wall 2B 50
Walkers La. WA5: Penk 6G 81
WA9: Sut M 4E 61
Walker St. CH42: Tran 6F 69
CH47: Hoy 2B 64
CH62: Port S 5B 88
L6: Liv 4G 53
Walker Way L9: Walt 5F 21
Wallace Av. L36: Huy 3A 58
Wallace Dr. L36: Huy 3H 57
Wallace St. L9: Ain 5G 21
WA8: Wid 3E 97
Wallacre Rd. CH44: Wall 3A 50
WALLASEY 2A 50
Wallasey Bri. Rd. CH41: Birke 6B 50
Wallasey Golf Course 1H 49
Wallasey Grove Road Station (Rail)
. . . . .1A 50
Wallasey Rd. CH44: Wall 3B 50
CH45: Wall 3B 50
Wallasey Village CH44: Wall 1A 50
CH45: Wall 1A 50
Wallasey Village Station (Rail) 2A 50
Waller Cl. L4: Kirkd 6E 35
Waller St. L20: Boot 5B 20
Wallgate Way L25: Gate 3B 74
Wallgate Way L25: Gate 3B 74
Wallingford Rd. CH49: Upton 5D 66
Wallis Dr. WA8: Wid 6G 79
Wallrake CH60: Hesw 6D 100
Wallsend Ct. WA8: Wid 6D 78
Wall St. L1: Liv 5D 4 (6C 52)
Walmer Rd. L22: Water 3G 19
Walmesley Rd. WA10: Eccl 6G 27
Walmsley Dr. WA11: Rainf 4G 17
Walmsley St. CH44: Wall 2E 51
L5: Liv 2C 52
WA8: Wid 3G 97
Walney Rd. L12: W Der 5E 37
Walney Ter. L12: W Der 5E 37
Walnut Av. L9: Walt 2A 36
Walnut Gro. L31: Mell 6E 13
WA9: St H 5F 43
Walnut St. L7: Liv 6F 53
(off Mt. Pleasant)
Walpole Av. L35: Whis 4F 59
Walpole Rd. WA7: Run 1F 123
Walsham Gdns. WA9: St H 1C 60
Walsh Cl. L5: Liv 3C 52
Walsh Rd. L14: Broad G 5G 55
Walsingham Ct. CH44: Wall 4F 51
(off Liscard Rd.)
Walsingham Dr. WA7: Nort 3F 115

Walsingham Rd. CH44: Wall 4F 51
L16: Child 6A 56
WA5: Penk 4H 81
Walter Beilin Ct. L17: Aig 4C 72
Walter Gro. WA9: St H 6B 44
Walter St. L5: Liv 2B 52
WA8: Wid 2H 97
Waltham Ct. WA7: Nort 1G 115
Waltham Rd. L6: Liv 1A 54
Waltho Av. L31: Mag 6D 6
WALTON 3H 35
Walton Av. WA5: Penk 4G 81
Walton Breck Rd. L4: Walt 6F 35
Walton Hall Av. L4: Walt 3G 35
L11: Norr G 2B 36
Walton Hall Rd. L4: Walt 3H 35
Walton La. L4: Walt 6F 35
Walton Pk. L9: Walt 1G 35
Walton Rd. L4: Walt 6E 35
WA10: St H 5B 28
Walton Station (Rail) 1F 35
Walton St. CH41: Birke 3G 69
WA7: Run 3E 113
Walton Va. L9: Walt, Ain 5G 21
Walton Village L4: Walt 3F 35
(not continuous)
Wambo La. L25: Gate 4E 75
Wandsworth Rd. L11: Norr G 4D 36
Wandsworth Way WA8: Wid 6D 96
Wango La. L10: Ain 2C 22
Wantage Vw. L36: Roby 1E 75
Wapping L1: Liv 6D 4 (1C 70)
Wapping Quay L3: Liv 2C 70
Wapshare Rd. L11: Norr G 4C 36
Warbler Cl. L26: Halew 1F 93
Warbreck Av. L9: Walt, Ain 4G 21
Warbreck Moor L9: Ain 5H 21
WARBRECK PARK 4G 21
Warbreck Rd. L9: Walt 5G 21
Warburton Hey L35: Rainh 3H 59
Warden St. L4: Walt 5E 35
Wardgate Av. L12: Crox 2A 38
Ward Gro. CH42: Rock F 3H 87
Ward Rake L30: N'ton 5D 10
(off Granams Cft.)
Ward Rd. L23: Blun 4C 8
Ward St. L3: Liv 3G 5 (5E 53)
L34: Presc 6D 40
WA10: St H 1E 43
Wareham Cl. WA11: Hay 4E 31
Wareing Rd. L9: Ain 5A 22
Waresley Cres. L9: Faz 1C 36
Warham Rd. L4: Walt 6A 36
Waring Av. CH42: Tran 1F 87
WA9: St H 3D 44
Warkworth Cl. L36: Huy 1A 76
WA8: Wid 6A 78
Warmington Rd. L14: Knott A 4G 55
Warmwell Cl. L24: Speke 2D 108
(off Cartwrights Farm Rd.)
Warner Dr. L4: Walt 5A 36
Warnerville Rd. L13: Liv 6F 55
Warnley Cl. WA8: Wid 6B 78
Warren, The CH49: Upton 4F 67
WA12: Newt W 2H 45
Warren Cft. WA7: Nort 6E 115
Warrender Dr. CH43: Bid 1B 68
Warren Dr. CH43: Bid 3G 67
CH45: Wall, New B 5B 32
Warren Golf Course 6B 32
Warren Hey CH63: Spit 4A 104
Warrenhouse Rd. L22: Water 1D 18
L33: Kirkb 5C 14
Warren Hurst CH45: New B 5C 32
Warren La. CH62: Brom, East 4F 105
(not continuous)
Warren Pk. CH45: Wall 6B 32
Warren Point CH45: Wall 5B 32
Warren Rd. CH47: Hoy 2A 64
L23: Blun 4C 8
Warren St. L3: Liv 4H 5 (6E 53)
Warren Way CH60: Hesw 4B 100
Warrington New Rd. WA9: St H 2F 43
Warrington Old Rd. WA9: St H 3F 43

Warrington Rd. L34: Presc 1D 58
L35: Presc, Rainh, Whis 1D 58
L35: Rainh 1D 58
WA5: Penk 5G 81
WA7: Cas 3A 114
WA7: Manor P 1C 114
(not continuous)
WA8: Bold H 1D 78
WA8: Wid 3G 97
Warrington St. CH41: Tran 5G 69
Warton Cl. L25: Woolt 1E 93
WA5: Penk 6H 81
Warton St. L20: Boot 5B 20
Warton Ter. L20: Boot 5B 20
Warwick Av. L23: Crosb 6F 9
WA5: Gt San 2F 81
Warwick Cl. CH43: Oxton 4E 69
L36: Huy 4A 58
Warwick Ct. L8: Liv 3G 71
(off Gwent St.)
Warwick Dr. CH45: Wall 1E 51
CH48: W Kir 3C 82
Warwick Gro. WA7: Cas 4B 114
Warwick Rd. CH49: Upton 4C 66
L20: Boot 1D 34
L36: Huy 4A 58
Warwick St. L8: Liv 3E 71
WA10: St H 2B 42
Wasdale Av. L31: Mag 5E 7
WA11: St H 3F 29
Wasdale Rd. L9: Walt 6G 21
Washbrook Av. CH43: Bid 1G 67
Washbrook Cl. WA10: Eccl 1H 41
Washington Cl. WA8: Wid 6D 78
WA9: St H 3C 60
Washington Dr. L33: Kirkb 3H 13
Washington Pde.
L20: Boot 1C 34
Washington Rd. L27: N'ley 5H 75
Washway La. WA10: St H 4D 28
WA11: St H 4D 28
Wastdale Av. CH46: More 6A 48
Wastdale Dr. CH46: More 6A 48
Wastdale M. CH46: More 6A 48
Wastle Bri. Rd. L36: Huy 2G 57
Watchfield Cl. L24: Speke 2D 108
(off Cartwrights Farm Rd.)
Waterbridge M. WA7: Cas 3C 114
Waterdale Cres. WA9: St H 6H 43
Waterdale Pl. WA9: St H 6H 43
Waterfall Dr. L4: Walt 2G 35
Waterfield Cl. CH63: Hghr B 6F 87
Waterfield Way L21: Lith 2A 20
Waterford Rd. CH43: Oxton 4B 68
L27: N'ley 3E 75
Waterford Way WA7: Murd 1E 125
Waterfront WA4: Pres H 1H 155
Waterfront Business Area L8: Liv 2E 71
Waterfront Business Area Parliament St. Nth.
L1: Liv 2E 71
(off New Bird St.)
L1: Liv 2D 70
(off Simpson St.)
Waterfront Business Area Parliament St. Sth.
L8: Liv 3E 71
(off Stanhope St.)
Watergate La. L25: Woolt 1D 92
Watergate Way L25: Woolt 1D 92
Waterhouse Cl. L6: Liv 1H 53
Waterland La. WA9: St H 3B 44
Water La. L35: Tar G 5C 76
WATERLOO 2G 19
Waterloo Cen. WA8: Wid 5E 97
Waterloo Cl. L22: Water 3F 19
Waterloo Ct. CH63: Beb 5A 88
L22: Water 3G 19
Waterloo Dock L3: Liv 1A 4 (4B 52)
WATERLOO PARK 2H 19
Waterloo Pl. CH41: Birke 4G 69
Waterloo Quay L3: Liv 1A 4 (4A 52)
Waterloo Rd. CH45: New B 4D 32
L3: Liv 1A 4 (4B 52)
L21: Sea 5G 19
L22: Water 3G 19

Waterloo Rd. WA7: Run 2D **112**
(not continuous)
WA8: Wid 6E **97**
Waterloo Station (Rail) 2G **19**
Waterloo St. L15: Wav 2E **73**
WA10: St H 2D **42**
Waterloo Warehouse L3: Liv 1A **4** (4A **52**)
Watermead Dr. WA7: Pres B 2H **125**
Waterpark Cl. CH43: Pren 2B **86**
Waterpark Dr. L28: Stockb V 5B **38**
Waterpark Ho. CH42: Tran 1D **86**
(off Storeton Rd.)
Waterpark Rd. CH42: Tran 2B **86**
CH43: Pren 2B **86**
Watersedge WA6: Frod 5H **123**
Watersedge Apartments
CH45: New B 4E **33**
(off Egerton St.)
Waterside L30: N'ton 4E **11**
WA9: St H 1F **43**
Waterside Cl. WA7: Run 2C **112**
WA9: St H 1F **43**
Waterside Dr. WA6: Frod 5G **123**
Waterside La. WA8: Hale B 6A **96**
Waterside Pk. L36: Roby 6F **57**
Waterstone Cl. L11: Norr G 2F **37**
Water St. CH41: Birke 3H **69**
CH44: Wall 3F **51**
CH62: Port S 6C **88**
L2: Liv 4C **4** (6C **52**)
L3: Liv 4B **4** (6B **52**)
L22: Water 3G **19**
(off Brunswick Pde.)
L23: Thorn 3B **10**
WA7: Run 2E **113**
WA8: Wid 6E **97**
WA10: St H 2D **42**
Water Twr. Rd. CH64: Nest 6A **118**
Waterway Av. L30: N'ton 6H **11**
Waterworks La. CH66: Hoot 6E **121**
Waterworks St. L20: Boot 2D **34**
Waterworth Dr. L7: Liv 6H **53**
Watery Ct. WA9: St H 5B **44**
Watery La. WA9: St H 5A **44**
WA10: Windle 4G **27**
WA11: Windle 4F **27**
Watford Rd. L4: Walt 6H **35**
Watkin Cl. L30: N'ton 2H **21**
Watkins Av. WA12: Newt W 2H **45**
Watkinson St. L1: Liv 2D **70**
Watkinson Way WA8: Wid 1D **78**
Watling Av. L21: Lith 2A **20**
Watling Way L35: Whis 1G **59**
Watmough St. L5: Liv 3E **53**
Watson Ct. CH41: Birke 2H **69**
(off Argyle St.)
Watson St. CH41: Birke 2F **69**
Watton Beck Cl. L31: Mag 5E **7**
Watton Cl. L12: Crox 3C **38**
Watts Clift Way WA9: St H 2F **43**
Watts Cl. L33: Kirkb 5C **14**
Watts La. L20: Boot 4D **20**
Wauchope St. L15: Wav 1C **72**
Wavell Av. WA8: Wid 3A **96**
Wavell Rd. L36: Huy 3G **57**
Waverley Dr. L34: Presc 2H **57**
Waverley Gro. CH42: Tran 1E **87**
Waverley Ho. L19: Aig 4D **90**
Waverley Rd. CH47: Hoy 2C **64**
L17: Aig 5A **72**
L23: Blun 6E **9**
Waverley St. L20: Boot 2B **34**
Waverly Ct. WA9: St H 4G **43**
Waverton Av. CH43: Oxton 1A **86**
WAVERTREE 1D **72**
Wavertree Athletics Cen. 2D **72**
Wavertree Av. L13: Wav 6C **54**
WA8: Wid 3D **96**
Wavertree Blvd. L7: Liv 6B **54**
Wavertree Blvd. Sth. L7: Liv 6C **54**
Wavertree Bus. Pk. L15: Wav 2D **72**
Wavertree Bus. Village L13: Wav 6D **54**
Wavertree Gdns. L15: Wav 2D **72**
(off Prince Alfred Rd.)

WAVERTREE GREEN 2F **73**
Wavertree Grn. L15: Wav 2E **73**
Wavertree Ho. L13: Liv 6E **55**
(off Binns Rd.)
Wavertree Nook Rd. L15: Wav 6G **55**
Wavertree Retail Pk. L7: Liv 6A **54**
Wavertree Rd. L7: Liv 6H **53**
Wavertree Sports Pk. 2D **72**
Wavertree Technology Pk.
L7: Liv 6B **54**
L13: Wav 6C **54**
Wavertree Technology Park Station (Rail)
. . . . .6D **54**
Wavertree Va. L15: Wav 1B **72**
Wayford Cl. WA6: Frod 6F **123**
Wayford M. WA6: Frod 6F **123**
Waylands Dr. L25: Hunts X 4D **92**
Waymark Gdns. WA9: Sut M 4F **61**
Wayville Cl. L18: Moss H 1F **91**
Weardale Rd. L15: Wav 3C **72**
Weates Cl. WA8: Wid 6A **80**
Weatherstones Cotts. CH64: Nest . . .6F **119**
Weaver Av. L33: Kirkb 3B **14**
L35: Rainh 4H **59**
Weaver Ct. L25: Gate 6E **75**
Weaver Cres. WA6: Frod 6H **123**
Weaver Gro. WA9: St H 2C **44**
Weaver Ho. L25: Gate 6E **75**
(off Ribble Rd.)
Weaver Ind. Est. L19: Garst 1G **107**
Weaver La. WA6: Frod 5F **123**
Weaver Pk. Ind. Est. WA6: Frod 5H **123**
Weaver Rd. WA6: Frod 6H **123**
WA7: West 1E **123**
Weaver Sailing Club 5H **123**
Weaverside Av. WA7: Sut W 3B **124**
Weavers La. L31: Mag 3D **12**
Weaver St. L9: Walt 2F **35**
Weaver Vw. WA7: Clftn 3G **123**
Webb Cl. L7: Liv 6A **54**
Webb Dr. WA5: Burtw 1H **63**
Webber Estates L33: Know I 1E **25**
Webber Rd. L33: Know I 2D **24**
Webb St. L7: Liv 2A **72**
WA9: St H 4H **43**
Web Complex, The L33: Know I 3E **25**
Webster Av. CH45: Wall 2F **51**
L20: Boot 1E **35**
Webster Dr. L32: Kirkb 1A **24**
Webster Rd. L7: Liv 2B **72**
Websters Holt CH49: Upton 3D **66**
Webster St. L3: Liv 2E **5** (5D **52**)
L21: Lith 5B **20**
Wedge Av. WA11: Hay 6C **30**
Wedgewood Gdns. WA9: St H 1H **59**
Wedgwood St. L7: Liv 5H **53**
Wedgwood Dr. WA8: Wid 5F **79**
Wednesbury Dr. WA5: Gt San 3H **81**
Weightman Gro. L9: Ain 5G **21**
Weirside WA9: St H 1H **61**
Welbeck Av. L18: Moss H 4D **72**
Welbeck Ct. L22: Water 2F **19**
(off Mt. Pleasant)
Welbourne Rd. L16: Child 6G **55**
Weld Blundell Av. L31: Lyd 3A **6**
Weldon St. L4: Walt 3F **35**
Weld Rd. L23: Blun 6E **9**
Welford Av. CH43: Pren 1B **86**
Welford Cl. WA9: St H 6H **43**
Welland Cl. L26: Halew 5G **93**
Welland Rd. CH63: Hghr B 6F **87**
Wellbank Dr. L26: Halew 2A **94**
Wellbrae Cl. CH49: Upton 4B **66**
Wellbrook Cl. L24: Speke 1F **109**
WA7: Brook 2E **125**
Wellbrook Grn. L24: Speke 2F **109**
Wellbrow Rd. L4: Walt 3G **35**
Wellcroft Rd. L36: Huy 3G **57**
Wellens Wlk. WA10: St H 2A **42**
Weller St. L8: Liv 4F **71**
Weller Way L8: Liv 5G **71**
Wellesbourne Pl. L11: Norr G 3E **37**
Wellesbourne Rd. L11: Norr G 2E **37**
Wellesley Gro. CH63: Beb 5A **88**

Wellesley Rd. CH44: Wall 3D **50**
(not continuous)
L8: Liv 5G **71**
Wellesley Ter. L8: Liv 5G **71**
Wellfarm Cl. L9: Ain 2B **36**
Wellfield WA7: Pres B 2G **125**
WA8: Wid 6E **79**
WA11: Rainf 5G **17**
Wellfield Av. L32: Kirkb 2A **24**
Wellfield Pl. L8: Liv 5G **71**
Wellfield Rd. L9: Walt 1G **35**
Wellgreen Rd. L25: Gate 2B **74**
Wellgreen Wlk. L25: Gate 2C **74**
(off Wellgreen Rd.)
Wellingford Av. WA8: Hale B 6H **95**
Wellington Av. L15: Wav 3B **72**
Wellington Cl. CH63: Beb 5A **88**
L10: Ain 6A **12**
Wellington Employment Pk. Sth.
L5: Kirkd 1C **52**
Wellington Flds. L15: Wav 3B **72**
Wellington Gdns. L22: Water 2F **19**
(off Mason St.)
Wellington Ga. L24: Hale 3D **110**
Wellington Gro. L15: Wav 1C **72**
Wellington Mans. CH45: New B 4C **32**
(off Atherton St.)
Wellington Rd. CH43: Oxton 4C **68**
CH45: New B 4C **32**
CH63: Beb 5A **88**
L8: Liv 5F **71**
L15: Wav 2C **72**
L21: Lith 4A **20**
Wellington St. L3: Liv 4D **52**
L19: Garst 5G **91**
L22: Water 2F **19**
WA7: Run 2E **113**
WA8: Wid 5E **97**
Wellington St. Ind. Est. WA8: Wid 5E **97**
(off Wellington St.)
Wellington Ter. CH41: Birke 4F **69**
L8: Liv 4G **71**
WA10: St H 6E **29**
Well La. CH42: Rock F, Tran 1G **87**
CH49: Grea 6A **66**
CH60: Hesw 1E **117**
CH63: Hghr B 5F **87**
L16: Child 2B **74**
L20: Boot 2D **34**
L25: Gate 2B **74**
WA5: Penk 6G **81**
(not continuous)
Well La. Gdns. L20: Boot 2D **34**
Wells St. L15: Wav 2D **72**
Wellstead Cl. L15: Wav 1E **73**
Wellstead Rd. L15: Wav 1E **73**
Wellstead Wlk. L15: Wav 1E **73**
(off Wellstead Rd.)
Welsh Rd. CH66: Chil T 6G **121**
Welton Av. CH49: Upton 4D **66**
Welton Cl. L24: Speke 2F **109**
Welton Grn. L24: Speke 2F **109**
Welton Rd. CH62: Brom 3D **104**
Welwyn Cl. WA9: St H 1D **60**
Wembley Gdns. L9: Walt 5F **21**
Wembley Rd. L18: Moss H 5F **73**
L23: Crosb 6H **9**
Wendell St. L8: Liv 2A **72**
Wendover Av. L17: Aig 6A **72**
Wendover Cl. CH43: Noct 5H **67**
WA11: Hay 4F **31**
Wendron Rd. L11: Crox 6H **23**
Wenger Rd. WA8: Wid 4F **79**
Wenlock Cl. L26: Halew 4G **93**
Wenlock Dr. L26: Halew 4G **93**
Wenlock Rd. L4: Walt 6H **35**
WA7: Beech 3C **124**
Wenning Av. L31: Mag 5D **6**
Wensley Av. L26: Halew 4H **93**
Wensleydale L9: Walt 4G **21**
Wensleydale Av. CH62: East 2E **121**
L35: Rainh 4B **60**
Wensleydale Cl. L31: Mag 5A **6**
WA5: Gt San 1H **81**

Wensley Rd. L9: Walt 4G 21
Wentworth Av. CH45: New B 6D 32
Wentworth Cl. CH43: Noct 5H 67
   WA8: Wid 4E 79
Wentworth Dr. CH63: Brom 2C 120
   L5: Liv 3F 53
Wentworth Gro. L36: Huy 5D 56
Wernbrook Cl. CH43: Noct 5H 67
Wernbrook Rd. L4: Walt 6A 36
Wervin Cl. CH43: Oxton 1A 86
Wervin Rd. CH43: Oxton 1A 86
   L32: Kirkb 2H 23
Wesley Av. CH44: Wall 2E 51
   WA11: Hay 4H 31
Wesley Gro. CH44: Wall 4G 51
Wesley Hall Gdns. WA9: St H 1B 60
Wesley Pl. L15: Wav 1D 72
Wesley St. L22: Water 3F 19
W. Albert Ct. L17: Aig 5H 71
W. Alfred Ct. *CH43: Oxton* *4E 69*
                (off Alfred Rd.)
West Allerton Station (Rail) 2F 91
WEST BANK 1E 113
Westbank Av. CH45: New B 6E 33
W. Bank Dock Est. WA8: Wid 6C 96
W. Bank Rd. L7: Liv 5C 54
Westbank Rd. CH42: Tran 6E 69
W. Bank St. WA8: Wid 6E 97
Westbourne Av. CH48: W Kir 1B 82
   L23: Thorn 3B 10
Westbourne Gro. CH48: W Kir 1B 82
Westbourne Rd. CH41: Birke 4E 69
   CH43: Oxton 4E 69
   CH44: Wall 3B 50
   CH48: W Kir 1A 82
Westbrook Av. L34: Presc 1B 58
Westbrook Rd. CH46: More 2A 66
   L25: Gate 4E 75
W. Brow Gdns. CH43: Bid 1G 67
Westbury Cl. L17: Aig 2A 90
   L25: Hunts X 3F 93
Westbury St. CH41: Tran 5G 69
Westcliffe Ct. WA8: Wid 5F 79
Westcliffe Rd. L12: W Der 6E 37
West Cl. CH43: Noct 4H 67
   L34: Eccl P 6G 41
Westcombe Rd. L4: Walt 6A 36
Westcott Rd. L4: Walt 1H 53
Westcott Way CH43: Noct 5H 67
Westdale Rd. CH42: Rock F 1G 87
   L15: Wav 1D 72
Westdale Vw. L15: Wav 1D 72
WEST DERBY 6F 37
West Derby Golf Course 1A 56
W. Derby Rd. L6: Liv 4G 53
                 (Low Hill)
   L6: Liv .2B 54
                (Orphan Dr.)
   L13: Liv 1D 54
W. Derby St. L7: Liv 5G 53
W. Derby Village L12: W Der 6F 37
West Dr. CH49: Upton 4E 67
   CH60: Hesw 6E 101
West End Gro. WA11: Hay 5B 30
West End Rd. WA11: Hay 5B 30
Westerhope Way WA8: Wid 6D 78
Western Approaches Mus.
   (Underground Wartime Mus.)
            . . . . .3C 4 (5C 52)
Western Av. CH62: Brom 2D 104
   L24: Speke 3E 109
   L36: Huy 4C 56
Western Dr. L19: Gras 4E 91
Westerton Rd. L12: W Der 1A 56
Westfield Av. L14: Broad G 5A 56
Westfield Cres. WA7: Run 4C 112
Westfield Dr. L12: Crox 3A 38
Westfield M. WA7: Run 4D 112
Westfield Rd. CH44: Wall 6F 51
   L9: Walt 5E 21
   WA7: Run 4C 112
Westfields Dr. L20: Boot 4F 21
Westfield St. WA10: St H 2D 42
              (not continuous)

Westfield Wlk. L32: Kirkb 1F 23
W. Float Ind. Est. CH41: Birke 5D 50
Westgate WA8: Wid 4H 95
Westgate Rd. CH62: Port S 1B 104
West Gro. CH60: Hesw 5D 100
Westhead Av. L33: Kirkb 1B 24
Westhead Cl. L33: Kirkb 2C 24
Westhead Wlk. L43: Kirkb 1B 24
Westhouse Cl. CH63: Brom 2C 120
WEST KIRBY 1A 82
West Kirby Concourse (Leisure Cen.)
              . . . . .6A 64
W. Kirby Rd. CH46: More 3A 66
West Kirby Station (Rail) 1A 82
West Knowe CH43: Oxton 5B 68
West La. WA7: Pal F 6A 114
Westleigh Pl. WA9: Sut L 2G 61
W. Lodge Dr. CH48: W Kir 6A 64
West Mains L24: Speke 2A 110
West Meade L31: Mag 5A 6
Westminster Av. L30: N'ton 5E 11
Westminster Chambers *L1: Liv* *3E 5*
              (off Crosshall St.)
Westminster Cl. L4: Kirkd 5E 35
   WA8: Wid 3H 95
Westminster Ct. CH43: Oxton 4B 68
Westminster Dr. CH62: Brom 6D 104
   WA11: Hay 4H 31
Westminster Gro. L34: Presc 2A 58
Westminster Rd. CH44: Wall 3D 50
   L4: Kirkd 4D 34
Westmoreland Rd.
   CH45: New B 6E 33
Westmorland Av. L30: N'ton 6C 10
   WA8: Wid 2F 97
Westmorland Dr. L3: Liv 1D 4 (4C 52)
Westmorland Pl. L5: Liv 2D 52
Westmorland Rd. L36: Huy 5G 57
W. Oakhill Pk. L13: Liv 5E 55
WESTON 1D 122
Weston Ct. L23: Blun 6D 8
   WA7: West 6D 112
Weston Cres. WA7: West 1D 122
Weston Gro. L26: Halew 5A 94
   L31: Mag 3B 12
WESTON POINT 6B 112
Weston Point Docks
   WA7: West P 6B 112
Weston Point Expressway
   WA7: Run, West 4C 112
Weston Rd. WA7: Run, West 5C 112
Weston Vw. WA7: Clftn 3H 123
W. Orchard La. L9: Ain 3B 22
Westover Cl. L31: Mag 6B 6
Westover Rd. L31: Mag 6B 6
WEST PARK 3B 42
West Pk. Gdns. CH43: Bid 1G 67
West Pk. Rd. WA10: St H 3B 42
Westport Bus. Pk. L20: Kirkd 6C 34
West Quay L3: Liv 2C 70
West Rd. CH43: Noct 4H 67
   CH65: Ell P, Hoot 4H 121
   L14: Broad G 5G 55
   WA7: West P 6B 112
Westry Cl. CH46: More 1H 65
West Side WA9: St H 3G 43
West Side Av. WA11: Hay 5C 30
Westside Ind. Est. WA9: St H 3G 43
West St. CH45: Wall 2D 50
   L34: Presc 1C 58
   WA10: St H 4B 42
West Twr. L3: Liv 2B 4
WESTVALE 1G 23
West Vw. CH41: Tran 5H 69
   L36: Huy 5B 58
West Vw. Av. L36: Huy 5B 58
West Vw. Cl. L36: Huy 5B 58
Westview Cl. CH43: Noct 5H 67
Westward Ho CH48: Caldy 5D 82
Westward Vw. L17: Aig 6G 71
   L22: Water 1D 18

Westway CH43: Noct 5H 67
   CH46: More 6C 48
   CH49: Grea 5B 66
   CH60: Hesw 1D 116
   L15: Wav 1F 73
   L31: Mag 5B 6
   WA7: Pal F 6A 114
Westway Sq. CH46: More 6C 48
Westwick Pl. L36: Huy 4D 56
Westwood WA7: Wind H 4E 115
Westwood Cl. CH43: Oxton 4B 68
   CH64: Nest 5A 118
Westwood Gro. CH44: Wall 3C 50
Westwood Rd. CH43: Bid 3G 67
   L18: Aller 3G 91
Wetherby Av. CH45: Wall 2A 50
Wetherby Ct. L36: Huy 2E 57
Wethersfield Lodge CH43: Noct 5A 68
Wethersfield Rd. CH43: Noct 6A 68
Wetstone La. CH48: W Kir 2C 82
Wexford Av. L24: Hale 3D 110
Wexford Cl. CH43: Oxton 5A 68
   WA11: Hay 4F 31
Wexford Rd. CH43: Oxton 5B 68
Wexwood Gro. L35: Whis 5F 59
Weybourne Cl. CH49: Upton 2E 67
Weyman Av. L35: Whis 4E 59
Weymoor Cl. CH63: Spit 3H 103
Weymouth Av. WA9: St H 4B 44
Weymouth Cl. L16: Child 1B 74
   WA7: Murd 1G 125
Weymouth Rd. WA5: Burtw 1H 63
Whaley La. CH61: Irby 5D 84
Whalley Av. WA10: St H 4C 28
   WA11: Rainf 3F 17
Whalley Cl. L30: N'ton 5D 10
Whalley Gro. WA8: Wid 6H 79
Whalley Rd. CH42: Tran 4F 69
Whalley St. L8: Liv 5F 71
Wharf, The WA7: Pres B 1H 125
Wharfdale Rd. WA5: Gt San 2H 81
Wharfedale WA7: Pal F 1D 124
Wharfedale Av. CH42: Tran 1D 86
Wharfedale Dr. CH62: East 2F 121
   L35: Rainh 4B 60
Wharfedale Rd. CH45: Wall 1B 50
Wharfedale St. L19: Garst 6A 92
Wharford La. WA7: Nort 2G 115
Wharf Rd. WA12: Newt W 3G 45
Wharf St. CH62: Port S 6C 88
Wharmby Rd. WA11: Hay 5G 31
Wharncliffe Rd. L13: Liv 4E 55
Wharton Cl. CH49: Upton 3B 66
Wharton St. WA9: St H 4F 43
Whatcroft Cl. WA7: Run 1H 123
Wheatcroft Rd. L18: Aller 1G 91
Wheatear Cl. L27: N'ley 5G 75
Wheatfield Cl. CH46: More 2D 66
   L30: N'ton 6H 11
Wheatfield Rd. WA8: Cron 4A 78
Wheatfield Vw. L21: Ford 1B 20
Wheat Hill Rd. L36: Huy 2G 75
Wheathill Rd. L36: Huy 2G 75
Wheathills Ind. Est. L27: N'ley 3F 75
Wheatland Bus. Pk. CH44: Wall 5F 51
Wheatland Cl. WA9: Clock F 3G 61
Wheatland La. CH44: Wall 4F 51
Wheatland Rd. CH60: Hesw 6G 101
Wheatlands WA7: Run 4A 114
Wheatley Av. L20: Boot 6E 21
Wheatsheaf Av. WA9: Sut L 1H 61
Wheeler Dr. L31: Mell 6F 13
Whelan Gdns. WA9: St H 1C 60
Wheldon Rd. WA8: Wid 4F 95
Whernside WA8: Wid 1A 96
Whetstone Ct. *CH41: Birke* *4F 69*
             (off Whetstone La.)
Whetstone La. CH41: Birke 4F 69
Whickham Cl. WA8: Wid 6D 78
Whimbrel Av. WA7: Beech 2B 124
Whimbrel Pk. L26: Halew 2G 93
Whinberry Dr. L32: Kirkb 2H 23
Whinbury Ct. WA9: Clock F 3G 61
Whincraig L28: Stockb V 6D 38

Whinfell Gro. WA7: Beech 2A **124**
Whinfell Rd. L12: W Der 2G **55**
Whinfield Rd. L9: Walt 5F **21**
 L23: Thorn 3A **10**
Whinhowe Rd. L11: Norr G 3F **37**
Whinmoor Cl. CH43: Noct 3H **67**
Whinmoor Rd. L10: Faz 4E **23**
 L12: W Der 2G **55**
Whinney Gro. E. L31: Mag 3A **12**
Whinney Gro. W. L31: Mag 3A **12**
WHISTON 4E **59**
WHISTON CROSS 4D **58**
Whiston La. L36: Huy 3A **58**
WHISTON LANE ENDS 5E **59**
Whiston Station (Rail) 4E **59**
Whitburn Rd. L33: Kirkb 5C **14**
Whitby Av. CH45: Wall 2A **50**
Whitby Rd. WA7: Run 4E **113**
Whitby St. L6: Liv 1B **54**
Whitchurch Way WA7: Run 1H **123**
Whitcroft Rd. L6: Liv 4B **54**
Whitebeam Cl. L33: Kirkb 3B **14**
 WA7: Wind H 4E **115**
Whitebeam Dr. L12: Crox 2H **37**
Whitebeam Gdns. WA9: St H 1A **60**
Whitebeam Wlk. CH49: Grea 1H **83**
Whitechapel L1: Liv 4E **5** (6D **52**)
Whitefield Av. L4: Kirkd 5E **35**
Whitefield Cl. CH49: Woodc 6F **67**
Whitefield Dr. L32: Kirkb 1F **23**
Whitefield La. L35: Tar G 4A **76**
Whitefield Rd. L6: Liv 3H **53**
 WA10: St H 6B **28**
WHITEFIELDS CROSS 6B **80**
Whitefield Way L6: Liv 3G **53**
White Friars WA10: Eccl 1G **41**
Whitegate Cl. L34: Know 1F **39**
Whitegates Cl. CH64: Will 6G **119**
Whitegates Cres. CH64: Will 6G **119**
Whitehall Cl. L4: Kirkd 4E **35**
Whitehart Cl. L4: Walt 4H **35**
Whitehaven Rd. L5: Liv 1F **53**
Whitehealth Way CH46: Leas 4D **48**
Whitehedge Rd. L19: Garst 4F **91**
WHITEHOUSE 3H **125**
White Ho. Cl. WA11: Hay 5D **30**
Whitehouse Expressway
 WA7: Brook, Pal F 1A **124**
Whitehouse Ind. Est. WA7: Pres B . .3G **125**
 (not continuous)
Whitehouse La. CH60: Hesw 4G **101**
 CH63: Brim 4G **101**
Whitehouse Rd. L13: Liv 5F **55**
Whitehouse Va. Ind. Est.
 WA7: Pres B 2H **125**
Whitelands Mdw. CH49: Upton 4C **66**
White Lodge Av. L36: Huy 4F **57**
White Lodge Cl. CH62: Brom 2D **120**
Whitely Gro. L33: Kirkb 3C **14**
White Mdw. Dr. L23: Thorn 4A **10**
White Oak Lodge *L19: Gras* 4D **90**
 (off Beechwood Rd.)
White Rock St. L6: Liv 3H **53**
Whiteside Av. WA11: St H 6A **30**
Whiteside Cl. CH49: Upton 5E **67**
 L5: Liv .2D **52**
Whiteside Rd. WA11: Hay 5D **30**
Whitestone Cl. L34: Know 3E **39**
White St. WA8: Wid 6E **97**
Whitethorn Av. WA5: Gt San 4H **81**
Whitethorn Dr. L28: Stockb V 5D **38**
Whitewell Dr. CH49: Upton 3D **66**
Whitewood Pk. L9: Ain 5B **22**
Whitfield Cl. CH42: Tran 5F **69**
Whitfield Gro. WA11: Hay 5C **30**
Whitfield La. CH60: Hesw 3E **101**
Whitfield Lodge WA8: Sut L 3H **61**
Whitfield Rd. L9: Walt 6G **21**
WHITFIELDS CROSS 6A **80**
Whitfield St. CH42: Tran 5F **69**
Whitford Rd. CH42: Tran 5E **69**
Whitham Av. L23: Crosb 6H **9**
Whithorn St. L7: Liv 1B **72**
Whitland Rd. L6: Liv 4B **54**

Whitley Cl. WA7: Run 5D **112**
Whitley Dr. CH44: Wall 2F **51**
Whitley St. L3: Liv 3B **52**
Whitman St. L15: Wav 2C **72**
Whitmoor Cl. L35: Rainh 6C **60**
Whitney Pl. L25: Woolt 1E **93**
Whitney Rd. L25: Woolt 6E **75**
Whitstable Pk. WA8: Wid 5C **78**
Whitstone Cl. L18: Aller 1A **92**
Whittaker Cl. L13: Liv 6D **54**
Whittaker St. WA9: St H 4H **43**
Whittier St. L8: Liv 2A **72**
Whittington Ho. *L21: Lith* 4A **20**
 (off Beach Rd.)
Whittle Av. WA5: Gt San 1H **81**
 WA11: Hay 6C **30**
Whittle Cl. L5: Kirkd 1E **53**
Whittle Hall La. WA5: Gt San 3H **81**
Whittle St. L5: Kirkd 1E **53**
 WA10: St H 4B **42**
Whittlewood Ct. L33: Kirkb 5B **14**
Whitwell Cl. WA5: Gt San 2F **81**
Whitworth Ct. WA7: Manor P 1F **115**
Wicket Cl. L11: Crox 6H **23**
Wickham Cl. CH44: Wall 5F **51**
Wicksten Dr. WA7: Run 3G **113**
Widdale Av. L35: Rainh 4B **60**
Widdale Cl. WA5: Gt San 2H **81**
Widgeons Covert CH63: Thorn H . . .2B **118**
Widmore Rd. L25: Gate 5E **75**
WIDNES 3F **97**
Widnes Crematorium WA8: Wid 6E **79**
Widnes Eastern By-Pass
 WA8: Wid 5D **96**
Widnes Golf Course 2D **96**
Widnes Rd. WA8: Cuerd, Penk 1B **98**
 WA8: Wid 4E **97**
 (not continuous)
Widnes Shopping Pk. WA8: Wid 3F **97**
Widnes Station (Rail) 6E **79**
Widnes Tennis Academy 1D **96**
Widnes Trade Pk. WA8: Wid 4G **97**
Widnes Vikings RLFC 3D **96**
Widney Cl. L7: Liv 1H **71**
Wiend, The CH42: Rock F 2F **87**
 CH63: Beb 6A **88**
Wigg Island Community Pk.
 Local Nature Reserve 1H **113**
Wightman St. L6: Liv 4H **53**
Wignall Cl. L32: Kirkb 4A **24**
Wilberforce Rd. L4: Walt 4H **35**
Wilbraham Pl. L5: Liv 2D **52**
Wilbraham St. CH41: Birke 3G **69**
 L5: Liv .2D **52**
 WA9: Clock F 4A **62**
Wilburn St. L4: Walt 4F **35**
Wilbur St. WA9: St H 6A **44**
Wilcock Cl. L5: Liv 2D **52**
Wilcote Cl. WA8: Wid 5G **79**
Wildbrook Dr. CH41: Birke 6H **49**
Wildcherry Gdns. WA9: St H 6H **41**
Wilde St. L3: Liv 2G **5** (6E **52**)
Wilding Av. WA7: Run 3F **113**
Wild Pl. L20: Boot 4E **21**
Wilfer Cl. L7: Liv 1A **72**
Wilfred Owen Dr. CH41: Birke 2A **68**
Wilkes Av. CH46: Leas 4F **49**
Wilkie St. L15: Wav 2C **72**
Wilkinson Cl. WA8: Wid 6E **97**
Wilkinson Ct. *L15: Wav* 1B **72**
 (off Willow Rd.)
Wilkinson St. CH41: Birke 4E **69**
Wilkin St. L4: Kirkd 6E **35**
Willan St. CH43: Oxton 5D **68**
WILLASTON 6H **119**
Willaston Dr. L26: Halew 5A **94**
Willaston Rd. CH46: More 6B **48**
 CH63: Raby, Thorn H 1F **119**
 L4: Walt 4H **35**
Willedstan Av. L23: Crosb 6G **9**
William Brown St. L3: Liv 3F **5** (5D **52**)
 (not continuous)
William Ct. CH64: Nest 5B **118**
William Harvey Cl. L30: N'ton 6F **11**

William Henry St. L3: Liv 1H **5** (4E **53**)
 L20: Boot 3B **34**
William Jessop Way L3: Liv . . .2A **4** (5B **52**)
William Morris Av. L20: Boot 6E **21**
William Moult St. L5: Liv 2D **52**
William Penn Cl. WA5: Penk 4G **81**
William Rd. WA11: Hay 6B **30**
William Roberts Av. L32: Kirkb 1G **23**
Williams Av. L20: Boot 6E **21**
Williamson Art Gallery & Museum . . .4D **68**
Williamson Ct. L25: Woolt 2E **93**
 L26: Halew 2A **94**
Williamson Sq. L1: Liv 4E **5** (6D **52**)
Williamson St. L1: Liv 4E **5** (6D **52**)
 WA9: St H 1G **43**
Williamson Student Village *L7: Liv* . .6G **53**
 (off Paddington)
Williamson Tunnels Heritage Cen. . .6G **53**
 (off The Old Stableyard)
Williams St. L34: Presc 1D **58**
William St. CH41: Birke 3G **69**
 CH44: Wall 5G **51**
 WA8: Wid 1G **97**
 WA10: St H 1E **43**
William Wall Rd. L21: Ford 1B **20**
Willingdon Rd. L16: Child 6A **56**
Willington Av. CH62: East 4E **121**
Willink Rd. WA11: St H 4G **29**
Willis Cl. L35: Whis 5D **58**
Willis La. L35: Whis 5D **58**
Williton Rd. L16: Child 4A **74**
Willmer Rd. CH42: Tran 4E **69**
 L4: Walt 6H **35**
Willoughby Dr. WA10: St H 5H **41**
Willoughby Rd. CH44: Wall 3B **50**
 L14: Broad G 5A **56**
 L22: Water 2G **19**
Willow Av. L32: Kirkb 6G **13**
 L35: Whis 4E **59**
 L36: Huy 5D **58**
 WA8: Wid 1F **97**
Willow Bank CH44: Wall 5D **50**
Willowbank Rd. L36: Huy 2E **57**
Willowbank Rd. CH42: Tran 6F **69**
 CH62: New F 5B **88**
Willowbrow Rd. CH63: Raby 3E **119**
Willow Cl. CH44: Wall 5D **50**
 L14: Broad G 5A **56**
 WA7: Run 6F **113**
Willow Ct. CH63: Hghr B 5F **87**
 WA9: Clock F 3H **61**
 (off Clock Face Rd.)
Willowcroft Rd. CH44: Wall 5E **51**
Willowdale Rd. L9: Walt 1G **35**
 L18: Moss H 4D **72**
Willow Grn. L25: Woolt 5B **74**
Willow Gro. CH46: More 2B **66**
 L15: Wav 1E **73**
 L35: Presc 2E **59**
Willowherb Cl. L26: Halew 1F **93**
Willow Hey L31: Mag 2C **12**
Willow Ho. L21: Sea 5A **20**
Willow La. CH63: Raby 4F **119**
Willow Lea CH43: Oxton 5C **68**
Willowmeade L11: Norr G 2F **37**
Willow Moss Cl. CH46: More 5E **49**
Willow Pk. CH49: Grea 5A **66**
Willow Ri. L33: Kirkb 6B **14**
Willow Rd. L15: Wav 1C **72**
 WA10: St H 2A **42**
 WA11: Hay 4G **31**
Willows, The CH45: Wall 6A **32**
 WA5: Gt San 4H **81**
 WA9: Clock F 3G **61**
Willow Tree Av. WA9: Sut L 3H **61**
Willow Tree Ct. WA8: Wid 1H **97**
Willow Way L11: Crox 6H **23**
 L23: Crosb 4G **9**
Wills Av. L31: Mag 5B **6**
Willsford Av. L31: Mell 6F **13**
Wilmere La. WA8: Wid 4E **79**
Wilmot Av. WA5: Gt San 3H **81**
Wilne Rd. CH45: Wall 1C **50**
Wilsden Rd. WA8: Wid 2H **95**

Wilson Av. CH44: Wall 3G 51
Wilson Bus. Cen. L36: Huy 6A 58
Wilson Cl. WA8: Wid 2H 97
  WA10: St H 2C 42
Wilson Gro. L19: Garst 5G 91
Wilson Rd. CH44: Wall 3G 51
  L35: Presc 4D 58
  L36: Huy 5H 57
Wilson's La. L21: Lith 3B 20
Wilstan Av. CH63: Hghr B 6F 87
Wilstone Cl. L6: Liv 3F 53
Wilton Grange CH48: W Kir 5A 64
Wilton Gro. L13: Liv 5E 55
Wilton Rd. CH42: Rock F 2A 88
  L36: Huy 6F 57
Wilton's Dr. L34: Know 2E 39
Wilton St. CH44: Wall 3D 50
  L3: Liv 1H 5
Wiltshire Dr. L30: N'ton 6D 10
  (off Simon's Cft.)
Wiltshire Gdns. WA10: St H 3D 42
Wimbald Cl. L25: Gate 4E 75
Wimbledon St. CH45: Wall 2D 50
  L15: Wav 2C 72
Wimborne Av. CH61: Thing 6E 85
Wimborne Cl. L14: Knott A 1D 56
Wimborne Pl. L14: Knott A 2D 56
Wimborne Rd. L14: Knott A 1C 56
Wimborne Way CH61: Irby 4B 84
Wimbrick Cl. CH46: More 1D 66
Wimbrick Ct. CH46: More 1D 66
Wimbrick Hey CH46: More 1D 66
Wimpole St. L7: Liv 5H 53
Winchester Av. L10: Ain 6B 12
  L22: Water 1E 19
Winchester Cl. L25: Woolt 4D 92
Winchester Dr. CH44: Wall 3C 50
Winchester Pl. WA8: Wid 3A 96
Winchester Rd. L6: Liv 1A 54
  WA11: Hay 2G 31
Winchfield Rd. L15: Wav 3D 72
Windbourne Rd. L17: Aig 1H 89
Windermere Av. WA8: Wid 5F 79
  WA11: St H 3E 29
Windermere Ct. CH41: Birke 4E 69
  (off Penrith St.)
Windermere Dr. L12: W Der 4G 37
  L31: Mag 5D 6
  L33: Kirkb 5H 13
Windermere Ho. L17: Aig 1B 90
Windermere Pl. WA11: St H 3E 29
Windermere Rd. CH43: Noct 4G 67
  WA11: Hay 5D 30
Windermere St. L5: Liv 1G 53
  WA8: Wid 5F 79
Windermere Ter. L8: Liv 4H 71
Windfield Cl. L33: Kirkb 3C 14
Windfield Grn. L19: Garst 2H 107
Windfield Rd. L19: Garst 1H 107
WINDLE 5H 27
Windle Ash L31: Mag 5B 6
Windle Av. L23: Crosb 5A 10
Windlebrook Cres.
  WA10: Windle 5H 27
Windle City WA10: St H 5D 28
Windle Ct. CH64: Nest 5A 118
Windle Gro. WA10: Windle 5A 28
Windle Hall Dr. WA10: St H 4C 28
WINDLE HILL 6E 119
WINDLEHURST 5D 28
Windlehurst Av. WA10: St H 5C 28
WINDLES GREEN 4B 10
Windleshaw Rd. WA10: St H 5B 28
Windle St. WA10: St H 6D 28
Windle Va. WA10: St H 6C 28
Windmill Av. L23: Crosb 4H 9
Windmill Cl. L33: Kirkb 4A 14
Windmill Gdns. CH43: Bid 1G 67
  WA9: St H 1H 43
WINDMILL HILL 3E 115
Windmill Hill Av. E.
  WA7: Nort, Wind H 3F 115
Windmill Hill Av. Nth.
  WA7: Wind H 2F 115

Windmill Hill Av. Sth.
  WA7: Wind H 4F 115
Windmill Hill Av. W. WA7: Wind H ..3E 115
Windmill La. WA4: Pres H 6H 115
  WA5: Penk 4G 81
Windmill St. WA7: Run 3F 113
Window La. L19: Garst 1G 107
Windsor Av. L21: Lith 3A 20
Windsor Cl. CH49: Grea 6B 66
  CH62: New F 4A 88
  L30: N'ton 4F 11
Windsor Ct. L8: Liv 3F 71
  (off Northumberland St.)
  L20: Boot 6E 21
  (off Windsor Rd.)
Windsor Gro. WA7: Run 5B 114
Windsor M. CH62: New F 4A 88
Windsor Pk. Rd. L10: Ain 6C 12
Windsor Rd. L9: Walt 5G 21
  L13: Liv 1B 54
  L20: Boot 6E 21
  L23: Crosb 4F 9
  L31: Mag 1A 12
  L35: Presc 3F 59
  L36: Huy 5C 56
  WA8: Wid 5E 79
  WA10: St H 2B 42
Windsor St. CH41: Birke 4E 69
  CH45: New B 4D 32
  L8: Liv 2F 71
Windsor Vw. L8: Liv 2H 71
Windus St. WA10: St H 2C 42
WINDY ARBOR 1B 76
Windy Arbor Brow L35: Whis 1C 76
Windy Arbor Cl. L35: Whis 1D 76
Windy Arbor Rd. L35: Whis 5D 58
Windy Bank CH62: Port S 5B 88
  (not continuous)
Wineva Gdns. L23: Crosb 6H 9
Winfield Way WA8: Wid 3F 97
Winford St. CH44: Wall 4F 51
Winfrith Cl. CH63: Spit 3H 103
Winfrith Dr. CH63: Spit 3H 103
Winfrith Rd. L25: Gate 5E 75
Wingate Av. WA9: St H 1B 60
Wingate Cl. CH43: Noct 5A 68
Wingate Rd. CH62: East 2E 121
  L17: Aig 1C 90
  L33: Kirkb 5B 14
Wingate Towers L36: Huy 3F 57
Wingate Wlk. L33: Kirkb 6C 14
Wingfield Cl. L29: Seft 1D 10
Wingrave Way L11: Norr G 4F 37
Wings Ent. Pk. L24: Speke 1D 108
Winhill L25: Woolt 5C 74
Winifred Rd. L10: Faz 4F 23
Winifred St. L7: Liv 6H 53
Winkle St. L8: Liv 4F 71
Winmoss Dr. L33: Kirkb 4B 14
Winnbourne Gdns. WA9: Sut M ...4F 61
Winnington Rd. CH47: Hoy 4A 64
Winnipeg Dr. L27: N'ley 4G 75
Winnows, The WA7: Run 4H 113
Winsford Cl. WA11: Hay 4H 31
Winsford Dr. WA5: Burtw 6G 45
Winsford Rd. L13: Liv 1D 54
Winsham Cl. L32: Kirkb 3B 24
Winsham Rd. L32: Kirkb 3A 24
Winskill Rd. L11: Norr G 4E 37
Winslade Ct. L4: Walt 3H 35
Winslade Rd. L4: Walt 4H 35
Winslow Cl. WA7: Nort 5F 115
Winslow St. L4: Walt 1G 35
Winstanley Ho. CH62: New F 4B 88
  (off Winstanley Rd.)
Winstanley Rd. CH62: New F 4B 88
  L22: Water 1G 19
Winster Dr. L27: N'ley 5A 76
Winster M. WA10: St H 5H 41
Winston Av. WA9: St H 3D 44
Winston Dr. CH43: Noct 4G 67
Winstone Rd. L14: Knott A 3C 56
Winston Gro. CH46: More 1C 66
Winterburn Cres. L12: W Der ...6H 37

Wintergreen Av. L11: Norr G 4D 36
Winter Gro. WA9: St H 2D 44
Winterhey Av. CH44: Wall 5D 50
Winterley Dr. L26: Halew 5A 94
Winter St. L6: Liv 4G 53
Winthrop Pk. CH43: Oxton 4A 68
Winton Cl. CH45: New B 5C 32
Winton Gro. WA7: Wind H 4F 115
Winward Dr. L24: Speke 1B 108
Winwick Vw. WA5: Coll G 4F 45
Winwood Hall L25: Woolt 2C 92
Wirral Beach Caravan Pk.
  CH47: Meols 5F 47
Wirral Bus. Cen. CH41: Birke 5E 51
Wirral Bus. Pk. CH49: Upton 6D 66
Wirral Cl. CH63: Beb 2H 103
Wirral Gdns. CH63: Beb 2H 103
Wirral Intl. Bus. Pk. CH62: Brom ..4F 105
Wirral Ladies Golf Course, The ...3A 68
Wirral Leisure Pk. CH62: Brom ...2E 105
Wirral Mt. CH45: Wall 2B 50
  CH48: W Kir 1D 82
Wirral Mus. 3H 69
Wirral Sailing Cen. 1A 82
Wirral Tennis & Sports Cen. 5H 49
Wirral Transport Mus. 2G 69
Wirral Vw. L19: Gras 5D 90
Wirral Vs. CH45: Wall 1A 50
WIRRAL WATERS 1F 69
Wirral Way CH43: Noct 4G 67
Wisenholme Cl. WA7: Beech 2A 124
Wisteria Way WA9: Bold 6C 44
Witham Cl. L30: N'ton 5G 11
Withburn Cl. CH49: Upton 3C 66
Withens, The L28: Stockb V 6D 38
Withensfield CH45: Wall 1D 50
Withens La. CH44: Wall 1D 50
  CH45: Wall 1D 50
Withens Rd. L31: Lyd 4C 6
Withert Av. CH63: Hghr B 3F 87
Withington Rd. CH44: Wall 4E 51
  L24: Speke 2H 109
Withins Rd. WA11: Hay 3G 31
Within Way L24: Hale 4E 111
Withnell Cl. L13: Liv 5F 55
Withnell Rd. L13: Liv 5F 55
Withycombe Rd. WA5: Penk 5G 81
Witley Av. CH46: More 6C 48
Witley Cl. CH46: More 6C 48
Witney Cl. CH49: Grea 6A 66
Witsun Dr. L4: Kirkd 6E 35
Wittenham Cl. CH49: Upton 5D 66
Wittering La. CH60: Hesw 5B 100
Witterings, The CH64: Nest 6A 118
Witton Rd. L13: Liv 1B 54
Witton Way WA11: Rainf 2F 17
Witt Rd. WA8: Wid 4E 97
Wivenhoe Ho. L19: Aig 4D 90
  (off The Spinnakers)
Wivern Pl. WA7: Run 2F 113
Woburn Cl. L13: Liv 3D 54
  WA11: Hay 4H 31
Woburn Dr. WA8: Cron 3B 78
Woburn Grn. L13: Liv 3D 54
  (off Woburn Hill)
Woburn Hill L13: Liv 3D 54
Woburn Pl. CH42: Rock F 1H 87
Woburn Rd. CH45: Wall 1D 50
Wokefield Way WA10: St H 1A 42
Wokingham Gro. L36: Huy 1G 75
Wolfenden Av. L20: Boot 6E 21
Wolfe Rd. WA9: St H 3A 44
Wolferton Cl. CH49: Upton 2F 67
Wolfe St. L8: Liv 4E 71
Wolfrick Dr. CH63: Spit 4B 104
Wolseley Rd. WA10: St H 6D 28
Wolsey St. L20: Kirkd 4E 21
Wolstenholme Sq. L1: Liv ...6F 5 (1D 70)
Wolverton Dr. WA7: Wind H 4F 115
Wolverton St. L6: Liv 2A 54
Womack Gdns. WA9: St H 1C 60
Woodale Cl. WA5: Gt San 2G 81
Woodall Dr. WA7: Run 4F 113
Wood Av. L20: Boot 6E 21

Woodbank Cl. L16: Child 1B 74
Woodbank Pk. CH43: Oxton 5B 68
Woodbank Rd. WA5: Penk 5H 81
Woodberry Cl. CH43: Noct 5H 67
    L33: Kirkb 3B 14
Woodbine St. L5: Kirkd 6D 34
Woodbourne Av. L14: Knott A 3H 55
Woodbridge Av. L26: Halew 1F 93
Woodbrook Av. L9: Walt 4F 21
Woodburn Blvd. CH63: Hghr B 3G 87
Woodburn Dr. CH60: Hesw 1D 116
WOODCHURCH 1F 85
Woodchurch Ct. CH42: Tran 6E 69
Woodchurch La. CH42: Tran 1D 86
    CH49: Woodc 3G 85
Woodchurch Leisure Cen. 6G 67
Woodchurch Rd. CH41: Birke 6E 69
    CH42: Tran 2F 85
    CH43: Pren 2F 85
    CH49: Woodc 2F 85
    L13: Liv 3E 55
Wood Cl. CH41: Birke 2F 69
    CH66: Hoot 6G 121
    L32: Kirkb 1H 23
Woodcote Bank CH42: Rock F 4A 88
Woodcote Cl. L33: Kirkb 5C 14
Woodcotes, The CH62: Brom 1D 120
Woodcot La. CH60: Hesw 4C 100
Woodcroft Dr. CH61: Hesw 3D 100
Woodcroft La. CH63: Hghr B 3H 87
Woodcroft Rd. L15: Wav 2B 72
Woodcroft Way WA9: Clock F 3G 61
WOODEND .5F 97
Woodend CH61: Pens 6D 84
    L35: Whis 1E 77
    WA7: Murd 6G 115
Woodend Av. L23: Crosb 3G 9
    L24: Speke 5E 93
    L25: Hunts X 5E 93
    L31: Mag 2A 12
Woodend Ct. WA8: Wid 1H 97
Woodend Ind. Est. L24: Speke 6F 93
Woodend La. L24: Speke 1E 109
WOOD END PARK 4D 90
Woodene Cl. L32: Kirkb 4C 24
Woodfarm Hey L28: Stockb V 5C 38
Woodfield Av. CH63: Hghr B 4G 87
Woodfield Cres. WN4: Ash M 1H 31
Woodfield Rd. CH61: Pens 1C 100
    CH63: Beb 2A 104
    L9: Walt 6F 21
    L36: Huy 5E 57
Woodford Cl. WA7: Run 1F 123
Woodford Rd. CH62: New F 3B 88
    L14: Knott A 3A 56
    WA10: Windle 5A 28
Woodgate L27: N'ley 3E 75
Woodger St. L19: Garst 6G 91
Wood Grn. CH43: Bid 1G 67
    L34: Presc 1C 58
Woodgreen Rd. L13: Liv 3E 55
Wood Gro. L13: Liv 5D 54
Woodhall Rd. L13: Liv 4E 55
Woodhatch Rd. WA7: Brook 2D 124
Woodhead Rd. CH62: Port S 5C 88
Woodhead Row CH62: Port S 6C 88
Woodhead St. CH62: New F 4B 88
Wood Heath Way CH62: East 6G 105
WOODHEY .4G 87
Woodhey Ct. CH63: Hghr B 3H 87
Woodhey Gro. CH63: Hghr B 4H 87
Woodhey Rd. CH63: Hghr B 4H 87
    L19: Gras 3E 91
Woodholme Ct. L25: Gate 5D 74
Woodhouse Cl. L4: Walt 6E 35
Woodhurst Cl. L36: Huy 1E 57
Woodhurst Cres. L14: Knott A 3C 56
Woodin Rd. CH42: Rock F 3A 88
Woodkind Hey CH63: Spit 3A 104
Woodland Av. CH47: Meols 6D 46
    WA8: Wid 2D 96
Woodland Dr. CH45: New B 1C 60
    CH49: Woodc 6E 67
Woodland Gro. CH42: Rock F 3H 87

Woodland Rd. CH42: Rock F 3H 87
    CH48: W Kir 1E 83
    CH49: Woodc 6E 67
    L4: Walt 5B 36
    L21: Sea 4H 19
    L26: Halew 4G 93
    L31: Mell 5E 13
    L36: Huy 1E 57
Woodlands, The CH41: Birke 4F 69
    CH49: Upton 3D 66
    L34: Eccl P 6F 41
Woodlands Dr. CH61: Barn 1G 101
Woodlands La. CH48: W Kir 2D 82
Woodlands Pk. L12: W Der 2E 55
Woodlands Rd. CH61: Irby 6B 84
    CH64: Park 6H 117
    L9: Ain .5B 22
    L17: Aig 1C 90
    L36: Huy 5D 56
    WA11: St H 5F 29
Woodlands Sq. L27: N'ley 5A 76
                                        (off Wood La.)
Woodland Vw. L23: Thorn 2A 10
Woodland Wlk. CH62: Brom 4C 104
    WA7: Cas 4C 114
Wood La. CH45: Wall 1A 50
    CH49: Grea 4B 66
    CH64: Park 5G 117
    CH64: Will 6A 120
    L27: N'ley 4H 75
    L34: Presc 2B 58
    L36: Huy 5B 58
    WA7: Beech, Sut W 2B 124
    WA7: Murd 1E 125
Wood Lea L12: Crox 2A 38
Woodlea Cl. CH62: Brom 2D 120
Woodlee Rd. L25: Gate 5E 75
Woodleigh Cl. L31: Lyd 2A 6
Woodley Fold WA5: Penk 6H 81
Woodley Rd. L31: Mag 3A 12
Woodpecker Cl. CH49: Upton 4B 66
    L12: W Der 4B 38
Woodpecker Dr. L26: Halew 1G 93
Woodridge WA7: Wind H 4E 115
Wood Rd. L26: Halew 4G 93
Woodrock Rd. L25: Woolt 1D 92
Woodruff St. L8: Liv 5F 71
Woodside Av. CH46: More 2B 66
    WA11: St H 3D 28
Woodside Bus. Pk. CH41: Birke 2H 69
Woodside Cl. L12: W Der 5F 37
Woodside Ferry App.
    CH41: Birke 2H 69
Woodside Rd. CH61: Irby 5C 84
    WA5: Gt San 2H 81
    WA11: Hay 4G 31
Woodside St. L7: Liv 6H 53
Woodside Walkway CH41: Birke 2H 69
Woodside Way L33: Kirkb 4B 14
Woodsome Pk. L25: Gate 6E 75
Woodsorrel Rd. CH41: Birke 2B 68
    L15: Wav 2F 73
Woodstock Gro. WA8: Wid 1B 96
Woodstock Rd. CH44: Wall 4C 50
Woodstock St. L5: Liv 2D 52
Wood St. CH41: Birke 2F 69
    CH47: Hoy 2B 64
    CH62: Port S 6B 88
    L1: Liv 5F 5 (6D 52)
    L19: Garst 5G 91
    L21: Lith 4B 20
    L34: Presc 1D 58
    WA8: Wid 2G 97
    WA9: St H 1G 43
Woodthorn Cl. WA7: Dares 1H 115
Wood Va. WA9: St H 1C 60
Woodvale Cl. CH43: Bid 1G 67
Woodvale Ct. CH49: Woodc 2E 85
                                        (off Childwall Grn.)
Woodvale Rd. L12: Crox 2B 38
    L25: Woolt 1D 92
Woodview L34: Know 2F 39
Woodview Av. CH44: Wall 5G 51
Woodview Cres. WA8: Wid 3G 95

Woodview Rd. L25: Woolt 5B 74
    WA8: Wid 3G 95
Woodville Av. L23: Crosb 6F 9
Woodville Pl. WA8: Wid 2B 96
Woodville Rd. CH42: Tran 5E 69
Woodville St. WA10: St H 1F 43
                                        (not continuous)
Woodville Ter. L6: Liv 2H 53
Woodward Rd. CH42: Rock F 3A 88
    L33: Know I 5E 15
Woodway CH49: Grea 5B 66
Woodwall Cl. CH62: Brom 3E 105
Woodyear Rd. CH62: Brom 6E 105
Woolacombe Av. WA9: Sut L 2G 61
Woolacombe Rd. L16: Child 3A 74
Wooler Cl. CH46: More 1A 66
Woolfall Cl. L36: Huy 3D 56
Woolfall Cres. L36: Huy 3D 56
WOOLFALL HEATH 2F 57
Woolfall Heath Av. L36: Huy 2E 57
Woolfall Ter. L21: Sea 5A 20
Woolhope Rd. L4: Walt 3H 35
Woolley Cl. WA6: Frod 5H 123
Woolmoore Rd. L24: Speke 5E 93
Woolston Rd. WA11: Hay 4E 31
WOOLTON .1D 92
Woolton Cinema, The 1C 92
Woolton Golf Course 3D 92
WOOLTON HILL 6A 74
Woolton Hill Rd. L25: Woolt 5A 74
Woolton M. L25: Woolt 1C 92
                                        (off Quarry St.)
Woolton Mt. L25: Woolt 6C 74
WOOLTON PARK 5C 74
Woolton Pk. L25: Woolt 5C 74
Woolton Pk. Cl. L25: Woolt 6C 74
Woolton Rd. L15: Wav 2E 73
    L16: Child 3G 73
    L19: Aller, Garst 5G 91
    L25: Aller 5H 91
    L25: Woolt 4A 74
Woolton St. L25: Woolt 1C 92
                                        (not continuous)
Woolton Views L25: Hunts X 3F 93
Worcester Av. L13: Liv 6B 36
    L22: Water 1F 19
Worcester Cl. WA10: St H 3D 42
Worcester Ct. L20: Boot 2D 34
Worcester Dr. L13: Liv 6B 36
Worcester Dr. Nth. L13: Liv 6B 36
Worcester Rd. CH43: Bid 1H 67
    L20: Boot 1D 34
Wordsworth Av. CH42: Rock F 2H 87
    WA8: Wid 3D 96
    WA9: Sut M 4E 61
Wordsworth Cl. L32: Kirkb 3G 23
Wordsworth St. L8: Liv 2A 72
    L20: Boot 6A 20
Wordsworth Wlk. CH48: W Kir 3B 82
Wordsworth Way L36: Huy 6G 57
World Museum Liverpool 2F 5 (5D 52)
World of Glass, The 2E 43
Worrow Cl. L11: Norr G 2F 37
Worrow Rd. L11: Norr G 2F 37
WORSLEY BROW 5A 44
Worsley Brow WA9: St H 5A 44
Worsley St. WA11: Hay 5B 30
Worthing St. L22: Water 1E 19
Worthington Cl. WA7: Pal F 6C 114
Wortley Rd. L10: Faz 3C 22
Wray Av. WA9: Clock F 3H 61
Wrayburn Cl. L7: Liv 1A 72
Wray St. WA9: Clock F 3H 61
Wrekin Cl. L25: Woolt 2D 92
Wrekin Dr. L10: Ain 1C 22
Wrenbury Cl. CH43: Oxton 1B 86
    WA7: Sut W 3B 124
Wrenbury St. L7: Liv 5A 54
Wren Cl. WA7: Pal F 1C 124
Wrenfield Gro. L17: Aig 1A 90
Wren Gro. L26: Halew 2G 93
Wright St. WA8: Wid 6E 97
Wrights La. WA5: Burtw 3G 63
    WA5: Cuerd 1B 98

Wrights Ter. L15: Wav 2E 73
Wright St. WA44: Wall 3F 51
  L5: Liv 2D 52
Wrigley Rd. WA11: Hay 5G 31
Wroxham Cl. CH49: Upton 4E 67
Wroxham Ct. CH49: Upton 4E 67
  (off Wroxham Cl.)
Wroxham Dr. CH49: Upton 5E 67
Wroxham Rd. WA5: Gt San 3F 81
Wroxham Way CH49: Upton 4E 67
Wryneck Cl. WA10: St H 5H 41
Wrynose Rd. CH62: Brom 5E 105
Wulstan St. L4: Kirkd 6D 34
Wycherley Rd. CH42: Tran 6F 69
Wycherley St. L34: Presc 1D 58
Wychwood CH49: Upton 4D 66
Wychwood Cl. L14: Knott A 4H 55
Wycliffe Rd. L4: Walt 6A 36
  WA11: Hay 4G 31
Wycliffe St. CH42: Rock F 1H 87
Wye Cl. CH42: Rock F 6H 69
Wyedale Rd. WA11: Hay 4E 31
Wye St. L5: Liv 1F 53
Wykeham St. L4: Kirkd 6D 34
Wyken Gro. WA11: St H 6G 29
Wyke Rd. L35: Presc 2E 59
Wyllin Rd. L33: Kirkb 1C 24
Wylva Av. L23: Crosb 6A 10
Wylva Rd. L4: Walt 1G 53
Wyncroft Cl. WA8: Wid 4A 96
Wyncroft Rd. WA8: Wid 4A 96
Wyncroft St. L8: Liv 5G 71
Wyndale Cl. L18: Moss H 6F 73
Wyndcote Rd. L18: Moss H 4F 73
Wyndham Av. L14: Broad G 5C 56
Wyndham Rd. CH45: Wall 2H 49
Wyndham St. L4: Walt 3F 35
Wynne Rd. WA10: St H 6C 28
Wynnstay Av. L31: Lyd 4C 6
Wynnstay St. L8: Liv 3G 71
Wynstay Rd. CH47: Meols 1C 64
Wynwood Pk. L36: Roby 6E 57
Wyre Rd. L5: Liv 6F 35
Wyrescourt Rd. L12: W Der 2H 55
Wyresdale Av. WA10: St H 4C 28
Wyresdale Rd. L9: Ain 4H 21
Wysall Cl. WA11: St H 6H 29

Wyswall Cl. L26: Halew 2G 93
Wythburn Cres. WA11: St H 3F 29
Wythburn Gro. WA7: Beech 2A 124
Wyvern Rd. CH46: More 1C 66

X

X Building L3: Liv 2C 4 (5C 52)

Y

Yanwath St. L8: Liv 2H 71
Yarcombe Cl. L26: Halew 2H 93
Yardley Cen. L33: Know I 1E 25
Yardley Dr. CH63: Spit 4A 104
Yardley Rd. L33: Know I 2E 25
Yarmouth Rd. WA5: Gt San 3G 81
Yarn Cl. WA9: St H 5B 44
Yarrow Av. L31: Mag 5E 7
Yates Cl. L34: Presc 2D 58
Yates St. L8: Liv 4E 71
Yeadon Wlk. L24: Speke 2E 109
Yellow Submarine 3E 109
Yelverton Cl. L26: Halew 2H 93
Yelverton Rd. CH42: Tran 6G 69
  L4: Walt 6A 36
Yeoman Cotts. CH47: Hoy 3C 64
Ye Priory Ct. L25: Aller 2A 92
Yew Bank Rd. L16: Child 2H 73
Yewdale Av. WA11: St H 7F 29
Yewdale Pk. CH43: Oxton 5D 68
Yewdale Rd. L9: Walt 1H 35
Yew Tree Av. WA9: St H 1G 61
Yew Tree Cl. CH49: Woodc 1E 85
  L12: W Der .1B 56
Yew Tree Ct. CH60: Hesw 5E 101
Yew Tree Grn. L31: Mell 5F 13
Yew Tree La. CH48: W Kir 1B 82
  L12: W Der .2A 56
Yew Tree Rd. CH46: More 5D 48
  CH63: Hghr B 1G 103
  L9: Walt 1F 35
  L18: Aller 6H 73
  L25: Hunts X 3E 93
  L36: Huy 1F 75

Yew Tree Trad. Est. WA11: Hay 3H 31
Yew Way CH46: More 6D 48
Yorkaster Rd. L18: Aller 2G 91
York Av. CH44: Wall 4F 51
  CH48: W Kir .3B 82
  L17: Liv 3B 72
  L23: Crosb 5F 9
  WA5: Gt San .2G 81
York Cl. L30: N'ton 4F 11
  WA10: St H .1D 42
York Cotts. L25: Gate 5D 74
York Ho. L17: Aig 4B 72
York Pl. WA7: Run 3F 113
York Rd. CH44: Wall 5F 51
  L23: Crosb 5G 9
  L31: Mag 2B 12
  L36: Huy 4A 58
  WA8: Wid 3A 96
Yorkshire Gdns. WA10: St H 3D 42
York St. CH62: Brom 6D 88
  L1: Liv 6E 5 (1D 70)
  L9: Walt 2F 35
  L19: Garst 1G 107
  L22: Water 3F 19
  WA7: Run 3E 113
York Ter. L5: Liv 1E 53
York Way L19: Garst 1H 107
  L36: Huy 4A 58
Youatt Av. L35: Presc 3E 59
Youens Way L14: Knott A 3A 56
Youth Court
  Liverpool 5D 4
Yoxall Dr. L33: Kirkb 4H 13

Z

Zander Gro. L12: Crox 2C 38
Zante Cl. L5: Liv 1E 53
Zara Ct. WA11: Hay 4E 31
Zenith Wlk. L25: Gate 2C 74
Zetland Rd. CH45: Wall 6B 32
  L18: Moss H 4D 72
Zetland St. CH41: Birke 4F 69
Zig Zag Rd. CH45: Wall 1D 50
  L12: W Der .2H 55
Zircon Cl. L21: Lith 3C 20

SAFETY CAMERA INFORMATION

PocketGPSWorld.com's CamerAlert is a self-contained speed and red light camera warning system for SatNavs and Android or Apple iOS smartphones/tablets. Visit www.cameralert.co.uk to download.

Safety camera locations are publicised by the Safer Roads Partnership which operates them in order to encourage drivers to comply with speed limits at these sites. It is the driver's absolute responsibility to be aware of and to adhere to speed limits at all times.

By showing this safety camera information it is the intention of Geographers' A-Z Map Company Ltd., to encourage safe driving and greater awareness of speed limits and vehicle speed. Data accurate at time of printing.

HOSPITALS, HOSPICES and
selected HEALTHCARE FACILITIES
covered by this atlas.

N.B. Where it is not possible to name these facilities on the map,
the reference given is for the road in which they are situated.

ALDER HEY CHILDREN'S HOSPITAL 3G **55**
Eaton Road
West Derby
LIVERPOOL
L12 2AP
Tel: 0151 2284811

ARROWE PARK HOSPITAL 2E **85**
Arrowe Park Road
WIRRAL
CH49 5PE
Tel: 0151 6785111

ASHTON HOUSE HOSPITAL 5D **68**
26 Village Road
Oxton
PRENTON
CH43 5SR
Tel: 0151 6539660

ASHWORTH HOSPITAL 4F **7**
Parkbourn
LIVERPOOL
L31 1HW
Tel: 0151 473 0303

BMI SEFTON HOSPITAL 5C **22**
University Hospital Aintree
Lower Lane
LIVERPOOL
L9 7AL
Tel: 0151 3306551

BROADGREEN HOSPITAL 5G **55**
Thomas Drive
LIVERPOOL
L14 3LB
Tel: 0151 7062000

CHESHIRE & MERSEYSIDE NHS TREATMENT CENTRE
....................................1B **124**
Earls Way
RUNCORN
WA7 2HH
Tel: 01928 574001

CLAIRE HOUSE CHILDREN'S HOSPICE
....................................4F **103**
Clatterbridge Road
WIRRAL
CH63 4JD
Tel: 0151 3344626

CLATTERBRIDGE CENTRE FOR ONCOLOGY 4F **103**
Clatterbridge Road
WIRRAL
CH63 4JY
Tel: 0151 3341155

CLATTERBRIDGE HOSPITAL 4F **103**
Clatterbridge Road
Bebington
WIRRAL
CH63 4JY
Tel: 0151 3344000

FAIRFIELD INDEPENDENT HOSPITAL 1C **28**
Crank Road
Crank
ST. HELENS
WA11 7RS
Tel: 01744 739311

HALTON GENERAL HOSPITAL 6B **114**
Hospital Way
RUNCORN
WA7 2DA
Tel: 01928 714567

HALTON HAVEN HOSPICE 2E **125**
Barnfield Avenue.
Murdishaw
RUNCORN
WA7 6EP
Tel: 01928 712728

LIVERPOOL HEART & CHEST HOSPITAL
....................................5G **55**
Thomas Drive
LIVERPOOL
L14 3PE
Tel: 0151 2281616

LIVERPOOL SPIRE HOSPITAL 4D **72**
57 Greenbank Road
LIVERPOOL
L18 1HQ
Tel: 0151 7337123

LIVERPOOL UNIVERSITY DENTAL HOSPITAL
....................................5F **53**
Pembroke Place
LIVERPOOL
L3 5PS
Tel: 0151 7062000

LIVERPOOL WOMEN'S HOSPITAL 1G **71**
Crown Street
LIVERPOOL
L8 7SS
Tel: 0151 7089988

MARIE CURIE CENTRE, LIVERPOOL 1D **92**
Speke Road
Woolton
LIVERPOOL
L25 8QA
Tel: 0151 8011400

MOSSLEY HILL HOSPITAL 6C **72**
Park Avenue
Mossley Hill
LIVERPOOL
L18 8BU
Tel: 0151 2503000

MURRAYFIELD SPIRE HOSPITAL 6H **85**
Holmwood Drive
Heswall
WIRRAL
CH61 1AU
Tel: 0845 6002110

NHS CHILDREN'S WALK-IN CENTRE (SMITHDOWN) . . .3B **72**
Smithdown Road
LIVERPOOL
L15 2LF
Tel: 0151 2854820

NHS WALK-IN CENTRE (BIRKENHEAD) 6F **69**
Derby Road
BIRKENHEAD
CH42 0LQ

NHS WALK-IN CENTRE (GARSTON) 1H **107**
70 Banks Road
LIVERPOOL
L19 8JZ

NHS WALK-IN CENTRE (KNOWSLEY HALEWOOD) 4H **93**
Halewood Centre
Roseheath Drive
LIVERPOOL
L26 9UH
Tel: 0151 244 3532

NHS WALK-IN CENTRE (KNOWSLEY - HUYTON) 5G **57**
Nutgrove Villa
Westmorland Road
Huyton
LIVERPOOL
L36 6GA
Tel: 0151 244 3150

NHS WALK-IN CENTRE (KNOWSLEY - KIRKBY) 1A **24**
St Chad's Clinic
57 St Chad's Drive
LIVERPOOL
L32 8RE
Tel: 0151 244 3180

NHS WALK-IN CENTRE (LITHERLAND TOWN HALL) . . .3B **20**
Hatton Hill Road
LIVERPOOL
L21 9JN
Tel: 0151 475 4667

NHS WALK-IN CENTRE (LIVERPOOL CITY CENTRE)
. . . . .4F **5** (6D **52**)
Unit 4, Charlotte Row
53 Great Charlotte Street
LIVERPOOL
L1 1HU
Tel: 0151 285 3535

NHS WALK-IN CENTRE (LIVERPOOL - OLD SWAN) 5E **55**
Old Swan Health Centre
St. Oswalds Street
LIVERPOOL
L13 2BY
Tel: 0151 285 3565

NHS WALK-IN CENTRE (MERSEY VIEW) 4F **53**
45 Everton Road
LIVERPOOL
L6 2EH

NHS WALK-IN CENTRE (ST HELENS) 2F **43**
Millennium Building
Bickerstaffe Street
ST. HELENS
WA10 1DH
Tel: 01744 627 400

NHS WALK-IN CENTRE (WIRRAL) 4D **50**
Victoria Central Hospital
Mill Lane
WALLASEY
CH44 5UF
Tel: 0151 678 5111

NHS WALK-IN CENTRE (WIRRAL ARROWE PARK) 2E **85**
Arrowe Park Hospital
Arrowe Park Road
WIRRAL
CH49 5PE
Tel: 0151 6788496

PARK LODGE HOSPITAL 2B **54**
Orphan Drive
LIVERPOOL
L6 7UN
Tel: 0151 3308901

PEASLEY CROSS 4G **43**
Marshalls Cross Road
ST. HELENS
WA9 3DE
Tel: 01744 458 459

PRIMARY CARE TREATMENT CENTRE 5G **91**
Church Road
Garston
LIVERPOOL
L19 2LP
Tel: 0151 330 8301

Hospitals, Hospices and selected Healthcare Facilities

RATHBONE HOSPITAL 5E **55**
   Mill Lane
   Old Swan
   LIVERPOOL
   L13 4AW
   Tel: 0151 4717810

ROYAL LIVERPOOL UNIVERSITY HOSPITAL 5G **53**
   Prescot Street
   LIVERPOOL
   L7 8XP
   Tel: 0151 7062000

ST CATHERINE'S HOSPITAL (BIRKENHEAD) 5F **69**
   Church Road
   BIRKENHEAD
   CH42 0LQ
   Tel: 0151 6787272

ST HELENS HOSPITAL (MERSEYSIDE) 4G **43**
   Marshalls Cross Road
   ST. HELENS
   WA9 3DA
   Tel: 01744 646461

ST JOHN'S HOSPICE IN WIRRAL 4G **103**
   Mount Road
   Higher Bebington
   WIRRAL
   CH63 6JE
   Tel: 0151 3342778

ST JOSEPH'S HOSPICE 1H **9**
   Ince Road
   LIVERPOOL
   L23 4UE
   Tel: 0151 924 3812

SCOTT CLINIC 2A **60**
   Rainhill Road
   ST. HELENS
   WA9 5BD
   Tel: 0151 430 6300

SMITHDOWN HEALTH PARK 3B **72**
   Smithdown Road
   LIVERPOOL
   L15 2HE
   Tel: 0151 33080

UNIVERSITY HOSPITAL AINTREE 5C **22**
   Longmoor Lane
   LIVERPOOL
   L9 7AL
   Tel: 0151 5255980

VICTORIA CENTRAL HOSPITAL 4D **50**
   Mill Lane
   WALLASEY
   CH44 5UF
   Tel: 0151 6787272

WALTON CENTRE FOR NEUROLOGY AND NEUROSURGERY
. . . . .4C **22**
   Lower Lane
   LIVERPOOL
   L9 7LJ
   Tel: 0151 5253611

WHISTON HOSPITAL 3F **59**
   Warrington Road
   PRESCOT
   L35 5DR
   Tel: 0151 426 1600

WILLOWBROOK HOSPICE 6G **41**
   Portico Lane
   Eccleston Park
   PRESCOT
   L34 2QT
   Tel: 0151 430 8736

WOODLANDS HOSPICE 5B **22**
   Longmoor Lane
   LIVERPOOL
   L9 7LA
   Tel: 0151 5292299

ZOE'S PLACE - BABY HOSPICE 2A **56**
   Yew Tree Lane
   LIVERPOOL
   L12 9HH
   Tel: 0151 2280353